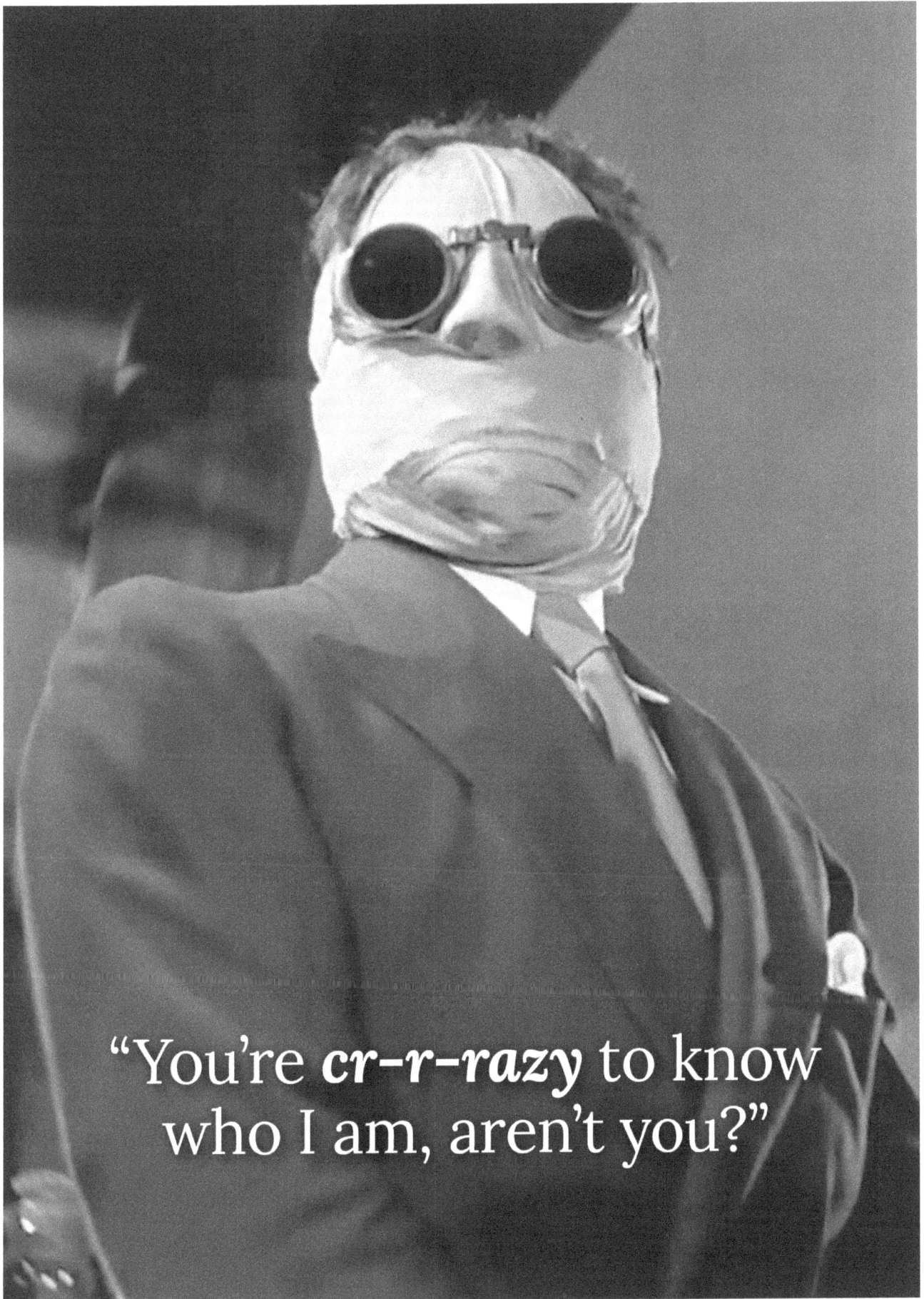

"You're **cr-r-razy** to know who I am, aren't you?"

CLAUDE RAINS:

AN INVISIBLE MAN

By
Toby I. Cohen

Published in the USA by:
BearManor Media
1317 Edgewater Dr #110
Orlando, FL 32804
www.bearmanormedia.com

Perfect ISBN 978-1-62933-991-7
Case ISBN 978-1-62933-992-4

BearManor Media, Orlando, Florida
Printed in the United States of America
Cover design by Karen Chacon, www.opmdesign.com
Book design by Robbie Adkins, www.adkinsconsult.com

Table of Contents

Preface

The first time I ever saw Claude Rains, I wasn't quite ten years old.

Growing up in West Philadelphia during the late 1930s, summer heat could only be overcome by fleeing to the "air-cooled" movie palaces. Thankfully, there were several of these within a six-block area of our working-class neighborhood. My mother went often, and when she took me along, I sat quietly absorbed by the images on the screen. Naturally I came to have favorite performers — not comedians nor cowboys, but actors like Bette Davis and Edward G. Robinson. I would imitate Robinson from his gangster films: No one could push that little guy around, and he had an unusual way of speaking. Davis — I was mesmerized by how she delivered lines with such authority. At school, I auditioned for every play and believed that someday I would become an actress.

It was quite safe in those days to allow children to take their dime and go off alone to attend a Saturday matinee. Newsreels, *March of Time* or another short, the latest serial chapter — all ran before the main feature. One Saturday, I wasn't interested in the horror film playing at my favorite movie house and decided to walk two blocks to another theatre. The one-sheet poster displayed in the front window depicted my favorite actress Bette Davis in a Warner Bros. film called *Mr. Skeffington* — perfect.

I knew I had never seen (or heard) the actor playing Davis' husband, the title character. I was so taken by the story, by this actor's performance, by his unique voice, that I could not leave the theatre. I sat through two screenings of *Mr. Skeffington,* and was well into the third, when my father, a policeman with a flashlight, came down the aisle. I was summarily yanked out of my seat, dragged home, and put to bed without supper. Crying, I tried to tell my mother about the wonderful actor with the marvelous voice. She assured me that she liked Claude Rains too, but that I must never repeat my escapade, or no more movies.

Mother believed my passion for Claude Rains was a childhood infatuation, as I learned to love another accent: Charles Boyer's. But Rains was my favorite and I told her that not only did I want to become an actress like Davis. I wanted to learn to talk like Rains. I joined neighborhood theatre groups while still in high school. My parents could not understand why, at the age of sixteen, when my peers were crazy about performers like Frank Sinatra and Van Johnson, I was so taken with an old Englishman who, as it happened, owned a big farm just outside of Philadelphia.

In the fall of 1950, I read that Rains would be performing in a new stage play that would preview in Philadelphia before moving to Broadway. I was determined to see *Darkness at Noon.* I wanted to meet Rains. I even read the original novel the play was based on, hardly understanding the complex politics and philosophical rhetoric. December 26, 1950, was opening night; my mother and I had front row seats in the loge. I couldn't believe I was seeing Rains in person. I was completely mesmerized. After the performance, I talked my way backstage to his dressing room. It was crowded, full of adults, most of whom knew him. He was seated in a small wooden chair and for just a moment, the crush of people separated, and I heard someone say: "Oh, here comes one of his young fans."

I stepped forward. He smiled very slightly. He looked completely drained: His eyes were glassy, and it seemed to me he might slip off the chair. I could only feel for him. Everything I had conjured up to say went out of my head, and what came out of my mouth was: "Oh, Mr. Rains, are you all right? You look really terrible." He answered me very softly, "Well, I am rather tired." Then someone came in between us and before I knew it, Mother and I were out in the hall among the stragglers still leaving the darkened theatre. I was numb. I hadn't said anything I had wanted to.

Because *Darkness* ran during my school's Christmas vacation, I was able to take my newly purchased camera and wait outside the theatre every night for my idol. Once I met his wife Frances and his twelve-year-old daughter Jennifer. I politely asked if

I could have a picture, and Mrs. Rains kindly permitted it. On the show's last night, still lurking around the stage door, I caught Rains himself, walking to the theatre from his hotel three blocks away, in hat and scarf, coat over his arm. I popped up to snap a photo, almost blinding him. We exchanged no words during this harrowing ordeal, for which I couldn't blame him. (My pictures are reproduced on page 259, at the end of the chapter on *Darkness at Noon*.) Afterwards, my mother wrote him a note on my behalf; I was still amazed he took the time to reply (though he misspelled my last name).

I continued to be involved in a little theatre work, and even had my father take me to New York City to see a man in charge of a summer stock program. I attended Hedgerow Theatre School in the evenings. I had no plan; I was daydreaming, believing I would somehow be "discovered." One Saturday afternoon in May 1951, I attended the annual Devon Horse Show on the Main Line outside of Philadelphia. Taking the Paoli local train to Devon, I walked to the grounds, and to my surprise, there in the admission booth was Mrs. Rains. She remembered me because I had forwarded copies of the photos I took during the Philadelphia preview of *Darkness at Noon*. She was pleasant but determined not to be annoyed by a fan of her husband's; she told her daughter to escort me around the grounds, which Jennifer obediently did. I didn't mention her father and, after about an hour, thanked her and went off to watch the horse show. I had followed news reports of *Darkness'* Broadway success and was thrilled that Rains won every award for his remarkable performance. I graduated from high school that June, the same month the play closed.

About 1954, I was working for the Vogel Music Publishing Co. in Philadelphia. One day I heard someone come up the stairs and in a booming voice call out, "Mr. Vogel!" My desk was around the corner, so I couldn't see who entered, but the voice sounded so familiar! After the door to Mr. Vogel's private office closed, I went into the anteroom and asked his secretary who had just arrived, because he sounded

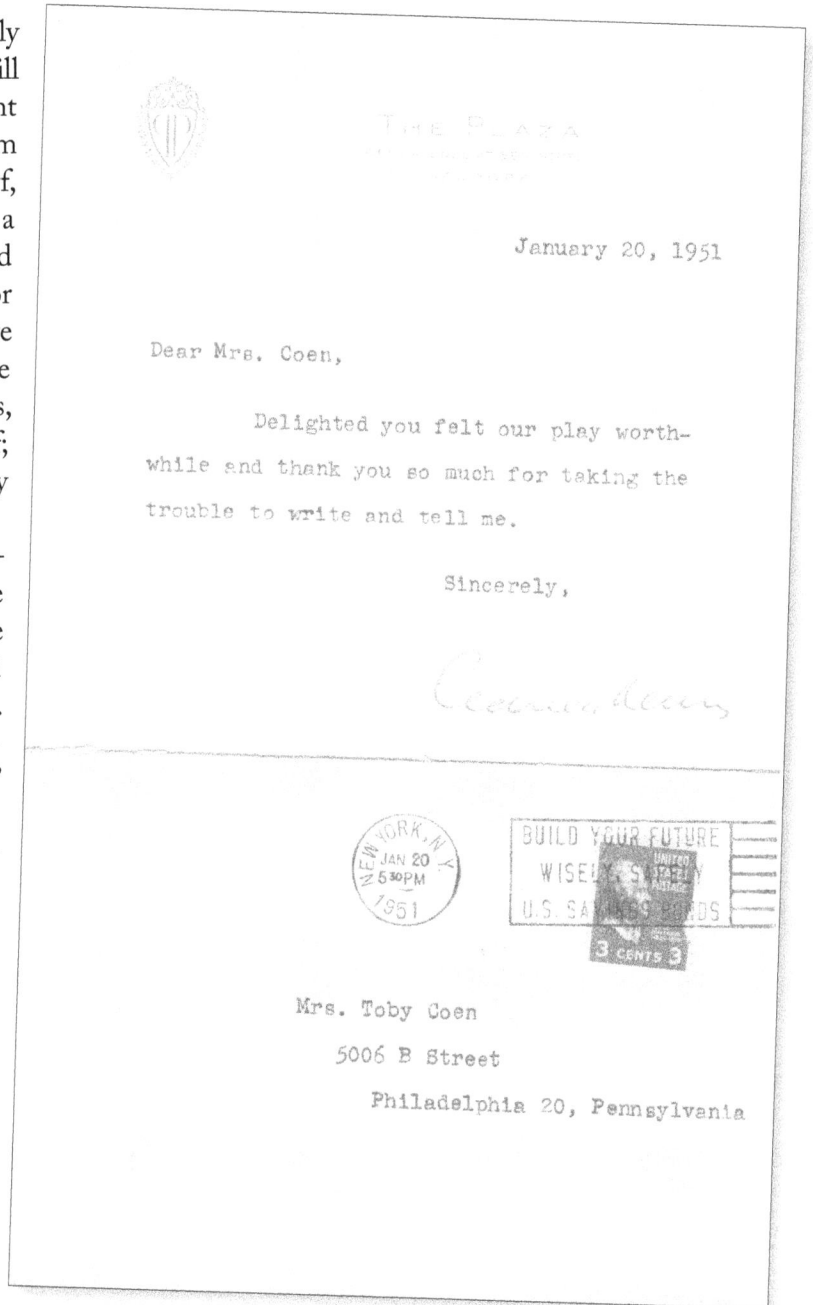

January 20, 1951

Dear Mrs. Coen,

Delighted you felt our play worthwhile and thank you so much for taking the trouble to write and tell me.

Sincerely,

Mrs. Toby Coen
5006 B Street
Philadelphia 20, Pennsylvania

just like Claude Rains. "That's because it is Claude Rains," she replied. "He and Vogel are friends." I had to sit down. She went on to say that Rains "wasn't very nice" because he had never said hello. Now was my chance to approach him — but say what? I've never been crazy about fans who annoy famous people with requests for signatures. And I'm usually calm around celebrities: I once enjoyed a fifteen-minute chat with Tennessee Williams when one of his plays ran in Philadelphia. But Rains was totally different. He was my god; I was so in awe of the power encompassed in his acting. The office door opened. As he left, I could only hear his final words to Mr. Vogel: "Not on

Jennifer Rains at the Devon Horse Show (photo taken by the author).

my beautiful old barn…" I wanted to run out after him. I wanted to say, "If I come out to the farm, will you show me your beautiful old barn?" But I couldn't manage it. I couldn't bear it if he dismissed me out of hand. Nor did I want to lose my job if Mr. Vogel took exception to my hounding a famous client. So I hesitated, and Rains walked down the stairs, and was gone.

Lacking direction, I endured a series of boring secretarial jobs, frustrated and not very happy, not knowing how to get started as an actress. Finally, I obtained a secretarial position with the NBC affiliate in Philadelphia, WRCV-TV. At last, I was working in "the industry," although in the business end since the sub stations did not produce any original programming. I'm certain my parents believed that like most girls my age in the 1950s I would eventually marry and live the usual suburban life — but that was not what I wanted. On my birthday in 1956, I asked my father to drive me out to Chester County to see Rains' farm, Stock Grange. I dressed up nicely — it

was my intention to knock on his front door and try to talk to him. It was a beautiful day, and when I saw the farm's sign and the spectacular surrounding grounds, I was breathless. But I was frightened too and I lost my nerve, still terrified of being rejected. Besides, I had no right to invade the man's privacy at home.

The next spring, I again met Mrs. Rains. Returning to the studio after lunch, walking down Walnut Street in downtown Philly, I happened to spot her. It was a chilly day, and she was wearing a black Persian lamb coat. She remembered me as we exchanged hellos. I inquired about Jennifer, then an undergrad at Bennington College. But when I asked how her husband was, she replied, "I don't know." I hesitated before I said, "You're not with him any longer?" And she shook her head. I didn't know what to say, other than, "How sad … well, it was good to see you again."

Our family left Philadelphia and moved to Columbus, Ohio. I had not made any progress in what I thought I wanted to do with my life: For the next two years, I worked in a couple of miserable jobs. I did meet someone who gave me an engagement ring, but I returned it and we remained good friends. Instead of getting married, I made the grand tour of Europe in 1961. I had lost track of Claude Rains' career. On my return, a friend took me to see *Lawrence of Arabia*. When I saw Rains on the screen, I was shocked at how much he had aged, but those old teenage feelings stirred again.

In the fall of 1962, I enrolled at Ohio State University. I sold my car, lived at home, and worked during the summers to pay my own tuition. A wonderful thing happened. I discovered I loved going to school, I loved learning. Absorbed in studies, I also kept active socially and went to movies and shows and concerts. I excelled, graduating *cum laude*, and making Phi Beta Kappa. Now I wanted to attend graduate school and teach history to college students. I sent applications to a few universities, hoping to obtain a scholarship, and just for the hell of it, I included Yale and Harvard. To my astonishment, I was awarded a partial scholarship to the MAT program at Harvard. With the safety net of a teaching certificate, I could go all over the country and perhaps even look into acting again.

But during my first semester in Cambridge, I immediately realized I was mentally exhausted and needed a break before getting back into intensive schoolwork. I requested and was granted a temporary leave of absence. I went to New York City in search of my "lost youth" — I thought I would go to a few theatre auditions and see if I still loved acting. With my secretarial experience and because I had worked at NBC, it was easy to get temp assignments to see me through. (Did I do anything about those auditions? No.) I was hired by *The Tonight Show Starring Johnny Carson*, and hearing the show was leaving for the West Coast, I asked to go with it. But when I mentioned relocation with a friend, who was the show's guest coordinator, she couldn't believe I would give up Harvard for a position like hers. She insisted I finish my degree and then rethink things — otherwise I would always regret it. She was right — and fortunately, I returned and earned my Masters in education.

May 30, 1967, was a seminal day in my life I will never forget. In a full two-column spread, *The New York Times* reported on the death of Claude Rains. I was devastated. It was over! I would never meet him. I would never be able to tell him why I loved his acting. And to be honest, I didn't actually understand myself why it was, from the time I was ten, that this artist and his work had meant so much to me. I thought about it for a long time — I tried to write about it. Obviously, I went on with life. With Rains gone, I assumed that I would just get over it what had been a childhood infatuation. But deep inside, I never did.

I taught junior high school social studies, I traveled a lot, never married. After some 20 years in academia, I left teaching for the antiques business, which was booming in the late 1980s and early '90s. I enjoyed this greatly and became quite knowledgeable, but when things slowed down, I became restless. I thought about concentrating on my hobby of writing short stories and poetry and trying to get something printed.

In 1993, browsing around the library, I discovered to my surprise that there was no comprehensive biography on the actor I considered one of the greatest of the 20th century. After reading Greg Mank's *The Hollywood Hissables*, a fun book with bios of multiple baddies, I phoned Mr. Mank and we had a delightful chat. I asked him why — at the time, it had been 25 years since Rains' death — nobody had written anything full-length. His answer was hard to dispute: It's tough getting answers to questions when most of the people involved are very elderly or have gone on to their just rewards.

It was then I decided how I would dedicate the next years of my life: researching my childhood idol. On my 60th birthday, I vowed I would complete my project whether or not it was ever published. But as the old saying goes: "Man plans — God laughs." Illness (myself, one of my younger sisters) and surgical procedures (a heart valve replacement, a pacemaker) intervened; after the death of my younger sister, there was her complicated estate to settle. I was still writing, still researching, but somehow, more than two decades went by. In the interval, a couple of books on Rains had come out, and while they covered his films, his stage work, his marriages, etc., I didn't feel they successfully investigated his complicated personality — what it was that made him a superb actor, and yet, a person no one really knew.

I believe one of the keys to the mystery of Claude Rains lies in the Pennsylvania farms he owned for nearly two decades. Rains' passion for the land, his unwavering commitment to restoration of historical properties, came from his soul. I visited the places that were so meaningful to him; I strolled under the now-spreading canopy of trees he himself planted, as both a naive girl of nineteen and a reflective woman of sixty. I believed I could feel what he felt and understand how it all spoke to him. I began to gain an understanding of why it was his heaven, why it brought such peace, and held such importance. And to understand why he deserted it, an act from which his soul never recovered.

In compiling the most detailed background to date on these rural havens, I believe I have found a way into the depths of Rains' heart. During his life, it was invisible to everyone.

Claude Rains deserves an in-depth analysis of his complexity as a person and an artist.

This is my tribute.

Introduction

"**W**ho is Claude Rains?" I was stunned by the question from the young man in the film department of the reference library where I had been conducting research — but then, he was only in his twenties. He and I grew up separated by five decades, maybe more; we were members of generations whose movie-going habits were entirely different. His exposure to motion pictures was nothing like what I experienced as a child and young woman during the "Golden Age of Hollywood." For him and his 21st century contemporaries, today's movies are saturated with mind-boggling CGI and special effects, chaotic cyberspace, in-your-face displays of sex and violence. My friends and I had grown up when pictures (predominantly black and white) often had leisurely stories, slapstick humor and, yes, tear-jerking pathos, reflecting charm, sophistication and class.

In responding to this young librarian, I wanted him to understand not just what made Claude Rains such an exceptional actor, but who he was off-screen. Since most movie buffs of any age are familiar with *Casablanca*, I explained that Rains played Captain Renault, the suave, charmingly corrupt French official with whom Humphrey Bogart's Rick begins "a beautiful friendship" at the finale. Immediately the young man responded with a smile, "That little guy stole the movie."

An integral element of the great films of Rains' era were the unforgettable performances of both the glamorous leads and the familiar ensembles of supporting character actors. Some had distinct style as well as exceptional skill. Others possessed unusual photogenic qualities while truthfully lacking genuine talent. A handful exhibited a mysterious, indefinable element which made them unique, individuals who embodied a special charisma. In some ingenious manner, they stimulated an audience's imagination. Not all the great Golden Age artists were spectacular-looking male and female stars. Many were memorable, sometimes oddly memorable character performers who were stars in their own right, and often commanded just as loyal a following. Claude Rains was one of the best.

Rains had a successful career on stage in both London and New York before he moved into films in 1933, at the age of forty-three, in *The Invisible Man*, a movie in which his face was completely bandaged. His fifty-four screen credits include such classics as *Now, Voyager, Casablanca, Mr. Smith Goes to Washington, Here Comes Mr. Jordan, The Adventures of Robin Hood, Notorious* and *Lawrence of Arabia*.

Claude Rains was an actor's actor: a completely focused professional who was dedicated to his work, taking nothing for granted and never resting on his laurels. Stocky, of less than average height and, despite a thick, tousled head of hair, not classically handsome; nevertheless, he had a powerful presence. With a scornful raise of an eyebrow and his penetrating stare, he demanded attention. The most sarcastic and suave of villains, he could also be sympathetic with ease and authority; or meek and humble and vulnerable. "Rains invested [his] roles with a slight but palpable air of mystery," said film historian Richard Schickel. "By never fully explaining himself, he commanded our wondering attention long after the film was over. It was a great, singular career."

And then there was his voice, low, husky, mellifluous, even sensual. "His power of investing even commonplace dialogue with smoldering conviction, is remarkable," said Graham Greene. "He can catch, as no one can, the bitter distrust of the world, religious in its intensity, which lies behind the heroic drama."

Although his acting often appeared effortless, Rains achieved success through hard work, severe discipline and perseverance. Nothing came easily, in either his personal life, or his career, as this book will show. Born in a wretched London slum during the last years of the reign of Queen Victoria, throughout his life he upheld and embraced many Victorian values. Although he lived during the first half of the 20th century and adopted American standards, he remained a product of his impoverished youth and his working-class background: hard-working, unnec-

he often unintentionally came across as intimidating. Even his only child admitted she occasionally felt uncomfortable, even somewhat afraid of her father, although he dearly loved her, spoiled her, and told anyone who would listen that she was his pride and joy. Rains was actually a very caring person, but his harsh upbringing made it difficult for him to express his emotions. He was inadequate, to say the least, in establishing permanent relationships: He married six times. A perfectionist in everything he undertook — his career, the preservation and restoration of the historical farmhouses he owned — he followed no formal religion, but almost devoutly lived by the Golden Rule. He harbored a profound sense of loyalty to colleagues at all levels. He disliked any form of pretense and, above all, could not forgive a lie. One tenet Rains held sacred was that integrity was the most important element of a person's character. When giving (infrequent) interviews, it was as if he were reciting a script of his life, frequently repeating the same stories, often in exactly the same way. Reporters found him to be mysterious but also friendly, intelligent, with a self-deprecating manner and a good sense of humor.

essarily thrifty, extremely prudent and very reserved. Yet while Rains' behavior and manner reflected those of a traditional Englishman in many respects, his attitude about fairness and his belief in equality were decidedly American: As soon as he was secure in his career and knew the luxury of a steady income, he became a citizen of his beloved adopted country.

Rains achieved unqualified recognition and admiration as an actor — he was nominated four times for an Oscar, and he was a recipient of the theatre's highest accolade for an artist, the Tony Award for Best Actor. Nonetheless, as popular as he was in his profession, personally he remained very much "an invisible man." He had few friends, and even those few people who considered themselves friends did so with qualification. An inability to be demonstrative often created the impression Rains was aloof;

Perhaps Rains was never to be "himself" in his acting because so many of the characters he portrayed with such conviction were the opposite of his real-life personality. In roles, Rains was often suave, confident, ironic, frequently cunning, occasionally unscrupulous and even deadly. He presented an image that was sophisticated and well-educated, most likely upper class. In reality, he was insecure, often tense, quite unpretentious, good-natured. Except for an expensive automobile, he lived quite simply with few luxuries, even after he was making money. As a young man, he had a potentially fatal flaw for an actor: a severe speech impediment and a strong Cockney accent. But he worked diligently to overcome this "class" stigma, developing impeccable diction with a pronunciation and tone that were unique and instantly recognizable. Having left school at age ten to go to work, he was completely self-taught, not just in academics, but speech and grammar as well.

There have been two previous works on Rains' life and career. While each provided interesting background information, I don't feel they captured the soul hidden behind the theatrical mask. The purpose of this book is different. My goal is to create a portrait, an examination, of a man who had no close friends but who convinced half a dozen women to be his wife; who was a respected, reliable, always-interesting artist whose work the public adored, but who remained an enigma to almost everyone who ever knew him. I wanted to bring Rains to life, as the man he was, with all his foibles, vulnerabilities and question marks. Rains' personality was much too complex to be entirely deciphered with complete assuredness so many decades on. Much of what I offer may be conjecture, but it is based on facts. I believe my speculations are sensible and informed, tied together by reasonable analysis of comments and actions. I hope I have even partially unraveled the

tangled knot of Rains' persona. What drove him to frequent self-destructiveness? To what extent did the lack of love in childhood dictate his inability to find love as an adult; his old-fashioned, even abusive philosophy about the duties of a wife? What influenced his strong, devoted, inflexible morality and strength of character?

While compiling accurate information was difficult, because I began this project three decades ago, I was fortunate enough to be able to contact Rains' few contemporaries still living—not just his colleagues in the entertainment business, but his Pennsylvania farm neighbors, his local postmistress, the son of the contractor who restored his farmhouse. I talked to the children of his sixth wife. His fifth wife told me I was the only person with whom she had discussed Rains. I received first-hand accounts from the local priest who talked with him, and the doctors who treated him in his final illness.

Claude Rains' professional *oeuvre* has enabled the movie-going public to establish with him a "beautiful friendship" that will endure "as time goes by." More than anything, I hope this book will enable fans to see, understand and appreciate the private side of this remarkable man.

CHAPTER 1
East End to West End

I can imagine an American filmgoer, seeing Claude Rains in one of his Hollywood roles, as an autocrat or smooth villain, feeling certain that here was a man who must have left an aristocratic family, somewhere in England, to amuse himself making films. Rains had that air, however sketchy the scenario or wooden the dialogue. But his early life is surprising. — J. B. Priestley

William Claude Rains was born Sunday, November 10, 1889, to Frederick William Rains and his wife, Emily Eliza, in a typical workingman's row house at 26 Tregothnan Road, Clapham, in the Lambeth section of London known as the East End. This district was London's version of the Lower East Side of New York: dirty, narrow streets harboring a conglomeration of working class poor, slaughter houses, docks, sailors and foreigners. It was plagued by crime and, most of all, extreme poverty. It was an area similar to the one so eloquently described by Charles Dickens in *Oliver Twist*, and hadn't changed all that much since that novel's publication some fifty years before. Queen Victoria was still on the throne – would be, for another dozen years – and although England was at the apex of empire, glory and power, the Rains family had little to do with such societal heights.

Claude Rains seemed to have little interest in his family's background or his lineage. A few handwritten notes outlining his father's side of the family are all that exist among his private papers, and he seems never to have made any effort to trace his ancestry. His grandparents were Alfred and Elizabeth Marley Rains; their son, Frederick William Rains, had been born on January 31, 1860. On the 22nd of October, 1884, Frederick married Emily Eliza Cox, who like him was twenty-four. The couple had a yearly succes-

sion of children over the next decade, and according to what Rains told his daughter, he was their first and only son. Several siblings didn't survive infancy, dying at birth or from causes prevalent at the time, and especially among their class – lack of decent food and an un-sanitized water supply harboring disease. It's probable these conditions had a pronounced physical effect on him, limiting his height and contributing to lifelong dental problems. There is no record of Rains being baptized into the Church of England or having any other religious orientation. He never attended formal church, nor did his parents give him any indication of the family's religious heritage.

CR's childhood home, 26 Tregothnan Road in London's East End. (Photo taken decades later.)

Much later, Rains told his daughter that he believed his father's side of the family was descended from traveling Sephardic Jews who had landed in England during the period of the Spanish Inquisition. Whether his father had passed on this information, or whether Rains concocted the story, is unknown.

At the time of his son's birth, Fred Rains listed his occupation as organ builder. Through the years, he held a variety of jobs, including boxing instructor, boiler maker and even actor. Evidently he would either fail or leave each job for something better. According to Rains, his father was the proverbial ne'er-do-well, a jack of all trades and master of none. Of the many vocations Fred held, Rains only remembered his father as an organ-maker and as a stoker at an iron works. The elder Rains' obituary notice in the *Hackney Gazette* stated he was once quite an athlete, having won a cycle championship at the age of forty when Claude would have been about ten. Fred's constant floundering about for work meant he was never able to earn a steady income, or provide his family with domestic security.

This environment, his father's lack of commitment to steady work, and genuine constant physical hunger had a deep psychological effect on Rains. In addition, Fred was cruel, with a vicious streak, welcoming any excuse to beat his son with a leather belt, which he did frequently starting when the boy was five. Not surprisingly, Claude hated his father, not for the beatings alone, but for the neglect of wife and family.

With this negative role model, Rains made it a point to cultivate the values and habits his father never possessed, starting with the ability to persevere and complete any task. Additionally, living as a youngster in an environment without financial security made him paranoid about money, a trait which greatly affected his professional decisions and lifestyle.

When speaking of the woman who bore him, Rains would say "my poor sweet darling Mother," an expression he employed more dramatically as he aged. Unfortunately, Emily would suffer from severe depression after losing so many children and Fred frequently took her to an institution where she remained for months at a time.

The relationship between Claude and his surviving siblings was strange and mysterious. Throughout the years, they did not correspond, and seldom met, even on the occasions when Claude returned to England for work. In 1948, when Rains' daughter Jennifer was ten, she met her father's only living relative: his sister, Aunt Tott. According to Jennifer, "I never understood that at all or why he even wanted me to meet her because he hated her, but he never said why." She described their brief visits as "bizarre."

Growing up in the East End of London, with such a family background and in terrible conditions, a young boy easily could have found himself destined to a hard-knock life. Great Britain was separated into strict social classes, based on a multiple of factors – birth, education, marriage prospects, profession and manner of speech. The latter could be especially stigmatizing, regardless of other achievements. That Claude Rains overcame all these social obstacles is quite a testament. As a child, he suffered from a speech impediment called rhoticism, difficulty in pronouncing the "r" sound. In a beautiful and popular American film star like Kay Francis, the trait sounded endearing. And today, the condition is no barrier to success as a performer (popular British television host Jonathan Ross and British historian Lucy Worsley have made it to the top of their respected fields, to name just two examples). But for a young boy who called himself "Willie Wains," and whose disorder was compounded by a severe Cockney accent and a slight lisp, life was tough.

When Willie was nine, his sister became ill and was sent to stay with their grandparents in Middlesex, under the assumption the "clean country air" would help her recover. Willie wanted to go too – he disliked attending school at All Saints Fulham, where his speech problems made him a target for ridicule. When his parents refused to allow him to accompany his sister, he decided to play hooky, convincing cohorts to inform the teacher that he was also sick and had been packed off to the country. This successful charade lasted for a rather astonishing six weeks, during which Willie meandered around the streets, stealing food or begging until it was time to go home for the evening.

During the time he was truant, a Mr. Smith hired the boy to sell newspapers. Willie met a youngster about his age who resembled a Little Lord Fauntleroy, outfitted in Eton collar and an elaborate suit. The two boys struck up a friendship. Willie learned that the dapper chap was dressed for choir practice; if he could also sing, there would be a place for him in Father Bernard Vaughan's choir in the chapel on Farm Street in Mayfair. Willie was not interested in music, but the fact that Father Vaughan supplied clothes and candy as payment for participation would have been enticing to any boy. Willie auditioned for Alfred Bellew the choirmaster, performing a heart-rending version of "I Am a Poor Blind Boy." To his delight, he was accepted. When not "employed" as a choirboy, young Willie continued to roam the streets, sometimes selling newspapers.

When the truancy was discovered, Fred gave his son a severe strapping and Willie returned to school accompanied by a policeman. It appeared his days as a Dickensian street urchin were over. While it was his mother's wish the boy receive a formal education, Fred only wanted to avoid problems with the law, especially if Willie was caught stealing. He couldn't care less that his son could sing; being a choir boy was not a real vocation and provided no income. Money was the factor that changed Fred's mind about Willie's education: A child could stop attending classes in order to work, but only with parental consent. If Willie could find a job and earn a few pennies to pass on to his mother, then Fred had no objections to his son leaving school. Even after being forced to return to the classroom, Willie often visited the choirmaster and remained in the choir for Sundays. Bellew liked the boy, and as Rains commented later, "[He] knew I was miserable both at home and in school — he had the impression I was competent." More important however, in addition to being choirmaster, Bellew acted as an agent for theatre managers, securing boys as extras for London stage productions. On one occasion, Bellew asked a few of the youngsters, among them Willie, if they would like to go to "the Haymarket." The boy assumed the reference was to a marketplace full of stalls displaying merchandise and was delighted by the prospect. When Bellew assured Fred that this was an opportunity for young Willie to earn a salary (involvement with a production in what was one of the most popular stage venues of the period), all thoughts of forcing his son to continue his education disappeared. Emily packed some apples for Willie's lunch and gave him two pennies for the horse-drawn bus trip to the West End, London's popular and thriving theatre district.

Perhaps Fred permitted this because he also had been an actor; his obituary notice actually described him as a British film industry pioneer, having appeared in over 500 films. However, while it is true Fred was quite active in early silent movies, it was usually as an extra and even a so-called producer of some one-reelers; he could hardly have completed five hundred films, even one-reelers. In 1917, Fred Rains produced a comedy film called *Bamboozled* under a company name of Swastika Films. (The symbol may have been inspired by Marshall Neilan's company in Hollywood which used the mark in the 'teens and early twenties.) The film was not a success

but, undaunted, in the next year Fred directed *The Haunted Hotel*, a one-reeler, and *Unexpected Treasure*, a two-reeler. In the 1920s, when his son was becoming active in the West End theatre, Fred appeared in fourteen films, the most memorable being *Nell Gwyn* (1926) starring Dorothy Gish and directed by Herbert Wilcox. Fred was also a monologue artist in a variety show and reportedly possessed a very good voice. (In its review of Rains' 1935 film *The Clairvoyant*, the newspaper *The Era* commented: "Claude Rains, it is of some interest to know, is the son of that fine old stage and film actor, Fred Rains. Claude undoubtedly inherits his excellent speaking voice and not a little of his acting ability from his father.") There is not much physical resemblance between Claude and his father, except for the dark, brooding eyes which made Fred seem commanding and at times even wild-looking. After his participation in the burgeoning film industry, Fred drifted back into various jobs, selling songs and teaching school. He even took a position as a manager of a boiler factory without knowing one thing about the trade, only to be fired three weeks later. This was another reason Rains grew up hating sham of any type, without respect for anyone, like his father, who lied about his abilities or skills, and especially, who seemed to lack any parental responsibility or integrity.

When Emily Rains died in 1942 during the war, Fred Rains married Mabel Lillian, known as "Babs," whom his son never met. During the 1940s, Rains dutifully paid for his father's upkeep in a rest home; when Fred died at eighty-five on December 2, 1945, Mabel had him buried in a common gravesite belonging to her family. Even in his later years, Rains seldom spoke about his parents, only occasionally mentioning his mother affectionately to his wives, and it seems he never forgave his father for keeping the family in economic jeopardy. Rains' daughter believed that even if her father had any emotional attachment to his parents, "he would have never shown it or revealed it to me."

Claude Rains' first "acting" job was in the original production of *Sweet Nell of Old Drury*, starring Julia Neilson and Fred Terry, John Gielgud's uncle. It opened on August 30, 1900, at the Theatre Royal, Haymarket. For running around a fountain dragging a wooden horse in a crowded street scene, Willie earned the handsome sum of ten shillings for the run of the play. Most of the money was commandeered by his mother for household expenses and food.

After *Sweet Nell* closed, Willie was placed in James Barrie's new play *The Admirable Crichton*, a perfect vehicle for its star Sir Henry Irving, at the Duke of York Theatre. As an extra, Willie received seven shillings six pence weekly which went to his mother; he was allowed to keep six pence for meals and bus fare. Quite frequently, he spent the extra penny for the bus trip on food instead and then walked the four miles home late at night. Of course, there was no extra money for clothes or shoes, so working in the theatre provided these rewards as well. On one occasion, Willie became the owner of a magnificent overcoat with velvet cuffs and collar: When leading lady Marie Tempest saw the small boy arrive at the theatre shivering and blue with cold, the brilliant, popular comedienne felt sorry for him, retrieved a fancy coat from wardrobe and told him to keep it.

During the run of *Crichton*, Willie was assigned the responsible position of page boy–callboy, the lowest job in the theatre; from such a beginning, few young men ever rose above the rank of stage manager. But at this point, Rains' life took a strange, lucky twist, as he recorded in the notes he prepared late in life for his unfinished autobiography. One of his jobs at the end of a performance was to straighten Irving's dressing room, putting away various articles and hanging up wardrobe. Unobserved, it was quite easy to pinch an occasional shilling left in a trouser pocket. One evening, Willie stole half a crown from the great man's discarded clothing. He was unaware he had been under suspicion for a while; the coin was marked and planted by assistant manager Lichfield Owen. Owen confronted Willie, reprimanding him, and reminding him, "Honesty is the best policy." The show's producer, Dion Boucicault, dismissed the boy on the spot, sending him packing with one shilling severance pay and the word **HONESTY** scratched on the coin. Willie was overcome with humiliation at being labeled a thief. When he reported the incident at home, his father was furious; it was bad enough to be sacked, but worse to steal. His mother, however, didn't believe Willie was a bad youngster, but merely that, like many a destitute boy, her son had been tempted beyond endurance. Emily was convinced he had learned his lesson and felt he deserved another chance. She also believed that the theatre might be the only viable avenue that would lead to Willie learning a trade. Plus, in the theatre, he would be

exposed to the greatest speeches ever written, spoken by actors with trained voices and perfect diction, an atmosphere that might possibly help him overcome his speech impediment. Lower-class speech could imprison a person forever; spending his adolescence in the slums, Willie would never improve his lot in life. The next day, Emily made a bold move: She went to Bellew with her son in tow and pleaded on his behalf, appealing to the choirmaster because he liked the youngster. Bellew had Willie swear he would never again steal anything. The boy complied, understanding that humiliation could be worse than any beating. With Bellew's help, Willie's position was again secured: He was a page boy by day (a general dogsbody, responsible for errands and small duties) and callboy by night (summoning the actors from their dressing rooms for places), at the prestigious His Majesty's Theatre, under the direction of the formidable Sir Herbert Beerbohm Tree, brother of Sir Max Beerbohm, noted writer and critic.

After Claude Rains became a star, this story was repeated ad infinitum; to nearly every reporter he ever spoke to, as well as to anyone who ever asked him how he became an actor. Some of the details were a bit fluid, altered in the telling by Rains himself or the secondary sources retelling it. For example, David Lean was told a slightly different version, which the director repeated to his biographer Kevin Brownlow:

> [O]ne of the people [Rains] looked after was Sir Herbert Tree, who liked the boy. Every evening when he came in, Tree would empty his pockets and put all his money on the dressing table. Claude used to tidy it up afterwards while [Tree] was on the stage. One day he noticed two-shilling silver coins. And Claude said, "I don't know what came over me, but I found myself thinking one of these wouldn't be missed and I took it and put it in my pocket. And this went on for several weeks. When there was a lot of change I took a silver coin and kept it." One day Tree said to Claude, "How much money have you got on you?" "I don't know, sir." "Well, could you see?" And Claude said, "I put my hand in my pocket and took out all my change and there was the silver coin I'd just pocketed." Tree picked it up and examined it and

said to Claude, "Look at this closely, will you?" On it was scratched a "T" [for thief]. [Tree] said, "I have suspected this for some time and so I have been marking the coins. This is a terrible thing, a great disappointment to me. I want you to come along and see me on Sunday morning at my house." [When Rains arrived], Tree said, "I've decided on your punishment. I think you might have a great future as an actor. The thing that's going to prevent it is that you don't speak properly. I've just written out a cheque. You're going to take that to Miss so-and so and every weekend you're going to talk to her and she will teach you to speak English. That is your punishment.

Another version was told to Anne Slavitt, who knew the husband of Iris Tree, the daughter of Sir Herbert. In this rendition, it was only "some actor" who caught young Rains stealing and dragged the boy to Sir Herbert. When Tree asked the boy why he stole the money, Rains replied: "It is what I need to buy some books on acting." At that point,

Tree pulled out his purse, peeled off a lot of bills and said, "Buy every book you ever wanted, and stay out of that idiot's sight until he's forgotten you." Not long after, Tree stayed very late in his office one evening and saw Rains center stage, talking to an empty darkened house. He was so impressed that he hired the young man as an actor in the company. A lovely story, and I am sure a true one, although everyone I know of who could confirm it is long gone.

This episode must be considered in the harsh reality of the times. Willie's being "allowed to work" was an affront to those fighting for child labor laws. The boy's position meant laboring from about ten in the morning to ten at night, and he was only eleven. However, the truth was, the young Rains was thrilled to be immersed in this exotic world of adults. Within three years, he decided he would make the theatre his life; he left home, sharing a flat with various members of the company or even sleeping in the theatre itself. In later years, when talking of his parents – to his daughter, or to others – the actor said he stayed with

his mother after his father abandoned her because she desperately needed the pennies he would bring to her.

Although lack of formal education was a handicap in many respects, the next six years of his life provided terrific training. Like many poor boys who later became successful, he was self-taught in reading and writing (although he never learned arithmetic beyond elementary levels). It was his determination and studying to improve himself which caught Tree's attention.

Sir Herbert Beerbohm Tree was a highly regarded actor and theatrical entrepreneur. Beginning in 1887, he managed the Haymarket Theatre for a period of ten years, until opening His Majesty's Theatre. In 1904, he founded the Royal Academy of Dramatic Arts (RADA). With a reputation built on overblown theatrics in the grand style of the period, he was also noted for producing first-rate plays. Rains remembered Tree, who was always addressed as "Chief," as "absent-minded and therefore very engaging, but at the same time officious, imperious. Very tall. He used to go to great pains to set up elaborate practical jokes." If Rains owed his future as an actor to anyone, it was to Tree; he never forgot his mentor and the influence the man had on his career.

There were others who helped young Rains turn his life around. One of these people integral in Rains' education was Walter Crichton, a public relations man for Tree's productions. Willie was generally well-liked by all in the theatre company, especially for his politeness and responsible attitude. Crichton knew the boy had a very limited formal education, and one day questioned him about his reading habits. Willie blurted out that in his spare time he read the lines in the plays (as callboy, it was part of his job). Willie added that he also read two popular boys' magazines. Crichton was horrified at Rains' inability to read well, since the boy could never advance without this skill, and so he started Willie on a learning regime by setting up a list of books which would educate as well as appeal to him. The first book Rains read was Robert Louis Stevenson's *Travels with a Donkey in the Cevennes*. But as the content became more difficult, Willie found there were words he could not understand, or pronounce, so he began reading with two books: the assigned work of literature and a dictionary. He would look up every word he didn't know to check the definition and proper pronunciation. According to Rains, it was in performing this process that he caught the attention of Sir Herbert.

The company was on tour, and on the train from Belfast to Dublin, Rains settled into an empty compartment and pulled out his current book. When Tree came in, he was astonished to find a callboy reading Thackeray's *The Newcomes*. Noting the second book beside the lad, Tree asked him how he could absorb two books at once, to which the youngster replied: "I can't read one without the other, Chief." Impressed, Tree began to take a personal interest in Willie's progress.

Of all the books, plays and poems which had a great effect on Rains, his favorite was Shakespeare's *Richard II*; he memorized the text, but never had a chance to perform it professionally. Any time he had to take a city bus, Willie would sit on the top level with Shakespeare in one hand and the dictionary in the other. He claimed it took him six months to learn the play entirely, as well as all the meanings of the archaic words. Why this particular work appealed to him, Rains never explained. Being responsible for calling the cast to places required Willie to know a play by heart, line by line, so he would be aware when an actor's cues were coming up. Knocking politely on the dressing room doors, he would announce, "Fifteen minutes, please." Tree noticed Rains' trouble with certain words, especially anything with the letter "r." Half a century later, in 1951, when Rains received the Medal for Good Speech on the Stage for his Tony Award–winning *Darkness at Noon* performance – an award he prized above all others – he told the gathering: "[As] a callboy I had to summon actors from their dressing rooms to the stage. It was difficult to be taken seriously because I had an impediment in my speech. I had no 'r's. If anyone asked my name, what I answered came out as Willie Wains. I had ideas that someday I would become an actor, and the important thing was to get rid of the impediment…. I discovered I had a lazy tongue, the muscle of which had never properly been used because my mother thought I talked 'pwittily'…."

Tree and Walter Crichton were impressed by Willie's consistent practicing of vowels and consonants to rid himself of his speech problems. Crichton approached a young actor who had recently joined the company, J. Fisher-White, for advice. It was decided to aid Willie financially for voice lessons to rid him of the "r" impediment. Fisher-White sent the boy to Lyall Sweet, a director at another theatre. On the first visit, Sweet handed Rains a book by Evelyn Millard containing a chapter that described Willie's problem — a lazy tongue. The book contained an exercise consisting of raising the tip of the tongue to the roof of the mouth and blowing over it, thereby strengthening the tongue muscles. As Rains recalled for interviewers: "I blew and blew and after eighteen months I succeeded, and I could say, at last, my name was Willie Rains! And then I was so proud that I annoyed everyone with it."

It began to be thrown about that Rains should consider becoming an actor, but the young man believed the position of stage manager was more financially secure. Besides, and of considerable importance, acting was "effeminate" – especially "putting makeup on one's face." He simply wanted to overcome a handicap which might hinder his advancement in life. When Tree questioned Rains about his goals, now that he was overcoming the speech problems, the young man stated he wanted to be a stage manager, as this would garner him the princely sum of five pounds a week. Tree told Rains to give serious thought to going on the stage, encouraging him to continue to develop his voice until he spoke the King's English perfectly. Tree closed the conversation by telling the young Rains to appear in his office the next day at precisely 1:00 p.m. Rains appeared as ordered, reminding the Chief of the offer to help, and explaining that he lacked the money to continue voice lessons and buy elocution books. Tree presented Rains with a check for fifty pounds. It was more money than the boy had ever seen in his life. He made a solemn promise that he would follow Tree's advice, leaving the office proud and full of gratitude that someone cared so much about his future. He was thrilled that the great man no longer regarded Willie Rains as a callboy or prompter or even a stage manager, but an actor. If Sir Herbert Beerbohm Tree believed in his prospects, then Rains knew he could and, by God, he would succeed.

During the next eighteen months of concentrated effort, Rains changed his entire manner of speaking, developing an accent that was, according to David Lean, "neither Oxford nor American, but proper English in its purest spoken form." In a 1935 magazine article, Rains himself explained:

Diction is of the greatest importance. An overly British accent should be avoided as much as an overly American one. The ideal accent is that of the actor who is readily understandable on both sides of the Atlantic. As an Englishman playing American roles, I often became confused with that other Rains who is the Englishman… The point is all my training and compulsion strains to make me say "gaar-ahge," but American audiences would not know what I mean unless I say "ga-rahge." The accent must be on the last syllable. The only thing that has become standardized in both countries is the broad "a." I can say "ahfter" in any character and get away with it.

But dare I say "clark" in an American role? No, I must say "clerk." And as an Englishman, the British fans would write vicious notes if I said "derby" instead of "darby." Take the word "police." In England, a bobby is simply a "pleeceman" but in America a cop is very definitely a "poolice-man." Also in England I would never stay in a hotel, but would always stop in a hotel.

Eventually, after months of self-discipline, Rains lost any trace of the accent which betrayed his East End upbringing. Gone too was the speech impediment. As he shaved each morning, the actor would repeat the phrase "oysters are proper for dinner," rolling the "r"s with great exaggeration and flourish. He still studied the dictionary diligently, page by page, learning the proper pronunciation of every word, and continued to do so for the next several years.

By the time Rains was sixteen, he was earning enough to live by himself in a Brixton rooming house. 1906 was an important year for another reason in his association with Tree: A seemingly insignificant incident would bring him to the notice of another celebrity of the period. Sir Herbert often produced and acted in the works of internationally renowned playwright George Bernard Shaw, who respected Sir Herbert because he always mounted a noteworthy production. One afternoon, the eminent playwright was present during a rehearsal of his play *The Admirable Bashville* and suddenly felt unwell. Sir Herbert dispatched young Rains to fetch a doctor. The matter was of little consequence, as Shaw was not seriously ill; Rains promptly forgot about the incident – until reminded of it by G.B.S., who recalled the episode in detail when the two men met again in 1944 for the filming of Shaw's *Caesar and Cleopatra*.

During the years prior to World War I, Rains never took any formal acting lessons. Instead, he had the best possible "on-the-job training," watching the greatest performers of the age, observing their body movements, facial expressions, what they did with their hands. His first opportunity to formally appear on stage, however, was in a small part with no words: As an opium addict, he thrashed about madly in a drug den in Tree's production of an adaptation of Dickens' unfinished novel *The Mystery of Edwin Drood*. (Rains would star in the film version when Universal adapted the story in 1935.)

As Rains' speech improved, so did his position; he was promoted from callboy to prompter, recording one amusing incident in the handwritten notes he made for his unfinished autobiography. During a rehearsal for a production of *Faust* in which Sir Herbert was starring, Rains was off in a corner of the wings with a small light on his script. Tree loudly ordered the light to be turned off, as it was destroying the illusion of shadows. After his outburst, the great actor forgot his lines and called out to the prompter (Rains), "What do I say?" The reply: "I don't know, Chief – I can't see the book because you told me to turn out the light." Bellowing that Rains was an idiot, Tree hit upon a fitting solution for the cheeky young man: He put Rains on stage as an extra with his back to the audience. Whenever Tree needed a cue, he would tap Rains with his foot. Rains was ordered to learn all the lines overnight. However, during the next day's dress rehearsal, it was Rains who, because of his sleepless night, forgot the dialogue. Tree exploded, but Rains was not dismissed; instead he was "relocated" as an assistant both to the electrician and, more importantly, to the stage manager. By June 1910, Rains was the assistant state manager for Tree's production of *Henry VIII*, which opened on September 1 and ran until early April 1911. As assistant stage manager, Rains spent most of each day compiling manuscripts, keeping records for future revivals, and in numerous other menial tasks which should have been taken care of by the stage manager. Feeling taken advantage of, Rains complained to the business manager and requested a raise, but was told "the Chief said no," and that Rains "had lost his senses in demanding the salary he did."

In those days, Rains had a short fuse. Stalking out of the theatre, he headed to the nearest pub where he met a friend employed at the Haymarket. After Rains explained his situation, the friend told him there was an acting position open at the theatre. And so on June 28, 1911, Claude Rains made his formal acting debut in a small role as Slag, a beggar, in Lord Dunsany's play *The Gods of the Mountain*. He was also given the position of assistant to the stage manager, Charles La Trobe, and a respectable wage for both jobs. La Trobe was sufficiently impressed with the young man's abilities to offer him the dual job of assistant stage manager and actor in Harley Granville-Barker's Australian touring company of Maeterlinck's *The Blue Bird*. To go abroad all expenses paid, earning

a salary, was indeed a thrill and Rains accepted immediately. He signed a contract and returned to His Majesty's to give his official notice.

When Rains told Tree why he was leaving, it became apparent that Tree had never been approached about Rains' request for a raise. The business manager, confronted with his lie, tried to justify his actions by saying, "The boy was becoming impossible." Rains argued that he wasn't "impossible" at all, in fact he was very grateful to Sir Herbert, but he had to stand up for his rights. Tree regretted losing the budding young talent, but Rains had already signed a contract with the Haymarket touring company. Besides, it was time to move on. It was another opportunity to rise above the ordinary.

CHAPTER 2
Love and War

When Rains left for Australia in June 1911, he was experienced in just about every aspect of working in the theatre, gaining an excellent reputation as he rose through the ranks of callboy, prompter, electrician, property man, assistant stage manager and finally stage manager. The last decade had been a thorough education. Because Rains still pondered Tree's suggestion that acting might be his real forte, he continued to read plays, practice voice recitation and perform before a mirror. While he served as stage manager for Harley Granville-Barker's company in Australia, he also acted in Maeterlinck's *The Blue Bird*, Shaw's *You Never Can Tell* and a 17th-century comedy, *The Antipodes*. But these small roles afforded insufficient experience for him to consider himself an actor. He found performing enticing but knew he still had much to learn. Rains was fortunate to be associated at various times with some of the most respected and brilliant talents of the period, as he later recalled: "I was the prompter with Mrs. Patrick Campbell and I was callboy for Ellen Terry. It was a treat to watch her in *The Winter's Tale*. I stood in a corner and wept. Mrs. Pat had beauty and magic. I adored Constance Collier as Nancy in *Oliver Twist*. When she played Cleopatra, she was the most beautiful woman on the stage. And I think [Johnston] Forbes-Robertson was the greatest Hamlet."

There were other valuable lessons to learn. Rains witnessed all kinds of bad behavior, unreasonable demands and childish tantrums from theatre "divas" of both sexes. He made himself a promise never to indulge in such unprofessional demonstrations. It was true he possessed a temper and was a very tense individual, but he learned never to display impatience or exasperation in the presence of anyone in the company.

After six months, Rains returned to London in December to serve as stage manager and play small roles in a variety of productions for different companies. Juggling the two positions kept him quite busy, running from venue to venue in the West End. He soon realized he had to make a decision and concentrate on one vocation or the other. While he liked being an actor, and it would bring welcome public recognition, employment opportunities were steadier as a stage manager. Acting was a much less reliable occupation, and Rains knew there was nothing romantic about poverty or constant economic deprivation and financial worries. His reputation as a responsible and versatile young man had impressed London's theatre impresarios, and he was continuously employed in some capacity. But he was still unsure about which path to take. Later, he told an interviewer, "I never really had any ambition – never really had a thought-out goal. I was a bit of a muddler, and I had no plan at all for life. I never had any kind of frantic ambition." This quote is confirmed by the notes he made while preparing his autobiography when he was in his seventies. Several scribblings stand out: He was "befuddled" because he had "no ambition – no ambition," and he "did not want to be a Sir Herbert." Still, Rains was greatly impressed by Tree's ability to hold an audience spellbound. Rains might not possess an inner drive to act, but he relished the idea he could become someone other than himself and hold an audience in his grasp. Additionally, acting enabled one temporarily to escape into another personality and into another "reality." In his sketchy remembrances, written in very tiny letters on yellow legal pads and pieces of cardboard, Rains indicated he was always "surprised" at his achievements; there is the question "What to do with life? Just go on — don't know." In an interview in 1947, when he was fifty-seven, Rains acknowledged: "I'm not ambitious in the sense that I have had a goal toward which I worked, but I must work, work, work." This aspect of his personality never changed throughout his life.

As an actor, Rains began to be hired for small parts, such as Grasset in *The Green Cockatoo*, and then in early April, he enjoyed his first substantial role as Omayi, a member of Paris' Japanese colony, in *Typhoon* at the Haymarket. The show was so successful that it was moved to the larger Queens Theatre, and then transferred to the even larger Globe Theatre to accommodate audiences. The show ran for 202 performances until August 23. For the first time in his life, there was the luxury of money to subsidize a decent, quality wardrobe; he became quite a dapper dresser. Tree then asked Rains to serve as assistant manager for his new production at the Haymarket, *Within the Law*, which would prove to be highly successful (a run of 426 performances).

Busy professionally during this period just before the first World War, Rains was finding personal involvements just as consuming. Feeling the pangs of what he later called "puppy love," he had his first serious relationship at age sixteen when he fell for a young walk-on actress named Elsie Rowbottom, herself only fourteen or fifteen. Saving up his money, he bought her a silver bracelet, but she resisted his advances and was wooed by Tree's wardrobe master. About the same time, according to the descendants of a twenty-year-old seamstress named Rachel Nelson, Rains got the young woman pregnant, but Tree made her a suitable "severance payment" on behalf of the capable employee he didn't want to lose.

While working for Granville-Barker, Rains was besotted by the company's leading lady, the talented, beautiful and sophisticated Isabel Jeans. She was flattered by his attentions; Rains was rather seductive-looking with his piercing eyes and his unruly thick brown hair, usually tousled romantically. He was no longer the naive teenager who might once have been irresponsible with a partner. However, he could be – and often was, as a track record of six marriages amply illustrates – rash. If Rains met a woman on Monday and decided he loved her and wanted to sleep with her, by Friday he would propose. His convictions about a woman's virtue, convictions he held throughout his life, were decidedly Victorian, and

LILLAH McCARTHY
GRANVILLE BARKER

PRESENT

"Iphigenia in Tauris"

YALE BOWL

MAY 15

MAY 15 1915

complicated by his own strongly developed integrity. Apparently, the young Jeans was equally impulsive, and intrigued by this talented, intense-looking man who begged her to marry him. The couple tied the knot on March 27, 1913.

In 1914, Granville-Barker sent for Rains, telling him: "I'd like you to take my company of *Fanny's First Play* to America. You'll act as my representative until I get there. All you have to do is watch the production, make sure that everything is all right on stage. Clock the audience as it comes in, in order to check the box office, handle finances – ah – make speeches about Mr. Shaw and me before different clubs and organizations – I'd like you to see to it that the publicity is good, too – and, oh yes – I nearly forgot, you'll play a small part." Accordingly, Claude and Isabel sailed for the United States the same month. For the remainder of 1914, he managed the Granville-Barker company as it toured the U.S.

In 1915, Rains made his American acting debut as Spintho in Shaw's *Androcles and the Lion.* He also played a herdsman in a performance of Euripides' *Iphigenia in Tauris* starring Granville-Barker and his wife Lillah McCarthy, which was performed at the Yale Bowl on May 15. This production was mounted twice more (May 31 and June 5) at the College of the City of New York Stadium. Even in small parts, Rains was beginning to be noticed. His performance at City College was reviewed: "Claude Rains seems to have modified somewhat the sheer physical vigor of his performance as the herdsman, but it remains an exceedingly effective contribution to the play...."

Not surprisingly, the Rainses' marriage was not going smoothly, probably due to the couple's immaturity and career clashes. Rains still embraced Victorian standards, which dictated that a wife subordinate her needs and desires to those of her husband without question. However, Isabel possessed a strong personality and felt quite differently. Then, too, with her beauty and talent, she was in great demand by theatrical producers in England and could afford to be independent. Rains later confessed to having little control over his short temper. Another important factor in the break-up may have been the fact that Rains liked America immensely and was not anxious to return to England, whereas Isabel was quite homesick. When world war forced the touring company to return to Britain, Isabel deserted her husband in America. Eventually the couple legally dissolved the short-lived marriage. Five years later, Isabel married barrister and playwright Gilbert Edward Wakefield, youngest son of the former Bishop of Birmingham. She became one of England's foremost character actresses, aged well and retained much of her elegance, evident in her performance as Leslie Caron's stylish aunt in *Gigi* (1958). She died in 1985. Though Rains would marry another five times, in 1962, when he was seventy-one years old, he remarked to fellow actor Frederick Rolf that Isabel Jeans had made it impossible for him to ever be happy with any other woman.

After only a short time in America, Rains felt great affection for the country. More than anything, he admired the opportunities it afforded, and the fact

Isabel Jeans

that, unlike England, the country wasn't controlled by a centuries-old class system. While obviously there were rich people and poor people, just as back home, in America, Rains did not feel the stigma of "minding his betters." In England, he believed he would never truly be able to rise above his lower-class background, no matter how well he spoke or how educated he became. Above all, he liked the open friendliness of Americans, as opposed to the formality and seeming aloofness of the English. He would have remained in the States, but for one important thing: the war. As a British citizen, Rains was subject to conscription, but he felt a moral obligation to return to his native country. He had no grandiose ideas of the nobility of war, or illusions about glory and honor, but he believed that it was his duty to serve. Sailing home, there was time to reflect on his life and immediate future: "I didn't particularly want to fight anybody, and I certainly didn't want to get hurt. So when a friend said he could fix me up with a commission in the Army Service Corps, as a second lieutenant working with supplies, I decided that was ideal." Perhaps another reason for his decision to enter the army was a general dissatisfaction underlying his life at the time. Even continuing a career in the theatre was still up in the air, since he felt he had relatively little to show for the more than ten years he had spent in the profession. Maybe it was time to try something different.

As it turned out, the friend couldn't be of assistance after all; early in the conflict, the British Army was overflowing with officers and what they needed was enlisted men. By February 1916, Rains was in a quandary: He knew sooner or later he would be conscripted, and he wanted to choose the type of unit in which he would serve so that he could remain in England. His request for officers' training was denied, and choice seemed unlikely unless he made his decision quickly. As Rains would tell the story, his predicament was solved one afternoon when he saw in the street "a magnificent big fellow about a foot taller than I was, and twice as wide, wearing seven yards of gorgeous tartan pleated about him. Below his military jacket, the tilt of his kilt was jaunty. It was a beautiful costume." Captivated by the heroic-looking, handsomely dressed Scottish soldier, Rains immediately entered the enlistment office of the London Scots, which then consisted only of volunteers, and gave the most convincing performance of his life. That day, the stage manager became a soldier, reflecting the young man's tendency to act impulsively and emotionally. Rains' military records gave his address as 37 Fairmont Road in Brixton Hill. Although they were no longer living together, the dissolution of his marriage hadn't been completed in the courts, so he listed Isabel Jeans as his wife.

Rains received the service number 5842 and was posted to the 3/14 Battalion. From February through April 1916, he was billeted at "The Angles" in East Sheen for combat training. Initially, Rains enjoyed his new role as a soldier, donning his dress kilt whenever opportunity permitted. He felt a sense of newfound pride as a stalwart man of the Hodden Grey kilt – the company known to the Germans as the "Ladies from Hell." It was drama at its highest and he was delighted. In June, he was transferred to the 2nd Battalion and

The London Scots, 1914.

three weeks later left for France from Southampton with the British Expeditionary Force. Twenty-six-year-old Rains had no idea how much this stint in the military would affect the course of his life.

The London Scots had a splendid history long before the Great War. Given their unique *esprit de corps* and reputation for exceptional bravery, it is not surprising this battalion was one of the first sent to France. It is also not surprising that within months, the unit was recognized for its extreme heroism and terrible losses. Though it's unknown if they ever met, Rains was literally in the "company" of several other young men who would also become famous film and stage stars: Basil Rathbone, Ronald Colman and Herbert Marshall (who would lose his left leg after being shot in the knee), all served in the London Scots.

The ordeals were horrifying: ineffective communication between headquarters and officers in the field, lack of up-to-date ground maps, outmoded or defective rifles, no warm food, little sleep and uniforms unsuitable for modern warfare. The footwear worn by the Brigade was totally inadequate, not insulated for the trenches and mud of Flanders. These soldiers had no boots, only shoes and spats, and the headgear was a cloth cap instead of a helmet. While all aspects of the war were terrible, chief among the horrors was the use of poison gas, a ghastly tactic for which the Allies were not prepared. In the early years, directives about mustard gas consisted of little more than the absurdly inadequate "Every man should carry a large handkerchief or piece of flannel, which in case of gas attack, could be wetted and fastened across the mouth and nostrils." The effect of chemical warfare was not understood until experienced. Additionally, after gas masks were issued, instruction manuals stated that "the mask was to be carried on the head so it could be rolled down over the face immediately." But once helmets became standard issue, this was impossible, and in actual combat a soldier soon discovered he could not retrieve his mask and adjust it to his face in time to avoid the poison fumes.

In his documented history of the London Scottish, Lt. Col. J.H. Lindsay described one skirmish between the canal near the Vimy Ridge and a town called Loos, in which losses were at 40,000: "Trench warfare seemed to have become a settled state of existence, in which toil, suffering and losses went on without any visible result." Soon after his arrival in France, Rains was posted to a position on that infamous Vimy Ridge. He carried his entrenching tool on his left side and a haversack (containing rations, washing and shaving materials and a cardigan) on his back. He did not wear the blue Glengarry bonnet he had in England, but a khaki tam o'shanter. It must have been a miserable experience. Trenches were often filled with water up to the men's knees; 600 soldiers had to sleep, eat and do any "business" in 300 yards of trench space. Lice, rats and dysentery were omnipresent, as was the stench of bodies decaying on the battlefield between trenches, or caught up on barbed wire.

On July 18, 1916, Rains was appointed lance corporal, a promotion made official on September 10. Drawing on the experience of his youth, he knew how to endure deprivations and squalor, and was never one to complain about hardships. Rains' recollections of the war focused on his fellow soldiers rather than the misery of the trenches. Many years later, in a speech he gave in Toronto, he related the following anecdote:

You know, way back in [September] 1916 I behaved very badly to a Canadian sergeant. I was in France with a Scottish Regiment, in a kilt at Vimy Ridge. We had been there some time and were to be relieved by the Canadians. Well, they came and the regiment went, and I was left behind acting as a conducting NCO. My job was to point out the bad spots to the Canadian Sergeant of the company that was to occupy my company's section – bombing platforms, consolidated craters, advance posts. When we had done, it was dark, and I had to leave to overtake the regiment the next morning. Sgt. Hunter, I think his name was, and I shared the same dugout that night, but before hitting the hay we had a talk and a smoke. I was smoking my best friend – a beautiful straight-grained briar pipe. The sergeant, a lover of pipes, admired it, polished it, and told me he would like to have one like it. We finished our talk. I took off my haversack and an apron we wore over the kilt. I blew out the candle and went to sleep. When I woke up in the morning, the sergeant had gone and I couldn't find my pipe, so being human I thought the worst. Well, I pulled myself together because I could not fool about with time – I put on my haversack and my apron, took up my rifle and made my way along the duck boards in the trenches to battalion headquarters where I was to be picked up by a truck…. I was hot, and I dove into the pocket of my kilt apron for my handkerchief and there I found a note. This is what it said: "Corporal Rains, in case you forget it in your hurry to get away, I have put your nice briar pipe in your haversack."

Although detailed information concerning Rains' military record is scanty, he was evidently a diligent soldier, and on November 4, 1916, was promoted to full corporal. Three days later, somewhere on the Vimy Ridge, Rains himself became another casualty of the infamous location: a victim of the dreaded poison gas, and sprayed additionally with shrapnel pieces. His vocal cords were burned, and he lost ninety per-cent of the sight in his right eye. After five months at the Front, Corporal Rains returned to England on a stretcher. The next three weeks were spent recovering in a military hospital. According to Rains, doctors were astonished by his "miraculous recovery." When he was finally able to speak again (many wounded soldiers weren't), his voice was huskier, deeper, with a more intimate timbre; Rains the performer considered it a change for the better. The damage to his eye, however, was unequivocally negative. While the physical appearance was normal, the ability to see was practically gone. In hospital, Rains learned how to maintain balance without depth perception, and for the remainder of his life, very few people knew about the handicap. Oddly, however, when his daughter asked him just how he came to be blind in one eye, he told her he had "stepped on a mine," and never related it to the gas attack. Released from hospital on November 22, Rains was posted back to the First Battalion, despite his injuries: the London Scots was a fighting unit. There was no question of Rains being returned to the Western Front, so once again he applied for a commission. He now had a much better chance: With the continuous and mounting loss of officers, there were more openings, especially for a wounded soldier from the London Scottish.

Enlisted men usually were required to attend officers' training school; as a corporal, however, written approval from Rains' commanding officer sufficed. While awaiting completion of necessary paperwork, he remained with the regiment, assigned to clerical work until May 4. Finally, transferred to the Bedfordshire Regiment with a temporary commission as a lieutenant, he was posted to the 13th Transport Workers Battalion at Croydon, Surrey. Ironically, this is exactly the type of position his friend had promised to secure for him in '15. Rains maintained this safe assignment for the remainder of the war. Evidently he did well, for on March 22, 1918, he was promoted to Temporary Captain with compensating salary, a position in which he remained, probably enjoying the status and privileges of a ranking officer as much as the increase in his monthly paycheck.

In a rather strange way, Rains had found a niche in the army. Service had given him respectability and security he had never known in the theatre. He was an officer, at a time when class could often count for more than merit in the British army, and he liked the camaraderie, discipline and associated status. After the military, acting seemed a "sissified" occupation: "Go back to the theatre? Put paint on my face? Nothing so effeminate." The army had made "a real man" out of him. Armistice was declared in November, but Rains did not receive his official release from active duty until February 1919. If he wanted to retain his commission, he could re-enlist as a captain, an idea which appealed to him. Years later, after Rains had become a film star, studio-issued press releases contained many exaggerations about his war record (as they did for most celebrities who had served). One claimed that Rains returned to England as soon as war broke out, when in actuality he waited nearly a year; another had him fighting for over three years on the Western Front in France; another had him "almost buried alive when a shell exploded and a number of trench sandbags were hurled on top of him." Rains himself never discussed the details of his war experiences, saying only that he went in as a private, emerged as a captain, and was gassed. His daughter once asked him if he had ever killed anyone during the war. "He never answered me and just grew very quiet," she remembered. "In fact, he did not speak to me or anyone for the remainder of the day," and went about the house, quite despondent.

Interestingly, Rains elected to remain in the military. He applied for and received papers for a post in British Somaliland. But it happened that his re-enlistment papers required the signature of his commanding officer who, on that particular afternoon, was not in his office. So Rains went up to the West End to enjoy a Beatrice Lillie show. By chance, he ran into an old friend who told him about an available acting role that had his name on it. The temptation was great: return to the environment which had been the only real home he had known since the age of ten, a place in which he felt comfortable and secure. Rains promptly forgot how dashing he looked in his Hodden Grey kilt; as an actor, he could wear any costume he wanted. In the theatre world, he was safe, figuratively and literally. More importantly, as an actor, he felt a sense of power; he could become anyone he wanted to be. Wisely, however, he decided to hedge his bets: He would return to the theatre for a trial year, and just to be certain, he did not relinquish his army commission. It was a risk, because as an active serviceman, he could be recalled for duty at any time. But it was a risk worth taking. He saw no need to be hasty – and after all, there was that monthly

As the mad poet in Reparation.

check from the military to consider for a young man who was practical and careful about finances.

Rains had not only survived the Great War, he had prospered. The potential for a life-threatening or disfiguring injury had been turned to his advantage for a career on the stage. He might not be the tallest actor in the company, or classically handsome, but he could boast of a remarkable speaking voice, like "gravel, coated in honey," which to many feminine fans reflected mysterious seductiveness.

There was one final change. Army buddies had teased him unmercifully about the name William

Claude, the initials "W.C." signifying, in the vernacular, "water closet." Far from seeing the joke, Rains considered such comments tasteless. When he returned to the stage, he made the decision to drop his first name. The truant boy Willie Wains was gone forever, banished back to the slums of the East End. From now on, theatre marquees, and eventually silver screens across the world, would credit the man he had become, the elegant, the urbane, the stylish – Claude Rains.

Returning to acting was not an easy road, especially since his experience consisted of only a few small roles. Although his reputation as an efficient and reliable stage manager was now five years in the past, he was still remembered by most producers. He checked out his friend's suggestion: American producer Gilbert Miller's new production, which would tour the northern cities. Miller was aware of Rains' background and offered him work as stage manager, but Rains insisted he also wanted to perform. It was agreed that Rains would take on the crew position on the condition he also could appear in small speaking parts.

After the summer, Rains returned to London for the new fall season, and was assigned as stage manager for a play (based on Tolstoy's *The Living Corpse*) titled *Reparation*, with a small acting role as Ivan Petrovich. Starring Henry Ainley, it opened at the St.

Reparation *program.*

Julius Caesar program.

James Theatre on September 26, 1919, and enjoyed a decent run through January 3, 1920. For the first time in his life, Rains saw his name mentioned by a critic in the *Times*. In reporting news from London, *Variety* noted, "The Army has done [Ainley] good, both physically and histrionically.... Marion Terry gives a fine performance...." Rains' name was listed among the seven "others who lend distinction to a long cast."

Rains next stage-managed Ainley's production of *Julius Caesar*, appearing as Casca. The play ran through March 20 with 83 performances, and Rains achieved his goal of critical notice: "The envious Casca of Mr. Claude Rains is full of first-class work," "An impressive Casca from Mr. Claude Rains," and, in *The Saturday Review*, "[The play features] notable new readings of individual parts, such as Mr. Claude Rains' Casca." Only the *Spectator* reviewer felt that Rains' portrayal was weak, the writer adding, "With a good deal more restraint and light and shade Casca might become an effective splenetic." This call for restraint was valid and constructive criticism, as Rains

did have the tendency to be dramatic. So while the early good reviews excited him, he began to recognize that at times subtlety was needed for effectiveness. Being "big" was acceptable during the Victorian period, but by the 1920s, as a style it was on the wane. Praise was, of course, delightful, but he did not learn as much from compliments as from comments that pinpointed a shortcoming.

Immediately following *Julius Caesar*, Gilbert Miller scheduled *Uncle Ned* in Sheffield, starring Ainley and Herbert Marshall's wife Edna Best, with Rains repeating his duties as stage manager and tackling the small role of Mears for 49 performances. One critic made a short but, for Rains, significant comment: "An excellent bit of work is put in by that clever young character actor, Mr. Claude Rains, as a detective." No matter how famous or talented the headliner might be, a good supporting actor could still shine.

This fact was highlighted in Rains' very next production, when two weeks later he appeared as Inspector Khlestakov in Gogol's *The Government Inspector*. Opening April 11 at the Duke of York Theatre, the show received favorable notices, especially for star

BRUTUS: "Was the crown offered him thrice?"
CASCA (MR. CLAUDE RAINS): "Ay, marry, was't, and he put it by thrice."
28

Julius Caesar.

CR and Stella Freeman in The Government Inspector.

Maurice Moscovich. Rains made a significant impression on the *Observer* critic: "Mr. Claude Rains … did an admirable job…. [S]lim and dapper and light, Mr. Rains looked as if he [might] have been blown away by this tornado of a man; but he held his own, and the contrast of his style with that of the Governor provided one of the most enjoyable exhibitions of comedy that we have seen for some time." Another critic stated, "Mr. Claude Rains plays the adventurer with the right air of impudence. … [He] was especially good as the half-drunken boaster in a scene that calls for exceptional acting." But even with such praise and consistently good performances, Rains could not land leading roles. The London theatre was still, more or less, tied into an "old chap" network which made things difficult for a newcomer.

During the summer of 1920, Rains decided to try his hand in the relatively new medium of motion pic-

tures, appearing in a silent titled *Build Thy House*, directed by Fred Goodwins. Quite possibly the role – a drunken loafer – was secured for him by the picture's male lead, Henry Ainley. As it turned out, making a movie did not excite him, probably because he was unable to utilize his most precious asset – his voice. The film made no impression on critics of the period. The experience was sufficient to convince Rains to stick with the theatre.

After *The Government Inspector* closed in London, Rains toured England as Cassius in *Julius Caesar*, a much larger and more important role. His summer season ended in August at Wimbledon when he appeared in *The Jest*, an Italian play set in the time of Lorenzo the Magnificent and once again starring Henry Ainley. (Rains' role of the poet, Gianetto, was played on Broadway with great success by John Barrymore.) Rains was singled out by several critics, one writing: "[The play is] memorable for the sinister figure drawn by Mr. Claude Rains as Gianetto. Mr. Rains gives a powerful portrayal of the vengeful poet. The character had qualities of introspection to which the actor gives admirable expression. Mr. Rains will probably go far in his profession." Such comments increased Rains' confidence and reinforced his approach in establishing a commanding presence on stage.

However, he was feeling dissatisfied in his personal life. While he always got along with his peers, he seemed unable or unwilling to establish any significant friendships. When he was an army officer, most of his companions were also in the military, and on the rare occasions when he did "make merry," undoubtedly it was in the usual pattern of carousing and drinking. But he disliked partying and all types of nightlife in general, so except for going to plays, his entertainment was limited to reading. Few people ever knew when Rains was upset, let alone in genuine emotional turmoil; he would never display or reveal his feelings except perhaps through one of his stage or film characters. Even those who liked and attempted to befriend him found his self-established barriers precluded intimacy. Throughout his life, he developed few deep relationships.

After the dissolution of his marriage to Isabel Jeans, the disappointment of losing the first woman he really loved had finally abated, with loneliness overcoming Rains. He seems to have been attracted to the companionship of very young women, so it is not surprising that he soon noticed a pretty eighteen-year-old co-star named Marie Hemingway. They had dinner together frequently; Rains was attracted by her good looks and taken by her "needing him"; he wanted to sleep with her, but not until they were legally husband and wife. In what would become a routine with women, Rains' hastiness did not allow time for any real relationship to mature. As with Isabel, he fell prey to his desires and acted impetuously by persuading Marie to marry him. They wed at St. Martin's Register Office on December 20, 1920. The couple resided at her small flat until they moved to 28A Camden Grove in London. Rains hated living in apartments and wanted a small cottage with a garden.

Whatever her personality, Marie was likely too immature to deal with a complex man like Rains. He could be moody and, when studying a role, would not let anyone or anything disturb his concentration. His narcissistic nature required catering, and sometimes he could be a fearfully demanding figure especially when he was in one of his moods. His predilection for whiskey, especially when combined with a short temper, often made him appear prone to violence. What could aggravate any unpleasant situation was his tendency for making spiteful comments; he could

CR's second wife, Marie Hemingway.

As the opium-smoking lead in Daniel.

also be facetious, or unaccountably quiet. In his strange way of showing affection, he would tease in a manner that was sometimes hurtful and insensitive. It is not surprising then that their marriage would fail to afford either Claude or Marie any real happiness or fulfilling companionship. The couple quickly became estranged.

At the beginning of 1921, Rains was fortunate to be cast in a role which became a turning point in his career. *Daniel* was an adaptation of the Louis Verneuil play originally written for the acclaimed Sarah Bernhardt, who had acted this male part during her last season in London. Over seventy, and recovered from a stage injury which had led to the amputation of a leg, the Divine Sarah still gave a performance of poetic masculinity and youth – a tribute to her great talent and well-deserved reputation. It was an exciting challenge and Rains relished the opportunity to display his skills.

The play opened in mid–January 1921 and had a successful six-week run. Rains was supported by an excellent cast, including Edith Evans and C. Aubrey Smith. The story was high melodrama, with young Daniel sacrificing himself (by smoking sixty pipes of opium a day) because he and his brother are in love with the same woman. The last act provided a great scene, when the young man makes a passionate speech about the triangle affair. The role was a dramatic triumph for Rains, even though his character is not seen on stage until the third act in a four-act play. One critic noted: "Mr. Claude Rains scores another marked success as Daniel. It is a difficult part, but Mr. Rains plays it brilliantly. He leaves an abiding picture of a queer, pathetic, lovable, but abnormal human being crushed." The *Illustrated London News* stated: "Mr. Claude Rains' tour de force in the act in which the morphinomanic [*sic*] runs through a veritable gamut of emotion – all revealed English stage-art at its best." Although such praise served to reinforce Rains' inclination for highly dramatic gestures and emphatic speech patterns, he was learning how to be subtle, as another review illustrated: "Claude Rains gave a superbly poetic rendering of Daniel, untheatrical, simple, and touching – as fine a bit of artistry as any audience could wish for." The *Stage's* critic felt the play's success was "due largely to the splendid work now done in the title-role by Mr. Claude Rains."

The genre of the drawing room comedy was quite popular in London and *Polly with a Past*, written by George Middleton and Guy Bolton and based on a Somerset Maugham comedy, gave Rains a small role as "The Stranger." Regardless of the wonderful cast – Noël Coward, Edith Evans and C. Aubrey Smith – the play lasted only a month. Rains again managed to get noticed. One critic "regretted Mr. Claude Rains wasn't on till the last scene." Another stated, "Claude Rains' character was unnecessary to the play, but we would not have [wanted to miss his] finished thumbnail sketch."

Instead of going out on the summer circuit, Rains elected to remain in London to work. His next production, Baroness Orczy's costume drama *The Legion of Honour*, was dismissed by most critics. At this time, he was still in the Army Reserve and receiving a monthly stipend for his officer's commission. If, however, he chose not to act in trite plays, he had to re-evaluate his situation. Having tasted artistic success, even on a limited scale, Rains had found acting a satisfying profession in many respects. Moreover, he was able to select parts, which put him in control of his life. If he decided to return to the army, even as an officer, he would have to conform and obey orders. Unquestionably, there was a sense of comfort in the theatre as well as satisfaction in receiving flattering reviews. He had established an excellent reputation with general managers and directors as an untemperamental and professional artist. Rains made the major decision to relinquish his commission; he sent in his letter of resignation on September 1 and staked his entire future on being an actor. Now there would no longer be a monthly check unless he found work.

In late January 1922, he secured a part in Mary Roberts Rinehart's thriller *The Bat*, which opened at

CR (*pictured above his signature*) in The Bat.

the St. James and ran for an impressive 327 performances through early November. Prior to its London success, *The Bat* had enjoyed a two-year stint on Broadway (and went on to remain a theatre "chestnut" for decades). Rains' small role of Billy, a Japanese servant (casting regarded as both ridiculous and inappropriate today wasn't given a second thought at the time), contributed to his lifelong professional philosophy of accepting small roles for a substantial paycheck, or if they afforded him a challenge.

Throughout most of 1922, Rains worked six nights and two afternoons a week, spending the balance of his off-time in rehearsals for his next play. For someone who claimed to have "no ambition," he kept up this rather frantic pace. He had no choice financially, and with plays closing sooner than expected, found himself in a touchy financial situation.

To supplement an inconsistent and meager income, Rains became a speech teacher at Herbert Beerbohm Tree's Royal Academy of Dramatic Art. Two years earlier, he had performed two scenes from Shakespeare for the RADA students and made quite an impression on the staff because of his excellent command of the English language. An effective instructor, he was a member of the auditioning panel who sat in judgment on young applicants. Two promising ones were Charles Laughton and John Gielgud.

During this period, Rains was "extremely attractive to women,"
according to his student at the Royal Academy of Dramatic Art,
John Gielgud.

In his autobiography *Distinguished Company*,
Gielgud recalled that Rains was

> already much in demand as a successful
> character actor. He lacked inches and wore
> lifts in his shoes to increase his height.
> Stocky but handsome, with broad shoul-
> ders and a mop of thick brown hair which
> he brushed over one eye, he wore beauti-
> fully cut double-breasted suits, starched
> shirts with pointed collars and big cuffs,
> and wide satin ties. He had piercing dark
> eyes and a beautiful throaty voice.... Need-
> less to say, all the girls in my class at the
> Royal Academy of Dramatic Art, where
> he was one of the best and most popular
> teachers, were hopelessly in love with him.

Laughton never gave Rains any
particular credit, but whenever Gielgud
was interviewed about his early days he
always complimented Rains: "[He] was
somebody who taught me a great deal …
and I am certainly grateful to him for his
kindness and consideration toward me…"
Another time he recalled fondly: "Rains
was an enormously favorite teacher with
us all – his vitality and enthusiasm made
him a delightful teacher … I worked as
hard as I could, and imitated Rains' acting until I became extremely mannered."
Also, as the young Gielgud understudied
for Rains several times, he recalled, "[A]s
Dubedat in *The Doctor's Dilemma,* [Rains]
was just the romantic boyish figure I
hoped to be…" But after 1925, they never
acted together again.

Decades later, in 1951, in a speech,
appropriately enough, about good speech,
Rains recalled his days at RADA:

> Like all teachers, I discovered that
> some of my pupils were more tem-
> peramental than others – some were
> more adept than others but nearly
> all of them had speech difficulties
> of one kind or another. So at some
> point during their studies, they could
> be sure of one particular assignment.
> It was a tongue twister – a series of verbal
> acrobatics from a book of nonsense titled
> *Grim Tales Made Gay.* American poet Guy
> Wetmore Carrly had evidently discovered
> it was more fun not to take things seriously
> and he had written a takeoff in rhyme of
> the Bluebeard story. That gentleman was so
> fond of severed heads as he called it "How
> the helpmate of Bluebeard made free with
> the door."

Being a teacher was a time-consuming responsibility, and since Rains felt no deep satisfaction in the
task, he left the Academy after one year. However, it
was at RADA, still wallowing in his estrangement
from Marie, that Rains noticed one of his students,
another 18-year-old who bore a remarkable resemblance to Isabel Jeans: a beauty named Beatrix

Thomson. Rains became (as he confessed years later) "prey to his emotions." Physical needs were obviously natural, but his stringent Victorian morals were thoroughly ingrained and, together with his high personal standards of integrity and/or morality, limited or probably even precluded philandering. He would not indulge in a casual affair; it was untenable to consider subjecting a woman one supposedly cared for to gossip for indulging in relations outside the boundaries of accepted social behavior. If Rains felt strongly attracted to a pretty woman, he seems to have acted on impulse – instead of carrying on an affair, rushing into holy matrimony. He threw aside common sense and fell in love with Beatrix while he was still married to Marie.

Beatrix was apparently one of those young RADA girls that John Gielgud amusingly remarked were "in love with Rains." In all likelihood, she was flattered by the attention lavished upon her by such a dashing figure, not just a highly regarded Academy instructor but one of the theatre's leading new artists. Beatrix was the daughter of an army colonel, spoiled by her family and a bit immature. She was not the type to appreciate Rains' penchant for teasing nor apparently did she realize it was his way of displaying affection. Several years later, during an interview, she claimed that when Rains was one of her instructors, "he made her life miserable, teasing her and assigning parts she did not want to perform." She felt he gave her "negative guidance" but, in spite of this, she prospered at school.

Beatrix and Claude wanted to marry, which meant a legal, official divorce from Marie. On March 15, 1922, Rains wrote to his wife, by this point certain he had made a dreadful mistake in marrying a woman so emotionally unstable. But despite her faults and immaturity, Marie loved Claude in her way. She believed his temper and occasional nastiness resulted from too much strain, and because he never relaxed or took a holiday. For a week she stayed with her parents, hoping Claude would calm down; evidently she had no knowledge of his new relationship. However, on her return, Marie discovered her husband was living at a club. On June 22, Rains went to their flat to gather his belongings and, according to Marie, to "make a scene" over the divorce. Because she would not acquiesce, he flew into a rage and broke a door panel (or threw a drawer at her, according to another version). A frightened Marie agreed to a legal separation and initiated proceedings, citing her husband's

violence and "cruelty," but then unexpectedly, withdrew her appeal. Rains realized the consequences of his actions and told Marie he "promised not to cause further difficulties."

He tried to continue his involvement with Beatrix, but with her proper middle-class upbringing, she refused to continue her relationship on an intimate basis while he was still married and made it clear he would have to marry her. These difficulties were increased by the fact that Rains had no money for settlements, alimony or barristers. At age thirty-three, his personal life was in a shambles, making his professional one precarious. He decided he must tackle the issue with Marie straight on. In a letter dated November 5, 1923, he literally handed over "evidence" of his adultery, making him entirely liable legally: "It is obviously impossible for us to go on through life in this unhappy way. I have not been true to you since we separated last year. I enclose a bill from a hotel where, if investigation should be made on your behalf, sufficient evidence for divorce can be obtained."

Perhaps Rains had come to the conclusion that he was at fault because of his hastiness in marrying Marie, and so he should bear the responsibility. By now he wanted to get out of the marriage by any means possible so he could marry Beatrix. The bill mentioned was from the Bangor Hotel in Torrington Square, stating the room had been let to "Mr. & Mrs. Rains." Although Beatrix was the co-respondent, she refused to become involved or appear as a witness in the proceedings.

This time the divorce went to court, where Marie claimed it was a most unpleasant marriage because of her husband's "bad temper" and "violence" and that he often "assaulted her." Rains probably did use "abusive language" and make accusations about her behavior. (Through the years, Rains rarely spoke of his marriages. His fifth wife, concert pianist Agi Jambor, stated that Claude told her that Marie was "a nymphomaniac." What exactly he meant by using that term is uncertain; a few newspaper clippings at the time of her death in the late 1930s mention emotional problems.) Yet even with his human faults and emotional outbursts, Rains remained a gentleman because he said nothing of her reputed sexual excesses during the proceedings. He would have considered doing so distasteful, much too private to discuss, even in a court of law. He would bear all the blame and pay for it heavily, both monetarily and socially.

In 1923, Rains appeared in five productions, with two earning him critical rewards but little money, causing the actor to quip he was an "artistic success, but a financial failure." A very positive experience was playing Louis Dubedat in George Bernard Shaw's *The Doctor's Dilemma*. Shaw revivals were frequent and, while often short-lived, very well-received by a select group of London theatre-goers. Because most critics and theatrical notables already knew the playwright's work, they tended to concentrate on the actors' interpretations. It was sheer joy for Rains; he loved Shaw's wit and usually gave an excellent performance. Likewise, although unbeknownst to Rains, Shaw admired the actor's work and was quite pleased whenever Rains was in one of his plays.

Some critics suggested that Rains' personality flaws interfered with his giving a convincing characterization. He heeded these criticisms. Like many talented artists Rains had an ego; however, it was more a personal handicap than a professional one, because as an actor, he never carried on like a prima donna and, in fact, earned the reputation of being quite humble. It was his all-consuming, narcissistic need for attention that often dominated his character, but he was learning how to control this tendency. Critics noticed: "Dubedat is a part that all young actors want to play. It is superbly actable and the death scene is one of the best things in modern drama. Mr. Claude Rains subdued his powerful personality and gave a very interesting rendering of this artistic scoundrel, overstressing, if possible, the unpleasant side of the character." Throughout his career, Rains would imbue many characters with an irresistible wicked charm that delighted audiences, and playing a scoundrel was the type of role he loved most. The production ran only 28 performances.

Rains' next play was also a failure, but ironically his involvement was not only noticed, but indirectly would be the catalyst for his future career. In early May, Josef and Karel Capek wrote a Swiftian commentary on society called *The Insect Play*, told in parable, using insect life to represent different phases of the human experience. It was adapted by Nigel Playfair, who would play an important role in Rains' life in the coming years. The critics scorned the play, calling it "a failure of fantasy." But among the cast, which included John Gielgud and Elsa Lanchester, was an actor of Rains' age named James Whale – who of course would emigrate to Hollywood and become a well-known and highly respected film director at Universal, making such classic horror films as *Frankenstein* and *Bride of Frankenstein*. Working in the play with Rains, Whale was taken by his colleague's talent and, above all, how he used his superb voice to suggest the inner thoughts of his character. It was this facility that Whale would remember, causing him to have a hand in bringing Rains to Hollywood, in order to direct the actor in his remarkable (talking) film debut, *The Invisible Man*.

Within three weeks of the *Insect Play* debacle, Rains was working again, and this time his acting earned him even more laurels than usual. Felix Aylmer played the title role in *Robert E. Lee*, with Rains as the young philosopher-soldier David Peel. John Gielgud understudied his former teacher and had a small part as an aide to General Lee. Gielgud idolized Rains to the point of imitation, but soon discovered his own voice and slight frame did not carry the same forcefulness of the stocky little actor. Even when he was not acting, Rains' natural demeanor could intimidate people and Gielgud was very much afraid of "the master," although Rains was gracious and helpful to Gielgud. The play ran through the summer of 1923.

Although Rains still felt he wasn't being adequately compensated, professionally things were going well. In late September, multi-talented actor-manager-writer Seymour Hicks was producing a new play at the Drury Lane titled *Good Luck*. He had met and cast Rains previously, and was determined to employ the actor as often as possible. *Good Luck* opened to mixed reviews, but struck a chord with the theatre crowd; it had a long run, until May 1924. It was a basically trivial work depicting the class of society devoted to horse racing, but its huge cast "offered all the attraction traditionally associated with Drury Lane autumn drama – a crowded stage, an involved plot, and thrilling incidents realistically presented." Among its supporters was *Spectator* critic Martin Armstrong, who wrote, "*Good Luck* is astonishing. It contains every human experience except an aeroplane crash. The play provides over three hours of crowded entertainment.... It is well worth a visit." Such a strong review helped keep the play running for 260 performances, even though a most influential critic, James Agate, vehemently attacked it: "I was not even moderately amused, and it is pitiful to me to see so fine a talent as that of Mr. Claude Rains

On the "Lee's Headquarters" set of Robert E. Lee: CR as David Peel, John Gielgud as an aide to Lee, Felix Aylmer as Lee and Tristan Rawson as Tom Buchanan.

As David Peel, "the philosopher and sniper" in Robert E. Lee.

struggling against masses of carpentry and willfully absurd heroics…."

Finally a divorce was granted in Rains v. Rains in May 1924. Wisely, the actor considered it was best to wait a respectable period of time before marrying again: He was now a public figure and the tabloid newspapers often wrote about the private lives of celebrities, with rumors circulating in theatrical circles about Rains the rogue and adulterer. (Marie Hemingway never remarried. After drinking heavily for many years, she took her own life.)

On November 24, 1924, Claude and Beatrix tied the knot at the Windsor register's Berkshire office. There was no formal wedding, Beatrix's parents were not present, and the couple did not go away for a honeymoon. It might have helped to escape for a while and begin his third marriage in a pleasant and relaxing atmosphere. Not a great actress, Beatrix was very attractive, and her entrance into the theatre was provided by prominent manager Basil Dean, who had seen her at the Royal Academy and offered her a two-year contract. She appeared in several of Dean's productions, once playing a small part opposite Rains in Shaw's *Getting Married*. One critic commented:

"Miss Beatrix Thompson [*sic*] will certainly not be an admirable Leo until she has contrived to master the elements of distinct stage elocution." Rains offered to help, and while Beatrix's acting did improve slightly, her husband's involvement might have caused tension and jealousy. The couple appeared together in several plays that year. Her career moved along well, helped by her demure beauty and her husband's coaching.

There may have been other strains, however, since Beatrix had been pampered and spoiled by her parents, and would not have relished life as a struggling artist – or life as the wife of a struggling artist. Since relinquishing his army commission and paying the lawyers, Rains' financial position was a bit precarious. The couple had moved to Camden Hill, an old-fashioned area where they found a charming little house with a garden. Beatrix was working steadily in small parts, or perhaps she was able to pay the rent from an allowance, because whatever money Rains earned went to pay for his divorce settlement and alimony. Beatrix created the impression that she could handle a difficult man, and initially may have found it very satisfying to be married to an actor so highly regarded.

CHAPTER 3
Crowning Achievements

In the summer of 1924, Rains appeared in several of Bernard Shaw's works in repertory in Hampstead. The Everyman was a small "off–Broadway–type" theatre which only devotees attended, simply because it was located in a rather inaccessible part of London. The manager, Norman Macdermott, initiated a series of two-week runs of what today are seldom-seen Shavian works, including *The Man of Destiny*, in which Rains appeared quite effectively as the twenty-seven-year-old Napoleon Bonaparte, to whom he bore a striking resemblance. As usual in repertory schedules, he repeated his role in the late summer for another two weeks. This play reflected Shaw's usual iconoclastic charges about established reputations of great men and institutions. *The Man of Destiny* was designed to upset all the conventional notions about military glory and martial courage. Several critics felt it was too wordy, thin and even tedious. Some considered Rains an additional weakness: "Mr. Claude Rains was good in the quiet moments, less good in the bombastic ones." By August, when the play was repeated, the actor apparently had made some refinements to his original approach, and/or become more comfortable in the role, because the same critic now wrote: "Mr. Rains improved his Napoleon 100%." Others agreed: "Mr. Claude Rains' Napoleon is a superb piece of acting. He carries off the long speeches with wonderful aplomb, and every moment and inflexion seems to be just right." When it came to Shaw, Rains seemed to understand instinctively what the author intended, insight which he demonstrated in his next role, John Hotchkiss, in the playwright's satire *Getting Married*. Again critics commented on the shortcomings of the play, but it benefitted from its strong, resourceful cast: "When Mr. Hotchkiss (Claud [*sic*] Rains) and Mrs. George Collins (Edith Evans) were acting, the scene became much more lively and the stage properly occupied." *The Observer* raved: "Mr. Claude Rains … is an actors' actor. He never does anything wrong."

Rains' next leading role was an actor's dream and he handled it superbly; however, it was not a play designed for the average London audience, being quite *avant garde*. In addition to producing popular revivals, the Everyman often introduced works of unknown authors offering unusual subject matter. *Low Tide* was written by German Expressionist Ernest George, but English theatregoers rarely accepted unusual forms of social commentary. Rains' character Pat Donovan was an unsympathetic lout and a ruffian; a clever man who might have contributed to society, but whose environment fostered a destructive personality overcome by poverty. In the squalor of London's slums, he represents an exponent of Nietzsche's philosophy of the instinctive cruelty of Man. Reviewers found the play exciting, and Rains earned unqualified praise for his performance. Audiences, however, were not convinced and dismissed the sordid story. Rains was bitterly disappointed by the public's reception; he had put his heart and soul into creating a foul-mouthed East End brute, who called to mind Dickens' immortal Bill Sikes. Noted reviewer James Agate, who had been supporting Rains' career for some time, wrote:

> Mr. Claude Rains played the part with a virility and power which it did one good to see. The actor looked six inches taller than he really is and was at times quite frightening. How is it that this fine player is not seen more often on the West End stage? …That Mr. Rains can convey the Beardsley mood [in *Low Tide*] and also portray the rough of our own today demonstrates that he is an actor of great accomplishment. There was not an inch of Mr. Rains that was not acting, from the muscles of his neck to the jut of his thigh.

Era's critic enthused, "[A]s Pat Donovan, Mr. Claude Rains has the chance of a lifetime. He gives a magnificent performance, firm, vigorous, and massive in conception. His cockney is irreproachable, and the whole performance is a carefully observed piece of creative acting. [An ironic compliment, given that the actor had spent years training himself to lose his native accent.] Compared with Pat, Bill Sikes is a cooing dove. Never has Claude Rains been seen to better advantage."

Low Tide seemed to glorify the despicable character, which must have put off audiences, and for all the raves, the play lasted only one week.

Rains was upset and despondent over what seemed to be a never-ending cycle, professionally. He understood Pat Donovan – he had experienced first-hand the squalor of London's slums. His brothers and sisters had died as a direct result of disease and malnutrition, and the filthy conditions of the East End. *Low Tide* demonstrated just how such an environment can eat away at a man's soul or turn him into a brute. The playwright wanted to make middle-class audiences aware of this social reality, in the hope it might ignite a stronger social conscience for reform. Shaw tried to do this as well, but with refinement and wit, whereas the German's play was too furious.

After a brief return as the Little Emperor in another two-week run of *The Man of Destiny*, Rains had another chance to interpret Shaw, as Richard Dudgeon in the popular *The Devil's Disciple*. During this production, Rains escaped injury in a stage accident which papers covered sensationally.

Actor "Hanged" on the Stage: Mr. Claude Rains in a Grim Misadventure

[A] well-known actor was almost hanged in full view of a London audience. The victim was Mr. Claude Rains.

The accident occurred in Shaw's play *The Devil's Disciple*, where, in the character played by Mr. Rains, he has to mount a wheeled scaffold and have a noose placed round his neck. Just as the scaffold is about to be wheeled away by the executioner, the real culprit arrives, averting the execution.

"But on Saturday night," said an Everyman Theatre official to-day…, "as a stage crowd was pressing round the scaffold, something or somebody touched it, and it started to move.

"Mr. Rains had the rope round his neck, and was jerked off his feet. In less than a second he would have been swinging in front of the audience.

"Happily the executioner grasped the situation in the twinkling of an eye, and grasped both the moving scaffold and the unfortunate actor, and saved him from being hanged.

"The condemned man has now insisted on brakes being fitted to his scaffold in future."

Another paper proclaimed: "Stage Execution Almost Became Real When He Lost His Balance," and quoted Rains, who gave a slightly different version of the story: "The steps leading to the scaffold rest on a little trolley, so that when I am about to die, the executioner pushes the trolley and the steps from under me. Just as the executioner had placed the rope round my neck, I lost my balance. The steps and trolley beneath me began to move, and if the executioner had not noticed it and acted quickly, I am sure my sins would have found me out."

Rains followed yet another Shaw (*Misalliance*) with an Ibsen (*The Philanderer*, which ran into the New Year and finished on January 10, 1925). The quick close of another disappointment, *Home Affairs*, enabled him to accept a role generally regarded as the pinnacle of his English stage career: Faulkland in Nigel Playfair's extravagant production of Richard Brinsley Sheridan's first play *The Rivals*, written in 1775 when Sheridan was only 24. Witty and stylish, it's still considered a classic romantic comedy of manners, from which we get the word "malapropism," for the humorous errors of speech made by the immortal character, Mrs. Malaprop. *The Rivals* opened at the Lyric Theatre, but because of its popularity was transferred to the Hammersmith, a larger venue where it enjoyed a run of 93 performances from March to May.

In the original production, the role of Faulkland was small; in some productions, it was cut entirely. However, in Playfair's version, the character was developed in importance. The best friend of the male lead Sir Anthony Absolute, Faulkland is moody and insecure, plagued by doubts that his lady love returns his great affection for her. Clad in an extravagant

First wife Isabel Jeans and second, current wife Beatrix Thomson, on stage together – in a play with CR (The Rivals)!

THE EIGHTEENTH CENTURY IN SHERIDAN COMEDY: "THE 'RIVALS' REVIVED AT THE LYRIC THEATRE, HAMMERSMITH.

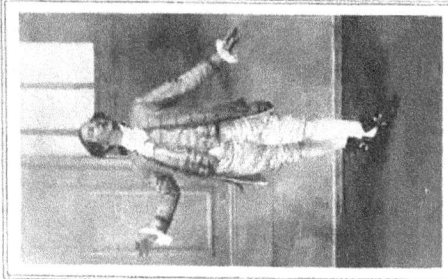

March 14, 1925, Illustrated London News.

costume, pointed shoes and a fop-
pish wig, Rains "[leapt] on the part,"
but not everyone was impressed. One
reviewer wrote that Rains played
Faulkland "as a fantastic, almost a
figure of burlesque, whose behaviour
is explicable only on the assumption
that he is insincere or insane." Another commented: "Mr. Claude Rains
overdid his acting of the now gushing
rather than melancholy Faulkland,
whose bombast he sought to indicate
by means of emphatic diction, as well
as exaggerated prancing and abrupt
Jack-in-the-Box–like movements."

Ivor Brown, the eminent *Saturday
Review* critic, saw the performance
very differently: "The effort to furnish
up the dingy part of Faulkland has
resulted in a brilliant burlesque of the
lovelorn fool by Mr. Claude Rains. This
actor, who seems to control a greater
impetus than any of our time, fairly
takes the part by storm and sweeps its
brain-sickly humours into a triumph
of the ridiculous." Equally enthusiastic
praise came from the *Times*:

We have left to the last the
most notable feature of the revival – the Faulkland of Mr. Claude Rains.
Faulkland is a notorious stumbling-block.
Did Sheridan mean his jealous vagaries
to be taken seriously…? However, we can
only take him ironically today. Mr. Rains,
then, is right to stress the irony. Indeed, he
almost burlesques the part – but he does it
with such sincerity and depth of feeling as
almost to turn the comedy to tragedy. Here
is a man who is at once ridiculous and suffering agonies. You laugh immoderately
and end by laughing on the wrong side of
the mouth….

Awkwardly, two of Rains' real-life loves were
both in the cast: first wife Isabel Jeans, "a rare young
beauty" whose performance "has that quality of natural artificiality which is the essence of the comedy of
the period," and current wife Beatrix Thomson.

CR and ex-wife Isabel Jeans in The Rivals.

Again James Agate berated the West End's play
producers (called "managers" in England) for their
lack of nurturing such talent. He began by stating:
"Let me seize the occasion to say again that Mr.
Rains is one of the very best actors in England…."
Then he continued with:

A Reproach

It is a standing reproach to West End
managers that Mr. Rains can only be seen
when one is on pilgrimage. This actor can
play nine or ten entirely different parts
superbly, therefore they think he cannot be
trusted to fill a middling role adequately.
He is neither a stock figure nor a tailor's
dummy. He does not look like your manager's pre-conceived notions of a lawyer's
clerk, bishop, publican, or prizefighter. He

happens to be that, from managerial point of view, supremely useless thing, an actor, and a very fine actor. Is he perhaps, not six foot tall? Mr. Rains is not a friend of mine, and I offer this paean out of simple duty.

Interestingly, one critic saw in the actor his need to dominate on stage; the analysis is perceptive. Writing "The World of the Theatre," a feature article in the *Illustrated London News*, J.T. Grine opined: "In [Rains'] conception, this strange person becomes a vociferous swaggerer with some grotesque mannerisms … He seemed to carry the day, but to me he burst the frame of the picture. It was a bizarre impersonation – Mr. Rains' work often is – and it was effective. But somehow he tried – unwittingly, of course – to sweep away his fellow-actors, to stand

The Rivals.

out alone in prominence…. Undoubtedly his performance will be admired and much discussed…." It was polite to include "unwittingly" but nothing Rains ever did in his acting was not carefully calculated. This trait remained with Rains, both personally and professionally; he just became more adept and tactful in his approach. On or off stage, he liked to be the center of attention. At dinner parties, if the conversation did not revolve around him, or he wasn't holding forth with one of his entertaining stories, or the topic of conversation wasn't one that interested him, he would grow quiet or even leave the room.

Rains followed up his 18th century fop in *The Rivals* with a character from the American West in *Salomy Jane*, a play based on a Bret Harte tale. Then he was in the Far East (*The Man from Hong Kong*), and to Italy for a Pirandello variously translated as *Right You Are (If You Think You Are)* and *And That's the Truth*. The latter received negative reviews, but as was frequently the case, Rains was singled out: "Mr. Claude Rains magnificently caught the intensity and excitability of the part of Signor Ponza."

That description – intense – began to be associated with the best of the actor's performances, and even with his personal persona. One reviewer saw the energy that Rains projected as being detrimental at times: "There is some brilliant acting in this play by Claude Rains who is probably the most dynamic and eruptive actor now before the public. I know of no other player more highly charged with electricity. The one danger is that he may sometimes make the sparks fly at the wrong moment. If anybody seems to be bursting to act, that man is Mr. Rains."

Rains was indeed bursting with passion and creativity but few plays of that period provided an appropriate release for his energy.

In late November 1925, the actor made contact with his old friend and colleague, Harley Granville-Barker. With his superb reputation, Granville-Barker had little difficulty securing funding and, like so many other producers, was concerned about the shortage of well-written plays. In the void, managers resorted to hit American shows or the stylized French plays which were out of date. Often tried-and-true vehicles of previous decades were resurrected. This was the case with

THE MAGAZINE-PROGRAMME

No. 575   TITLE REGISTERED

AMBASSADORS THEATRE

West St. - Shaftesbury Avenue

Proprietors, AMBASSADORS THEATRE LTD.   *Licensee,* MARGERY JAY
Sole Lessee, H. M. HARWOOD

The Madras House 4D.

A Comedy in Four Acts

by

HARLEY GRANVILLE-BARKER

PROGRAMME

SEE THE TWO COMPETITIONS WITHIN

The Madras House, a West End success fifteen years earlier. Rains played an American businessman; the play, largely because of the producer's name, had a solid run of 97 performances.

The following March, Rains appeared in *From Morn to Midnight* by German Expressionist George Kaiser, translated by Ashley Dukes. On only fifteen performances, the actor again received astonishing reviews for a play that was a convoluted recounting of a single day in the life of a bank cashier who, love-smitten, steals 60,000 pounds from his bank. The audience is subjected to the spiritual experience of the man as he spends all of the money in one day, and ends up committing suicide. The play was quite fantastic, bewildering and yet exhilarating at the same time. The *Times* reviewed it as "noisy, garish and tiresome. Mr. Claude Rains shouted himself hoarse (and thereby gained the applause of the usual crowd which mistakes

'slogging' for cricket with a zeal worthy of a better cause). He is a true artist, as playgoers well know, and it was disconcerting to find him on this occasion at a disadvantage...." One headline proclaimed "Actor's Triumph in New Play" with the subhead "Audience Spellbound by Claude Rains": "Claude Rains scored the triumph of his meteoric career in last night's production.... In this savage indictment on materialism [he] gave an intensely dramatic performance which held the audience spellbound. The reception at the close was wildly enthusiastic. A fine play beautifully acted." This predicament summed up Rains' career: He had only outstanding reviews to show for all his artistry, working for "next to nothing," and it was wearing him down.

Rains' last play upon the London stage was Phillip Morris' *Made in Heaven*, which ran during the first two weeks of October 1926. He played a violin genius who becomes involved in a triangle love affair. Critics felt the play uneven – parts of it were "banal and trite" while some of it was "witty" – and once again sprang to the actor's defense as a brilliant performer whose talents were wasted. The finest compliment came from *The Nation*, which called him "a really fine imaginative actor, who can adapt his technique to a small or large theatre, and whose smallest intonations and gestures come over with extraordinary effectiveness. He is one of the few people on the stage who have a real command of voice, and who realize that the small still one is infinitely more powerful than the roar." Reviewers faithfully sprang to advocate on Rains' behalf. *The Spectator*'s Ewan Agnew com-

REGENT THEATRE, KING'S X.
Museum 9015.

Commencing TUES., Mar. 9, at 8.   Thereafter 8.15.

GEORG KAISER'S

FROM MORN TO MIDNIGHT

A Play in Seven Scenes.

TRANSLATED by ASHLEY DUKES.

Caste will include:

CLAUDE RAINS.

Mats. Thurs. & Sat., 2.30.   POPULAR PRICES 1/2 to 7/-

mented: "One grows almost tired of praising Mr. Rains. For the last three years every critic of importance has said that Mr. Rains is in some respects our most brilliant actor. What then, is the matter with the London Theatre that it does not see to it that he is never unemployed?" A colleague concurred: "There must be something radically wrong with the London Theatre that it can find no permanent employment for this consummate actor." *Made in Heaven* closed after thirteen performances.

Rains could take no more of this uncertainty and failure. Noteworthy critics were equally frustrated with the state of the London theatre. Time and time again, eminent writers such as J.B. Priestley attacked the managers and berated the tasteless theatre-going crowd. It was shameful, they lamented, that talents like Rains and other artists were being wasted on shallow productions concocted by thoughtless theatre owners. For some reason, Rains did not like repertory work. He might have refused to become entangled with a "permanent" company because it meant doing the same plays and would not permit him to experiment with new and innovative works by which he could increase his theatrical knowledge and experience.

While her husband's career was suffering, Beatrix agreed to appear in the American production of *The Constant Nymph*, a traditional play which had always attracted audiences. Producer-director-actor-writer Basil Dean, equally disgusted with the London theatre environment, decided he would do well to take the production to Broadway with Beatrix in the lead.

Gossip columns reporting on the New York theatre, and specifically the casting of *The Constant Nymph*, indicated that Dean would find a "suitable American actress" for the part made famous by Edna Best in London. He decided to feature the 22-year-old Beatrix, and felt sure he would have a hit.

Initially, Rains was angry, but not jealous. He wanted to remain in London and he felt it was preposterous for his wife to leave him alone for her own career. (Ironically, if their positions had been reversed, he probably – like most men of the period – would have expected her to dutifully follow him.) The couple decided she would accept the offer on the condition that Rains also be given work; the actor was offered the position of tour stage manager as well as a small role in the play, Roberto. His wife was now the star, which must have been difficult, if not outright humiliating, for a man of his temperament. Rains accepted the situation since he could not bear to endure loneliness; he also wanted to return to America to ascertain if his positive impressions were still as strong as they had been in 1914-15.

Perhaps this period in Rains' stage career is best summed up by John Gielgud: "Though he won praise from the critics for several years in plays of many different kinds, Rains never achieved big star position in London. He finally left England…. 'I cannot eat my notices,' he once said to me rather sadly, just before he went away. He acted with striking virtuosity and the London stage suffered a great loss when he deserted it forever."

England's loss would prove to be America's gain.

CHAPTER 4
The Englishman in New York

On November 30, 1926, Cunard liner *Mauritania* docked at the Chelsea Piers on the Hudson River, New York. Two of her passengers were Mr. and Mrs. Claude Rains. Years later, the actor recalled for *Silver Screen* magazine: "I came over then as a passenger, you might say, to play in a play with my then-wife. And that play was the forerunner of my joining the Theatre Guild as they were pleased to designate me, their 'leading character [actor].'"

The Constant Nymph, adapted from the Margaret Kennedy novel, had a successful Broadway run, largely due to its exceptionally fine cast. Beatrix Thomson scored very well with both audience and critics: *The New York Times* reviewed the play as one of the "most sustained and moving emotional drama[s] of the season [with] Miss Thompson [*sic*] as Teresa giving a notably fine performance." Her husband, however, suffered through not being noticed. After all the praise and recognition he'd achieved in London – and given his ego – undoubtedly the situation caused a strain on the marriage. "A special word of praise should be reserved for the Roberto of Claude Rains," was all the *Times* could muster. It was as if he were a bit player, as if he were starting all over again. Because Beatrix was young, beautiful and the star of the show, she was the subject of many interviews and news items in the New York theatre columns. Some of her remarks to reporters make it appear that Beatrix enjoyed her husband's plight; she made rather mocking comments about his (past) behavior towards her when she was a student at the Academy. Rains' ego was too insecure to remain long in Beatrix's shadow. Whatever his reasoning, he decided to leave the production.

Rains was excited by what he saw happening in the New York theatre world, especially in Greenwich Village, where experimental plays were eagerly attended by audiences who, unlike Londoners, patron-ized the *avant garde*. He was offered and accepted the title role in *Lally* at one of these off–Broadway venues. This was a gamble, moving from the comparable security of Broadway, but he needed recognition, he survived upon it. The play wasn't a success but it turned out well for Rains: Its author Henry Stillman also directed for the prestigious Theatre Guild. Stillman invited Guild manager Lawrence Langer and Guild producer Theresa Helburn to come see Rains' work. Langer and Helburn were impressed by the actor's forcefulness and unique style.

Beatrix was doing quite well in *The Constant Nymph*, which had been moved to a larger theatre to accommodate audiences. With his wife busy, Rains toured for several months with East Coast theatre companies, including the Guild. When *Constant Nymph* ended its run in early December, Beatrix and Claude had a chance to (briefly) co-star in a four-act play titled *Out of the Sea*. Beatrix, now a successful Broadway ingénue and a celebrity, was often interviewed by the New York press. Rarely did she say anything flattering about her husband. She continued to joke about the "nasty treatment" she received from him when he was her teacher, describing his influence as "more or less negative," and commenting that she "married him out of spite."

At the start of the 1927-28 season, the Theatre Guild formed a repertory company with permanent players to be known as the Acting Company; Rains was invited to join as a leading performer. The project, the brainchild of Lawrence Langer, was a unique undertaking. A play would be produced for a week, then the same actors would be used in a second play for a second week, then back to the first play. Although the schedule was demanding, it alleviated the boredom of performing the same role night after night. Rains was delighted with the prospects of steady work and in the company of such splendid actors as Alfred Lunt, Lynn Fontanne and Edward G.

FORD'S THEATRE

Direction STANLEY COMPANY OF AMERICA

This Theatre, under normal conditions, with every seat occupied, can be emptied in less than five minutes. Look around now; choose the nearest exit to avoid the dangers of panic. WALK (DO NOT RUN) to that exit.

Week Beginning Monday, Nov. 19, 1928

Matinees Wednesday and Saturday

Third Production of the First Baltimore Subscription Season

The Theatre Guild of New York Presents
THE THEATRE GUILD ACTING COMPANY

—IN—

"MARCO MILLIONS"

By EUGENE O'NEILL

Production Directed by Rouben Mamoulian
Settings and Costumes Designed by Lee Simonson
Incidental Music Composed and Supervised by
Emerson Whithorne

CAST OF CHARACTERS
(in order of appearance)

CHRISTIAN TRAVELER ....Vincent Sherman
MAGIAN TRAVELER ....Sanford Meisner
BUDDHIST TRAVELER ....Louis Veda
A MOHAMMEDAN CAPTAIN OF GHAZAN'S
    ARMY ....Albert Van Dekker
A CORPORAL ....George Lester
PRINCESS KUKACHIN, Granddaughter of
    Kublai ....Margalo Gillmore
MARCO POLO ....Earl Larimore
DONATA ....Ruth Chorpenning
TEDALDO, Papal Legate to Acre.....Philip Leigh
NICOLO, Marco's Father ....Henry Travers
MAFFEO, Marco's Uncle ....Whitford Kane
A DOMINICAN MONK ....Albert Van Dekker
A KNIGHT CRUSADER ....Philip Foster
A PAPAL COURIER ....Harry Wise
ONE ALI BROTHER ....Felix Jacoves
OLDER ALI BROTHER ....Louis Veda
THE PROSTITUTE ....Teresa Guerini
A DERVISH ....John Henry
AN INDIAN SNAKE CHARMER ......John Henry
A BUDDHIST PRIEST ....Vincent Sherman
CHAMBERLAIN OF THE COURT....Philip Foster
KUBLAI, the Great Kaan........Morris Carnovsky
CHU-YIN, a Cathayan Sage ....Claude Rains
BOATSWAIN ....Albert Van Dekker
PAULO LOREDANO, Donata's Father.John C. Davis
A BUDDHIST PRIEST ....Vincent Sherman
A TAVIST PRIEST ....Louis Veda
A CONFUCIAN PRIEST ....Harry Wise
A MOSLEM PRIEST ....Sanford Meisner
GHAZAN, Kaan of Persia ....Sanford Meisner
MESSENGER FROM PERSIA.....Peter Morrison
PEOPLES OF CATHAY, COURTIERS, NOBLES,
    LADIES, WIVES, WARRIORS OF KUBLAI'S
    COURT, DANCERS, CHORUS OF MOURNERS:
    Lota Bonner, Phoebe Brand, Gladys Leuba, Na-
    dine Miles, Helen Brown, Frances Propper,
    Ruth Bluestone, Jean Swiller, Harry Wise, John
    Henry, George Lester, John C. Davis, Lucian
    Scott, Hiram Sherman, Sidney Little, Sydney
    Dexter, Walter Williams, Gervaise Butler,
    Karol Rembov, Peter Morrison, Paul Yost, Wal-
    ter Franklin, Francis Ward, Lawrence Tuck,
    David Bunn, Philip Foster, George Lamar.

TABLE OF SCENES

Prologue: A sacred tree in Persia near the confines of India, toward the close of the Thirteenth Century.

ACT I

Scene 1—Exterior of Donata's House, Venice—Twenty-three years earlier.
Scene 2—Palace of the Papal Legate at Syria at Acre. Six months later.
Scene 3—Persia—Four months later.
Scene 4—India—Eight months later.
Scene 5—Cathay—The Grand Throne Room in Kublai's Palace at Cambaluc—One month later.

(OVER)

Program for Marco Millions.

Robinson. The Theatre Guild's innovative idea kept production costs to a minimum while giving good actors work on a continuous basis.

During the summer of 1928, Rains appeared in the touring company of *Marco Millions*, another reliable box office attraction. It did well, but without a steady female companion, Rains was often quite lonely. During one rehearsal, he noticed a young, attractive dark-haired ingénue. "Who is that beautiful extra in the white dress over there – what's her name?" he asked. The reply, "That's Frances Propper," made Rains laugh: "I don't believe it. No one could have a name as silly as that."

At 37, Rains was quite attractive with his thick head of hair and dark brooding eyes. To his credit, he paid little attention to infatuated bit players and remained faithful to his wife. However, this new, shy girl never displayed any immature adoration of him. As Rains recalled later when discussing how he met the woman who would become his fourth wife:

"No, it was not 'love at first sight' with me. Or if it was, which is a debatable point, it was entirely in my subconscious. We never had a date, Frances and I, during the whole of the tour. I was married. I wouldn't look at anyone..." Frances herself remembered: "I certainly knew he was there ... I certainly had an awareness, I certainly looked at him! Yes, I think I did fall in love with him then.... I had a special girl friend on that tour, Phoebe.... She knew how I felt about Claude. She'd warn me, 'He never pays any attention to anyone.' She'd say, 'Give up, Frances!'"

A confident Frances insisted: "I bet you five dollars that I'll be successful before this tour ends!" But at the end of the tour, Frances had to pay out the five bucks: "I gave up! He really was a man apart, during that tour ... he never joined in any of the company's festivities. He never seemed to be fully conscious that we were there, at all..." Rains concurred: "I'd do my job and go straight back to my hotel room. Now and again, I must confess, I'd tramp the streets of Cleveland or Baltimore, or wherever I'd be, all night long."

While her husband was out on the road, Beatrix phoned to say she was dreadfully homesick; furthermore, she had been offered a play back in London. Rains may have sensed that Beatrix did not love him, but he had a strong emotional investment in the marriage, and this turn of events affected him quite deeply. Part of Beatrix's decision was due to the rise of Actors Equity. In the beginning, the union fostered economically based resentment against "foreign stars" who took lead roles away from Americans, especially glamorous ingénues who often were cast for looks more than talent. Good character actors, like Rains, were welcomed with little objection. Beatrix also missed her friends, family and the social stability of the English middle-class life to which she was accustomed. She returned alone to England in October 1928.

Late in the year, Rains finished his touring and returned to New York, still a Guild employee. Financially he felt more secure: He had earned more than $4,000 from work in the city and another $3,000 on the road. After deducting expenses, his net was over $5,000, a comfortable salary at the time. But he was alone. In reflection, he probably realized his third marriage had not developed or matured on a stable basis. Moreover, he and Beatrix had met at a rather vulnerable time when he was going through a difficult period with his second wife. Rains admittedly had begun the new relationship while married to Marie. Although the flesh had been weak, he felt morally obligated to legalize it and had the integrity to make the situation "right." Perhaps he and Marie never truly loved each other; it was an impetuous decision to marry; on her part, Beatrix was immature and spoiled and may have confused infatuation with love. At the time, Rains was quite a celebrity in London, a dapper dresser, younger looking that his years, the perfect gentleman. However, their priorities about their professional and personal lives were decidedly different.

Perhaps Beatrix assumed that the combination of her husband's dependence on companionship, and his reluctance to engage in an extra-marital affair, would make him lonely enough to return to England. However, while he may have been dejected, Rains was proud and stubborn: A man with a shred of dignity did not run to a woman who deserted him. Also, he was comfortable in America, a feeling he never quite experienced in England. He liked New York, he liked the Broadway theatre crowd, and he liked his American success. He was making a decent living for the first time in his career.

He had also found that American performers interacted differently than their English counterparts. Instead of an "every man for himself" attitude, a company worked for the good of the production. The entire concept of democratization, especially within the Theatre Guild, had great appeal. Most

importantly, he was attracted to the lack of class consciousness. Rains had always been extremely sensitive to the British social structure, and sensitive about his perceived place in it. This was a significant factor in his eventual decision to make his future life in the United States.

Rains did apparently return to England for a brief visit, although the exact dates of his sailing are uncertain. If Beatrix had indicated she wanted a reconciliation and would give up her career, he might have remained, but she made it clear she no longer had any real feeling for him. Evidently, she indicated she had been seeing other men, which Rains considered unforgivable; however, without evidence of infidelity, there was no legal grounds for divorce. If her husband desired his freedom, Beatrix wanted a hefty settlement and alimony. Rains did not want to become involved in something that would cost both time and money, and there was a job waiting for him with the Theatre Guild. He left England, quite despondent about yet another failed marriage. There seemed to be no satisfactory resolution: "I didn't want to see anything break up, anything to which I had given so much."

In New York, the Guild's managers were delighted with his return; they had always felt Rains' style, talent and professional attitude were especially well-suited for their organization. For the 1929-30 season, the Guild again decided on a permanent circuit program to tour the eastern part of the U.S. in addition to their Broadway schedule. The circuit crew would revitalize the reliable old plays at reasonable ticket prices. Production costs, including actors' salaries, were kept to a minimum. But even with a reduced income, Rains wanted to continue his association with a company with which he had established a good reputation. Rains once again performed in *Marco Millions*, and after understudying the title role, eventually went on in a production of *Volpone*. He also toured with the play.

Rains remained depressed about his emotional dilemma and found himself occasionally thinking of the young woman with the silly name, Frances Propper. Frances was only eighteen. She wanted to spend her summer in the theatre; he had seen her again when she was escorted by a friend to a cocktail party the actor threw at his 34th Street apartment. With her quiet manner and easy laugh, she was hard to resist, even for a still-married man: "I thought that I was thinking of her only as a charming and pleasant

The Camel Through the Needle's Eye.

young person … that was a time to which I can only refer as 'torn' …"

In early spring, Rains was rehearsing his role as the butler in *The Camel Through the Needle's Eye*, written by František Langer and adapted for the stage by the principal director Philip Moeller. The play was to open at the Martin Beck Theatre on April 15, 1929, but the actor playing the lead shockingly suffered a fatal heart attack on his way to rehearsal. As understudy – and because Lawrence Langer and Helburn had such confidence in his ability – Rains took over the role:

> I'd worked out the butler pretty carefully, with the director; we decided he should be a very well-mannered sort of butler, the kind Oscar Wilde wrote about.
>
> On Thursday evening, four days before the play was to open, the director said he wanted to speak to me after rehearsal. My heart sank. Here it is, I thought they've had enough of Rains' butler. It sank still further when I heard orders being given that the stage was to be set for one scene; and that this was going to be pretty tough for Rains.
>
> I'll never know whether they had enough of my butler. They got rid of him; but not as I feared. What they asked me to do was to read the English actor's part. He had died two hours before. Of course, I read it.
>
> Four days wasn't long enough to study the character, to build him from the inside out. So I decided, as a short cut, to work from the outside. I'd made up my mind how the man looked; I didn't have time to decide how he would think. I'd ask myself, "What did he wear? What about his movements? Would they be quick or slow? Would he wear glasses? Did he part his hair on the side? Did he comb it straight back? Did he strut?" …
>
> The scheme worked, after a fashion. It got the curtain up on schedule. But that performance was a phony, a hollow shell. The man was a clotheshorse, not a real person. You must begin inside. But you can't begin inside anything you don't understand. That's why it's always easier to play a heel than a sympathetic part. One bad trait can make a man evil; it takes a lot of fine ones to make him admirable…. It takes the experience of maturity to analyze virtue. …You can't play an emotion if you haven't experienced it; you can't portray a trait that's entirely foreign to you…. You can't play understanding and tolerance unless, to a certain extent at least, they are a part of you.

Critics dismissed both the play – light-hearted "intelligent hokum," quite unsophisticated – and Rains' performance: "Claude Rains makes a capital figure of an irate continental father by the device of playing as if someone had shoved a ramrod down his back."

Rains made it a practice to learn the script of anything he acted in so he could understand how his character fit. He was approached by a young actor, Jules "Julie" Garfield, who was an unofficial assistant in the production crew. Garfield would later come to Hollywood, change his first name to John, and become a huge film star. (And, incidentally, make six films with Rains.) According to Larry Swindell's biography *Body and Soul: The Story of John Garfield*, Rains taught the up-and-comer a valuable lesson during a scene: "Claude Rains confronted Julie with a near smile that spoke amusement, and it threw Julie; he forgot his lines and stood there sputtering. Rains calmly ad-libbed a little speech incorporating all of the lines [Garfield] was supposed to say, then calmly waved Julie off the stage…. Julie was awed by the polished Guild actors he observed. This included Claude Rains who later would be of capital importance to Julie's film career…." The two men liked each other's personality. Both detested hypocrisy in life and in acting. Although they never became close, when together they discussed plays and occasionally had dinner. Garfield was fascinated by Rains' skill and wanted to learn all he could from the English actor.

Rains' breakthrough on the American stage came with a Guild production of Romain Rolland's *The Game of Love and Death*, a three-act drama which opened in late November 1929. He had a small but significant role and received rave reviews in what was otherwise a rather pedestrian and wordy drama. At last he made his mark on several members of the powerful critics' circle: "[T]he outstanding performance is that of Mr. Claude Rains as Lazare Carnot who, according to the author's stage direction is: supercilious, bitter, haughty and sarcastic, suggesting a sneering common sense. It is heartening to look on as Mr. Rains gives life to M. Rolland's puppets…." The *New York Times* echoed these sentiments and further stated while the play was unsteady and of narrow interest, "[it's] almost saved by one performance – the precise dominating acting of Claude Rains, who, as Carnot, contributes magnificently to one scene." Another described the actor's performance as "[c]risp, sure, incisive, shading each meaning with gesture and eye and lip, Mr. Rains in his quarter-hour on the stage gives a performance such as this season is not likely to be lucky enough to see again."

It was admittedly unusual for an actor to be on stage for only fifteen minutes in a production, and yet catch the eye of every reviewer. The dean of Broadway critics was John Mason Brown, at that time writing for the *New York Evening Post*. Brown recognized Rains' talent and understood how the actor used precise and selected techniques to build a completed characterization. After seeing Rains in the role, Brown became as avid a supporter of the actor in America as James Agate had been in London:

> The play ran a tepid talking course. It continued in this static, unexciting way until well within the second act, when because of the appearance of Claude Rains as Carnot … it suddenly leaped into memorability … because of what Mr. Rains did for it during the all too brief interval he was on the stage. With a voice that cut like steel, with hands that carried in their fingertips the whole threat of the Committee, and with a fine control of pauses that were electrifying in their intensity, Mr. Rains brought the quality of complete persuasion…. In short, the evening as a whole was not a very happy one…. Had the rest of the company equaled Mr. Rains, however, it might have all been a different story.

While the Theatre Guild also recognized Rains' abilities, they could not pay him what he might have been worth; the stock market crash of 1929 had its effect on Broadway and layoffs were beginning. Many of the organization's better artists were deserting the theatre for the movies, where salaries were astounding. Rains did not care for films, especially silent ones, and decided to remain in New York.

In late February 1930, he enjoyed another triumph as the prime minister, Proteus, in Shaw's *The Apple Cart*. Ordinarily, Americans would find Shaw's highly stylized declaration that democracy was impractical hard to digest. However, the Shavian wit struck a chord in Depression America, questioning its political system's ability to solve economic problems created by uncontrolled capitalism. In just two months, the play was moved to a larger theatre and then, running even longer than expected, went on to the Alvin Theatre. The art deco set was striking, Shaw's dialogue clever and amusing as always, especially with Rains' biting delivery. Actor and playwright were made for each other as New York critics quickly recognized. Even the *New York Times*' hard-to-please Brooks Atkinson observed, "Claude Rains finds the right mixture of master and charlatan as the prime minister." John Mason Brown called the play an enjoyable addition to the 1930 season "and one

Claude and Frances.

The actor had decided to make the U.S. his permanent home; during the summer, he briefly returned to England to secure a quota number to gain legal admission as an immigrant, applying for citizenship rather than remaining as an alien. Back in the States in the fall of 1930, he rejoined the Theatre Guild's touring company, and his excellent reputation could reasonably have been assumed to keep him in New York for the foreseeable future. In fact, in December, one critic wrote that the actor's work "definitely stamps him as a stage force that must certainly be reckoned with during the next decade."

If Rains was now starting to achieve real professional success, his personal life was still in a shambles. Without his wife, he may have been lonely and sexually deprived, but he was not bored; he was constantly meeting new people, and he continued to keep company for the next few years only with Frances Propper. The couple was extremely careful and discreet: She was under twenty-one and he was still married. In 1940, Rains told an interviewer that on their first date, he took Frances to the Caviar Restaurant in New York. "I discovered that she loved pâté de fois gras, caviar, all rich food, and so she had it … instead of orchids and bottles of 'Temptation' and other perfumes and trinkets, such as other girls enjoy. I brought Frances pâté de fois gras sandwiches and delectable, imported antipastos!" Because she lived in the Bronx, they were able to get together frequently. The fact that she was seeing a thrice-married older man must have been appalling to her family, but Frances always had a mind of her own, and eventually her parents came to trust her judgment and Rains' integrity. Whatever their objections to the profession of their daughter's erstwhile lover, they were impressed by his propriety and manners. Although the next few years were very difficult for the couple, they remained loyal to each another.

Rains began to "supervise" Frances' life as if she were already his wife. "He always noticed my clothes," she stated. During those first years, and throughout their eventual marriage, Rains had a great influence

of which the Guild can well be proud." He singled out Rains, "whose excellence as an actor becomes increasingly clear with each new part and every larger opportunity he is given at the Guild. With the quietest means Mr. Rains manages to dominate the stage and lend authentic theatricality to each scene in which he appears." "Dominating the stage" was exactly what Rains was learning to do.

in selecting her outfits. "There were lovely ventures into the shops in New York," remembered Rains, "lovely … we always bought her hats together. I once had a coat made for her at Fortnum and Mason, too … without even consulting her. And on another occasion I bought some lingerie for her from Miriam Hopkins, fancy that! Miriam had got some made at a convent or somewhere … anyway, she was disposing of some of it and I was one of the buyers!" Each felt very comfortable in the other's company and they had dinner together whenever possible. Somehow Rains even bought a car for their "mutual enjoyment" and they made excursions into the countryside on Sundays.

To Rains' great satisfaction, Frances gave up the idea of being an actress: "It was wonderful to me, having been married to a woman with a career, to find a woman who didn't care anything about a career, who just wanted to hold my hand…" They would go to the movies and see plays, recalling for one interviewer that in the spring of 1929 they saw Ruth Gordon in *Serena Blandish* and were "ecstatic" about it. They also remembered in 1930 sitting in the last row of the last balcony and weeping together while watching R.C. Sherriff's *Journey's End*, a film directed by their former acting colleague from the West End, James Whale, now making a name for himself in Hollywood.

After a while it became evident to Frances' family that although she was quite young, her feelings were much more than immature infatuation. But until they were legally married, it was a very difficult and harrowing period for the couple, who often felt hopeless. Rains was now an established Broadway actor, but the economic realities of the Depression nullified any hopes of his obtaining a salary commensurate with his talent.

In their January 1931 issue, *Theatre Arts* magazine asked well-known critics to name the truly great actors of the period, those "who have mastered their art." Every list included Claude Rains. One contributor went further: "I can think offhand of only a half dozen actors and actresses who can be other than themselves when needs be," naming Rains along with George Arliss, Lunt and Fontanne, Laurette Taylor and Katharine Cornell.

The Great Depression was also a great leveler: An impressive reputation did not translate into an impressive salary. As the economy worsened, so did the Theatre Guild's financial problems; in 1931, it was on the verge of bankruptcy. Only revivals of Shaw attracted large-enough audiences for the group to remain solvent in its 13th season. Box-office receipts were dwindling, actors were being paid less, with some working at barely subsistence level. (In mid–May, Rains was so badly in need of funds, he had to request an advance of $250 to tide him over the summer months.) There were those who tried to make it through the hard times, but many more left for Hollywood studios and guaranteed paychecks.

Rains remained in New York, though the Guild's tendency to produce plays with limited audience appeal must have exasperated him on occasion, such as the gloomy, anti-war drama which was its fifth entry in the 1930-31 season. The American public might have wanted to be entertained, but the Guild felt an obligation to enlighten and educate. *Miracle at Verdun* by Hans Chlumberg was a serious drama with intricate scenes and a huge cast. The play had been well-received in Germany, where the anti-war playwright stirred the audience's conscience by having the dead of World War I return to see the result of their supreme sacrifice. Perhaps realizing that American and German audiences differed in their reaction to the conflict, the Guild mounted an elaborate production with music by Aaron Copland, and intermittent talking motion pictures scenes. Two directors were assigned to the undertaking, Philip Moeller and Herbert Biberman. Cheryl Crawford (later to become an outstanding Broadway producer) served as casting director and contracted Rains for three roles: a messenger, a German survivor and the Belgian prime minister. Writing in the *Times*, Brooks Atkinson, usually a Guild supporter, opined that the production was "overwrought, disjointed, and attempted too much." However: "Claude Rains … makes himself heard over the general din, and gives a splendid, potent performance."

Rains himself respected the general attitude of the American theatre-going public:

> Playgoing is taken so much more seriously as an intellectual pastime in New York than it is in London…. English audiences are, naturally or not, more demonstrative, but theatre-goers in London simply walk down the street in the evening and go into the Theatre with the most attractive bills

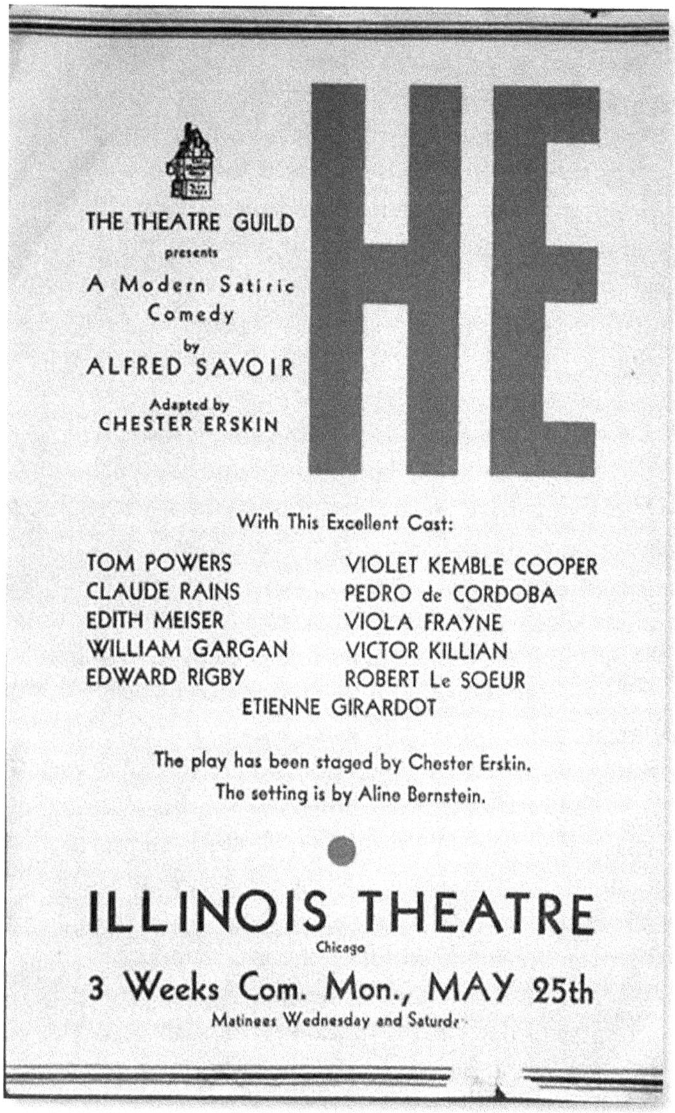

THE THEATRE GUILD
presents

A Modern Satiric
Comedy
by
ALFRED SAVOIR

Adapted by
CHESTER ERSKIN

HE

With This Excellent Cast:

TOM POWERS   VIOLET KEMBLE COOPER
CLAUDE RAINS   PEDRO de CORDOBA
EDITH MEISER   VIOLA FRAYNE
WILLIAM GARGAN   VICTOR KILLIAN
EDWARD RIGBY   ROBERT Le SOEUR
          ETIENNE GIRARDOT

The play has been staged by Chester Erskin.
The setting is by Aline Bernstein.

●

ILLINOIS THEATRE
Chicago

3 Weeks Com. Mon., MAY 25th
Matinees Wednesday and Saturday

ship remained limited. Rains easily attracted women, so it was a dangerous time for him, but he was not inclined to indulge himself recklessly. In a way, acting was his salvation; he became so intently involved that by an evening's end, he was exhausted. It was as if he had an "invisible" comrade to alleviate the loneliness.

In mid–September, Rains toured in a play by Alfred Savoir titled *He*, a modern satire which, after tryouts in Princeton, Chicago and Philadelphia, opened the Guild's 1931-32 season. It closed shortly thereafter. Once again, a short-lived production was, for Rains, a personal success. The plot revolved around a group of people stranded in a hotel in the Swiss Alps during a brutal storm. "He" appears, claiming to be God. Miraculous things occur, but the stranger denies any responsibility, and eventually it is revealed that "He" is an escapee from a mental hospital. As the Napoleonic elevator man who interprets the miracles for the audience, Rains was singled out: "Claude Rains comes very close to 'stealing the show' as the elevator operator of Corsican ancestry and the Bonaparte philosophy…. Rains scored in every one of his scenes, 'folding up' the allegory of the play in his own capacious abilities…. [T]he character has a

posted … "just to see a show." They really don't care what the play is on the stage or who is in the play. They patronize the theatre with impartial intent. In New York it is all very different. The evidence that the public taste for legitimate attractions is becoming refined and classified as the circumstances that they go to the theatre at all. Otherwise they'd just go to the pictures. Here the theatre is a serious and intelligent institution rather than just an agency of amusement.

Rains' loyalty to the Theatre Guild during these difficult times – he was to remain with the company for another two years – was costly emotionally as well as financially. Being alone in New York was, to a degree, rough psychologically, since he found himself feeling deeply for Frances, but their relation-

THEATRE
· GUILD ·
PROGRAM

THE MOON
IN THE YELLOW RIVER
by
DENIS JOHNSTON
at the
GUILD THEATRE

CR (seated), Egon Brecher and Henry Hull in The Moon in the Yellow River.

decided dramatic achievement, thanks to Mr. Rains' superlative performance." Photographs depict Rains as dark and brooding with a remarkable physical resemblance to Bonaparte.

Rains did not work again until February 1932 when he gave one of his finest performances as an Irish philosopher in *The Moon in the Yellow River*. (The title comes from an Ezra Pound poem about a self-deluded Chinese man named Li-Po, who is drowned on a night when, having had too much to drink, he tries to embrace the moon reflected in the Yellow River.) This three-act drama, written by Irishman Denis Johnston, dealt with the political situation in Ireland. It had been well-received in Dublin, performed by the Abbey Players, who were able to illuminate its dark and hidden meanings. It was a handsomely styled production and the characters were provoking, eccentric and sentimental. Rains

THE
THEATRE GUILD
MAGAZINE
for MARCH 1932

CLAUDE RAINS

Rains does everything that can be done to ... lend life to Mr. Johnston's symbolism. Among Mr. Rains' many gifts must be numbered his lively faculty of lending interest to almost anything he says. He is a cerebral player, whose means are as quiet as they are commanding. His diction is as pure as any to be heard behind our local footlights."

The Guild next produced another Shaw work, hoping to ensure good box office. The most memorable aspect of *Too Good to Be True* was the cast, which included Beatrice Lillie, Leo G. Carroll, Hugh Sinclair, Hope Williams and Rains as the atheist hermit called "The Elder." Critics were dismissive; they had neither the reverence or enthusiasm for Shaw's utopian Socialism and labeled the play "talky and with errant ideas." It closed within the month.

Rains was now forty-two, again without a steady income and living alone in an East 33rd Street apartment. He had to face reality. By the early 1930s, many established and talented theatre artists had left New York for Hollywood; but like the Lunts, Rains still elected to

symbolically represented Irish complexity, poetry and wit in his engineer, Dobelle, who returns home in a neutral state of mind after Ireland has won its independence from England in 1927. Because he cannot align himself with any of the quarrelling political factions, he is the brunt of cruel taunts from all sides, especially the Republicans. Several critics felt the play timely and a "fascinating study of the tangled political and national philosophy of Ireland" but another called it muddled and meaningless, especially to American audiences, blaming uneven direction. "As one of the best actors in our theatre, Claude

remain. All these failed productions had one virtue at least: Each reaffirmed for the actor that given the right character, he could rise above even the poorest work.

That summer, Arthur Hammerstein and Lawrence Weber offered Rains an unusual part in an unusual play. *The Man Who Reclaimed His Head* was an anti-war drama by Jean Bart and directed by Herbert Biberman. The action starts with the aftermath of a gruesome murder, and then utilizes a series of flashbacks to explain the genesis of the crime. Rains played the lead character, Paul Verin, a physically disfigured, exceptionally intelligent writer who shuns

any kind of social interaction. Verin is also a committed Socialist, but because he adores his beautiful but money-hungry wife Adele (played by Jean Arthur), he agrees to become a ghost writer for an ambitious newspaper publisher, Henri Berthaud. This debonair figure is a womanizing, people-pleasing politician who intends to use his paper as a stepping stone to public office. Because of Verin's scathing anti-war writing, Berthaud becomes a popular spokesman for the Socialists just prior to World War I and is elected premier. Verin is filled with resentment and anger at his puppet's political success. Berthaud suffers from his own demons: He is incensed that a physically grotesque man like Verin should be married to such an attractive woman. Wooed by right-wing political factions, Berthaud becomes a sudden advocate of war with Germany. He no longer needs the idealistic Verin, who is shipped off to the killing fields of Verdun. But Verin overhears soldiers gossiping about Berthaud's current sexual escapades; he deserts, returns to his home in Paris and walks in on Berthaud attempting to rape Adele. In an insane rage, Verin murders Berthaud and (off-stage) decapitates him: Verin has "reclaimed" his voice, his mind and his spouse, all in one feral and symbolic act. It was a bizarre, morbid production, but a tour de force for Rains. To depict Verin's physical disfigurements, the actor wore extensive makeup, building up his cheekbones and nose, and walking at an angle, left shoulder dropped severely, his arm hanging limp as if paralyzed.

From the reviews, it appears the audience in Philadelphia was overcome less by the drama and more by the superb acting by the cast of fifty. Critics felt the play was interesting but admitted intermittent bewilderment. Nevertheless, they were ecstatic

Four glimpses of the grotesque stage makeup for
The Man Who Reclaimed His Head.

about Rains' performance – he alone, they all felt, made the play seem plausible. One headline banner proclaimed: "Rains impressive in Newest Role," continuing: "[H]e plays a part that is intensely fascinating, a fascination that paradoxically grips while at times it repels. It seems to have been the fortune of Mr. Rains for some time past to stand head and shoulders alone in his medium…. He is an actor who inspires enthusiasm, and he has again scored decisively in the present production." J.H. Kean of the Daily News was most enthusiastic: "Rains, thru this performance, wins the right to lay claim to the designation as one of the greatest of the younger

CR and Romaine Callender in The Man Who Reclaimed His Head.

Hirschfeld artwork depicting CR and Stuart Casey's characters in The Man Who Reclaimed His Head.

generation of character actors…. He has that voice that would make him the most satisfactory Disraeli of the younger generation of stage luminaries. He knows the fullest extent of his talent and he doesn't make any effort to over-step his bounds. That is why we like him. For Rains has the ability to tear a passion to tatters without making the sound of the rending apparent." The producers were pleased by the ovations in Philadelphia, but felt the play was too long and physically taxing for the actors to present during a blistering New York summer. The opening was delayed until September, with all concerned believing they were in for a long run.

However, as sometimes happens after successful out-of-town tryouts, when the play opened in New York, the reviews were entirely different. It's remotely possible Rains' ego overcame his original approach to his character; he might have made an actor's greatest mistake, overacting in the belief it would enhance his performance. However, it's more likely that the (notorious) New York critics simply saw the production differently: They tore the play and the performances to shreds. Even Rains' ardent admirer, John Mason Brown, was disappointed:

[U]ntil last night's disclosure, Mr. Rains' record has been almost too good to be true. But last night, Mr. Rains seems, at least to these hitherto admiring eyes, to have succumbed to all those frailties to which even the best actors, I suppose, are natural heirs. In other words, in *The Man Who Reclaimed His Head*, he has found himself in the sort of part which few actors can resist, and he has overplayed it just as badly as almost any actor — certainly any talented actor — would do. It is a hokum role in which Mr. Rains finds himself, and he acts it in an even more hokum style than it is written, which is saying a great deal. He has his good, even his excellent, moments; bizarre, driving moments similar to those at which he has always excelled. But the part gradually gets the better of him … and when it wins its final victories, Mr. Rains does almost everything but bite the people sitting in the first two rows.

As *Wang Lung in* The Good Earth.

The Man Who Reclaimed His Head closed before the end of the month. So much for the long run all had anticipated.

Rains returned to the Theatre Guild, and Helburn and Langer were glad to have him back. For the production of Pearl S. Buck's Pulitzer Prize–winning novel *The Good Earth*, the actor was assigned the lead role of Wang Lung, with a huge supporting cast including Sydney Greenstreet, Henry Travers and Alla Nazimova as O-Lan. (In this period, of course, the casting of white actors to play roles of color wasn't considered inappropriate as it is today.) Opening night in mid–October, it was raining – an omen.

Brooks Atkinson diagnosed the major problem to be Buck's writing style and the dramatic time shift within the story, both difficult to transform into a stage play. (The book later became a successful MGM movie with all-white stars, including Paul Muni and Oscar winner Luise Rainer.) After appearing in another unsuccessful Guild production in February 1933 (*The American Dream*), Rains, perhaps not surprisingly, turned down the offer of the lead in a road company of *The Good Earth*. He finished the year playing Georges Clemenceau, the statesman and journalist who was a major contributor to the Allied Victory in World War I, in a play titled *Peace Palace*, which had a successful run at the Westchester (New York) County Center. The Guild decided not to bring it into the city.

It was a rather dismal year professionally, and Rains' personal life was still unsettled: "I had been, I suppose, an artistic success, but I had not been able to support myself, really. I … was tethered to my apartment for fear some producer would offer me a part." On one of his drives in the countryside in New Jersey near Lambertville, he saw a FOR SALE sign advertising a farmhouse with ten acres. Perhaps surprisingly for a man who seemed so "urban," Rains harbored a boyhood memory: deep feelings for the soil he had inherited from what he later described as "the cherry orchard section of England." He had always wanted to live in the country, and northern New Jersey was just a short train ride to New York City. Justifying his decision on the fact he could buy the property cheaply and grow his own food while having a roof over his head, he purchased the dilapidated place for $2,600 of his $3,000 savings. On June 17, 1933, William Claude Rains became a resident of New Jersey, a farmer as well as an out-of-work performer. Still not legally free to remarry, he lived frugally, artistically demoralized from the failed plays of the past year. Life revolved around the need for security, emotionally and financially. He had no way of knowing that events were unfolding almost three thousand miles away which would change his life forever.

Chapter 5
Invisible Star

Out of work, morose over the state of both his professional and personal life, Rains poured his energy into his small farm: "I kept busy putting the place in shape, and I thought if worse came to worse, I could go into the little drugstore in town and shake up sodas." It would have been easier, of course, if he and Frances could have been together more often, but he would not involve her in a public affair. While they continued to meet with great discretion, he spent most of his time alone.

Everything on the farm needed repairing, updating and cleaning out. There was no electricity, no central heating, no indoor plumbing. Rains immediately began work on the most important building: the outhouse. While he was putting shingles on the roof, a neighbor with a telephone (Rains had none) came by to tell the actor that his agent, Harold Freedman, had been trying to reach him. Rains learned that Universal wanted him to test for a film. He was astonished. After his Broadway success in 1932, he had recorded a screen test for RKO at a Long Island studio. It turned out very badly. In performing a part he knew well, the mentally ill father in *A Bill of Divorcement*, Rains expected to breeze through without difficulty. However, "[the test] was terrible! I was all over the place! I knew nothing about screen technique, of course, and I just carried on as if I were in an enormous theatre. When I saw the test, I was shocked and frightened..." In relating the incident later to Hollywood gossip columnist Hedda Hopper, Rains stated: "I really chewed up the scenery, and after seeing myself on the screen, I assumed that my Hollywood career had ended before it began."

Rains wasn't crazy about the film industry, but the truth was, he knew very little about it – in fact, he had actually seen only a handful of movies. The single silent film in which he had appeared, 1920's *Build Thy House*, had not afforded any real satisfaction. A medium in which he was unable to depend on his crowning glory, his wonderful voice and the precise diction he had worked so hard to perfect? Now, however, he needed both work and money, and so he agreed to go to Hollywood. He had nothing to lose, especially since Universal was paying for the trip. So he boarded the train to Los Angeles, unaware of what had transpired at Universal to instigate the summons, much less any idea that his life was about to change forever. This single experience would give him everything he wanted (and deserved): the start of a three-decade career in motion pictures, financial security and public recognition as a beloved movie character actor.

Rains arrived in Hollywood at the height of the Depression. In 1930, some 1300 banks had closed and over 26,000 businesses failed. In 1931, over one million people were on the dole; by 1932, there were twelve million unemployed people in America. In New York City, the financial capital of the country, former bankers and college professors were desperately selling apples on street corners for a nickel. In Los Angeles, however, movie producers with fourth grade educations were confidently charging five cents admission to their films and making a fortune.

One such successful mogul was Carl Laemmle, Jr. His studio, Universal, founded by his father Carl Laemmle, Sr., had had an unexpected hit on its hands in 1931 with *Frankenstein*, starring a relatively unknown English actor named Boris Karloff and directed by James Whale. Realizing the bonanza that lay in thrilling horror pictures, Laemmle acquired the rights to H.G. Wells' classic 1897 novel *The Invisible Man*. The studio chief was anxious to begin production on his movie adaptation, but there were problems. The picture was handed to Robert Florey, who was enjoying elevated status as the script writer of *Frankenstein*. Florey was to both write and direct the new movie. But when Wells sold the film rights to Universal, the author insisted on script approval,

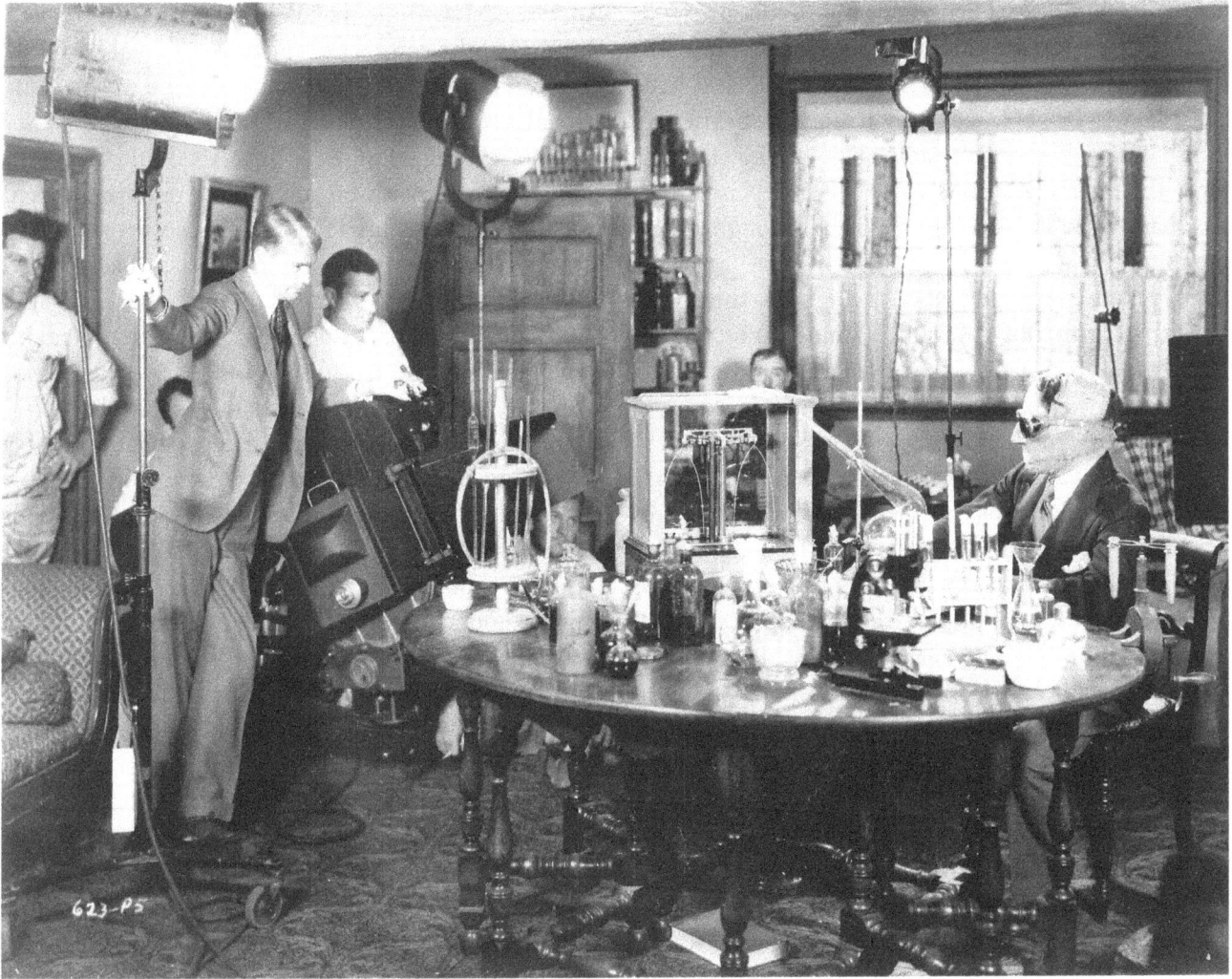

On the set of The Invisible Man, *director James Whale on the left (in suit and tie). (Photo courtesy John Antosiewicz)*

and between April 1932 until May 1933 he had already dismissed as unworthy twelve adaptations. The project went through the hands of four different directors before Laemmle finally decided only James Whale could bring to the film what was required; Whale was given the directing assignment in June 1933. Whale then requested that R.C. Sherriff, who had written the director's previous films *Journey's End* and *The Old Dark House*, take over the writing task and produce a screenplay which was faithful enough to the original story to please the author. This turned out to be lucky number thirteen.

Whale was already well-respected in the film industry. Astute and intuitive, he understood that good movies were a combination of clever film-making techniques and solid performances. Based on his own first-hand experience in the West End,

Whale usually cast as many British theatre actors as possible, considering them to be better trained. After relocating to Hollywood in 1929, he was responsible for persuading colleagues like Charles Laughton, Elsa Lanchester and Una O'Connor to follow him. Because of his success with *Frankenstein*, Whale not only had an excellent reputation but also leverage at Universal. Cinematographer Arthur Edeson, who had worked with Whale previously, was hired. The concept of creating an "invisible man" on film was technically challenging, requiring both extraordinary photographic knowledge and the ability to incorporate reliable stage trickery. Universal now had a well-written script, a good supporting cast, an experienced director, the best cameraman, and all the necessary technical facilities to make the movie — but no leading man.

The story of *The Invisible Man* begins with a poor but dedicated chemist discovering a drug – the wonderfully named Monocane – which renders him invisible. Before he can find the antidote, side effects transform him into a dangerous megalomaniac, and he initiates a reign of murderous terror before he is finally tracked down and killed by police. The lead actor had to be able to portray the chemist's mental deterioration without the advantage of showing his face. The ultimate success of the film depended on a superbly skillful execution solely through vocal technique.

When Laemmle purchased the rights to the novel, he did so with Boris Karloff in mind; anticipating the actor's acceptance, Universal printed advertisements with Karloff's name. However, after learning he would not be seen throughout the entire film, Karloff was less enthusiastic about the project; plus, there were salary disagreements. Whale was also coming to the conclusion that a relatively unknown actor would be more effective than the now-famous star, so audiences would not "see" Karloff each time they heard the "invisible man." He considered Colin Clive, who had played Henry Frankenstein, but Clive was anxious to return to England. Other stars offered the part turned it down once they learned their face would be bandaged from start to finish.

Then Whale remembered someone he had known for fourteen years and with whom he had worked in the theatre. Whale remembered the intensity, intelligence and unusual insight that Claude Rains projected in every part. Above all, he remembered the actor's distinctive voice. That was the sound he wanted for his unseen protagonist. Whale convinced Laemmle to view the actor's RKO screen test – that theatrical disaster, with all the ranting, raving and scenery-chewing. The producer was appalled. Rains was too short, much too flamboyant for films, plus he was completely unknown to movie-goers. Whale understood that Rains had duplicated in his screen test the same style he employed so effectively on stage. But the director knew that Rains was an intelligent and hard-working actor who could quickly learn, and utilize, appropriate film techniques. According to Rains, Whale insisted: "I don't give a hoot what the man looks like. That's how I want him to sound." To confirm his hunch, Whale scheduled another screen test, this time filming a scene from *The Invisible Man*. Already wearied by all the delays, Laemmle relented and telephoned Rains' agent.

For this second screen test, Rains played the scene in which Griffin explains how he became invisible, and glories in his newfound power. His performance

convinced Laemmle that Whale had been right, and he offered the actor a two-picture contract. Not only was Rains going to make money, but he was personally pleased to be working with his old friend – they had both come a long way since 1923 and *The Insect Play*! The two men were alike in many ways. Born in the same year, each had risen from poverty and was acutely sensitive about his lower-class background and painfully aware of status limitations in England. Each had served on battlefields in the Great War and emerged from the ordeal as an officer. Both men presented as aristocratic and learned; Whale deliberately assumed this affect as part of his personality to give him more authority and respectability. Each had left England to work in America where skill and talent counted far more than family background.

Professionally they differed in that Whale thoroughly understood the power and future of films and was already established in the new industry. Luckily and most importantly for Rains, Whale respected intelligent actors and understood their ego-driven compulsions. Rains was more traditional and held fast to the artistry of the theatre and the independent creativity it afforded the actor. Nevertheless, he was always willing to listen and learn from people he respected, and Whale was certainly one of them. Rains would learn a great deal about the art of film acting from making *The Invisible Man*.

Ready to sign his Universal contract, Rains was unsure about salary; he asked Whale for his opinion and the director suggested $3,000 per week. When Laemmle agreed, Rains was overjoyed; that was nearly as much as he had earned in an entire year on the stage. He would now be working under a director he liked and admired and making a great deal of money. He also insisted on top billing, an issue which would remain a concern throughout his film career, often more important than salary. In this case, he received name above the title, the ultimate honor, and in the complete credits list, his name is larger than those of the other players.

Until production was actually underway, Rains was idle. Whale encouraged his friend to increase his knowledge of film composition, and what was and was not effective acting on screen. "James kept talking about this and that in pictures, about actors and pictures of whom I'd never heard. When he learned I'd seen only about six films in my life, he told me to go right out and see pictures – to see three a day until

The February 1934 issue of Everyday Science and Mechanics *divulged a few of* The Invisible Man's *special effects secrets.*

I knew something about them."

By the beginning of the summer, Rains was assigned to his first day on the set. He still knew very little of what was expected of him, as Whale had not told him anything about the making of the picture; and Rains never thought to inquire about his character's invisibility or how it would be accomplished. "I'd never read *The Invisible Man* when I got the call to play him, and it came as a shock to discover that throughout the movie my face was to be swathed in bandages, right up to the very last scene." Dumb-

founded, Rains asked, "Not even at the beginning? Not even my eyes?" Whale replied, "No, Claude, you're here for your voice." This was an extraordinary challenge for an actor. "I would want to do more and thought at least I could try to express something with my eyes. Then [Whale] would say, 'But Claude, old fellow, what are you going to do it with? You haven't any face.'"

The special effects, extremely imaginative for the time, involved a great deal of effort on the part of crew and cast. (The detailed technicalities have been covered in multiple books and articles. The best are noted in the bibliography.) Rains worked with remarkable fortitude performing some very complicated maneuvers under difficult circumstances. For example, in each scene in which the Invisible Man unwraps his head and undresses, the actor had to disrobe in such a manner that his hands never crossed between the camera and parts of his body, because they would immediately photograph as black objects. These remarkable tricks were accomplished by legendary special effects supervisor John P. Fulton, in coordination with cameraman Edeson. Together they created startling illusions with remarkable results: a bicycle glides by without a rider, glasses are spilled, pieces of furniture slide about, and money is scattered over the street as if someone is throwing it — all seemingly under some mysterious power.

It was an extremely uncomfortable film to make during a hot California summer. The story was set in winter, so the actors had to wear appropriately heavy clothing. Then, too, there was the heat generated by the giant klieg lights, and no air conditioning in the sound stages. Rains worked with bandages on his face, his body sheathed in the black velvet under his clothes. It was dark and claustrophobic. In spite of his physical discomfort, the actor continued to

CR and Gloria Stuart in The Invisible Man. *(Photo courtesy John Antosiewicz)*

enjoy the technical aspects of filmmaking and even remained on the set when he was not needed. He remarked later that doing *The Invisible Man* was "a lark." Such a comment, however, belies the fact that Rains remained uncomfortable and apprehensive about being in films. For an artist of his experience and ability, it was a most incongruous way to get into the film business. He was a tense actor by nature and his anxiety was heightened by Whale's constant yells of "cut." He tried not to become distracted by the director's interruptions, necessary as they were for the technical intricacies involved, but the ordeal of performing such a complicated role in such a zoo-like atmosphere made him extremely nervous. He was always serious while working; he was even more so during this shoot because he was learning a new craft. Rains could not easily relax, and his own strict, self-imposed attitude about work contributed to making him appear introverted and self-absorbed.

Playing Rains' fiancée Flora, Gloria Stuart already had a dozen pictures to her credit, although she was twenty years younger than her co-star making his talkie debut. Stuart described Rains as "completely cold, only thinking of his performance," and found the actor's "unbending professionalism and serious-ness a little hard to take."

I think he was very anxious about it — many times [in discussing the film], I describe Claude as an actor's actor, and by that I mean completely self-engrossed and very accomplished; however, it was difficult working with him.... I know he was nervous.... We never had any conversation of any kind and often Whale would have to remind him and say, "Now, Claude, let's stay on our marks." I don't think his aloofness was directed towards me, but it was due to the fact he was so uptight about making the film.

Perhaps Rains felt somewhat inadequate because his ingenue co-star knew more about film acting than he did. Stuart conceded the possibility: "I don't think he was difficult [to work with] because it was *me*; it was the situation. James was very, very…pernickety about Claude's interpretation of this man." The two artists did not always agree, but Whale ruled.

Much has been written about Whale's creative genius; his quirky use of humor, even comedy, to defuse, or perhaps emphasize, horror (epitomized in 1935's *Bride of Frankenstein*); his imaginative eye for camera angles and scenic design. All of that is in evidence right from *The Invisible Man*'s opening scenes which set the tone and atmosphere of the picture. A figure clad in heavy overcoat, hat and muffler battles a blinding snowstorm as he staggers through the drifts to the Lion's Head, an English pub full of beer-swilling, darts-playing villagers. The door is flung open with a whirling sound of rushing wind and Griffin is framed in the doorway. Quick close-ups of his bizarre visage, a face made up of bandages, dark goggles, an oddly artificial nose. At the bar, Rains delivers his first line on film, his voice deep and husky, rolling his "r"s, announcing imperiously "I want a rrrroom – and a fire." The audience is immediately captivated by this mysterious figure. And because there actually is no mystery – the film is, after all, titled *The Invisible Man* – we may not be surprised, but we experience an ecstatic thrill shortly when the innkeeper's wife (Una O'Connor) barges into the stranger's sitting room while he is having dinner. Before he can quickly raise his napkin in front of him, she sees that the bottom half of his face is … missing.

A policeman is summoned to oust the crazy occupant. Griffin is talking out loud to himself, each word clipped and staccato, gesturing rather wildly as he mixes chemical potions almost in a frenzy. Griffin's mutterings through the bandages and exaggerated movements emphasize his increasing madness. When he cries desperately, "There must be a way back! God knows, there's a way back!" the audience pities the chemist even though his Fate is sealed because he "meddled in things that man must leave alone."

As the policeman attempts to evict him, Griffin becomes furious: "I'll show you who I am – and *what* I am!" He throws away the fake nose, unwraps the bandages, disrobes and becomes "invisible" except for

"E's all eaten away!"

an empty white shirt "dancing" around the room as he shrieks with insane laughter.

Later, Griffin blithely explains his plans to Dr. Kemp, the scientist he intends to make his partner in crime: "We'll begin with a reign of terror, a few murders here and there. Murders of great men, murders of little men, just to show we make no distinction." Only when Flora implores him to given himself up does Griffin momentarily become calm. Rains speaks gently, conveying tenderness in deep, soft

The last paragraph of the Invisible Man *script describes the reappearance of Jack Griffin's body.*

CASE NO. 15975

JOHN GRIFFIN

SCOTLAND YARD

G. R.

John Griffin

Class *Maniac – Murder*

Classification No. 44 63 18 CC 12

RIGHT HAND

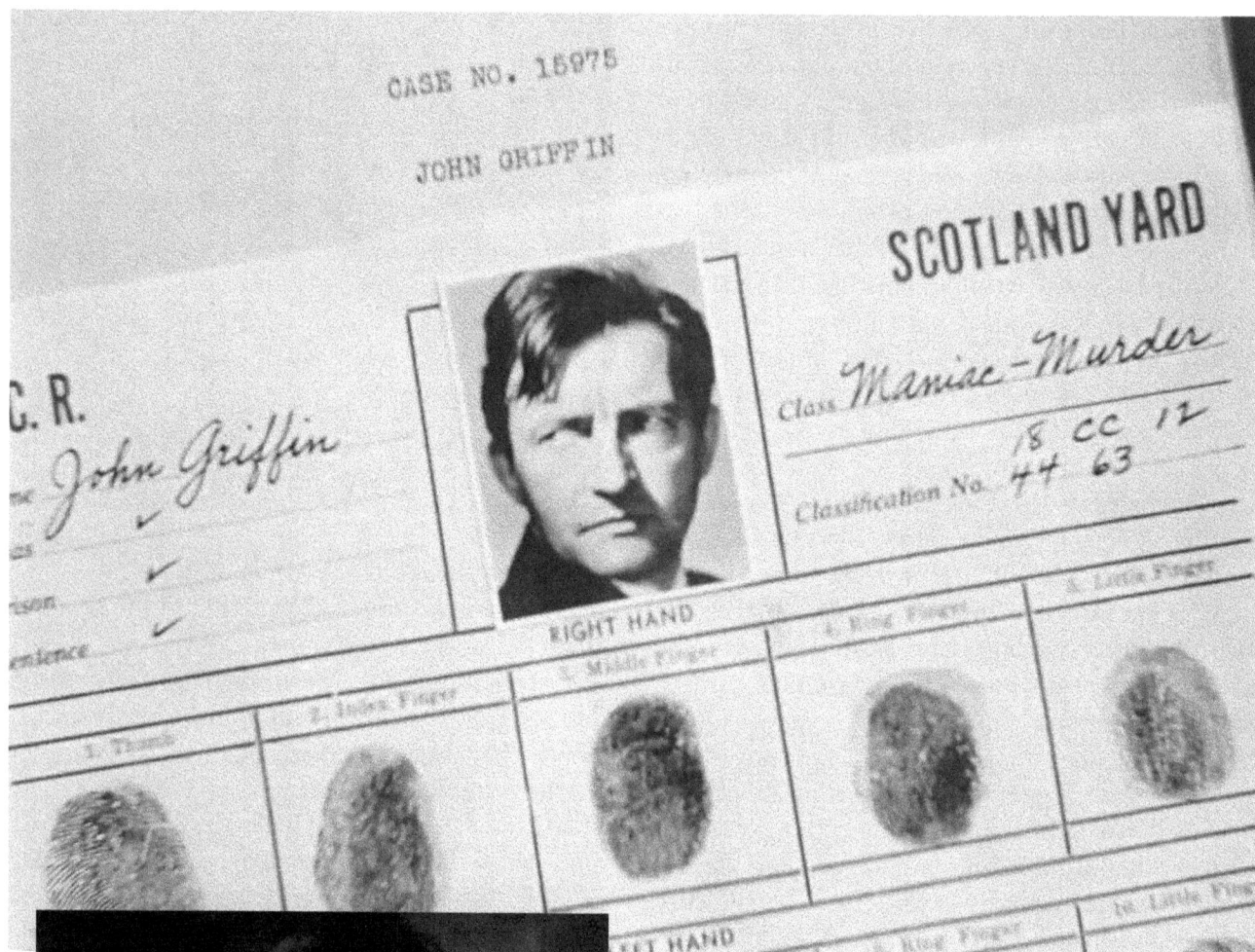

Universal's Invisible Man sequels usually referenced Rains' Jack Griffin from the original. The Invisible Man Returns (1940) also showed viewers the photo of Griffin in his Scotland Yard file (above), while Abbott and Costello Meet the Invisible Man (1951) gave us a look at Griffin's picture on the wall of a colleague's laboratory (at left).

tones, clearly demonstrating Griffin's sensitivity and genuine love for Flora. This scene is one of the most poignant in the film as Rains soars through a swing of emotions. Bewildered, Flora asks him why he did such a thing: "For you, my darling. I wanted to do something tremendous. To achieve what men of science have dreamt of since the world began. To gain wealth and fame and honor. To write my name above the greatest scientists of all time." But as he begins to lose stability, his body becomes tense; he raises a gloved hand to hold his head in frustration and pain. His agitation builds as he tells her his plan to take over the world. He is panting, the gauze across his mouth sucked in and out with each frenzied breath. Then he rises up, arms folded across his chest in the self-conscious pose of a conqueror; Whale's camera shoots him from below as he pronounces the famous line: "Even the moon's frightened of me – frightened to death. The whole *world's* frightened to death!"

In the exciting finale, the police set fire to the barn in which the Invisible Man is sleeping. As he runs from the burning building, one footprint after another appears in the snow, and a policeman is able to shoot him. And because "the effect of the drug will die with him," the audience gets its single, much-anticipated glimpse of a visible man – a darkly attractive Claude Rains, a pale corpse in the hospital bed, looking a decade younger than his forty-four years, hair artfully tousled even in death.

What is interesting about Rains' first movie is the manner he handles his character. He makes no judgment about Griffin; he plays the part as humanly as possible – no monster, but a mortal man, reduced to madness not by some outside force or circumstances, a curse or a deformity, but by his own intellectual curiosity, and perhaps a bit of hubris. What makes *The Invisible Man* different from many other films in the genre – *The Phantom of the Opera, Dracula, Frankenstein* – is that it's not dependent on frightening the audience with horrifying actions or grotesque makeup. Therefore, it is not really a "horror" film as much as a fantasy.

On November 13, 1933, *The Invisible Man* was officially released, playing at the Roxy Theatre in New York. Audiences and critics were fascinated by the cinematic trickery, and by Rains' faceless performance. "No actor in movie history has ever made his first appearance on the screen under quite as peculiar circumstances as Claude Rains does in *The Invisible Man*," exclaimed the *New York Times* reviewer. The movie was an unqualified success. Critics unanimously agreed that Rains was splendid in the title role, that his astonishing voice conveyed every emotion. "[His] performance offers a character of towering vengefulness, impatience, conceit, wit and sarcasm…" wrote one critic. Recognizing the man

Ninety years after its initial release, The Invisible Man still inspires toys for today's kids.

behind the infamous deeds, another wrote: "[Rains] is deliciously mad and endearing in a most furious way when he is supposed to be a monster." At the beginning of 1934, *The New York Times* called *The Invisible Man* one of the ten outstanding hits of 1933.

Rains learned a great deal while making *The Invisible Man*: Film acting was very different from acting in a theatre, where all movements were exaggerated to play to the back of the house. Now the reverse was true: The camera captured the tiniest change in facial expression. In this medium, less was more. But at times, words alone were not the critical aspect of a scene or a character. A turn of the hand and an expressive look could be more effective. But one thing remained the same regardless of the medium: Rains possessed an uncanny ability to lose himself in a role, to dissolve his own personality into the character. In that respect, Claude Rains, the person, was always an "invisible man": Like a figure on a black-and-white negative, in real life he was the reverse of the image – cosmopolitan, suave, educated, self-assured – he portrayed. With this self-created aura of sophistication, he created an on-screen persona which he wanted people to believe off-screen, and in this way was able to hide his true self.

The Invisible Man was artistically and financially successful, but Carl Laemmle still had doubts about its leading man. James Whale tried to convince the studio head to sign Rains long-term, emphasizing his potential as a reliable character actor. "It's a pity to type him as a monster," Whale wrote, "as he has a curiously romantic appeal." When Rains asked for $3,000 per week for his next film, Laemmle used the extension clause to drop him. But the actor's great reviews made an impression at other studios and he soon received numerous offers. While (discomforts notwithstanding) he had enjoyed the film experience, and especially the money he received, Rains' first love was still the theatre. Despite this spectacular launch as a film actor, he elected to return to New York and the Theatre Guild for one more attempt to be a stage star. And more than anything, he wanted to marry Frances.

CHAPTER 6
Movie Star–Farmer

After his *Invisible Man* success, Rains was in a much better financial situation, but because there were no other immediate movie offers, he returned to his Lambertville farm in the fall of 1933 in a depressed state of mind. "I was not married then — I was alone, so I wept and waited and carried on all by myself. An actor is a very emotional fellow, and when he's not working, he gets very depressed, very frustrated, and is apt to feel that the next step is the poorhouse or the actors' home." Rains refurbished the farmhouse by putting in a bathroom and fixing up the kitchen, and he made sure his New York producer knew he was available for any Broadway work. Because his reviews for his last two plays, *The Man Who Reclaimed His Head* and *The Good Earth*, had been negative, he was anxious to reassert his stage reputation.

The 1933-34 New York season seemed promising: Tallulah Bankhead in *Dark Victory*, Judith Anderson and James Stewart in *Divided by Three*, and Katharine Cornell in *Romeo and Juliet* with Basil Rathbone, Brian Aherne and Edith Evans. Attempting to aid live theatre in its bid to remain competitive with motion pictures, many actors agreed to accept lower salaries.

The Theatre Guild had confidence in its new season, which offered Eugene O'Neill's *Ah, Wilderness!* and Maxwell Anderson's *Mary of Scotland*. However, they also decided to produce a controversial social protest drama, John Wexley's *They Shall Not Die*. True to its mission, the Guild felt it had a moral obligation to shine a spotlight on social injustice in America. The play was based on the infamous Scottsboro case, in which nine young black men were convicted of raping two white girls. With few hard facts to go on, the jury of twelve white men arrived at a guilty verdict based on highly questionable circumstantial evidence, especially testimonies from the girls, who had been intimidated by the district attorney into pressing charges. It was pre-war Southern "justice" at its most contemptible. Rains was offered the small but important role of the boys' Northern defense attorney, Nathan G. Rubin.

Rains felt optimistic about the drama, believing it had a chance for a successful run, given the sensational trial on which it was based and because Northerners had been so outraged by the outcome. Like many artists, Rains sympathized with the Guild's aspirations of raising theatre-goers' social consciences. Most of all, however, he believed the role was an opportunity to "rehabilitate" his Broadway reputation. In preparing for the part, Rains visited with the real-life famous trial lawyer his character was based on, Samuel Leibowitz, to observe first-hand any notable mannerisms or speech patterns (he wanted to use a New York accent). When Leibowitz left the room to get some refreshments, Rains took a pipe from the lawyer's desk and stuffed it into his coat pocket, with the idea it would lend authenticity to his characterization. After seeing the play, Leibowitz was impressed enough to comment: "That Rains, an Englishman, could thrill the man Leibowitz, is alone an accomplishment." The actor also attended local trials, making notes on how the attorneys got across points to a jury, with both vocal theatrics and grandiose gestures.

During rehearsals, Rains kept to himself, avoiding informal cast gatherings. His was a difficult role, requiring a lot of energy. The cast, however, was feeling uneasy about his behavior, especially since the play's success depended on his performance in the third act. As Ruth Gordon observed in her autobiography: "Claude Rains had the long part ... In rehearsals, Claude was colorless; it could sink the play. [In] his seven-page speech, he droned. Everybody worried. He was the pivot of the whole play. [On] opening night ... Claude's summation blew the roof off! Even that frosty Guild first-night list had to loosen up and cheer. It's the only time I ever saw an actor wait till opening night to wrap up a show."

They Shall Not Die opened at the Royal Theatre on February 21, 1934, receiving mixed reviews. While there was overall approval of the Guild's attempt to deal with the inflammatory issue, several critics felt that Wexley's drama was too strong an attack on the Southern justice system. The play offered a valid indictment of the injustices committed against the accused, but critics condemned Wexley's approach as grim, harsh and much too theatrical (for example, Rains' recitation of the Lord's Prayer as the curtain fell). Two reporters who had attended the original trial agreed that ninety-five percent of the play recreated the actual events, but felt the playwright's dialogue sounded at times like yellow journalism. And so the public didn't go – they wanted to be entertained, perhaps informed, but certainly not lectured.

However, on a personal level, Rains scored extremely well, especially with some notable critics like John Mason Brown, who considered the actor's performance alone worth a visit to the theatre: "His clipped speech is charged with meaning. His voice is possessed of a melodious vibrancy which centers the attention upon every word he speaks. His abrupt gestures are filled with significance. And his short, pigeonish body is alive with energy." *The New York Post* was also a rave: "Rains had seized upon his role with all the conquering power of his voice and dynamic force. It is a passage of brilliant inflection sharply defined and deeply felt…. [Rains achieved reality by] watching Samuel Leibowitz … visiting East Side restaurants and listening to Jewish lawyers talk."

A few critics found fault with his early scenes, describing his antics as "histrionic flamboyance," and that he "struts amusingly and none too convincingly" and was "attitudinizing." But when it came to the final courtroom scene, all agreed that the actor had "eloquent moments of magnificence." *The New York Times'* Brooks Atkinson encouraged the public to attend the play just to see Rains:

> In the last act Claude Rains as the defending attorney gives one of the most electric performances of the year…. Mr. Rains can be a gaudy actor when his part is Faustian. *The Man Who Reclaimed His Head* and *The Good Earth* exposed the worst of him. But he is also an actor of great power

and latitude; and his playing of the New York attorney in the courtroom scene is magnificent and moving. What a tremendous scene that is!

The usually understated Robert Benchley of *The New Yorker* extolled the actor's performance: "[T]he third act, after creating a strangely unsympathetic character in the person of the cocksure Jewish attorney who finally takes the case, is given over to the trial in all its terrifying hopelessness, and here Claude Rains gives a remarkable exhibition of sheer physical stamina…."

Given all this praise, the Guild was bewildered that the audiences were not buying tickets. After it closed, a *Theatre Arts* magazine critic suggested why *They Shall Not Die* had failed: "Everything was condensed into the last act and fell on Rains' role." It was just too much to ask of one man. John Mason Brown thought so highly of Rains' performance, he published a longer article in the *Saturday Review* in a desperate effort to keep the actor in New York City and the play alive. Brown admitted that in the past, Rains had been given to bouts of being overdramatic, but felt this fault was due more to an "overwritten script" than to the actor's ability: "There is no one in our theatre at the present time who can rise more brilliantly to the acting opportunities of a scene than Mr. Rains can…. Having been given very little assistance by the text, his instinct persuades him to overact as a means of assisting the author…." But even this eloquent appreciation could not convince patrons to attend the play.

The failure of *They Shall Not Die* meant that the Theatre Guild could not pay its talent or meet other financial obligations. Ruth Gordon, who played one of the accusing girls, remembered vividly the final days of the run: "[T]he house receipts were going down and Claude along with the others was told the cast was getting half their salary but the leads would have to work for nothing. Rains' reaction was bitter — he had literally made the play come alive and his notices were superb but he had nothing to show for it. Furious, he told the Guild's manager, 'Remind me never to go in a play with you — next you'll ask me to pay to act.'"

The organization's predicament was summarized by one theatre historian in a stinging commentary: "[L]ay the blame as you like on movies and motors and radios and what-not rival distraction, what has alienated many thousands of theatregoers … through the land has been the loss of confidence in the value of the stage entertainment sent to them." This may have been true, but neglects to acknowledge the full impact these "distractions" had upon the public, and ignores the sociological and economical changes the nation was going through, that affected the public's choices.

Rains relished the critical recognition, but he had literally worked for almost nothing. It made him bitter and frustrated, not only with the Theatre Guild but Broadway overall. He realized he could no longer depend upon the stage to provide him with a steady income. Except for redeeming his reputation with the New York critics and satisfying his ego, Rains' return to Broadway accomplished little for his career. But in fact, his performance had attracted the attention of two very important people: Ben Hecht and Charles MacArthur, well-known writers in both New York and Hollywood with sterling reputations. Impressed by Rains' work, they were considering him for a part in their new film.

In addition to collaborating on plays and film scripts, Hecht and MacArthur each wrote short stories, and Hecht's "Caballero of the Law," published in the May 1933 issue of *Saturday Evening Post*, had an unusual and ironic plot. The team decided to expand the clever story into a motion picture, and in early 1934 negotiated a contract with a friend of Hecht's, the head of Paramount, George J. Schaefer. MacArthur and Hecht were to write, produce and direct four pictures at Paramount's Eastern Service Studios in Astoria, Queens, which was under the supervision of Walter Wanger. Paramount also took responsibility for the films' distribution throughout their movie houses.

The pair didn't want a big name for the lead in their first independent film production, believing that a star personality often distracted audiences. With only *The Invisible Man* to his credit, Claude Rains was still virtually unknown as a film actor. However, he was talented and experienced, and could and did bring in theatre audiences, the type of people Hecht and MacArthur were trying to reach. They felt Rains would excel as the sly, clever scoundrel in their movie. On his side, Rains liked the men's style: Their stories permitted escapism within a semi-realistic framework, such as their successful stage play made into

a successful movie, *The Front Page*. Rains accepted Charles MacArthur's dinner invitation to his home in Nyack, New York, to discuss the project.

The actor read and liked the original short story; he also liked being courted by two such famous men, and being encouraged by MacArthur's equally famous wife, Helen Hayes. After dinner, the pair read aloud the script, now titled *Crime Without Passion*. Rains immediately fell in love with his role of a brilliant and arrogant criminal defense attorney. The salary offered, low by Hollywood standards, was decent; to compensate, Hecht enlarged the part and gave Rains top billing on a solo card. It was a terrific opportunity to be formally introduced to the movie-going public. Rains also liked the fact that he did not have to go to Hollywood, but could work in the Astoria studio close to his farm in New Jersey.

There were other reasons for Rains' excitement. By now a few film offers had come his way, but he refused them because they came with the condition that he sign a long-term contract. While he wanted the benefit of a guaranteed, larger salary, maintaining his artistic independence was essential. Rains had enjoyed making *The Invisible Man* because he respected James Whale and the challenge of the part, but a long-term contract was too confining and limiting. He was convinced that, "to make a name for myself on the screen, I must accept only worthwhile parts in worthwhile pictures. It was no good just taking the first offer that came along." Finally Rains relished playing an incredibly smug cad, overly dramatic in court, calculating and devious with women.

Ruthless and self-absorbed, Lee Gentry mocks authority during his trials, even manipulating evidence to get his clients acquitted; his unscrupulous tactics have resulted in exoneration for thirty undoubtedly guilty men. Disliked by his peers for his disregard for justice, Gentry is the darling of the newsmen who love to cover his sensational cases. But he has a fatal weakness: women. His current mistress, a nightclub dancer named Carmen Brown (Margo), cares deeply for him, but Gentry has grown weary of her and is already involved with another woman, socialite Katy Costello. The lawyer's desire for Katy drives him to create fights with Carmen to force her to decide to leave him. Carmen threatens to commit suicide; as she and Gentry struggle over a gun, it goes off. Carmen slumps to the floor; reaching for her, Gentry comes away with blood on his hands and believes she

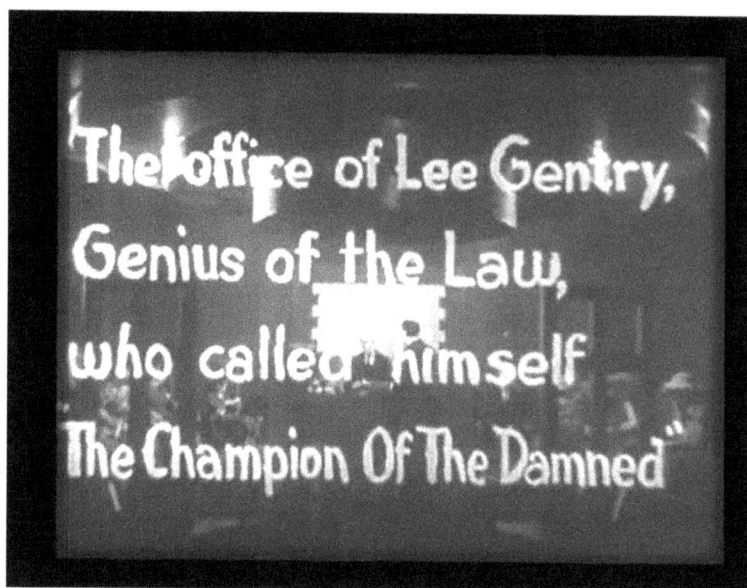

This on-screen foreword characterized Rains' character in Crime Without Passion.

is dead. In a clever use of split screen, Gentry's "alter ego" appears, almost ebulliently instructing his terrified other self how to cover up the crime. In the film's ironic ending, Gentry's plan has him pretend to wait for Carmen at the nightclub where she dances, but he has too much to drink and gets into a fistfight with Carmen's old boyfriend, Eddie. Losing control, he reaches into his pocket for Carmen's gun and shoots and kills Eddie. As the police take Gentry away, Carmen comes out for her dance routine! (The bullet had only grazed her.) All of Gentry's conniving was for nothing, he will go to the chair for murder after all. And when his alter ego suggests cheerfully that he use the gun on himself, Gentry raises it in trembling hands, but can't go through with it. "Coward! Coward!" shouts the vision.

During pre-production, Rains approached Hecht about his character. The actor felt that no man was entirely all good or all bad; he always projected the gray area in between, allowing for human weakness. As written, Rains explained, the role was too unsympathetic, too much of a scoundrel. Rains recalled Hecht's reaction when he suggested toning it down a bit: A tirade of four-letter expletives which instantly settled the disagreement: "That guy's a heel! I know he's a heel. And that's my idea of a hero! Play him as he is — and don't take the edge off anything." As an artist himself, Rains knew better than to argue. Even though both MacArthur and Hecht had reputations as cynics, Rains found "they were also sentimentalists

at heart." He liked their manner and, unlike many in the Hollywood scene, "they lacked any sense of self-importance." Unlike James Whale, these men created an easygoing atmosphere and maintained a nonchalance on set, sprawling on the floor playing backgammon between takes.

In addition to the sophisticated dialogue they had written, Hecht and MacArthur wanted to make a fast-paced film that was different, utilizing the new industry's technical innovations. Hecht persuaded his friend David O. Selznick to send him Lee Garmes, a top cameraman, and special effects genius Slavko Vorkapich. The producers-writers-directors rounded out their crew by engaging the young, rather outrageous pianist Oscar Levant to compose the background music. Even the opening credits were *avant garde*: animated shards of glass form the letters in the titles. Three veiled women in flowing white garments fly through the air; representing the Furies, they descend, shrieking and laughing. Subliminal images of skulls can also be detected.

The supporting cast included teenage Mexican actress Margo, who had been appearing at the Waldorf Hotel's Rainbow Room, as Carmen. Whitney Bourne, a Park Avenue model, made her film debut playing Gentry's new love Katy. To keep expenses to a minimum, a host of famous friends and associates volunteered as "extras." MacArthur's wife, Helen Hayes, and Fanny Brice, the Ziegfeld star, appeared in a hotel lobby scene, and the two writers themselves played reporters and other parts.

Production began in May 1934 and remained on schedule, shooting nine-to-six daily. But the summer months approached, and maintaining such a pace was difficult in record-setting heat. The arc lamps were blistering, and in order to keep out noise and light, there were no windows in the stage. Finally, Rains exploded:

> One day we had a lot of difficulty with one of my scenes. It was the tricky double-exposure sequence in which my logical mental self argues with my illogical emotional self. I played it through once and something went wrong with the lights. I played it through again and something

CR with Margo in Crime Without Passion.

went wrong with the camera. I played it through a third time and something went wrong with the sound. And then I started making mistakes. I became mechanical. There was no feeling in my expressions, no meaning in my lines. I blew up. "I'm not going on with this!" I shouted. "I'm not a puppet!" There was an awed silence. Everybody waited respectfully for me to cool down. Then Charlie, quite unperturbed, said quietly, "O.K., puppet. Let's take a rest." From then on, he always called me his "little puppet." How can you get temperamental with a man like that?

There were other pressures, such as several financial backers visiting the set. In normal times, Hecht and MacArthur would have little difficulty in obtaining funding based on their excellent reputations, but 1934 was the worst year of the Depression. Even with successes such as *Twentieth Century*, *Scarface* and

Rasputin and the Empress, the two found themselves hampered by a tight budget. Because they had to keep their costs within $150,000, neither took a salary.

As filming continued it, became a relentless battle with perspiration as a *New York Times* reporter on the set noted: "Every few moments a man with an eyebrow pencil, powder puff and comb went to work on [Rains and Margo] and fortified them temporarily against the heat." Scenes were rehearsed and then shot with constant interruptions or comments by Lee Garmes to Rains: "More profile, Claude" or "Claude, try to turn. Your hair's so thick and unruly that it covers your face." As Gentry, Rains was dapper and attractive with a trim little mustache and hair falling softly over his forehead, wearing natty three-piece suits and a gardenia in his buttonhole. He exhibits an attractive cockiness in his theatrical demeanor in court, with movements that seem almost choreographed, and when he seductively woos the resistant Katy.

Hecht and MacArthur liked working with Rains. He seemed to know without much direction how his character would behave in any given situation; neither man ever had to explain Gentry's attitude in a scene. Rains was especially effective in voicing his "alter ego," cooing approval at Gentry's shrewdness or chastising him for being careless. But as Gentry finds himself in a web of circumstantial entanglements, the actor still manages to create sympathy for the character. Rains always brought something extra to his unscrupulous characters. His villains were never totally evil: They were devious, calculating, smug, weak, obnoxious, even once or twice a little nuts, but still, they were human beings. Creating a sympathetic bad guy became one of Rains' trademarks.

Crime Without Passion was completed on schedule within 28 days; however, there was an unanticipated stumbling block. After a pre-release screening, the film was deemed in violation of the Production Code. Among other complaints, "The prologue emphasizes illicit sex relationships which are unnecessary to plot motivation," and "[T]he costumes of the Furies are so light as to constitute indecent exposure prohibited by the Code…." Additionally, the original ending, in which the humiliated Gentry did kill himself at the police station, had to be altered because it "cheated justice." A compromise was reached; the writers agreed that Gentry would not escape retribution by suicide. Instead, the law would triumph over the unscrupulous lawyer. As for the love affairs, MacArthur was able to persuade Breen that they were an integral part of the story, and the movie was issued a certificate of approval.

Crime Without Passion opened at New York City's Rialto on August 21, 1934. Rains' association with *The Invisible Man* was played up with one ad describing his unscrupulous lawyer as "a mental Dracula." Another claimed: "Frankenstein was a sissy compared to this fiend." *Crime Without Passion* was a clever story with unusual camerawork and superior acting, but Depression-weary audiences were not interested in artistic films. The absurd ads misled audiences, who understandably expected a spooky horror movie. The sophisticated, occasionally *avant garde* drama was not exactly the type of entertainment most of the public wanted in 1934. Many film critics, however, liked what Hecht and MacArthur had created, calling it a film of exceptional artistry. Just as with *The Invisible Man*, reviewers were most intrigued by the innova-

tive film techniques, insisting that the superimposed shots and the double images stole the film. As gossip columnist for the powerful Hearst papers, Louella Parsons was never known for artistic insights, but she probably understood why the film would have a limited audience: "It is an interesting experiment [but] *Crime Without Passion* is not a picture for the people. It's a picture for the highbrows and for the intellectuals who like their entertainment the hard way." She felt Rains gave a great performance and urged people to see the movie. Throughout the years, Parsons remained a loyal supporter and admirer of the actor's work.

Crime Without Passion did succeed in establishing Rains as a film actor. *Film Daily* described his performance with one word, "immense," and *The New York Times* enthused, "Mr. Rains handled his role in a masterly fashion. He gets full effect out of the cleverly written speeches and gives an extraordinarily clear characterization." The *Tribune* couldn't resist bringing up the actor's previous cinematic tour de force:

> I suspect that in great part Claude Rains is to blame for the failure of the drama to be properly convincing in its forcefulness. Mr. Rains is, of course, a brilliant actor, one of the best in the country, but he has a definite tendency toward extravagance and in *Crime Without Passion* he is often too extravagant for comfort. In fact, the suspicion arises that Mr. Rains, who played a part in which he couldn't be seen in *The Invisible Man*, was grimly determined that no such fate should overtake him here. Thus we see him indulging in gesticulations that make for attention but not for dramatic reality.…

However, the "extravagance" in Rains' representation of Lee Gentry was part of the lawyer's personality and not just Rains' acting style. Those gestures and expressions were just what MacArthur and Hecht wanted.

In cities like New York and Hollywood, the picture played to capacity crowds and reviewers were extremely enthusiastic. But outside of these large metropolitan areas, audiences did not patronize the movie. Louella Parsons was right – the film was far too sophisticated for its time. Writing in 1980, critic Herman Weinberg explained the film's un-

Notice atop the door to this theater showing Crime Without Passion, *a sign heralding,* "THE INVISIBLE MAN UNMASKED."

derlying problem: "Thirty years ago … when I first saw the Hecht-MacArthur *Crime Without Passion*, I thought [then] it was ten or fifteen years ahead of its time…. Seeing it recently again, I feel we still haven't caught up with it."

Rains was astute enough to heed the criticisms that his stage experience was interfering with his film technique. He still had a great deal to learn and continued to attend and study movies of exceptional quality. As Rains' daughter commented: "Claude was a method actor before it became such a big deal in films, but he would be the first one to deny it." *Crime Without Passion* furthered Rains' new standing in the picture business, and as Lee Gentry, he began creating the screen persona for which he is best remembered: suave and debonair, intelligent and calculating, sometimes manipulative, cruel and unscrupulous. But often with a smile twisting his lips and an irresistible purr in his voice. He had earned a considerable salary while working with top-notch creative people. Claude Rains was now a movie star.

CHAPTER 7
Growing Tensions on the Farm

While Rains was filming *Crime Without Passion* on Long Island, his farm in Lambertville, New Jersey, was struck by lightning. All of the buildings burned to the ground. It was a devastating loss – everything of value he possessed, including career memorabilia and recently acquired valuable antiques. This dreadful event was due in part to his own obstinacy in refusing to put up lightning rods because he considered them unattractive. An insurance policy covered the buildings only, valued at $4,000. Having spent half his salary from *The Invisible Man* on improvements to the house and barn, Rains elected not to rebuild in the same area; he wanted a larger house and more land in a different location. A few months earlier, he had attended the Pennsylvania wedding of a friend near the historic Brandywine area around Valley Forge and decided that was where he wanted to live. The New Jersey farmstead was not easy to sell because of low land values; even when he did find a buyer, in June 1935, Rains was only able to get $1200, a further loss. He took up temporary residence at the Players Club off Gramercy Park, but never intended to establish permanent residence in New York City. Divorcing Beatrix and marrying Frances was now his number one priority. According to his 1934 income tax papers, he had grossed close to $30,000; however, expenses incurred in the fire (nearly $8,200) caused him to net a much lower figure of $21,600. (Six thousand dollars of that was from *Crime Without Passion*.) He felt he was in a financial position to move forward with his new life; he could not foresee that the divorce from Beatrix would become an exceedingly expensive ordeal.

Before 1934 ended, Universal offered Rains a contract to make two films in the coming year for $10,000 each. He accepted; the security would assist in providing Frances with a comfortable lifestyle befitting her upbringing. Looking for property in the Brandywine area of Chester County, Pennsylvania,

he couldn't find exactly the right place, but he did locate something in adjacent Delaware County, about thirty miles southwest of Philadelphia: a forty-acre farm called Glen Mills. Although the old Colonial farmhouse needed repairs and restoration, it was a decision he made happily and with great expectations. Rains was finally in a position financially and emotionally to make it the perfect home for his fourth bride.

Rains had known Frances for seven years, but there were multiple reasons for the long delay in making things permanent, including the obvious, that he was still legally married to Beatrix. Frances' family objected to their daughter's involvement with an actor (not a profession held in the highest regard by society) whose future prospects were questionable and therefore insecure. Frances herself initially was hesitant about marrying a man who did not have a reliable income. Rains, too, was a bit apprehensive; his three failed marriages left him very uncertain as to whether he could maintain a relationship. "I have been kicked around an awful lot — professionally and emotionally.... I suppose I was somewhat of a prey to my emotions, and they can be awfully misleading. You can get hurt — and you can hurt other people. I had something of both." Now both he and Frances had to be certain of their feelings for each other. He dismissed the age difference: "A man can't possibly know the first thing about romance until he has had twenty years' experience with it.... I still say that until a man is at least forty, he is unqualified to become a great lover, either on or off screen. When I met Frances, I had given it all up as a bad job. I had always wanted children, a home, but I had just about decided all that was not for me."

Everything about their backgrounds and personalities suggested a mismatch. In addition to being twenty years older, Rains came from a lower-class background and had worked hard for everything he had. Life had been much easier for Frances. When she and Claude first met in 1928, the Proppers, a Czech-Jewish family, lived on Prospect Avenue in the Bronx, then a fashionable middle-class area. She was the youngest child, with two older brothers and three sisters. The Proppers were well-to-do, and Frances had grown up in a comfortable environment. She had completed high school but decided not to go to a university. As a young woman, she was quite popular socially and pursued by a number of eligible young men, most of whom were in stable professions. Oddly, the family's objections did not include the fact that Claude was not Jewish. (Although the family members were not religious, they were members of the Reform sect.) Rains never actually practiced or claimed any formal religion.

The Proppers liked Claude very much, but were concerned about how different in temperament he seemed from Frances. He had a good sense of humor but was extremely intense; Frances was easygoing. He was shy and introverted; she was very sociable and had lots of friends. While their attraction puzzled her family, Frances herself had little doubts. Above all, there was his honesty and integrity and, most importantly, she trusted him. Unlike so many other people, she never seemed intimidated by Claude's commanding persona, and felt comfortable with him, enjoying his sense of humor, admiring his tenacity and perseverance, his diligence, his reliability. He never lied to her, he was courteous and considerate; he seldom used foul language, did not gamble and was very neat. Although he did drink socially, he never drank to excess and always seemed to be in control. Unlike many other successful actors, he never forgot his struggles. The most important criterion was that she and Claude both valued having a loyal and steadfast companion more than "romantic" involvement or excessive physical intimacy. They got along because Frances usually catered to Claude's whims and fussiness; she adjusted her desires to meet his. She also seemed to understand and accept that, given his artistic temperament and exceptional talent, he could be moody and difficult at times. Frances was quietly strong and never appeared ruffled, and Claude admired this. While she was not a beautiful or glamorous woman, her face and demeanor had a softness, a gentleness, that he found appealing and comforting. Each of them seemed to possess what the other lacked, and

their contrasting personalities somehow fostered compatibility.

Obviously there was enough chemistry between them to keep them committed to each other over the years. Frances could have ended the relationship easily and found another husband from among her many suitors, but she chose not to and was "fatalistic about it," believing that eventually they would be together. In many respects, their long courtship was much harder on Claude than Frances. She was socially active. She dated other men on a platonic level, mostly to maintain peaceful relations with her family, and must have made it perfectly clear to any prospective wooer that she was not serious about them. For Rains, the wait had to have been difficult, emotionally and physically. When he was away from Frances, he had no close friends he could turn to for comfort and to ease his loneliness. He could not see Frances as frequently as he would have liked, and when they did get together, they had to be discreet, so intimacy was limited. In a contemporary fan magazine interview, he recalled one period when he was overcome with depression and guilt at having put Frances into such a situation:

> [T]here was only one interim, one eternity of eighteen months when, because it all seemed so hopeless, and she was a young girl and I, an older man, and I felt the beastly unfairness of tying her young life to mine when nothing might ever come of it…for that eighteen months, we were apart, didn't see one another…even now [*he said with a shudder*] those eighteen months have the power to haunt me, each day of each one of them, separately, like ghosts walking over my grave…

The strain of the unfulfilled relationship played havoc with Rains' nerves during this long delay, and he admitted to another fan magazine that at times he was deeply lonely: "I was a married man, with few — and sinister prospects — of getting unmarried. For seven, long years we waited and hoped and hoped and waited [for the] great happiness that comes out of long unhappiness…."

Whether the couple was intimate prior to their marriage must be left to speculation. Given the long period of their courtship, it is probable. Years later,

Frances related facts to her daughter which indicated she had spent time with Claude at the first farm properties. However, most of the details of their seven-year relationship were never revealed to anyone, not even to Jennifer when she was older.

To follow their story to its happy conclusion …

In early April 1935, Rains' lawyer filed divorce papers in New Jersey, still the actor's legal domicile (the farm at Lambertville had not yet been sold). Rains was granted a decree of desertion by Beatrix, recognized by the New Jersey court. While waiting for the formal papers, and believing the matter legally settled, Claude married Frances in a civil ceremony on April 8, 1935, at the Bronx County Courthouse. Judge Harry Stackell, a relative of Frances, performed the ceremony, and her brothers Karl and Walter attended. Neither Claude nor Frances wanted a formal or religious wedding; both felt a civil ceremony was sensible and economical. It also avoided any possible family objections and publicity. Immediately afterwards, the couple left for their new home in Pennsylvania — Claude's wedding present to his bride.

Their farmhouse, situated on forty acres known as the Reinholt place, was located near the towns of Glen Mills and Cheyney, Pennsylvania, about thirty minutes from Philadelphia. Cheyney was a crossroads in the early 18th century and the stone farmhouse was one of several owned by the wealthier persons in the Chester Creek valley area of Delaware County. Nearby was a grist mill called "Locksley" and Rains occasionally referred to his place by this name (an amusing coincidence, relative to his association with the English folk hero Robin Hood who was known as Robin of Locksley).

Four original buildings were on the site: an early stone farmhouse, a barn, a spring house and a carriage house. One part of the two-sectioned farmhouse was built by Thomas Cheyney in the early 1800s and consisted of a kitchen and "great room" with a bedroom on the second floor. The second and older, larger section was built in 1747, prior to the Revolutionary War, so the building had quite a history which greatly appealed to Rains.

When Rains bought the farm, all of the buildings needed restoration and repairs. For two months prior to the wedding, a great deal of work was done on the house and barn. It was an idyllic setting; the couple delighted in country living and both adored the old farmhouse. They took pleasure in searching for Co-lonial antiques to furnish their home. Frances liked to cook, so the kitchen was equipped with modern conveniences. Given her background, it's surprising Frances came to like country life in such a short time. She confessed that, before meeting Claude, she "loathe[d] the country, and I would never live in it. Claude always loved it, cities tire him…. [N]ow we have a farm in Pennsylvania … and I am a country girl and love it…" A few years later, Rains remodelled the carriage house into a guest house and added a four-car garage. He restored the stable to its original specifications of 1750; perhaps unusually, considering he was born English, he developed a keen interest in the history of American farmhouses and barns, especially of the Revolutionary War period. Rains restored any building in which he lived to its original condition, ensuring historical authenticity.

Rains acquired an Irish setter named Patience and two male English setters whom he called Toby and Tim. In short order, the household increased by twelve puppies. There are photos depicting the award-winning stage and screen star driving a horse-drawn hay gatherer. Evidently Rains did some actual work, but he knew his limitations and hired an experienced farmer to manage the holdings. Farm life, however, seemed second nature to him; he relished dressing in old pants and work boots and undertaking odd jobs around the place like painting the barn, or tending to his large vegetable garden, as well as caring for the chickens, pigs and a few cows. By Hollywood standards, life was simple.

With more Hollywood offers coming in, Rains needed to establish a second residence in Los Angeles; frequent three-day train trips across the country were both tiring and expensive. Furthermore, he didn't like leaving his wife alone on the farm; Frances belonged at his side, and she wanted to be with him.

Unfortunately, problems with Beatrix were not so easily solved. Her former wife, perhaps jealous at his success, had always felt slighted and was understandably irritated that he was seeing another woman while still married to her. She was determined to obtain a financial settlement, which was one reason she had not initiated the divorce. By now, Rains had established himself in America as an eminent stage actor who had recently added movies to his résumé. After consulting her lawyers, Beatrix decided to bring suit against Claude on the grounds of bigamy, claiming that his divorce decree granted in a New Jersey court lacked jurisdiction. It was invalid in Great Britain because, at the time of the marriage and the separation, Rains was legally domiciled in England. Then she claimed she had not "deserted" Claude: In choosing not to return to England with her, it was he who had deserted her. The British lawyers further countered that Rains was not a U.S. citizen and announced that they would bring the matter before an English court of law.

Rains argued that he was a bona fide resident alien who worked and paid taxes in the United States. His attorney considered that position legally justifiable and urged the actor to fight. He did, but it was a costly battle, since he was forced to pay for an American lawyer as well as an English solicitor. Neither he nor Frances could possibly foresee the duration and expense of these divorce proceedings.

For the next two years, the attorneys sent letters back and forth across the Atlantic. It was all extremely stressful. While he was hesitant about becoming a contract studio actor, the financial strain of these legal expenditures, along with maintaining two homes, made a reliable, steady income a necessity. Facing the reality of circumstances in 1936, Rains signed a seven-year contract with Warner Bros. This now meant he would be unavailable to travel to England to resolve issues expediently and so his attorney had to make the trip, adding to the costs. The need for funds during this divorce was undoubtedly a contributing factor to Rains not remaining independent.

On top of everything else, English newspaper articles began suggesting that Rains was a bigamist. Such scandalous negative press was detrimental to his new career, but fortunately, he had Frances' complete understanding and support. Then, too, they were anxious to start a family, especially because Claude was older. But if the New Jersey divorce were invalidated, they would be forced to annul their marriage. So reluctantly it was agreed to reduce complications by not having children until there was a legal resolution.

In July 1936, Rains received a letter from his American attorney who was in Berlin attending the Olympic Games. A careful and discreet man, he did not cable his client from London, because the case was causing quite a stir in the British tabloids, and he feared a press leak might aggravate the situation with an additional suggestion of adultery. By this time, the tone of the case was one of vicious innuendo. He advised Rains that a British court would regard the matter of legal domicile at the time of the marriage as the crucial point in the case. If a decree was awarded to Beatrix, she could then institute a separate action suit for costs and maintenance. Rains' attorney planned to counter that Beatrix had deserted Claude when she left America, and additionally had committed adultery during their separation, which he indicated he could prove. Rains, however, objected to this approach, fearing it would only make the situation uglier. Should the case reach such levels of argument, the press could play havoc with the story, and the actor felt he simply could not afford to chance such notoriety, regardless of the truth as his attorney stated it: "There is certainly nothing that even hints of immorality in your conduct and nothing in it that is subject to criticism." Rains' lawyer further assured him that even if the court decreed in Beatrix's favor, she could not enforce the issue as long as he remained in America. This meant, however, that Rains could never again perform in England, because Beatrix could then secure a court order to attach his earnings and possibly cause him to be detained by the authorities.

It was a messy situation and Rains wanted it resolved. He had done nothing morally wrong or illegal according to American law, but he was paying heavily for "extenuating circumstances." It was all harmful to his career, his health and his relationship with Frances. He decided it might be more expedient to settle things financially, and Beatrix agreed. She would give a general release to Claude from any and all future liability if he paid her 4000 British Pounds Sterling plus her attorney fees; by today's standards, she wanted almost a quarter of a million dollars. Rains' lawyer disagreed with the actor's decision and advised his client "to continue the fight," insisting he had letters proving Beatrix had committed adultery and had no intention of reuniting with her husband. But Rains remained firm in his decision to settle, writing his lawyer to "get him out of the predicament" as quickly as possible and avoid any court appearances. In early November 1936, a letter arrived advising that the case would be on the docket of the British courts by the end of the year. Maddeningly, Beatrix changed her mind and decided not to accept the offer; instead, she wanted to take the matter to court, evidently more interested in yearly alimony payments. In mid–November, Warners began to apply pressure on Rains because the newspapers were pestering the studio's publicity department regarding the case. On November 30, the actor's lawyer let him know that the case was delayed and would probably not be resolved until year's end.

This entire ordeal had been like an anvil hanging over his head and Rains must have felt dreadfully edgy. Yet none of this was apparent when he was working. On the set of a film, he never discussed his problems with anyone; even in the midst of emotional upheaval, Rains could feign calm. Because of this, very few people knew the details of the couple's problems.

Early in January 1937, Rains' attorney advised him that under the English court system, the proceedings to award Beatrix a decree nisi would take another six months, during which time her attorney intended to apply for permanent alimony to be paid until she remarried. Rains' attorney countered that the 4,000 British Pounds Sterling originally demanded was the complete award. He expressed great confidence that the matter would be settled completely by June 1937 – and it was. Beatrix actually fared well, given that Claude had received little affection or support from her. In all probability, she did not love him when she married as a young girl in 1925, but instead was infatuated – he was quite attractive and a noted stage actor, and the young, spoiled and immature Beatrix was charmed by his attention. Unquestionably, when she returned to England in 1926, both of them knew the marriage was over and most likely neither one of them remained celibate during the interim seven years.

By mid–1937, Rains' financial problems had increased as the divorce and settlement cut into his earnings considerably. Now Frances was pregnant; the upcoming birth meant hospital and doctor expenses, while he was still maintaining the Pennsylvania farm as well as paying rent for the house in L.A. These financial burdens compelled him to go from one picture directly into the next; except for short respites on his farm, there is no evidence he had any time off. Frances did realize, to some extent, that the psychological scars inflicted by his harsh childhood and uncertain life as a poorly paid and often unemployed actor created great emotional and economic insecurities in her husband. She believed that time and a steady income might overcome his fears. However, she did not realize to what extent these insecurities controlled not only his professional decisions, but his overall behavior.

On July 4, 1937, Rains had two announcements for the press: He was celebrating his "Independence Day" with all legal problems resolved, and his present wife was due to give birth to his child in late January 1938. On July 27, 1937, the divorce proceedings were at last finalized by the courts, and Rains was happy for the first time in a decade. He now had everything he wanted in life: recognition as an actor, a steady income, a farm and the woman he loved. That all of this turmoil had not caused a rift in their marriage is a credit to Claude and Frances. A child would only strengthen their bond.

CHAPTER 8
Horror Stardom at Universal

Returning to the timeline of Rains' story ...
The movies offered financial security: In a single month making *Crime Without Passion*, he had earned $6,000, a very considerable sum. But the sweetest satisfaction came from Universal's executive, Carl Laemmle, Jr., who reversed his former position and offered Rains a contract – though it was to make several more films within the horror genre. The actor accepted, even if agreeing meant working in Hollywood, and appearing in pictures that might be of questionable quality. There were other factors motivating his decision to return to Universal: He desperately wanted to marry Frances, and he liked the idea of owning land and having a farm. These goals necessitated steady employment at a good salary. It was sweet to taste the "good life" and the happiness and financial security it offered, after so many years of struggling.

Accustomed to the theatre's operating environment and artistic freedom, Rains found making a movie quite different and difficult in several respects. A day's work consisted of ten hours, Monday through Saturday. Actors arrived at the studio about seven or eight in the morning, depending on makeup and costume requirements, and reported to the set promptly at nine, fully prepared and ready to begin work. The costly time factor made the system rigid and quite intense. The atmosphere of cooperation – presented to the public by manipulative publicity departments – was occasionally true, but it was the exception. Unlike most theatre companies, movie set crews and casts were not usually one big happy family. Talent, in front of and behind the camera, was assigned to a given production; as in any artistic working environment, personalities clashed and there were interpretive differences. Tempers were short and outbursts were frequent, especially from "stars" with large egos and demanding personalities, who had to be accommodated in order to avoid any hold-ups in produc-

tion. There were often disagreements between actor and director over how a line should be delivered, or how the lighting was affecting the actor's face.

Rains wanted to make all the films he could while his luck was holding out, so although he and Frances loved living on the Pennsylvania farm, more often than not they found themselves in Hollywood. The couple eventually realized this constant travel and separation was upsetting their lives too much and that it would be more practical to rent or even buy a place in Los Angeles. This meant the expense of maintaining two residences, but it would allow them to feel more relaxed and, more importantly, to have more time together. When Rains bought the Glen Mills property, it was with the idea that he would remain with the Theatre Guild, requiring only travel to New York (about two hours). He could return to the farm every evening if he wished. At this stage, living permanently in Southern California never entered Rains' mind. He disliked the environment, especially in the summertime when it was brown and barren, and he missed the lush Pennsylvania greenery that reminded him of England's countryside.

While Claude made movies, he and Frances led a quiet, unobtrusive life, seldom attending the glamorous affairs which were such a part of the Hollywood scene. The couple enjoyed going out occasionally, but never went to nightclubs or large parties; small, intimate gatherings were more to their liking. Moreover, when he was making films, Rains retired quite early. He often went to bed by eight in the evening and was up at four or five in the morning ready to work. Frances, however, stayed up later and enjoyed the luxury of breakfast in bed, which she often did whether in Hollywood or on the farm. That was one morning ritual over which they never agreed but never argued about. Claude commented once that he and his wife did not have breakfast together because he refused to have it in bed. Frances refused to get up to have it at the table, stating "I think it's barbarous!" In other ways, they were in agreement about their social life. "We never see very much of people, anyway," Claude stated, "probably because we have a grand time doing nothing, absolutely nothing, together…"

Making Hollywood movies created emotional conflict for Rains since he loved to be on the farm, but he also loved to act; However, once he was home in Pennsylvania, within six weeks he would start to fidget and anxiously wait for his agent to telephone. He would become moody when not acting, but tense and exhausted when he was. Rains was never driven by the desire for fame or great wealth and he frequently admitted he lacked serious ambition. Like most entertainers, performing allowed Rains to become what he could never be in reality; for that reason, he especially loved playing a rogue or a scoundrel. Rains repeatedly stated in interviews that he believed human beings wanted to escape into their primitive and basic instincts, but that living in a society teaches people to modify their desires and "behave." Being an actor allowed him the privilege of throwing off the constraints of societal and institutional mores, but in a safe, make-believe setting. He knew that being a perfectionist caused stress, but acting was an outlet for his undefined frustrations and inhibitions. His reserved English manner and his inability to reveal his feelings to anyone created an inner tension for which acting provided psychological relief.

Much as he loved the theatre, there were artistic advantages in making a film: "For sheer acting possibilities, I believe the screen has an unrivaled future." Rains believed if an actor performed in a controlled manner, an image on the screen, filmed properly, could project much more insight about a character. He disagreed with those theatrical actors who openly voiced disdain for motion pictures; and believed that he could broaden his abilities as an actor in this powerful medium that was shaping popular culture and even modern society.

In the late summer of 1934, Rains approached Universal's Laemmle, Jr., about the first of his two-picture contract. The actor wanted to make a film version of *The Man Who Reclaimed His Head*, a play he felt had never received the recognition it deserved when he appeared in it on Broadway with the Theatre Guild. With war drums pounding in Europe, he believed the story's pacifist message would touch audiences. Laemmle couldn't have cared less about

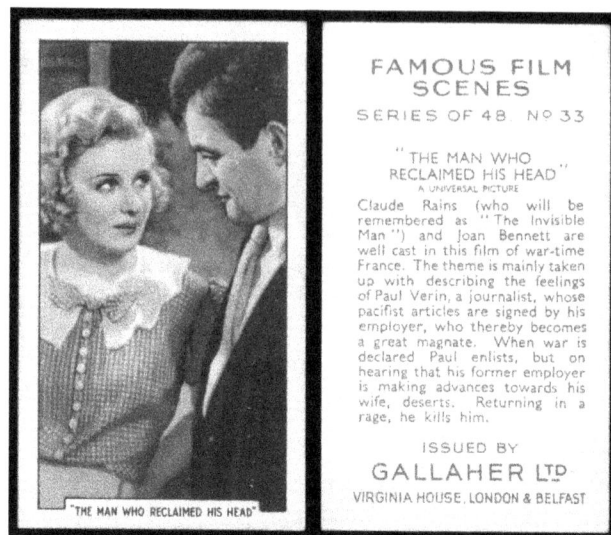

CR and Joan Bennett on a cigarette card advertising The Man Who Reclaimed His Head.

any moral message, but he liked the title (it sounded horrific), and the decapitation at the finale could be played up to attract movie-goers. He saw the film as perfect melodrama and instructed his publicity department to create press releases using the title as a selling device, associating Rains with his previous famous role: "Carl Laemmle Presents Claude Rains (The Invisible Man) in…" Newspaper ads underscored Rains' previous movie identity: "The Invisible Man Becomes The Man Who Reclaims His Head." Universal's press kits to movie house managers contained distorted newspaper ads, all with ghoulish artwork and suggestive one-liners: "Others stole his brilliant mind, but when they tried to steal his beautiful wife, one man lost his head and the other reclaimed his own." Another ad exclaimed: "To you who love murder mysteries – see the most fantastic sensational crime ever committed!" This publicity approach was probably annoying to Rains, but after the commercial failure of *Crime Without Passion*, he understood such means were often necessary to entice audiences. Universal's publicity machine never once advertised the film's anti-war element. Generally the play was easily adapted, but Rains did stipulate one significant alteration: He would not wear makeup to appear deformed. With all the subtleties afforded by the film camera, in close-ups, Rains knew he could make the audience understand the insecurities and true tragedy of the character.

Production began in mid-September. Rains received a salary of $10,500 with an extra allowance of

CR *and Joan Bennett behind the scenes on* The Man Who Reclaimed His Head. (*Photo courtesy John Antosiewicz.*)

$288 for travel expenses. Supporting Rains as Paul Verin were Lionel Atwill as the corrupt editor-publisher Henri Dumont and Joan Bennett as Paul's wife Adele. Again the story stressed Paul's aspirations to put his eloquent and dramatic words in the newspaper (even under another's byline) to warn the world about the "merchants of death" (arms manufacturers) who are the instigators of war.

As in the play, the film emphasized Paul's deep love for Adele, as he sacrifices his creative integrity to obtain money to make her happy. Although a faithful and dutiful wife, she has little interest in her husband's intellectual work (which requires financial sacrifice), and she longs for the bourgeoisie life, its trappings and parties. Paul has negated his principles

by ghost-writing pacifist editorials for Dumont. The articles are brilliant and make Dumont popular with the public. Realizing this, the munitions makers present the editor with political opportunities and he soon becomes their puppet. When the public mood turns in favor of war, Dumont easily changes his position. Appalled at this betrayal, Paul leaves the newspaper and tries to fight both the politicians and Dumont, but his attempts are useless; World War I breaks out. Dumont uses his new political power to have Paul sent to the Western Front. Now the editor can pursue Adele, whom he desires; he does not really love her but wants to take advantage of her loneliness. As much as he is a success, he is also bitterly jealous of Paul's intelligence and talent. At first Adele is flattered, but soon realizes Dumont's shallowness and how superior her husband really is.

Paul learns of Adele's situation in a train station where he awaits transfer to the death fields of Verdun. Enraged and distraught, he deserts his unit and makes his way to Paris. He arrives home to find Adele struggling as she attempts to spurn Dumont's advances. Paul draws his bayonet. There is a scream as the two men scuffle and in a crazed rage of emotion, Verin decapitates Dumont (not shown on screen), thereby reclaiming his "mind" and his wife. After a fadeout, Paul is seen carrying a satchel and his child to the home of an eminent lawyer to whom he has been relating the story we have seen in flashbacks. Adele arrives along with the police and Verin is led away. Because it was a crime of passion to defend his wife's honor, the lawyer assures Paul that no jury in France will convict him.

Rains' performance was praised: "The acting for the most part is excellent…. Rains gives the picture much of its conviction, portraying his role with intensity and simplicity." The film was classified as a "tense drama accentuated by the fine performance

CLAUDE RAINS

"THE MAN WHO RECLAIMED HIS HEAD"

A UNIVERSAL PICTURE

REPRESENTED BY

HAROLD FREEDMAN   OR   **HAWKS-VOLCK**
BRANDT & BRANDT   CORPORATION
                                                      Agency
NEW YORK   BEVERLY HILLS

Rains spent $100 on this full-page "want ad" in the December 6, 1934, Variety.

of Rains…." A critic for the Hearst papers syndicate stated: "If it were not for the fact that it serves to introduce Claude Rains, an exceptionally competent stage actor in a role which gives him wide opportunity to show his ability, I might call the picture dull and heavy."

Despite the shocking actions of the main character, Universal's press releases tried to play up Rains' attractiveness to women:

In real life the head of this specialist in eerie portrayals on the screen is topped by a thick lock of forward falling jet black [*sic*] hair undisciplined by comb or brush.

It is a huge head set firmly upon powerful shoulders. His eyes are dark brown and commonly have a commanding penetrating expression which in moments of excitement becomes wild looking, almost…. [His] hands are large and powerful. When he talks and becomes interested in the conversation, one eyebrow arches nervously. Though rather short and stocky in build, he is a handsome man and radiates sexual attractiveness. Each of his wives has been an outstandingly beautiful woman.

Although inappropriate for this particular picture, in fact none of this description is exaggerated, for Rains did often exuded a strong sensuality, especially when he smiled his mischievous little smile. There was an air of mystery about him, which many women found quite alluring. *The New York Times* noted: "[O]nce Rains invests himself with heavy drama and strangeness, [and] then he assumes a kind of virtuoso terrorism that makes it difficult for you to breathe when he is on the screen."

Rains remained apprehensive about making movies full time; a clause in his contract permitted him the right to return to New York for stage work. But Rains had no real intention of sacrificing his new career on the altar of Thespis: He merely shifted his goal somewhat. Now if a movie script was not to his liking, he still considered doing it. If the role was something he could work with, then a weak or contrived storyline mattered less.

Laemmle knew Rains was now a box office draw, especially in villainous roles, and decided to put the actor immediately into another thriller. Shortly after *The Man Who Reclaimed His Head* was finished on October 23, production began on the actor's next project. He would work six weeks, from mid–November until December 15, at the salary of $2,000 per week.

Lionel Atwill and CR in The Man Who Reclaimed His Head. *(Photo courtesy John Antosiewicz)*

Mystery of Edwin Drood was based on the famously unfinished novel by Charles Dickens. Rains was familiar with the story because years earlier he played a bit part in a stage adaptation, thrashing around wordlessly as one of the drug addicts. (This was the performance that prompted Sir Herbert Beerbohm Tree to describe the young Rains as the best overactor in the trade.) In the movie, he plays the lead, John Jasper, choirmaster of the cathedral town of Cloisterham, England, and secretly addicted to opium. Jasper, who gives voice lessons, has a fanatical love for his beautiful young student Rosa (Heather Angel), but the intensity of the slightly sinister man frightens her. (Rains is dubbed the several times Jasper sings in the choir.) His unholy passion for Rosa leads to death – for his beloved nephew Edwin Drood, whom Jasper murders, and for himself, when he tries to flee his crime.

CR and Juanita Quigley in The Man Who Reclaimed His Head. *(Photo courtesy John Antosiewicz)*

Mystery of Edwin Drood's *tormented choirmaster John Jasper. (Photo courtesy John Antosiewicz)*

Production proceeded smoothly except for the climactic scene in which Jasper, pursued by the police, scrambles to the top of the church's bell tower, from which, distraught and unbalanced, he leaps to his death. The set had an eight-foot drop and Rains elected not to use a stunt man. He hit the floor groaning. Filming was halted while his twisted right ankle was wrapped in ice and he rested for half an hour. Still in pain, he then went back to shooting; there were still six short scenes scheduled to be filmed on that set before it could be struck. After a night in pain, he went to the hospital the next morning for an x-ray. It transpired he had torn several ligaments and was on crutches for two weeks.

In *Edwin Drood*, Rains gives one of his better performances. His choirmaster is less monster and more flawed mortal, beset with inner demons over which he has no control. It is not explained why Jasper has become an addict, but it seems logical that he turned to drugs to relieve his mind of the evil obsession tormenting him, frequently leaving his sleepy little village to skulk off to London to indulge his habit. Rains has a couple of great scenes, combining both horror and pathos. In one, he lies on a makeshift bed in an opium den, hallucinating under the influence of the narcotic. Jerking and writhing, he relives strangling nephew Edwin with a scarf; eyes wide, face contorted, his mouth twisted. In another, Jasper learns that Rosa and Edwin had no intention of marrying, meaning that he murdered the boy for nothing. Overcome with terrible disbelief, he tries to speak, but stutters uncontrollably, almost as if having a seizure; his eyes well with tears. He tries to raise himself out of his chair but faints in a state of shock.

As would be expected, Universal press releases played up the horror: "gripping with suspense," "a thing to bewitch your senses for days." Handsome, atmospherically filmed, *Mystery of Edwin Drood* opened on March 21, 1935, and was a commercial success for the studio. *The New York Times* commented: "Mr. Rains, who has become the devil's own brother during his brief and hair-raising screen career, is brilliantly repellent. His searching eyes and malignantly arched eyebrows are tainted with mania. In the opium den after the murder, when he wrestles with his conscience during his drugged stupor, Mr. Rains makes your flesh crawl...."

There was no denying that what Rains could do, and do well, was impart "a wealth of weirdness

and intensity" both to his character and a film. But it had to be done judiciously, with restraint. Rains understood that when he was excessively flamboyant, it could come across as unbelievable. He began to see that understatement was far more effective. He learned that the slightest lift of an eyebrow could convey more than a page of dialogue. That said, it was clear he had an asset that set him apart: Within a few years, Rains established an identity through his slightly stylized technique, and more than anything else, his flexible, mellifluous, remarkable voice.

As Rains became more famous, devotees of movie magazines clamored for articles about this mystery man who remained "invisible" to fans. Always private and reluctant to let anyone invade his life, he still understood that publicity was a part of being a Hollywood figure. Interviewers found the actor rather difficult to describe and some felt there was always "a fascinating air of unreality and overstatement about his work ... which comes from the Rains personality. He is a charmingly unreal person in private life." During the release of *Mystery of Edwin Drood*, a Universal press release was entirely accurate about the subject's private life: "Most of Hollywood cannot understand Rains, for he goes to no parties, does not mix socially in any way and prefers to remain at home. Those who know him say this is not aloofness but shyness. Rains, an unusual actor, talks so little about himself on acting, but will talk hour after hour about his farm and antiques and becomes positively excited by a well-preserved piece of furniture of mid–Victorian era."

Of course, it is very difficult to know how accurate the published quotes attributed to Rains and the stories about him actually are; for example, three different London areas were reported as his birthplace (Camberwell, Clapton and Brixton). Frequently misrepresented was the duration of his World War I service. Rains was in France for only five months, but many articles quote him as claiming he spent three or four years there. It's not credible that an ex-soldier, who had endured what Rains had endured, would have lied, so in this case, the reporter was embellishing.

On the other hand, various aspects of his life story are consistently retold correctly, such as his youthful speech impediment, how he became involved in the theatre, and his lifelong gratitude to Sir Herbert Beerbohm Tree. Surprisingly, other aspects of his past that would surely have interested fans are never covered at all, such as his multiple marriages and his

THE GREATEST MYSTERY-THRILLER SINCE "INVISIBLE MAN"
PREMIERE SHOWING. PANTAGES THEATRE TOMORROW

The MYSTERY of EDWIN DROOD

CARL LAEMMLE PRESENTS
A   UNIVERSAL   PICTURE   WITH
CLAUDE RAINS
DOUGLASS
MONTGOMERY
HEATHER ANGEL — DAVID MANNERS
FRANCIS L. SULLIVAN — VALERIE HOBSON
Directed by STUART WALKER
An Edmund Grainger Production

relationship with his parents. The only subjects he discussed freely were the farm, Frances' companionship and his "simple pleasures": "I don't know whether I should confess it or simply state it as a fact … but it is true that I am perhaps the most retiring individual in recent history [in Hollywood]. I have no social life, and I know nothing about Hollywood. I have been accused of being a studious type, but I do little reading, though I do apply myself quite intensely to the study of the role and the picture in which I am appearing." This comment was reported in quotation marks, but it appeared in a film pressbook, a notorious instrument well-known for misrepresentation. For example, given the fact that Rains had an extensive library on the farm, with floor-to-floor shelves filled with books, it is difficult to believe he did "little reading."

But Rains concealed anything truly personal, and his identity remained enigmatic. Writers found the actor knowledgeable about literature, history, the craft of the theatre, and very interested in his work. They also found him evasive. Undoubtedly some of Rains' comments about his past were exaggerated, and in this way the line between fact and fiction became muddled. He never explained why acting was his chosen profession, or why it gave him satisfaction,

and he never discussed his opinion of his peers. Not only was there little introspection, there seemed to be actual avoidance of it. Rains refrained from giving too much importance to his poverty-stricken and lonely childhood, or that he had taken to the streets at age ten. Perhaps he felt that to dwell on such things would be to acknowledge the lasting effects on his psyche and behavior. Rains had a clever gift for carefully arranging his answers to interviewers' questions and being able to deviate from an unwelcome query with a story from his theatrical life.

The general public had no idea that, even though his salary was nearly $5,000 a week during the Great Depression, the actor remained emotionally as insecure as ever, despite a healthy ego. Financially comfortable, he was still cautious about spending money and at times was overly frugal, probably because of the scars from his childhood poverty. In 1930s Hollywood, when many stars bought extremely lavish homes and expensive automobiles, Rains' simple lifestyle appeared odd to his colleagues. This was an era when ostentation was expected from film idols – it was all part of the fantasy world they were seen to live in. Often interviewers were bewildered because Rains was an actor who presented such a debonair, sophisticated aura in his films, but his tastes were unabashedly plain. To a large extent, his manners and morals were still a reflection of Victorian-Edwardian decorum, and they remained fixed even while he incorporated into his lifestyle many American attitudes and mores. Hollywood never influenced Rains' values and he continued to embrace his own way of doing things — sometimes to extreme measures. When he lived in Pennsylvania, he usually purchased only used cars; when in Hollywood, he rented them. The only symbol of extravagance and status the actor ever wanted was a Rolls-Royce, which to him displayed position more than wealth, but he eventually settled on a Bentley, and even that he did not buy until he was sixty-five years old. When it came to managing household expenses, Rains was totally in charge of the checkbook, providing his wife with an allowance for necessities, and usually purchasing anything she requested that he felt was reasonable. However, he was very tight about anything he considered frivolous, such as an extensive wardrobe. Frances could not buy a dress without Claude's approval, which may have caused resentment. When daughter Jennifer was a teenager, her father refused to give her an allowance and yet he would not hesitate to buy expensive items for her. She could have anything she asked for, but not money.

Rains chose not to associate with the glamorous Hollywood. Although there was a large, established set of ex-pat British actors in Hollywood who met frequently on a social basis, Rains never felt comfortable or at ease with the "English colony." As he saw it, their affairs seemed to represent an impractical frolicking he abhorred, much like the upper-class social gatherings in England.

Possibly, this attitude was reinforced by an early incident in his film career, when he had a chance meeting on the Universal lot with former student Charles Laughton. When Rains had been a Royal Academy of Dramatic Art instructor, Laughton was one of his very talented pupils. In the years since, the portly character actor had achieved great success, and in 1933 won the Best Actor Oscar, playing the title role in the English film *The Private Life of Henry VIII*. In 1935, Rains spotted his former student in a studio commissary and attempted to congratulate him on his achievements. With no acknowledgment, Laughton turned away and continued his conversation with a companion. Although Rains seldom

mentioned the snub, he vowed never to behave that way to a colleague, and it appears he never did.

A reporter once asked Rains if he regretted leaving the Theatre Guild and then noted that the actor "took over" the interview as if he were on stage, but in a humorous manner, all to create an effect:

> His eyes flashed with the loftiest artistic aspirations. "I spurned their offers!" he shouted. (He has two voices — one a shout and the other a whisper; both make you edge away slightly.) "They told me they wanted to take me away from my art, from the stage, to play in their beastly movies. I wouldn't listen! I resented the mere suggestion! Then they cabled to say how much they would pay me — and you couldn't see me for dust. I had my bags packed and was in Hollywood the next morning." Then followed another gust of Rains laughter. The nice thing about that story is that I still believe that both bits of it are true. [Rains] probably did work himself into an artistic frenzy....

Though often aloof on the set, Rains could actually be very funny. His co-star in *The Clairvoyant*, Fay Wray, commented: "[Rains] was a very quiet most of the time, but sometimes his sense of humor would come to the forefront." In various studio "blooper reels" (many available on YouTube), Rains is completely uninhibited: In an outtake from *The Prince and the Pauper*, palace guard Alan Hale anxiously asks of Rains' Earl of Hertford, "What's to be done?" Rains hesitates, obviously blanking on his scripted reply, and then wails in a teeny falsetto voice, "I don't *know* what's to be done, I don't know-w-w!" Twice he muffs a *White Banners* line to Fay Bainter: The first time, he throws back his head and barks out a litany of amusing British profanities; the second time, he makes an over-the-top horrified face and whirls around, playfully biting his fingers. In a *Kings Row* outtake, he walks toward Robert Cummings on his line, "Of course, you can never tell," and then abruptly turns to the off-camera crew, shouting with exasperation, "I'm not talking the *dialogue*, for God's sake!"

On the other hand, Rains could easily intimidate anyone either quietly or with an explosive command:

"Anyone studying a portrait of Rains is reminded of the resemblance to an exceedingly alert and sometimes deadly tiger. He has terrific vitality which with his sure sense of acting, makes him an exceedingly dangerous person for another actor to oppose in a scene. His stern manner is modified by a rare – a very rare – smile, which shows the tender side of this very amazing man."

At times it bothered him that those people he cared about misread his personality: "Some people say I have a belligerent walk, a belligerent attitude. They must be wrong… It isn't belligerence. It can't be. It's an inferiority complex…" Apparently this behavior was a device, instinctively developed not only because of his short physical stature, but because of his insecurity. "Belligerence" was the protective cloak Rains assumed when it was needed.

As much as he disliked the climate of Southern California and the social environment of "Tinsel Town," Rains now used his Los Angeles address as his legal residence, since he was spending more than six months a year making movies. However, he remained apprehensive about his recently acquired good fortune, admitting to a reporter, "I have to keep my fingers crossed." As a film actor, the one thing that bothered him was the fear he would be typecast too quickly if he made another Hollywood movie, especially for Universal. Consequently, when an offer arrived to make a picture for Gainsborough Productions in England, Rains accepted. A trip abroad would also afford the opportunity to rethink permanent residency in America. *The Invisible Man* was showing all over the world – Claude Rains would return to his native land in triumph.

CHAPTER 9
A Return to England

When Rains arrived in England in early 1935, *Picturegoer* magazine interviewed him for an article titled "Why I Left Hollywood." "England is my home," he replied, adding he felt British films were just as worthy as those produced in America.

Rains had returned to London to play the title role in *The Clairvoyant*. His leading lady was another Hollywood import, Fay Wray. The actress was intrigued by Rains' approach to his work: Sixty years later, she remembered his technique vividly in an interview with Kevin Brownlow: "I liked [Rains'] style, he was always ready, always stretched himself to be taller than he really was. …He never made you feel that he was casual, or that he tossed anything off ever, no. He was deeply sincere about his work."

Rains stars as the Great Maximus, King of Mind Readers, who performs his (fake) act with his wife in English music halls. The role gave the actor a rare opportunity to run the gamut of emotions: humorous and affectionate as he teases the wife he adores; theatrical as he performs his mind-reading act; and then horrified and guilt-ridden when he finds that his pretense to see the future has now somehow become genuine. He is especially effective when he awakens from a trance and realizes he has no control over his own mind. Wray admitted that the actor's trance scenes were chilling: "There was no artificial creepiness about his trance. It was simply straightforward acting on his part. But every time he went through these scenes, he was so intense that I felt a horrible cold shiver run all the way down my spine."

Only twenty-seven when she worked with Rains, Wray wrote an article about her experience for a British publication. (Although Wray and Rains were both at Universal at the same time, they had never met previously.) Wray described Rains as a "psychological actor" with "amazing intensity" when working on the set, "fascinating" to watch: "I found him to be a rather unexpected mixture of boyishness and seriousness. He is, without a doubt, one of the most meticulous actors I have ever known.… Several times he would ponder quietly over a scene, then say he felt that the character's reaction would be different from those described in the scenario. And he would always be psychologically correct."

Although she had been in the industry since her teens, Wray thought Rains was different from many of her colleagues. Most stage actors considered their talents diminished by the medium of film, but Rains found making movies intriguing, especially as he learned to take advantage of a benefit the camera afforded an actor: the close-up. Wray commented that Rains' eyes "seemed to me all the while to reflect the actual thoughts of the character." They were as asset off-camera as well. "If anyone is talking to him and he is tired of the conversation, he will not trouble to interrupt. He will simply look at the person in a way which seems as if he is looking right through him. And the conversationalist will falter, forget what he is talking about, and bring the tedious talk to an end."

Wray was very keen about Rains' artistic ability, meticulous, always prepared, with a style that was very elegant. Above all, she was impressed because he wanted to understand what he was doing and why. She obviously admired Rains as a colleague: "It was a relief to have him be so certain and right about what he did, so you could depend upon that strength, keeping things together." She knew he was uncomfortable about his height and that he wore elevated heels. She was quick to add that although Rains was short, he was sturdily built and that he was sexually attractive because of his mysteriousness manner.

The Clairvoyant received modest reviews in England. When it opened in the States in June 1935, it was less successful, dubbed by *The New York Times* as a "meandering melodrama which would be utterly unimportant except for Mr. Rains' presence.

Maximus, "King of Mind Readers," in The Clairvoyant. According to Kinematograph Weekly, Rains, "equipped with just the right personality, ...imparts the essential touch of uncanniness to the part, yet always remains human...."

Fay Wray, who played Rains' wife in The Clairvoyant, *remembered him as a "fine" and "dedicated" actor.*

His vigorous and sensitive performance is about all that holds a faulty story structure together." Another reviewer wrote: "Claude Rains in the title role gives a haunting performance in his complex character.... It is refreshing to see him exhibiting light-hearted shenanigans with [his wife] only because he usually plays such serious and heavy parts. It is apparent that Rains romps and moves easily from a carefree spirit into a troubled man burdened with a 'gift' of insight which is causing him more grief than wealth."

Clairvoyant screenwriter Charles Bennett told film historian Tom Weaver that he was writing just ahead of the cameras: "I was in the studio, and the assistant director would come up and say, 'Have you got any more pages?' He'd take them down to Maurice Elvey, the director, and they'd shoot them." Regarding Rains, he recalled:

> One day, Claude Rains came up to my office and said, "By the way, Charles, have you noticed this girl [Jane Baxter] who's playing the second part?" I said, "Yes, she's quite lovely." He said, "I only ask because she keeps on saying, 'That writer up there, he's so good-looking, I can't put him out of my mind.'" I thought, "*This* is very in-

teresting!" So I went down to the set, met Jane Baxter, and we became very close friends. After the picture was over, one night we were having dinner on the lawn at the big hotel in Bray, and she said, "Do you know, Charles, how I met you?" I told her what had happened. She said, "No, it wasn't quite like that. Claude Rains used to come up to me every day and say, 'Have you noticed this writer? He can't put you out of his mind...!'" Rains was a practical joker [*laughs*]! He was on his way back to America on the *Normandie* and we sent a telegram to him that night, thanking him very much.

Rains enjoyed filming in England and relished the recognition he received. More articles were written about him for this one picture than appeared in a year's time in the States. During the actor's brief stay, J.B. Priestley and other noted critics speculated a possible return to the English theatre. Priestley later wrote that, had Rains done so, there was no doubt that he could have reached the levels of Ralph Richardson, Laurence Olivier and former student John Gielgud. But Rains was now more comfortable in the States with his American wife and her large extended family; additionally, there was his desire to have his children born in America.

In mid-March 1935, when Rains returned to the U.S. following the completion of *The Clairvoyant*, *Variety* reported that the Universal contractee was set for the title role in the studio's announced *Hunchback of Notre Dame* remake (ultimately never made), "but may go into a Broadway legit in the interim." Rains wanted to do everything he could to ensure he would not be typecast in his new career, so when Paramount offered him a very different part in a picture titled *The Last Outpost*, Rains cabled his agent to accept. The deal was only for the single project; Rains still believed a long-term contract would inevitably make him the slave of a studio's demands. In the 1930s, this was a difficult position to maintain. Agents were in the early stages of developing their positions of power as negotiators, and while Rains was irrefutably an actor of quality, intelligence and skill, he was middle-aged, not particularly handsome, and too short to be a classic leading man.

In the years to come, Rains would make several films at Paramount. *The Last Outpost* was the first, and sadly not one of the best. While the script, written by Philip MacDonald, lacked substance, Paramount's studio boss, Adolph Zukor, felt it was a good time to release a film similar in mood and locale to the recently successful *The Lives of a Bengal Lancer*, a fact largely played up in the publicity campaign. Basically it was a love triangle interwoven into the British Army's efforts to protect the Empire in the Middle East during World War I.

The picture afforded Rains a large and meaty role and saw him undertaking actions very unlike his usual persona (trekking through the untamed jungle, struggling across a desert). John Stevenson is an undercover British Intelligence Officer who joins forces with star Cary Grant's character, Michael Andrews. The story opens in the Turkish Theatre of War against the British during World War I when the Kurdish government was allied with the Turks to help destroy the Armenian Balkari peoples, securing their cattle for a food supply. Both Andrews and the audience are uncertain of the motives of the ambiguous Stevenson, who is a strange, silent man. Andrews is injured and, back in a Cairo hospital, falls in love with his nurse (who

The Last Outpost.

vast numbers of the enemy, the two men realize one must leave to try and warn the column. Andrews swears to Stevenson that "nothing happened" and that Rosemary remained faithful. Stevenson then struggles across the blistering desert until he finally reaches the relief column. Andrews, with only a single revolver, is holding off about twenty natives, but just in time Stevenson leads the army column back to save Andrews for the third time, only to be shot by the enemy. He dies in Andrews' arms, selflessly muttering, "Better this way...her happiness..." His head drops. In this version, we have the heroic husband dying to save his wife's loved one as well as the men at the fort. Stevenson makes the noble sacrifice which will allow Andrews to marry Rosemary. It is an "honorable ending," and it was unadulterated corny melodrama. Graham Greene summed it up: "Half of *The Last Outpost* is remarkably good and half of it quite abysmally bad..."

turns out to be Stevenson's wife). Finally on leave after two years, Stevenson returns and discovers their affair. Enraged, feeling betrayed by both his friend and his spouse, Stevenson follows Andrews where he is assigned at "the last outpost" in the Sudan. Confronting Andrews with "You ruined my life, now I'll end yours," Stevenson draws his revolver, but true to Hollywood's idea of melodrama (especially in the 1930s), at that moment the outpost is attacked by "savages." (The picture presents the completely racist picture of all indigenous peoples that was unfortunately habitual and acceptable for the time.) In a flash of patriotism, the two British officers set aside their personal differences to warn the relief column coming to their rescue. During their escape, Stevenson saves Andrews once again, this time from a stampeding herd. Because of Andrews' leg injury, and the

Prior to release, Paramount ran into trouble with the Production Code enforcers because of several suggestive sexy scenes that the studio was told to change or eliminate in order for the film to obtain a seal of approval. One objectionable scene took place in a bedroom in which Rains gives his wife a diamond bracelet, caressing her and kissing her rather seductively on the neck. Shockingly, he is clad in pajamas and she is dressed in a negligee. A fadeout follows. This innuendo of intimacy was seen as much too explicit.

Production began on April 29, 1935; Claude and Frances arrived in Hollywood on May 7 and he started work on May 15. He was paid $4,000 per week and ended up being on the film 26 days; he also received the round trip train tickets for $300 plus $100 for miscellaneous expenses. Star Cary

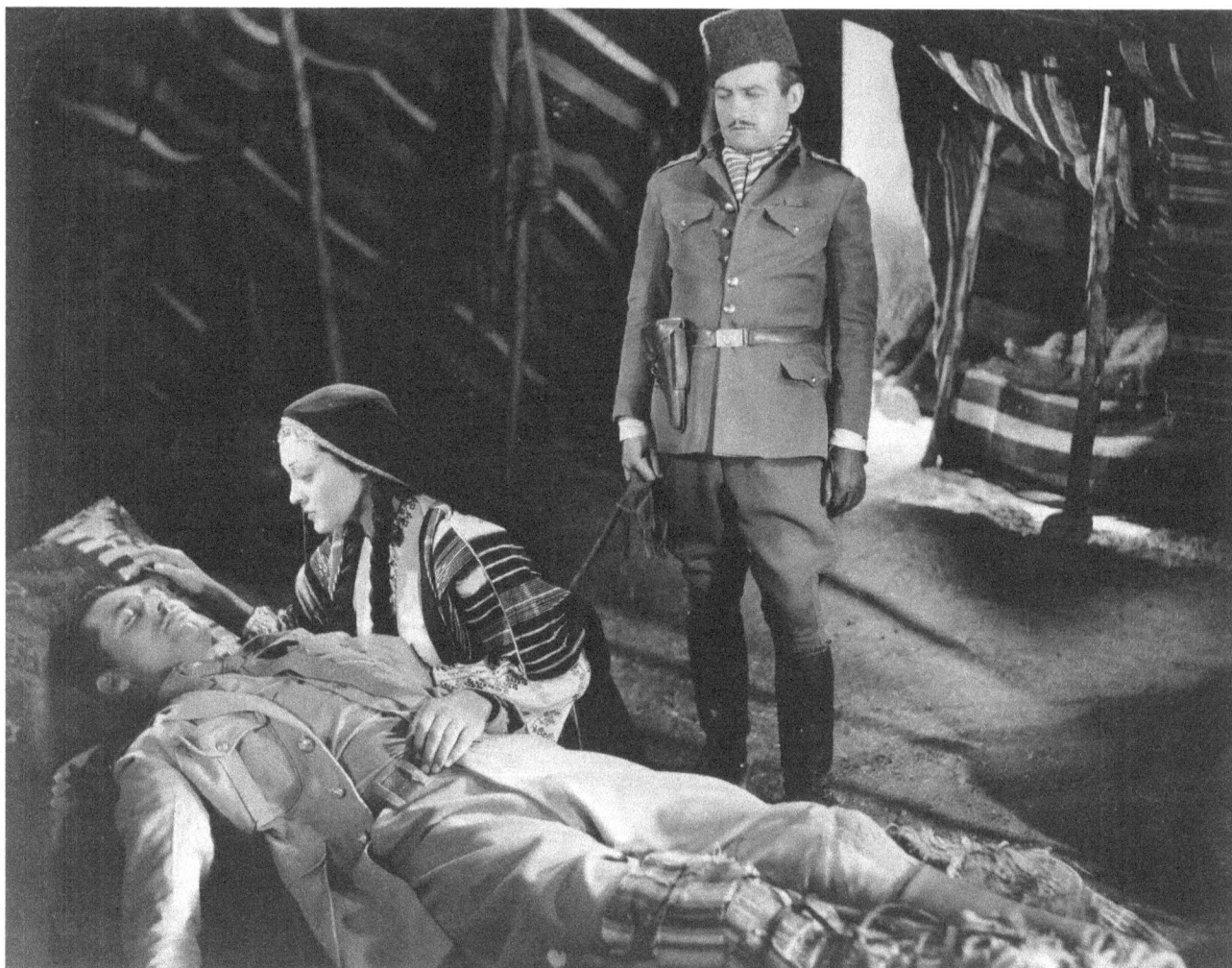

Rains (right) with Cary Grant and Kathleen Burke in The Last Outpost.

Grant, who was under a Paramount contract, made a grand total of $12,500 no matter how many days he worked. This just reinforced Rains' determination not to become the "property" of any studio. He noticed other things about how a studio conducted its business: It was all managed like a factory. Careful time sheets and records were maintained. Daily memos went back and forth between production head and director as well as the studio boss with every dollar being accounted for. Actors were not even called by their name on the daily shoot sheets; they were assigned numbers indicating who was to be where on any given day. This number usually corresponded to their billing status. Grant was number one and Rains was number two.

The changes made to the script extended production until September; Rains had to work an additional four weeks and one day. The death scene and the desert treks were shot in the blistering heat of August in the desert of Yuma, Arizona, where the temperature ranged from 105 to 120 degrees. Sometimes filming had to begin at 4 a.m. and production closed down between 11 a.m. and 2 p.m. to avoid the worst of the heat. Added to this, the entire company suffered stomach ailments, as well as further misery when the area became infested by crickets which got into everything – food, bedding, clothing. It was a deplorable working situation. Rains was miserable, but took everything in stride and never complained. A September 9 memo indicates that that the scene in which Rains is shot, and falls mortally wounded from his horse, would have to be reshot the next day. The reason: "Rains' eyes were so badly inflamed from sand and wind," he could not see.

Rains had to demonstrate horsemanship in several scenes. Prior to this picture, he had never ridden in his life. Frances recalled that he rushed home one day, beside himself with nerves about getting on a horse. The couple went straight out to a riding school. Eventually he grew comfortable enough

The Last Outpost.

CR and Cary Grant in The Last Outpost.

in the saddle that he and Frances would ride each morning in the Hollywood Hills before production began. But evidently he gave it up, because daughter Jennifer doesn't remember ever seeing her father on a horse. However, Frances delighted in the sport and continued it for many years, even when they moved to a much larger farm in Pennsylvania. Records from Glen Mills show that in 1939, Rains purchased a horse for Frances' birthday.

The Last Outpost opened to the mediocre reviews it deserved. The *New York Herald Tribune* said it was "second-rate imperialism" and nowhere near the quality of *The Lives of a Bengal Lancer*. But the reviewer did cite Rains, who "has a chance to act all over the screen with characteristic fervor and does it very well indeed."

The Last Outpost was the sixth film Rains made and it was also his last taste of freedom as an independent artist. Astute studio heads like Jack Warner realized exceptional talent beyond a bad script, and Rains was just the type Warner wanted: not a glamour boy like Cary Grant but a forceful actor who did not need looks to attract an audience. A new venture for Rains was on the horizon — that of a contract player for one of the best studios in Hollywood, a professional association that would last for ten years.

CHAPTER 10
Property of Warner Brothers

In the 1930s, a long-term contract with a major studio was both a blessing and a curse: a godsend financially, but often a kind of death sentence when it came to artistic freedom. Studios were listed on the stock exchanges, beholden to shareholders and boards of directors; studio chiefs were astute, shrewd, ruthless businessmen. They sold dreams – their "product" was a world of fantasy – and the Depression was the perfect soil to foster the blooming of the Golden Age of Hollywood. Going to the movies was different than attending the theatre. Theater-going was an activity usually associated with the upper middle class, with intellectuals. A movie ticket was cheap, and cinemas were springing up in little towns across America. Unlike the artificial distance the stage created between the audience and the players, the motion picture camera could zoom in for a close-up of an actor's face, sharing every nuance of expression. This created a pseudo-familiarity between movie patrons and the artists, which in turn also created a loyal following of fans who would attend any film featuring their favorite stars.

There were several major drawbacks inherent in becoming a studio's "property." If an actor was under contract, he could be assigned to any film and had little opportunity to refuse a part. As an artist, Rains had difficulty getting into a role if he felt he was unsuited for it. Also, he felt the arrangement played havoc with creativity: "I don't believe in long contracts because I think one is apt to become 'typed' for one thing. And for another thing, you can very easily become stale and tired working too long in one studio. I am convinced that the public becomes tired of seeing your face too many times in one year."

There were other negatives. If a contract player was offered a role by another studio, a deal had to be worked out between legal departments, with the final decision made by the studio chief. (In return, the studio would receive a sum of money or a per-centage for the use of their "property.") Even worse, studios could arrange to loan out an actor to another studio without the actor's consent. Added to all these entanglements was the *coup de grace*: If a contract actor wanted to work at another studio, he could be "temporarily released"; however, the time spent away from the home studio was added on to the original agreement. With such arrangements, a seven-year contract could easily become a ten-year obligation. This is exactly what happened to Rains during his association with Warners.

Even though he was well aware of all these issues, by the end of 1935, Rains felt he had no alternative but to ally himself with one of the major studios. He was forty-five years old. His new young wife was accustomed to a comfortable lifestyle. The couple intended to keep their Pennsylvania farm but knew they also would have to maintain a Hollywood home. Most importantly, they wanted children. Because Rains was still a British subject, he had to pay income tax to the British government in addition to U.S. Federal and California state income tax. He was still a member of Actors Equity; if he returned to Broadway for a job, he would have to pay taxes in New York state as well. On top of everything else, about this time Rains became financially responsible for his mother's upkeep in a senior living residence in London.

So if he was going to become an indentured servant, the question was, where?

Despite his success at Universal, Rains did not want to be associated with a studio whose reputation was based on its (admittedly successful) horror films. Although Paramount head man Adolph Zukor was a powerful force, his studio lacked a concrete artistic philosophy.

But Warner Bros. was not afraid to handle highly volatile social issues of the period: inequality, gangster violence, political corruption, prejudice and the anti-hero. Studio topper Jack L. Warner wanted strong, forceful personalities who could act – immortal "tough guys" or "heavies" like Cagney, Robinson, Muni, Bogart – to round out a roster of romantic, handsome leading men like Errol Flynn. The studio also had one of the most talented and most admired actresses in the business under contract, Bette Davis. In addition, Warners executives understood the advantage of a supporting company of reliable character actors.

Jack Warner was impressed by what he knew about Rains. By now the actor had established an excellent reputation as a dedicated and highly consummate artist who would be an asset to any studio. On October 31, 1935, Rains' L.A. lawyer, Ralph Lewis, received correspondence from Warners' representative, R.J. Obringer, regarding a seven-year contract. After ironing out several differences, inserting certain clauses respective to billing, detailing provisions for working in the theatre, and sufficient advance notice of assignments, Rains signed the instrument on November 27 to be effective on December 2. While he could have demanded a high salary, Rains felt he needed to be more concerned with other matters which were of extreme importance to him such as billing. The specified salaries would cancel on March 11, 1940, at which time Warners could pick up on its first options to renegotiate. Rains received $4,000 per week for his first and second pictures, then $4500 per week for his third and fourth. He was guaranteed four weeks on each film, but if retakes were necessary, he would work the fifth without additional compensation. However, if the production went into a sixth week, he would receive his weekly allowance. All this meant that by the end of the sixth year, Rains would be receiving $38,000 per film.

The clause that confirmed freedom to perform in a theatrical production but without a "run of the play" contract meant he could be in a play only about two months. It was unlikely that any producer would enter into negotiations with an actor with such a sword of Damocles hanging over his head, but initially this arrangement satisfied Rains because he had seldom been in a play that ran as long as eight weeks. However, as the years passed, he regretted the wording which prevented him from sticking with a long run. Warners met Rains' demands, but kept him on a leash. The contract also allowed the actor to accept radio work, but only within conditions specified by

the studio and only with pre-approval. Especially demeaning was the clause granting Warners the right to lend or transfer Rains to another studio, whether or not the actor agreed. Further, Warners could, subject to the approval of the artist, sell or transfer his contract to another major studio. But if Rains refused or declined, then the studio could terminate his contract and take legal action.

One aspect of major concern to the actor: billing. The contract stated: "Artist shall not have less than second featured billing and the size of type in the ad shall be the same as the first featured artist." When it came to illness, the studio was especially parsimonious. If Rains was sick for more than a week, he could be replaced in his current film, or substituted into another picture when he recovered. To be certain of "genuine" illness, Warners, like all the studios, had their own physicians. If an actor was absent from the set due to anything other than illness (for example, personal leave), causing delays in the production schedule, he would pay the studio for time lost. (Rains never took any personal time, not even when his child was born. There were several occasions when he worked with a fever or some other health issue, in order not to lose a day's pay. Given the fact he was prone to colds and the flu, it is remarkable he was not absent more often than production records indicate.)

In 1936, Rains' agent was William Hawks (brother of renowned director, Howard Hawks) of Hawks-Volck Corporation in Beverly Hills. Generally the actor was satisfied with the contract Hawks drew up for him, with the exception of one item, and on this issue letters went back and forth for several weeks. Rains insisted that Warners pay for his transportation to and from Pennsylvania. The amount involved was negligible (about $300), but it was a matter of principle: The actor reasoned that if the studio failed to notify him of his next project while he was still in Hollywood, and he left for the East, then it was due to their negligence. If Warners wanted him to return to Hollywood, it was the studio's responsibility to reimburse him for the expense involved. This return of expenses to an actor was unheard of, but eventually Warners conceded. A clause stated the studio would reimburse for the cost of a single first-class railway ticket from New York to Los Angeles and return, including a Pullman compartment, but they were required to pay for only two journeys in each direction during any year. Because Jack Warner already had a

CR and Anita Louise in Anthony Adverse.

film in mind for the newest member of his stable, contract negotiations were rushed through within a week – just to save the train fare. A final stipulation Rains insisted upon was inserted: that his voice could not be dubbed in English for any overseas companies showing the film. He knew the value of his most prized asset. By December 2, 1935, Claude Rains was the property of Warner Bros. Studios.

On November 27, even before his contract went into effect, Rains was assigned to his first picture. Because he was anxious to begin, he waived his right to thirty days' notice and reported on December 2 for costume fittings. He had a four-week guarantee but did not finish the film until February 1936. It was the first of sixteen films Claude Rains would make for Warner Bros.

Anthony Adverse was a sprawling costume extravaganza, following the dramatic and romantic adventures of its late-18th century eponymous hero. Based on the epic novel by Hervey Allen and starring Fredric March in the title role, it had an enormous supporting cast, including Olivia de Havilland, Edmund Gwenn and Gale Sondergaard. (The latter was an accomplished theatre actress known for her portrayals of manipulative and forceful women; Rains had appeared with her in several Theatre Guild productions. *Anthony Adverse* was her film debut, and for her performance as a wily woman who blackmails her way to the top, she won the first Best Supporting Actress Oscar.) Rains was pleased to be working with one of the outstanding young directors of the time whom he admired very much: Mervyn LeRoy, known as the boy wonder of Hollywood.

Producer Hal B. Wallis had considered Edward G. Robinson and Basil Rathbone before casting Rains as the Marquis Don Luis Da Vincitata. As the scheming, vain, lecherous, cruel grandee of Spain who is envoy to the king of France, Rains made the absolute most out of a meaty role. The movie opens with a coach bearing the marquis and his new young bride Maria (Anita Louise) speeding towards a chateau near a health spa. To his chagrin and annoyance, Don Luis is afflicted with a painful seizure of gout, which renders him unable to claim his marital rights on his honeymoon.

Above: CR and Anita Louise in Anthony Adverse.   Below: CR with Anita Louise and Louis Hayward in Anthony Adverse.

CR as the aged Don Luis in Anthony Adverse.

CR as Emperor Napoleon and Dick Powell as his younger brother in Hearts Divided.

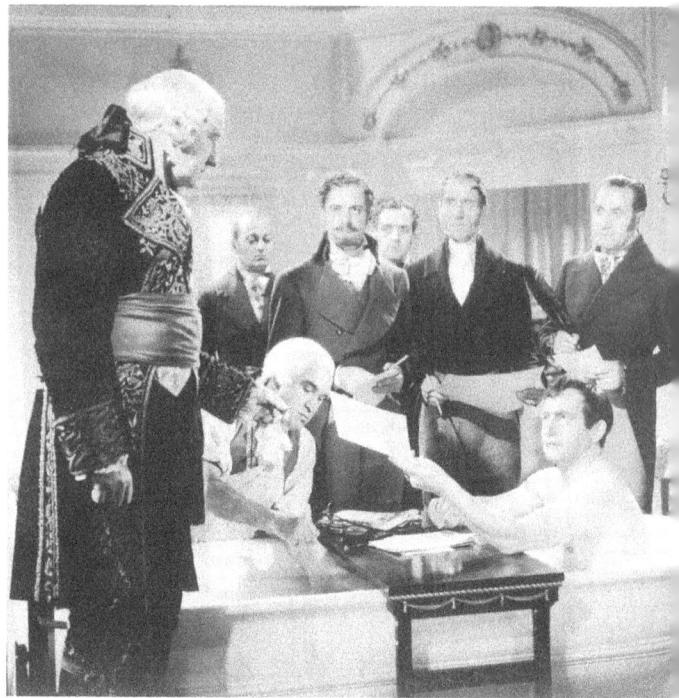

Halliwell Hobbes (left) and CR in Hearts Divided.

While he undergoes three months of treatment in the baths, the demure Maria, whose marriage was arranged by her wealthy merchant father, is courted by a dashing, handsome officer (Louis Hayward). Cured, Don Luis is ready to enjoy his role as a husband. After strutting about in his satin finery, he primps in front of a mirror, smoothing out his mustache and goatee, spraying on scent. When her lover attempts to save Maria from Don Luis, the marquis kills the young man in a duel. Rains plays to the back of the house in the scene in which Don Luis waits for his wife to deliver her lover's baby: Sprawled in a chair, he drains a tankard as the liquid dribbles down his chest, and chews a chicken leg with his mouth open. When his servant announces the birth of a boy, he dissolves into maniacal laughter worthy of the Invisible Man. Throughout, Rains is resplendent in an array of fabulous period outfits. As the story progresses, his looks change over the decades (facial hair to clean-shaven, permed dark curls to a flowing white wig). The actor's technique was intense: A makeup man who worked on the picture remembered: "The first time I ever saw him, he sat down at a dressing table and he looked

at himself for a moment and suddenly his face changed. Without touching it, he'd aged 30 years. Rains actually makes up with his mind."

Anthony Adverse was a Best Picture Oscar nominee that year. *Variety* wrote: "Rains gives an extraordinary fine version of Don Luis, sinister grandee." The role was an excellent Warner Bros. debut for Rains and established him as an exceptional asset for the studio.

By the time Rains finished his work in *Anthony Adverse* on February 6, 1936, he had already been assigned to his next film. Eventually Rains would, like other members of the studio's "permanent stock company," become accustomed to taking on new roles quickly.

In mid–January, at the direction of Jack Warner, studio lawyer R.J. Obringer sent a memo to Hal Wallis suggesting that Rains' next role would be Napoleon. There was some disagreement concerning the wording of his original contract as Rains was not to be forced to complete two movies within a twelve-week period. Wallis issued an angry memo to Arnow and Obringer: "I want to get the Claude Rains situation straightened out immediately and I want it definitely established that he is going to play the part of 'Napoleon' in *Hearts Divided* the basis of eight weeks out of twelve, as we discussed. Get this thing cleared up and let me know." Eventually the legal knots were worked out and the actor was assigned to make *Hearts Divided*, starring Dick Powell

Hearts Divided.

the screen or stage. One of the most delightful scenes in which he figures is the bath episode where he issues commands while in the midst of his ablutions." And the *Morning Telegraph* noted: "It is Mr. Rains, indeed, who practically runs away with the picture…. A bow for Mr. Rains." Yet the most astute review was that of the *Herald Tribune*: "Anyone who saw Mr. Rains play Napoleon in *Napoleon's Barber* here in 1928 will remember the short, slight man with his bank of black hair over the troubled brow, hand in bosom and burning eye. During his impassioned appeal to the heroine to give up his brother for the sake of France … he delivers himself once more of oratory…. In fact … when his ministers convene with him at his bath, he is equally hypnotic, though shorn of his medals (and clothes)." After this film, Rains decided never again to play Napoleon: After four stints, he had had his fill and felt he could no longer present a new and different dimension to the historic figure.

In real life, Napoleon was able to come between Jerome and Elizabeth Patterson and annul their marriage, but the movie ends with Napoleon's mother (Beulah Bondi) coming to the rescue, taking Jerome's side and giving a pouty Napoleon a gentle chastisement. (The exasperated mom: "When you were a little boy, playing with tin soldiers in the vineyard, I never dreamed it would all come to this!") Rains' scenes are amusing as he makes ironic references to Waterloo and to Josephine's penchant for expensive jewelry. Even non–Hearst papers saluted his performance: *The New York Times* called him "a capricious yet superbly ruthless Napoleon" and *Variety* gave him "top acting honors": "He creates an outstanding characterization of the man in his less imperialistic moments, deft, witty, shrewd and persuasive in his dealings with his brother and the girl the latter would marry."

Stolen Holiday, Rains' next assignment, teamed him with one of Warner's top female stars, the beautiful and statuesque Kay Francis. The picture was based on the Stavisky Affair, a real-life financial scandal in France that ended with the mysterious death of

and Marion Davies, the charming and funny actress who was also the acknowledged mistress of William Randolph Hearst.

Even the talented screenwriting of Casey Robinson and Laird Doyle couldn't create interest in the comedic story of the historical romance and subsequent marriage of Jerome Bonaparte, brother to the great Napoleon, to an American commoner. The movie's resemblance to reality was almost non-existent. Rains recognized that the story was ridiculous and, having played the Little Emperor several times on stage, this film version offered no special challenge.

Nonetheless, nearly all the movie critics (whose columns appeared in every Hearst-owned newspaper), including the influential Louella Parsons, went overboard praising Rains: "Claude Rains [is] probably the best Napoleon who has ever been seen on

CR and Kay Francis in Stolen Holiday.

the man at its center, Serge Alexandre Stavisky, and which purportedly implicated the legendary designer, Chanel.

Rains was on his Pennsylvania farm when he received notice to report to Warners; he sent the studio a telegram requesting railroad tickets for himself and Frances. The studio refused, and once again there was disagreement about transportation costs, a matter on which the actor would not budge. Jack Warner complied simply because he knew he could make Rains "pay" in other ways in the future. Claude and Frances arrived in Hollywood in late June, renting an apartment at the Château Élysée, a well-known celebrity dwelling with a storied Hollywood history.

Assigned to direct the film was Michael Curtiz, a fixture at Warner Bros. from 1926 through 1953 and already one of the industry's most prodigious talents. *Stolen Holiday* marked the beginning of an amiable and fulfilling relationship for the director and actor,

who made a total of eleven films together. Rains was one of the few actors in Hollywood capable of working well with the Hungarian-born Curtiz, who had a reputation not only for erratic English and personal idiosyncrasies, but for rude behavior on a set, especially to minor players. Curtiz was respected for his filmmaking expertise; he nearly always produced a good film and could work reliably in any genre; but he frequently went over schedule, exceeded budgets and exasperated the studio execs.

Scriptwriter Casey Robinson's plot for *Stolen Holiday* (which had the working title of *Mistress of Fashion*) begins in Paris with clever confidence man Stephan Orloff (Rains) selecting, and convincing, equally confident Parisienne model Nicole Picot (Francis) to be his escort at soirees where he will mingle with the important business people he intends to swindle. With the (unwitting) assistance of the ravishing Nicole, Orloff secures the support of ministers and highly placed political officials as well as a prominent newspaper editor and has free rein for his nefarious "business affairs." Nicky believes Orloff is a legitimate businessman, and their mutual ambition becomes the basis for an affectionate friendship. In gratitude for her help, Orloff establishes Nicky in her own salon, and she soon becomes famous as a fashion designer of haute couture. The pair both enjoy unqualified personal, and financial, success. When Stefan's schemes begin to unravel, he takes advantage of their understanding and asks Nicole to marry him in a society wedding to ward off governmental scrutiny of his activities. She agrees, even though she has fallen in love with a British diplomat (Ian Hunter). But the police close in on Orloff; to make sure *his* scandal doesn't ruin *her*, there is only one way out for him.

From the very first day, things did not proceed smoothly. There were continuous changes to the script; the film quickly exceeded its allotted shooting schedule; and the weather that summer was particularly unbearable (there was no air conditioning in the Burbank studios). Rains detested being in California in the stifling heat anyway, and costuming required him to wear an overcoat in many scenes. Records indicate that on August 24 it was so sickeningly hot, the actor was forced to leave the set, feeling ill and dizzy. (This action meant he "owed" the studio an additional day of work or he would be docked a day's pay.)

In other respects, this was not an easy project for Rains. His character was difficult to interpret because of the constant script changes: He would learn his lines, plan his moves, only to discover the scene was to be thrown out or altered. All of this caused problems, frustration and disagreements, especially concerning his character's interaction with Francis' Nicole. While the drama of the scandal was an intricate element of the storyline, Jack Warner wanted the script to heighten the picture's romantic triangle.

Additionally, there was the disparity in height between Francis (five foot nine) and Rains (around five foot six), not the last time Rains would have to make adjustments when filming with a taller leading lady. Warner sent off a confidential memo to Hal Wallis: "There's one thing we want to warn Mike Curtiz about, and that is we should arrange our setups so that Kay Francis won't tower over Rains…. If Mike is smart, he can move them around and put them in certain positions so that this won't even be noticeable. If necessary, on the close shots we can set Rains up on a couple-inch board, or something…." Warner

added: "That's a good idea of Rains playing this with a mustache; it gives the thing punch. In looking at Rains with his mustache and his modern wardrobe, he certainly can do everything, and do it right…. We want to keep him in mind."

Orloff is a clever and persuasive man who desires power and wealth at any cost. Rains plays him as a self-serving but roguish manipulator, with the sophistication and distinguished looks to make Nicky's feelings for him believable. (This personality type was Rains' forte: suave, urbane, totally unscrupulous, and yet charming and agreeable, even sexually attractive.) For the first half of the film, the story is brisk and sophisticated. Francis and Rains are delightful and engaging in their clever, witty repartee; the two fit neatly into their roles and make the characters genuine and likable. When the good-natured, if pedestrian, Hunter shows up as "the other man," the main storyline is sidetracked from the delightful flirtatious relationship between Stefan and Nicole. In 1992, when New York's Museum of Modern Art screened the picture, a *New York Times* writer described the ambiance perfectly: "[A]s Francis floats across a ballroom floor in a white turban and a beautiful backless dress while Rains lifts a mocking eyebrow beneath the brim of his shiny top hat, it seems as if glamour and irony had just been invented."

Rains' last scene is his finest moment in the picture, as he reveals Orloff's true soul with extreme sensitivity. After he has betrayed Nicole's faith in him, he ponders: "Perhaps there is some way I can balance the scales. I may yet prove that your friendship was not wasted – that you saw qualities in me that even I did not suspect existed. If I can do this, you'll know the whole truth about me…" Although Orloff's emotions are overpowering, he forces himself to conceal them from Nicky. Controlling his desperate desire to embrace her, instead he squeezes his hands together tightly. Leaning over her, with exceptional tenderness he gives her a kiss on the forehead. In that restrained gesture he is saying not only "thank you" but "goodbye." It is a graceful moment – a soft, quiet display of affection, delicate and humble. And he turns and exits, knowing that when he tries to leave, he will be gunned down by the policemen surrounding the house (his death sparing some very important people a great deal of embarrassment over their collusion).

Like Nicole, the audience cannot hate Orloff, especially after he makes his supreme sacrifice. One

CR, Errol Flynn and Bobby Mauch in The Prince and the Pauper.

critic wrote: "[T]he role of a financial swindler is a part ideally made for Rains … but the plot labors under a poorly devised script. Claude Rains carries off honors with his unexpected restraint in this more obvious Deep Dark Villainy Role. The key word here is 'unexpected' in that a more genuine human being is portrayed with more restraint." Another commented that Rains "does a superb job." According to *Variety*, Rains "executes a forceful performance and dominates many of the scenes by the sheer power of his characterization. He plays with delicate restraint, giving the part conviction and sincerity."

In late November, Rains' agent called Warner Bros. to obtain permission for his client to appear in the *Lux Radio Theatre* broadcast "Madam Sans Gene," starring Robert Taylor and Jean Harlow and hosted by Cecil B. DeMille. Rains had a contractual right to do this, but such requests had to be approved by Jack Warner, who of course knew that any Rains appearance was good publicity for the studio. Such minor matters only serve to indicate just how restricted a contract player was within the system. Rains was considerably less trouble than many of the studio's bigger stars; nevertheless, it must have been annoying that his every move required studio approval. The appearance was okayed, with the

stipulation that the sponsors give credit to Warner Bros. and mention Rains' forthcoming picture *The Prince and the Pauper.*

To bring Mark Twain's historical fiction to the screen was a large undertaking for Warners. The film was placed in the capable hands of director William Keighley.

Set in Tudor England, the action begins with the death of King Henry VIII and the subsequent coronation of his young son Edward VI. (Warners was betting the film would draw large audiences in an America infatuated with the British royal family, eagerly anticipating the upcoming real-life coronation of George VI after years of obsessing over the drama of "Edward and Mrs. Simpson.") To help ensure box-office returns, Errol Flynn was cast as the nominal lead but his role was limited. Starring in the title roles were Billy and Bobby Mauch, twelve-year-old identical twins. Mistaken identity ensues when the prince and the pauper happen to meet under odd circumstances in the palace. Astonished by their resemblance, the boys exchange clothing as a prank. Inevitably, Prince Edward is mistaken for the pauper and ejected from his palace by his own guards, later to be aided by Flynn's cocky adventurer. Meanwhile, the court nobles assume Tom is the prince. When

As the scheming Earl of Hertford in The Prince and the Pauper.

Between takes on The Prince and the Pauper.

the honest lad tries to explain the truth, no one believes him – except the wily and scheming Earl of Hertford (Rains), who seizes the opportunity to have the impersonator crowned and himself appointed as his powerful guardian. With Flynn's patriotic desire to serve his king, the entire mix-up is straightened out and the rightful heir assumes the throne. The earl's crimes call for him to forfeit his head, but a merciful King Edward banishes him instead. "May I learn generosity from you, sire," the earl says grimly, Rains' delivery making it clear that he regrets nothing but being caught.

At first Rains wasn't pleased about playing yet another scoundrel but he soon realized that this role was decidedly different and was delighted with it. While Hertford is a conniver and a knave, he is not an evil man. With his hair permed into tight curls and sporting a full pointed beard, Rains struts and swaggers in his period costume of doublet, balloon pantaloons and stockings, bedecked with furs and jewelry. His plumed hat, worn (as he always did) at a jaunty angle, adds to his charisma.

Production began in early December 1936 and was completed by early February 1937; Rains started in mid–December and was finished in mid–January. This meant that the Rainses had to spend Christmas in Hollywood, away from their beloved farm. As per his contract, Rains was paid $4,500 per week.

On January 11, about eight days before he finished the film, Rains caught a bad cold which turned into a serious case of influenza. Weak and feverish, he was unable to work for several days. This meant a salary and time adjustment because obviously he would exceed his four-week commitment. He was still far from well when he returned to the set. The film premiered simultaneously in several cities on May 11, 1937, the day before George VI's coronation in London. At a gala at the Boyd Theatre in Philadelphia, Rains was guest of honor — his attendance ordained by Jack Warner.

CHAPTER 11
Three Films and a Baby

Within three years of making his first movie, Rains had become a recognized and respected film actor. He had taken James Whale's advice seriously, and while on a set closely watched and noted everything that went into the creation of a good scene: not just dialogue and blocking, but how the lighting and the position of the camera could create dramatic impact. Rains possessed a quality that was to prove highly beneficial in his career: a ceaseless willingness to improve. Even in the most tedious film, he was never uninteresting. He thoroughly understood one of the secrets of a good performance: It's not necessary to speak in order to draw attention. A slight movement, a quick glance, a wry smile or, often in Rains' case, a raised eyebrow could convey so much more than words. Rains' stance, his stride, the sweep of an arm, the turn of a head, the twitch of a lip, created a unique presence that was intelligent, subtle, irresistible. And yet when it came to the words, almost anything delivered with his impeccable timing and diction, in that superb, velvety voice, that raspy, seductive purr, was believable. Perhaps it stemmed from the actor's love for classical music and the fact that to him, words were like notes to be orchestrated and combined in a cadence. A movie script is just words on paper until a good actor interprets them in much the same way a conductor leads a great orchestra. Rains choreographed his dialogue, giving it a lyrical shading by using either gusto or andante cantabile. Every inflection created a kind of sensuous excitement. Rains was passionately in love with the English language and its subtle nuances. Often his delivery transcended commonplace meaning; a single monosyllabic "oh," even just a "hmmm," could convey volumes.

As important as performing was to Rains, he needed to escape from the atmosphere of Southern California which both he and Frances found quite suffocating. For a man who embodied such a debonair, sophisticated film persona, Rains was decidedly simple in his tastes. If he seemed to want to assume the role of an English squire, maintaining his country estate, it was due more to his love of the land and the peace of country life than any affinity for the landed gentry. He loved the lush greenery of his farm and the change of seasons which was vital to his emotional well-being. Living in the country provided an essential simplicity. He still adhered to an Englishman's view of a genteel evening at home by the fireside, perhaps an intimate dinner with a few friends, or settling down with a pipe and good book. The actor who could be so much larger than life on stage was too shy to indulge in or even attend gaudy parties or nightclubs which he considered vulgar. While many Hollywood stars had notorious reputations for abusing alcohol in public, Rains confined his drinking, which at times was considerable, to his own home. Sadly, he was a big drinker most of his life, but always a model of sobriety when working. At this early time in his life, he could control his desire for whiskey and no one ever saw him inebriated.

During the entire period he worked in Hollywood, he never indulged in excessive spending. Not for him the fancy car, expensive clothes or useless frivolous luxuries. He didn't live in a lavish home and didn't host formal parties. The Victorian-Edwardian sensibilities of his youth never left him. They probably contributed to what appeared to be an active dislike of many of the inventions of the mid–twentieth century: gadgets, especially radios and televisions, which he never owned. No air conditioning was installed at the farm. As for "night life" – there wasn't any. He seldom went to the movies or even the theatre for entertainment. Unless he was ordered to go to a film's opening, he hardly ever saw himself on screen. For Rains, acting in films was a means to make a decent and creative living which he found enjoyable, and at times vital to his existence, but it was not an all-embracing philosophy.

Somber and possessed of an exceptional high sense of morality, Rains was nevertheless tolerant of views that did not correspond with his thinking and was usually liberal-minded, especially in politics. Living in Hollywood meant publicly exhibiting oneself, always being "on" for newspaper and fan magazine reporters, and he seemed to have been uncomfortable with anything that was an invasion of his privacy. It was much better to live some three thousand miles away. He seldom socialized with other members of the cast when filming and often took himself to a corner — not being antisocial, but he just felt more comfortable being by himself.

As genuine and admirable as many of his attributes were, Rains could be selfish. He always felt his wife should adapt to his lifestyle and to his values. Fortunately, on most things they were in agreement, but if they weren't, he would seldom compromise. Undoubtedly, Frances found the marriage more compatible and life easier to handle by giving in to her husband's dictates, and for a long time she was comfortable and satisfied. Given Rains' formidable manner (whether as a husband, father, friend or actor), any reasonable person would hesitate to question his decisions or behavior. While he was very respectful and polite in a formal way, he often could not display or exhibit any sense of sensitivity about other people's needs. This unfortunate trait, and his inability to become intimate with people, could be considered his greatest shortcomings. He seemed unable to display trust by revealing his deepest feelings or fears.

Now that Rains was a Hollywood actor, he couldn't escape the public's demand for background and information about his life. As previously explained, when interviewed by the popular movie fan magazines of the period, he usually told the same tried-and-true stories; there were always two themes in every article written about him, acting and/or his farm. He seldom discussed a film except to promote a few personal favorites and he never discussed his co-workers. In his few letters, or in comments he made to friends, there is little evidence of intellectual analysis and no revelations about his philosophy of life. When he spoke of loving the farm, he never explained why it was he found such a life so meaningful; he never defined exactly what pleasures engulfed him when he was digging in the soil.

Nonetheless, Rains remained respected by the press because of his lack of phoniness. He had an expressive vocabulary from his years of studying the dictionary and "his general attitude of complete interest and vital response, bore all the marks of gentlemanliness." Yet as early as 1938, an English interviewer noted a strangeness about him; not that he was odd as much as rather fascinating:

His dark eyes flash a trifle wildly and as he fires question after question, staccato fashion, they seem to reflect firmly the note of urgent demand in whatever it is he has just said. In those eyes I have read time after time the everyday world and all its people. His questions will always seem to be charged with a certain bitterness. It is not malice, though it could often be mistaken for it. It could even pass for downright malevolence if you were meeting the man for the first time and had heard nothing of his personal make-up.... [T]he first time I met him ... I thought Claude Rains was merely being rude.... [F]or quite a time, Rains remained something of a puzzle to me.

Rains liked working at Warners because of the type of films being produced and the opportunity the studio provided to be able to work with top writers, directors and actors. Over the years he would see the biggest stars, like his friend Bette Davis, become wildly famous and adored by audiences – but in the process, become overly demanding. And even when artistic acts of defiance could be justified, he still felt such behavior was unfortunate, if not inappropriate, because it made things difficult for the crew. Jack Warner liked Rains' attitude because he was a "good boy" and did as he was told without causing difficulty, hardly ever complaining about assignments. Moreover, Rains was a consummate professional and never ego-driven or temperamental. His rare disagreements were almost always over financial matters rather than artistic ones. Rains also realized that if he wanted to stay in films, he had to acknowledge that the studio had the final say. Yet with some justification, actors of great skill and stature like Bette Davis, among others, felt their only weapon of retaliation was to walk off a set in an attempt to force studio executives to compromise over

CR (right) with Don Briggs and Allyn Joslyn in They Won't Forget.

a given problem. Rains never did this during the term of his contract with Warner Bros., wisely noting that actors who irritated Jack Warner would be targets of revenge. Rains regarded his boss not so much a tyrant as a businessman, and while he did refer to the studio head as the "old son of a bitch," was never afraid of him.

Although there were some negative aspects to being under contract, Rains was pleased he had selected Warner Bros. He continued to like the studio's general philosophy of producing pictures which displayed, as Neal Gabler wrote in his 1988 book An Empire of Their Own, "a host of forces [which] prevented one from easily attaining virtue … a world that daunted and dared – a world where one's only hope and only meaning lay not in higher morals, not in love, not in family, not in sacrifice, but in action." Generally speaking, during Rains' early years of his association with the studio, their working relationship was amiable – mainly because the actor rarely displayed artistic temperament about assignments. Yet Warner harbored misgivings about casting Rains as a lead, believing that, with his unusual looks and short stature, the actor lacked the charisma to carry a film. Even though actors such as James Cagney, Paul Muni and Humphrey Bogart were also neither tall nor particularly handsome, their screen persona seemed to radiate a quality which commanded attention.

One young producer believed Rains was effective and capable enough to be given the chance to headline.

Mervyn LeRoy had been building a stellar reputation on such instant classics as Little Caesar (1931) and I Am a Fugitive from a Chain Gang (1933). He had directed Rains in Anthony Adverse the previous year and was a big fan of the actor. Late in February 1937, he wrote to Roy Obringer: "Would like to give Raines [sic] a starting date of March 1, 1937, for part of Andy Griffin in the picture, In the Deep South." The fact that LeRoy was considering Rains for the role of a Southern lawyer, given the actor's style and British accent, indicates LeRoy's confidence. It was a controversial condemnation of lynch law and prejudice, but within a year and with a new title, LeRoy's They Won't Forget would be voted by critics as one of the best films of 1937. Daring for its time, it's still considered by many film historians as one of the most important and overlooked works of the period.

(It is perhaps best remembered for the brief appearance of a sixteen-year-old Lana Turner. At the time, Rains told an interviewer: "I won't forget the way she looked the day she walked onto that set, wearing a sweater! None of the men who were on the set that day – neither cast nor crew nor visitors – will forget." He added that he still liked to look at a pretty face, prompting his wife to say, "Well, thank Heaven, you'd have one foot in the grave if you didn't!")

The story was based on Ward Greene's novel *Death in the Deep South*, the true account of a mob lynching of a Jewish northerner accused of raping a young girl in 1915 Atlanta. Greene had covered the trial and, appalled, wrote a novel about the proceedings. The case became a cause celebre for political and social figures in both the North and South, and it stirred up the deep feelings between the two regions.

In the novel, mill superintendent Leo M. Frank, recently relocated to Georgia, is accused of murdering a factory girl. An ambitious anti–Semitic politician seizes the opportunity to stir up prejudice. In a mockery of the justice system, Frank is convicted purely on circumstantial evidence, receiving the death

CR with Edward Norris in They Won't Forget.

sentence. A young black janitor was also involved, but most of the hatred is directed at Frank because of his religion. Repelled, risking his own career, the governor reduces Frank's sentence to life imprisonment, but a furious redneck mob kidnaps Frank from the train carrying him to prison, lynches him and dumps his body on the steps of the governor's mansion.

Making a picture about such a touchy subject was risky, but LeRoy and Warner Bros. agreed that the story represented an indictment of all prejudice and hate. However, Jack Warner was sensitive about the religious angle (being Jewish himself, as were most of the European movie moguls). He insisted the anti–Semitism motivation be replaced by "Northern hatred," which would attract a larger, more sympathetic audience. The script ultimately followed a Northern teacher, Robert Hale, who teaches at a Southern business college and comes under suspicion of murdering a student (Turner) simply because of his background. The three-ring circus of his trial turns the town into a powderkeg. Aspects of the actual story were altered

A behind-the-scenes look at They Won't Forget's *crowded courtroom set.*

to avoid legal issues, and the anti–Semitic politician became Andy Griffin, an ambitious Southern district attorney who wants to use the case to advance his political ambitions.

By the end of February, Claude and Frances had returned to Hollywood, renting an apartment at 1354 Club View. For Rains, a great deal of hard work lay ahead, beginning with rehearsing to play down his impeccable pronunciation and clipped speech. Talking like a Southerner (or at least, minimizing his English accent), and incorporating the swaggering mannerisms of a "good old boy," (e.g., thumbs in suspenders, cigar in his teeth), Rains wanted to appear authentic but not obvious. Always a perfectionist, he reread the book several times, immersed himself in the history of the South, and made it a point to learn about prominent reactionaries like Huey Long. A dialect coach was hired to supervise the cast, and Rains diligently practiced his drawl. "[The vocal coach] and I spent the better part of a day together. We drove for hours through California, and as he read the lines to me, emphasizing the way a true Southerner would speak certain words, I repeated them back to him." Nevertheless, he admitted, "During the first two days'

work … I was most self-conscious about the dialect problem. However, as time went on, I found myself growing into the role, feeling more and more that I really <u>was</u> Andy Griffin, the bantam little lawyer with the Napoleonic complex…" It was an irony that the actor "had to unlearn the clear and precise English, including the richly articulated 'r's I had been at such early pains to master, going through the picture with the broad Georgia accent of a lawyer from the Cracker country."

They Won't Forget opened in July at New York's Strand Theatre with Rains in attendance (at the request of the publicity department, not of his own volition). Congratulations went to all concerned: "a masterpiece of cinema production" and "Warner Bros. at its violent best … one of those smashing fascinating brutal melodramas that seems to have been taken straight off the front page." Howard Barnes of the *New York Herald Tribune* called the film "imaginative and … compelling in its distinction by splendid acting. It is an honest, moving and provocative photoplay…. Chief acting honors must go to Claude Rains … it is the finest performance he has ever given." *The New York Times* agreed: "Great praise [to all] but notably to Mr. Rains for his savage characterization of the ambitious prosecutor." *Variety* stated, "Rains especially stands out in one of the very best parcels of

Prop poster from They Won't Forget.

playing he has yet delivered in films." (Kudos for an excellent performance, but no mention of his accent. Whether playing a Southern boy like Andy Griffin, a hard-boiled New Yorker [*They Made Me a Criminal* in 1939], or a French prefect of police [*Casablanca* in 1942], Rains' unmistakable voice was always British.)

Not only did Rains gain professional satisfaction from his reviews, but personally, members of Frances' family finally came around to believe she had made a good marriage. Her oldest brother Henry liked Claude very much and the two men became friends; Henry's sons visited the farm during many summers. In fact, Henry was so impressed with Rains' performance in the picture, he created a scrapbook for the actor to pass on to his children. He collected every newspaper in New York City and cut out the *They Won't Forget* reviews. To put the film in context,

he included some advertising and news items from July 14 and 15, reflecting the political and social climate of the time. The scrapbook is a time capsule; there are ads for Lucky Strike cigarettes, a LaSalle automobile, the current Broadway offerings, and the fact that it cost twenty-five cents to see the film at the Strand until one p.m. The scrapbook was a beautiful gesture, and although Rains never collected articles about himself, he treasured the gift for the rest of his life.

Following the wrap-up of *They Won't Forget* on April 15, Claude and Frances immediately retreated to their farm. The actor was exhausted and looked forward to spending the summer there, and truly relaxing, but working with his hired hands and planting crops. That spring, a miracle happened.

For three years, Claude and Frances had tried to have a child. He submitted to fertility tests, but the difficulty seemed to be Frances' inability to carry a child full term. Several times the couple anticipated the arrival of a baby only to experience the tremendous heartache of another miscarriage. Other than this, the marriage was stable and the couple quite compatible. For the first time, Rains could believe the union was for life, and he looked forward to growing old with his wife. Then, in May, Frances was again pregnant. Doctors ordered her to spend considerable time in bed and limit all unnecessary activities. The couple was gloriously happy as each month passed with the pregnancy progressing well. Rains had already applied for U.S. citizenship so that his naturalization papers would be finalized within six months of the baby's arrival. This was to be his gift to his child.

Rains loved America passionately. The U.S. had given him everything he wanted: recognition, money and success. Here he never felt he had to "mind his betters," a credo he heard repeatedly as a youngster. While he no longer should have felt inferior to anyone, there were too many ingrained complexes in his personality. Although he was secure in many respects, he never truly felt the peace of mind his position in life should have afforded him.

But now life seemed to be going splendidly. For the first time, he was deeply happy: he was respected in Hollywood, financially secure, owned an estate

CR and Otto Kruger in They Won't Forget.

was married to a devoted wife, and now he was going to become a father.

When not shooting a film, Rains supplemented his income by performing on radio, work that he enjoyed immensely. Such assignments were even convenient if the show was being broadcast from New York; because of the proximity of the Brandywine area to Manhattan, he could travel to and from the city on the same day. He had made his radio debut back in 1932, appearing with Alla Nazimova in a segment of *The Good Earth* on September 13 of that year; the Broadway show was not doing well and the extra publicity helped with promotion. All through the 1930s, Rains appeared in both drama and comedy programs, alongside such stars as Bing Crosby, Bob Hope, Jack Benny and Fred Allen. He appeared in an abbreviated adaptation of *They Won't Forget* with Fay Wray. He read Edgar Allan Poe's "The Tell-Tale Heart" on the *Fleischmann Yeast Hour* and "Cask of Amontillado" on *James Melton's Sunday Night Party*. In an interview, Rains recalled: "The NBC studios in the RCA Building were convenient to the Broadway theatre where I often appeared – and I relished performing in radio drama as a kind of 'relaxation' from the strain of the stage's continuing demands. The same situation applies in Hollywood, where I'd often commute between movie lots and radio studios."

The relaxing summer of 1937 ended when he received instructions in mid–July to report on August 9 for a new film, *Gold Is Where You Find It*, a story of conflict between wheat ranchers and gold mining companies in the upper Sacramento Valley of the 1870s. In early August, Rains and his wife returned to Hollywood to take up their usual residence at the Château Élysée. Frances' pregnancy was going smoothly; the baby was due in late January. Rains hoped to get back to Pennsylvania by then so that Frances could recuperate from the birth at the farm. He was happy and excited, worried and apprehensive. In the event they couldn't make it back to the farm in time, he had already made other preliminary arrangements. As Frances laughingly recalled for an interviewer: "We used to have 'The Drills' before the baby was born; that is, we called them Fire Drills. They were Claude's idea. Actually, they were drives from the Château Élysée to the Cedars of Lebanon Hospital, so that Claude could know, to the minute, how long it would take him to get me there when the baby came…. [W]e had a Fire Drill every night for about ten nights … he was so afraid for me, so terribly anxious and worried … you might have supposed that I was the first woman ever to have a baby…" Her husband's reaction was as expected: "I felt as though I *were* the first man and I still feel so. I never expected to have a baby of my own…"

Gold Is Where You Find It started shooting in mid–August. The cast included Olivia de Havilland as Rains' daughter and George Brent (who received top billing) as the love interest. George Hayes, later "Gabby" Hayes in Roy Rogers Westerns, added some comic relief. There was a special objective behind the project: Warners had wanted to experiment with a new color processing system, outdoors and on location, before using the expensive film on their upcoming spectacle *The Adventures of Robin Hood*. *Gold* would be the studio's first-ever three-strip Technicolor release. It was shot in Weaverville, California; location set-ups were difficult and caused many delays and retakes, especially given that production crews were not yet experienced working with the effects of natural light on color film. Moving large, cumbersome camera equipment around the rough countryside was a formidable task. Also, Curtiz was always a fussy director with crowd scenes and he was particularly determined to do a good job because he wanted to be assigned to *Robin Hood*. The dramatic flooding of the valley with some nice stunt work as men are swept away by the torrents, plus great miniature work of the debacle, was impressive. As usual, Curtiz ran up expenses and wore everyone's nerves to a frazzle. The picture also went over schedule and therefore, on completion, Rains immediately needed to go into his next assignment. Because of this, he and Frances would not be able to return to Pennsylvania in be-tweeny. Much to Rains' dissatisfaction, his first child would be born in California.

Why Warner Bros.' casting director, a young Steve Trilling (who would become Jack Warner's right hand man), chose Rains for the part of Colonel Chris Ferris is difficult to decipher; perhaps it was simply that Curtiz liked having Rains in his films. Curtiz knew Rains wasn't happy with the part and tried to placate him by having the writers enlarge the importance of his character. As leader of the valley's wheat ranchers, Colonel Ferris insists on avoiding bloodshed by battling the greedy gold miners in the courts rather than with guns. Warner files indicate that in the picture's climactic flood scene, Ferris was

As *Colonel Ferris in* Gold Is Where You Find It.

to have been fatally hurt. Production stills depict a shirtless Curtiz standing on the banks of the Trin-ity River directing Rains as the dying Ferris, pinned under a log in the rush of water; George Hayes (who is not in the scene as it appears in the final film) in the river with his arms around the actor. However, this sad ending was discarded and instead George Brent heroically pulls the colonel to safety so he can be present in the crowded courtroom when the California Supreme Court pronounces a victory for the ranchers.

It's interesting to see the usually sartorially splen-did Rains sporting various kinds of Western hats, and carrying a Henry-type rifle. Because he had practiced beforehand, Rains appears reasonably comfortable the few times he's glimpsed on horseback, and he valiantly flattens out his "a"s in a vain attempt to sound less English. But when he has to trade retorts with Hayes and stomp about in cowboy boots, it's a bit awkward. Reviewers were quick to notice: In the *New York Herald Tribune*, Howard Barnes described

The Gold Is Where You Find It shooting script called for Colonel Ferris to drown at the end; Ferris (CR) and his loyal ranch hand Enoch (George Hayes) are seen in this photo from that unused footage.

Rains as "strutting around as a phenomenally well-to-do rancher and ranting…. [He] plays the role right up to the hilt…." *Variety* more kindly noted, "Rains does by far the best job in the film as the sincere fearless, justice-seeking planter. It's a nice break for him, getting away from the unsympathetic roles he has been doing on end."

Late in September, Rains learned that his next assignment would be the Technicolor extravaganza *The Adventures of Robin Hood*. Before Rains even began work, the sensitive question of billing arose – again. Basil Rathbone, a free agent, insisted on third position; Jack Warner persuaded Rains to accept fourth in return for a salary of $5,000 per week. Rains' contract was to expire on December 1, but since he was already assigned to *Robin Hood*, this meant the actor would have to carry over one 1937 picture into

1938; this was fine with him, providing he received compensation for the picture prior to the expiration of his contract.

An ambitious project, *Robin Hood* was budgeted at a hefty $2 million – Warners' biggest outlay to date. Understandably, Jack Warner wanted to be certain the film was in capable hands. Initially, the picture was helmed by William Keighley, who directed the location scenes, but he was replaced by Michael Curtiz. Executive producer Hal Wallis wrote in his autobiography that he had found Keighley's action scenes ineffective. (Both directors received screen credit.) Rains was pleased to again be working with the demanding Curtiz; the two men respected each other, with the actor once remarking, "I've done a lot, taken a lot, from Curtiz."

In the swashbuckling 12th-century tale, Rains was cast as the wily rascal Prince John, brother of King Richard. While "The Lionheart" is off fighting in the Crusades, John grinds England's Saxon peasants under his heel through violent subjugation,

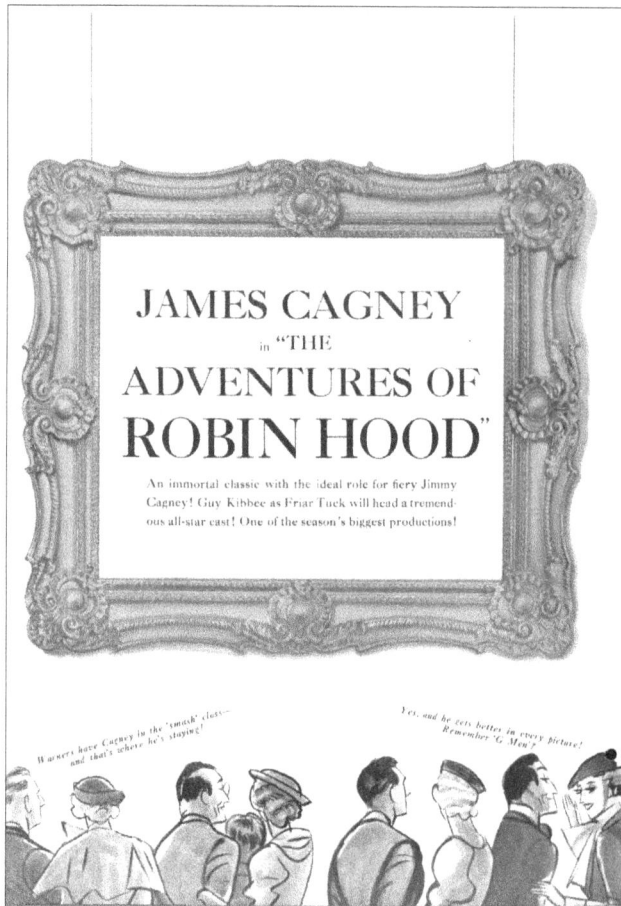

Warners' original (hard-to-imagine) casting, according to this Warners announcement in a September 1935 Variety.

As *Prince John in* The Adventures of Robin Hood.

all the while scheming to usurp the throne. He is aided in this reign of terror by the unscrupulous Norman knights, headed by Sir Guy of Gisbourne.

Whenever he played historical figures, Rains conducted thorough research, reading profusely about the real-life individual, and what he learned was reflected in his cinematic portrait. He was especially delighted with what he discovered about Prince John: Vain, fastidious, cunning as well as heartless, he loved rich, elaborate clothing and was bedecked in jewels; he enjoyed delicate fruits. On screen these characteristics are all brought to life. Effete and haughty, John admires in a handheld mirror the sumptuous picture he presents draped in coronation robes. His orders and proclamations are issued with hammered consonants, every "r" rolled; but he can also purr his clever speeches, vocal pitch soaring up and down the scale. Clearly, there is a steely raptor's brain conniving within the languorous, feline exterior.

Rains explained:

It has always been my contention about character acting, that each part is based on one single idea. If you can discover that idea for yourself, or if the director finds it for you, the person you are playing comes alive. It's as simple as that…

When first I read the script of *Robin Hood*, I shook my head over it. Here were all these people, lovable, picturesque, romantic, except for a couple of heavies. … Where, I thought to myself, does Rains fit in? I was unhappy about it. I couldn't feel Prince John; couldn't seem to make anything of him. I was so unhappy that the office said I needn't do the part. So I gave a long sigh of relief, and forgot about it. A week later they came back to me with a revised script. Wouldn't I reconsider? Prince John was changed a little. But I still couldn't see him as a person. He was just another heavy. I couldn't see what I could make of him.

The Adventures of Robin Hood.

But I'd begun to be interested. I did some research; I read all these books I could find about the period, I studied its costumes. All of a sudden I saw light. I found a book which told about John; which said that, in that robust, hard-drinking, heavy-eating period of English history, he never ate meat nor drank wine; that he loved clothes and had thousands of costumes; that, when they were married, he gave his wife three dresses. Just three. He became real to me, then. There was the one idea that made him. He loved things, and he was mean. He was precious, selfish, small. The sort of precise, fussy man who would nibble at a grape, and plot unkindness. A vicious sort of person, in a cold, pedantic way. Then I found out that he had red hair. That, in a Technicolor picture, was another important thing about him; that, too, gave him his place ... a red-haired, fussy sort of man who loved clothes! I saw him now. The costume department saw him too, and designed a whole magnificent wardrobe for him, built with the color of his hair in mind. Greens, golds and blacks.

Most of the picture's outdoor scenes were filmed in Chico, California, 460 miles north of the Burbank studio, at a place called Bidwell Park, which at that time had a forest of 2400 acres. Except for the large archery tournament, nearly all of Rains' work was filmed on sound stages on the Warners lot. The actor made $25,000 for this six-week assignment, almost as much as star Errol Flynn, who received $30,625. Ironically, Basil Rathbone, the outsider, was the highest paid member of the cast, making $37,000.

The Adventures of Robin Hood was an Oscar contender. While it failed in the Best Picture category, the spectacular Art Direction, Film Editing and Original Score won awards. A timeless tale scripted with witty dialogue, beautifully shot, boasting a perfect ensemble cast and one of Erich Wolfgang Korngold's most rousing scores – there are countless reasons *Robin Hood* remains a favorite with film fans.

Contemporary critics raved. The *New York Daily News* enthused, "[T]he picture abounds in lusty action. It sighs with romance and is full of the sort

The Great Hall in The Adventures of Robin Hood.

of high adventure that catches the breath of the beholder and makes his spine tingle with suspense and pleasure. ...In short, the film has everything that a picture-loving public could desire in the way of screen entertainment." *The Philadelphia Inquirer* saluted everyone associated with the picture, including "the technicians, the stunt and bump men, who fought, bled and all but died for the film's sake, the research department, which spent a couple of years burrowing through Robin Hood lore, and Erich Wolfgang Korngold, who supplied the rich, rousing musical score." "Here's the ticket for the human who has refused to outgrow his love for high adventure," promised the *Chicago Tribune*. "[Errol Flynn] is excellently supported by an intelligently assembled cast. Claude Rains is perfect as the villainous John." *Variety*'s review included the comment: "Claude Rains' splendid impersonation of John, the intended purloiner of the throne, does full credit to this actor's seasoned talents." Despite only some 22 minutes of screen time, Prince John remains one of the actor's most memorable performances.

It was now very clear to Rains what the difference was between acting on stage and acting for the camera:

On the stage, you have four weeks to build a part in rehearsal, before the curtain goes up. In the movies, you have four days. Camera technique is quicker, more concentrated in a shorter space of time. And, in a way, it demands less. On the stage, you must not only build your part, but you must

Above: Three bad men: Robin Hood's Sheriff of
Nottingham (Melville Cooper), Prince John (CR) and
Sir Guy of Gisbourne (Basil Rathbone).

Below: Behind the scenes on Robin Hood.

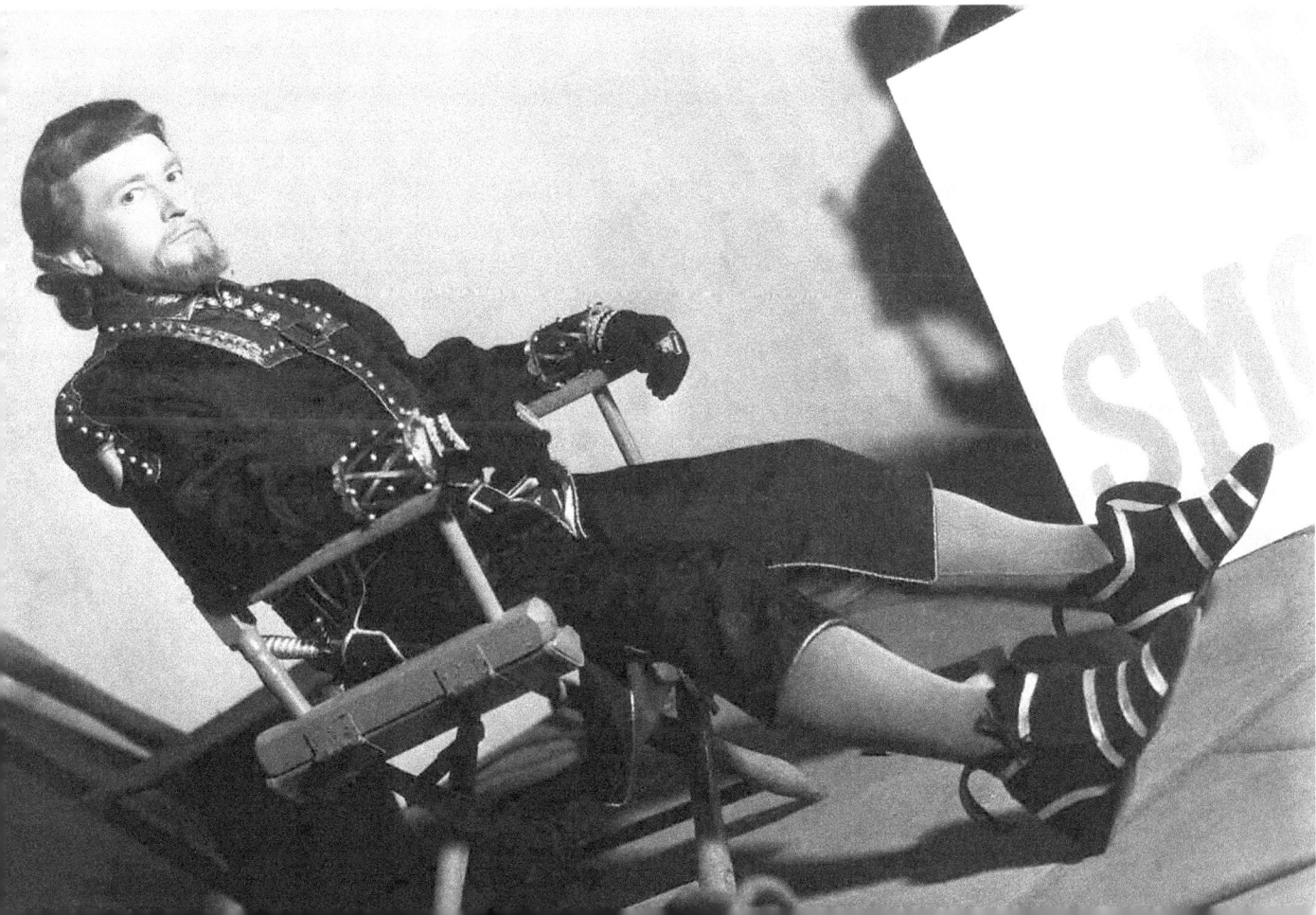

also put it across the footlights, give it the force that projects it to the audience. On the screen, the camera does the projecting for you. Your only job is to be inside the character's mind, thinking his thoughts, showing his emotions with your eyes, your facial expressions, rather than with gestures. The minute you start thinking of the camera as an audience, and start trying to project him, your time has come to pack your bags and leave.

And always, on stage or screen, your time has come to pack when you begin to enjoy a part too much. That means you've identified yourself and your own emotions too far with your character. It means, from the point of view of the audience, that Prince John is disappearing and Rains is creeping in. Nobody cares about Rains. You have to keep a part of your mind aloof and impersonal, to judge the other part – to see that, like a trained seal, it does its job.

So you must identify yourself with your character, but not so closely that you lose yourself in him. You must be inside of his mind. But not too far…

Sometimes that part of you aligned with the character has a nasty trick of going right home with you from the studio. This can be hard on those near and dear, especially if it's an unpleasant character. My wife threatened to divorce one of them once, if I couldn't leave him on the set. I think it was the lawyer in *They Won't Forget*. I wouldn't have blamed her. He was an insufferable, opinionated sort of show-off.

The article was titled, "He's Never Himself."

While Rains was still shooting *Robin Hood*, he received the standard thirty-day notice assigning him to *White Banners*, in the role of Paul Ward, a totally different type of part: a doting father who is both a small-town schoolteacher and an amateur inventor. On December 22, Rains' agent notified him that his new start date would be between January 10 and 24. With Rains so busy and Frances in no condition to house-hunt, the couple had remained at the Château Élysée. Coming off of one film and moving straight into another, while concerned about his wife's con-

CLAUDE RAINS
as
"PRINCE JOHN"

THE ADVENTURES OF
ROBIN HOOD

A First National Picture—Presented by Warner Bros.

From the May 20, 1938, Variety.

dition and excited about becoming a father, made Rains anxious and nervous.

Based on anticipated medical and hospital expenses, the actor requested a salary advance. On January 6, 1938, Obringer issued a memo to the Warner Bros. accounting office indicating that Rains was to receive $24,000, constituting his salary for the second of the four films he was to complete during 1938. Rains was now making $6,000 per week with four weeks guaranteed. Notwithstanding, the actor obviously had other things on his mind, as a studio memo proves: "On Saturday and again today, Monday, we have shot sequences without Claude Rains who has been with his wife at Cedars of Lebanon where she is awaiting their baby. Mr. Rains advised us that if he was on the set when he got word the baby was being born he would want to leave immediately to be with Mrs. Rains, and under these circumstances [director Edmund] Goulding preferred to work without him instead of having to run the risk of changing from

CR and Jackie Cooper (in glasses-and-mustache disguise) and two other students in White Banners.

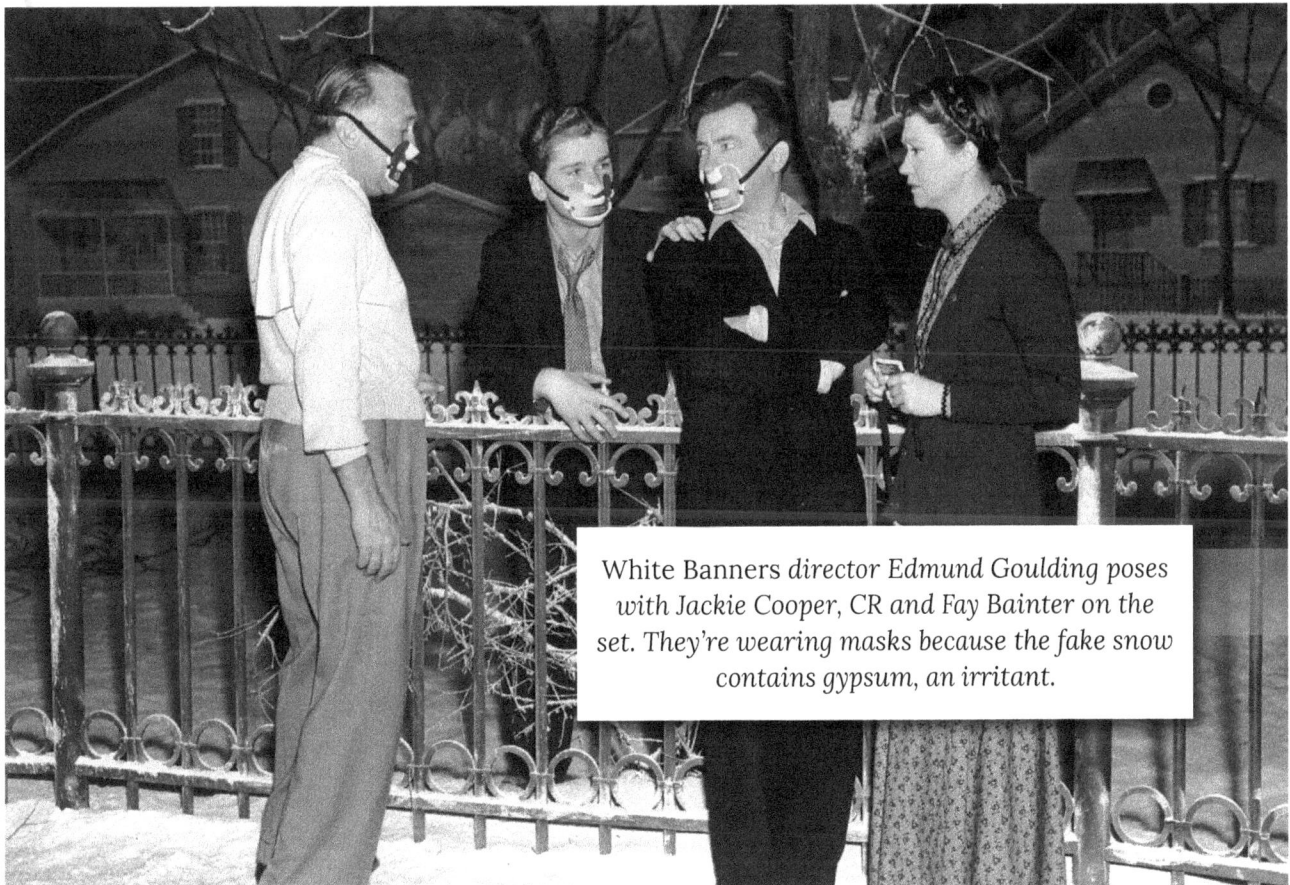

White Banners *director Edmund Goulding poses with Jackie Cooper, CR and Fay Bainter on the set. They're wearing masks because the fake snow contains gypsum, an irritant.*

one sequence to another in the middle of the day."

As fate would have it, Rains was on the set of *White Banners* on January 24 when Frances went into labor and was rushed to Cedars of Lebanon Hospital. Fortunately, everything went well and the eight-pound baby daughter they named Jennifer was born at 5:10 p.m. (Decades later, when she became a professional actress, Jennifer changed her first name to Jessica.) Rains remembered vividly that Frances "never looked lovelier than when [the baby] was coming, she was more beautiful then than she ever was – much more beautiful…"

Claude Rains was finally a father at age forty-eight. He was overcome with joy.

CHAPTER 12
Contract Numbers and Historical Figures

Becoming a father changed Claude Rains, as one perceptive interviewer noted after visiting with the actor:

[O]ne day we happened to steer the conversation away from films and politics; away from the shams of Hollywood and the whims of the movie public. We started talking family, children, our children. And Claude Rains became a different man. His eyes softened yet did not lose their hold. He was going to become a father for the first time in his life — a hope held sometimes strongly, then again faintly, through many years and several chapters of marital history, and like any man at such a time, he was caught off his guard.

Rains is not the kind of person to become over-sentimental, but I saw that day how strong a game sentiment can play with him. The aggressiveness which forms his chief superficial characteristic had for once been drawn aside and the real man unmasked for me. And in the deep happiness he failed to conceal, I found the key to the mystery which had up to that day seemed to clothe his whole personality. Hidden behind the actor with a substantial share of theatrical ego, I found the man who abhors sham, whose unflinching eyes are constantly on the look-out for yes-men upon whom he may lose the scourge of his natural sarcasm.... It appeared to me that I had found, all at once, the complete answer for so many things.

In this April 2, 1938, *Film Weekly* article, "He Hates Humbug," W.H. Mooring suggested that Rains was caught between two passions. He could not incorporate the lifestyle of a Hollywood actor into his private world; and while he loved his craft, he needed to escape back east to his farm. Rains' "design for living," or lifestyle, was not shaped by his profession.

When at last he became a father, Rains wanted to shower his child with affection and love. But because he had never been the recipient of such emotions when he himself was young, was he now, at nearly 50, capable of exhibiting them in a way a child would understand? His first gift to his newborn was to become an American citizen. (Jennifer, born in the United States, automatically had dual citizenship with Great Britain.) While filming *They Won't Forget* the previous year, he had begun the application process, an act that was notable enough for *Variety* to print an item about his intent on March 15, 1937. On April 13, 1938, in Philadelphia, Rains took the required oath, and was as proud as if he had won an Oscar. His next gift was to his wife: the purchase of a house, a beautiful white frame and gray stone dwelling surrounded by great trees and set up against a hill off Sunset Boulevard at 1240 Stone Canyon Road. At that time, the neighborhood was remote and far from the busy world of Hollywood; it still remains one of the lovelier drives in the midst of a sprawling city. However, moving into and furnishing the new house would not come until several months later.

White Banners had a fine cast featuring Jackie Cooper (sixteen, but still two inches taller than Rains) and Fay Bainter (whose performance earned her an Oscar nomination for Best Actress). The sentimental script was based on a novel by Lloyd Douglas, author of *The Robe* and *Magnificent Obsession*. Set in 1919, the story concerns a mysterious middle-aged woman (Bainter) who enters the lives of an affable high school science teacher (Rains) and his wife. As their new housekeeper, she keeps everything tidy while dispensing wisdom and emotional support of the teacher's efforts to invent an iceless ice box. She encourages him to allow his clever student (Cooper), a budding scientist-engineer, to work with him. Eventually, it is revealed that the boy is actually the son Bainter gave up after an early affair. All ends happily. It was a pleasant, tender, sentimental story, but it did little at the box office and little for Rains' career.

The production of *White Banners* – and every other Hollywood movie in the works on March 2, 1938 – was disrupted by one of Southern California's worst rainstorms in decades. Over an area of 30,000 square miles there was destruction and an estimated 118 deaths, many of them victims of landslides and collapsing bridges. The *White Banners* troupe began work that day but soon quit; by 4 p.m., *all* production on the Warners lot had stopped due to rising water and power outages. Perhaps some of the departing *White Banners* personnel paused in the downpour to witness the spectacle of a giant rubber whale prop, swept off a Warners loading dock, floating off the property and disappearing down the fast-flowing L.A. River.

Discussing *White Banners* in later years, Rains recalled that the director had wanted him to learn the chemical jargon in the script so it would appear he really understood the workings of refrigeration: "The technical language wasn't so hard, although my knowledge of chemistry was skeleton sketchy, but, when director Edmund Goulding insisted that I really learn something about machinery — valves, compressors, reduction coils and such, I — well, profanity being unprintable, let's say that I did learn, and now know how to operate a compressor and hook up a reduction coil although what to do with this particular 'know-how' remains, to this day, beyond me."

As *"Papa" Lemp, head of the household in* Four Daughters.

Just prior to completion of the film, Samuel Goldwyn notified Warners and Rains' agent that he wanted the actor for a picture with Gary Cooper. At this point, all Rains wanted to do was return to Pennsylvania, but what the actor longed for and what Jack Warner would dictate ran along two different paths. Nevertheless, Rains was so happy with events in general that he decided to treat himself and Frances to a luxury befitting a "star." He bought a LaSalle convertible coupe for the princely sum of $1,538.50 — the perfect symbol of a successful Hollywood actor.

As Rains was preparing to return to the East Coast, he was given his next assignment, to begin April 23. The actor agreed to waive the contractually required 30-day notice on the condition that at the conclusion of the picture, he would receive a six-week leave. He was exhausted, but he needed the money because of the expenses of the new Hollywood house, a baby

CR and Rosemary Lane in Four Daughters.

and the upkeep of the farm. Jack Warner hesitated, but realized his man had been working steadily, going from one production to another for over a year and a half, and it was apparent he was drained. In every likelihood, the actor's small part could be completed in less than the usual five weeks. Then he could return to Pennsylvania and get his crops planted.

Based on a story by Fannie Hurst, *Four Daughters* was quite a departure for the actor, cast as a rascally but lovable widowed music professor raising four beautiful, musically talented daughters. Director Michael Curtiz wanted cuddly Charles Winninger for the role of the father, considering Rains too strong for the part of a lovable old codger; however Jack Warner and Hal Wallis were relying on Rains for his reliable box-office appeal. Wearing baggy clothes and a loose tie, a curly unruly wig and a white mustache, Rains spends his limited amount of screen time acting gruff, but with a grin on his face. Here was an opportunity to overact and remain within character since the old man himself is a "ham." After the heavy

drama and intellectual plunges of his first few movies, and a couple of unmitigated villains, a comedy role was a relief. Rains handles the shenanigans of "Papa" Lemp in a sometimes undisciplined manner which causes him to be a caricature more than a real person. We first see him using a flute as a conducting baton, and later looking silly in a big kitchen apron; Lemp doesn't mind being playful and making himself an object of fun any more than Rains' character of Prof. Ward did in his previous film, *White Banners*. Yet it comes across pleasantly as he recites his lines with gusto, teasing his daughters with a mischievous grin. Such a movie could have easily been overdone, but as always, Curtiz managed things effectively, balancing the unexpected heart-rending moments with the romance and comedy. *The New York Times* critic wrote, "It may be sentimental, but it's grand cinema." It proved so popular that Warners successfully produced two sequels featuring the Lemp family, *Four Wives* and *Four Mothers*.

Most noteworthy about the film was the debut of a then-unknown stage actor from New York, John Garfield. Rains had known Garfield in New York,

CR with Lola Lane, Priscilla Lane, Gale Page and Rosemary Lane in Four Daughters.

and suggested Curtiz view the test the young man had made for the pivotal part of Mickey Borden. Up until now, Garfield had been a freelance player and eagerly signed a Warners contract for $1,000 for five weeks of employment. The role of the cynical, failed musician with a defensive chip on his shoulder was ideally suited to his talents. Garfield, known to friends as Julie, having changed his first name from Julius, had the knack of playing a seemingly smart-aleck tough guy with a sentimental streak. Much like Bogart, he excelled at the down-and-outer who is likable, clever and talented, but who has been short-changed by life's circumstances or lost opportunities.

Rains admired Garfield's honesty, remembering him from the Theatre Guild; likewise the young actor respected Rains tremendously. Rains liked Garfield because he had qualities similar to Humphrey Bogart — the American anti-hero, brutally honest, a lack of pretentiousness and a desire to learn and grow. And then, too, Rains felt flattered when Garfield asked for advice. Larry Swindell, Garfield's biographer, wrote extensively about their relationship:

> An unexpected benefit was Garfield's association with Claude Rains, whose performances for the Theatre Guild Julie had admired. Their socializing began and ended at the studio, but they were usually seen together during idle moments on the set…. He and Julie talked about actors and the differing styles of their craft; and when he felt he had won Julie's confidence, Rains offered a tip that brought Mickey Borden's character into a better screen perspective. Informally rehearsing an early

scene, Julie asked, "How'm I doing?" and Rains said, "Rather theatrically, I believe." …As Claude Rains explained, "You were addressing May Robson as if she were seated in the last row of the balcony. The movie critics will like that — they approve of anything done big. But if dramatic truth is your aim…" Julie muted his scene — he said: "Claude Rains taught me things some people never learn about acting in films. He warned me about Mike Curtiz and his mania for close-ups. That's when you have to underplay (Rains had told him). No two screen directors are alike, so an actor must always make adjustments."

On release, *Four Daughters* raked in $1 million in profit, a considerable sum at the time. *The New York Times* put the picture on their list of the year's ten best, and it was recognized by the Academy with a nomination for Best Picture. Garfield became an overnight star, deservedly so, and received an Oscar nod for Supporting Actor.

Finished by the first week of June, an exhausted Rains returned to the Glen Mills farm. As promised, he was permitted six weeks leave. On July 23, after being at home for three weeks, his agent, Bill Hawks, conveyed the good news that *Four Daughters* was well-received at a sneak preview. However, the publicity department wanted to bill the sisters as a group on a single line, dropping Rains' name to the second line, for which they needed his permission. The actor replied succinctly: "Dear Bill: If you think it wise then let Warners have their way this time…"

Producers and directors now recognized Rains' ability to deliver, and by the end of 1938, director Frank Capra, the genius behind *It Happened One Night* (1934) and *Mr. Deeds Goes to Town* (1936), advised Jack Warner he was seeking Rains' services for an upcoming picture. But Warner wanted to re-team Rains with Garfield before he would agree to loan out the actor for Capra's project. Warner wanted his studio associated with better-than-average films, and he employed better-than-average artists to do it, but the bottom line had to be the dollar sign. Since Rains was a box-office draw, Warner had no hesitation in putting him into any picture, regardless of its substance. It was this reason that for the first and only time in their long association, Rains formally protested an assignment. When he received the script for *They Made Me a Criminal*, Rains was appalled: The part, though a lead, was all wrong for him. He felt so strongly about being miscast that he sent Warner a telegram, something he had never done before:

> Dear Jack,
>
> Having thoroughly enjoyed my association with the studio and toed the line to cooperate to the best of my ability, I feel that you should know of my inability to understand being cast for the part of Phelan in *They Made Me a Criminal*. Frankly, I feel that I am so poorly cast that it would be harmful to the picture. You have done such a good job in building me up that it seems a pity to tear that down with a part such as this, and I am confident that your good judgment will recognize this. Dogs delight to bark and bite and I think I have been a good dog for three years, so perhaps you will give me five minutes to talk it over.
>
> Claude

Gloria Dickson, John Garfield and CR in They Made Me a Criminal.

Warner ignored the actor's instincts. The studio wanted to promote John Garfield by immediately casting him in another film to keep his image before the public. However, an established and popular supporting actor was still a necessity, and by this time Rains was a box-office draw. Rains was angry, but astute enough to realize that Jack Warner had many methods of ruining a career. Such was the artistic pitfall of a contract player. What went up could come down.

They Made Me a Criminal went wrong from the beginning, when the studio assigned a director who must have been one of the most ill-suited possible: musical genius Busby Berkeley. Warner did this only to be economical, as Berkeley was drawing a high salary but was not currently working on a project. Supporting John Garfield were Gloria Dickson and the group of popular young knock-about actors known as the Dead End Kids. Except for working with Garfield, Rains was miserable. He could not get into the character. Nevertheless, at a salary of $6,000 per week for a four-week assignment, the actor decided he could get through the experience.

Garfield stars as a New York boxing champion, on the run after being framed for the killing of a reporter. Looking like a tramp after a cross-country hike, he lands on an Arizona date ranch where a gaggle of New York street kids have been sent for rehabilitation. He has a positive influence on the delinquents, and agrees to a boxing match to earn money which they need. This brings him to the attention of a savvy New York cop (Rains) who is seeking his own redemption after putting an innocent man in the chair. He tracks Garfield down and makes the pinch but, realizing the good influence Garfield's devotion has had on the kids, and theirs on Garfield, he pretends he's got the wrong man and leaves without him. *They Made Me a Criminal* was a remake (sometimes scene for scene and line for line) of an earlier Warner melodrama, 1933's *The Life of Jimmy Dolan*, with Douglas Fairbanks, Jr., as the boxer on the lam and, of all people, the studio's resident specialist in playing rustic

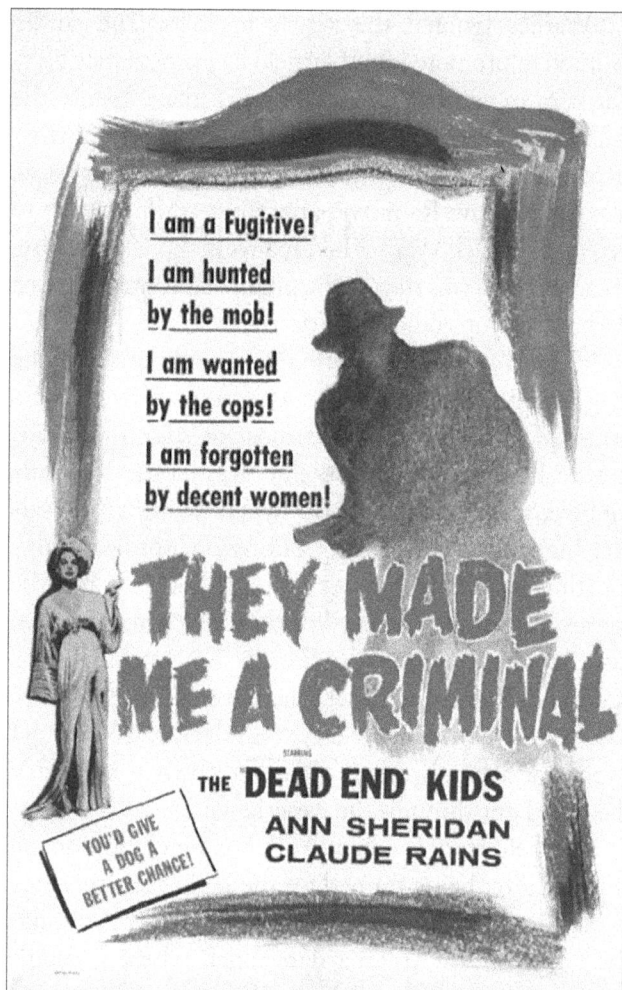

I am a Fugitive!
I am hunted by the mob!
I am wanted by the cops!
I am forgotten by decent women!

THEY MADE ME A CRIMINAL

STARRING

THE DEAD END KIDS
ANN SHERIDAN
CLAUDE RAINS

YOU'D GIVE A DOG A BETTER CHANCE!

boobs, Guy Kibbee, as the cop. (In *Jimmy Dolan*, the boxer *did* kill the reporter – but the cop could still cut him loose in the closing scene, because the movie was pre–Code.)

The shooting schedule illustrates how erratic Berkeley was. On September 15, Rains was kept on set twelve hours for a single take. Four days later, Berkeley kept the actor until 6:15 p.m. with four takes. Left to his own, Rains could always give a credible performance, but if he was told how to act a part, he went through the motions as ordered. To a degree, it became a test of egos and one day, September 20, Berkeley was determined to make Rains do the scene as commanded; the actor was held for six takes on a scene that lasted nineteen seconds on screen. Three days later, another episode required nine takes. The two men were not antagonizing each other deliberately — each was miscast — and the outcome was a poorly made film. Throughout October, the movie haunted Rains as he was called back repeatedly for retakes. As late as December 21, there was more reshooting while the studio tried to doc-

tor the film before release. Finally in January 1939, *They Made Me a Criminal* opened to mixed reviews, with positive comments reserved for John Garfield. Garfield tried to help the situation, telling reporters that "Rains, as the hounding detective, contributed the strongest performance." Rains did his best, but one reviewer got in a clean hit with his comment: "[W]ith an American drawl, a slouch, and a cigarette permanently drooping from his lips … [Rains is] unable to subdue his English accent and never really convinces. But it [was] fascinating to watch the intelligence and conscientiousness with which he seeks to build up and sustain the characterization."

To further assert his authority, Jack Warner had his public relations department use the experience to impress other actors on the lot. A lengthy advance press sheet serviced by the studio contained quotes attributed to Rains; whether he actually made the comments is up for debate. In general, Rains had little respect for PR, which he considered a sort of "Let's pretend" game for the press.

"Actors should stick to acting," is the opinion of Claude Rains, one of the screen's better players, and leave such things as story selection to their studios. No actor, Rains believes, has any sensible right to express a binding decision on the matter of whether or not he will play in a picture selected for him by his producers. Rains, who has acted with distinction in numerous pictures for Warner Brothers … declares observation has convinced him that less than one percent of the present day film stars have the sense of showmanship to qualify them to say what pictures they should or should not take.

To have a say in the selection of his stories is a freelance actor's privilege. It is part of the risk he runs by not attaching himself by contract to any one studio. However, I firmly believe that the moment an actor contracts with a studio for his exclusive services, he sacrifices the right to choose his stories. It seems obvious that the producers are going to do their very best to satisfy the public appetite and it seems equally obvious that they are not going to chance destroying or hurting a personality they have spent thousands of dollars building up.

Then abruptly in the middle of the quote, the writer interjects his own thoughts:

> Rains, incidentally, practices what he preaches. Not once in several years under contract to Warners [actually only two years] has he refused to play in a picture to which he was assigned. Perhaps that is one of the reasons Rains goes on year after year in various character roles at one of Hollywood's top salaries. His philosophy is best summed up in the remark: "It's their money they're spending. Who am I to tell them how to spend it?
>
> In *They Made Me a Criminal*, Rains plays a role which he considers much better than any he might have pictured for himself if he had been given the choice. He is cast as a detective trying to redeem a career which was stymied when he sent an innocent man to the chair.

This last paragraph is not true — Rains did not have a "choice," but he said nothing to contradict. It hardly seems plausible the actor would have expressed such views as these. This type of studio PR was a way for Jack Warner to make sure his stable "got the message." Nevertheless, the actor learned a valuable and painful lesson from this incident, one which he didn't forget when including options in his next contract the following year, such as the right to refuse two pictures if he felt his role was unacceptable. His integrity as an actor was at stake and, insecure as he was, he decided he would never again compromise. It was an empty triumph because throughout the ten years of their association, Jack Warner always had the upper hand. Rains once told his daughter the studio would send at least two terrible scripts at the beginning of each year, knowing he would refuse the parts, thereby ensuring he had to accept any future scripts sent within the contract period. Yet the studio head also learned a lesson. The actor had undeniable box-office appeal: Warner Bros. was receiving a great deal of fan mail addressed to Rains even as the third featured player, and it was senseless to upset him by casting him in a role in which he could not give a credible performance. By now, other studios, directors and producers wanted the versatile character actor for their own projects, and Warner knew that Rains would have no difficulty finding other assignments.

As 1938 drew to a close, Warners had to take up the options of Rains' original 1936 contract, providing for a substantial increase in salary. If the studio refused to grant Rains his demand of two film refusals, the relationship would have ended. Generally speaking, Rains liked working at Warners — he admired most of the directors, producer Hal Wallis, and he especially liked how James Wong Howe photographed him. Perhaps it was his insecurity or his new responsibilities as a father, or perhaps he received advice from his agent; whatever the reason, he chose to remain with Warners rather than taking the risk of being a freelance actor.

Accordingly, on November 3, 1938, Warners picked up his option for another year at $6,000 per week with four weeks guaranteed per picture. This made Rains one of the industry's highest paid character actors, and because he was "in demand" at other studios, he was able to enhance his position in the negotiations. Furthermore, this figure represented the highest weekly salary Rains ever earned as a contract player; however, with the freelance clause injected, he would be able to make more money per picture with other studios. He also obtained the right to make three films for other studios or producers as long as he still met his obligations with Warners.

There remained one point not yet settled: his upcoming assignment in *Juarez*, a picture he did not particularly want to do. Warners was bent on making this movie with elaborate historical details, but shooting in black and white dimmed its effectiveness. Rains was cast as the cocky, imperious Napoleon III. The rest of the cast was impressive: Paul Muni in the title role, the 19th century Mexican president, Brian Aherne as Maximilian of Austria, "emperor" of Mexico during the Second Franco-Mexican War, Bette Davis as Maximilian's wife Carlota, and the rising John Garfield miscast as Juarez's boldest general. Rains' character would appear only in a few scenes, just over ten minutes of screen time. This would hardly require four weeks of work. But knowing that Rains' name added cachet to the project, Warner appealed to the actor's weakest spot: money. Obringer sent Hal Wallis a memo stating there was to be a special arrangement whereby Rains' scenes would be shot within one week, for which he would be paid not $6,000 but $7,500. Rains agreed, because the part was short and would not count as one of the four roles he was contracted to complete.

While he waited to shoot *Juarez*, Rains appeared on several radio broadcasts from Los Angeles, including *Lux Radio Theatre*, hosted by Cecil B. DeMille. Many radio programs were broadcast in front of live audiences, exposing the actors to their fans as the announcer or host expounded on their background and current activities. DeMille, reading from a Warners studio press release, announced that Rains was a former member of the famous "Ladies from Hell" Battalion in World War I and rose to be a captain. He had worked with the Theatre Guild in New York and then, finding himself without a play, decided to buy a farm in Lambertville, New Jersey. Now he was an "ex-farmer appearing in Warner Bros. films." After the performance, the cast reappeared for a five-minute chitchat before sign-off. This trivial banter promoted a "homey" quality not just with the studio audience, but with listeners across the country. It was an atmosphere created and popularized by FDR during his famous fireside chats. On this particular show, Rains corrected DeMille by stating he was "still a farmer of 40 acres in Delaware County, Pennsylvania." He went on to say that he was thinking of introducing some Western steers on his eastern estate, and then closed with a bit of forced humor that he was referred to as the "invisible boss" of the farm, because of his starring role in *The Invisible Man*. Interestingly, on all these shows and in all chats, Rains never talked of his acting and most conversation revolved around the farm.

The strained relations with Warner Bros. did not improve. Disagreement over the billing for *They Made Me a Criminal* pushed the usually amiable Englishman over the edge. Moreover, it turned out that *Juarez* could have been counted as one of the four Warners pictures he was required to make that year, and therefore, instead of $7,500 for the one week's work, the actor could legally and rightfully have insisted on a $24,000 guarantee.. This December 9, 1938, memo from Obringer to Charlie Enfield underscores how sensitive this issue was with the actor:

> We have received considerable concessions from Claude Rains, inasmuch as he really had us over a barrel for two unproduced pictures which we were to have produced by December 1st, this year, and Rains was in a position where he could easily have collected $48,000. I got out of this embarrassing situation, and also, we were able to get Rains to treat the *Juarez* picture as an outside picture, thereby paying him a small flat price for this picture instead of $24,000, the guaranteed price for one of his regular pictures. The billing clause of Rains was quite an issue, and Rains only made the above concessions with the understanding that he would get the billing which I outlined to you in my recent note, and it would be useless to try to ask Rains for any further concessions, as I know that he would definitely not grant them.

As usual with such an involved production, Rains' starting date on *Juarez* was delayed (until December 27). While the picture would have little impact on his career, it marked the first time Rains would meet and act with Bette Davis — the beginning of a lifelong friendship.

She might have been only play-acting in *Juarez,* but at the time, Bette Davis was the real-life Empress of Warner Bros. Still, she claimed that when she met Rains, she didn't feel like one. In her 1962 autobiography, tellingly titled *A Lonely Life,* she wrote: "I was in awe.... It must be clear that I was hardly a meek or obscure young actress. Still [Rains] scared the life out of me. When he looked at me during our scene as Napoleon would look at Carlota with loathing, I thought he, Claude Rains, held loathing of me, Bette Davis, as a performer! We have laughed about it many times since."

With an outstanding cast and crew, *Juarez* should have been successful. But the picture was overly long, the players awash in excess verbiage. Rains' resemblance to portraits of Napoleon III was striking, with his black wig, stylized waxed mustache and goatee emphasizing smug cockiness. His emperor was highstrung and quick to display his temper, but just as quick to purr approvals of devious, clever schemes. It was a convincing performance of a little man with big ambitions — an unscrupulous tyrant, easily given to sulking when confronted with the slightest setback to his plans, easily misled by his equally ambitious consort, the Empress Eugenie (Gale Sondergaard, reuniting with Rains after their terrific teaming in *Anthony Adverse*). One reviewer called his performance "the best rendition ever of that upstart nephew of the original Napoleon.... Rains makes him proud,

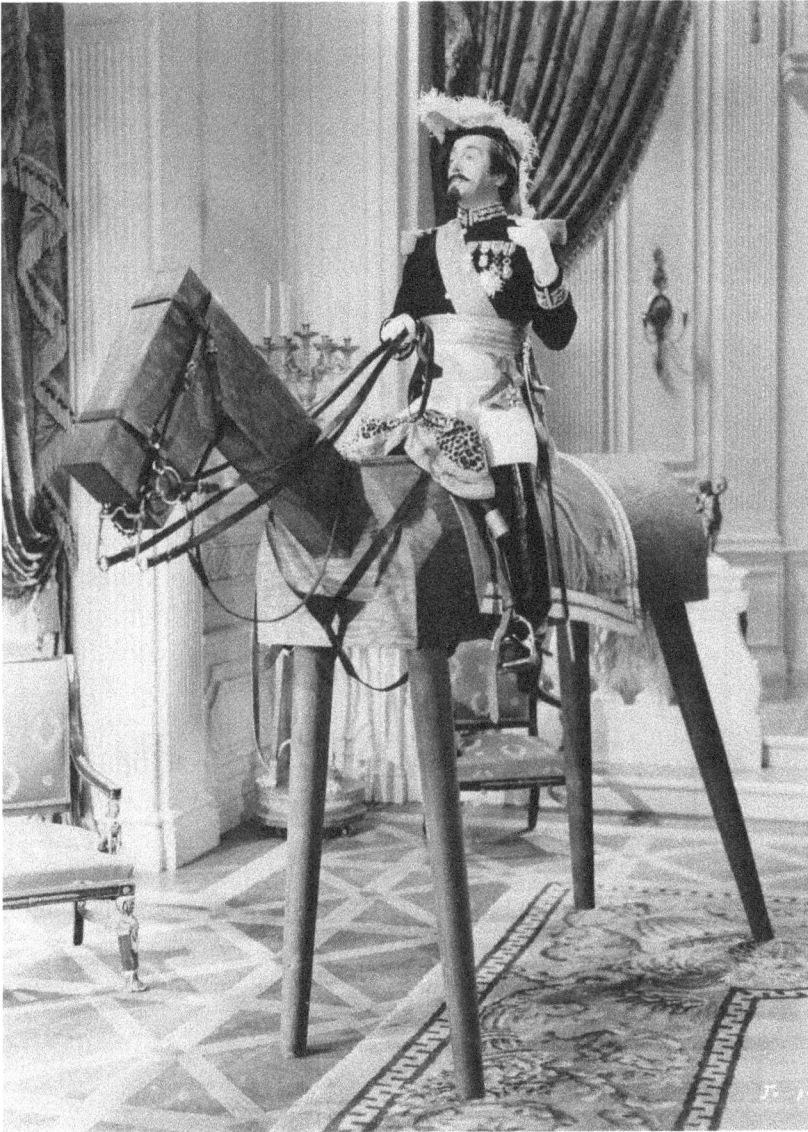

As Napoleon III, the "bourgeois Napoleon," in Juarez.

beyond friendship — or at least, she would have liked it to go beyond. She was greatly attracted to him (as she was to so many men). He always knew how deeply she felt about him, and that she would have taken their relationship further, both emotionally and physically. Bette was a strong and possessive woman, but she needed a man who would fawn over her. Rains could never have been this type of companion. Ironically, his needs were similar, but as the saying goes, opposites attract. She recalled shooting a scene in *Juarez* and staring at him intently. When he asked her if anything was wrong, she replied: "Thank God you're married." The next day, the actor reported to the set with Frances and Jennifer in ·tow, perhaps to emphasize his status as husband and father. Nevertheless, Davis made her feelings clear when late in life she commented: "I think he was basically enormously sexy, it reeked." In the end, Bette wanted more than Claude was capable of giving; she came to understand and accept this. Because Frances was secure, there was never any jealousy or tension between the women, and they all got along quite well.

vain, crafty, elusive, and cowardly. His scenes are relatively few, but Rains makes them vivid." *The New York World-Telegram* was succinct: "perfect."

As she later wrote, Davis was impressed with Rains and felt he was one of the only actors in Hollywood who had the dramatic strength to equal hers. Whenever she could, she used her influence to have him assigned to her pictures — they made four together. Both were talents of extraordinary qualities and temperaments; both were so exceptionally skillful that each could recognize in the other a deep commitment to craft and profession. "When Claude played a character, he was the consummate actor," Davis said. "It was always monumental theatre with him."

To some degree, Davis' interest in Rains went

The year 1939 would be one of Rains' best. His popularity was at a high point; the studio was sending out hundreds of photographs in answer to letters from fans young and old. He was an American citizen with a lovely white stone house in one of the nicest areas of Los Angeles. He was living the American Dream. It was all a very far cry from the dirty little boy from the slums of London who had little to eat, no overcoat and slept at the theatre.

Even though his income had increased, Rains still maintained a very simple life in comparison to most Hollywood stars. Yet he was happy. Frances was respectfully "obedient" in kowtowing to her husband's little whims, but she did so out of love, not in fear. Rains insisted in one interview that he was not "the Head of the House or anything so smacking of tyranny, but I am well aware of all the things done for my comfort, the meals at the times I want them, the things I like to eat, the thought of me…" Nevertheless, he was head of the manor in every respect, but fortunately their relationship remained compatible. Frances always felt it was easier to go along with this arrangement than to create unnecessary spats. Photographs show a happy family with Rains smiling warmly as Jennifer rides on his shoulders. He now had everything he ever wanted.

While Rains was respected by his peers and most professionals associated with the movie business, he remained very private and reserved. He maintained a commanding and forceful presence and, even in the most casual of conversations, came across as either brusque or restrained. Because of this, Rains was never the most popular actor on the Warners lot. He seldom chatted with anyone, never went to lunch with co-stars, never socialized after the day's work, and kept to himself — in short, a real-life invisible man, a man no one ever knew. An article from the mid-1930s explained: "It isn't that he's 'aloof' or anything like that, nor that he Goes Into The Silence when he's working, like Muni, but somehow you do have a feeling that he…well, that he doesn't want to be disturbed."

What it was that truly motivated Rains is difficult to decipher, especially what it was that moved him spiritually. That he loved his work is irrefutable; that he found his daughter a great joy was obvious. When interviewed around this time, he seems open and honest, but nothing is ever said about his likes or dislikes on subjects such as art, music, poetry or politics. There is nothing about what he truly desires from life. Rains could be as proud of his garden of Jerusalem artichokes and cabbages as he was of any critical recognition. He often created what one interviewer called a "fascinating air of unreality and overstatement." Yet this is what made his performances so unusual — just as one is often fooled into thinking that the ventriloquist's dummy is quite "real." Yet those who knew or worked with Rains found this expressiveness a part of his personality and that he was a charmingly "unreal person."

Most directors considered Rains a solid performer who studied every role with utmost thoroughness. Only on rare occasions did he misinterpret and when this did happen, he would then take an entire day to review the scene and get into a different mental frame of reference. Rains didn't merely walk in and out of a character. He had to be inside the man's brain, inside

his soul. He understood the secret that working with a camera reflected what the actor was thinking. (This type of personal involvement created great strain and tension and it's not surprising, returning home after a day's work on a set, that Rains would turn to whiskey to relax.) Long before his first scenes were shot, Rains analyzed the complexities of his character. In a letter to the author, esteemed *Los Angeles Times* critic Charles Champlin commented: "Claude Rains could do that paradoxical trick that actors must bring off: to be the actor that the customers want to go and see, and yet to be able to disappear into the character he is playing, so that you are at once the actor and not the actor." Rains knew he was short and not classically good-looking, but he could nevertheless come across as attractive both through his strong presence and seductive, underplayed mannerisms. He could bellow and he could purr with equal effectiveness. By this time in his film career, Rains had developed his own style. While a superb and skilled craftsman, he was never a natural actor. Rains studied hard, learning his lines and moves, pacing the floor and intoning various accents on different words or syllables.

Separate from the financial rewards, being a "star" character actor had its disadvantages: it meant Rains had to spend more time in Hollywood than on his farm. With expenses mounting, he arranged on January 6, 1939, for an advance of $24,000 which enabled him to make renovations on the Stone Canyon Road house. Nevertheless, disagreements with the studio over salary and billing continued. Irritated, the actor began to voice his concerns more often, so that when he did make a request, it was granted.

On January 23, the studio issued a freelance contract to the actor, covering his services in a Technicolor short called *Sons of Liberty*, starting work about January 25 at $5,000 with a one-week guarantee, with the proviso: "This engagement is separate from his contract." Rains could have demanded and probably received his going rate of $6,000 per week, but the budget for *Sons of Liberty* was limited.

By late 1938, the fever of patriotism was going strong in America. While the country was still not officially engaged in the world war raging in Europe, there was little doubt that eventually America would be drawn into the conflict. Earlier in the year, the Patriotic Foundation of Chicago launched a public campaign for recognition of a little-known hero of the American Revolutionary War: Haym Salomon

CR and Harry
Cording
in Sons of
Liberty.

(1740-1785), a Jewish businessman whose dedication to the colonists' cause literally saved General Washington's army. Warner Bros. wanted to assist in some way.

Their initial plan, according to the *Variety* column "Inside Stuff — Pictures" (June 21, 1939), was a full-length feature; "Later the Jewish angle was to be subordinated to a story around George Washington. Then it was to have been a four-reeler and later a three-reel feature." It ended up a two-reeler. With Rains top-billed as Salomon, it was shot in late January 1939.

The fact that a movie, even a short one, about a Jewish hero was produced at all was a surprise to many. Although the studio moguls of the time were nearly all Jewish, there was an unwritten contract among them not to make movies with overly Semitic overtones. Harry and Jack Warner were violently opposed to Hitler and his Nazis, but felt constrained to tackle the sensitive issue. The short gave Rains another chance to work with Michael Curtiz, and paired him for a third time with Gale Sondergaard, playing Salomon's devoted wife.

An emigre from Poland, Haym Salomon was

a prosperous Philadelphia merchant who raised money and moral support for the colonists' rebellion against Britain. Learning that the American side could lose because the long-unpaid troops were deserting, he provided a large sum of money for the cause and encouraged other businessmen to raise over $400,000 for Washington's needs. In retaliation, the British seized his property, and the patriot was thrown into prison until the war ended. (The young American government never repaid him and he died in poverty.) Historians agree that without Salomon's efforts, the army of the United States would have been defeated. But his name is seldom mentioned in the history books, unlike Christian heroes such as Patrick Henry and Paul Revere. In filming Salomon's story, Warner Bros. was aware of the sensitivity of the Jewish elements of the storyline, and downplayed Salomon's religion, limiting it to one scene in which Rains wears a prayer shawl to synagogue services. Partly because of the patriotic theme, reviews were quite favorable. Some were unreasonably superlative, the writers doing all they could to convince independent theatre managers to book the short film.

Whether or not Rains' portrayal of Salomon was

accurate historically is unknown because so little was written about this exceptional man. It's likely the actor had strong personal feelings about playing Salomon, especially after becoming a U.S. citizen. As he stated: "Every actor likes to play a heroic part now and then, but my feeling toward Haym Salomon was deeper than that. The story of his contribution toward the cause of freedom and tolerance is especially timely…" Additionally, Rains wanted to contribute to the awareness of what was happening to Jews in Europe. First, his wife's family were Jews from Czechoslovakia, a country brutally overrun by the Nazis. Although they were far from devout, this *was* their heritage. Also, according to Jewish law, lineage descends from the mother, which meant that his daughter Jennifer would be recognized by other Jews as Jewish.

There was another potential reason, one that remains as mysterious as everything else in Rains' life: his own background. Rains told Frances and Jennifer that his father had made comments which indicated his own heritage was Jewish. He told Frances that his father once suggested the family was descended from Spanish Jews fleeing the Inquisition of the late 15th century when England was one of the few countries permitting immigration. Jennifer stated that her father often repeated this story to her, and that he thought it was true, but had no proof. There's no indication Rains ever expressed belief in any formal religious denomination or pronounced his feelings about God. He declined to be married in a church, always going to justices of the peace, and he and Frances raised Jennifer without devotion to any specific creed.

Variety ad.

In the end, the actor was pleased with his contribution to *Sons of Liberty*, which in 1940 received an Oscar for Best Short Subject, Two-Reel. Twenty-one years later, in 1960, Rains himself was honored: *Variety* reported from Philadelphia that he was to be the recipient of the First Covenant Award from Old York Lodge B'nai B'rith for his portrayal of Haym Salomon.

CHAPTER 13
Mr. Rains Goes to Columbia

While Rains was making *Sons of Liberty*, Warners started production on a film with the working titles *Fly Away Home*, *Family Reunion* and *A Family Affair*, and ultimately released as *Daughters Courageous*. It had its basis in *Fly Away Home*, a three-act comedy that ran on Broadway for six months in 1935. (The cast included Thomas Mitchell, Andrea King, Sheldon Leonard, Albert Dekker and Montgomery Clift.) Warners bought the screen rights in 1938 and Kay Francis was set to star. But their plans for it later changed. The huge success of *Four Daughters*, and the breakout performance of John Garfield, had Jack Warner clamoring for a sequel to keep the young actor in the public eye. There was a slight problem: Garfield's character died in a car crash in the final reel. The studio came up with an unusual solution: Have the exact same cast play basically the same characters in a new film, but with a completely different storyline. That meant Fay Bainter as the mother, the Lane Sisters and Gale Page as the daughters, May Robson as the housekeeper, Jeffrey Lynn, Frank McHugh and Dick Foran as suitors. And bring Garfield back as a sullen rogue who captures the heart of Priscilla Lane. But there wasn't much similarity of the one-dimensionally comic papa of *Four Daughters* in Rains' new role: The actor often said that the well-rounded character of Jim Masters was one of his favorites.

After the actors completed the obligatory costume tests, Hal Wallis wrote a memo to Jack Warner to confirm Rains' participation: "The new test of Claude Rains with that old trench coat, and without the mustache, is much better. It is more like that character we want." (Rains wore his usual Homburg hat as a prop, and even though Wallis initially objected, the actor insisted it enhanced and added to the "chicanery" of his character.)

Under the direction of Warners workhorse Michael Curtiz, for whom Rains turned in a couple of his best performances, *Daughters Courageous* is the

Rosemary Lane, CR, Gale Page, Lola Lane and Priscilla Lane in Daughters Courageous.

eternal fable of the prodigal. Growing up in Carmel, California, the four bubbling daughters of Nan Masters (Fay Bainter) are preparing for her marriage to Sam Sloane (Donald Crisp), a financially secure, pleasantly dull pillar of the community. Unexpectedly and to everyone's astonishment, the girls' father Jim Masters, who deserted them twenty years earlier, appears, a sort of Enoch Arden who has been on a "rendezvous with the universe." The family gives him a chilly reception, but Jim's subtle humor and obvious good heart disarms nearly everyone, and awakens

CR and John Garfield in Daughters Courageous.

affectionate feelings in the daughters for the father they never knew. Moreover, his stories of vagabond travels conjure up a life they will never experience, cocooned as they are in their small-town family life; he opens up the possibility of new horizons. However, Masters realizes that he can't simply swan back into their lives as if he never left, nor can he win Nan back from Sloane. And when he sees the wanderlust in his daughter Buff's beau Gabriel (top-billed Garfield), he knows that to save her from herself, he must somehow prevent their ill-conceived union.

Each of the three male figures represents something all people desire: Sloane, the businessman — security; Jim, the vagabond traveler — adventure and romance; Gabriel, the fisherman's son — impetuous youth. For all his faults, Jim has integrity. Realizing Gabriel is a younger counterpart of himself, he warns the young ne'er-do-well that he will end up hurting Buff just as he himself hurt Nan twenty years earlier. In the end, the two kindred souls leave town together, rather than be caught up in the conformity of the middle-class world they cannot adjust to. Nan marries Sloane, and we know the daughters will settle into a replica of their mother's pleasant, if unexciting, world. The audience can't help but like Jim and

Gabriel and, even while tending to side with Nan's more realistic outlook, they will always wonder how Jim and Gabriel fared. Yet in this finale there is no firm resolution: it is up to the audience to decide who was "right or wrong." This intelligent film was far ahead of its time in presenting a story whose main theme is that marriage offers choices and risks, and the right choice isn't necessarily right for everyone. The film's artistic intelligence might have hurt it at the box office. In the 1930s, with life as difficult as it was, most audiences wanted clear-cut resolutions with no unknowns.

Rains' role represents the scalawags of the world, who cannot conform to society's norms, as sympathetic and poetic. Even though at times they are irresponsible, such people possess their own insight and a charm that is hard to resist, and can be regarded as a viable alternative to the so-called virtuous middle-class life. Rains recognized the attractive nature of the role:

> I'm a bum in this role, but a charming bum at that. Even though the story tells you that Jim Masters has been everywhere he oughtn't and done everything he shouldn't … even the audience itself can't help having

CR and Fay
Bainter in
Daughters
Courageous.

a certain liking for the irresponsible fellow. He never pretends to be other than he really is, you see, and that is very disarming…. There is a little bit of admiration for the irresponsible fellow in every one of us. He sometimes does what we all would relish doing, if we just didn't see so clearly the consequences that would follow.

Even those critics who found the story somewhat implausible acknowledged it was Rains' skill in portraying the character that caused confusion in audiences accustomed to movies providing cut-and-dried solutions to Life's problems. A lengthy article in the *Hollywood Spectator* commented:

Regarded abstractly, the action of Claude Rains returning so casually to the wife and children he had abandoned twenty years is a story element not easy to accept; but Rains so quickly establishes his personality, so quietly acquaints us with his philosophy and thought process, that while we still feel no other person would behave that way, we must admit such a man undoubtedly would. If Rains had acted all

over the place, read his lines as most are read, his characterization would have been lacking in plausibility.

Describing the film itself, Garfield's biographer Larry Swindell noted that it "merited distinction as one of the American classics of the late thirties." Kay Francis, set for the lead when Warners acquired the rights to the play, starred with Walter Huston in the studio's 1942 remake *Always in My Heart*.

During the making of *Daughters Courageous*, other incidents in Rains' relationship with Warners would have strong ramifications for both the actor and the studio. Financial quarrels persisted. Memos went back and forth until Jack Warner realized that he must write personally to Rains, hitting on the most sensitive issue with the actor:

March 9, 1939

Dear Claude:

It has come to my attention that you have expressed dissatisfaction with respect to the billing which has been accorded you in connection with some of your recent pictures…

While I am satisfied there has been no intentional disregard by any of our departments as to our contractual obligations with respect to billing, it is possible that some inadvertencies may have been committed. Therefore, I am again impressing upon the minds of all of the officials of this studio who play any part in setting up the billings on our various pictures to adhere strictly to the obligations established in our contracts…

In closing may I personally express my appreciation of the splendid performance which you gave in the portrayal of the character "Haym Salomon" in our picture *Sons of Liberty* and which I am sure will contribute largely to the success of this picture.

Warner closed with a statement that the relationship between the studio and the actor would be one of "mutual benefit." This letter (curiously, the only personal communique from Warner to Rains preserved in multiple library archives) placated the actor; he continued his stint with the studio with no further difficulties. Whatever he may have thought of the studio head on a personal level, Rains liked working at Warner Bros.

In early 1939, Rains was in great demand, with both Samuel Goldwyn and Columbia wanting him for projects. To keep Rains on their own lot, Warners sent him a thirty-day notice on March 14 scheduling him for *The Knight and the Lady*, eventually made as *The Private Lives of Elizabeth and Essex*, and starring Bette Davis and Errol Flynn. (The role Rains was up for, Elizabeth I's advisor Sir Francis Bacon, ended up being played by Donald Crisp.) Among those desiring Rains' services, Frank Capra especially wanted the actor for his new film *Mr. Smith Goes to Washington*. Columbia contacted Trilling about the actor, but Warner told Trilling to "kill that off by saying Rains was 'all tied up.'" However, Rains knew what was going on, so he and his agent went to see the highly regarded director on March 23. Warner hoped that the required thirty-day notice would prohibit Rains from being available, but Capra was determined to wait. On the same date, Rains' agent William Hawks called the studio to obtain permission for the actor to appear on the Rudy Vallee radio program on March

30. Hawks also contacted Trilling, who in turn immediately got off a memo to Hal Wallis:

Bill Hawks 'phoned — they had been over to see Frank Capra, and the part in *Mr. Smith Goes to Washington* was the best thing Claude Rains has ever been offered since he has been in pictures — equally as important as James Stewart's and Jean Arthur's roles, and they were therefore loathe to pass it up. They thought that "Warners would probably prefer Rains doing it anyway to add to his prestige and name value for Warners' own future benefit."

I told him we had already served the thirty-day notification and we had always planned, ever since I spoke to him two weeks ago, that Rains play the part of Bacon in *The Knight and the Lady*, which we naturally were going to be terribly upset if anything interfered with it.

Rains has to give us a definite reply within three days after receipt of the notification, so we should have his legal answer by Monday; but from the way Hawks spoke I am sure Rains is going to take the Capra picture, which leaves us only the right to extend our contract.

The very next day, Rains mailed notice, registered and special delivery, that he had signed with Frank Capra to make his picture, commencing on April 4 and shooting until July 5. If Jack Warner did not like it — the hell with him. Since this was the actor's first independent movie since the February dispute, Warner did not want to aggravate the tense situation. The entire fiasco had been created to prevent Rains from going to Columbia. It failed.

With the advent of material contributions to the Allies, the Great Depression's economic stranglehold on America's psychology began to ease and movie attendance increased. Many cinema historians consider 1939 a watershed year for the industry: releases included *Goodbye Mr. Chips*, *Stagecoach*, *Dark Victory*, *Ninotchka*, *The Wizard of Oz*, *Of Mice and Men*, *Gunga Din* and *Gone with the Wind*. Even with the rumbles of war in Europe, it seemed that "happy days were here again." The people's faith in the democratic process had been restored. Few films represent this

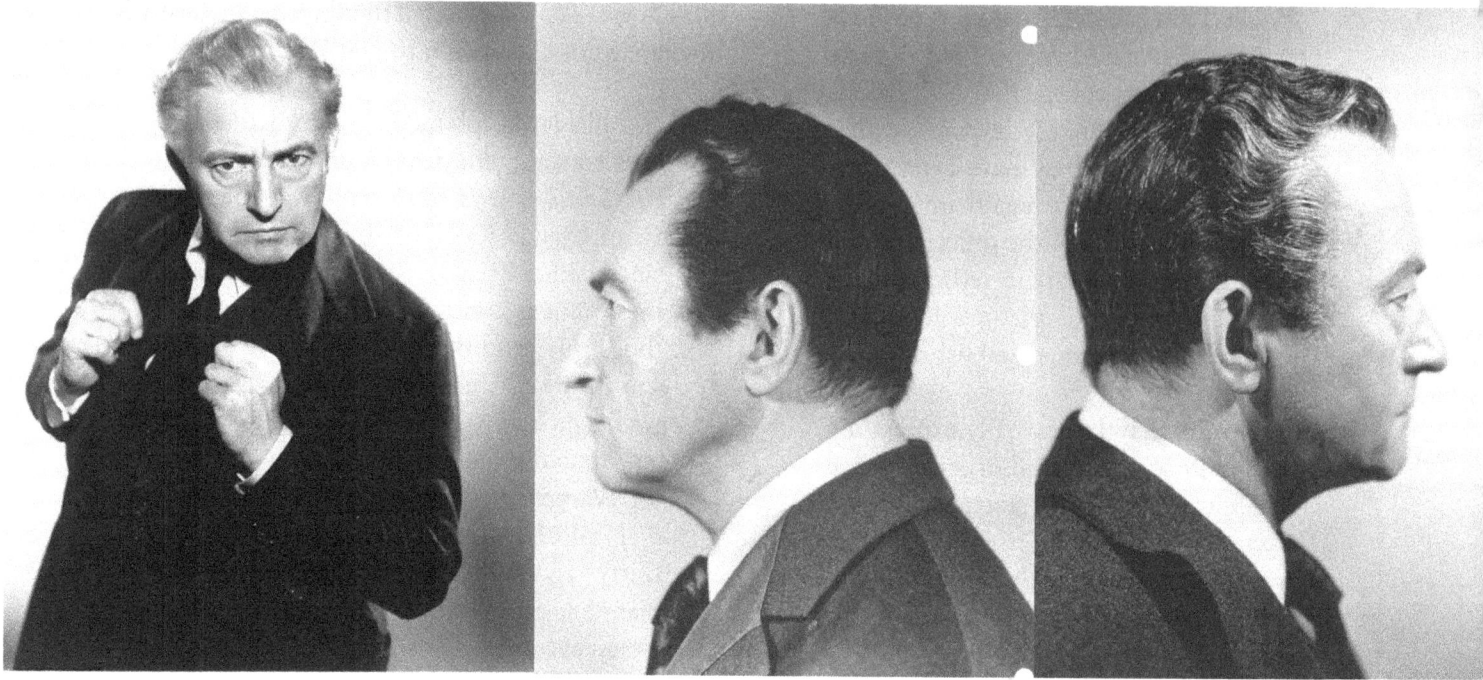

These shots from Mr. Smith Goes to Washington illustrate various hair and makeup tests that were made in pre-production.

better than Capra's *Mr. Smith Goes to Washington.*

The simple, classic story follows James Stewart as a naive country boy from an unnamed state who overnight becomes its junior Senator. Arriving starry-eyed in the nation's capital, Jefferson Smith is determined to carry out his duty to his country. He is completely unaware he is only in Washington because a corrupt political "machine" needed a know-nothing in "their" seat in Congress — one who won't question an upcoming crooked bill that serves their ends. Also under their crooked control for years has been the state's much-admired senior Senator, Joseph Harrison Paine (Rains), whom Smith idolizes.

The elder statesman, having compromised too often in his lengthy career, has lost sight of ideals that earned him the faith of constituents and the sobriquet "The Silver Knight." (Pre-production photos depict Rains in several different character hair and makeup combinations, both with and without glasses, before the final look: a white wig combed elegantly back and professorial rimless frames.) Rains' conniving characters were usually deliberately devious and under-handed, but in Senator Paine, the actor creates a man who believes the end justifies the means, and that he can do "good" within the boundaries of his corrupt political office. Nonetheless, as he admits to Jeff, in Washington, "you check your ideals outside the door like you do your rubbers."

In addition to the salary — a total of $41,000, basically $8,000 per week – *Mr. Smith* provided Rains

with a real opportunity to display his talent. Years later, Capra wrote: "[Rains] had the artistry, power and depth to play the soul-tortured idealist whose feet had turned to clay...." The audience's emotions run the gamut as the actor makes us warm to Paine as Jeff's caring mentor, then be completely disillusioned when he calls for the young man's (manipulated) Senate expulsion — but then, at the end, stand and cheer as Paine regains his integrity in the most dramatic way possible. Driven to the brink by Smith's dramatic, selfless filibuster, Paine tries to shoot himself, but storming back into the chaotic chamber, he desperately shouts at the top of his lungs to be heard, beating his breast:

> I'm not fit to be a Senator! I'm not fit to live! Expel me! Expel me, not him! Willet Dam is a fraud! It's a crime against the people who sent me here — and I committed it! Every word that boy said is the truth! Every word about Taylor, and me, and graft, and the rotten political corruption of our state! ...I'm not fit for any place of honor or trust! Expel me!"

The movie ends on a riotous note, leaving Senator Paine's fate up in the air. However, the original script

As *Senator Paine* in Mr. Smith Goes to Washington.

Academy Awards, including Best Picture, Best Director, Best Actor (Stewart) and Best Writing–Screenplay. It won for Best Writing-Original Story. Rains himself earned the first of his four nods for Best Supporting Actor, losing to *Stagecoach*'s Thomas Mitchell. In 1977 when *Mr. Smith* was remade by producer Frank Capra Jr. as *Billy Jack Goes to Washington,* its writer-director-star Tom Laughlin offered the Claude Rains role to … James Stewart (who said, "Thanks, I've already done it").

On June 15, Rains received notice from Warners that he would next appear in the studio's *Four Wives.* The original plan was for the film to continue the story thread of *Daughters Courageous,* but then it became a sequel to *Four Daughters* instead, with Rains returning as Adam Lemp, the "Doctor of Music," lovably grumpy as ever. ("Was it the Chinese [who] used to drown their girl babies? What ever happened to that beautiful custom?!") His part was small but he received his full weekly salary of $6,000 with four weeks guaranteed. Rains gets the first laugh in the movie: In the opening scene, "Papa" Lemp is resplendent in a feminine kitchen apron, compelled by his sister May Robson to help with the spring cleaning. As a Beethoven symphony plays on the record player, he washes windows unhurriedly; Robson surreptitiously puts on a fast-paced swing record, and as a reflex Rains shifts into a comically high gear. Annoyed at the way he was manipulated, he glares at the record and snorts, "Benjamin Goodman – *bah*!" Warners made the family film a Christmas week (1939) release.

answers that question with an additional scene not included in the film: A hometown parade, confetti and cheers, a hero's welcome for Smith who rides in an open car with Clarissa. Smith sees Paine watching the parade and leaps from the car. Paine fearfully starts to move off, but Jeff insists: "I say it's your parade, sir. You've got to come!" Smith takes Clarissa and Paine home to his mother who warmly greets them. The crowd outside is clamoring for Smith to speak, but he says, "Not me! Joseph Paine is the man they ought to be listening to!"

The film's powerful message garnered it raves: "[A] totally compelling piece of movie making, upholding the virtues of traditional American ideals." *Billboard* labeled it "The Great American Picture." *Mr. Smith Goes to Washington* was nominated for eleven

Back home on the farm during the summer of 1939, Rains aggravated a previous condition and needed surgery. In those days, it was difficult for stars to keep their names out of the papers when scheduled for any procedure, but so far away from the West Coast, it wasn't surprising that only a small notice

Mr. Smith Goes to Washington.

appeared in the *Philadelphia Evening Bulletin* of October 13 reporting that "the naturalized English Actor was in the University Hospital and was resting following a hernia operation." Ordered to rest for six weeks, he spent the remainder of October and all of November at the farm, much to his enjoyment.

As 1939 ended, Rains had a lot to be thankful for. In addition to the $41,000 he earned at Columbia, he received $66,000 from Warners; salaries from his many radio appearances brought his gross income up to just over $112,000. Tax forms indicate the usual ten percent paid to his agent Hawks, and also a large investment loss. On May 10, 1940, when Hitler invaded Holland, Rains' accountant in New York wired the actor advising him that all stock investments were sold except U.S. Savings Bonds. What exactly the loss was remains unknown, but it must have been considerable given his tax was barely $2,256 against a salary of over $100,000.

Rains felt content and happy. He and Frances had a stable relationship, and she grew more and more to love living in the country, as much as he. Both of them disliked the West Coast, and even though they had a nice home on Stone Canyon Road, they felt more comfortable on the farm. Whenever Rains returned

to Hollywood for a film, his wife and daughter went along, until Jennifer reached school age. Publicity photos depict a proud papa giving his two-year-old daughter piggy back rides and beaming with happiness. He was especially delighted when his little girl, unable to pronounce "Da-Da," called him "Fa-Fa," an endearment she continued until she was in her early teens. Her father took to signing notes and postcards to her in the same way, a sweet habit he continued until his death. His life was a total joy in so many respects, it seemed to frighten him. As usual when not shooting a film, Rains contracted for as much radio work as he could, and throughout the 1940s he was featured in several episodes of NBC's *Cavalcade of America*. This series featured stories about such historical figures as Benedict Arnold, John Paul Jones and Thomas Paine. These appearances were relaxing to Rains: Next to farming and reading, performing on the radio was a favorite "pastime."

While he loved the farmhouse at Glen Mills, there were problems with the soil; the acreage was not sufficient to grow surplus crops needed for steers. Meticulously kept record books show that while Rains was not losing money, neither was he making any from the farm. Then, too, there was no longer any

Top: CR and Rosemary Lane in Four Wives.

Bottom: The cast of Four Wives: back row, Lola Lane, Eddie Albert, Frank McHugh, Dick Foran, Jeffrey Lynn and Gale Page; front row, Rosemary Lane, May Robson, CR and Priscilla Lane.

another location nearby, since both he and Frances loved the Brandywine area. For Rains, "home" was where his heart was and that meant a farm. All in all, his life was on an even keel. He would have liked to have had another child, but at age 50, he felt it wasn't wise, and it was much too risky for Frances. Besides, given his devotion to his work, there may not have been sufficient time to meet greater family needs.

As 1939 ended and as Rains recuperated from the hernia procedure, Warners scheduled him for *Saturday's Children*, a script the Epstein brothers adapted from the 1927 Pulitzer Prize–winning play by Maxwell Anderson. The studio was continuing their successful theme of working-class families and the financial hardships of young newlyweds — in this case, John Garfield and Anne Shirley. In his *New York Times* review of the film, Bosley Crowther wrote: "No studio in Hollywood seems to have a more consistent regard for the American middle class, with its myriad little sorrows and triumphs, its domestic delights and dissensions, than Warner Brothers…."

challenge in the restoration of the farmhouse — all was complete. Finally, and perhaps most importantly, Rains preferred to live in rather remote areas, and the population of Delaware County seemed to be increasing. For all these reasons, as well as the fact he was now making more money, Rains felt he could afford a larger estate, one on which he could be a real country squire. Starting in 1940, he began to look for

In *Saturday's Children*, Rains essayed yet another American dad, a soft-spoken, meek but good-natured Washington Heights (New York) store bookkeeper. With wire spectacles and hair parted in the middle, he ruefully admits he "stopped living" at 43, when he realized what the end of his life would be: exactly what it *had* been up to then, repetitious and dull.

John Garfield, CR and Anne Shirley in Saturday's Children.

And he is determined to help keep this from happening to his daughter (Shirley). Shirley marries a co-worker (Garfield) but the couple's financial woes lead to squabbles and their break-up. Feeling that he has failed his child, Rains arranges a potentially fatal workplace accident for himself, so that Shirley and Garfield can use the compensation money to make a new start.

Vincent Sherman, Rains' young friend from his Theatre Guild days, was assigned to direct. Unlike the generally tense atmosphere on a Michael Curtiz set, Sherman and staff created an air of ease on *Saturday's Children*, but there were scheduling overruns. Voluminous memos went back and forth, expressing concern: "It was 4 o'clock yesterday afternoon before the Director had covered the ground we had scheduled him to cover by noon. Practically every scene up to that time with Claude Rains and Elisabeth

Risdon [playing Rains' wife] was rehearsed at least 5 or 6 times and then retaken 5 or 6 times before being okayed to print." Rains appreciated the more relaxed pace under Sherman, and was complimentary: "This man is precious … one of the best directors of actors I've worked with." Sherman possessed an ability to see moviemaking from the actor's point of view (he himself had been an actor). Years later, Sherman acknowledged that Rains was the most "astute craftsman" he ever knew. He also maintained that the actor was not cold or aloof as so many thought, but basically shy.

Although separated by age difference, we became good friends [in the Theatre Guild days]. He was gracious and kind to me at a time when I needed it…. We would spend hours talking or playing chess. He rarely discussed any personal matters, although I did learn he had been

married two or three times in England....
Most of our conversations, then and later,
were about theater and films — he was a
man of mystery otherwise, who guarded
his privacy....

In 1937 ... I found myself working on
the same lot as Claude. By this time, we
were both married and soon to be fathers.
He seemed happier than I had ever seen
him, had a lovely home in Bel Air, and his
career was moving ahead steadily.

[Warners] made me a director, and in
my second film, *Saturday's Children*, Claude
was cast as the father of Anne Shirley. It
was a gentle role, warm and sympathetic....
While we were friends and I felt he respected me, I was nevertheless worried
about how he might react to my directing
him. After all, he had been a star on Broadway when I was just a bit player, and he
was now a well-known Hollywood figure,
while this was only my second directorial
effort. I had no cause for fear or doubts. On
the first day of shooting, he was on the set
on time and was letter-perfect in his lines.
Early that morning, we rehearsed a long
and substantial scene, and after I finished
explaining what I hoped to accomplish to
the cast, I glanced over at Claude. He was
smiling and gave me an imperceptible-to-
all-but-me nod of approval. I will always
be grateful for that gesture. It gave me the
courage and confidence I needed.

On January 26, Rains became quite ill with fever
and a cold, for which poor Vincent Sherman was
blamed, as an internal memo indicates: "Director
has been carrying his rehearsals to extremes.... From
11:00 o'clock yesterday morning until 6:20 p.m. last
night, only five print takes were made, and only two
of them carried more than one line of dialogue. After
working on the last scene of the day for one hour, and
making seven takes, the director refused to OK any
of these takes for a print. It was on the seventh take
that Claude Rains informed the director that he was
tired and not feeling very well, but that he would go
through the scene once more, which he did and then
went home." Rains had reported that day at 8:00
a.m. for makeup and costume and then left at 6:20

The Sea Hawk.

p.m. — he was then out quite ill for two days. On
the release of *Saturday's Children*, Bosley Crowther
cited Rains for "turn[ing] in another of his tender,
understanding father roles" while *Variety* said that he
was "as agreeably cast as ever he has been ... as the
kindly but self-deprecating father."

Having wrapped *Saturday's Children* on January
31, 1940, Rains reported for work the very next day
on Errol Flynn's latest swashbuckler, *The Sea Hawk*.
Set in Elizabethan England, the adventure tale had
Queen Elizabeth (a wonderful Flora Robson) weigh-
ing the threat posed to her country by the impending
Spanish Armada. Devoted to "Queen Bess," Flynn's
Captain Thorpe (patterned after real-life English
naval hero, Sir Francis Drake) and his seagoing band
of Merrie Men clash with King Philip's fleet in a
series of well-staged and exciting battle scenes. Rains
plays the Spanish ambassador, Don José Alvarez de
Cordoba, guardian to his niece Doña Maria (Brenda
Marshall) who, of course, falls in love with privateer
Thorpe. As usual, Rains wore the period costum-

CR owned a beautiful Bel Air home, with sycamores out front.

The living room, decorated in beige and henna tones.

Ladies-in-waiting, CR, Flora Robson and Brenda Marshall (on the floor) in The Sea Hawk.

ing handsomely and convincingly, as opposed to colleagues who were just too contemporary to look anything but uncomfortable in cape, starched ruffled collar, and doublet and hose. Rains always appeared born to such resplendency; he may not have been tall, but he was surprisingly muscular, especially considering he was 50; he cuts quite a dashing figure. To "look Spanish," his naturally auburn brows were darkened, a touch of eyeliner added, and he sports a stylish trimmed goatee and curling mustache, with a rather bouffant black wig. He gives a polished, characteristically sly performance as the devious envoy.

The Sea Hawk reteamed Rains with several old colleagues, in addition to Flynn: director Michael Curtiz, Donald Crisp, Una O'Connor, Montagu Love and more. It also provided his one opportunity to share the screen with another English specialist in velvety villainy, Henry Daniell, playing the queen's treasonous lord chancellor. Because his role was small, Rains assumed he would be finished within a couple of weeks, but Flynn was not the most reli-

able actor for appearing on set sober and there were numerous delays.

The Sea Hawk was the last film Rains made under his initial Warner Bros. contract, which was set to expire on April 10, 1940. Warners elected to pick up his option with modifications made to the original November 27, 1935, agreement. Now the actor was required to make two pictures at $6,000 per week, with a five-week guarantee and the one additional week free, if needed. Again included in this contract was his right to make two pictures for other studios as a freelance. However, a new clause was inserted stating that Rains could not commit himself to any outside engagement until he first advised Warners of the start and completion dates. Obringer also wanted a limitation on the number of weeks Rains could work on outside pictures, and the proviso that these weeks would extend his Warners contract. This was a crucial factor, because it meant that Rains' contract could continue almost endlessly at the same salary. This was the price he had to pay to be a semi-freelance.

The positive aspects of the new contract were that he could now make more films and work with different producers and directors. He had more leverage, and a guaranteed salary of $60,000 whether or not Warners made their two films. The crucial negative aspect of the contract was that Rains would owe Warners for time away from the studio. That is exactly what would happen.

While Warners appreciated having a box-office draw like Rains on the payroll, they were constantly worried about directors keeping him on their sets beyond his guaranteed period, because he now was an "expensive" talent. If the studio had to pay him $6,000 per week, it sought to control his schedule on a fixed salary. Rains wanted to include an extension in the new contract that in the following year he would earn $6,800 per week. Warners agreed to the new figure, but only as a future option. Caught up in these legal maneuverings, Rains would never make more than $6,000 per week with yearly increases after the first two years. Jack Warner had gambled on permitting the actor to engage in outside work, in order that the contract would be extended at a controlled rate, and it worked. Finally, there was the issue of billing: Rains insisted he was never to have less than second featured billing in any Warner Bros. production.

On March 19, 1940, a new agreement was signed. There is no indication that Rains sought or received legal counsel. He seemed fully aware of all ramifications, and the security of earning the then hefty sum of $6,000 per week was satisfying. But, in truth, Warners had made the better deal, which the actor would not realize until it was too late. For now, he had had enough of contract shenanigans and left Hollywood to return to the peace and quiet of Glen Mills.

Rains' personal and professional lives seemed to be going quite well, especially after the depressing divorce from Beatrix. "Until I married Frances, I was getting to think [there was] something so untidy in my life…I couldn't find happiness or give it." In his fourth marriage, he did find those things that had eluded him — fulfillment professionally, working his small farm, and his daughter and his wife at his side.

However, his lack of sensitivity as to what created happiness for others remained one of the greatest shortcomings of his personality. He deeply loved Frances and Jennifer, but what was lacking in his adoration for the two women in his life was an ability to display his affection, especially physically. Much of this was most likely due to his Victorian English upbringing; he felt it improper to overwhelm a loved one with demonstrative behavior, and he was embar-rassed by it. It was easier to buy a gift to symbolically show what he wanted to express, and while for some people such an approach is adequate, others require more. This may have been true for Frances since she came from a very loving family and as the youngest was pampered and fussed over. Nevertheless, Claude and Frances were compatible, seldom disagreed and seemed content in each other's company.

Without doubt, Frances propped up her husband's emotional and mental stability. Rains appreciated the calming influence she had on him. Above all, he loved her quiet honesty and always believed he could trust her. This was an extremely crucial factor in their marriage, trust, because Frances had influence in shaping the environment of his home life. Jennifer remembers that there was much laughter in the house during her childhood. What Claude owed Frances is best revealed in his own words: "She is so calm, Frances, she has a beautiful calm that is one of the qualities that has made us so happy together. She is never the prey to her emotions. She is sound and she is sincere. She never says 'yes' when she means 'no,' a very rare thing in a woman. She is like a healing hand to me. You never see any of the temper I used to have, do you, Frances?" he asked.

The conversation reported in an extensive interview Rains granted to *Silver Screen*, one of the many dime movie fan magazines flooding the market, rings surprisingly true (surprisingly at a time when publicity was rampant and such pieces were often completely fabricated). However, the title, "A Villain's Love Story," reflects the one difficulty in his career the actor could not overcome: typecasting. In the article, Rains defined the relationship he and Frances enjoyed: "I never make any important decision without first consulting her. She's wise, she's awfully wise…she knows. And in all the small ways, too, I am dependent on her. She drives me to the studio every morning, when I am working. And on the few occasions when she doesn't drive me, the day never afterwards seems so bright and warmed." He revealed how she waited for him during the terrible ordeal of his divorce from Beatrix:

> Twelve years ago, we met … five years ago, we were married and I am just as crazy about her now as I was then. More so, if that be possible. I haunt the mailbox when she is away, I write to her every day, long

letters, too, I, who loathe correspondence and never write to another soul.... [O]ccasionally, she stays on our farm in Pennsylvania for a few weeks after I come back to Hollywood to make a picture. I get frantic without her, frantic. I can't read, can't sleep, can't enjoy having people around. In fact, I see less of people when she is away than I do when she is here. I seem to get more out of our relationship in her absence, when I am alone.

When asked if there were never quarrels, Frances responded:

Claude loves music and I don't love it at all, don't understand it, don't even like it. But otherwise … I think we are really singularly alike in all that we like or dislike … not temperamentally the same, as he has explained, because I am naturally calm and he is not naturally calm, I am relaxed and he is very tense … but even our temperamental differences seem to be the right differences, they balance. Neither of us cares about a lot of money, but we both care a lot about security, especially Claude. He's really fanatic about it, especially since [Jennifer] came … and of course we want other babies, of course we do … we both dislike the same people which is even more important than liking the same people … we both detest insincerity… So there aren't really many differences.

As for arguments, quarrels, no. You see, if any disagreement does come up and you don't talk, there just can't be a fight. If you talk, if you begin to argue with a man, you never gain a point anyway and you lose a tremendous amount of ground … and so, if ever we do feel irritated, I just put a gag in my mouth and keep quiet. I had to learn plenty of self-control during all that time when Claude was married and I didn't know what was going to happen. We were on edge in those days and, without the exercise of considerable control, we would have gone right over the edge.

Time and events bore out the truth of Frances' comments — this was an accurate description of their relationship and remained so for nearly twenty years. (There were to be no more children after Jennifer, who recalled that her mother endured several miscarriages. There was some discussion of adoption, but Claude's advancing age, coupled with the uncertainty brought on by the coming of the war, were concerns.)

The age gap remained a sore point for Claude, and of course only became more of an issue as the years passed. Frances found it exciting to be married to a man as dynamic as Rains, and admitted that when she saw him on the screen, she got shivers up and down her spine. But for the actor, there were the inevitable awkward and embarrassing moments, and while he learned to live with it, there was anxiety: "Sometimes when the cashier at the bank or the man in the garage says to me, 'Your daughter was in this morning,' I have a slightly peculiar sensation, but like to think I know how to preserve this lovely thing called love better than I might have known in my younger days…"

While Claude treated Frances with respect, by his nature he tended to be the dominant figure in the household, and at times could be ignorant of the needs of others. Yet she put up with his whims for a variety of reasons. If Claude was not always physically warm and demonstratively loving, he was totally faithful. In an industry in which it was easy to have an affair, it appears that Rains remained faithful. He never needed to prove himself as a man outside of his relationship with Frances; all his faults and idiosyncrasies were secondary to his qualities of loyalty and honesty, and his love of simple joys. Most importantly, he acknowledged Frances' tempering influence on his explosive outbursts; he credited her with making him realize that he used the pronoun "I" too often and "we" never enough. But the greatest need of this profoundly talented artist, but extremely insecure man, was to be loved and respected. In acting, he found both.

That early respite on the farm was short as Rains was required to spend another hot summer in the Burbank studios. By July 15, he was on the set of *Four Mothers*, the third and final picture in the *Four Daughters* series. By this time, the actor had left the Hawks agency and signed with another agent, Mike Levee; the actor remained with Levee for over six years. Although Rains plays the same character as the previous two films, with a curly wig softening his

CR on his farm in 1940.

features, a character mustache and twinkle in his eye, Rains personifies the ideal tolerant and loving parent. The new storyline focused more on the father than the daughters, and Rains' part was larger: Lemp talks up one son-in-law's Florida real estate development to the point that many of the Briarwood townsfolk invest; and when it's wiped out by the one-two punch of a hurricane and tidal wave, the whole town holds him responsible. Even the local music foundation, to which he has devoted his life, shows him the door. Intending to reimburse his neighbors, Lemp sells the house, which is to be torn down and replaced by an apartment building. But then the organizers of a world-famous Beethoven festival come to Lemp, "the best authority on Beethoven in America," and invite him to conduct the orchestra at a Cincinnati concert. Papa is center stage throughout much of the movie and *literally* center stage in a lengthy scene at the end, as he wields the baton in a Hollywood Bowl–type amphitheater before an audience of thousands. The maestro returns to Briarwood by train where scores of cheering citizens give him a hero's welcome. (Rains: "What *is* all this racket? Is Roosevelt coming?").

The filming of *Four Mothers* progressed slowly and went into the sixth week mainly because Rains

became quite ill. Given the heat of the Burbank studios and the frantic pace the actor had been working in the last year, it is not surprising that on August 23 he suffered a severe throat infection and a high fever. In all probability it was strep throat, for he was off the set for several days. Studio policy demanded if an actor was absent more than a day, the studio doctor had to attest to the legitimacy of the illness and this is exactly what happened. It must have been humiliating, but the doctors confirmed Rains was quite ill and ordered not to return to the set until August 27. All business, Jack Warner sent a memo to the payroll department stating the actor was not to be paid for these four days and the studio was to "obtain the proportionate number of days free at the termination of the sixth week." *Four Mothers* was a successful finale to a harmless film series that had pleased American audiences for several years, but by 1940 it was wearing thin and Warners decided to bring it to a close.

On September 3, Rains received his new assignment. However, instead of resting for thirty days between films, as was his contractual right, Rains again waived notification before commencing work on *Lady with Red Hair*. Even though he had not fully recovered from his illness, Rains started on the new project on September 11, fearing his plum part might be passed on to another actor — that of real-life theatre impresario David Belasco (1853-1931). The script was based on a memoir by the celebrated stage actress Mrs. Leslie Carter; her autobiography appeared in *Liberty* magazine in January 1927 as "Portrait of a Lady with Red Hair." Warners purchased the story as a vehicle for the delightful and talented Miriam Hopkins.

While Mrs. Carter had acted for Belasco from 1890 to 1928, the film concentrated only on her early (pre–World War I) career. Playing Mrs. Carter's mentor gave Rains the opportunity to rant, rave, employ wild, flourishing gestures and enjoy himself immensely. Belasco had been known as a Broadway Svengali: excitable, demanding, obstinate, devoid of

CR and Miriam Hopkins in Lady with Red Hair.

Lady with Red Hair. *According to a* Variety *columnist: Rains "does catch the spirit of David Belasco, especially in the years when the famous producer had snowy locks."*

warmth, highly emotional and flamboyant, but nevertheless a creative genius. (Rains' strong physical resemblance was augmented by a wig even more bouffant than the actor's own hair.) As Jeanine Basinger noted in her 1993 book *A Woman's View: How Hollywood Spoke to Women*: "Actors who play impresarios are usually dominant figures, men like Claude Rains, Conrad Veidt and John Barrymore, who have beautiful voices, great panache, and strong camera presence. They are to be seen as too old or too experienced for the young[er] woman, but not as ugly or totally unlikable. They represent a viable alternative…. [T]hese men, whether ghost, angel, mysterious stranger, doctor, or psychiatrist … help a woman to be what she really wants but cannot achieve on her own.

They liberate her, take her out of herself. They empower her, and can represent anything and everything accordingly." Unfortunately, Curtis Bernhardt was not a particularly hard-driving director, and he was prone to shooting an exasperating number of takes for scenes lasting only a few seconds. There are multiple memos from Jack Warner in the production file, with indications that the director made no attempts to accelerate shooting. Rains was still weak from his infection, and in the days before antibiotics he would have been highly vulnerable to getting sick again, which is exactly what happened. On September 24, the unit manager wrote to the production manager: "Have just been informed by Mr. Rains that he is not feeling well, contracting a cold, and may not be able to appear for work tomorrow Thursday [September 26] (he at least gave us a little warning)." At 6 a.m. Thursday morning, the production head called Rains to see if the actor was coming to the set. Although he had a fever, Rains did not want to cause problems by prolonging the shoot; he reported at 9 a.m. and worked straight through until 6:20 p.m. Both he and Hopkins again worked late and until shooting ended at 5:55 p.m.

because "Miss Hopkins was so exhausted she was in tears." Hopkins then refused to report to the lot for a full week and by October 5 the production was fifteen days behind. Meanwhile, Rains was held on set for three days doing nothing; the entire company was laid off awaiting the return of the leading lady.

Undoubtedly Rains was exasperated by this experience. Because the film was expected to be wrapped by this time, his agent arranged for the actor to appear on a CBS radio broadcast with Shirley Temple, performing "The Littlest Rebel" for *Lux Radio Theatre*. Warners released Rains for rehearsal on October 10 at 2:30 p.m. Following the broadcast, Rains reported to the studio on Saturday at 1 p.m. to finish a scene with Hopkins.

It was not uncommon for actors to juggle several projects at once, even while shooting a picture. On October 9, Rains gave an address presented by the "Hollywood for Roosevelt" organization. He stated that the event was special to him because it was his first presidential vote, and that he truly admired the manner in which FDR had alleviated the conditions of the Great Depression: Rains always wrote his own speeches. In this one, he commented: "Ladies and Gentlemen: I am an actor, not a politician — this is the third time in my life that I have made a speech of this kind, but times of crises do arise and I believe I need to speak out in a sincere conviction. I am heart and soul for the reelection of President Roosevelt, and the Roosevelt campaign committee has asked me to come here and tell you why. I intend to vote for him because he has battled unceasingly during his seven and a half years in office for democracy and freedom both at home and abroad." He went on to list all the remarkable things FDR had accomplished, including the WPA, the NRA and other programs. The speech was about nine pages long, but Rains was so proud of it and what it represented, he kept the draft among his papers for the next thirty years.

Rains was probably relieved to complete his work on *Lady with Red Hair* on October 12. When the picture opened in early December, critics were kind, and as usual praised Rains' performance. *Variety*, which had a few reservations about the picture as a whole, wrote: "Claude Rains provides a standout characterization as David Belasco.... [It] will be tabbed as one of the season's best portrayals." The *New York Herald Tribune*'s reviewer wrote: "These characters are brilliantly interpreted by Miriam Hopkins and Claude Rains. It is this teaming and conflict of personalities that makes the ... film one of absorbing interest." *The Hollywood Reporter* was even more enthusiastic: "[It] is to Claude Rains for his magnificent and powerful delineation of temperamental David Belasco that top performance honors must be accorded. It is, by all odds, the finest work Rains has ever done before the camera." Another critic in the same paper commented: "Claude Rains in the Belasco role has what I consider to be his best opportunity to date. So to say that he makes the most out of it is to speak truth. He dominates the picture just as Belasco dominated the New York theatrical stage. It is one of the finest characterizations I have seen. *Lady with Red Hair* is important not because of the central figure in the story, but it is important because an excellent actor takes a supporting role and makes it the central figure."

On November 4, 1940, Mike Levee advised Warner Bros. that Howard Hawks wanted Rains for a role in an independent project about Old West icon Billy the Kid that Hawks and millionaire producer Howard Hughes were preparing. Any plans for the actor's involvement (possibly as Billy's friend, the English rancher, Tunstall) apparently fell through. The picture was made and finally released nearly three years later, becoming notorious under the title *The Outlaw*.

Back in Pennsylvania, Rains wanted to use his star status to help FDR get re-elected. In one speech delivered in Philadelphia for the Democratic National Committee, he made a personal appeal:

This vote means a good deal to me, if you will permit me a personal moment. As some of you may know, I was born an Englishman. I lived in this country before the last war and after serving nearly four years [*sic*] in England and France during that war, I came here in 1926 and I have lived here ever since. I have an American wife and an American child and I own a farm not far from Valley Forge where Washington and his Continental Army starved. A few years ago, I became an American citizen and on November 5th I shall cast my first Presidential vote for Mr. Roosevelt. I have abiding faith that a great many people will say to Franklin Delano

Roosevelt tomorrow: "Well done, thou good and faithful servant."

Rains' heartfelt address stirred up great enthusiasm. He was asked to go to Chicago along with the Governor of the State and the Democratic National Committee to make another passionate address.

> Up till a short time ago I am going to say what I did not have the right to say. I was an Englishman and any expression of mine regarding a Presidential preference would have been mere impudence on my part. But ladies and gentlemen, I am an American now. I love America and I love to do this and I love her enough to want to fight for her welfare… The things that you hold dear, I cherish also and I also want to help preserve them… This is not merely a presidential election we are facing. What we do on November 5th may change the history of the world and the face of the nations. Before becoming an American citizen, I had, as you know, to study quite thoroughly the American system of government. It is the most democratic system in the world…

He then elaborated on the New Deal which he viewed as an investment in the country:

> [T]here is one thing in this world of ours which is quite indispensable to the dignity of man — integrity — without integrity no single man, much less the leader of one of the great nations on earth is worth a single vote. It is my profound and considered opinion that FDR is above all else a man of one hundred percent integrity. It is my belief that because of that integrity as a leader, the president of the U.S. has accepted the demands of people that he run for his third consecutive term in a man-killing office.
>
> He and the people know in their hearts that his task, well begun and valiantly executed, is not yet finished.

As winter passed into early spring, there were no calls from his agent; Rains couldn't handle the lull and became moody and nervous. Waiting for the phone to ring, he resorted to whiskey in the afternoons. For seven months, instead of relaxing, he grew more and more edgy and restless. He came to realize that the security he longed for, and the work he desperately needed, would conflict with his desire to become a completely freelance actor. Being tethered to Warners now appeared to have its advantages. His taxes reveal that his finances were becoming very complicated: He still had a contract with Warners, but he had freelanced for two films, made numerous radio broadcasts, owned a house in Bel Air and the farm, paid a salary to his farm manager, had travel expenses, made investments for Jennifer's future, maintained an agent in Los Angeles. He always needed money. Most of his investments went into annuities and U.S. Savings Bonds. He paid dues to the Players Club in New York, to AFTRA, to Actors Equity and the Screen Actors Guild. There were property taxes both in California and Pennsylvania. In addition to daughter Jennifer, he declared his mother and father, now in their 80s, as dependents, since he was sending them money for their rent and food; but the IRS declared such a deduction illegal since his parents resided in England. From the $100,000 he earned in 1939, his income dropped to a net of $42,128.75 and his debt to the government came to $10,643.05. H.H. Pike and Company in New York served as his accountants, and he hired Price Waterhouse for the same job in California. Rains kept all his own records for the income tax people, but because he lacked schooling and did not know the complexities of involved arithmetic, Frances had completed the calculations. Now, however, it was clearly time for tax accountants. This $32,000 net represented the lowest amount he made since becoming a screen actor and it unnerved him greatly.

If running the farm added to his expenses, it was reasonable to believe that, with the prospect of world war looming, even with price controls he could make a profit growing food, especially wheat. But none of this could be accomplished on a forty-acre farm. While at home in late November, Rains made a momentous decision: He would look for another, bigger place. He contacted several local real estate brokers with two absolutely non-negotiable points: He wanted to remain in the Brandywine valley, and

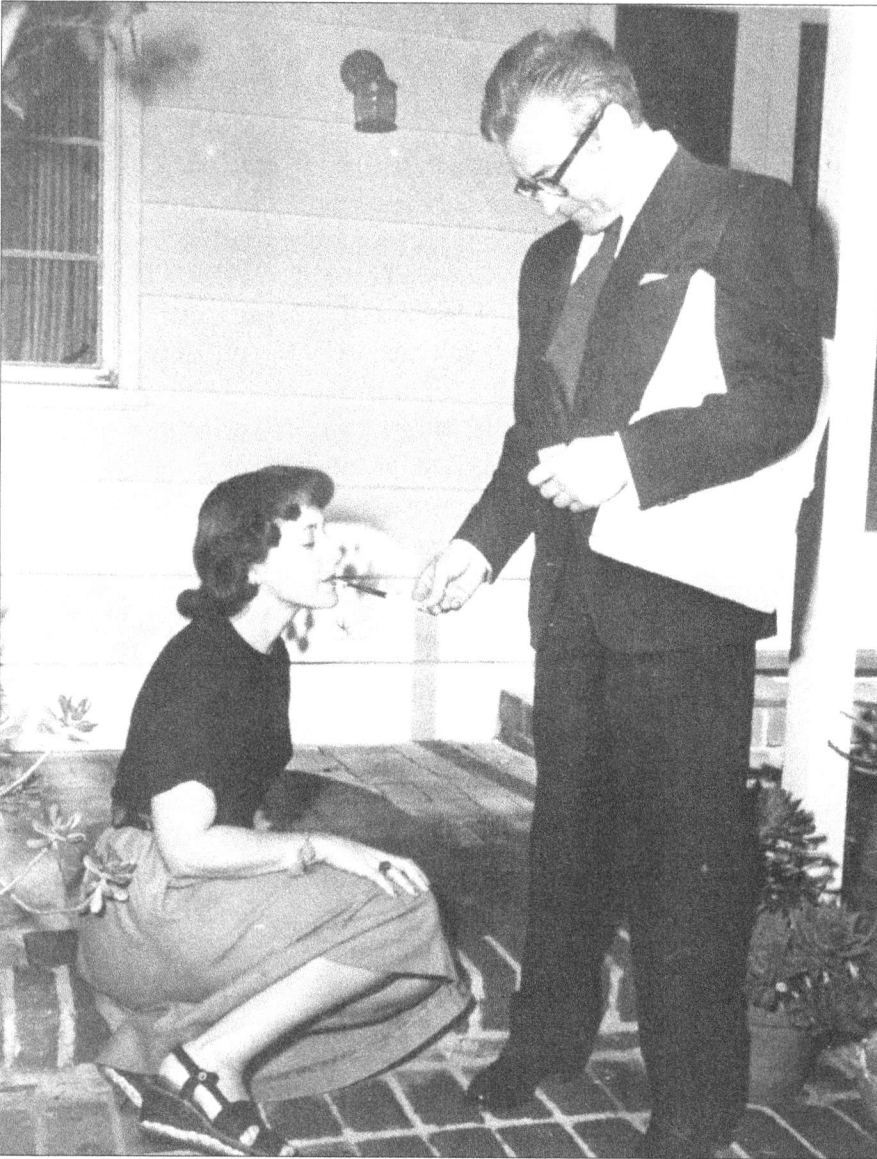

Claude and Frances at home.

the buildings on the property had to have historical significance.

On a cold winter day in December, a broker called about a secluded place not too far from West Chester. It was located near Downingtown, about 50 miles west of Philadelphia. However, he cautioned, the 330 acres had lain fallow for many years, the land and buildings had been severely neglected, and in general the farm was very run-down. However, it did have the desired acreage and met the other criteria. Initially things did not sound promising, but when Rains visited the property, it was love at first sight. He had found Shangri-La, and its restoration became like a religious experience for him.

CHAPTER 14
Sanctuary

Sometimes a man hits upon a place to which he mysteriously feels that he belongs. Here is the home he sought.... Here at last he finds rest.

W. Somerset Maugham, The Moon and Sixpence, 1919

Rains took Frances to see the old farm known for over one hundred years as Stock Grange. She was aghast at its dilapidated condition, realizing it would take a vast amount of money and time to restore. Just like her husband's other two farmhouses, it had no electricity, no central heating and lacked adequate plumbing. She also knew that once Claude made up his mind, there was no changing it. But the setting was idyllic. In 1907, acclaimed artist N.C. Wyeth wrote about his life in Pennsylvania's Brandywine Valley, describing the serenity and pervasive gentle mood which overtakes a person living in its midst: "Never have I appreciated nature as I have in this place … this is a country full of Restraints. Everything lies in its subtleties, everything is so gentle and simple, so unaffected."

Stock Grange resonated deep within Rains' heart. He saw well beyond its broken-down physical condition, the result of shameful neglect. Eventually it became a reflection of the man who would love and care for it from 1941 until 1956.

The history of Stock Grange dates back to 1747, but no owner preserved it with the integrity it deserved like Rains did. His dedication to the restoration reflected his values. Apart from collecting antiques, Rains' passion and inner joy was returning old farmhouses and barns to their original condition. To him, the task was a kind of tribute, sanctifying something of beauty and value which had long been neglected or abused; restoration was a renaissance undertaking which touched his soul, providing a deep sense of fulfillment. His efforts on the forty-acre Glen Mills farm made him realize that his spiritual calling came from the land.

As with many Brits, Rains longed for a place with green rolling hills and pastoral views reminiscent of the English countryside. This he found in the Brandywine area, when fate brought him there in the mid–1930s to attend the wedding of a friend. He assumed it was the same destiny that brought him to Stock Grange, which could boast of all the criteria he longed for, beginning with its long and significant history in Chester County during the American Revolution War. This was genuinely important to Rains: His home had to have heritage. Secretly he harbored the aristocratic notion of being a country squire and claimed that his family was descended from a long line of farmers, but nothing substantiates this. To truly understand Rains the man, it's necessary to understand what he did for, and felt for, Stock Grange.

The large farmstead was located in West Bradford Township near Romansville, not far from historic Valley Forge. It was also within ten miles of the famous Wyeth family farm at Chadds Ford. In her brief history of West Bradford, Barbara Ayars wrote: "Stock Grange is an outstanding landmark of Chester County and knew several owners, all of them colorful." While the farm did indeed have numerous owners, everyone in the area agrees that it was Claude

Rains who did more than anyone else to restore it.

The original site consisted of nearly 350 acres and a log house, built around 1740. The property was first sold to a Tory, Philip Marchington. After the Revolutionary War, it was confiscated by the new United States government and sold to a General Humpton, who had been a commander at the Battle of Brandywine. Around 1767, he erected the original stone building, a structure which still stands today, and called the place Stockport. The land had lain fallow for decades, utilized as pasture by the neighborhood farmers who brought their stock (cattle and sheep) to graze.

The most important ancestral family to claim Stock Grange was that of John D. Steele, who in 1805 purchased the land and its 1767 stone house for $8,000, a large sum for the time. By 1811, Steele had erected a five-story barn and added a large two-story building to the original stone house. All additions were made in stone 20 inches thick, dug from the surrounding fields. The Steeles and their dependents lived at Stock Grange throughout the entire 19th century and into the 20th. One local resident was Dr.

Charles H. Stone, eventually chief physician of the hospital in nearby Coatesville, a man who became friendly with Rains. In March 1928, the property was sold to Charles Elkington, who had his "fifteen minutes of fame" as unexpected host to Charles Lindbergh when the aviator was caught in a fog on his way to Washington D.C. and was forced to land on a dirt road in the vicinity. (That road right by the farm now bears the name of Lone Eagle Road.)

During the Great Depression, Elkington lacked the funds to maintain the farm and gradually the large empty house fell into disrepair. Unwisely, he rented out the fields to tenant farmers who, in need of cash crops, abused the soil with the planting of corn, which depletes it of nutrients and lime. By the late 1930s, Stock Grange had fallen on hard times, neglected almost to ruin. To rid himself of the property taxes and costs, Elkington sold the deed to the Central Pennsylvania Conference of the Methodist Church, Inc. When Rains first saw the dilapidated place in December 1940, it was at its nadir.

On page 147 of the deed book N-20 at the Court House in West Chester, it is recorded that on January 20, 1941, Rains purchased the entire property from the Methodist Church for $1. However, the deed document also had a $22.00 Internal Revenue stamp which was equal to $22,000: In this way, the church did not have to pay any taxes on the sale. Originally the parcels of land totaled 328 acres, but as the years passed, Rains acquired more field acreage for a total of 477.

The actor became almost fanatical in his determination to preserve the history of the property, proudly boasting "I never remodel — I restore." In charge of the overall project was Lowell Gable, a builder from the town of Paoli. Rains' orders were simple: "Fix it up, but don't change anything — instead make it like it was." Both men were very exacting in their approval of individual contractors who had to be excellent craftsmen and understand the trust placed in them. Only those Rains felt were as committed to historical accuracy as he were hired, such as contractor C. Ashton McDonnell, who became one of Rains' friends, as much as any man could be.

The original 1747 section of the house, which had been built into an earthen bank at the rear, was largely intact: its twenty-inch–thick wall, the large 12 foot by 16 foot kitchen, a large great room. Photographs taken by a local newspaper show Rains smiling enthusiastically as he points to the huge, rough-hewn ax beam, twelve inch by twelve inch, positioned over the deep open-hearth cooking fireplace. A door in the great room opens to an extremely narrow curved stairway which leads up to a bedroom area. Between the original house and the 1811 addition were two large bedrooms. A bathroom was added by taking part of the second bedroom.

Rains had the rotting wood of the old kitchen floor removed and, to his delight, discovered the original green flagstone flooring of 1747, stones which had been quarried right from the farm's fields. If Frances was going to actually use the kitchen, she insisted modern appliances be installed; in nearly all other issues, she had bowed to his husband's wishes, but not that. 20th century conveniences were anathema to Rains' sense of authenticity, so the couple compromised: Frances would have all updated appliances, but everything would be hidden behind faux wooden pine cabinets, and additionally the electric range had to have a front iron piece replicating a wood burning stove. For this job, Rains hired an ironmonger in Lancaster. Though daughter Jennifer was only five years old at the time, she remembered the many Saturdays she accompanied her father as he went to see how the stove cover structure was progressing. From January until April, workmen incorporated the modifications so that the family could move in by spring. Just three weeks before the old farm at Glen Mills was sold on April 29, 1941, the Rainses moved into their new home. It was well-hidden along the back gravel dirt roads of Chester County, with an entrance lined with beautiful old chestnut trees, and the new sign swinging off a post proclaiming that Stock Grange stood at the entrance of the home's private lane.

While the thick walls of the great room were in good shape and only needed a coat of plaster and whitewash, the interior flooring — laid in 1767 — had to be replaced; alas, there was no vintage flagstone to be had. Rains had the contractor use the boards from the barn's granary, which were black oak and tu-

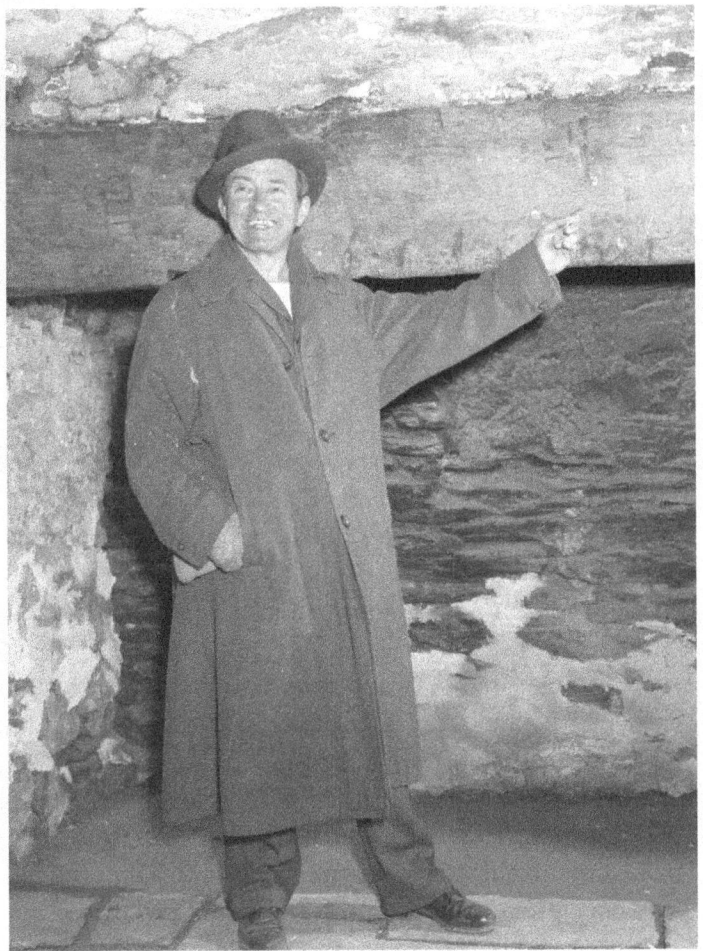

CR proudly shows off an original, centuries-old beam at Stock Grange. (Photo courtesy Temple University Archives)

lip poplar. When Ash McDonnell suggested that the sloping floors should be leveled, the actor "shrieked at the very thought," insisting that everything was to be repaired in exacting original detail. To be certain, the builders visited and studied structures of old 18th century farmhouses in the nearby area. Expense was no object. Ceiling beams were put back in place using traditional mortise and tenon. Doors, windows and door frames were pegged — all modern nails removed. Rains told Gable to hire a blacksmith to forge nails that were exact duplicates of the original ones used in the 18th century. Luckily, there remained one original door and window which were used as models for the rest of the house's original iron hardware. There were no doorknobs; instead, the original latches were found from another site, made workable and attached. Jennifer recalled a two-year search for the proper hinges that had originally been used. Rains could have very easily had an ironmonger make up copies that resembled the genuine article, but he adamantly refused. Instead, he instructed local antique dealers to track down 18th century hinges, which eventually they managed to do.

There was new stucco paint, a new roof; the two sections of the "old 1767 house" and the "new 1811 house" were joined when an old hallway was unsealed. Steps were replaced with authentic hand-hewn boards from the trees on the land. The 1811 section had a broad central entry with a sturdy but graceful staircase with a hand-carved railing, leading to a landing which extended across the width of the hall. To the left of the downstairs hall was a grand large dining room with a Greek-inspired fireplace. The windows each had a small seat, and panes of 18th century handblown glass with the contours sending a sort of shimmering fantasy light into the room. Where panes were broken, Rains replaced them with new ones, but manufactured in the same 18th century fashion. Upstairs were four large bedrooms, each with a fireplace, but only the guest room had its own bathroom. Installing additional bathrooms and central heating proved quite difficult. To bring in a furnace with pipes extending to the radiators, channels had to be cut into the stone walls; then the radiators were concealed with a false cabinet front. All of this took many years to complete, and a great deal of money. Although Rains was generally very frugal, when it came to the farm, being true to the original design of the architecture was crucial for him.

Work continued through the 1940s; scarcity of materials due to the war caused delays. Rains put in a new granary and stalls and replaced the decaying entrance with a dirt "bridge" connecting the old house with the barn. New rafters were added to boost up the weakened top floor and a hog house adjoined the side of the area near a new silo. Everything on the farm was of importance to Rains, but his "beautiful old barn" was his pride and joy, for there were no others like it in the area. It was indeed a grand, dignified and imposing structure, noted in the region for its historical configuration of five stories and twenty-inch–thick walls.

The exterior showcased a flagstone terrace and a gracious lawn and garden. Outside the living room was a small open cantilevered arch, a lovely spot to sit on an old-fashioned swing, especially when the wisteria was in bloom, and look out over the spring house, the hen house, the windmill, the pastures — no matter where the eye would look, there was serene beauty. The many trees lining the pastures nestle together like amiable neighbors wanting to live in harmony with no fighting for space.

Rains' private quarters for studying his lines were in the large room over the great room in the 1767 structure. Here, he was no longer himself, but instead whatever character he would inhabit for his next film or play. He would shut himself off and diligently rehearse, never allowing anyone or anything to interfere. His daughter recalled often hearing his voice bellowing lines of dialogue – the habit of shouting for dramatic effect to be heard in the back of a theatre would remain with him, often exhibited in his everyday speech pattern, if he were frustrated or agitated, even when volume was not necessary. Everybody in the house had to be quiet while he was "working."

Rains' wife's nephew Eric recalled visiting him in 1956 or '57. Eric and his new wife found the actor pacing up and down reciting his lines from a script. "It was astonishing, and I never saw anything like it. At first we thought we were being ignored and then we realized he was rehearsing and truly did not see us." He did not acknowledge their presence for about ten minutes.

It wouldn't be until after the war that Stock Grange was finally restored to Rains' exacting specifications. At times, when Hollywood summoned her husband, Frances supervised the work, with many phone calls and correspondence back and forth. Frances shared Claude's love of country life, and for a city girl, she surprised all her relatives with her understanding of her husband's commitment to the restoration, agreeing with him that Stock Grange would be furnished with genuine antiques whenever possible. They both loved the location near the Paoli local's train stop on Philadelphia's Main Line. It was only a thirty-minute train ride to Philadelphia to transfer to the ninety-minute train to New York City.

Here Rains found the greatest happiness of his life. Here was sanctuary and peace and where his daughter would grow up until she went off to college, and where he planned to spend the rest of his life with Frances.

Sensibly, the actor realized his limitations: Even though he was muscular and strong, not to mention dedicated, he was, after all, in his fifties. Additionally, he knew his profession would often necessitate weeks away. Hiring some experienced help was imperative. Charles Brown, a local African-American man in his mid- or late forties, came highly recommended. Charles and his wife Lucille (called Lily) eventually came and lived at Stock Grange in a small cottage Rains built for them. A natural farmer who loved the land, Brown was to manage everything connected with planting and harvesting (although extant original documents refer to "two hired farmers during the planting and harvesting seasons").

In addition to farm duties, Charles often acted as Rains' driver, especially when the actor had to go into Philadelphia on business. Rains simply was not a good driver, especially in a city; he had accidents frequently, but seldom reported them in fear of problems with the insurance company. Locally, he had the (deserved) reputation of being reckless behind the wheel. Neighbors would see him barreling down roads in his Jeep with one foot hanging out. "When you saw him coming down the road," remembered one neighbor with affectionate amusement, "you gave him wide berth, because he only drove in the middle of the road and wouldn't get over." The joke in the area was that he kept one foot outside the Jeep in case he had to jump clear.

The Browns were the only people Rains employed, eschewing "servants" in the literal sense. Just as Charles managed the farm, Lily did the general household chores, but she was not regarded as a maid. Frances did the cooking for most of the dinners, especially when there were guests, and she also learned all about canning. The Browns remained with the Rains family for the entire sixteen years the famous couple lived at Stock Grange. They lived in the small colonial cottage adjacent to the farmhouse just across the private dirt road, receiving room and board and a small salary at the going rate. The Philadelphia Naval Yard was close to Chester County and seriously in

need of workers during the war; Charles would have made much more money employed there. But he genuinely liked being a farmer, loved Stock Grange, and in his own way, regarded Rains with affection.

As different as the two men were, each was very respectful of the other's skill. Rains was the "squire" in name and ownership, but he always deferred to Charles' knowledge and expertise. Rains' daughter remembered a conversation between the two men, Rains asking, "Isn't it time to start planting, Charles?" Brown replied, "No, Mr. Rains, not until next week perhaps." Yet often Rains could be impatient. Charles once told a neighbor, "Mr. Rains always pushed hard — he wanted things done and right away — he expected a lot."

Charles could not help but respect his boss: Rains studied as religiously to be a successful farmer as he had studied to become an actor. He devoured books and bulletins from the Pennsylvania Agriculture Bureau; he talked to the farmers in the area, asking all kinds of questions and listening intently to the answers. Rains would insist that he ran the farm, but it was Charles who kept Stock Grange going. As much as Rains was book-learned, the actual physical labor of chores was in Charles' very capable hands. Eventually, and with Charles in agreement, Rains acquired more land, enlarging Stock Grange to nearly 500 acres. He had sworn he would make his farm sustainable, but qualified himself by stating, "If the farm did not become profitable, then I'll quit," meaning he would quit hoping.

Within a few years, Rains had earned the genuine respect of his neighbors: not for being a celebrated

actor, but for the industrious way he tackled making Stock Grange into a working farm with high yields. Originally, when the neighbors learned it had been purchased by a Hollywood star, there were raised eyebrows and general viewing with skepticism. What did he think he could do with that land, some fields badly eroded, others barren from years of abuse? With the same thoroughness that characterized his professional career, Rains made a study of erosion, contour plowing and drip farming. He conferred with the county agent, with soil conservation experts, read catalogs and farm journals voraciously even when on a movie set. Fellow actors remembered him, quiet and aloof, with his head buried in some seed or fertilizer magazine. "When he talked about his estate, talked about the farming, you had the feeling that he was talking about something he loved," said Leonid Kinskey, who played the "crazy Russian" bartender Sascha in *Casablanca*. "Otherwise, you couldn't squeeze a word out of him."

With the help of the federal government and the Agricultural Bureau, Rains received advice and financial aid to replenish the worn-out soil. By 1942, documents indicate livestock ownership of: forty-two steers and four milk cows, twenty-seven pigs, fifty white pigeons, and two dozen chickens. Frances seldom went to the grocery store or butcher, since nearly everything was sustainably produced on the farm. At harvest time in 1942, farm records could boast an inventory of eight tons of hay, eight hundred bushels of oats, eleven hundred bushels of balmy, five hundred fifty bushels of wheat, thirteen bushels of corn and two thousand one hundred eleven bushels of soybeans. According to documents prepared around the first part of 1950, "[T]he farm is sectioned off into 150 acres of farming land, 150 acres of pastureland, and 100 acres of wooded land, on which grow black oak, walnut, hickory and pine." The farm raised "corn, wheat, barley, hay, vegetables for home consumption, as well as up to 100 head of either or both hogs and beef."

The neighbors agreed it was Charles who did the manual labor and who was always seen on board the tractor. Despite printed stories to the contrary, Rains was seldom, if ever, seen working the fields, though he would not hesitate to dig in the dirt and feed the livestock. More often than not he was observed with a foot up on a fence rail, learning his lines for his next film. (Driving farm vehicles is difficult under the best of circumstances and having vision in only one eye would have made the task actually dangerous.) To reporters, Rains would claim that "he farmed" and "did chores," but even his daughter never recalled seeing him on the tractor in the fields. To this extent, his "farming" consisted of the large ninety-foot by fifty-foot garden which he alone plowed, planted, cultivated and maintained. It was Rains' chief pleasure; his personal project "was the family truck garden where he grew everything from artichokes to zucchini. His tomatoes neatly poled, beans well sprayed and not a weed in the lettuce beds. But his real enthusiasm was root crops: turnips, parsnips, carrots and Jerusalem artichokes."

Frances and Claude liked to brag that almost everything on their table came from their farm, "from the paper-thin slices of ham to the whipped

"Gentleman farmer" Rains genuinely did enjoy getting his hands dirty on his farms. "Whenever I find one of my black moods coming over me, I dig." (Photo courtesy Temple University Archives)

cream on top of the peach shortcake." Breads, ice cream, vegetables, meats, fruits, milk, eggs — the Rains family was remarkably self-sufficient. Of course, the butchering was professionally done, but Rains was justifiably proud that the meat before him came from a steer he raised, fed on grain he grew, and was prepared by his wife or Lily. Frances was so well-known to be a good cook, the Blue Bonnet Margarine Company asked her to appear in one of their advertisements.

Frances learned to can the harvested vegetables and felt a sense of pride in maintaining a well-stocked homemade pantry. She was a good cook and enjoyed making elaborate dishes and rich desserts for their infrequent dinner parties. As a rule, though, her daily preparations were simple since Claude liked plain food and rarely indulged in the pastries and other delicacies she concocted. Rains' passion for farming grew as the years passed. He liked the idea that a farm could be self-sufficient, providing food staples not only for the family but livestock as well. His farm served another, equally important purpose: it was a respite. "Whenever I find one of my black moods coming over me, I dig – often from five a.m. until sundown." What exactly the moods were, he never revealed. But after a day in the soil, or engaged in other related tasks around the farm, Rains would change into clean clothes and, with his pipe clenched between his teeth, sit in a deck chair on the lawn and contentedly watch his Jersey cows graze over his meadows.

Rains liked his neighbor in nearby Chadds Ford, famous artist Andrew Wyeth, son of N.C. Wyeth. He understood what Andrew meant when he wrote: "One must go deeply inside something you know and bring it to the surface." As an actor, Rains went deep inside his dreams, fears and desires in all the characters he portrayed, but it was only at the farm that he could be himself and quietly restore his soul. In direct contrast to his sophisticated film persona, the environment of Stock Grange was like its owner: unassuming, unaffected, dignified as it blends into its surroundings rather than imposing itself on the land. Somehow the sensitive aspect of Rains' nature seeped into the walls. Unassuming, unaffected yet possessing a quiet dignity. Rains, a man who made his living with his voice, had a silent communion with this place and what it meant to him. After working in Hollywood, Rains went "home," and a calmness overtook him when he was imbued with the prevailing spirit of Stock Grange.

Within a year, much of the heavy work on the farmhouse was completed. An old cesspool was filled in with stones and dirt; it eventually became part of Frances' flower garden. The only new buildings (in addition to the Browns' cottage) were designed to fit into the scheme of the Colonial architecture: a hen house, a pigeon coop, a root cellar, a machine shop and garage for the tractor and other equipment. Near the Browns' cottage across the road from the main house were the kennels for Rains' English Setter dogs. Together Claude and Frances searched for original furnishings of the period; everything blended together seamlessly. In the 1950s, a cinder block building was built to accommodate the growing inventory of heavy farm equipment, including a combine for use in crop harvesting. Rains repaired the roads, built new fencing, and planted an apple orchard. He added a pen for the steers and pigs along the side of the barn and a corn crib. Eventually there would have to be a new silo.

Yet all of these additions nestle into the surroundings and are unobtrusive in the lush, roiling acres, with their avenues of trees lining the large pasture lands for cattle, the huge fields crossed by two shallow streams.

Jennifer grew up sharing her parents' love for Stock Grange. In addition to summer visits by Frances' nieces and nephews, her friends spent time there and she cherished fond memories of the place where she spent her childhood. During the war years, her father, an early riser, would drive Jennifer to the Quaker school she attended, and Frances would pick her up in the afternoons. Because Rains was not a particularly good driver, due to his blind eye, Jennifer admits she was often apprehensive on these morning trips. What made it more unsettling were the times that he added to the tension by giving her a script and ran lines with her. Between his swerving of the car, the bumpiness of the dirt road, and trying to keep her eyes on the words, she often arrived at school sick to her stomach. But she didn't dare say anything to her father — simply because it would not have made any difference. Rains commanded and his wishes were to be obeyed. Perhaps such behavior went back to his youth, when he was always being ordered about in the various low-level jobs he held in the theatre. He had been taught not to question superiors or elders.

After the war, expenses mounted: When materials

once more became available, more repairs were made, including some very necessary restoration to the slate roof of the old house and barn. Even when he was on a film set, things had to be attended to. In a letter dated December 11, 1945, Rains indicated he was repairing the barn and sent instructions for the work to McDonnell. But so exacting were his details for authenticity that a sample of the slate had to be mailed to him in Hollywood along with a sample of the original mortar ingredients to ensure the mixture would be genuine. In October 1945, a new slate roof adorned the house. In addition, locust posts were put in several areas, one being along Chestnut Lane for a new split rail fencing. For 1944 and 1945, expenses for Stock Grange repairs amounted to nearly $6,000, the actor's full salary for a picture.

Nineteen forty-seven was the farm's best year of production. Rains inventoried over 34,000 pounds of wheat, 1,600 bushels of oats, 2,500 bushels of corn and 80 tons of silage. On paper was a gross profit of $8,500, but Rains took this money and immediately "plowed" it back into the farm with purchases (equipment or more cattle) within the same year. The actor tried to maintain his own bookkeeping, but demands on his time, as well as the complications of maintaining two homes, soon necessitated an accountant. (But Rains, to his dying day always maintained control of his checkbook.) In 1948, the farm increased production of wheat to 40,000 pounds and 3,000 bushels of corn; a new baler was purchased for $2,400. In 1949, 54 steers were added.

Rains had an unusual relationship with his neighbors. Asking one to take him to the blacksmith, "Can't today-- tomorrow." Rains said he could not go tomorrow because he was leaving for California. "Listen," was the reply, "Why don't you stick around here and tend to your own business?" There is an amusing, and charming, consistency to neighbors' description of Rains: "A strange figure—a character you might say, but we loved him and respected him and his privacy, maybe we respected the privacy too much, for we would never bother them." "He was a character and we all loved them—they had their lives and we had ours—to us he wasn't a celebrity, just another farmer." "He was a character—a nice man, gentleman, and we all liked him a lot." Rains, it was agreed, "was not a snob—just a regular person who had a great sense of humor." One recalled him coming up to their farm often to talk to her brother, Bob, about farm-related matters. "Yet he wasn't the kind of man who would just stop in and have a cup of coffee, nor could you enter Stock Grange of your own liking—one had to be invited." There were sometimes parties hosted by Frances and Claude: "Oh, they entertained all right, but 'their crowd' you know, doctors or lawyers or people like that."

Just as in Hollywood, Rains remained distant; privacy and solitude were parts of his persona and made him feel safe. It wasn't until December 1951 that he made his first public appearance in Chester County; by then, he had been a resident for twelve years. Only a handful of neighbors ever saw him, wearing jeans like any other farmer, with the dirt of Stock Grange still clinging to his shoes. He was not a snob, and his aloofness was not a pretense at modesty — it was just that Rains preferred to fade into the landscape of the rolling hills. He emerged for a recitation at Coatesville High School on a subject close to his heart: a reading of the poems of Dr. Charles H. Stone, a direct descendent of the Steele family who had previously owned Stock Grange. Frances had become quite active with the Women's Auxiliary of the Coatesville Hospital and probably coaxed her husband into making the appearance. Rains told a *Philadelphia Evening Bulletin* reporter: "I have done this out of deep interest in the Coatesville Hospital and affection for its chief Dr. Stone and his associate, Dr. Julius Margolis." The latter was the actor's friend and personal physician well into the 1960s.

With all the care and love Rains put into Stock Grange, the greatest legacy he bequeathed the farm – one he knew he could never live to enjoy himself – was the planting of thousands of trees throughout the estate. As he explained in 1962: "I had 20 acres of downgrade land, and I planted thousands of trees on that downgrade, alpine and blue spruce. When I moved into town, what I hated most was giving up those trees." The grove is located about a half-mile from the farmhouse, and in the decades since they were so tenderly planted, the fragile young saplings have soared into the air, their treetops forming a living Gothic arch. The feeling while walking through them is like being in a cathedral. Silence permeates,

allowing no intrusion of the outside world in this sanctuary. Sunlight glitters between the pines, like stained glass, the diffused light creating a softness which enhances the quiet. Then shadow and light flicker, creating an atmosphere of spirits beckoning, and inviting one into the tranquility. It is as if the air were peace itself, to be breathed into the soul, enabling one to emerge clean, refreshed, calm, reborn. This is a place of timelessness. Walking in this place, there is no need of identity, of ambition, of cares — it is being completely aware of the self within the cosmos of just being. Perhaps here Claude Rains felt like a true creator in a way he could nowhere else … as if he too had become a pine tree.

More than anything else he achieved in life, Stock Grange made Rains proud. It represented his simple expression of life, within a richly historic framework. His restored buildings were among the finest example of Colonial architecture found in the Brandywine Valley. By May 1948, the couple had done such an impressive job, the place was written up in *Country Gentlemen* magazine. The article stressed that Stock Grange was the only farm in the area to have underground wiring, in order than no poles would interfere with the views of the countryside. Rains had created an alliance among his neighbors to have eleven telephone and electrical lines installed underground, so the farm would continue to have the same look it had more than a hundred years earlier. Those neighbors who could afford it went along with replacement; those who were unable to do so at the time were very appreciative of the gesture, and eventually became part of the project after the war.

For Rains, the satisfaction gained from acting was temporary, lasting only from one role to the next. Although he loved being a performer, to look out over a field of oats or wheat swaying in the wind, or to watch over his livestock, or to dig out in his garden — all this made him feel more in tune with life and with himself. Acting was a livelihood, a way to earn money, success and recognition, but Stock Grange offered a spiritual foundation.

Ash McDonnell understood what Stock Grange meant to Rains. It was Ash and his son Terry who planted the pine and blue spruce in the grove. Terry remembered there was a big old ash tree (with a huge cavity) which Rains and his father tried to save, and he remembers Rains was at the McDonnells' house often for supper. What struck Terry was Rains' lack

of pretentiousness: "He told us to call him Claude — not Mr. Rains. This was his way of showing people he accepted them as friends."

Remembering the devastating fire at his Lambertville, New Jersey, farm, Rains went to extremes for fire prevention and protection at Stock Grange. He had more rods on his barn than anyone else in the area and maintained a large insurance policy costing $8,000 in 1942 dollars. He insisted on organizing fire drills with rope ladders. In the main bedroom was a large ring bolted to a piece of oak on the floor; the family would practice throwing the rope ladder out the window (although he never climbed down). To make certain of an ample water supply, Rains had a natural spring swimming hole dug, with a mud bottom, and in later years Jennifer spent many a summer day playing in a "pool" made from damming a nearby brook. Nothing was to be artificial, like it was in Hollywood. Thus, almost as if in a movie, Rains established his fiefdom in which he was the lord and master. In fact, a noted cartoonist of the day painted a picture of Rains the artist titled "The Squire"; it remained one of Rains' favorite drawings.

Frances wasn't as enamored with the solitude of Stock Grange as her husband. She enjoyed socializing with friends, especially when Rains was in Hollywood for weeks on end. As one neighbor remembered:

Frances and I would ride together whenever I could get away — she loved horses — but wouldn't talk much. Once she called me and asked me to go blackberry picking with her. I think at times in later years, she was bored and lonely, but she loved Stock Grange and told me she'd never live anywhere else. Now, looking back, I think she was groping for friendship and didn't know how to … well, I am just sorry now … I was so busy with my own life, but she needed friends. Once she took me through the house and showed me Claude's library upstairs in the old house — they were his quarters so he could rehearse his lines. She said he would shout a lot and needed the room to himself. But other than that, she never talked about him. I remember that she seemed strict with the child — several times I saw this — and yet in truth [Jennifer] was spoiled. Oh, she was a beautiful, lovely girl, but spoiled. Claude really spoiled her.

As if he were retreating to a monastery for contemplation and a renewal of the spirit, so Claude Rains would retire to Stock Grange. The farm became synonymous with peace and privacy. Most importantly, it became a place to gather memories — wonderful, happy memories with laughter and good times, and eventually, sad ones too. As Rains himself put it twenty years later: "I loved the farm. It was something to come home to. When the play closed, or the movie was finished, I went right back to the farm. Knowing it was there sustained me."

CHAPTER 15
The Route to *Casablanca*

In the second half of 1940, Rains had been pre-occupied, happily busy putting Stock Grange in shape, but by late fall, he had not heard from his agent with any new film offers. Many actors would have relished freedom after having worked so hard, and to have time to deal with the multiple responsibilities of a new property. Not Rains. For him, being out of work for seven months was unsettling and affected his mood. Frances did all she could to calm him but knew Claude would never feel secure emotionally; he was set in his ways. Oddly during this time, Rains made no effort to contact the Theatre Guild, but this may have been due to his uncertain obligations with Warner Bros, since the studio could "request" (demand) his return at any time.

In the spring, Rains traveled to Hollywood to test for a new project, but the director thought him unsuited and he wasn't offered the part. To alleviate his client's disappointment and anxiety, Mike Levee handed Rains another script for Columbia Pictures. Rains read it through that night and the next day told his agent to accept. It was a godsend. Amusingly, a year that began with *Variety* reporting that Rains would play the Devil in RKO's *The Devil and Daniel Webster*, found him instead playing an agent of Heaven.

Some eight decades after it was made, *Here Comes Mr. Jordan* remains a delight, proving that comedy is timeless. The unusual story begins when a heavenly messenger (Edward Everett Horton) too hastily snaps up the soul of boxer Joe Pendleton (Robert Montgomery) seconds before the plane Joe is piloting crashes. This miscalculation creates a problem for Celestial Registrar Mr. Jordan (Rains), when it is discovered that in fact Joe would have survived and has another 50 years allotted to him. To make

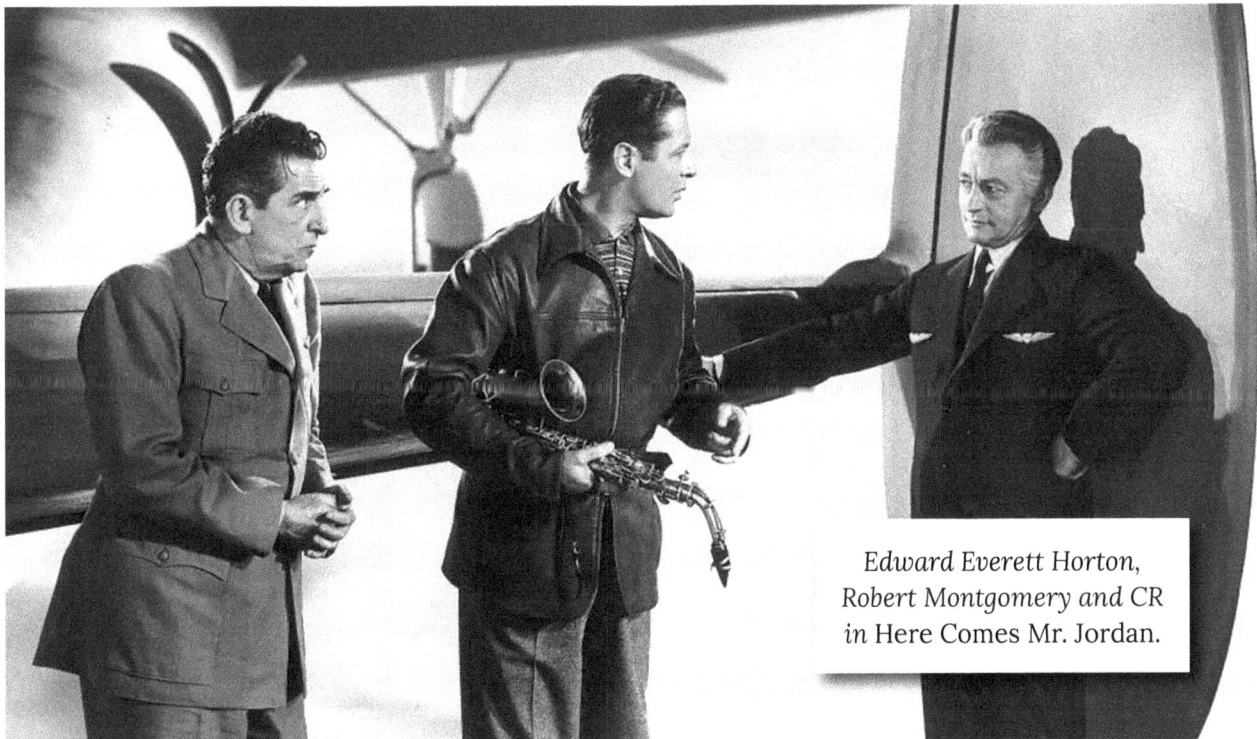

Edward Everett Horton, Robert Montgomery and CR in Here Comes Mr. Jordan.

Here Comes Mr. Jordan.

Robert Montgomery and CR in Here Comes Mr. Jordan.

things right, Mr. Jordan and Joe return to Earth to find another body, one that the prizefighter insists must be "in the pink." Joe agrees to assume the flabby form and corrupt life of a playboy millionaire named Farnsworth when Joe falls for a young woman whose innocent father the millionaire was maligning. With Joe "in charge," the millionaire turns over a new leaf, hiring the deceased Joe Pendleton's manager Max (James Gleason) to get him "in the pink" so he can win the championship title Joe has been promised. But when Fate steps in, seeming to separate Joe from his girl, Mr. Jordan assures Joe that, confusing as events are, this is "[your] destiny… Eventually all things work out — there is design in everything. Don't worry, Joe. You'll have everything that was ordained for you…"

As Mr. Jordan, Rains is outfitted in a somber suit coat with some kind of generic flight wings on the pockets, and a silvery wig that is considerably more tamed than the actor's own hair. Lines are delivered quietly, gestures kept at a minimum. Not the comedic element — that job is more than ably performed by Horton and Gleason. Instead, he is warm, kind and patient, reminiscent of Dr. Jaquith in *Now, Voyager*. Rains plays Mr. Jordan as subdued but giving the impression that he truly does know all things in Heaven and Earth, Horatio. We trust him. We believe him when he promises the distraught prizefighter: "You remember I said you wouldn't be cheated? Nobody is, really … This is your road, Joe … and everything's going to be all right." It is one of Rains' most reassuring performances. He is the reality of Heaven. And when he stands in the shadows of the stadium corridor, watching Joe and The Girl go off together, his final little wave of a salute and "So long, champ!" can't fail to bring a lump to the throat.

Here Comes Mr. Jordan was nominated for five Oscars, including Best Picture, Best Actor (Montgomery) and Best Supporting Actor (Gleason). It won

CR and Anna Neagle in Forever and a Day.

CR attacks the painting of C. Aubrey Smith in Forever and a Day.

for Best Writing, Original Story, and Best Writing, Screenplay. The film was also a box-office success; so much so that *The Hollywood Reporter* ran a news item that Columbia was planning a sequel entitled *Hell Bent for Mr. Jordan.* The project had to be shelved until original cast members Montgomery, Rains and Gleason could be re-assembled, which unfortunately never happened. When a follow-up was finally made in 1947, it was titled *Down to Earth*; Gleason and Horton returned as their original characters, but Mr. Jordan was played by English actor Roland Culver. Rains did recreate his role in a *Lux Radio Theatre*

program on January 26, 1942, which ironically starred Cary Grant, Columbia's original choice to play Joe. In 1978, the film was remade as *Heaven Can Wait* with Warren Beatty as Joe and James Mason as Mr. Jordan. It received nine Oscar nominations.

It was in the middle of making *Mr. Jordan* that Rains filmed his contribution — as another baddie — to a unique "star-studded" production. *Forever and a Day* was helmed by seven different directors; its even larger writing team included several renowned names (C.S. Forester, James Hilton, Christopher Isherwood, R.C. Sherriff, John Van Druten); and the cast, prominently promoted on all advertising, consisted of 78 "name" players. Everyone worked without pay. Originally conceived by a group of British and French nationals living in Hollywood as a way to raise money for war refugees, the movie went into production at RKO-Pathe under the title *This Changing World* on Sunday, May 18, and continued on-and-off shooting through January 1943. In episodic flashbacks, the story follows the history of an English manor house and its inhabitants. Rains was cast in the first segment to be filmed, under the direction of Herbert Wilcox. In this segment, construction on the mansion begins in 1804; when it's finished, blustery admiral C. Aubrey Smith refers to the house as "she" and, noting that it is built to last, predicts it will see lots of people, "good and bad. Aye, and strange happenings too, no doubt." His prediction instantly comes true when a woman emerges from the storm raging outside and collapses on the doorstep. Susan (Anna Neagle [Mrs. Herbert Wilcox]) has fled her creepy guardian, Ambrose Pomfret (Rains), because he has promised her hand in marriage to an older, equally creepy man. When Susan instead marries Smith's dashing, devil-may-care son Ray Milland, Rains vows revenge. Fourteen years later, after Milland's death in the Napoleonic War and the birth of his son, Rains follows through on the vow, secretly paying Neagle's debts in order to seize the house. In an unexpected supernatural twist, Neagle predicts that the house will hate his presence every moment Rains is in it – which it does. One night, in a drunken rage, Rains takes a sword to the portrait of Smith above the fireplace. Smith's ghostly voice is heard, telling Rains he can do nothing to make the house his. Shocked, Rains drops his weapon and then fatally falls on it. *Forever and a Day* was eventually released by RKO on March 26, 1943. Profits were distributed to British and American charities connected to the United Nations war effort.

Rains often referred to Hollywood as an actor's heaven, even if it meant relinquishing real choice over his roles. His next project gave him genuine pause. *Kings Row*, based on the controversial best-selling novel by Henry Bellamann, depicted the ugly realities and often hidden prejudices of life in small-town America at the turn of the 20th century. The story dealt with serious, taboo subjects: incest, sadism, unethical medical practices and homosexuality. It would be extremely difficult to make a movie from this social indictment in an effective and suitable manner, and only Warners would have dared to try. Some of his industry colleagues advised Jack Warner not to make the film; Joseph Breen, head of the Production Code office, warned the studio that the material as written in the book would be unacceptable in a movie. In that respect, bringing the story to the screen became a kind of challenge to everyone involved.

Set in the 1890s, the intense movie follows the lives and friendships of several inhabitants of the seemingly placid American small town of Kings Row. ("A GOOD CLEAN TOWN," according to the sign at the city limits.) Kind and noble Parris Mitchell (Robert Cummings) prepares for medical school by working under the mentorship of Dr. Alexander Q. Tower (Rains). Since childhood Parris has been sweet on Tower's daughter Cassie (Betty Field), even though Dr. Tower is a man of mystery and Tower's wife is tucked away upstairs in his home and never seen. "There's something crazy about that house," Parris' friend Drake (Ronald Reagan) muses while chomping an apple. But Dr. Tower eventually warms up to Parris: "If I had a son, I'd want him to be as nearly like you as possible."

After Mrs. Tower's death, Cassie acts irrationally and runs hot and cold on marrying Parris. Shockingly, Dr. Tower fatally poisons Cassie and then commits suicide. Afterwards, Parris learns from Dr. Tower's notes that Cassie suffered from incipient hereditary insanity; Tower had decided to end her life before she could go completely insane like her mother. And perhaps he was also preventing Parris

– for whom he had such high hopes – from making the same mistake he (Tower) did when he married an unbalanced woman. "Maybe he was just looking into my future," Parris tells Drake. "He thought more of me than I ever knew...."

As the story continues, Drake is ruined when his trust fund is stolen; forced into a railroad yard job, he has a serious accident that results in a doctor (Charles Coburn) amputating his legs. He withdraws from the world but feisty working-class Randy (Ann Sheridan) never loses faith, marrying him and encouraging him. Ultimately they learn that Drake's doctor may have needlessly amputated in an effort to render him undesirable to the doctor's daughter, whom he considered above the carefree playboy. Nevertheless, love conquers all and the human spirit can't be extinguished.

English actor James Stephenson (whose exceptional performance in *The Letter* was Oscar-nominated) was originally cast as Dr. Tower, but early in production he died of a heart attack in his home. He was only 52. Hal Wallis immediately thought of an alternate: "After a midnight emergency [conference], we decided to replace him with Claude Rains, who could match Stephenson, even surpass him, in the role. We called Rains at his home in Chester County, Pennsylvania, and he declined instantly. But we tried again, rushed him the book, and he finally agreed to break off his much-needed vacation and make the long train journey west. His refusal to fly meant a considerable delay in our schedule."

It's not surprising that Rains initially declined the part, given that the novel had stirred so much controversy. He was hesitant to be involved with questionable subject matter, but his reluctance subsided when he discovered that the always reliable Casey

As Dr. Tower in Kings Row.

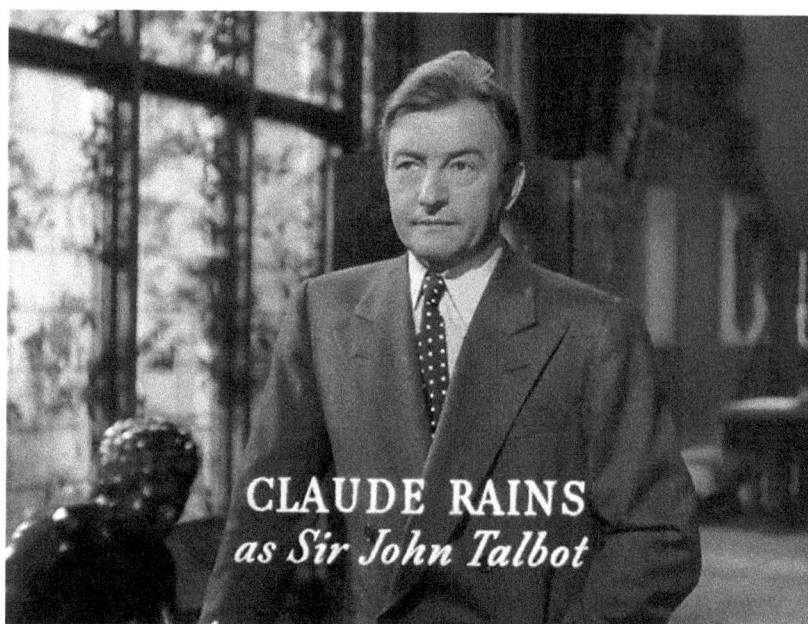

From The Wolf Man's *opening credits.*

51 *Lon Chaney, CR and Evelyn Ankers in* The Wolf Man. *(Photo courtesy John Antosiewicz)*

Robinson had vastly modified the novel to secure Production Code Office approval. Robinson's sensitive script made Rains realize there was a tragic aspect to Dr. Tower. (In the novel, Tower is engaged in an incestuous sexual relationship with his nymphomaniac daughter.) Rains reported for work on August 13, and finished up by the end of the month, at a guarantee of $5,000 per week.

Much of Dr. Tower's actions and comments are mysterious, but while remaining aloof and a bit morbid, Rains breathes humanity into the brief role. Portraying the torment of a father helpless to cure or even treat his mentally ill daughter, Rains suffers in silence, going deep inside himself to reflect the bitterness of a failed life. From personal experience, he understood how terrible it was to know loneliness and to be unloved.

Beautifully photographed by James Wong Howe under the direction of Sam Wood, with powerful acting from Sheridan, Cummings, Field and Reagan (undeniably his best work in his best role), and a glorious score by Erich Wolfgang Korngold, *Kings Row* foreshadows future overheated dramas like *Peyton Place*, in which a lovely little town is revealed to be a snake pit of passion and perversion. The film failed to establish itself with audiences because it was morbid and gruesome: ironically, as one critic summed it up: "Its very excellence in production and acting make the malevolence of its story the more terrible."

During August, while he was filming *Kings Row*, Universal contacted Rains to play the father of Lon Chaney, Jr., starring in the title role of *The Wolf Man*. Possibly Universal desired Rains because the public still associated the actor with *The Invisible Man* and his name attached to that kind of picture still had cachet a decade later. The offer presented the actor with a dilemma. A horror film would do little for his career, but it was work; never again did he want to experience being in the wasteland for seven months. And if he often turned

down offers from other studios, he might not be considered in the future. The crux of the matter was that he needed money. Restoration of Stock Grange was costing a small fortune. And for the first time since 1935, he would receive top billing over a strong supporting cast, including Ralph Bellamy, Bela Lugosi, Maria Ouspenskaya and Warren William.

As Sir John Talbot, Rains represents the voice of reason in the story — until he discovers that lycanthropy actually exists and his own son is a victim. His strongest acting comes at the very end when, tragically, he is the one who destroys the Wolf Man: The Monster attacks him, and he beats it with a silver-headed cane. Previously reserved and self-assured, a man of words not action, Sir John launches into a brutal frenzy, his face distorted, his hair hanging in his wild eyes as he strikes the creature over and over in the eerie, fog-enshrouded wood (a deliciously spooky recreation on a Universal soundstage). Then he watches as the dead Wolf Man transforms back into his son. As he kneels beside the body — his beloved boy, no longer a cursed child of the night — he strokes Larry's face with great tenderness. Rains'

Top: CR, Lon Chaney and Evelyn Ankers in The Wolf Man. *(Photo courtesy John Antosiewicz)*

Middle: CR is horror-struck after he realizes he's beaten his own son to death in The Wolf Man.

Bottom: The dramatic finale of The Wolf Man: *CR stands over the body of Lon Chaney, flanked by Warren William (kneeling on left) and Ralph Bellamy (standing on right). (Photo courtesy John Antosiewicz)*

As Nutsy in Moontide.

CR and Jean Gabin in Moontide.

expression sends a message that maybe with more understanding and a willingness to listen (qualities he lacked as a father), Sir John could have helped his son overcome his fate.

The Wolf Man was released two days after December 7, 1941. While it was dismissed by the critics as a B-monster flick, it was the perfect distraction and delighted matinee audiences, providing Universal with a big hit. It remains a favorite today, deservedly — it is fast-paced, exciting, and Larry Talbot's transformation from man to wolf still astonishes. It was accomplished not by two-dimensional computer imaging but clever camera effects and the wizardry of makeup expert Jack Pierce. The character made several more appearances in Universal's other franchise series, featuring Frankenstein's Monster and Count Dracula — and even the most frightening series of all, Abbott and Costello.

Immediately following *The Wolf Man*, Rains was tapped by 20th Century–Fox's production chief, Darryl F. Zanuck, for *Moontide*, a moody romance written expressly as the English language debut of noted French actor Jean Gabin. In the early 1940s, Gabin was largely unknown to American audiences, although he had wide appeal in Europe, especially

following his excellent performance in Jean Renoir's award-winning *Grand Illusion* (1937). Gabin was considered a French Spencer Tracy or Clark Gable, but casting him in a Hollywood picture was still a risk, since it was a period of intense Americanism and there was a tendency to shy away from anything or anyone foreign.

Screenwriter Nunnally Johnson was enthusiastic about the story and felt the lead was an excellent role in which to launch Gabin. However, the film's producer, Mark Hellinger, sent Zanuck a ten-page memo criticizing John O'Hara's screenplay, adapted from Willard Robertson's best-selling novel. Then Gabin fussed about the script, creating further delays. In fact, the Frenchman's insights were astute. His character, originally called "Frenchy," was too stereotypical as written; Gabin felt he had to have more depth and needed to be called by the name he has in the book, "Bobo." Nearly all of the actor's suggestions were incorporated. Johnson substantially reworked O'Hara's script beginning in November and revising it as late as April (but took no screen credit). Filming finally began in November and lasted fifty days.

Initially Fritz Lang was assigned to direct, but after less than three weeks of shooting, illness forced him to withdraw and Archie Mayo, an equally strong director, took his place. Mayo was better liked by the actors, including Rains. Zanuck knew that even a star of Gabin's talent could not carry the movie alone; the addition of several well-respected American character actors skilled enough to enhance a moody, artistic film was crucial. Zanuck decided to cast Rains as "Nutsy," the character who serves as the voice of reason throughout the story, and Thomas Mitchell as the crude and dangerous parasite, "Tiny."

Until required to report to the set, Rains rehearsed his character at Stock Grange. Because "Nutsy" was original to the screenplay, the actor had free rein in developing the character: a night watchman with a philosophical bent; well-read but shabby-looking. Worldly-wise, engaging and easygoing, he is a man of integrity. Instead of his usual evenly paced, turn-on-a-dime stride, Rains gave "Nutsy" a shambling walk and let his beard grow so that by the time he arrived on set, he looked every inch a tramp, with a rough-looking stubble as well as a broad, untrimmed mustache. Wire-rim round glasses completed the picture. "Nutsy" is well-educated, suggesting he may have been an academic, a philosopher who became disillusioned with life in the Depression. He has let the world go on without him, as he creates his own. Delighted with Bobo's kindness, manliness and principles, he sees it as his mission to save the Frenchman from the dangerous "Tiny." When Rains and Gabin are together, there is real chemistry, reminiscent of that between Rains and Bogart.

Much creativity went into the making of *Moontide* and it seems a pity that the film never received the recognition it deserves. When first planned, early in 1941 prior to America's involvement in World War II, it was to be filmed in the harbors of Los Angeles and San Pedro. However, security and military issues following Pearl Harbor led the government to ban any filming at the location. Many of the scenes take place on a waterfront, which had to be created on a

CR, William Halligan (bartender) and Thomas Mitchell in Moontide.

stage, with stone breakers, waves and a dock (in front of a rear-projection ocean) — all built from scratch and costing some $40,000.

Director Mayo followed Lang's style in creating a gray atmosphere in nearly every outdoor scene, enhancing the ambiance of the story. The film's score was by Alfred Newman, who incorporated Irving Berlin's "Remember" into the theme. (Legal squabbles over the use of the song delayed the picture's release; a vast amount of correspondence and legal documents about royalties went back and forth, and in fact continues today, with the Berlin estate. This is one reason the film is not broadcast on television.)

Moontide was released the first week of May 1942 and some astute critics recognized its merits, but for the most part the American public did not appreciate the somber mood. Audiences were not accustomed to the foreign, natural style acting employed by Gabin. Finally, it might have been that many misinterpreted the intended exaggerated sequences and even the characters. Some critics felt it was Hollywood's attempt to make an "artsy" movie or a "French melodrama." Others commented that while the cast was excellent, the film as a whole lacked depth, and an undefinable quality prevented the viewer from relating to, or feeling compassion for, the characters.

Critics had a difficult time deciphering the enigmatic "Nutsy" because they, like the audiences, had come to associate Rains with the roles he usually played: suave, sophisticated, usually villainous. Nevertheless, *Variety* cited his "memorable performance, quietly human and wholly admirable."

Rains' tax returns for 1941 showed a gross of over $75,000 from Universal, Columbia and 20th Century–Fox, $15,000 coming from Warners for *Kings Row* and $8,000 from various radio performances. His net income, however, was only $65,567 — a far cry from the $100,000 he earned in 1939. As advised by his accountant, Rains sold the Stone Canyon Road house. America's entry into World War II made train travel extremely difficult, so until the Rainses could find another location, he and Frances decided to stay at the Château Élysée. It became evident fairly quickly that the arrangement was too inconvenient, but it was nearly impossible to find and rent apartments, so the couple decided to look for another house, at least for the duration of the war. Between the restoration of Stock Grange, the start of school for Jennifer and the need for an L.A. home, Rains needed every dollar he could earn.

Rains' mother died on May 13, 1942, and the war made getting to England for the funeral problematic.

While Rains had been out on loan to other studios, the estrangement between the actor and Warners did not diminish. But by the end of April 1942, Jack was finally ready to have one of his best and most reliable character men return.

In 1942, Bette Davis was *the* leading lady at Warner Bros., and according to many — critics and public alike — the best actress in Hollywood. The role of Charlotte Vale in *Now, Voyager* would be one of her greatest achievements (earning her the seventh of her astonishing eleven Oscar nominations). Professionally a success in every respect, the actress had, nevertheless, earned the reputation of being difficult on a set and prone to arguments with directors. In addition to her temperament, she was often late or ill, so Warners tried to prepare ahead of time for delays on her pictures. While others might have issues working with Davis, Rains never did; as a theatre stage manager, he had learned to endure all kinds of behavior, especially from very talented actors. He also had a sympathetic understanding of Bette's insecurities.

Now, Voyager was directed by Irving Rapper, one of the few directors who got along well with Davis.

CR and Bette Davis in Now, Voyager.

The production was supervised by Hal Wallis, with Casey Robinson scripting from the recent bestseller by Olive Higgins Prouty. The cast included Paul Henreid in one of his first major roles as Charlotte's married lover and elegant, venerable Gladys Cooper as Charlotte's domineering mother. Production was already underway when Rains reported on April 24 for tests and makeup, beginning work the next day.

From the very first scenes in the massive mansion of the Vales of Boston, we see how victimized and repressed thirty-something Charlotte (Davis) has been by her cruel, haughty mother (Cooper). As a last resort, one of the country's foremost psychiatrists is summoned, and Dr. Jaquith (Rains) shocks the family with his diagnosis that their almost sadistic "ragging" has driven Charlotte to the brink of a nervous breakdown. He stages an intervention, spiriting the tormented young woman away to his Vermont sanitarium. Three months of treatment at Cascade puts Charlotte on the road to recovery, both mentally and physically. Slim, well-dressed, shy and uncertain, Charlotte embarks on an ocean pleasure cruise where she meets Jerry (Henreid), an unhappily married architect. Romance blossoms. Back at home, the newly independent Charlotte quarrels with her mother, who suffers a fatal heart attack. Consumed with guilt, Charlotte flees again to the sanctuary of Cascade, where she sees a lot of herself in Jerry's twelve-year-old daughter Tina (Janis Wilson), herself a lonely, emotionally unstable patient. Bringing Tina out of her shell helps the girl, her father and the now-confident Charlotte, who has become her own woman at last — even if she and Jerry cannot "ask for the stars," since they "have the moon."

Despite his third billing, Rains' role of the understanding, humane Dr. Jaquith wasn't large, but the character is pivotal: His warmth, support

CR and Bette Davis in Now, Voyager.

and professional care help transform a tormented neurotic spinster into a strong, independent woman able to find love. The actor's agent sought a salary of $5,000 per week ($25,000 guarantee); Warners countered at $25,000 for six weeks' work.

Again, Rains represents the nurturing, but (as scripted) asexual figure; the masculine support system has helped the woman overcome her inhibitions with no overt romantic motives. He makes his nonchalant entrance into the film and the Vale mansion knocking out his pipe against a large, rare Chinese urn in the foyer. Then, not knowing what to do with the ashes, he says to the butler standing beside him in amazement, "Messy things, pipes. I love 'em." Less a medical doctor and more caring friend, Jaquith visits Charlotte's bedroom and admires the little boxes she has carved. "Did you do these?" he asks in wonder. "They're really professional…. Now, this is *very* good detail. I have a great admiration for people who are clever with their hands. I was always so … clumsy with my own." The captivated Charlotte — a twitchy little sparrow he has talked down from isolation in the treetops to perch happily on his finger — can respond in no other way than: "I should think you were the least clumsy person I have ever met." In short order, he creates a genuine bond with the emotionally battered woman — one that we suspect will be lifelong. Critics responded to his warmth and sensitivity. "Claude Rains is the high spot in the casting," wrote one, with another stating: "[He] brings delightful depths to his friendly psychiatrist and makes it one of his best roles."

In fact, Davis described the scene near the end of *Now, Voyager* in which she and Jaquith discussed the expansion of the hospital as "reeking with sex," despite the fact that the two never touch. It was the way Rains looked at her. In her 1981 article for

American Screen Classics titled "A Dual Portrait of Bette Davis and Claude Rains," cinematographer Anne Etheridge agreed: "Without indulging in any of the conventional demonstrations of love, Rains could portray, by a look, a tone, a gesture, any of its nuances from shy adoration to smoldering passion, with greater effect than is ever produced by kisses or clinches."

Neither Davis nor Rains bought the maudlin direction the story took, and especially the film's ending. As Davis told Etheridge, "Claude and I used to talk by the hour about the ending. I know Charlotte finally married him because he was strong, and she had become strong. …That scene where they were planning the new wing together — brother! It was so obvious!" She had made the same assertion in 1971 on Dick Cavett's talk show: "Of course [Jerry] was never going to be right for her, he was too weak. I always felt that eventually she married Dr. Jaquith, my gorgeous Claude Rains. I always felt that after the movie was all over, she went and worked with him."

However, having committed the "sin" of a one-night affair with Jerry, there was no way Charlotte could be "allowed" to live happily ever after with him, not in 1942. There had to be repercussions, and repentance, at least to appease the Hays office, which additionally argued that it would "dishonor" the medical profession for a psychiatrist to marry a former patient, especially a woman who had a one-night stand with a married man. This was not a story about a woman's independence but rather a woman's sacrifice. Either way, Production Code Board objections notwithstanding, 70 years later, *Now, Voyager* remains a beloved film classic.

On some level, emulating their characters, Bette Davis would have liked to have ended up with Claude Rains in the final reel. Often she openly admitted her strong feelings; she even joked with him about his marrying so many other women and ignoring her. But whenever she would hint at or suggest anything beyond a friendship, Rains would smile but not respond. As much as he admired her professionally as an artist and personally as a strong, clever woman, and as genuinely fond as he was of her, Rains knew their temperaments were too much alike for them to ever be compatible as a couple. Many personality traits strengthened their mutual admiration. Flamboyant in their mannerisms, each needed to be the

CR and Bette Davis in Now, Voyager.

center of attention. In addition to their talent, both had unusual patterns of speech and weren't considered attractive by classic standards. However, they both possessed the quality to attract with dynamic presence and formidability.

Both loved acting and also knew that it alone could never satisfy their deepest needs; both needed companionship of the opposite sex desperately. Sadly because of their temperaments, both lacked the ability to maintain solidarity with a spouse and had devastating disappointment in the failure of their frequent marriages.

Yet they instinctively understood each other's talent and ego-driven qualities. It may have been that Bette understood Claude on an equal basis, especially as an actor — on his need for perfection, his moodiness, his mysterious manner. Above all she understood Claude's struggle in his rise to stardom which had taken such a long time. He had worked very hard

to achieve his status and had known so many years of insecurity, whereas Bette rose to stardom in only a few years. He knew he was a good actor, but always felt he had to prove himself; Davis never doubted her talent.

Their behavior and interaction as friends came to reflect a brother-sister relationship more than anything else. Frances undoubtedly understood because she accepted the actress into her home, became her friend and was quite unperturbed by her presence on the farm for long periods. As Claude's wife, Frances never felt intimidated by Bette's open admiration for her husband and the two women got along well. Bette trusted the couple and the friendship lasted for over a decade mainly because Claude and Frances never pried or advised and just accepted her. Bette adored country living and the East Coast as much as Claude did; whenever it was possible, she would telephone and announce she was coming to Stock Grange, especially after a divorce or an affair. Jennifer Rains recalled that the actress' arrival at the farm was usu-

ally very secretive; she was told never to mention the famous actress' presence at school. Claude or Frances (or Charles) would meet Bette at the train station or drive into Philadelphia as she arrived incognito and was whisked away to the sanctity of the farm. "She might stay for weeks," according to Jennifer, "but then she was like one of the family and I used to call her Aunt Bette when I was younger." Davis had her own guest room, which came to bear her name, and she would lounge around the grounds as the days fell into weeks. When she was there, Bette became a part of the family.

More than anything else, Bette Davis was one of the few women who understood Rains' complexity and respectfully honored his desire for distance. She might have loved Claude with more emotion than Frances but could never have offered the same sense of tranquility in his domestic life or been what he required in a wife.

While Rains was still on the set of *Now, Voyager*, he received notification assigning him to a new film within 24 hours, which meant he was memorizing two scripts at the same time. No one involved with *Everybody Comes to Rick's*, the picture's working title, knew it would become one of the most famous and highly regarded movies ever made. In it, Rains would walk off through the fog with Humphrey Bogart and into cinema history.

Casablanca has been designated by the American Film Institute as the second greatest Hollywood movie of all time, behind *Citizen Kane*. It's the most famous film in which Rains ever appeared. And the character of Captain Renault, the suave, wily Prefect of Police, is probably the one for which the actor is best remembered. (Ironically, Renault was not one of Rains' favorite parts; he insisted he never saw *Casablanca*, not even after it received the Best Picture Oscar. Rains was hardly sentimental about most of his films: Acting was work, something he loved to do, but he saw no purpose in watching himself on the screen when he could no longer change or improve a performance.)

Entire books have been written about the film, with innumerable analyses, conflicting stories, differing opinions and even a few misconceptions.

However, even before there was a script, producer Hal Wallis knew that Claude Rains was a perfect choice for Captain Louis Renault. Wallis had always appreciated the actor's work, his easy adaptability to any role — not to mention his box-office appeal — and cast him whenever possible. While it's been suggested that the Epstein brothers, the writers of much of the initial screenplay, "envisioned the role of Renault to be played by one of their favorite actors, Claude Rains, and gave him more witty lines, the type of material they knew he could play to perfection," studio memos contradict this assertion, indicating they preferred an actual Frenchman and were supported by Jack Warner. Wallis insisted that Rains' sophistication and charm were what was needed for character; and both Wallis and Warner agreed that polish was more important to the role than a French accent. Early in the filming, Hal Wallis received a letter from co-worker Jack Moffitt suggesting that Rains modify his characterization to be more of a "baddie." "Wouldn't we get a better character if the Prefect was a literal embodiment of Vichy, cowardly ... constantly willing to make small bargains. Always trying to make the Germans hope for something..." Wallis ignored the suggestion.

On May 22, 1942, while Rains was still shooting *Now, Voyager*, he received notice to report on June 4 to the *Casablanca* set. This left no opportunity for any rest between projects. The actor's contract for the picture included first featured billing with letters of his name to be no more than fifty percent smaller than those of the three main stars. Guaranteed a minimum of five weeks, he actually worked five and a half, earning $22,000. (Retakes brought his final paycheck up to $28,000.) Ingrid Bergman's salary for the film was only $25,000.

Director Michael Curtiz focused on the characters more than the plot, an important decision with which Wallis agreed. The dialogue was exceptionally clever, but the lines alone could not have carried the sketchy plot. It was the high level of combined talent that elevated the final product, the exceptional chemistry and interplay between the actors. Julius Epstein once commented he felt the entire story was "schtick and hokum." Each screenwriter changed, added, deleted or altered scenes and dialogue. These extensive and frequent changes made it very difficult for the players who had to learn new lines almost daily. This made for a frustrating and tense work environment. Nevertheless, the dialogue remains one of the film's greatest and most memorable assets. Several lines (two of them Rains') have entered popular culture: "Play it, Sam" (almost always misquoted as "Play it again, Sam"), "Round up the usual suspects!," "I'm shocked, shocked!" and of course, "Louis, I think this is the beginning of a beautiful friendship."

Curtiz enhanced the interaction of the players by having the camera focus on the actors' expressions, with cinematographer Arthur Edeson using long focal lenses and shadowing to create a heightened sense of intimacy [by] keeping the faces sharp while softening everything around them. As usual, the director was relentless in perfecting the scenes, whatever the cost in money or time. Wallis became furious about the cost overruns.

Production notes for July 2 indicate that Rains worked for two hours on five takes which amounted to only thirty-five seconds of screen time. Even though nerves were frayed by constant reshoots, the actors got along well. For relief of the tension, the cast sometimes turned to humor and practical jokes, some initiated by Peter Lorre.

Many fans of *Casablanca* see the poignant love affair between Rick and Ilsa as the primary focus of

As Police Captain Louis Renault in Casablanca.

CR and Humphrey Bogart in Casablanca.

the movie, but most film historians agree with the analysis of Howard Koch, the final scriptwriter who probably had the most impact on the filmed version: "The most provocative relationship in the story was that between Rick and Capt. Renault, because it was ambiguous and its denouement unpredictable. The resolution of their relationship was closely tied into the fate of Ilsa and Laszlo. For this reason, I concentrated on the cat and mouse game between Rick and the French prefect, cutting down to a large extent Renault's seductive pursuit of the refugee girl."

While audiences probably didn't care one way or the other if the Prefect of Police got the girl, they desperately wanted him to get the boy: the interplay between Renault and Rick is one of the most enjoyable aspects of the film. Cohorts of sorts, their verbal sparring and cynical joking at each other's expense reveal genuine admiration. Rick's actions reignite in the Frenchman his long-dormant sense of values, with the result that he joins Rick in his "mutiny" against the forces of evil. Each man's true character is in limbo in Casablanca; both actors skillfully capture that ambiguity.

Debonair in his impeccable uniform, his cap set at a jaunty angle, Renault is obviously quite the "player," a quality which could come across as crass, but Rains makes him so charming the audience can't help but

allow Renault his enthusiasm for "breathtaking blondes," and his wicked, wicked ways in general, because they are presented with so much style. In fact, until the very end, it's tough to decipher Renault's motives.

Until … "Major Strasser has been shot." And after a perfectly timed dramatic pause, he utters the famous line "Round up the usual suspects." With this order, any moral ambiguity about Renault is dispelled. As the plane carrying Laszlo and Ilsa takes off, he knows that, like his American friend, he has reached the point of no return. It only required the final straw, the perfect impetus, for him to give up security, his career, what was always going to be an untenable life in Casablanca, and, like Rick, sacrifice it all for the greater good. Bogart and Rains, backs to the camera, stroll off together into the fog. Both had longed for what they seemed to mock — honor and purpose. Both hide their integrity under veneers of nonchalance. At the end, each has reestablished honor, so nearly lost forever.

On November 26, *Casablanca* opened at the Hollywood Theatre in New York City. This review sums up the audience reaction: "*Casablanca* has everything — excitement, suspense, ill-fated love, tenderness, humor … not to mention a cast so superior you wish each role had been given twice the footage." *The Hollywood Reporter* agreed: "Here is a drama that lifts you right out of your seat. [A] surefire box-office smash …. But in addition to its present timeliness, the picture has exceptional merits as absorbing entertainment, reflecting the fine craftsmanship of all who had hands in its making. Certainly, a more accomplished cast of players cannot be imagined, and their direction by Michael Curtiz is inspired."

Nominated by the Academy for multiple Oscars, *Casablanca* won for Best Picture, Best Writing, Screenplay, and Best Director. Bogart, nominated for Best Actor, and Rains, up for Best Supporting Actor, both lost. Instead of Bogart's complex performance as the cynical anti-hero who drinks too much, the win went to Paul Lukas' virtuous, less ambiguous

Paul Henreid, Ingrid Bergman and CR in Casablanca.

anti–Nazi agent in *Watch on the Rhine*. Rains was passed over for Charles Coburn's sly matchmaker in the improbable romantic comedy *The More the Merrier*, a film rarely seen, and a performance hardly remembered. Perhaps it would be some satisfaction if Rains knew that Captain Renault, and his portrayal of "a poor corrupt official," remains beloved by each new generation of filmgoers, more than 75 years after Rick and Louis began their "beautiful friendship."

Chapter 16
An Opera Ghost and Mr. Skeffington

Rains went from one of the most outstanding films of his career to one of the most unusual. By the 1940s, the multi-faceted Arch Oboler had made a name for himself as a playwright, screenwriter, novelist and producer-director in almost every entertainment medium. He had created the immensely popular "spooky" radio series *Lights Out*.

Like many Americans, Oboler was appalled by Hitler's growing empire in Europe and feared that democracy was in peril. He also believed, quite accurately, that many complacent Americans had little conception of the political issues involved and of the menace of fascism in general. To promote a deeper gratitude for democratic liberties, he reworked a story — most famously known as "This Precious Freedom" — several times, on various airwave series. With each re-telling, he tweaked the plot of a family man, John Stevenson, coming home from a vacation in the middle of nowhere to discover that his town has been taken over by Nazis. It was a chilling warning about what could happen to a single American citizen who experienced the sudden loss of his liberties.

Barbara Bate, Paul Hilton, CR and Bobbie Stebbins in Strange Holiday. (Photo courtesy John Antosiewicz)

In 1940, after the Nazis invaded Poland and Great Britain was fighting for its life, Americans remained greatly divided about becoming involved in another "European" war. Oboler and people like him tried to make Americans understand that it was a "world" problem — a fact that was brought home on December 7, 1941. By early 1942, as nearly all major American factories were converted into war plants. General Motors wanted to create an effective propaganda piece for its employees that stressed the importance of each individual worker's commitment. The company's vice-president feared that many workers would begin to feel America was impregnable to Nazi influence. They were impressed with the effectiveness of "This Precious Freedom" and decided to make the radio story into a film, not for feature release, but as propaganda to be shown to the thousands of GM employees. (GM had already made one such patriotic picture, *America Can Give It* with Walter Huston.)

The film was supervised by L.M. Corcoran and produced by Frank Donovan of General Motors. The giant corporation had its own studios for the production and recording when management wanted to promote a project or workplace safety. The two men hired Oboler to write the screenplay as well as direct. He was informed he could select any actor he wanted to play the role of Stevenson and that General Motors would pay all costs involved.

Claude Rains had just wrapped *Casablanca* at Warner Bros. and was preparing to return to his farm when Oboler approached him about the project. The actor had been working hard during the past several months, and *Casablanca* had proved particularly difficult, with all of the last-minute rewrites and reshooting. Nevertheless, Rains agreed to make this new, unusual picture.

First, he truly believed that he would be contributing something important to the war effort by making such a pro-democracy film. He felt a sense of obligation to be involved personally in patriotic service, just as his farm crops were committed to the war effort. Also, the actor was always intrigued by *avant garde*, bizarre plots. He liked young Oboler and the message of the story and believed he could bring something special to the role, which called for an average, middle-aged American. However, the executives at GM, as well as Rains, felt the film should end differently than the radio version — on a positive note, with a sense of timely awareness.

Playing John Stevenson was a demanding role, both physically and as a test of the character actor's ability to control his style. The actor wanted the opportunity to impersonate an "average Joe," a guy as far removed as possible from an English Tudor lord or a historical figure like Napoleon or a tragic mad scientist. More importantly, the script echoed some of his deepest feelings about his adopted country. He was living proof of the American dream and believed he could convince others to realize what freedom really meant. Like Oboler, he felt Americans tended to take democracy for granted.

Everyone involved with the production was highly enthusiastic. *This Precious Freedom* was shot on the General Service Studios lot in Hollywood. All through the hot summer of 1942, they worked hard and put in overtime so that the film was completed by late September. Some sources listed it as a two-reeler (15 to 24 minutes), others as a four-reeler (30 to 48). According to *Variety*, it would be shown in GM plants and in theatres rented for private showings.

Then, for undocumented and unknown reasons, the General Motors top executives shelved the film. Since the corporation was both producer and owner of the finished product, there was little Oboler could do. He and Rains were bitterly disappointed. Oboler tried to obtain the rights and finally, presumably with Rains' help, was able to raise enough money to buy it from GM. The two men then discussed reworking the production, making it longer and distributing it commercially. But during wartime, such a venture wasn't really feasible; independent filmmakers found it almost impossible to secure the necessary space, equipment or funds. And so it sat on the shelf.

It wasn't until February 1944 that the short film was expanded with additional scenes shot by Elite Pictures. In the middle of that year, Rains was in England to make the extravagant film adaptation of Shaw's *Caesar and Cleopatra*. By the time the actor was able to devote any time and money to the little project, it was September 1945. The war was over; both Rains and Oboler knew the story was dated but felt the basic message was timeless. Oboler knew a large studio name was essential for proper distribution and promotion, and convinced MGM to purchase the film, which they did in a mood of patriotic zeal. However, deciding it was a tough sell, they too stuck it on the shelf. In truth, *Strange Holiday*, the final title, did seem passe: Americans were weary of propaganda and there had been other, more effective

Strange Holiday.

films, like Frank Capra's series *Why We Fight*, which captured the essence of patriotism and the dangers of letting down our guard against men like Hitler.

Rains and Oboler obtained the rights from MGM for $5,000. The original short version made for GM ends with Stevenson in prison, soon to die, and lamenting how he lost his precious freedom. For the extended version, these scenes were reshot, and the overall concept changed to "what if the Nazis had won the war." In the 1945 version, it's all a nightmare: Stevenson wakes up and he rushes home to his family with a new awareness of his dream's message.

Bette Davis visited the set and was very excited by Oboler's creation, requesting that he write a screenplay for her. It is likely she may have been one of the investors. However, in addition to its bad timing, the finished film had other major drawbacks. It was produced on an extremely limited budget; the sets only exaggerate their artificiality. Rains struggled with the confusing and illogical script and once again, he and others noted that whenever he played the "common" man, his performance seemed less inspired, lacking that unique spark that glimmered within his odder characters.

After the long version was completed, Elite Pictures arranged for its release through a company called Producers Releasing Corporation. The time lapse between composition and release date hurt the picture's credibility: It was not until 1946 that the film was finally shown in movie houses, and then it was usually part of a double feature, considered a "B" film because of its sixty-minute length. The company did not have enough funds or friends to promote the film, but just as John Stevenson was tired of hearing about the war, so was the U.S. public. By 1946, Americans had done the job of safeguarding our liberties and did not need to be lectured about freedom's price. But both men still believed in the project. Reviews dismissed the work as "confusing" and "too arty."

Rains learned a painful lesson about producing, releasing films and his own "stardom." Just how much of his money he invested is unknown, but he lost it all, and by the end of 1946, Elite Productions ceased to exist. However, Rains continued to admire Oboler

Frances, Claude and Jennifer.

and maintained contact with the writer.

Strange Holiday was a work of love for Rains in many respects: He was not only the star, he was in effect a producer. Most importantly, it reflected what he truly felt about America.

In the 1930s, Rains had commanded $5,000 to $6,000 a week, especially when working for other studios. Ironically, now that his star status was growing with a hit like *Casablanca*, his salary was not. Warners was now paying him $4,000 a week — quite a comedown from the $7,500 he earned for seven days on *Juarez*. Yet the actor couldn't fault the studio: They had both agreed on a lower contractual salary in exchange for the right to make films for other studios. Additionally, Warners was using him less than they had — a bitter pill to swallow.

In examining Rains' financial papers, it appears his net worth never surpassed $1 million. He would never apply for a mortgage, kept cash

Phantom of the Opera. (*Photo courtesy John Antosiewicz*)

CR and Susanna Foster in Phantom of the Opera.

CR and Susanna Foster in Phantom of the Opera.
(Photo courtesy John Antosiewicz)

reserves in his bank account and, like most Americans in the '40s, bought war savings bonds and treasury bonds. He also dabbled in safe securities which paid substantial dividends, like General Motors, but these were hardly profit-making ventures, especially during the war years. He lacked business astuteness, and his multiple divorce proceedings had been extremely costly. His agent Mike Levee was involved with complicated contract negotiations with Warners over the usual issues (salary, weeks worked, guarantees, advance notice, options to do radio work, no loanout without the actor's consent and finally, if he refused an assigned role, he could not be suspended). Warners' attorneys felt they needed time to study these complex matters and decided to wait until Rains finished his current film before committing to a new contract.

By January 1943, Universal had started preproduction on a remake of their 1925 silent hit *The Phantom of the Opera*. This new production would be shot in Technicolor and have substantial footage of the performance of an opera, composed especially for the film. To play the tortured title character, some studio executives suggested casting Lon Chaney, Jr., who very much wanted to replicate his father's famous performance as a deformed monster; Chaney let it be known around the studio he was very upset when Claude Rains was cast. The script was still going through rewrites when Rains, supported by director Arthur Lubin, agreed to the assignment, because in this version, the character was going to be driven to madness by circumstance. Additionally, because he wanted no ordeal along the lines of *The Invisible Man*, Rains insisted his face not be completely covered in his guise as the Phantom.

The cast of the remake include Nelson Eddy and Edgar Barrier as the male leads, and Susanna Foster as the Phantom's muse, Christine. The final script was again based on Gaston Leroux's 1910 novel, but more freely than the silent version, and many loose ends dangled. The silly escapades of Christine's suitors provide unwelcome comic relief which detracts from

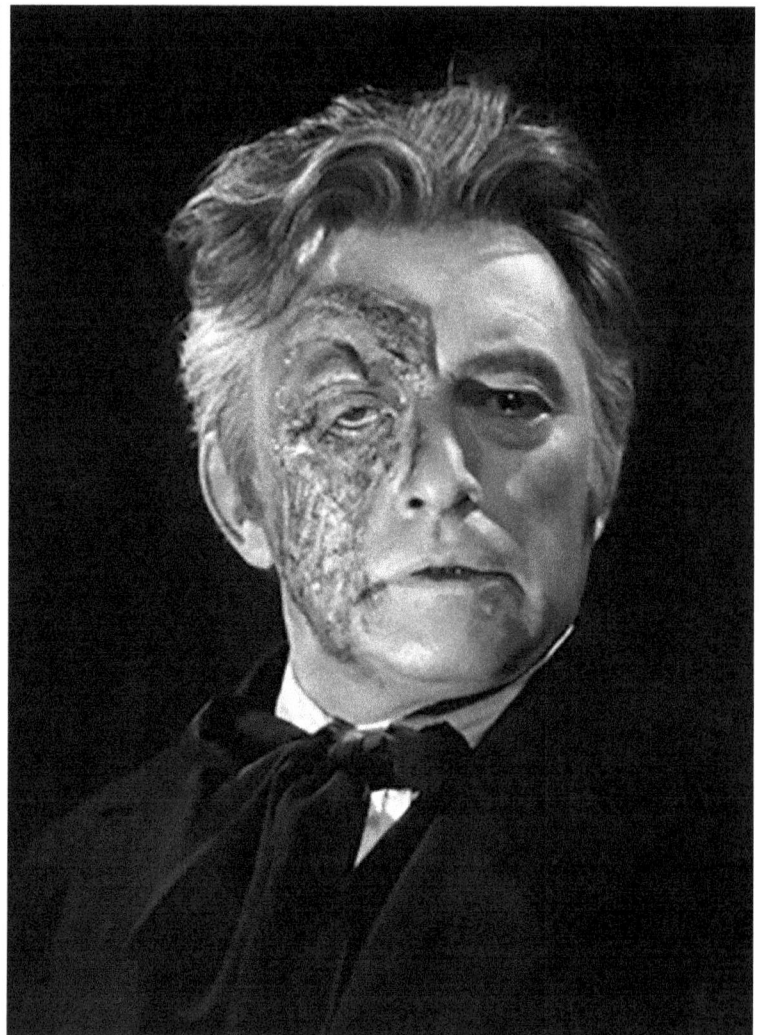

The two faces of the Opera Ghost

the seriousness of the story. Comparisons between the original and the remake were inevitable. The Chaney film had tremendous impact on audiences and remains a classic. The 1943 version is well made and beautifully filmed, with extraordinary sets and a lovely score, but it can't compete for thrills and chills.

The story is set in the last quarter of the 19th century. For years, Erique Claudin has been a violinist in the Paris Opera orchestra. When some difficulty with the fingers of his left hand causes him to miss notes during a performance, he is reluctantly dismissed by the manager, but under the assumption that the musician has saved his considerable salary against retirement. The truth is, the older man has been living in abject poverty and has no savings at all, because for three years he has been the anonymous benefactor of a young member of the Opera chorus, paying for her singing lessons from a high-priced teacher.

One of the plot problems is inherent from the get-go. It is unclear if Claudin has romantic feelings for the girl, if he is simply a worshiper of her great talent, or if perhaps he is actually her father. Along those lines, Rains' performance is a bit confusing: At times, he seems like a caring, paternal figure, and at others, there is a definite sensuality in his behavior. In a scene near the end, he leads the beautiful young woman by the hand into the dank underground catacombs, calling her "my darling" in a very seductive manner. No explanation is offered as to why he will do anything to ensure the singer's success. Apparently this rather important plot point fell victim to various disorganized rewrites and script cuts. Regardless of motivation, Rains creates terrific sympathy for his tragic character. Alone in his cheerless garret, he plays his piano concerto's haunting melody, based on a lullaby from his hometown, with tears glistening in his large, soulful eyes. He is humble and meek, stammering when he quietly speaks, walking with a bit of

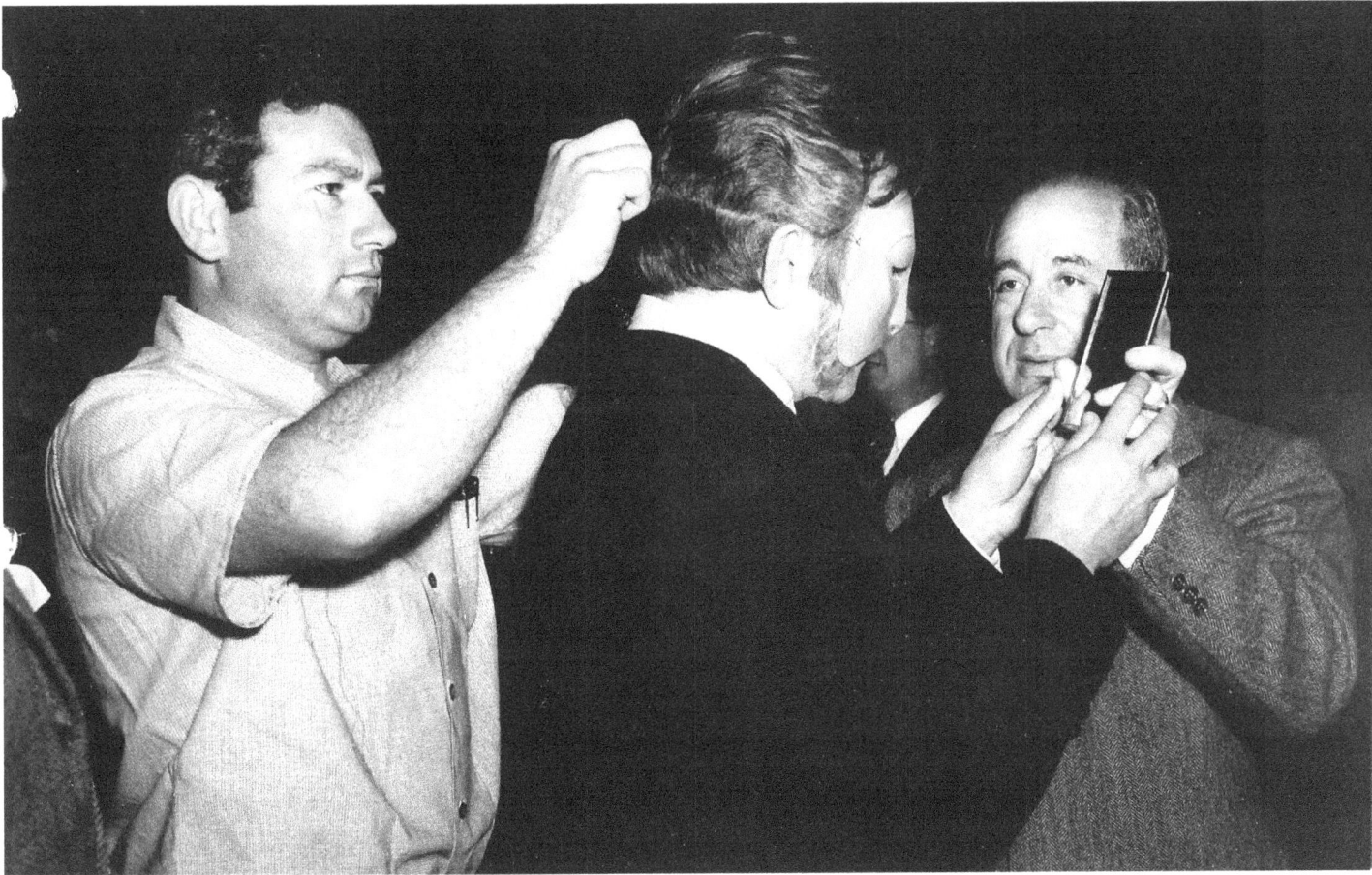

CR dons his Opera Ghost mask as Phantom of the Opera *crew members Julius Rosenkrantz (property man) and Samuel Kaufman (makeup) provide other finishing touches. (Photo courtesy John Antosiewicz)*

a defeated shuffle. An "absent-minded artist" look is emphasized by a navy jacket that is old and threadbare, and the actor's magnificent head of hair, longer than usual (with net extensions at the temples to add silver to the auburn color), falling over his forehead.

Claudin's only chance to make money is dashed when a rude music publisher discourteously refuses to buy the concerto Claudin has put his heart and soul into; there are no options left for the devastated musician. He begs the publisher for the return of the only copy of his magnum opus, unaware that, in a neighboring office, the great Franz Liszt is playing the work and praising it highly. Hearing the beautiful theme, the distraught Claudin mistakenly believes his music has been stolen; he argues with the publisher, then leaps on him violently, hands around the man's throat in a fit of temporary insanity. Alas, that insanity becomes permanent when the publisher's assistant tosses a (convenient) tray of etching acid into Claudin's face. In agony, his features horribly disfigured, he blindly staggers out into the streets, to find refuge from the police down in the Paris sewers.

Driven mad by both physical and psychological pain, Claudin now becomes the Phantom of the Opera, attempting to further his protege's career by getting rid of everything — and everyone — he believes stands in the way of her success. In the climax, down in his catacomb lair, Claudin plays piano for the terrified young woman, urging her "Sing, Christine, sing!" Curiosity compels her to tear off the Phantom's mask, revealing the acid-scarred face beneath. Christine's erstwhile suitors burst into the Phantom's lair. A gunshot is fired, causing the ceiling to cave in. The Phantom is crushed but Christine and her suitors escape the collapse of the musical underworld around them.

According to Susanna Foster, who was 18 when she made the picture: "It was such a happy, classy set…the crews were great. It was the middle of World War II and soldiers, and Marines often came on the set to visit. Rains was a great gentleman. He always had a twinkle in his eyes and was very flirtatious…" According to Foster, Rains accomplished many of

Renee Carson, Miles Mander (on the floor) and CR in Phantom of the Opera. *(Photo courtesy John Antosiewicz)*

the action scenes without a double, such as when he had to throw himself into the sewer water. She remembered him as very reserved on the set and not a talker. The extras often stood around and watched Rains while his scenes were being filmed:

> I felt he helped me in the scenes without saying anything. He never said, "Do this or that or try this." Never. He just accepted me, and I played with him and we worked together. When Christine pulls off the mask — that scene when I backed up was so good — it was because of him; I really was stunned and terrified....

He was an actor from the word "go" and his twinkle was wonderful. He sorta flirted with me and I think he liked me. I would imagine he liked music. They didn't know what to do in the picture — how to handle it — where he [Claudin] had this crush on this young girl — not a sexual love — just a love....

It was wonderful to act with him because you could react to him, and he taught you without your realizing it. He never, ever demanded anything. He was a gentleman with everyone, even the grips. Claude didn't give interviews — he did his work and that was satisfying for him. I remember he would smile a lot.

TOBY I. COHEN   193

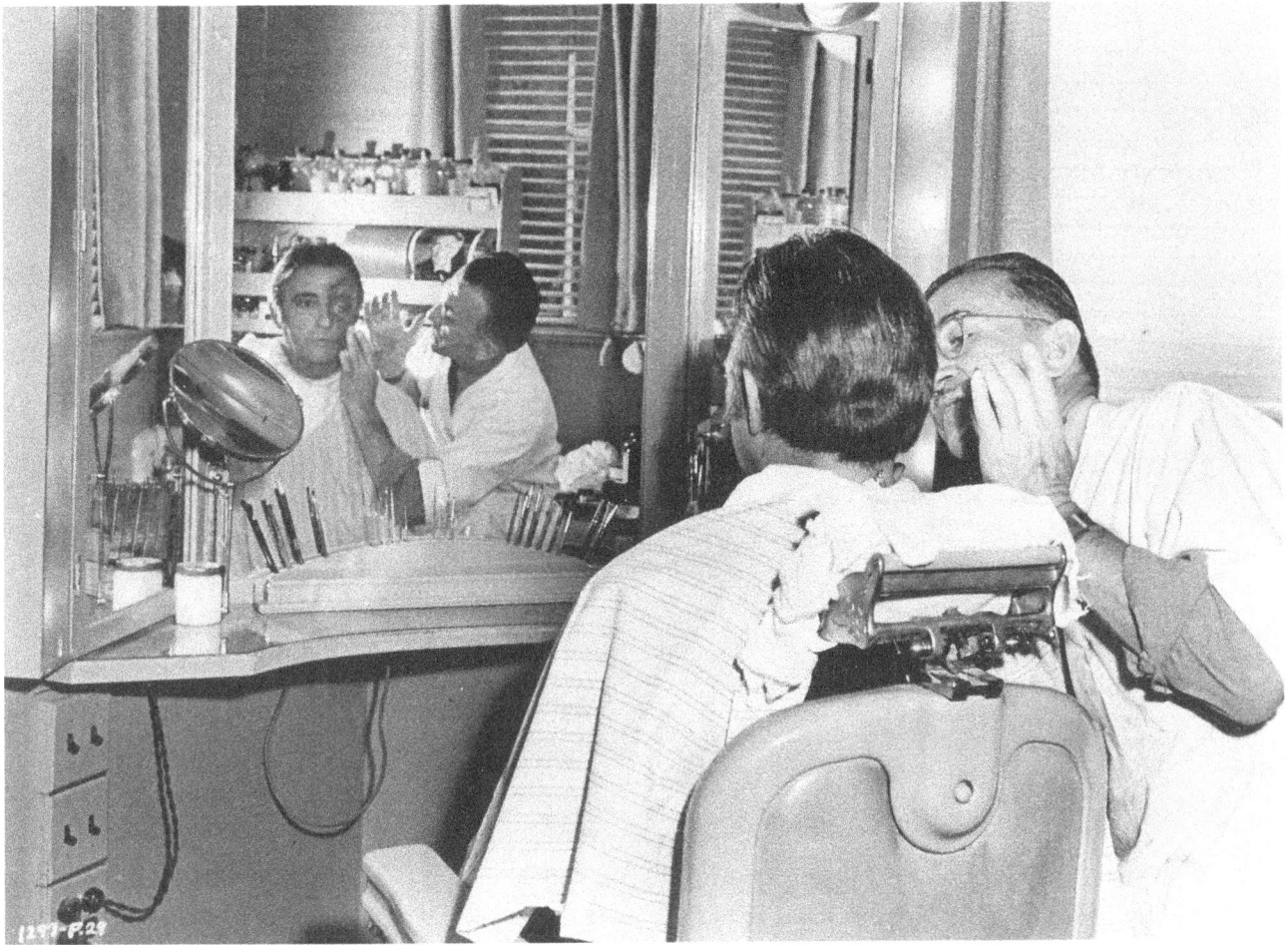

Jack P. Pierce applies CR's spectacular makeup for Phantom of the Opera. *(Photo courtesy John Antosiewicz)*

In the thrilling scene in which Claudin receives the acid in his face, Rains' reaction is so excruciatingly real, one can almost feel the searing of his flesh. The eerie green liquid drips from his hair and the sleeves of his coat as he stiffens erect with a searing cry, then doubles over, hands clutching at his face like claws, uttering cringe-making, high-pitched whimpers of agony.

Decades later, Susanna Foster agreed: "I will never forget that cry and moaning — it was like a hurt animal — it was marvelous." Some critics weren't happy with Jack Pierce's makeup, but HD broadcast and/or Blu-Ray prints reveal it in all its Technicolor glory: the right eyelid pulled down, eyebrow gone, the textured skin of the forehead, the side of the nose, the cheek down to the jawline a ghastly florid pink and purple.

Phantom was released in August 1943 and while it didn't receive terrific reviews, it was successful at the box office (Universal's biggest moneymaker of the year). It also won two Academy Awards, for Art Direction/Set Direction - Color, and Cinematography - Color. The *New York Herald Tribune* wrote: "It could not have been an easy task for Rains to

fill Chaney's boots with the title role. He does so splendidly…. [T]he progressive stages of insanity which cause his lethal exploits in the opera house are interpreted with skill and considerable horror." A unique compliment came from *Look* magazine in the form of a full spread: "Although Claude Rains' Phantom may disappoint some old Chaney fans, it is only because there is less ham in Rains and more actor." Remembering the production half a century later, director Lubin still praised Rains: "I cannot give him enough accolades as an actor. He was determined not to frighten people in the role."

As soon as he completed *Phantom*, Rains left for the East Coast. An April 15 news article mentions his appearances at war bond rallies in Philadelphia and Toronto; on April 22, he contributed his talents to a mass memorial in Philadelphia for stricken Jews in Europe. Although he received little publicity for his war efforts, and never bragged about them, Rains did his part in

Humphrey Bogart, Philip Dorn, CR, George Tobias, Helmut Dantine and Peter Lorre in Passage to Marseille.

raising money for war bond drives, but usually on a local level and not in the limelight of Hollywood.

Finally, all differences between the actor, his agent and Warners were amicably settled, and another two-year contract signed, with *Variety* reporting on May 13 that the actor's first appearance under the new deal would be as the second lead in *Passage to Marseille*. It seemed logical that, following the overwhelming success of *Casablanca*, Warners would elect to recast their prime contract players in another sentimental propaganda action-drama, although this time without a major romantic storyline. Again, hero Bogie would battle Nazis, again assisted by Rains, and this time aided by Peter Lorre. Sydney Greenstreet, only marginally shifty in the earlier film, was now unabashedly a bad guy.

Passage to Marseille begins in the present day, at a camouflaged airfield in the English countryside, where a wartime journalist is interviewing Rains, a colonel in the Free French air force, about the daring pilots in the England-based squadron. The tale is told in flashbacks (within flashbacks) about a group

of convicts from a French Guiana penal colony, led by Bogart, who escape in order to return and fight for France. All except Bogart, a disenchanted newspaperman who's now out for number one. After much derring-do, tearful patriotism and run-ins with Nazis, Bogart's true nature comes to the fore and he makes the ultimate sacrifice. The film ends at Bogart's funeral service, with Rains reading aloud to his buddies a sentimental letter Bogart wrote to his young son who still lives in France with his mother.

On July 20, Rains reported to location in Victorville, California, where the Army Air Force Training School was transformed into the camouflaged English airport. Similar to his appearance in *Casablanca*, he wears natty dress whites and dark military uniforms, cap at his habitual jaunty angle, with a trim mustache and an eye patch (over his right eye, not surprisingly the one in which he was virtually blind from war injuries).

The shooting schedule was grueling: On one day, the actor worked twelve hours, from 2:00 p.m. to 2:24 a.m., on just two takes amounting to forty seconds of screen time. Many of his scenes had to be shot in the evening or early dawn. On July 22, he was shooting from 8 p.m. to 2:45 a.m.; on July 23, 8 p.m. until 3:05 a.m. Rains wasn't used to being up so late, and he required a number of takes. His behavior was so unusual and irregular, it prompted a memo from the unit production manager: "For your information, the company was unable to photograph the last shot last night due to the fact that it was after 6 o'clock by the time the cameras were ready and the company had two rehearsals and Mr. Rains was 'blowing his lines' and Mike [Curtiz] decided to start it first thing in the morning."

To compound these problems, Bogart had been unable to begin work until August 30; since several crucial scenes required the two actors, Rains had to be held over until September 11. In one instance, he sat on the set for an entire week without shooting a single scene. Even though he was being paid, Rains must have felt exasperated, and the schedule took its toll on the usually good relationship between Rains and director Curtiz. The actor had worked through the hot summer and was now well beyond his five-week scheduled commitment. Shooting dragged on through September 29 and everyone's nerves were frayed. Hal Wallis became equally exasperated, as an internal memo indicates:

> As explained to you yesterday, Mr. Curtiz is going to try and concentrate on Claude Rains which might mean he will return to the boat [location] next Wednesday, after having left it for one day in order to prepare certain explosions and stay on the boat concentrating on Rains, and by doing this, Mr. Rains will be through in the picture with the exception of a certain trick or process shots that I cannot schedule or give you dates on at this time.
>
> As I told you, Mr. Wallis is very mad and feels that once Rains leaves the company and goes into another picture, we can never get him back. I told him that I felt he should discuss this problem with Mr. Warner.

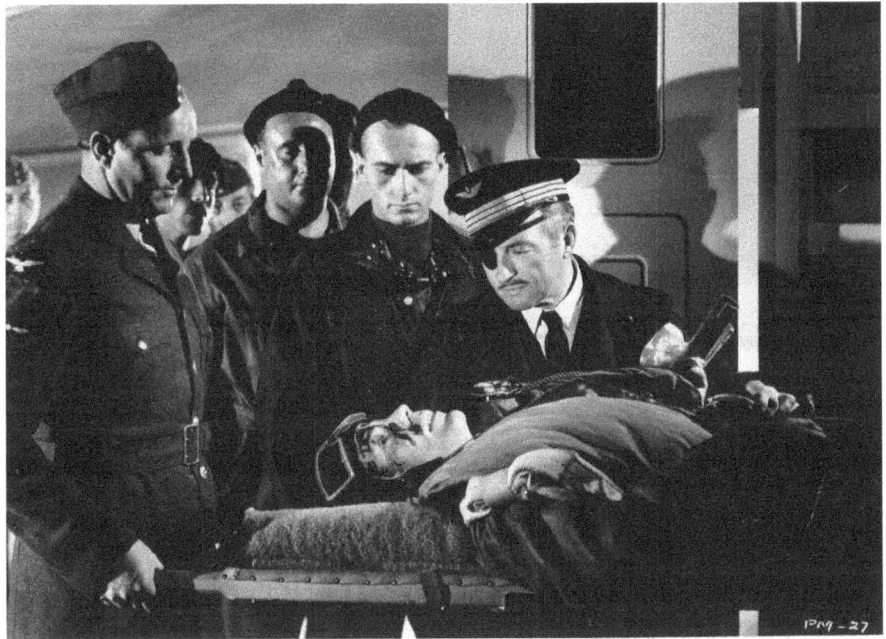

CR and Humphrey Bogart (on stretcher) in Passage to Marseille.

Evidently this is exactly what Wallis did — on October 9, when *Passage* was in its fifty-first day of shooting and six days behind schedule, Curtiz was ordered to complete the scenes with Rains by October 15. It was the longest the actor ever spent on a set. The only saving grace was the fact that, because it was summertime, Frances and Jennifer had been able to be with Rains, living at their new Brentwood house.

Slightly improbable in plot, *Passage to Marseille* was nevertheless a well-made movie, and audiences were caught up in the emotional impossibility of the heroism and jingoism, including film expert, historian and author Richard Schickel, who wrote: "This dour and insanely complicated film remains so memorable to me [because of] the energetic conviction of Curtiz's direction; James Wong Howe's moody, deep focus cinematography; and Claude Rains' intelligent civility as the audience's surrogate, that character, vital to traditional movie narrative, through whose eyes we apprehend the story."

Warners did not want to see Rains working for another studio, and he was obligated to make one more movie for them under the present contract. In the title role of *Mr. Skeffington*, he delivered one of his most sensitive performances, and earned a third Academy Award nomination. Warner Bros. had purchased the rights to Elizabeth von Arnim's novel in

Mr. Skeffington.

I action, Fanny bitterly sobs, "I married Job so I could take care of Trippy. And now Trippy is gone – and all I've got is Job!" — at which point a blast of Max Steiner music underscores a shot of Job standing right behind her, hearing all. Job at last rebels and begins a series of meaningless flings, prompting Fanny to file for divorce. In a stand-up-and-cheer moment, he is unrepentant: "Do you think I ever would have <u>looked</u> at another woman if I'd received one grain of affection from <u>you</u>?" Even though his Mr. Skeffington is the title character, Rains then vanishes for most of the remaining film, relocating to Europe despite the danger there to Jews like himself. The ending is a three-hanky reunion: Fanny, a caricature of her former self, after her looks have been destroyed by diphtheria; Job, blinded by his Nazi captors in a concentration camp. Job will always "see" her as young and beautiful, and Fanny has accepted the truth in the axiom "A woman is beautiful only when she's loved." Fanny tenderly takes her husband's arm, announcing to her servant that "Mr. Skeffington has come home."

Making the film proved taxing for all concerned, because Davis was dealing with tremendous personal problems and stress. A month prior, her second husband Arthur Farnsworth, only 35, had collapsed on a Hollywood street, dying two days later. An autopsy determined that the cause of death was a skull fracture, but nobody, including his wife, could explain how he suffered such an injury. Davis was distraught, and Jack Warner suggested postponing shooting. But like Rains, Davis found working a tonic, and within time incidentally began an affair with Vincent Sherman. Hal Wallis knew that Davis and Rains were extremely compatible and that their two names on a theatre marquee would attract audiences. However, when Rains read the script, he was less than enthusiastic: Job Skeffington was a "stupid man" who let a woman, who didn't deserve his loyalty, destroy him.

His personal derision of the character reveals a serious character fault: Rains' inability to understand human weaknesses in certain emotional relation-

1939, but scriptwriters found the story cumbersome, and the project was shelved. Bette Davis had always wanted to play the female lead and approached Jack Warner, who initially tested Irene Dunne, Claudette Colbert and Katharine Cornell before succumbing to Davis' entreaties. Paul Lukas tested for the part of Skeffington, and even Paul Henreid was announced as having landed the role, but the assignment went to Rains at the request of Davis and director Vincent Sherman. Production began in October, while the actor was still on *Passage to Marseille*. On October 18, Rains reported for work for the new picture.

Screenwriters Julius J. and Philip G. Epstein had changed the setting of the decades-spanning soap opera from England to Manhattan. The saga begins in 1914 with men swarming her Gramercy Park mansion to vie for the attentions of Fanny Trellis (Davis). Shallow, selfish and extremely vain, men mean nothing to Fanny — until her brother Trippy embezzles $25,000 from the Wall Street firm of Job Skeffington (Rains). Fanny irresponsibly makes the decision to marry the sedate, older financier to keep her wastrel brother out of prison. Job sincerely loves her but knows it's not reciprocal; Fanny even continues to encourage her former beaux. The birth of a daughter changes nothing, but Job remains patient and hopeful. When Trippy is killed in World War ships. Job may be foolish, but he is not stupid. Perhaps what Rains really felt was that it was "stupid" to let people see one's vulnerability, the reason feelings were to be subjected to strict discipline and kept secret. After his ordeals with Isabel Jeans and especially Beatrix Thomson, Rains may have felt that any individual who allowed himself to submit to such indignities and humiliation was deserving of them.

The performance is from the heart. Knowing Rains as she did, Davis suggested that perhaps part of his intensity might have stemmed from an incident during filming, when Rains brought Frances and Jennifer to the set. He and Bette overheard a crew member refer to the actor's guests as his daughter and granddaughter. "It was," Davis stated, "one of the most embarrassing moments I ever went through. You could see it was killing Claude…" It was one of the few times that he let his feelings show while working, and he was so bothered that he rarely permitted either his wife or child on one of his sets again.

A major story arc of *Mr. Skeffington* revolves around Job's Judaism. Anti-Semitism was a subject that was assiduously avoided early in the war years by all the Hollywood studios. It was an extremely touchy issue to tackle and even caused the Office of War Information to raise questions about the script. Jack Warner stood firm. One scene poignantly depicted Job's relationship with his young daughter. Now divorced, he tells the girl he must leave America without her, trying to explain what would happen if she accompanied him to Europe — the difficulties she might encounter because they are of different religions. She wants to know why people don't like Jews, and why is there intolerance. Rains is unable to answer. Quietly and with restraint, he simply replies, "I don't know," but the words underlie how bigotry has affected his life. In the face of her innocence and sweetness, he relents and agrees to take her with him; when father and daughter embrace, Rains' eyes well up with real tears.

CR and Bette Davis in Mr. Skeffington.

According to Vincent Sherman:

Directing [Claude] was only a matter of giving a slight suggestion here, a gentle nudge there. He was an immaculate actor, clean, precise, and exact in everything he did. There was no floundering about until he got the feel of a role, but a studied analysis with a design in the background that built bit by bit until the total architecture became visible. It was not consciously Stanislavsky, but he was doing precisely what Stanislavsky had formulated in connection with building a character. [Claude] knew what he wanted and why; Claude had great concentration, knew his attitude in each scene, played *with* his partner, and created an inner life for his character.

He was a professional in the best sense of the word. While he came on the set prepared, he always allowed room for the director to create with him. Having adapted to picture-making, he was aware that the film director must stage scenes with the camera in mind; he was always ready to make any adjustment in terms of

movement and positions.

Sherman credited Rains with "saving my life in that picture," noting that he was "marvelous to work with…. One word described Rains: 'elegance.'"

[Claude was] the kind of person who would get along with anybody — he did his job and never allowed personalities to annoy him. He was so into what he was doing — a consummate professional and a warm human being, too. He knew his lines; he never went to any director and said this or that bothers me. Once he accepted a role, that was it. When he walked onto the set, he would stand still and never make a move unless it felt natural for his character to do so. His instinct was always so right about everything and he never got moody on the set. And he had the irony that his character needed.

Rains received rave reviews and his third Academy Award nomination for *Mr. Skeffington*. Once again, he lost on Oscar night (to Barry Fitzgerald in *Going My Way*). Perhaps by now Rains was practical about the Academy's politics and Hollywood's partiality; but he must have felt disappointed, if not hurt. Then, too, he could reasonably have believed, or hoped, that there would be more opportunities in the future. The movie's avoidance of dealing directly with anti–Semitism was criticized by some: "The dignified, gentlemanly appearance and behavior of Claude Rains as Skeffington are doubtless packed with splendid pro–Semitic implications. But the circumstances seem to call for more than implications, if there not to be left an unsettled and unsettling residue… The subject should have been treated with much more completeness."

The dramatic final scene of Mr. Skeffington.

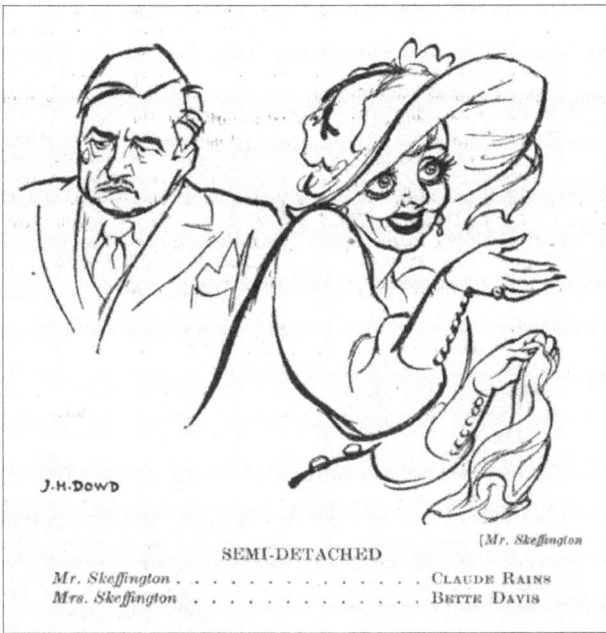

J.H.DOWD

SEMI-DETACHED

[Mr. Skeffington

Mr. Skeffington	CLAUDE RAINS
Mrs. Skeffington	BETTE DAVIS

With the wrap of *Mr. Skeffington*, Rains had completed two of four films required in his 1943 contract. His second two would be at the higher salary of $5,000 per week, and would end his long-term agreement with the studio, initiated nine years previously. Knowing that Warners would not pick up his option — another four films within two years at $6,000 and $7,000 per week respectively — Rains prepared to become a freelancer at age fifty-four. Actually, he was looking forward to selecting his own parts and negotiating his own salary. Within a few months, due to some erroneous publicity and some miscalculated mathematics, he would be known as the highest paid actor in Hollywood history.

CHAPTER 17
The Million Dollar Man

For a considerable time, Britain's largest film studio, the J. Arthur Rank Organization, had wanted to produce a lavish spectacle along the lines of a Hollywood Cecil B. DeMille epic. Not only would such a picture bring prestige to the studio, but it would also boost the nation's morale by giving notice that England was still a viable movie capital, even in the midst of World War II. Because the works of George Bernard Shaw had always been popular with the theatre-going public, Rank decided to film his 1898 historical play *Caesar and Cleopatra.* Shaw had been approached by Hollywood producers on numerous occasions, but the venerable playwright had a strong dislike of the studio system and the way scripts were often bastardized from famous sources. However, a friend of his, producer-director Gabriel Pascal, proved more persuasive, convincing Shaw that if he (Pascal) were in charge, any film version of a Shaw play would be in safe hands. Shaw agreed and Pascal secured the rights to *Caesar and Cleopatra.*

The story covers the nine months that the legendary Roman spent in Egypt, consolidating his local power by setting up pro–Roman puppet governments. Caesar, who at the time would have been fifty-plus years old, enthroned as queen the sixteen-year-old Cleopatra. In Shaw's fictionalized version of their relationship, the mighty conqueror becomes her mentor and lover as he teaches her how to behave with dignity and to rule effectively. With its grand spectacle, it was a perfect subject for a prestigious Technicolor extravaganza. However, as producer-director, Pascal proved to be problematic for the project.

A Hungarian who spoke with a thick accent, Pascal was then living in England. Known for making lavish films, he was disliked by many of his industry peers; nevertheless, by the summer of 1943, he was able to secure financial backing for the project in Britain and the United States, as well as distribution contracts.

Unfortunately, when it came to actual production, Pascal knew little about the technical aspects of filmmaking. He had a tendency to run way over schedule and appear on sets demanding immediate changes long after a scene had been rehearsed and even shot.

Casting proved difficult; in addition to his professional notoriety, Pascal had a sketchy personal reputation as a "wicked old beast," among other labels. Many top artists refused to work under his direction. (Even Rains, who was always careful not to let personal feelings interfere, found working with Pascal difficult and exasperating at times.) Oscar-winning Vivien Leigh, still stunning in her early thirties and married to Laurence Olivier, was selected to play the queen of Egypt who beguiles, as well as learns from, the elderly Roman emperor. Some felt she was a bit too old for the role, but Leigh proved her critics wrong as she created a striking Cleopatra, impish, devilish, coy and charming.

When it came to the male lead, Shaw had always considered Caesar the play's pivotal character and demanded final approval over casting. Pascal first approached John Gielgud, but the highly regarded actor refused on two points. At that time, he was primarily a theatre actor, but he also harbored a low professional regard, and a high personal dislike, for Pascal. Following Gielgud's rejection, it took nearly three months for Pascal to convince Rank that Claude Rains was right for the part, even if it meant the expense of bringing him over from the United States. Shaw agreed, remembering that, of all the actors who had performed his works, only Rains brought enlightenment to his words and seemed to exemplify Shavian wisdom with great skill. Later, the playwright explained: "Professionally, [Rains] is not an easy man to deal with. One has the impression, indeed, that he has never found himself easy to deal with! …But out of his personal and histrionic struggles there emerges a genuine power."

Caesar and Cleopatra.

The offer was made to Rains, and after several delays on the shoot of *Mr. Skeffington*, the actor went back to Pennsylvania to consider it. Several considerations caused Rains apprehension. It not only meant being away from his wife, his child and his farm for some time, but working on the film would literally put him in harm's way. In early 1944, England was no longer suffering from almost daily air raids; instead, it was the even more frightening V-2 rockets, the "buzz bombs," that were causing havoc. Later Rains would recall: "All the time I wondered when I would see my wife and daughter — and if ever I'd get back!" Every promise was made to assure the actor of his safety, but still he hesitated. It was Frances who persuaded her husband, as he later admitted that "going over [to the U.K.] created a certain amount of prestige. I didn't want to go but I agreed with her that I couldn't

do that particular part any place else." Both Rains and his wife hoped and anticipated that *Caesar and Cleopatra* would be one of the actor's crowning achievements, enabling him to command larger salaries in starring roles when he returned to Hollywood. It was undeniably exciting to be in demand by the leading film studio in England, to have been selected to interpret his work by one of the leading playwrights of the century. Frances and Claude could never have imagined that, when Rains left the States in April, he would remain abroad for the remainder of the year.

In truth, Rains was quite eager to tackle a Shaw play again, remembering with fondness when he appeared in *Misalliance* as a young actor in London, a production which Shaw attended. Afterwards, the actor received a postcard which simply asked, "My dear Mr. Rains: Must you be so char-r-ming? Sincerely, G.B.S." From then on, whenever Rains performed in a Shaw play, the great man would inscribe the actor' s manuscripts with a personal notation and his signature.

Because of wartime restrictions and travel intricacies, the British government orchestrated all necessary arrangements for Rains' transportation with the cooperation of the Canadian and American authorities. All was done secretly and took a few months to prepare. Some time in May, Rains was taken to a designated city in Canada to board a British bomber for the long flight to Scotland. From there, he was transferred to a flight to London. On the trip over, he met an intelligence officer, Major John McQuade, who spoke of his summer cottage in the village of Sandwich, New Hampshire. Eighteen years later, they would become neighbors and friends.

Pascal took Rains to his own farm until rehearsals began at Denham Studios. The actor had been away from the country of his birth since 1936, and took the opportunity to visit his sister, who lived in Purley on Velum Avenue. She was then Mrs. H.V. O'Connor, married to an editor of *Punch* magazine. The *London Times* reported her as stating: "We were all ready for

CR and Vivien Leigh in Caesar and Cleopatra.

him a fortnight ago. I was just bursting with anxiety about his visit. He is my only brother and I am dying to see him again after all this time. He is a very shy man, and he doesn't like publicity." The accompanying photograph showed brother and sister arm in arm, but in fact, the picture had been taken in 1936 on the set of *The Clairvoyant*. During the war, Mrs. O'Connor worked as a volunteer for *The American Outpost*, a monthly paper which reported the news to the U.S. servicemen in England.

Later, Pascal took the actor to Shaw's estate, Ayot, St. Lawrence in Buckinghamshire. Entering the house's great room, Rains saw G.B.S. attired in his usual knickerbockers, his shoes off and standing before a blazing fire, poking it. The playwright did not take his eyes off the blaze and there was an awkward silence. Pascal introduced Rains and began to jabber about the film. Shaw shook hands with the actor but then turned away to continue gazing into the fire. Rains was unusually nervous, recalling: "I was terrified by this business of his not looking at

me … I thought he was so disappointed in my non-classic appearance that he couldn't bear to face me." Shaw then abruptly turned around and said, "Do you remember when we first met, Mr. Rains?" Rains stammered that he was under the impression that this was their first meeting. Shaw pretended annoyance: "Oh no! Don't you remember in 1905 at His Majesty's Theatre in London, and a rehearsal of my only verse play, *The Admirable Bashville*? I collapsed in the theatre and a young sixteen-year-old boy — you, sir — went for the doctor." The incident came rushing back to Rains after nearly forty years — he was a teen working for Sir Herbert Tree's company and blurted out to his own astonishment, "The doctor's name was Matthews and he lived on Suffolk Street." They both laughed and Shaw complimented the actor on his prodigious memory.

The trio spent the afternoon chatting pleasantly. They toured the writer's estate and looked over Shaw's cattle, a breed which impressed Rains, and discussed their commonality of being farmers. The actor still felt uneasy because all during the afternoon, Shaw made no mention of his playing Caesar. Afterwards, when Pascal took Rains back to his own farm, the actor commented on his uncertainty about Shaw's feelings. Pascal mentioned this to the playwright, and within a few days there was a letter with reassurances that Shaw was pleased about the selection of the cast, especially Rains: "I remembered him and was perfectly satisfied in the first split second."

Marjorie Dean, Pascal's scriptwriter, assistant and friend (and ultimate chronicler of the ordeal that was to come), was also enthusiastic about Rains' casting.

> [T]he moment I heard the news I knew that there was no question any longer. [Rains] had the quietness, the authority, the humorous touch of faintly eccentric humanity. As soon as I read Gabriel's cable mentioning his name as a casting possibility, Claude Rains, was, for me, Caesar.

Bernard Shaw was pleased and interested when he heard that Claude Rains had agreed to play the role. Shaw remembered him as a young callboy who had grown up into a stage manager of the Tree-Terry productions at the Haymarket Theatre, and later as a London stage actor of some standing. His more recent fame as a Hollywood screen actor had passed practically unnoticed... It was "Ah yes, I remember him well. A very promising young actor..." It was something of a surprise to discover that he was now old enough to play the middle-aged conqueror.

Shaw had been right; with Rains' impeccable timing and dry wit and inner vitality, he was ideally suited for the part. His age (56) and experience supported understanding of the great conqueror's inner misgivings about fame, as well as regret for his failures. Rains had lived, and thrived, in two different eras: the old-world formality of Shaw's Edwardian theatre, and the exciting new world of an innovative film industry. One of the criticisms at times leveled at him was that, on the set, he was "all business," never joking, never sociable or friendly, always quiet and studying. But to observant critics and writers like Shaw and Graham Greene, Rains' diverse characterizations demonstrated a power that emerged from personal inner struggles. Always at war with himself in many respects, he hid his inner conflict; unresolved,

it undoubtedly promoted his drinking problems. The fact that he was able to utilize this tension in his performances was his genius as an actor, as well as his saving grace. This is demonstrated right from the film's opening scene, in which Caesar stands world-weary before what he believes is the Great Sphinx and confesses his weaknesses and self-doubts. Speaking so softly, so seductively, this imperious conqueror is just a man, an older man, a tired man, conflicted and unsure — much like Rains himself.

Pascal was elated with Rains' interpretation, referring to him as "my splendid Caesar," and insisting to everyone, after hearing Rains recite the Sphinx speech before filming began, that the actor was already the embodiment of the Roman emperor:

> His Caesar has recognizable greatness. Here is the small, aging, heroic man, happiest in action and the brotherhood of military comradeship, yet most truly himself in solitude, in the half-melancholy philosophy of a declining age...The whole performance builds up an unforgettable personality. Whether he is gay and carefree, wasting time over Cleopatra's childish pranks ... or reluctantly romantic at the Sphinx ... he is always the same vital, utterly characteristic Caesar, a man we know and can understand even when his actions momentarily defeat us. And underlying everything he says and does is a fundamental quality of humorous resourcefulness, expressing itself in the lifting of an eyebrow, a quickly suppressed grin, a sudden mock solemnity. This is Shavian acting of a high order... I rejoice to have seen Claude Rains' Caesar for its dry subtlety and strength, the curious sense it gives one of a great man's essential loneliness and isolation.
>
> Claude Rains was in the nature of a *sine qua non* for the film ... because it is so hard to imagine who could have played Caesar if he had not done so.

Marjorie Deans kept a journal of the day-to-day progress and of the many problems that occurred. The actual building of the Sphinx replica took longer than anticipated due to the shortage of materials. Rains spent the better part of April and May going

CR and Vivien Leigh in Caesar and Cleopatra.

relations between him and the people he had come over here to work with but it may have accounted for the heightening of his sensibility as an actor in playing Caesar.

Between Claude Rains' arrival, and the start of production, there was a maddening seven weeks' interval through every day of which Rains fretted audibly. Wartime production delays were so incalculable that nearly every picture coming out of the Denham Studios was behind schedule. We were waiting for the release of the big Number Five stage, in which our Sphinx-in-the-desert set had to be built for the opening of the picture.

To alleviate everyone's frustration while the Sphinx set was being constructed, Pascal decided to conduct rehearsals in the ballroom at the Bull Hotel in Gerrards Cross. It didn't help Rains, who was "visibly moping, and protesting that he didn't want to get stale on his interpretation before shooting started, scowled his way through his part in a barely audible mumble." Adding to this tension on the set, the German Luftwaffe renewed air raids on London and the suburbs. Unable to get a decent night's sleep, Rains became even more unraveled. (In London, he had a room at the Savoy Hotel; on several occasions, when the raids were in progress, he slept in the corridor to avoid flying glass from broken windows.)

The first day of shooting was scheduled for Monday, June 12. However, in response to the D-Day invasion of June 6, that week the Germans began their infamous V-2 rocket attacks. The terrifying aerial bombardment continued unabated for six weeks. Rains recalled that the night before one scene, he was unable to sleep. "When I walked on the set, the cameraman said: 'How am I going to photograph a face like that?' And sure enough, when I went to the mirror, I discovered I didn't look like the same person. My face was a tight as a drum."

over and over the script and trying to relax on Pascal's estate. Initially he loved the environment, but inevitable thoughts of Stock Grange caused him to brood and become morose. He walked around rather glumly, tromping through the spring mud outside the cow sheds, smoking his pipe, hands thrust deep into his pockets while he surveyed operations. As Deans found, "He was a curious, moody person, not much in harmony with life or with himself." Moreover, according to Deans, from the day of his arrival Rains was profoundly homesick.

The two people who were essential to his mental and emotional well-being, his wife and small daughter, had been left behind in America, and were the subjects of an incessant brooding homesickness from the moment of his arrival in England. This did not always make for amicable

As director, Pascal's personality did little to lessen the tension. He wanted everything to be perfect, his heavily accented English was difficult to understand, he was indecisive about trivial matters. Rains, homesick and suffering from lack of sleep, was increasingly irritable. Usually, he could maintain a cool professionalism even when things were chaotic. But this was unlike anything he ever experienced. A cast and crew photograph was taken on the set; under each figure, Rains later inscribed the person's name, but by his own figure, he scrawled: "Me in one of my black moods." These "black moods" had serious effects, on his personality and sometimes on his acting. Rains was never a superficial artist and at times, what affected him internally could interfere with his usual exacting control of characterization. Normally he was known for his congeniality and professionalism on a set but working with Pascal was especially disheartening for him. Vivien Leigh was affected as well; she began to argue with Pascal to the point where she refused to talk to the director.

Every day of the first six weeks of shooting was spent on the atmospheric Sphinx set for Caesar and Cleopatra's first meeting. The tension was lessened for a day by a visit from Shaw; he had a healing effect, especially on Rains. However, things went from bad to worse when Leigh revealed she was in the second month of a pregnancy. In addition to being frequently sick, she had to be extremely careful to avoid any possibility of miscarriage. Production now became hogtied by the shooting schedule. Originally, work had been arranged so that any scene of Leigh's in which Rains did not appear would be held until October, after the actor left. This was a financial necessity; under British law, Rains could only remain in England for six months, and extending his stay would result in an additional, enormous tax on his salary — an expense which would be borne, as per contract arrangements, by the production. The deci-

CR and Vivien Leigh in Caesar and Cleopatra.

sion was made to keep to his original departure date, which meant that Leigh had to shoot all her scenes before she began to put on weight.

During the remainder of July, the Memphis Palace scenes were were filmed. The picture was behind schedule. In mid–August, things were further disrupted when Leigh suffered a miscarriage. The loss of a baby would have devastated any woman, and at this time in her life, the actress was already becoming a bit emotionally unstable. Blaming Pascal and his erratic shooting schedule, she demanded he be replaced as director. Of course, this was impossible, since it was he who held the rights to the play. By

"Smooth and satisfying!

MILLIONS SAW CLAUDE RAINS AS CAESAR on the screen. Caesar took many chances—but *not* Claude Rains! A star is expected to serve the best. "I choose Schenley, of course!" says Mr. Rains. "I like its richer, finer taste. I am sure you will, too!"

IN HOLLYWOOD'S FINEST HOMES, Schenley gets star billing. Here Claude Rains enjoys a mellow highball served in the home of screen star Louis Hayward. Both celebrities prefer smooth, sociable Schenley for an enchanted evening.

now, Rains was also exasperated to the point that he was avoiding contact with Pascal. On Rains' own copy of a production still, depicting Caesar's triumphal march into the Egyptian capital, Rains wrote in pencil: "Caesar and Co. enter the Palace steps for last scene ... Just before the take, Pascal said, 'When you make the entrance, think of Mussolini.' Jesus!!!!"

Added to these emotional troubles, a V-2 rocket destroyed part of a set; then the weather became rainy and dreary, forcing outdoor shots to be rescheduled. It seemed to be another disaster when cinematographer Robert Krasker became very ill and had to be replaced. Unexpectedly, this worked out well for Rains. An old friend, Freddie Young, took over as director of photography. On loan to Rank from MGM, he was one of the industry's most experienced technicians. Young, a "first class disciplinarian," insisted that Pascal stay on schedule and stop interfering with shooting. This was practically a lifesaver for Rains, who was sinking into serious depression.

It had now become clear that Rains could not complete his work on the film and leave the country until some time in December. His agent Mike Levee tried to explain to Warner Bros. that the actor now

would not be back in the States until probably the early part of January 1945. Fearful of having another extension tacked onto his contract, Rains desperately approached Freddie Young for help. Fortunately, the British government agreed to extend the actor's visa for another twelve weeks, waiving the additional tax liability because of "circumstances beyond control," and Young promised to move things along as briskly as possible so that Rains would finish within two days of his December 15 deadline. In gratitude, Rains sent Young a stunning 14K gold Dunhill lighter.

When all was said and done, and after nine months of editing, *Caesar and Cleopatra* cost a staggering $5 million, an unbelievable sum for the day. It became the target of severe criticism, lambasted as the largest financial failure in British cinema history. Even the British Parliament criticized such wastefulness in a country at war and fighting for its life. Rains couldn't even bask in the glory of making an artistically successful film: When it came down to it, Shaw's work didn't require the trappings of an expensive spectacle. His plays were hardly known for their action, romance and drama — all essential elements of a colossal Technicolor production involving the entire production to Egypt for the exterior scenes. This added to the expense, took up a good part of 1945, and did little to enhance the film's quality. One reporter quipped: "What do you get for a million pounds in people, action and entertainment — a film that is full of ah-h-h's!" The same reporter went on to praise Rains: "As Caesar, he is worth every dollar of the 15,000 pounds he has been paid, even in these days of austerity. This mighty man, nose and all, is memorable."

To the surprise of many, American critics were far more impressed, calling the film "wonderful to look at," "visually thrilling" and "a colorful spectacle." Adjectives like these were enough to entice an audience now tired of war dramas. The picture did a brisk business, but American audiences didn't share the same opinion as the American critics, finding it tedious despite the sparkling performances. *Life* called it the "Movie of the Week," devoting several pages of photos to it along with the comment, "As played magnificently by Claude Rains, Caesar is a worldly

Caesar and Cleopatra.

man, humane, cynical, and full of confidence." The magazine declared it "a gorgeous pageant in the best DeMille tradition with an added bonus of fine acting and Shavian wit." Bosley Crowther of *The New York Times* acknowledged: "Mr. Rains is delightful ... manifesting with arch and polished grace all of the humor and tolerance and understanding that Mr. Shaw saw in the man. ... Mr. Rains also handles with sympathy and moving delicacy the poignant and fleeting intimations of a middle-aged man's yearn toward youth." Writing in *Esquire*, Jack Moffitt was even more impressed: "Claude Rains IS Caesar. His is one of the finest performances in the history of the talkies...There is power and authority in almost every Rains inflection and movement. His Caesar is a man who is world-wise in the true sense..." Even accolades like this did not soothe Rains: Whether on

hundreds of extras. The film lacked the liveliness necessary to entertain filmgoers. The main reason for its failure lay in the script itself: The adaptation didn't have the panache to "translate" Shaw's witty prose, so effective on stage, to a movie projected on an enormous screen.

To compound the scathing condemnation by both the industry and the government, the British movie critics were overwhelmingly negative in their reviews. Most agreed that *Caesar and Cleopatra* was superbly acted, with first-rate sets, but all in all, it was a "boring, silly film." What exasperated the most was Pascal's totally unnecessary extravagance. Because of the constant disruptions caused by rocket attacks (after Rains left), Pascal had persuaded Rank to move purpose, or because the opportunity didn't present itself, he never again performed in a Shaw play.

On top of the reviews, press on both sides of the pond went completely mad over Rains' fee for the picture. While the figure was large even by Hollywood standards, it had to be highly inflated due to the enormous wartime taxes demanded by the British Government. Headlines claimed Rains was receiving $1,280,000 — the largest salary ever paid to any actor for a single role — and labeled him "the first American actor to receive over a million dollars." Hollywood reporters had a good time practicing their math: "Rains is being paid at the rate of $213,333.33 a month. That makes $7,111.11 a day, or $296.20 per hour. That'd be good even in Hollywood."

The reality was quite different. Rains had worked well beyond the time stated in the contract, time for which he was not paid. Rank had agreed the actor would be compensated at the equivalent of his Hollywood salary for his four months on the film. In American dollars, that $7,500 per week was estimated at approximately $125,000 gross, but in order for him to net that figure after British taxes, the check had to be for $1,280,000. After additional U.S. taxes, in the final computation, the net was only $48,000 for a job that lasted eight months, during which time, of course, he wasn't accepting other work. The actor's returns for the year showed that — after taxes — he made a total of $79,000. Rank itself explained: "If we didn't pay him that kind of money, he would have practically nothing left by the time he had paid tax on his salary here and also in America." Nevertheless, the press played up the figure and barely mentioned the ruthless taxes. It was very embarrassing for Rains and his agent, and both became defensive when giving interviews. No mention was ever made about the fee Vivien Leigh received. As the star of the film, she probably netted twice what Rains did. Her astute agent simply kept the figures secret.

All this publicity concerning his salary had one upside: It impressed the heck out of the Hollywood moguls, who saw the million-dollar price tag without reading the fine print. It also put the actor in a much better bargaining position back home. By the time *Caesar and Cleopatra* reached the States, he was labeled the "Little Caesar" of 1946 and one of Hollywood's "hottest" character actors, with newspapers articles claiming: "Rains now Reigns." Additionally, he learned a very valuable lesson: The next time he

made a film in England, his contract would stipulate that he was to be paid in U.S. dollars instead of British pounds.

It's the height of irony that the next time the press had such a field day with an artist's salary, it would again stir up the sands of Egypt. In October 1959, *Variety* ran this story, and dragged Rains back into the spotlight:

> Elizabeth Taylor will receive $1,000,000 for undertaking title role in Walter Wanger's production of *Cleopatra* for 20th-Fox, first femme star to command such a figure for a single pic. Strangely, the other thesp ever to have received such a salary for a single performance was Claude Rains, for his appearance in *Caesar and Cleopatra....* This previously unheard-of sum was paid to Rains because of the British income tax, so star could salvage the amount of his regular stipend for a picture, $100,000.

When Rains at last returned to Stock Grange in time for Christmas 1944, he had a lot to reflect upon. Meeting Bernard Shaw was the highlight of the experience. However, financially, he had done no better than he did in Hollywood with considerably less stress and anguish. He had lost precious time which would now be added to his "servitude" at Warners, binding him to the studio for an additional forty-one weeks until January 21, 1946.

Rains suddenly became aware of how deeply his life revolved around his wife and child. He realized just how much Frances and Jennifer meant to him. Acting alone could no longer sustain him. He had never longed for wealth; he had all he needed to provide for his family in comfort and security, to send Jennifer to a good Quaker school near home. This is what happiness meant to him. The sole object of flamboyant ostentation he still coveted was that Rolls-Royce, but during wartime, such an extravagance it was out of the question, even if he could have afforded it. Besides, it would have been a ludicrous sight, a farmer tooling around the dirt and gravel roads of the countryside area in such a vehicle. That one symbol of success would wait for a while. Meanwhile he contented himself with a fine group of Black Angus steers just like Shaw had, and a new couch for his grand hallway.

CHAPTER 18
Farm Over Films

Clifford Goldsmith, writer of the highly popular weekly radio series *The Aldrich Family*, purchased a place near West Chester and, like Rains, was renovating his vintage pre–Revolutionary War farmhouse. He consulted the actor on historic restoration, and in sharing information and advice, the two men became friends. Doris Hall, Goldsmith's eighteen-year-old assistant, recalled that when Jennifer Rains was attending the Westtown Quaker school about four miles from West Chester, she would often play with Goldsmith's son. Hall's memories of Rains included that he was always polite and dignified. While he had a good sense of humor and was a gentleman at all times, the actor talked a lot about himself and showed little interest in others. Because of his commanding voice and manner, he often dominated dinner parties, bemoaning that whenever he went into West Chester, it was unbearable because he was noticed and pestered by people. Hall had the distinct feeling that Rains actually encouraged such attention and was feigning annoyance. After all, she explained, he dressed to be noticed, wearing a necktie around his camel hair coat, a homburg hat and dark glasses — very curious attire for a small farm town like West Chester.

The Goldsmiths and the Rainses continued to socialize and enjoyed many get-togethers. For Doris Hall, one incident typified the actor's personality. The group was having cocktails, and Rains was talking with great gusto and precision, gesticulating, paying a great deal of elaborate attention to her. She felt quite flattered that this noted artist would spend so much time with a woman not out of her teens. Afterwards, Goldsmith thought it best she knew the truth, even though it meant raining on her parade: With his understanding of actors in general and Rains in particular, her boss revealed that Rains had been performing the entire time. Goldsmith explained he had noticed that, where Rains was standing, the actor's

form was reflected in a plate glass window — and he had been watching himself the entire time. Though disappointed, Hall wasn't angry, taking the incident in stride. Based on her observations, she believed that Frances and Claude really cared for each other. "He seemed to adore Frances, you could tell by watching them. She was bubbly and outgoing, and he was rather formal."

As Jennifer approached her fifth birthday, Claude and Frances began to think about her education. Neither considered a private institution, nor putting their daughter in boarding school. They considered enrolling her in the country school close by in Downingtown, but their neighbor Mrs. Jeffers, a teacher for the local system, suggested the couple consider the Quaker school near West Chester. As the daughter of a celebrity, Jennifer might feel more comfortable in that setting than being among only farm children. While this institution wasn't free, there wouldn't be any pretension that might have been associated with a private school, and the institution was well advanced in its educational programs. Both Claude and Frances respected everything about the Quakers and were well aware that their area schools were renowned for excellent teaching methods, tolerance, strictness and non-denominational atmosphere. Being an early riser, Rains usually drove his daughter to school in the morning and Frances picked her up in the afternoon. When Claude had to be in Hollywood, Frances – to keep her gasoline use within the required wartime limit – took Jennifer in the morning and remained in West Chester (visiting friends or shopping) until it was time to pick Jennifer up.

Frances became active in the area's social affairs, especially with riding groups and hospital organizations. If anything bothered Frances about her life, it was not detectable to most people who knew her, but according to Jennifer, it was always disappointing to her mother and father that there were no more children. To make up for this, Frances often invited her nieces and nephews to spend summers at the farm. Because he had no extended family in the States, Rains adopted the Propper clan and became quite close to his wife's relatives. Never one to display emotion or physical affection, Rains had other ways of showing he cared. While his manner was cordial, his gifts often demonstrated thoughtfulness in selecting an item that had special meaning for the recipient. Most of Frances' family liked him, especially her brother Walter, and he got along especially well with Walter's son Eric and with Martha Propper Partridge's son Dirk. The boys loved spending summers at Glen Mills and then Stock Grange, and their happy memories remained quite vivid even decades later. Dirk recalled falling off the hay wagon and responding with a profanity in front of a very young Jennifer. Rains admonished the boy sternly but fairly, explaining that such language was not permitted on the farm and especially not in front of ladies. The lad took the lecture seriously: "Claude was always very proper. He may have cursed, but I never, ever heard him utter improper language when women were present." Dirk had made other pleasant memories:

When I was about 14, he and I went to see the movie *This Is the Army*. It was his idea — it was at the Mastbaum Theatre in Philadelphia and Irving Berlin appeared on the stage. I was too young to appreciate it, but Claude — well, he loved his adopted country and in retrospect it was a very moving thing for him.

Then there are other things. He learned about my railroad interest, and if the Rainses had to go to California by train, once or twice he allowed me to plan the trip and book it. I was only fifteen years old. The tickets, fares and schedules attracted me, and he would say to me, "Now, I want to leave L.A. on a certain day and be in Paoli on a certain day. What trains are there?"

Later, when I was with him in my teens, he would tell me off-color limericks like: "There was a girl, and her name was Charlotte. Born a virgin and died a harlot. For sixteen years, she kept her virginity. A remarkable thing in this vicinity."

In spite of my withdrawn ways and shyness, he put up with me and all of his wife's in-laws.

Dirk also remembered that the Rains family was on the local telephone party line, quite common in those days especially in the rural areas where the cost of rigging up a private line was very high during the war. Rains didn't feel there was any issue about being on a party line with three other farmers. The fact that the neighbors might listen in on his "Hollywood talk" never concerned him. Besides, a party line was much cheaper, and that's what was important to him.

All in all, Rains treated his wife's family as if they were his blood. Dirk remembered how his Uncle Claude would talk to him, which is actually surprising, given Rains' reluctance to become intimate with anyone. The boy was pleased by the trust, and never forgot anything said in this confidence between them. "Once in a great while, he would take me aside and confide in me as a kid. He told me when we were driving somewhere in the car that he had taught himself English from the ground up because the English he spoke from his own parents was Cockney. He just started from square one and the English he spoke on screen was not his native tongue. That to me is amazing, that a person can do that."

Rains did other things that endeared him to the Propper clan. Whenever a family member married, he sent a gift; when someone was ill, he sent flowers. He attended the college graduations of the nieces and nephews when possible. To Dirk who loved trains, he mailed postcards from each station as he traveled across the country to Hollywood, adding a few lines of personalization. The youngster felt this was truly thoughtful — that a famous actor should take the time to buy cards, write and mail them. In these little things, Rains was very considerate — in his way. In other matters and especially with Frances, he seemed unable to gauge a situation and respond to it appropriately. As kind as he could be, several family members agreed Claude could also be inconsiderate and curt at times. Sadly, there were instances when Rains didn't realize he was adopting such an attitude, and while it appeared deliberate, it was without intention or meanness. It was just "his way," a behavior not always understandable to others.

The idea of more children, even through adoption, seemed remote and impractical. To anyone who knew the couple, they seemed compatible and accepted each other's little foibles, with Frances continually giving into to her husband's pronouncements. Claude insisted that he seldom did anything without asking her advice, especially concerning his career. However, while he may have asked her opinion, he was the type of man who would not necessarily concur with it. Jennifer remembered one occasion in which Frances told Claude she did not think his agent Mike Levee was effective enough, and that an actor of his standing should be commanding a higher salary than he was. However, money was important to Rains only as a necessity, not as a desire. He merely wanted enough to feel secure. Mike's loyalty as a friend meant more; Rains would not leave his agent over money.

Rains spent every spare minute at Stock Grange, but the couple retained their elegant home on Evanston Avenue in Brentwood. To find an apartment in Los Angeles during World War II was next to impossible, and if Rains were going to spend lengthy periods in Hollywood, he wanted Frances and Jennifer with him, especially in the summertime. Also, because of the severe restrictions on train travel, it was more convenient and economical to maintain a residence on the West Coast. At that time, the Brentwood area was a haven for celebrities: the Rainses' neighbors included James Stewart, Lee Strasberg, Henry Fonda and Joan Crawford. However, except for an occasional hello, the couple wasn't socially active with the Hollywood set; they rarely attended lavish dinners and never went to nightclubs. An evening out meant a dinner party with a few friends and early to bed.

There were comforting little things in their lives, with quiet evenings on the lawn or in his library. Rains enjoyed a pipe in those days, and she smoked cigarettes. If they differed on anything, it was his love for, and her dislike of, classical music, but as with most things, they seldom fought over it. Rains would spin tales of the ghost living in the farmhouse until Jennifer felt she could see it; once he put tacks on her chair but denied he did so, proclaiming dramatically that it was the ghost.

Prior to *Casablanca*, Rains had accepted nearly every role he was offered, but the tremendous recognition he received for that film, not to mention the Oscar nomination, had a dramatic impact on that situation. From then on, even though he appeared in some box-office failures and outright poor pictures, his film career was assured, as well as his status as a top character actor. Studios clamored for him. During the war years, Rains was to make his most memorable pictures, with no thought of ever returning to Broadway; he was content to work in Hollywood, repeating frequently that shooting a film was "intensely stimulating. [The] camera, it's like a gun! It galvanizes you into tremendous emotional and mental activity." With its interruptions and restrictions, constant yells of "cut," scene and wardrobe changes, with endless technical issues confounded by shooting scenes out of sequence — film work was an enormous challenge, demanding much from an actor. Rains was completely able to give it. In 1948, he was candid with an interviewer (although which films he is referencing isn't clear):

> A few years ago, I played in pictures in which I was said to give representative performances. They were both box-office flops, and for seven months after them, nobody in this town asked whether I was alive or dead. Because of that, I have managed to stay normal… However well-established you are, things can happen over which you have no control. One mustn't get smug about it. All you can do is choose carefully, so that the pictures you're in have an average chance of being popular and be sure you have the kind of part that you can make a good job of. To be perfectly frank, I've just got my fingers crossed.

Outside of work, he also felt fortunate in his marriage. Frances had given him something vital to his life: commitment and a sense of order. In the early years especially, her companionship reduced his selfishness and subdued his ego. "Before Frances, I was getting to think something was so untidy in my life, I couldn't find happiness or give it. [She] taught me to say 'we' instead of 'I,' and I had to learn to give more than you take, learn to say 'no' and not being a prey to my emotions…" Frances, he insisted, changed his life, because he had been so moody and mercurial in his first three marriages. In one interview, he admitted going to jail over a fight he had in a rage of jealousy (probably during his marriage to Marie Hemingway). Before Frances, although his life was busy, it was also unrewarding. Frances had the ability to change his moodiness: "Like teaching a backward child to walk and talk, she taught me the alphabet and the ascending steps of happiness." More than anything, she was able to instill in him a desire for, and a love of, a home; to "find a satisfying and at the same time, or so I believe, an uncompromising course between artistic and financial success in my work."

In addition to a solid companionship with Frances, Claude had a deep love for his daughter. It was, he explained, "wonderfully satisfying that I can do for my daughter what couldn't be done for me: the nothing, nothing, in short — that was all that could be done for me. So deeply, indeed, did this nothing, nothing of my childhood scar me that, up to four or five years ago, I saved so hard, my wife rebelled." Even though Frances won a battle over the money, she never won the war and Rains remained unyieldingly tight when it came to financial matters. "He could squeeze blood from a penny," his daughter remembered, and yet he bought her everything she wanted in terms of material things and paid for all kinds of lessons. She could have anything — except money.

As previously mentioned, Rains insisted on having a say in Frances' wardrobe. Claude's taste may have been old-fashioned to a point, but he knew quality; and in 1954, Frances was named one of the ten best dressed women on the Main Line of Philadelphia.) As to his own wardrobe, while on business Claude's attire was always proper — suit and tie even at rehearsals. "My father," Jennifer stated, "was impeccable about his clothes." Unlike many male stars in Hollywood during this time, Rains never flirted with younger starlets on the set. Once married, he was faithful and expected the same behavior from his spouse. He still liked "to look at a pretty face," and Frances agreed it was only natural for a man to notice a beautiful woman. Because of his degree of loyalty, Frances never worried when he was in Hollywood without her.

Exhausted by the experience of *Caesar and Cleopatra*, Rains decided to avoid all Hollywood commitments and rest at Stock Grange for several months. He kept busy in other activities, including speaking at war bond drives. American patriotism seemed to be waning a bit, as European victories increased, so the War Department encouraged celebrities to promote sales. There were appearances in the Chester County and Philadelphia areas: The City of Brotherly Love not only housed the large U.S. Naval Yard, but also several Army supply centers. In late April, the Quar-

termaster Depot launched their seventh War Loan drive to encourage its 9,000 employees to invest their wages in war bonds. Rains spoke from the heart at an employee luncheon: "All of us should get behind this campaign, and with our individual purchases make sure that the national goal is reached. And I know we will."

There was radio work: In March, *Philco Radio Hall of Fame* on the ABC Blue Network, and the CBS *Theatre of Romance* (in A.J. Cronin's *The Citadel*). The following month he was on the airwaves, but without pay and with a heavy heart: President Franklin D. Roosevelt died on April 12, and on the day of the funeral, Rains was at the NBC studios in New York City to read several of FDR's best speeches. The actor's voice shook with emotion. Like many in Hollywood, he admired the late president and had stumped for his reelections in 1940 and 1944.

Rains continued offering his services for bond drives throughout the spring. In May, after V-E Day, he was invited to speak at the "I Am an American Day" rally in Springfield, Massachusetts. This celebration was the brainchild of newspaper magnate William Randolph Hearst who in 1939 promoted a Presidential Proclamation for a day when all naturalized citizens (which to Hearst still meant "foreigners") could pledge their allegiance once again to the United States. Rains accepted for two reasons: First, there was always the possibility that slighting Hearst could result in the actor's work receiving retaliatory pans in Hearst-owned publications. Secondly, Rains took his obligation of American citizenship very seriously; he wrote out his own speech, explaining the reasons he left England and why he loved America. Though lengthy, it is important to quote these charmingly personal words almost in full:

> I have a personal definition for the word "American" – personal, but one in which I am sure you will find an echo in your hearts and minds. American, I often say is the place where everyone may feel at home....
>
> When I was a boy of ten years, I went to work after school hours. Very soon there were no school hours at all, and I found myself alone wandering on the streets of Glasgow and London with no money in my pockets and large holes in my shoes. Throughout this time, I was told that the

upper classes were different — that I must mind my "betters."

Now, here in America, no one can tell my seven-year-old daughter that…. I was always conscious of my "betters." When I first came to America in 1912, I was amazed at [the fact] there were no "my betters" here. I might have stayed here but the first World War broke out, and I went back to join a Scottish regiment, and although by the time I was demobilized in 1919 I had become a commissioned officer, I found I still had to mind "my betters." I went to work in London as stage manager and part actor and I always had to mind "my betters" and I thought of America. When I returned to this country in 1926, I discovered I could say and do as I wished and here there were no "betters." It was in this country that in 1928 I met my wife … a typical American which means she is part Czech and part Jew. In 1935, I went back to England to work, but more importantly to find out if there might still be some latent nostalgia, some feelings for my native land, some reason to remain my homeland. I walked up St. James Street in London and the first thing that hit me were my "betters." I could tell who my "betters" were — I could tell by the way they looked at me and through me, by their reserve, which I could understand, and by their disdain which I

could not forgive. And while I am a rather reserved person myself, I have a good feeling for the greeting that an American gives that tells you how little he cares who you are, provided you are a fellow human being. "Hi ya, Mack" — I could not get back to America fast enough. I could not become officially an American fast enough, to live here not among my "betters" but among my equals.

Perhaps this recital will give you some idea as to why I call America the land where everyone may feel at home. Whether it be Professor Einstein, or a bewildered ten-year-old victim of the London Blitz — anyone with any claim to human sympathy may feel at home in America. That is why on "I Am an American Day," so many of us naturalized citizens wave a little flag and speak little words with a big meaning…

The timing was ideal when Rains' agent found a part for his client in Universal's upcoming picture *This Love of Ours*, which would not require his services until late in June. School would be over, so Frances and Jennifer could be with him in Hollywood at their lovely Brentwood house. Though the role was nothing special, the pay was good: a guarantee of eight weeks at $5,000 per week.

Based on a play by Nobel Prize winner Luigi Pirandello, *This Love of Ours* starred Merle Oberon and Charles Korvin as a Paris couple whose marriage

This Love of Ours director William Dieterle (right) prepares to shoot a scene.

In *This Love of Ours*, CR is a caricaturist who produces this drawing of himself.

CR and Merle Oberon (left) are visited on the This Love of Ours *set by Rains' wife Frances (right) and daughter Jennifer (holding dog).*

implodes over a misunderstanding; Korvin leaves and takes their small daughter with him. Years later they run into each other in Chicago, by which time Korvin is a top scientist and Oberon the piano-playing accompanist for a nightclub sketch artist, the Great Targel (Rains). The daughter, now a teenager worshipping the mother she was told had died, creates complications. Living up to *The New York Times'* description of his performance as "altogether delightful," Rains has a good line of patter for each patron who poses for him (jocular for a stout woman, soft and sweet for an elderly one) and describes himself as "a caricaturist … something of a psychologist … and a bit of a mountebank!" He even spends part of the final reel entertaining at a children's party and plays Pin the Tail on the Donkey. However, the picture was

dismissed as "designed for the weeping trade."

Rains was now anxious for a devil of a good part — which is just what he got in *Angel on My Shoulder*. The picture was scheduled to begin filming in June, but star Paul Muni's other commitments pushed the start date another five months, which meant — if Warners had nothing to offer him — that Rains could accept an outside assignment. Jack Warner saw this as an opportunity to remind Rains that he was still bound to the studio; in order to ensure he could make *Angel on My Shoulder*, Rains felt obligated to sign yet another six-month extension of his 1943 contract. This scheming infuriated the actor, who had been bound to Warner Bros. since 1936.

His consolation was one of the best opportunities in his career. Within days, RKO offered Rains the role of Alexander Sebastian in *Notorious*, Alfred Hitchcock's new film with Cary Grant and Ingrid Bergman. Although he wasn't pleased about playing a Nazi, even a postwar Nazi, it was a superior part in

CR (who often worked with taller leading ladies) and
Ingrid Bergman in Notorious.

what would clearly be a superior film, with outstanding co-stars and a director (of both financial and artistic successes) with whom Rains had always wanted to work. His start date of September 17 meant he would be finished well before *Angel on My Shoulder* needed him.

Just before Rains reported to RKO for *Notorious*, contract issues with Warners resurfaced. Columbia wanted Rains for *Down to Earth*, a musical follow-up to *Here Comes Mr. Jordan*, with Rita Hayworth as the leading lady. Rains had become synonymous with Mr. Jordan just as he had with the Invisible Man; Columbia offered him $50,000 for eight weeks work, beginning in late February. Rains liked the idea — it would be exciting to be in a musical — and Jack Warner liked it too, because he saw yet another opportunity to force Rains to sign another six-month contract extension. He ordered Rains to report to the Warner lot on February 4; the actor's only alternative was to sign. Rains, however, finally elected to end the vicious cycle and Warners' hold on him, and he refused. Rains was determined to leave Warners: Without it costing them one penny, the studio had successfully extended his original contract

by an additional three years at the original salary. It had been a steep price to pay. For too long, the studio had held the trump card and Rains wanted to fold, finally becoming a free agent.

When he directed *Notorious*, Alfred Hitchcock was still contracted to David Selznick. Even though the film was made through RKO in a complex loan-out, Selznick initially ran the project. Both men agreed on pairing Cary Grant and Ingrid Bergman, but it was Selznick who thought Rains was right for the role of Bergman's eventual husband. Hitchcock had wanted Clifton Webb, but Selznick wouldn't back down, making things clear in a memo: "Rains offers an opportunity to build the gross of *Notorious* enormously....Do not lose a day trying to get the Rains deal nailed down." The actor's contract guaranteed eight weeks work at $5,000 per week, only $10,000 less than star Cary Grant was receiving. When Selznick became financially and artistically embroiled in his infamous production of *Duel in the Sun*, Hitchcock was more or less independent of any interference from the producer. Consequently, Ben Hecht wrote the literate screenplay together with the director, incorporating an idea Hitch wanted to use: The hero indirectly forces the woman he loves to sleep with another man.

On the surface, *Notorious* is a sexy spy story following Alicia (Bergman), the innocent daughter of a convicted Nazi who is recruited to help in the American investigation of a group of Nazis sequestered in postwar Rio de Janeiro. Alicia's agency contact, Devlin (Grant), though cold and unflappable, begins to fall for her in spite of himself. The Nazis are suspected of collecting uranium ore for nefarious purposes. Believing Devlin has nothing but contempt for her, Alicia offers to become the bad girl he mistakenly thinks she is and marries the group's sophisticated ringmaster, Alexander Sebastian (Rains). Infiltrating the organization, she is embraced by all except Sebastian's suspicious mother (a superb Leopoldine Konstantin, in her only American film appearance). In passing details of their scheme to the Americans, Alicia's duplicity is detected, and Devlin must make a bold move to rescue her.

Rains decided to emphasize Sebastian's desperate love for the woman who will betray him. Sebastian's politics are nebulous and in fact at times he even seems uncomfortable with his involvement. One reviewer wrote, "Rains comes across as an appealing figure and

One of Notorious' *most famous shots, as the camera descends toward CR and Ingrid Bergman.*

one of the most fascinating and fully characterized of Hitchcock's villains…. [A]ppearing genuinely in love and eager to marry [Bergman] … we can't help but feel a bit of sympathy for him at the end…."

When the issue of a German accent arose, Rains felt any dialect would comprise his characterization. He had not employed a French accent as Capt. Renault and declined to apply German inflection as Sebastian. As in several previous films, Rains' height was an issue; Bergman was not the first leading lady who was a few inches taller than the actor. A ramp and other devices were designed to occasionally accommodate blocking. Everyone else tried to be discreet, but whenever the elevated platform had to be used, Hitchcock would quip, "There goes the shame of Rains."

Sebastian's marriage to Alicia would appear to be the middle-aged man's first attempt to break his mother's stranglehold. Subservient to the powerful and domineering woman, he feels manly and exhibits inner strength when Alicia accepts his proposal. He is not weak as much as he is insecure — short, ordinary-looking and aged in contrast to his rival, the tall, handsome, virile Devlin. Rains portrays this jealousy like a pitiful adolescent, and it's hard not to feel for him. As Francois Truffaut told Hitchcock during his famous interview with the director: "Claude Rains

was undoubtedly your best villain. He was extremely human. It's rather touching: the small man in love with a taller woman."

To his horror, Sebastian realizes Alicia's betrayal threatens not only his marriage but his very life. He turns to the only person strong enough to help him, making the chilling, quiet admission to his mother: "I am married to an American agent." Humiliated, he again becomes like a child; Hitchcock accentuates the moment by filming Rains from above, making him even more insignificant, seeming to shrink as his mother towers over him. Devlin rescues Alicia in front of Sebastian's fellow conspirators, and Sebastian knows his fate is sealed. Rains had always been capable of creating ambiguity in his characters' persona; the audience should hate Sebastian, but Rains makes it difficult. As his crumpled, diminished figure re-enters the enormous house, toward his doom, and the door closes behind him, the moment is full of pathos.

During the making of *Notorious*, word came from London that Rains' father had died on December 3; the news appeared in a few American newspapers. Rains made no overtures about attending the funeral. Fred had shown very little interest in his son; his son obviously, and not surprisingly, felt the same.

Notorious is considered one of Hitchcock's masterpieces, with its complex, psychological undertones in a tightly controlled script and emphatic memorable camera angles. The 1946 Oscar Ceremony was held on March 13, 1947. Again nominated for Best Supporting Actor, Rains was up against Clifton Webb for *The Razor's Edge*, Charles Coburn for *The Green Years*, William Demarest for *The Jolson Story* and Harold Russell for *The Best Years of Our Lives*, the epic drama about servicemen returning from the war which would win seven Oscars, including Best Picture. No viewer, or Academy voter, could fail to be moved by the honest, down-to-earth performance given by the disabled-in-real-life sailor. And no actor could compete with a war hero who made such a sacrifice. Russell was honored with a special award for "bringing hope and courage to his fellow veterans…," and then also took home the year's award for Best Supporting Actor. One writer lamented: "Claude Rains richly merited, but did not win, the Oscar … He gave the performance of his career as Alex Sebastian, a complex man who is both victim and victimizer of the woman who he very likely loves more deeply than [Devlin]."

Cary Grant, Ingrid Bergman, Leopoldine Konstantin and CR in Notorious.

citizen." Lacking anything in common with the industry crowd, he seldom socialized, an attitude which was misinterpreted as disdainful, his personal reserve often mistaken for snobbery. Rains was old-fashioned in his work ethic and often sided with management in any disagreements; he always felt a sense of gratitude to producers and studios for the opportunity to work, and he felt actors had a "duty" to be loyal to their employers. Finally, the Motion Picture Academy has been faulted for "overlooking" many fine artists: the list of Golden Age "never-wons" is astonishing (including Cary Grant, Judy Garland, John Barrymore, Marilyn Monroe and Hitchcock himself).

Following the success of *Notorious*, it's not surprising that Hitch wanted Rains for a second picture, offering him the role of the licentious, sadistic Judge Horfield in *The Paradine Case*. The part went to Charles Laughton when Rains turned it down, writing Hitchcock in a note that it was "not quite my dish." Even to make another film with one of the best and most powerful directors in the business, Rains wouldn't play such a character. He would have to be content with multiple — five, in fact — guest appearances on the director's 30-minute television series, *Alfred Hitchcock Presents*.

While Russell's portrayal was undoubtedly deserving of recognition, there was the undeniable overhanging shadow of politics. In 1996, Patrick Goldstein wrote a piece for the *Los Angeles Times* in which he commented: "In Hollywood, awards are often about something bigger than the sum of [one's] work; they are rewards for good show-business citizenship, symbols of the entertainment community's cozy shared values…" This was a critical strike against Claude Rains, who had never been a true "Hollywood

Work and repairs continued to keep Rains busy when he wasn't making a film. In October 1945, he had a new slate roof installed, to match the 1767 section of the house. In 1946, he redid the barn's roof and had a new split-rail fence erected along Chestnut Lane (using locust wood for the posts). By the end of 1946, Rains took more pride in his farm than in his last few films.

CHAPTER 19
Artistic Freedom at Last

Having explored the heavens for Columbia with *Here Comes Mr. Jordan*, screenwriter Harry Segall, the picture's co-writer, descended to the lower depths for an romantic fantasy, *Angel on My Shoulder*. The clever plot followed the afterlife of a murdered gangster, Eddie Kagle (Paul Muni), laboring in Hell, who strikes a deal with a trustee guard going by the name Nick (Rains) to return to Earth and take possession of the body of an incorruptible trial judge. Unbeknownst to Eddie, Nick is actually the Devil,

and the judge has been a long-time virtuous thorn in his side, his positive influence on crooks and would-be crooks creating a manpower shortage in Hades. Eddie's "mission" is to be his old, despicable self in the judge's body, ruining the judge's chances of becoming the state's governor. Eddie agrees, provided he gets the chance to rub out the former partner who murdered him and sent him to Hell in the first place. What Nick doesn't anticipate is the effect that Love has on a soul, even of the damned. Eddie falls for the

CR and Paul Muni in Angel on My Shoulder. (*Photo courtesy John Antosiewicz*)

Angel on My Shoulder. (Photo courtesy John Antosiewicz)

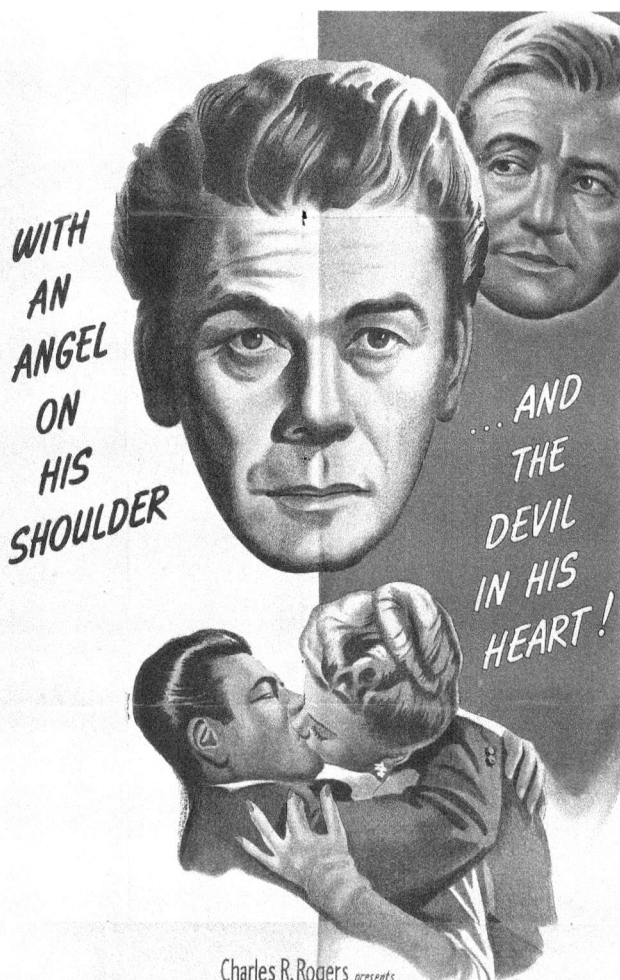

WITH AN ANGEL ON HIS SHOULDER

... AND THE DEVIL IN HIS HEART !

Charles R. Rogers *presents*

PAUL MUNI ★ ANNE BAXTER ★ CLAUDE RAINS IN

Angel On My Shoulder

with ONSLOW STEVENS · GEORGE CLEVELAND · ERSKINE SANFORD
Associate Producer DAVID W. SIEGEL · *Original Story by* HARRY SEGALL · *Screen Play by* HARRY SEGALL *and* ROLAND KIBBEE
Music Composed and Directed by DIMITRI TIOMKIN
Produced by CHARLES R. ROGERS · *Directed by* ARCHIE MAYO · *Released Thru* UNITED ARTISTS

judge's fiancée (Anne Baxter). Instead of the Devil's bidding, he begins to do good deeds but of course, in the rough manner of a gangster, all of which causes great confusion to those who knew the judge before his body was possessed. Realizing what life could have been like if he had not gone down the wrong road, Eddie reforms, nobly gives up the girl he loves, and secures a life free from harassment for the real judge and his future family. The film ends with Eddie and Nick going all the way "down" in a cellar elevator. Eddie suggests a job as a trustee will encourage him to keep his mouth shut about the Devil's embarrass-

ing failure. Nick explodes: "This is sheer, unblushing blackmail!" Eddie replies: "You oughta know, brother, you oughta know."

As Rains purrs through his playfully sinister performance, it's understandable why he wanted the role. Who better could personify the charming tempter, whispering in ears with such twisted cunning, a voice of infinitely fine shadings, making the Devil's arguments sound so sensible? (Eddie to Nick: "You got a way of puttin' things which makes sense … although inside me, I know that I shouldn't follow your advice.") In addition to the plum part, Rains liked working with director Archie Mayo and co-star Muni, even though the latter was a moody and quiet man.

Variety called Rains' delightful performance as the Devil "one of his smoothest impersonations, and he scores solidly.…" When the independently made *Angel on My Shoulder* was released by United Artists in September 1946, Rains' name was emblazoned across three Broadway movie marquees at the same time: for *Angel, Notorious* and *Caesar and Cleopatra*. This caused Bosley Crowther to quip, "It never Rains, but it pours."

In retrospect, these three films, while providing Rains with good parts, a good salary and increasing his prestige with the critics, had come at a cost: the length of his Warners contract. The studio knew the actor would refuse to sign any further extensions, so they decided to use him in one last movie. Bette Davis and Rains had made three successful films together for Warners, *Juarez, Now, Voyager* and *Mr. Skeffington*. The actress knew that once her friend's contract expired, the two of them might not have another opportunity to work together, so in the spring of 1946, she asked him as a favor to co-star in her next project, *Deception*. Steve Trilling remembered Davis insisting that Rains be in the cast. On March 20, Henry Blanke, now a prominent Warners producer, notified Obringer that Davis wanted Rains to read and learn the script between April 8 and 15, waiving any salary for the week. Correspondence over such a trivial matter indicated the standoff between Rains and the studio. Rains could hardly refuse: While the picture was definitely a "woman's film," his part was an actor's dream – a grand way to end his relationship with Warner Bros.

In *Deception*, Rains plays Alexander Hollenius, a world-renowned composer-conductor who is egotistical, manipulative, scheming and magnificently

Deception.

over the top, with his flowing mane of hair, white satin opera cloak and gloves, his fine taste in food and wine, and finer taste in women. His is a grand entrance in the picture, sweeping into Christine Radcliffe's (Davis) fancy rooftop apartment with his cloak over his shoulders, instantly silencing the hum of Christine's guests, commenting: "A party indeed!"

Hollenius' mentorship of accomplished pianist Christine has included an affair with all the trimmings: the apartment, a mink coat and more. When Christine marries an old boyfriend, aspiring cellist Karel Novak (Paul Henreid), Hollenius is furious … and then determines to annihilate either the marriage, or the groom, or both. His offer to have Novak solo during the debut of the composer's newest concerto is the first move in a deadly battle of wits between the older man and Davis, who is desperate to prevent her husband from learning that she was once Hollenius' mistress. The screenplay was written by John Collier and Joseph Than, based on *Monsieur Lambertier*, a 1927 two-character play by Louis Verneuil. The play was first filmed in 1929 as *Jealousy* and starring Jeanne Eagels (the overwrought lead of the original

version of *The Letter*) and Fredric March.

Returning to the Warners lot after a two-year absence, Rains was welcomed "home" by everyone from directors to electricians. *Caesar and Cleopatra* had made quite a stir; Davis plastered the walls of his dressing room with placards and show bills headlining his triumph in the British film. Unfortunately, the actress' personal life was in an upheaval. Just as filming was about to start, she found herself pregnant; her bouts of uncontrolled crying and frequent illness played havoc with the production schedule. She was often on edge, her temper quickly provoked by the slightest thing. Never the easiest actor to work with, she now made life on the set miserable for cast and crew. All this was reflected in her appearance; she looks tired, older, and because of the pregnancy, slightly overweight. According to director Irving Rapper: "From beginning to end, the making of *Deception* was a nightmare, relieved only by Claude Rains' brilliantly exaggerated playing of the composer." Rapper warned Davis that Rains was running away with the movie. "Rains was a prize actor [who] by whispering could undercut anybody! … Claude Rains rightfully stole the picture. It was up to him to work against the dialogue and to make the

A poster from a Hollenius concert (featuring artwork of CR) in Deception.

audience believe, through his jealousy, that they had been having a hot affair.... He worked like ten men in that movie."

Rains, as Davis' loyal friend and a consummate professional, never commented on the many delays, nor did he give any indication he was irritated, even though Bette's tantrums were preventing him from returning to his beloved farm. When crew members shared their disgruntled feelings, Rains would withdraw from the discussion. The picture went over schedule by forty-six days, which enraged Jack Warner, who had only reunited the three stars of *Now, Voyager* in the hopes of a good box-office return. Whatever problems Bette initiated with anyone else on the set, she never fought with Rains. The two instinctively understood each other's temperament.

Problems were caused by the Production Code demands to alter, rewrite or eliminate crucial lines, weakening the script by trying to get across story elements through innuendo. Christine's illicit relationship could not be explicitly stated, and she had to be punished for her immorality (and for committing homicide). The script became a shambles of what it originally was. It was still a handsomely made production with elegant set designs, particularly the composer's home with its enormous master bedroom, and Christine's swanky penthouse apartment, with its skylight view of New York rooftops. To one of his always perfect film scores, Erich Wolfgang Korngold added a dramatic original cello concerto.

Rains played his death scene to the hilt, remembering that even a dead actor can command attention. After Hollenius is shot, he falls headfirst down the grand staircase, lying spread-eagled at the bottom, his eyes open, a small sardonic smile on his face. Rains relished being murdered on screen: "When there is murder — that is where the attention of the audience, every audience member, is riveted. It's a good place for an actor to be because it is almost certain to be the best-remembered scene of the picture and the people involved are usually the longest remembered as well. I don't object to killing or being killed in a picture. It's usually the actor's big moment either way. It's insurance against being forgotten or ignored."

Louella Parsons loved *Deception*, praising the music and lavish sets, and heralding it as Bette's "best picture in years." In all probability, she knew better, but she had a great admiration and fondness for both Davis and Rains. At least she was right in her exaltation over the actor: "What a performance Claude Rains gives as that composer! Suave, haughty, playing with his erstwhile mistress as a cat plays with a mouse. Torturing her with the fear he will betray her to the husband… I have seen Rains in many a picture, but *Deception* is his top performance. His cruelty to the girl, his pretense of helping her husband … are all done with typical Rains finesse. Claude Rains can't be ignored as a supporting star, if you could call his stellar performance 'support.'" She wasn't alone. Another critic wrote: "Claude Rains carried the show. He turns in a portrayal of the temperamental composer who is an all-round practitioner of the art of living … that can be classed among the very best things he has done. His lines and his actions sparkle, and his performance is a tremendous challenge to Miss Davis in every scene they share. For his fans, this portrayal will be a real treat." Bosley Crowther agreed, but to Davis' detriment: "[T]he Mephistophelian performance of Claude Rains in this villainous role makes [Davis] look completely childish and absurd." Rains was pleased. He received outstanding reviews and, because the production had gone over schedule due to Davis' illnesses, he had worked an additional five weeks at $5000 per week, earning a $50,000 salary. He had also often enjoyed himself on the set, despite the turmoil.

Hollenius (CR) conducts in Deception.

Deception was the last film in which Rains and Davis worked together. Over the next two decades, the pair didn't correspond often, but they exchanged short notes, phone calls and visits. Even after Rains died, Davis maintained that he was her favorite co-star. Over the years, both demanded too much from their careers, hoped for too much from their relationships with others, were frequently disappointed and, eventually, disintegrated into ghosts of what they had once been. Fairly soon after the release of *Deception*, the actress visited Stock Grange to greet her friend with the affectionate pronouncement: "You son of a bitch! You stole the picture."

After ten years with Warner Bros., Rains had become disenchanted with the studio and felt an almost desperate need to be free. Throughout the filming of *Deception*, his agent Mike Levee had lengthy discussions with Warners lawyer Roy Obringer concerning the many extension clauses. Memos flew back and forth. In addition, there was the annual issue of whether or not to renew. As Obringer spelled it out for his boss:

> Rains' contract started April 7, 1943, and the seven years will end April 6, 1950 [with extensions and options]. We have two further options under the contract; the first being two years, four pictures, $6,000 a week, 5 weeks guarantee; the second being two years, four pictures, $7,000 a week, 5 weeks guarantee. Therefore, the outside termination of the contract, if the options are exercised, would be November 16, 1950.

It must have seemed an eternity to an indentured servant.

Warner had to decide whether or not to pick up the actor's options at the higher salary. Mike Levee

Bette Davis and CR in Deception.

used the opportunity to address a letter directly to the studio boss demanding his client receive star billing, emphasizing how many other studios were offering major roles to the actor. He noted that the contract stated: "In the event no one is starred, then he [Rains] is to receive featured billing in second position with nobody's name larger than his."

In view of the fact that Mr. Rains has been co-starred with Vivien Leigh in a five million dollar picture, *Caesar and Cleopatra*, and is being co-starred with Paul Muni in *Angel on My Shoulder* in the same size type as Paul Muni, and because it is my intention that I will not, in the future, commit him to any other outside picture without receiving co-star billing, I wonder if I cannot prevail upon you to grant him the assurance that when *Deception* is released that he will be co-starred with Bette Davis and Paul Henreid.

You have Mr. Rains' services for a period in excess of four years, and because his compensation with you is at the very nominal figure of $25,000.00 guarantee, and because I am being offered in three different studios 75,000.00 for his services, and in one instance $100,000.00, I thought it would be good business on your part to agree to this request with respect to the billing which I am making on Mr. Rains' behalf....

Jack Warner knew Rains was very sensitive about his billing and, at times, that factor was as significant to him as salary, so the studio boss wisely told Levee he would "bear [it] in mind," in order to placate him.

A decade earlier, Rains looked younger than his late forties; by 1946, he looked older than his late fifties. Although he kept his impressive head of hair, it had lost some of its wavy thickness, and gray was replacing the chestnut color. The lines in his face were deepened, with bags under his eyes. By the time he was wrapping *Deception*, he became ill due to exhaustion; he needed and requested three months leave. Warners agreed, providing the actor signed yet another three-month extension. This time Rains refused; he had had enough of extensions and wanted to be free of Warners entirely.

This legal hassling became further complicated because Rains and/or Levee were unaware of serious loopholes in the actor's contract. Unfortunately, Rains relied entirely on his agent's judgment and experience, seeking no outside legal advice. On October 3, Rains and Warners agreed to a sixty-day

Claude and Frances Rains out to dinner with
Deception *director Irving Rapper.*

"postponement" of his last contract picture with the studio. Since his current contract was to expire on November 16, Warners now wanted another extension for these two months. Reluctantly, but tired of the constant arguing and needing the rest, Rains signed. Legally the studio had first option rights to sign Rains as long as it abided by the figures stated in the option clauses, which were a part of the original contract Rains signed in 1943. Although his salary would now be $30,000 per picture, that rate wasn't truly representative of the pay scale for stars of Rains' stature. If he had been freelancing, he could have commanded more. Levee had not exaggerated in the amounts being offered the actor, and Jack Warner knew it. The situation seemed hopeless unless Rains bought his way out, an extremely expensive option. All this aggravated and aged him, especially because he had always been straightforward with the studio and expected the same, a naive assumption consider-

ing the nature of the business.

These legal and financial matters continued well into 1947. Rains had achieved great popularity with the movie-going public and outside studios, so timing was a critical factor, especially given that the studios' stranglehold on talent was changing drastically. This fact only made bosses like Warner tenacious in attempts to keep artists like Rains under control.

One of Warner Bros.' best directors, Michael Curtiz also wanted to become independent, but release his films through the studio. Such an arrangement would avail him of Warners' stable of talent, their sound stages, etc. His first such picture, the mystery thriller *The Unsuspected*, was adapted from a Charlotte Armstrong story by Curtiz's wife Bess Meredyth. The Warner Bros. contract actors were miffed when Curtiz decided to go "off the lot" for his stars. First, he arranged to borrow Samuel Goldwyn contractees Dana Andrews, Virginia Mayo and Cathy O'Donnell, but when Andrews walked out ("reportedly because he felt he would be playing second fiddle to Claude Rains," *Variety* revealed),

The Unsuspected.

Curtiz decided not to take the others. Rains was back in Pennsylvania when he received an offer; he responded on November 25, agreeing to be in Hollywood on December 27. Production was slated to begin on January 2, 1947.

Trusting no one at Warners and wanting to be certain of the commitment, Mike Levee demanded written assurance that his client would be the male star of the picture. Warners offered an amendment to the original April 1943 contract: The word "starring" would precede the artist's name but, in exchange, Rains had to agree to a provision that he could be loaned out as a part of his obligatory four-picture commitment. Wisely, the actor refused and demanded a new document. After ten years under Jack Warner's ruthlessness, Rains' professional dedication had waned; he'd had enough of the studio's manipulations. On December 26, he left Stock Grange to fly to Hollywood to take care of the situation. Levee also felt this was the time to terminate the 1943 contract without the extra cost of lawyers' fees to extricate the actor. Jack Warner soon realized that dangling the carrot of star billing would no longer work. On January 2, 1947, Obringer sent a cable to the studio head advising that Rains would not report to a set until something was worked out:

> Re: Claude Rains. As you know we have no loan out clause in contract.... Mike Levee today proposed following in connection Curtiz picture: Give Rains star or

co-star billing and ten weeks guarantee at $5,000 per week. Following Curtiz picture make new contract, basic term two years four pictures at $6,000 per week ten week guarantee and further option two years four pictures at $10,000 per week ten-week guarantee. This new contract would give us new start on seven-year statutory provision and Levee claims Rains getting $100,000 for ten weeks on outside pictures. New contract would provide we can loan Rains' services to any producer as long as we release picture. Also have arranged Rains' starting date on Curtiz picture January 6, 1947. Rains has right to do outside pictures without limitation, radio, stage work, etc. but we have preemptive rights. Please advise your reaction.

In short, this meant that on completion of *The Unsuspected*, Warners' 1943 binding contract would be terminated, on the proviso that Rains signed the agreement as outlined above. Two days later, Rains agreed. Like everything else in his life, artistic freedom had been a long time coming, and then, ironically, and almost cruelly, it happened at a time when Hollywood would soon go through the worst economic crisis in its history.

It been a three-year hiatus since Rains worked with Curtiz; this, their eleventh collaboration, would sadly be their last. Production on *The Unsuspected* finally got underway on January 20, with Joan Caulfield, slinky and sexy Audrey Totter, Hurd Hatfield and the always reliable Constance Bennett supporting. A relative newcomer named Michael North played the hero. With theatrical leonine hair and the attractive wire-rimmed round glasses of an intellectual, Rains stars as "your genial host," Victor Grandison, a sly, grandiose radio performer who lives in an enormous mansion outside of Manhattan. A devotee of true crime stories, Grandison narrates each episode of his popular series in his famously plummy tones — and manages to bump off a few minor players during the course of the movie. The role of the "unsuspected" villain was a delight: When a reporter asked how Rains liked playing a murderer, the actor replied with a smile and a twinkle in his eye:

I think it's lovely! After all, we spend most of our lives trying to be good, trying to do what we know is right, don't we? We try not to hurt other people, or to give in to our wicked impulses. But at heart, we are primitive, like children. Often, we'd secretly like to do the very things we discipline ourselves against. Isn't that true? Well, here I can be as mean, as wicked as I want to — and all without hurting anybody…

In his new role as producer-director, Curtiz was especially desirous that everything proceeded smoothly on his first independent project. Because he was spending his own money (and that of investors), he was extremely cautious and tight about his schedule, which made him more demanding. Thankfully for all concerned, Rains was accustomed to the director's methods and took the high-strung behavior in stride. Unusually, Rains held up filming a few days because he became ill with a very bad cold. Another day, he had one of his frequent auto accidents on his way to work, and while no one was hurt, it caused another delay. Nonetheless, Curtiz brought the production in thirteen days early, in mid–March, then post-preview scenes were added in June.

As was his usual manner, Rains did not socialize on the set, but he was amiable. Audrey Totter, then twenty-nine, remembered him as a quiet man who did not mingle a great deal. She thought Claude and his wife Frances seemed quite fond of each other and got along very well. "I always found them charming people. When I went to their home in Brentwood, Claude would always say, 'Will you please choose a drink?' and not 'What will you have?'" While reserved, the actor had a wonderful sense of humor, but never at the expense of anyone's ego. When he held a conversation, it was usually about his colorful youthful life in England (his usual script). In one offhand moment, Rains mentioned to Totter that he had had such a bad temper as a young man that he once threw a dressing table drawer at one of his wives. (This is reminiscent of the time he said he once went to jail because of his temper — it may have been the same incident. Although he did not mention the woman's

name, it can be assumed this occurred during the marriage to Marie Hemingway.)

In *The Unsuspected*, Curtiz employed some imaginative camera angles with unusual shadowing effects, but there were too many implausible aspects to the plot which even Rains' panache could not overcome. Although the audience knows from the start that Grandison is guilty, Rains gives a convincing performance which critics found to be of his usual high caliber, even if he was relying on his tried-and-true theatrical style. Columnist Herb Cohn wrote: "Claude Rains is the kingpin in this glittering set-up. He is so firmly implanted at the top of the hoity-toity heap that he can even get away with a tuxedo that's a little crushed and a hair-do that keeps flopping sloppily into his eyes." Released in October 1947, the picture received average reviews; on *Variety*'s list of the year's 75 top domestic grossers, it squeaked in at #75 with $2,000,000. The starring role, coming on the heels of his successful string of hits that year, put

The Rainses at home.

Rains on every producer's "most wanted" lists.

In March, Rains returned to Stock Grange in time for spring planting. His only professional work for three months was performing on CBS's *The Radio Reader's Digest* in a fairy tale called "Many Moons." In early June, Warners wired the actor that he needed to return for eight days of reshoots on *The Unsuspected*. Arrangements were made for his train expenses on the Broadway Limited and the Super Chief. Since this request was coming well after the obligatory contracted "one week after completion" of the film, Rains could have refused to make the journey for such a short stint, but the actor was never petty when it came to his work and he wanted the film to be a success for his friend Curtiz.

The rest of the summer was spent relaxing at Stock Grange, a welcome change of pace. He took more pride in his crop production than he did of his films and as he would tell reporters: "I am satisfied here. I take great pride in my farm. We have 400 acres, 50 head of cattle and 50 hogs; raise everything we need…. But I hope, on the strength of these recent films, that some favorable, nice thing will come along and then I shall go back and paint my face again." Now nine years old, daughter Jennifer resembled both her parents. She was enjoying life on the farm, especially in the summertime with visits from her friends and cousins. She continued to fascinate her father who adored her; Rains spoiled her terribly by giving her everything she wanted, including dancing and piano lessons. A neighbor remembered her as a nice and polite child, and added that her mother was more strict with her than her father. As is usual on most farms, there were dogs. Jennifer had her own puppy, usually of a different breed than her father, who kept English Setters. They were more farm animals than pets; Rains never permitted them in the house. They roamed freely outside and had to rely on themselves for their food in the form of squirrels and rabbits, plentiful on the vast acreage. Eventually Rains built and stocked dog kennels with the intention of breeding Setters, but nothing ever came of the project.

In the early fall of 1947, Rains reluctantly signed another short agreement with Warner Bros. — a fifteen-week extension of his contract — simply because there were no other offers of substance and he wanted an income. This time, however, the actor purposely initiated the extension to avoid playing a role he considered distasteful and which he adamantly refused to do; it was the price he had to pay for artistic freedom. Ethically, it might have been the right decision; professionally, it was not. Warners had assigned Rains to *Johnny Belinda*, an intense drama starring Jane Wyman as a deaf-mute girl who is raped. His character, Black McDonald, was an iron-willed farmer who viciously abuses the handicapped daughter whose birth led to his wife's death. Rains felt he simply could not portray a parent who was intentionally brutal towards a handicapped child. After his uncomfortable experience playing Dr. Tower in *Kings Row*, the actor was leery of a role he found personally repugnant. Rains' "bad guys" were usually so suave and well-mannered, it was difficult to truly hate them. Whatever his reasoning, the decision caused Rains to miss out on a huge professional opportunity: The film was nominated as Best Picture of the year, and Charles Bickford, who played the father, was himself nominated for Best Supporting Actor. Because of Rains' refusal to accept the assigned part,

HONORABLE WM. S. LIVENGOOD, JR.
Secretary of Internal Affairs
Commonwealth of Pennsylvania

CLAUDE RAINS
Distinguished Actor

Claude Rains delivers the Gettysburg Address on the spot where President Abraham Lincoln originally spoke those words exactly 84 years earlier, in 1863.

his contract was extended until January 10, 1948.

Unfortunately, there was another lost opportunity. In 1946, Jack Warner had purchased the screen rights to a provocative drama called *Flamingo Road*; but numerous censorship issues delayed production for a year. Originally Vincent Sherman was scheduled to direct, and he, of course, wanted Rains to play the conniving and despicable sheriff who runs the town. The script was sent to Rains at the farm, and after reading it, the actor wanted to accept, especially since it meant working with his old friend Sherman. However, there were further production delays, and Paramount offered Rains an untitled picture which he accepted instead. When production finally did get underway on *Flamingo Road*, Michael Curtiz was at the helm and Sydney Greenstreet played the sheriff — and got great reviews. Rains had now missed out on being in two critically acclaimed films.

As of 1947, Rains still was not completely a freelance actor, but his position was now stronger than previously, and his salary was much greater. The critical "right" that Warners held was that the studio could preempt any outside offers from other studios, if they had a firm assignment for Rains within an explicit timeframe and with a ten-week guarantee of $60,000. Temporarily Rains was satisfied with his situation. Throughout the year, he kept busy with projects that kept his name before the public. One was a rally to welcome the Freedom Train in Philadelphia at Independence Square, where the Liberty Bell is housed. There, on September 16, the actor addressed 5,000 schoolchildren in the Freedom Pledge: "I am an American, a free American. Free to speak — without fear. Free to worship my own God. Free to stand for what I think right. Free to oppose what I believe wrong. Free to choose who governs my country. This heritage of Freedom I pledge to uphold. For myself and all mankind."

Rains took this type of event seriously. His strong feelings for his adopted country were quite genuine, and whenever possible, he contributed time and services to civil or charitable events such as this without compensation. On this occasion, he was rewarded in another way: first by the wild cheering of the children after his dramatic delivery, and secondly by the fact that the ceremony was nationally broadcast. With his thunderous voice, he created a stirring patriotic moment. On November 23, he delivered speeches from his role as Haym Salomon in *Sons of Liberty* for the Philadelphia Women's Division of the American Jewish Congress in an Equal Rights Rally.

This time off offered another advantage; it allowed Rains the opportunity to review play scripts sent to him by New York producers who knew he was interested in returning to the stage. Lawrence Langer remained in touch throughout the actor's years in Hollywood, and whenever the producer was in Los Angeles, Langer, Claude and Frances got together for cocktails and dinner. By 1947, the Theatre Guild was once again becoming active in the revitalized postwar theatre scene. Langer wrote to Rains on November 7: "I have always thought that you would make a wonderful Voltaire, both on the stage and on the screen. We recently had a play sent to us on this subject, and I am sending it to you to ask your opinion on it…" Ten days later, Rains returned the script to Langer: "Voltaire as a part really intrigues me, but this play is dull and it seems to me utterly lacking in charm…" Langer suggested that Rains and the playwright meet to discuss the script, but the actor was persistent in his refusal. "I have finally given up hope of a play this season and so I am going to do a picture. Maybe by next summer an exciting play will come along. I don't think it would be a good idea for me to get together with the author for I have absolutely no sense of play construction. Like some of the critics, I know when a script is wrong, but I don't know how to put it right. If you have the right play, I'd love to do a job for you." In 1947, Stock Grange had its best year of production. Rains could boast that — with the indisputable help, and under the direction, of Charles Brown — he had raised 34,000 pounds of wheat, 1,600 bushels of oats, 2,500 bushels of corn and 80 tons of silage. Stock Grange made a net profit of $8,500, which Farmer Rains used to purchase more equipment and cattle. He did have paper losses amounting to $12,000 which helped to lower his federal taxes. By now the accounting was becoming excessively complicated so he hired Price, Waterhouse to prepare his taxes. Yet to his dying day, Rains always maintained control of his checkbook and never employed a money manager. His salary checks were sent to Mike Levee, who would in turn credit Rains' checking account with the Guarantee Trust Company in New York.

Surprisingly, Rains' financial worth (excluding his property) came down to only $65,000 in government bonds, a woefully small amount given his status. His largest income for 1947 was the $63,000 he was paid for *The Unsuspected*. Even though Rains lived very modestly by Hollywood standards, there were always expenses: salaries for Charles and his wife, Jennifer's schooling and lessons, the upkeep of the farm, the house in Brentwood and of course Federal, Pennsylvania and California incomes taxes.

In the meantime, there was a new film project which would eventually take him back to London. Director Ronald Neame had sent Rains a script for a picture David Lean was directing titled *The Passionate Friends*. Lean's previous movies, fine productions of *Great Expectations* and *Brief Encounter*, had both been well-received in the United States. Rains made sure a condition was added to his contract, that all financial transactions (salary, taxes, travel and hotel expenses) were in U.S. dollars, not British pounds. Never again did he want to go through the financial ordeal he had experienced making *Caesar and Cleopatra*. He was particularly happy about returning to his native country, and the opportunity to show his wife and young daughter the land of his youth. Frances had never been to England and, after listening to her husband's stories for so many years, she was eager to make the trip. Extensive arrangements had to be made for hotels and a lengthy stay; Rains decided to let the English movie studio handle all the details.

Meanwhile, Rains was obligated to complete the Paramount film, shot as *Abigail, Dear Heart* and released a year later as *Song of Surrender*. He left Stock Grange for Hollywood right after Christmas 1947; production commenced on January 5, 1948. Claude and Frances had kept the second home on Evanston Street, in Brentwood; he still hesitated to sell it, since they both liked the convenient location, found the place comfortable and had enjoyed their years there. It was much more pleasant than staying at a hotel or scrounging around for a furnished apartment every time he came west. Now, however, it was becoming

Song of Surrender.

more difficult for Frances to accompany her husband; Jennifer was twelve and attending the Quaker school in West Chester. The couple didn't want to leave their daughter alone (even with a guardian — who would have to be paid), and she definitely didn't want to go to boarding school.

For *Song of Surrender*, Rains received a handsome salary to play a substantial role. He was the highest paid actor in the cast, at $7,500 per week, his biggest paycheck ever for a single film assignment, greater even than the highly publicized and inflated salary for *Caesar and Cleopatra*. (As it turned out, Rains reported for work on January 12 to finish on March 1, but because of various issues, he was only used for twenty days and sat idle for twenty-one. This meant

Paramount presents
WANDA HENDRIX
CLAUDE RAINS
MACDONALD CAREY
in
"SONG OF
Surrender"
with **Andrea King**
A **MITCHELL LEISEN** Production

Produced by Richard Maibaum
Directed by Mitchell Leisen

Screenplay by Richard Maibaum
From a Story by Ruth McKenney
and Richard Bransten

A SIREN SONG OF SELLING ANGLES!
Listen:

It's rich in that basic audience ingredient—rapturous romance.

It's startling in its drama of a wild temptation that whispered to a duty-bound wife, "Surrender — Surrender — Surrender!"

It's scored with enchantment by a new Hit-Parade-headed sensation, "Song of Surrender," written by famous composers Victor Young, J. Livingston and Ray Evans — and sung by Buddy Clark.

It's irresistible as it brings back the voice of Caruso to thrill a new generation as he sings the songs the whole world loved.

Another Golden-Autumn Hit in
PARAMOUNT'S GOLD RUSH OF '49
to add to "Top O' The Morning" and those two big ones from Hal Wallis, "Rope of Sand" and "My Friend Irma"

that he received $75,000 for only three weeks of actual work.) This factor soothed any irritation that his billing would be subordinate to 20-year-old starlet Wanda Hendrix.

The story was set in rustic Connecticut in 1906. Museum curator Elisha Hunt (Rains) is a pillar of his church but a grim and puritanical husband to Abigail (Hendrix), who is little more than a child. When his music-loving wife has a relatively harmless rendezvous with an attractive New York playboy (Macdonald Carey) visiting the village, Elisha foolishly denounces her as an adulteress in their church. When she inevitably leaves him, Elisha goes into a state of shock. Abigail feels obligated to return and care for him, and one day he recovers sufficiently to ask for her forgiveness. When he expires, his death leaves her to follow her heart and make a new beginning with her young man — permitting the clichéd, trope-wracked script to reach its predestined end. *Variety* hailed the performances of Hendrix and Rains, but called the story "drab, melodramatic sub-

ject matter than makes for dismal entertainment."

Unpleasant though the character was at times, Rains couldn't help but see a lot of himself in the well-read and scholarly Elisha, especially the man's views of marriage. Just like the actor, the character was old-fashioned in manners and values. Elisha won't permit a gramophone in his house; Rains wouldn't permit a television, and the radio could not be turned on in his presence. (And yet he did have a record player to listen to the classical music he so enjoyed – and Frances didn't.) That he loved Frances was irrefutable, but it was hardly a physically passionate relationship. Elisha was a proper husband who gave his young wife an allowance and supervised the clothing she wore, as Claude did with Frances. In many ways, this character was a kindred soul, but it's difficult to feel sympathy for such a stiff-backed and authoritarian figure. Rains had proved himself capable of creating sympathy for many of his villains, but couldn't manage it for Elisha.

Immediately upon completion of *Song of Surrender*, Rains returned to Stock Grange to arrange the planting season with Charles. His Paramount contract had been suspended for six months so he could shoot *The Passionate Friends* in Europe. The actor was granted leave on the condition that he again extend his contract for the same period of time, meaning he would still be obligated to the studio until December 29, 1949. Such arrangements made it seem as if he would never become a freelance actor.

Because the Rainses lived near the social elite of Philadelphia's Main Line, Frances was conscious of her position as an eminent actor's wife; she was always a very well-dressed sophisticate. Frances' dressmaker in New York was Madame Pola, the same woman who had recently made the inaugural dresses for both Mrs. Truman and daughter Margaret. For the trip to England, Frances would travel with minimal luggage, so Madame Pola created two interchangeable suits, with accessories, all in black, brown and gray woolens, with silk blouses, one dressy for dinners and the other for day wear. Frances wore them handsomely, even when she and Jennifer went to Paris, where she attended a Dior showing.

Then, assured that the farm was in Charles Brown's extremely capable hands, Rains and his family left for England in late March 1948.

CHAPTER 20
A Looming *Darkness*

Ronald Neame's production of *The Passionate Friends*, directed by David Lean and co-starring Ann Todd and Trevor Howard, had the backing of the J. Arthur Rank Studios. The script was by noted writer Eric Ambler, based on a 1913 novel by H.G. Wells. Neame and Lean had been close friends and associates for ten years, achieving great success together via critically acclaimed films such as *In Which We Serve*, *Great Expectations* and *Oliver Twist*.

Originally Lean wasn't planning to be involved on *The Passionate Friends*. Neame had decided to direct the film himself, and shooting had been underway about six weeks before Rains arrived in the country. But Neame, who had run into difficulties working with Ann Todd, had also made the inadvisable decision to begin with only fifty pages of completed screenplay. Consequently, Eric Ambler, along with J.

Arthur Rank, felt the film should be given over to Lean to direct, with Neame remaining on board as producer. (Lean was, in fact, having an affair with Todd, whom he would marry the following year.)

In late March, Rains and his family arrived; it was a wretched flight over, with a nine-hour delay due to engine trouble, but the actor had used the time to study his lines. Neame met them at the airport. The weather was cold and wet, and Jennifer immediately caught the flu, followed by her father.

The ex-pat actor was home again, in peacetime, back to his memories. He was going to work with exceptional, skilled artists, in a wonderful role, and was receiving a good salary. In a way, he looked upon the trip as a vacation, and in some respects it was. As much as he considered himself an American, he still loved the English countryside, British manners, and Great Britain's respect for tradition.

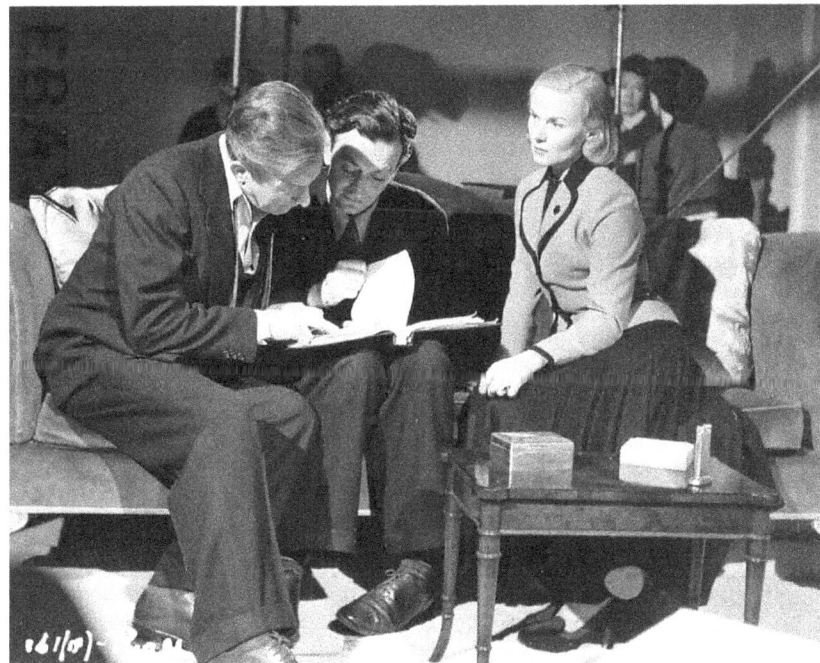

Behind the scenes on The Passionate Friends *with CR, David Lean and Ann Todd.*

The Passionate Friends bears similarities to *Brief Encounter*, a film which brought recognition to both Neame and Lean. Because of this, perhaps, the two felt they could take Wells' complex romantic psychological plot and have a good writer give it a contemporary setting. The focal point is a love affair outside of a stable but mundane marriage, and the woman's resolution to accept security over romance.

Mary Justin (Todd) is the wife of Howard Justin (Rains), an older, wealthy banker and financier, whom she married for security, confidently relinquishing her deep romantic love for a struggling young academic professor, Steven Stratton (Howard). Mary and Steven meet again and renew their friendship on a platonic

The Passionate Friends.

level, but things escalate while her husband is out of town on business. Caught out, Mary plans to run away with Steven. But, coming to the conclusion they can't be together, she remains with Howard, who has given her another chance. Nine years later, Mary again runs into Steven, now happily married, on holiday in Geneva. They spend a lovely day together reminiscing — though Mary can't help but fantasize what might have been. Catching Mary waving goodbye to the man he believes is still her lover, Howard sues for divorce. Naming Steven as co-respondent will ruin the professor's own marriage and career. Fearing for his reputation, Mary arranges one last meeting with Steven, assuring him that her husband has dropped the suit and all will be well. Then she returns home to find Howard alone and broken-hearted. She insists that there is nothing between her and Steven, but Howard is humiliated, convinced his trust has been brutally violated. He angrily smashes a lamp and turns his back on her. She runs from the room and doesn't hear him confess that, in a marriage of mutual convenience, he hadn't counted on falling in love with his wife. In despair,

Mary wanders to the Underground, and just as she is about to throw herself in front of a train, arms reach out to pull her back. It is Howard. She is weeping and shaking; he offers her his handkerchief, murmuring, "It's all right now … Shall we go home now, Mary — if you want to?" The distraught woman understands she is forgiven for her transgressions, and the stoic businessman realizes he is capable of great passion.

This ending was just a bit too contrived and, although neatly handled, melodramatic. Wells' original story dealt more with the way in which Mary's compulsive behavior and inability to choose led to her destruction. But when Lean took over as director, he rewrote Ambler's script, stressing the love triangle. The film creates the impression that Mary is just bored with her life with Howard and wants to recapture the passion she once knew with Steven.

Nevertheless, while the production was sensitively handled, the film lacks clarity. (Flashbacks within flashbacks don't help.) The final resolution leaves one uncertain. Is adultery ever justified? Can a man and a woman have a deep friendship without passion? And instead of it being clear that Mary has grown from the experience, it's Howard who has learned from the ordeal and become a more compassionate person. Whether Mary will respond to his love, we will never know.

As the astute, wealthy businessman, Rains portrays the only character in the film who displays "passion" in a realistic manner. Initially, Howard may seem boring, even awkward, unable to unbend and enjoy the festivities when he and his wife attend a raucous New Year's Eve masquerade ball. Later, discovering unused theatre tickets which confirm his suspicions of her infidelity, his coy and merciless game of cat and mouse with the lovers is a masterwork of underplay. According to Lean:

> I wanted the scene played very coldly. Claude had learned it on the boat [*sic*] coming over and he was word perfect.... I was scared stiff – my first encounter with a Hollywood star. Here I was telling this great actor what to do. I said, "You're having them on toast. You've got them where you want them. It's a rather sadistic scene. You are, in a way, being very cruel. The wife gets it, the lover doesn't. It's got to be played in quite a different way."

But through the action, he is transformed into a man of enormous feeling, whose true love for his wife surprises even him. Perhaps there was some genuine personal feeling underneath the performance. After three divorces, Rains was extremely sensitive on the subjects of marriage and fidelity. Howard Justin on surface seems a cold-hearted man, but he wants everything for his wife, and, although not demonstrative about his feelings, he does love her. In a way, Rains was exactly the same: He could be very formidable and seldom physically demonstrated his feelings. Stifled in his youth, denied parental affection in his formative years, the only way he could show how he felt as an adult was in the form of gift-giving. Then, too, in the British tradition, Rains learned to maintain a "stiff upper lip." At age 58, as one reporter put it, "[h]is face showed the expressive lines of a man who had been an actor all his life, and when he enjoyed a conversation, he would put the same great intensity into a discussion, using his facial gestures and his eager voice to great dramatic effect." Because of this, when he was not on stage, his approach was misinterpreted as "acting" or putting on a show. Few people could know this was his manner at home and even with friends.

Lean had enormous admiration for Rains long before he met the actor, and after working with him, developed a deep affection. In later years, he lamented not using Rains in more of his pictures. "I loved Claude. He was one of the very special people in my life," he told film historian Kevin Brownlow. "Claude always amused me because he carried timing to an almost absurd degree. You can almost put a Claude Rains scene to numbers: 'Yes,' pause of one, two, three, 'I'm not so sure.' Cross legs, two, three. 'What do you think?' And so on. It was that sort of technique, which is the basic technique of all acting, whatever anybody likes to say. You ain't got timing, you ain't got anything. It's tremendously important. I go in for it a lot myself."

Neame concurred:

> When you are a great and consummate film actor, which Claude became, it is something you see *behind* the eyes; it is something you see that isn't really a positive expression that is being used — you see some kind of truth behind the eyes .... [Claude] always wanted to be the center of attention and like most great actors he did have a very large ego, but he also had humility. In other words, his ego was large, but his sensibility and his understanding of not being arrogant but being receptive.... Sometimes actors with big egos can't take direction.

When working, Rains was extremely strict with himself, turning down any invitations to parties and all social activities, instead concentrating on his script. Then on weekends, he would go off with Frances to the countryside. As was his practice in Hollywood, Rains refused to see the day's rushes, believing that if he were pleased with his performance, he might get lazy with his characterization. *The Passionate Friends* was completed in fifteen weeks; Rains worked during April and May.

Rains loved his daughter deeply and when he was not talking about himself, he always talked of her. According to Neame: "When she was back in Pennsylvania, presumably at boarding school, Rains wanted to send or take her back a present and I remember we drove him something like 40 or 50 miles to a place that had antique spinets and clavichords. The love and care he put into choosing this gift he

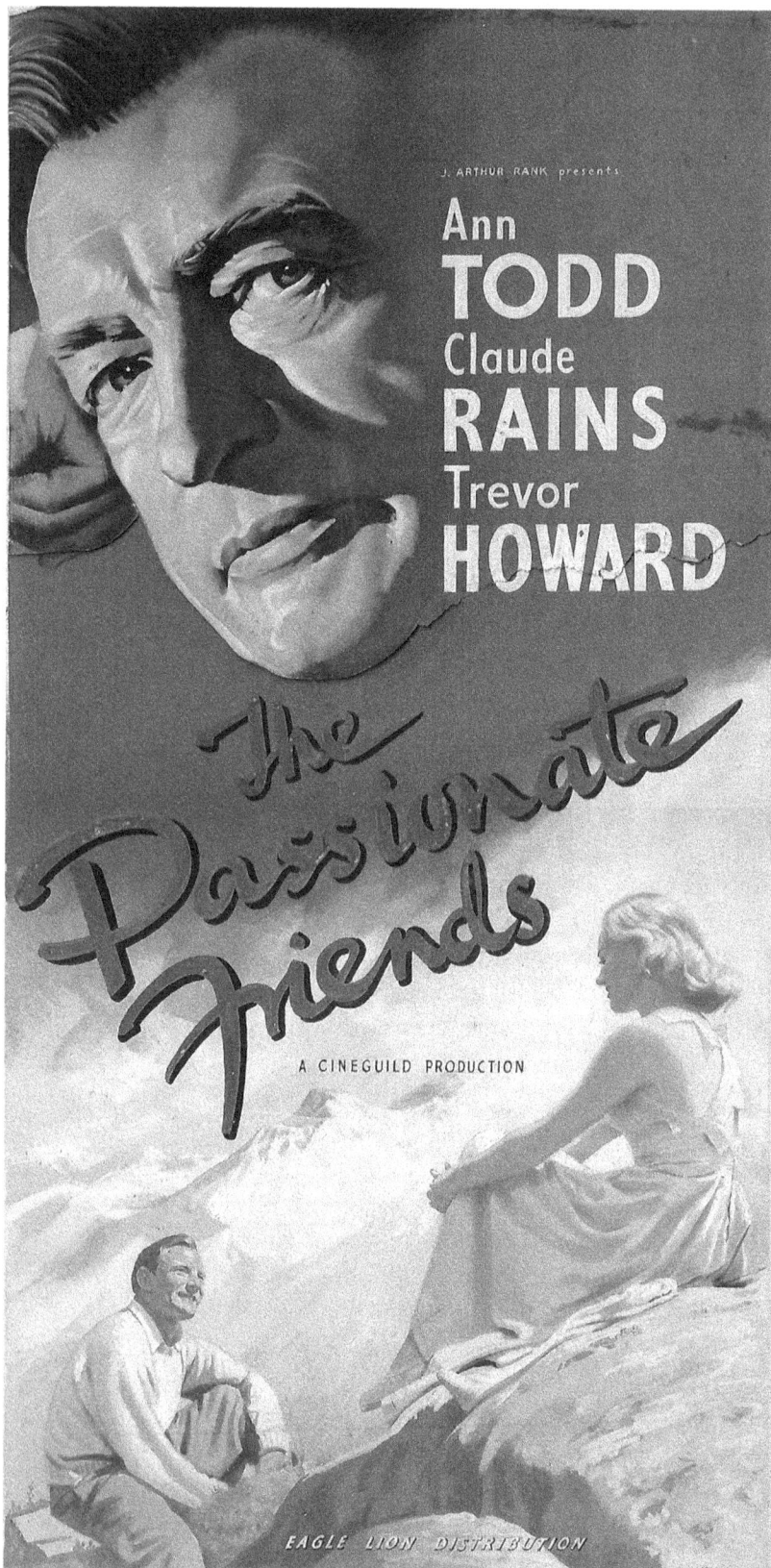

J. ARTHUR RANK presents

Ann
TODD
Claude
RAINS
Trevor
HOWARD

The Passionate Friends

A CINEGUILD PRODUCTION

EAGLE LION DISTRIBUTION

According to Neame, "Claude was always very, very friendly, and in the case of my wife and me, sometimes he would let his hair down. He did drink quite heavily … and we got along well simply because we both enjoyed a drink together, but he never, never went too far. He was a discreet drinker." Afterwards, whenever Neame was in New York or Hollywood, he and the Rainses got together, but oddly, the producer was never invited to Stock Grange.

In early May, after Jennifer went home to Pennsylvania to return to school, Claude and Frances spent several enjoyable weekends on short motoring excursions, especially around the countryside of the Cotswolds. These were pleasant trips (except for the actor's terrifying driving), but although both enjoyed themselves, they were anxious to return to the States. This they did in June, crossing over on the *Queen Mary*.

During the remainder of 1948 and well into 1949, Claude was active in radio as much as possible. He created his own NBC series, *Presenting Claude Rains*, in which he recited famous stories about historical figures. Broadcast weekly, the show was scheduled in a terrible time slot — 3:30 in the afternoon — just when many mothers were listening to the soaps. Rains' delivery of the monologues was intensely dramatic, and the show was well-received by the trades; nevertheless, *Presenting Claude Rains* had a limited audience and failed to attract a sponsor. NBC carried it by using the ad time to call attention to other network programs. As good as it was, without a sponsor the network had to cancel it.

The Passionate Friends was released in London in late January 1949. Generally, the English critics found the film fairly credible, if only because of the excellent acting, and Rains received good notices: "Claude Rains, with his calm deliberation and his slow, enigmatic smile … came across well as the banker. [He] hammers home with beautiful timing, every chance the script gives him." Another reviewer faulted the script, but not the actor: "Mr. Claude Rains is forced by the plot into melodramatic

wanted to send her was really quite moving in itself." Neame also stated he could see the "obvious" affection Claude and Frances had for each other. He befriended both and remained friends with each even after they were divorced.

attitudes and sustains them with authority," referring to the actor as "that powerful little giant…" It was not until the spring of 1949 that the film was scheduled for release in the United States. Rains had promised to attend the New York premiere but couldn't because he had to undergo another emergency hernia operation. Rains was embarrassed about the "location" of the injury and requested that the PR people state he underwent "abdominal surgery." This was his second hernia repair in ten years, and as before, he was ordered to spend at least six weeks in recuperation. Even during his surgical recovery, if the telephone didn't ring with a call from his agent, he became agitated.

Early in 1948, Warner Bros. had contemplated producing a full-length film of Sidney Kingsley's stage hit *The Patriots*. Kingsley wanted Rains for the role of Alexander Hamilton. While nothing came of that project, Kingsley used the opportunity to call the actor and invite him and Frances to spend a weekend at the playwright's Oakland, New Jersey home. Kingsley presented his idea for a new play based on Arthur Koestler's acclaimed novel *Darkness at Noon*. Rains showed some interest and agreed to read the script when it was ready. Rains stated honestly and bluntly that he was frightened, having been away from the stage for so long, and hesitant to leap into just any production. He remained in contact with Kingsley about the project, reading the book several times while remaining busy with radio and recording work. Stage actors are accustomed to being left hanging by excited producers, brandishing carrots of promised work, when no show ever materializes.

One of Claude's friends, a Chester County neighbor named Harl McDonald, was the manager of the Philadelphia Orchestra. McDonald suggested the actor consider performing some recitations in conjunction with renowned conductor Eugene Ormandy, under whose baton the orchestra had earned a reputation as one of the world's finest. Ormandy was currently preparing the premiere of Aaron Copland's "Lincoln Portrait" and McDonald persuaded Rains to read the president's speeches. The program was scheduled for the nights of October 15 and 16; guest artist Rains performed without a fee so that all proceeds went to the benefit of the orchestra. Rains loved classical music; several of his friends, such as McDonald, were active in this field. As usual, the actor scored a big hit with both the audience and the

musicians — so much so that he was invited back for another performance of *Lincoln* the following April. During the October performance, a bad cold forced Rains to use a microphone, but critics praised both events: "Mr. Rains spoke the words of the Great Emancipator with impressive dignity and well calculated reserve." He performed a second time at the Philadelphia Academy of Music on November 14 in a Theatre Guild production of *Valley Forge*, which was carried on the airwaves. Portraying George Washington during the winter ordeal at Valley Forge in 1777-78, Rains told a reporter: "This play could not be more timely coming so close to Armistice Day. And I am proud and happy to portray the role of General Washington. It is a part into which I can inject my sincerest characterization of a great man." (For all his patriotism and strong feelings for his adopted country, Rains did maintain many ingrained British traits, such as a love of tweeds, the smoking of a clean pipe, enjoying kippers for breakfast, a good cup of tea and, above all, refraining from ever displaying one's feelings.)

That fall and early winter, Rains was busy working on the farm, but he also had time for reflection. He was both fascinated and frightened by how quickly his daughter was growing up, and that within a decade she would be going out on her own. He confessed to an interviewer: "When my daughter says 'Goodbye' to me, I shiver all over — isn't that awful? Hate to see the dark come. Love my life so… I love the minutes of my days shared, as they are, with those I love, filled as they are, with things I love to do."

While he loved being at Stock Grange, the actor was restless to get back into harness. He still read most plays sent to him but remained most interested in Sidney Kingsley's project. He waited for the playwright to contact him again.

By now, Rains' professional relationship with Warner Bros. had taken on a distinctive and familiar pattern. The studio would assign him to a project, anticipating he would, in all likelihood, refuse it. In that way, the studio could then extend his contractual obligations to make other movies. In mid–November 1948, Rains received notice for a picture called *Task Force*, commencing later in the month. The role was wrong for him and he asked to be excused. This time, the studio only wanted to be due three movies instead of four, strongly indicating a desire to reduce ties with the actor and that they probably had no intention of picking up future options at a higher salary. This could not have been a surprise to Rains, who had not worked for them since *The Unsuspected* in 1947.

Although Rains was working steadily, his annual income never exceeded $120,000. His 1948 taxable income was $118,795 and even with the farm loss of $9,090, there was $39,000 due to the IRS. In preparing the annual tax forms, his accountant attempted to deduct everything possible, including the cost of taking Jennifer and Frances to England, which the IRS did not allow. (One expense that was permitted: the $1,400 wardrobe he purchased in London for *The Passionate Friends*: three suits, two coats and a large number of shirts. In this way, each year Rains maintained a limited but updated tax-deductible wardrobe as long as he wore the clothes in his films.) Even though the farm's yields were increasing, commodity market prices were lower. There were constant expenses: a new pick-up baler for $2,400; the pond cleaned and repaired for $625, replenishment of his cattle with the purchase of fifty-four steers at $6,500. Buying such items for the farm gave him pleasure.

His stringent and frugal attitude never wavered. He controlled the checkbook, giving Frances a $500 per month allowance to run the house. (There were few food expenses since everything came from the farm.) In 1948, he owned an old Ford convertible, an old Ford station wagon, and a used Jeep with a snowplow. He finally sold the 1941 Buick station wagon which had taken them all through the back roads of Chester County during the war.

To further supplement his income as well as to keep busy while waiting for the right play to come along, Rains made his first vinyl recordings. The set of 45 rpm records on the Capitol label, *Bible Stories for Children*, were five-minute tales from the Old Testament. The albums sold over 44,000 copies, but Rains only netted $2,670 in royalties.

Then Hal Wallis, who by this time was independently producing for Paramount, offered his favorite character actor a decent part in his next project, *Rope of Sand*, starring a relative newcomer of growing popularity, Burt Lancaster. Without any wrangling, Warner Bros. released Rains to make the film. Until just days before the start of *Rope of Sand* production, Kirk Douglas was set to co-star. When he bowed out to fulfill another commitment, he was replaced by Paul Henreid; Henreid's addition to a cast that already included Rains and Peter Lorre practically

The cast of Rope of Sand *clockwise from top: CR, Paul Henreid, Corinne Calvet and Burt Lancaster.*

made *Rope of Sand* a *Casablanca* reunion. Shooting began at Paramount on January 24, 1949, with Rains scheduled to work ten weeks at $6,000 per week — a salary larger than Burt Lancaster's. Director William Dieterle also did a lot of shooting in the desert outside of Yuma, Arizona; luckily for Rains, who never liked working outside the studio, most of his scenes were shot on sound stages.

As described by film expert Richard Heft: "In *Rope of Sand*, Rains is given the opportunity of a reunion with two of his co-stars from *Casablanca* (Paul Henreid as a sadistic mining industry cop and Peter Lorre as a philosopher-diamond fence), but it's really just another acting exercise as a high-status villain in a perfect tuxedo, as the wealthy head of a diamond mine, whose scruples are flexible — another paycheck job. However, Rains purring slyly at starlet Corinne Calvet is reason enough to spend 90 minutes of viewing time."

In the thin storyline, set in a stretch of South African desert owned by the Colonial Diamond Co., where diamond fields lie just beneath the sand, pretty much everyone involved is in search of a famous diamond shipment, cached by Lancaster some years

her unless he pays up. Amused — and impressed by her panache — he offers her a job: masquerade as the daughter of a company stockholder, make Lancaster fall in love with her, and find out where the diamonds are hidden. The interplay between Calvet and Rains is fun and sexy. Lighting a cigarette, she accepts his proposal and slips into his lap, inquiring if he wants to kiss her. Rains purses his lips as he mulls over the proposition, but oh-so-reluctantly demurs. Unknown to anyone but Wallis, Calvet had performed these antics in her screen test. She decided to incorporate them into the scene, and neither director Dieterle nor Rains had any idea she was going to slide over the back of the sofa directly into the actor's lap. Looking back on the filming, the actress recalled: "He was astonished — he didn't expect it, but the director also liked it very much and after three takes it was filmed."

Calvet described Rains as: "always polite. He was one of the few actors who didn't flirt or make any advances — the only leading man who never did. It was magic when we worked together…he was marvelous." She continued:

> He was sweet. It was my first American film and he kinda let me know after every take whether he liked it or not — with his eyes — like a glint in his eyes. He would wink, but it was a Claude Rains wink. If you didn't look for it, you wouldn't notice it. If he didn't like it, he'd keep his eyes straight.
>
> He was a man to himself. He considered himself a very sophisticated man in a way, and here I was this young, French, gorgeous thing who was the leading lady. …He didn't make any jokes. Very professional.

Reviews for his performance were classic Claude Rains: "Rains is smooth and silky as the agile conspirator" and "There is no actor who can surpass Rains at smiling wickedness."

Rope of Sand.

back. Lancaster is the one person who knows its location, but a deluxe beat down by police commandant Henreid and his men doesn't loosen his tongue. Also ineffective are the feminine wiles of a sexy lass (Calvet) turned loose on Lancaster by diamond company manager Rains. But Rains has more tricks up his sleeve: As Thomas M. Pryor wrote in his *New York Times* review, Rains "is artfully sinister in fanning the hatred between [Lancaster and Henreid]. Like a master puppeteer, he twists them this way and that, but always contrives to separate them short of killing each other until such a development best serves his own selfish purpose."

Hal Wallis had selected Calvet, a seductive young French brunette who resembled, and whom he billed as the successor to, Rita Hayworth. Early in the picture, she attempts to extort Rains by snaking her way into his hotel room, then tearing her own dress and announcing she will claim he attacked

Corinne Calvet and CR in Rope of Sand.

At last, Warners decided to take action regarding Rains' contract. The situation was becoming very trying for both parties; it was time for the long association to come to an end. A mutual agreement containing a legal release was drawn up to terminate it. On March 17, 1949, it was signed, and the amazing association between Warner Bros. and Claude Rains came to a cordial conclusion.

Now the actor was truly a free agent, but this freedom had come quite late in his career and at nearly 60, Rains found himself in an era with new young directors, hot new leading men and women, and postwar audiences wanting something different. The studio system and what had been the "Golden Age of Hollywood" were "gone with the wind." It was not just changing social attitudes, but also the growing competition of television, which was having a solid, advancing impact on movie-going. An actor like Rains — suave, sophisticated, with precise timing and clipped pronunciation — was, to some degree, out of step with the approaching 1950s.

It was at this time that RKO offered the actor a contract for three films. While his weekly salary remained the same $5,000, the length of hire was extended to a guaranteed ten weeks. There were other compensating factors, such as the enticement that the first project would be shot on location in the beautiful area of Chamonix, France, near Mont Blanc, with the studio paying all expenses, including a ticket for Frances.

The first project was *The White Tower*, based on a 1945 novel by James Ramsey Ullman. RKO had paid $175,000 for the screen rights to this mountain-climbing adventure story back in 1946, when it was still scaling the New York bestseller lists. The company's initial plans were for Ullman to script and Edward Dmytryk to produce and direct in the French Alps. But when Dmytryk ran afoul of the House Un-American Activities Committee, RKO fired him and abandoned their plans for the picture. Then, a year and a half later, the project was resurrected by producer Irving Allen and actor Franchot Tone, who proposed to shoot it independently for RKO. Tone also intended to play the role ultimately played by Rains. The new director was Ted Tetzlaff, who Rains would have remembered as the director of photography on *Notorious*. The studio assembled a large and impressive veteran cast: in addition to Rains, Glenn Ford, Oscar Homolka, Sir Cedric Hardwicke and Lloyd Bridges, and a new starlet, Italian actress Valli.

In mid–July 1949, with Jennifer off to summer camp, Claude and Frances sailed on the *Queen Mary*; Glenn Ford refused to fly and therefore most of the cast were sent over on the grand liner.

The film begins in a Swiss village where a young woman (Valli) is under a compulsion to climb the White Tower, the mountain on which her father died attempting to be the first to attain the peak. She assembles a veritable United Nations of a climbing party comprised of happy-go-lucky American loafer Ford, French author Rains, English doctor Hardwicke, Swiss guide Homolka – and German Bridges, who wears his Nazi past on his sleeve. During the ascent, a "World War II in miniature" develops.

The cast of The White Tower *en route to location in France: CR, Valli, Glenn Ford and Lloyd Bridges.*

Rains' character Paul Delambre is an alcoholic novelist afflicted with writer's block and married to a cold and catty wife (June Clayworth) who despises her husband's intellectualism. The script even gives us a hint that Paul is impotent when she drones, "Do you think you will 'come alive again,' as you call it, by breaking your neck on a mountain?" During the climb, he develops mountain sickness which he combines with drinking until he is in a complete stupor. Left behind to rest by the other climbers, he finishes his novel in his tent, carries the manuscript outside into the teeth of a fierce snowstorm, tears it up and willfully wanders away to perish in the cold. *The New York Times'* Bosley Crowther called Rains' character "a garrulous weakling" and "something of a bore."

The film script fell quite short; Lloyd Bridges remembered that "as a result, everyone went their own way with their parts." Most medium shots of the actors making their way up the mountainside were shot back in the studio and completely lack authenticity. Additionally, it was totally implausible that men the age and physical condition of Rains, Hardwicke and

Homolka would even have attempted, let alone been capable of, making such a challenging and dangerous assent. (For any rigorous on-screen athletics, Rains' stand-in, Leo Snell, took over.) Despite the fact that Bridges had been in the business for some 15 years, he recalled being overcome at performing with his

Lloyd Bridges, Oscar Homolka, Valli, Glenn Ford, Cedric Hardwicke and CR prepare to make a vertical ascent in The White Tower.

The White Tower.

veteran colleagues. He discussed theatre with Rains, of whom he was in awe, describing the actor as "a classic gentleman" and Frances as "attractive and charming.... Claude was very concerned about how he appeared on camera, and he was very pleasant to work with — always had a gleam in his eye."

Chamonix was a glorious place to be on location. Rains reported for work on August 10, sporting a handsome Vandyke beard which he had started to grow back in June. After so much time on the farm, he was in good health, eyes sparkling, complexion ruddy. The movie was melodramatic nonsense, but doing it meant a nice vacation in the Swiss Alps and $50,000 in the bank. When not shooting, Rains hunted around the small villages for antiques. A "Just for *Variety*" column reported that on an RKO *White Tower* set, "I found Claude Rains champing at the bit to get back to his Bucks County farm and try out a newfangled corn picker." Rains was especially interested in old farm implements: In addition to the corn picker, he purchased a primitive wooden plow which he found on a farm near Chamonix. He intended to

hang it over his fireplace, but it never found its way there. This impulsive and sometimes excessive antique-buying became habitual. The actor considered himself quite an expert, but while he was somewhat knowledgeable about American antiques of the Colonial period, more often than not the price he paid was exorbitant. He would never stoop to bargaining, which he felt was beneath his dignity.

By mid–October, Claude and Frances had returned to the States. Because Rains was now spending so little time in Hollywood, his accountant advised the actor to sell his Brentwood house and avoid California property taxes. During his absence, Rains had rented the place to his colleague Richard Widmark; Widmark expressed interest in buying and a sale was concluded, at a substantial profit. Rains spent some of the proceeds on more steers for the farm.

With the realization that within a month he would be sixty, Rains decided to make formal arrangements for financial security for his wife and daughter. His major concern was establishing a trust fund for Jennifer. His good friend and lawyer in Philadelphia, Judge Nochem S. Winnett, reassured Rains this was a sensible plan, even though Frances did not seem the type of woman to take advantage. Rains also expressed the wish that, if he should die first, Frances should not hesitate to marry again. While there was no longer a deep or profound emotional attachment, Claude always assumed Frances maintained a loyalty and integrity in the marriage. Giving his widow "permission" to marry again is quite Victorian, but also quite in character. In fact, Rains was in good health and the prospect of his advancing years didn't seem to concern him.

In 1948, Rains took an inventory of his estate. The farm and all of its property was valued at about $150,000. There were annuities to the value of $160,000, life insurance of $48,000, $80,000 in government bonds and $50,000 in cash. Comfortable, but even by 1949 standards, Rains was far from rich given his reputation as "a Hollywood star" and the amount of work he had done through the years. Nevertheless, many people assumed the actor was wealthy, an error he did nothing to correct. Money to him was not about accumulating wealth for its own sake or for material possessions; it was a matter of security. He needed to know he would have an income no mat-

CR's character tears up his manuscript before perishing in a blizzard in The White Tower.

ter what happened. This was his reason for investing in annuities for both himself and Frances. Annuities were the main financial instrument of security in those days when there were no IRAs, 401(k)s or other such plans. When it came to finances, Rains gave his wife's input little consideration. His neighbor, Mrs. Jeffers, remembered Frances saying that her husband "would listen to her opinion, but then do just as he wanted," which she may certainly have resented as time went on.

Frances was maturing into her forties and was still attractive, retaining a classic look about her figure and appearance. Although she loved Stock Grange as much as her husband, the farm was in a remote area and she had few friends close by; most were either in Philadelphia or the city of West Chester. Her family was still in New York; she stayed in touch daily by telephone with her older sister and confidant Martha. It is not difficult to understand that Frances began to feel isolated and lonely, especially when her teenage daughter went off with girlfriends. Most of Frances' local friends felt that although Claude was a "dear man," he could and often did become very moody. One friend remembered Frances saying frequently, "Claude is under stress right now," and interpreted this to mean that things were tense in the household. During the war years, Frances' life had

been busier, and she was more occupied with social affairs, but she never seemed to become involved with Claude's work.

When Jennifer was young, summers on the farm were usually a very busy time especially when Frances' nephews and Jennifer's companions visited. Frances' nephew Eric remembered his aunt introducing him to two of Claude's actor friends, Morris Carnovsky and George Coulouris. "Claude was like a lot of men I know who rely on their wives. Also, we were not 'close' as a family, but Claude liked everyone and he loved my father" (Walter Propper, who was once the sole member of the Propper family who approved of Frances' marriage).

I was kind of withdrawn as a youth, but I enjoyed Stock Grange and my Aunt Frances whom I adored — and Claude, but I had difficulty relating with them. I tended to stand off. And Claude had a very strong voice and expressed himself in a forceful way compared to my father who was mild-mannered. I was kinda scared. My mother [Martha] and Frances were extremely close ... so that relationship cascaded down to me, you see. She had a combination of severity or firmness with children, and she had a knack for personal relations. She attracted a lot of friends and was the cause of people coming to Stock Grange. She had a way of not fussing over guests and yet making them feel at home.

Another friend of Frances who knew the couple from their days at the Cheyney farm said: "Claude was completely self-involved and liked the conversation to be around him, yet he was unaffected and could be charming. He also could become very moody." She also remembered a visit to Stock Grange when Bette Davis was there, and that the actress made no secret of her fondness for Claude even in front of strangers. Rains seemed to enjoy the attention.

CR and Robert Mitchum in Where Danger Lives.

Toward the end of 1949, Sidney Kingsley began to work earnestly on his play, contacting Rains about every change. It was a remarkable relationship, the playwright working so closely with his male lead apparent. After *Darkness at Noon* had opened and was a hit, Rains gave *The New York Times* an interview about its genesis: "The telephone bill mounted between [Kingsley's New York] apartment and my film studio or my Chester County retreat. If I were on the Coast, he would outline a scene over the telephone. I would ask him to consult Frances on the farm: She would come see him in New York and they would work it out. When I'd arrive east, there'd be an outline of this scene, a development on another. It was an exciting time for all of us and a rare experience for an actor to work hand in hand with an author during creation, to feel his ideas respected, hear them challenged, argued over."

Never before in their marriage had Frances and Claude worked so closely, collaborating on an acting project; it was a new experience for both. Frances met the challenge quite well, but as to what degree he actually did listen to her suggestions is unknown. Regardless, in every subsequent interview about the project, Claude paid Frances homage for her contribution and her commitment in helping him in what became one of the most difficult and trying experiences of his professional life.

While Kingsley was still working on his play script, Rains agreed to make a second movie for RKO, the film noir *Where Danger Lives* with Robert Mitchum and sexy, new-to-the-screen Faith Domergue, a discovery of eccentric billionaire Howard Hughes. Mitchum is a San Francisco hospital doctor who falls for a patient (Domergue), a mysterious girl who tried to take her own life. Their fast and furious courtship hits a speed bump when she tells him that her father disapproves – but when Mitchum goes to Domergue's palatial home to confront him, he doesn't find the elderly father Domergue described, but an urbane, unflappable Rains, who sets Mitchum straight: "I wish you'd stop calling her my daughter.

Faith Domergue, CR and Robert Mitchum in Where Danger Lives.

She happens to be my wife." She married him for his money, Rains married her "for her … youth," as the old scoundrel puts it; Mitchum and Rains fight, and the scene ends with Rains dead and a concussed Mitchum unsure how it happened. The names of Mitchum, Domergue and Rains fill the screen before the title but Rains' part is actually quite small, just the one six-minute scene. It was not a great film, but that didn't seem to matter when such a large salary was involved: Rains was paid a flat rate of $25,000. But the more he performed in these weak efforts, the more apprehensive he became about his future in movies as he grew older.

CR, *Dana Andrews and Philip Dorn in* Sealed Cargo.

Rains realized, as he contemplated a return to the stage, that he had never extended himself as an actor in films to the degree he had done while with the Theatre Guild. Not until he read the completed script of *Darkness at Noon* did Rains recognize that the project would be the ultimate challenge of his career. In April 1950, Rains signed a conditional contract with Kingsley that if the play and the salary met with his satisfaction, the actor would commit himself for the run. He would not appear in any other stage play until the situation had been resolved. With the actor's signature on the contract, Kingsley now set about finding backers for the production, as Rains spent the remainder of the spring at Stock Grange.

In a couple months, because he still had not heard from Kingsley, Rains contacted his agent about completing the third movie due RKO under his contract. *Sealed Cargo* was a World War II melodrama set in the waters off Newfoundland. Dana Andrews starred as a New England fishing boat captain with Rains supporting as master of a Danish square rigger who claims to be a trader but is actually a German naval officer with a hidden cargo of torpedoes meant for Nazi U-boats. Again, he sported his own Vandyke beard and looked quite debonair in naval uniform (costuming he particularly enjoyed). The size of the part was hardly commensurate with third billing, but Rains made his appearances count, with *Variety* noting that he "[gets] across his menacing aspect underneath his quiet, cultured front."

The actor must have been relieved when, in the early fall, he at last received word from Sidney Kingsley: *Darkness at Noon* was a go. He knew it was "a damn good play and a damn good part and after sixteen years it would be good to be on the stage again." So much turned on the success or failure of the project: his career, his reputation, his family life, his relationship with Frances, even his health.

CHAPTER 21
"A hell of a fine thing to come back to the stage with..."

With such dramas as *Dead End*, *The Patriots* and his 1934 Pulitzer Prize–winning *Men in White*, Sidney Kingsley had become a highly successful playwright. During the war years, he produced little; then in 1948-49, he again received raves for his powerful *Detective Story*.

About the same time, the playwright decided that Arthur Koestler's intriguing 1940 anti–Communist novel *Darkness at Noon* had the makings of a gripping stage drama. With the Cold War at its chilliest in the United States, the story seemed timelier than ever. Kingsley discussed the matter with prominent theatre colleagues in the Playwrights Company, a group which had achieved respectability in American theatre circles (membership included Maxwell Anderson, Elmer Rice, Robert Sherwood and Kurt Weill). The subject of Koestler's book was deemed socially and culturally significant, albeit controversial, and therefore it would probably be difficult to obtain financial backing. In February 1951, after the show was a hit, *Variety* ran a list of backers, with contributions ranging from $10,000 down to $500. In addition to Kingsley (only $2,000) and his wife, actress Madge Evans (also $2,000), it included Kingsley's sister May Kirshner (who received "Associate Producer" credit on the show) "representing several assignees"; theatre party agent Lenore Tobin; film executive Joseph Moskowitz; producer Roger L. Stevens; Herman Jerome Berns and Mac Kriendler, co-owners of New York's 21 Club; Jack Entrator, owner of El Morocco; general manager Herman Bernstein (who owned the Alvin, the Broadway theatre at which *Darkness* opened, representing producer Leland Hayward); film director Anatole Litvak; producer Richard Aldrich; Mrs. Edward Look, wife of the lighting technician; Walter Vincent, president of

CR with Darkness at Noon *playwright Sidney Kingsley.*

the Actors Fund; Irwin Kramer, the operator of the Hotel Edison; author-playwright Irwin Shaw; and film producer Samuel Goldwyn, Jr. According to the trade paper, "The $100,000 production is presented by the Playwrights Company and the sole partner is Miss Kirshner."

Darkness at Noon was based on the shameful 1930s show trials of Soviet officials, when Stalin eliminated old comrades on trumped-up treason charges. Like Koestler's book, Kingsley's play, set

CR and Philip Coolidge in Darkness at Noon.

has become a casual sacrifice. It is a portrait of a tragic figure who becomes a victim of his own false philosophy; destroyed by the moral vacuum he helped create. The terrible irony is that his nemesis and torturer, the young guard Gletkin, represents the new order created by Communists like himself. The old commissar realizes he is guilty because he never questioned the corrupt means used to achieve the (bitter) shining end. Unjust hearings lead to Rubashov's execution.

On October 14, 1950, Rains began rehearsals; by the 20th, the trades carried items announcing the production and its additional cast of Alexander Scourby, Kim Hunter, Philip Coolidge and a new young actor, Walter J. Palance, whose big break had come a couple of years earlier when he understudied, and eventually replaced, Marlon Brando in *A Streetcar Named Desire*. He later achieved Hollywood fame as Jack Palance.

What attracted Rains to the part was his take on the character: that Rubashov was a "tragic villain," never outright evil, but a victim of his own character flaws, his own self-deception. It was an exceptional artistic challenge. The actor was well-aware that the art of making movies provided an inherent artistic safety net. If he forgot his blocking or couldn't remember a line, the director simply called "cut" and he could begin again. Stage acting necessitated sustaining a character for two plus hours, and the impassive lens of the camera would be replaced by the unforgiving stare of a thousand eyes. There would be no sensitive microphone to pick up every whisper; he would again need to project all the way to the back of the house. And when it came down to it, responsibility for the success or failure of the venture would rest on the shoulders of its aging star — quite a challenge for a man who hadn't been on

in an unnamed country, covers six weeks in the life of powerful Commissar Rubashov, now imprisoned, a victim of the purges. Rubashov's errors include developing feelings for his secretary and misspeaking at a crucial moment. Still an ardent supporter of Communism and convinced that the end justifies the means, Rubashov believes that an individual Communist should be willing to be sacrificed to the overall cause and the Party. As the weeks pass, Rubashov's frustration is heightened by limited interaction with fellow inmates and his own isolation. He reluctantly reexamines his convictions and, after insidious psychological torture, his faith in the Party's objectives crumbles. He realizes that he too

Kim Hunter and CR in Darkness at Noon.

stage in sixteen years. Plus, returning to the theatre meant the time-old schedule of eight shows a week, every week. However, even at 61, Rains was in good physical condition; his habits were temperate (apart from the drinking), and work on the farm had helped keep him strong and trim.

Added to the physical challenge would be the difficulty of working with a playwright who was also serving as director, and believed he was a good one. It quickly became clear that although Kingsley was a superb writer, he knew little about communication with actors on stage. He was fussy and difficult and, worst of all, vague about exactly what he wanted from the cast. As a result, rehearsals were very tense, especially when he and Rains clashed over their concepts of the Rubashov character.

As Kingsley saw it, anyone who became a Communist and enforced the party's dictatorship had to be evil. Rains had a different view of author Koestler's intent: Rubashov was a man who believed in a cause and was willing to sacrifice everything for it,

even his own life, if he felt it would make the goal obtainable. Such an approach to the character would enable Rains to create, as he had with other complex personalities, a sympathetic protagonist, all too human. However, it was exactly this that Kingsley feared, because of the political climate of the time. In the 1950s, McCarthyism was rampant. The Senator from Wisconsin had all too successfully initiated a genuine "Red Scare," and unfortunately, many members of the theatre and Hollywood communities were targets. The House Un-American Activities Committee hearings had become a witch hunt, destroying careers and even lives. Kingsley was worried his new play might also become a target.

As Kim Hunter explained it to author–film historian Tom Weaver:

> Sidney was terribly insecure about that particular play of his; I talked to him before we started rehearsals, and he was a perfectly reasonable, intelligent, gentle, nice man. Then we got into rehearsals!

> Because of the McCarthy idiocy during that period, he was terrified that people might think the play was slightly pro–Communist, so this beautiful play that he'd written he damn near ruined by insisting that everything be either black or white — no grays.

> And he'd written a lot of lovely grays but didn't allow any of them to be on stage for fear that people would get the wrong impression. So, he was very difficult during rehearsals.

Even before Rains got involved with *Darkness*, an incident hit home which reflected the tensions of the time all too well. Daughter Jennifer never forgot an unscheduled visit to Stock Grange one evening in 1948 from two FBI agents. The Rainses' housekeeper, Lily Brown, answered the door and then returned to the dining room as the meal was being served. In a very agitated state, almost trembling, she told Rains that the men wanted to talk to him. The actor rose from the table, instructing that the men join him in the library. After about fifteen minutes, the men left, and he returned to the dinner table. Nothing more was said about the matter. It was only later, when she was older, that she learned the reason for the "visit": a dinner party her mother and father had attended in the late 1930s, at which a Chinese woman had been one of the guest speakers. As the evening progressed, Claude and Frances discovered that the sponsors of the speaker were members of a Communist organization; the couple became apprehensive and decided it was wise to leave. The FBI agents had come to the farm to ask Rains to name the other individuals present at that dinner, or any persons he knew who were involved with the organization. The actor simply said it was too long ago and he could not remember. He understood and disliked "McCarthyism" too much to want to get anyone into trouble.

Working on a play as difficult as *Darkness at Noon* was a trying ordeal for everyone concerned, and interpretative differences caused friction which worsened the environment. Sacrificing everything to his own fears, Kingsley's direction took on the form of chastisement. Hunter recalled his childish routine of sending typewritten notes to torment the cast about their mistakes: "Niggling little notes — they were incredible, and we were all just absolutely uptight…" According to Hunter:

> Claude was a dear to work with, absolutely marvelous. He was so generous to the entire company because Sidney Kingsley — bless his heart — was a beast [*laughs*]!
>
> I think Claude and he had a lot of controversies and disagreements, but Claude kept them absolutely private so that the rest of the company was not involved in their fights. Whatever Sidney said during rehearsal, Claude just went ahead and did, and then had this fight with him afterwards, away from the company. Which was very generous of him, believe me, because everybody was so on edge.

Hunter, the only woman in the play, was having her own difficulties:

> When I discussed Luba with Sidney, she had her good and bad points, but because she became a "victim" of the party, she had to be lily-white — I could not make her a human being. Sidney kept fighting with me. Poor Claude bore most of it — he had one hell of a time. That much we all knew, but he was such a dear. We weren't quite sure what was going on between the two of them except I remember one time: when Sidney wanted Jack Palance, during one of the interrogation scenes, to offer Rubashov a cigarette and Claude said, "No, I can't take it." (Meaning that his character in that situation would not accept it.) And Sidney said, "Oh, don't be silly, it looks fine from out here," but Claude insisted that he would not take it.

The exhausted and frustrated actor decided to appear to give in. This meant adjusting his performance in daily rehearsals to show Kingsley something of what the director wanted, and then at night in his hotel room, working on what he knew was right. It was beyond arduous. Making notations in his script, Rains scribbled "aloneness" at the top of a page, and on another "fever" and "shiver." He accented certain words and underlined others. He added the description "self-appointed Messiah" and, interestingly, the name "Hollenius," the manipulative, imperious conductor he had played in the film *Deception*.

Prior to the show's Broadway opening, Rains never publicly talked about his differences with Kingsley — that would have been unprofessional and might have put the play in jeopardy. Only later did he describe the situation in a *New York Times* article under his own byline:

> Rehearsals were difficult, for values had curiously shifted. Sidney no longer was an author collaborating with an actor who was to realize his leading character: He was a director maneuvering his company like chessman. I was one of the pawns, and our personal friendship suffered the perhaps inevitable thousand little tensions. Of what intangibles are these! Conditioned by Hollywood and the farm for years, I am an early riser and am at my best in the mornings; conditioned by Broadway, Sidney is a late riser and drives his hardest

in the late afternoon. I found it physically exhausting to go three times through an act highly charged with shifting emotions in an afternoon and then do a run-through at night. My voice couldn't take it.

At her husband's request, Frances attended rehearsals, proving to be both Rains' most reliable critic and loyal supporter during this difficult period. She enjoyed sharing in his work because she knew how much it meant to him. This was the first time she had an opportunity to work with Claude professionally and he was impressed by her input:

A quiet collaborator, who whom I'd like now to pay proper homage, was my good and patient wife. Always Sidney attempted to depart from the novel in terms of theatrical effectiveness. I was for adhering strictly to the book. Frances was somewhere in between. I began to look on her in a new light, to realize for perhaps the first time in our seventeen years of marriage how sound, how constructive, above all in what great taste were her suggestions. As I listened, I learned to respect even when her honesty hurt.

CR and Jack Palance in Darkness at Noon.

As the Philadelphia preview neared, tensions mounted. Given his anxieties about returning to the theatre and his high standards for perfection, Rains found it difficult to sleep or relax, becoming "like a vegetable." Relations with Kingsley continued to deteriorate, and the actor felt "spent" and "worn out." He would talk about his character and the timeliness

of the play when questioned by reporters, but more often he would chat about Stock Grange, his wife and daughter. When asked about rumored friction with Kingsley, Rains smiled and simply said that working in a play written and directed by the same person caused unanticipated problems: "Actors have a natural tendency to gripe about the men behind the scenes. Well … I can't very well talk to the director about the author, nor can I talk to the author about the director. It's frustrating…"

Rehearsals went all through the day and late into the evening. Compounding all this was another serious problem which the actor never discussed, although everyone in the cast was aware of it: his relationship with the young man playing Rubashov's sadistic interrogator and guard, Jack Palance.

An old-school artist, Rains had always been meticulous about learning and delivering lines precisely. Palance worked in an altogether different style, prevalent at the time: method acting. At times, he would alter his movements or, more unpredictably, alter his lines such that they ended differently. Not receiving his scripted cues completely threw Rains off. According to Kim Hunter, during one rehearsal, Rains asked Palance to please be more consistent, so that the older man would know what cue to expect. Palance exploded in anger and went after Rains, who made a fast exit to his dressing room, locking himself in. Hunter vividly remembered Palance pounding on the door and yelling. No one knew what to do. Rains remained virtually barricaded in until he was assured that the young actor had left the theatre. After this incident, the two never spoke to each other, except in character on stage. The inevitable lingering pall even manifested itself during performances. As scripted, Palance's vicious guard, Glenkin, takes every opportunity to bully Rains' Rubashov. Palance, thirty years younger than Rains, athletic, and six foot three, was a very physical actor; at the time, he let personal animosity enter into his performance. To an audience, it was part of the play. Others knew better.

On December 26, a miserable icy evening, *Darkness at Noon* opened in Philadelphia. The balcony of the Forrest Theatre was practically empty, the mezzanine half full and the orchestra only three-quarters; many in this section were backers and well-wishers; there were also reporters from New York, New Jersey and Pennsylvania. Friends and family in attendance included John and Ann Wyeth McCoy, and the sons of Frances Rains' sister Martha, Dirk and Tony Propper. This author was also there. During one particular scene, Palance slammed Rains against the wall of the cell with such force that there was an audible thud and the scenery shook. A few days later in the run, when Palance was arriving for that evening's performance, the author (a brash 16-year-old) stopped him for an autograph as he reached the stage door and asked why he had used such force in the scene. The author has never forgotten Palance's reply: "Mr. Rains is a little man — he ought to grow up."

Forty years later, Kim Hunter confirmed the bad feeling which existed between the two men during the entire run of the play. Another member of the company, Allan Rich, just 23 years old when he played Prisoner 202, believed that Palance may have felt inferior because of his professional inexperience, and that he resented how much everyone deferred to Rains as the star. Rich contended that Kingsley, as director, should have defused the situation early on; but Kingsley refused to become involved. "Kingsley was complaining to everyone that Rains, who had frequent colds during rehearsals, was 'jeopardizing the play,' by being ill so often."

As playwright, Kingsley had constructed a tightly composed work in three acts, each one contributing to a haunting set of climaxes. It was difficult for any adaptation to match the literary artistry of Arthur Koestler, but the theatre piece was extremely effective as a chilling tale of the destruction of a famous revolutionary. The trickiest aspect was to incorporate several flashback sequences within each act, to provide the audience with details on Rubashov's past. Rains portrays the character at different ages over three decades, and changes in set designs reflected the time periods. These exceptional sets revolved around the main "cell" positioned center stage, with the other prison cells in a tier stage right. In one transition, Rubashov lies on his cot, suffering from a fever, until he drifts away to a night he spent with his mistress (Hunter) just before he denounced her.

Following the Philadelphia opening, *Variety* reviewed the tryout dispassionately, accurately pinpointing the pluses and minuses:

[*Darkness at Noon* is] almost certain to add artistic laurels to the playwright's already large collection. Claude Rains … will surely reap a crop of complimen-

tary citations. It seems equally certain that the Playwrights Company will also add to its luster and reputation as a producer of worthwhile and provocative plays. Whether all this will add up to a commercial success for the drama is something very much else again. It impresses as having an even chance for a moderate NY run …

The stagecraft is a highlight of the show. Rains won a well-deserved ovation for his work in a long, tough role. Kim Hunter, Walter J. Palance, Alexander Scourby and some others of the carefully selected cast are also outstanding. Though grim, unrelenting, without light relief, and certainly not ideal Christmas fare, there's no denying the excellent writing and theatrical power.

The *Evening Bulletin* reviewer wrote, "Rains gives his finest performance in a memorable career. On the stage virtually all of the time, he is called upon constantly to indicate profound but suppressed emotion. He never fails. The only criticism of his work is occasional inaudibility, a fault common to most actors returning from the movies." In fact, Rains was ill with a serious case of laryngitis. The doctor had advised him not to perform at all. The actor later described the opening weeks for *The New York Times*:

The morning after was a terrible one. My sense of responsibility to Sidney, to the Playwrights Company, especially to my fellow actors drove me to a decision. I went to my author-director and volunteered to give up my run-of-the-play contract and step out of the role. He said simply: "There's no time for that." We delayed the Broadway opening a few days in order to try out our changes with a new crew on preview audiences, and that made all the difference. And I had encouragement that I can't put into words without getting emotional about it from Maxwell Anderson and Robert E. Sherwood.

The exchange between Kingsley and Rains was probably composed for the benefit of the press. Both Kim Hunter and Rains' friend, producer Henry

Darkness at Noon contact sheet

Denker, stated that Kingsley actually wanted to replace Rains before the play went to New York; in fact, he had even contacted agents to secure another star. Hunter wondered if the agents who had been contacted weren't "on Claude's side," since all the actors Kingsley requested were (coincidentally) reported by their reps as "unavailable." Kingsley remained churlish, continuing to try and unnerve Rains. Set designer Frederick Fox's son recalled his father talking about the fact that Kingsley, who didn't understand actors, was quite demanding and didactic. Instead of keeping differences between himself and Rains private, Kingsley began to complain to anyone and everyone that the actor had lost the discipline of stage acting during his years in Hollywood. He accused the veteran of psychosomatic illness, contending that Rains threatened not to go on if he did not get his way. Few believed such nonsense. Allan Rich regarded Rains as a consummate professional who would go on with a fever, while Kingsley was a "kvetch" and did not trust anyone with his play.

Darkness at Noon concluded its Philadelphia run on Saturday, January 6. On Thursday, January 11, an audience of invited guests and backers attended a private preview in New York. Rains felt more confident than ever in his interpretation of his character: "A basic change came about at that time in my conception. From the moment I began to realize the importance of communication with the audience, [Rubashov] ceased to be the cold, still philosopher he is in the book, and became the frustrated man of action." Kingsley was furious. The two men finally confronted each other backstage after the opening night performance. "Just before the curtain went up," Rains explained, "well, I just said to myself, 'Fuck Sidney Kingsley!'" According to Hunter, "Sidney's jaw dropped and he didn't come back after that [*laughs*]!"

Rains told the story with a slight variation (eliminating Kingsley's name) to *The New York Times*:

> I was paralyzed with fright as I faced the first New York audience. Even before the play started, I was looking forward to its end… I would have welcomed the death sentence at that moment – the moment I speak of was at 8:04 p.m. on opening night, at that low morale point immediately following the last clammy handshake of a

well-wishing associate in the enterprise and a flat sixty seconds before the curtain rise. Could I do it? Under my breath I muttered two sentences: "To hell with them out there. To hell with everybody!" That seemed to do it. I felt better. The stage manager called "Curtain!" As I went on — I had to cross the stage in silence — a tribute I shan't forget rose from the expectant audience out front. There were friends and foes out there. I was brought to sharp recollection that I was an actor when I bungled my second line. I had to say, "I've been dragged from my sick bed." With my mind until this moment on the word 'sick,' the "s" dominated everything. I fumbled, and the line came out "snatched." But no one noticed it. From then on, Rubashov took over.

When the curtain came down, the audience exploded into thunderous applause and rose for a standing ovation with sixteen repeated curtain calls for the star, who wept openly. If Rains had exhausted himself in undertaking the strenuous role, critics exhausted their supply of adjectives to describe his performance. Calling *Darkness at Noon* "the finest play of the season," Whitney Bolton wrote in the *New York Telegraph* that Rains was "magnificent in one of the most exhausting roles in modern theatre, as well as the longest. Mr. Rains' performance is of vast size and he gives it every resource he has. I think it the best performance of the season." Some headlines praised Rains to the detriment of the play. "Despite the vivid and generally absorbing writing and despite the author's adroit direction of his scattered scenes, *Darkness at Noon* would have failed without the inspired aid of the other folk called into the enterprise, most of all Claude Rains in the leading role." Another reviewer remarked that Rains,

> absent from Broadway these 16 years … is recalled as a rather flamboyant actor and some of his screen efforts also have been in the too-showy manner. It's different this time. On stage nearly every minute, Rains is always a quiet and repressed Rubashov, showing in his face rather than in his words the suffering confusion, the struggle to

cling to wilting willpower and the ultimate surrender of an unhappy, disillusioned revolutionist. By his superb performance, Rains almost succeeds in closing the gap between a playwright's dialogue and a novelist's descriptions to provide a mood of evil and of terror.

The New York Times' Brooks Atkinson commented: "When Mr. Rains last played in New York … he was inclined to be a pompous actor — that is, the acting was imposing but on the surface. There used to be a tradition that Hollywood destroyed good actors, but Mr. Rains is not the first stage actor who has come back from Hollywood improved in technique and enriched in spirit." John Mason Brown of *The Saturday Review* wrote something similar after commenting that Rains' Rubashov turns out to be one of the major performances of the season.

"Always a good actor, Mr. Rains has sometimes in the past been tempted to be too much of an actor. His Rubashov, however, never gets out of hand. It is beautifully controlled and modulated, underplayed rather than overplayed, and doubly effective for this very reason. The demands of the part are backbreaking. Quite aside from what it represents as a feat of memory, its other requirements for concentration are merciless. Yet Mr. Rains manages to meet all these tests triumphantly. The iron of Rubashov is in him, the knife-like quality of his mind, the habit of command, and the force that is his. The human being is also there, alive though submerged…"

The actor so well known for his remarkable voice, the voice he had proved could still reach the back of the house, hadn't forgotten the subtleties he had learned for the camera. According to the *Sunday Herald Tribune*,

Rains' face registers total despair which cannot be put into words. After a brutal inquisition, his faith and soul have been crushed. With his facial expressions alone, Rains' acting displayed more than what any words Kingsley wrote could demonstrate — the complete and gradual disillusionment and breakdown of a man's belief. The actor succeeded in bringing to life what Koestler wrote about years later — the "dangers of devotion … and the impulse

to surrender oneself out of loyalty to others" … only to realize there is "a difference between what is understandable and what is right."

William Hawkins, critic of the *New York World-Telegram and The Sun*, praised the director as well as the star:

> Sidney Kingsley has done an amazing job … it almost seems an undramatizable story. Right on the par with the extraordinary production is the performance of the control role of Claude Rains.
>
> It is difficult to play a character who is moving neither toward triumph or failure but toward submission and despair … but Mr. Rains gets a grip on the play, its elaborate maneuvers and the leaden finish with the ideals he portrays that somehow makes his realization of the truth suggest an ultimate peacefulness. He makes you feel that knowing why he is damned is more important than hell's fires. He is sincerity from scalp to toe.

Critics came from out of state to review the play that was making national news. While calling Rains "truly magnificent," an Ohio reporter amusingly wrote: "Going backstage to see him after the performance, I had to apologize when we shook hands, for my palm was still moist from the tension of the show. But his was, too." Perhaps the banner that pleased the veteran actor more than any was the *New York World-Telegram and The Sun* proclaiming: "Alvin [Theatre] has a Hit! Mr. Rains, Farmer."

In addition to all the critical praise, some distinguished "civilians" were greatly impressed. Eleanor Roosevelt went to see the play twice. Backstage to congratulate the actor, she said: "I'd like to kidnap you, Mr. Rains, and have you perform all over." (Another version of this story has the First Lady saying: "I'd like to kidnap you, Mr. Rains, and have you do this play behind the Iron Curtain.") In her syndicated column, Mrs. Roosevelt wrote that Rains was overbearingly powerful and his portrayal haunting: "I was really more impressed on the second visit than I had been at the first. Claude Rains' acting is simply an extraordinary feat. I do not see how he

does it night after night." Even the fashion magazine *Vogue* marveled at Rains' "astonishing performance of almost unbearable emotion," and granted him a full-page side view photograph which was considered the ultimate rave for the chic fashion periodical.

Rains' old friend from the Theatre Guild, Theresa Helburn, wrote a note: "It is really magnificent, and we should all be grateful to have you back in the theatre. Please stay." To which the actor replied: "Dear Terry, bless you and thanks for taking the trouble to tell me. It was quite an ordeal after sixteen years (Leibowitz came back and wanted to know if I still had the pipe I stole from his office) but God was good to me and the rewards are sweet." His longtime friends from Chester County, John and Ann Wyeth McCoy, also wrote congratulations. In acknowledging them, Rains bragged: "Thank you for thinking of me opening night. It went off very well and in spite of some of the critics, we are (up to this point, anyway) packing them in. If you ever get to New York, do let us know, Love…"

While the play was a financial success, the cost had been high for Rains. He always gave fully and completely of himself in any production, and nothing else mattered. Because he focused so intently on his work, he could become withdrawn and often inconsiderate of others. Claude had relied on Frances more than ever during this project and at the start she, like her husband, had become friends with the Kingsleys. Then, because of the artistic disagreements between the two men, and especially after Kingsley attempted to replace Rains, that all ended, and Frances was caught in the middle of their feud. Rains imposed such a strict mental and physical discipline on himself, even Frances confessed to some friends that he was not the same man, that he had changed during the year he had worked on the role. When she stayed with her husband in New York, he behaved as if he were in a stupor most of the time, preserving his energy for the performance. The run of the play necessitated a change in some long-time habits: Instead of arising at four or five in the morning as he did on the farm and in Hollywood, he was now up later, at seven or eight. After taking a little breakfast and getting his throat sprayed, he'd return to the hotel and rest. He'd eat dinner at two o'clock and by five or six was at the theatre. He described for the *Herald Tribune* how taxing it was:

"a Fine play" ... and I recommend it to you heartily."
—WOLCOTT GIBBS, THE NEW YORKER

THE PLAYWRIGHTS' COMPANY
presents
SIDNEY KINGSLEY'S
Brilliant Play
CLAUDE RAINS
in
DARKNESS
AT NOON
Based on the Novel by
ARTHUR KOESTLER

ALVIN THEATRE, 250 W. 52 St. Mats. Wed. & Sat.

First, I get no rest from this terrifically demanding range of emotions. Second, I have to depend mostly on my eyes, face and posture to add or subtract the thirty years of the switchbacks. Third, I am constantly contending with other players who have been taking turns relaxing backstage and are now coming on, rarin' to go. Many of them are mighty fine players, besides being mighty fine people.

I wanted Rubashov, above everything, to be honest — as honest as in the book. I read all the Moscow purge trial accounts and almost memorized the book. At first, I made the mistake of regarding the stage Rubashov as more the philosophical character of the book than the strident character he has turned out to be in Act I.

There was a good reason for this modification of his character. We found out in the try-out in Philadelphia that the philosophical Rubashov could not be dramatically projected to the live audience. So, with Sidney Kingsley's and my wife's agreement, I made Rubashov much more — shall I say — defiant, shouting, pacing about. The reaction of the audience proved this was right. In a large theater before a large audience, Rubashov has to be stepped up. In doing so, I run the risk of indulging in over-histrionics with the result that in every performance I must walk a hair line.

When I crumble under torture, nobody really knows how I almost break with restraint.

It's a grand experience for me....I never would have stayed away as long as I did except that I was afraid I had lost my touch after all the years in movies. That's why I had to pick a tough role, the toughest I could find.

And in a *New Yorker* interview, he ended by saying: "It has all been wonderful, wonderful...What a hell of a fine thing to come back to the stage with."

By February, when Rains had hit his stride in the role, the strain was taking more and more of a toll on his mental and physical well-being. If he had any regrets, he never spoke of them. Initially he had wanted to do the play for two seasons, but by the spring he began to realize the physical ordeal was too much. On February 28, *Variety* ran a short item: "When Claude Rains was out of the cast of *Darkness at Noon* last Tuesday night (2/20), the fact was announced to the audience via loudspeaker from backstage, with no one coming before the curtain to explain the situation in person. An estimated three-fifths of the house immediately walked out, getting refunds. The slim patronage that remained gave understudy Will Kuluva an ovation at the final curtain." The actor was out "with a cold" on May 16, with Kuluva again going on. Not unreasonably, Rains refused to perform during the summer in a theatre without air conditioning and wearing the heavy winter coat required in Act II. For now, *Darkness* would run until June.

In mid–March 1951, *The New York Times* reported that the Voice of America would broadcast *Darkness at Noon* in its entirety. Never before had the organization aired a Broadway play. Never before had the Voice broadcasts pre-empted any of its programming, except for important presidential addresses. Now it would cancel all regular programs for two hours so that *Darkness at Noon* could be carried to an estimated radio audience of 100 million. NBC provided the studios. To ensure a static-free transmission, Voice of America sent out emergency procedures to its six relay stations. Originally the governmental agency had planned on using its own cast, until the Playwrights Company allowed Rains and the entire company, as well as all the unions involved, to volunteer their time for the broadcast on April 6 and 7.

DARKNESS AT NOON

Just before the end of the run, because of contractual commitments, *Darkness* relocated from the Alvin Theatre to the Royale. Half of the moving cost was borne by Howard Cullman, owner of the Alvin and the largest single investor in the play (at $16,000). Originally *Darkness* was to close on June 23, but ticket sales jumped at the new, smaller venue and the run was extended through June 30. *Darkness at Noon* closed after 186 performances. It would never return to Broadway.

Three months later, Edward G. Robinson — who, like Rains, had been long absent from the stage; in his case, 21 years — toured with the show. *Variety* reported that a film version starring Robinson would follow. In fact, it was another four years before *Darkness at Noon* made it to a screen — the small screen. When a ninety-minute version was broadcast as a special on NBC's *Producers' Showcase* on May 2, 1955, Lee J. Cobb played Rubashov. Sidney Kingsley had vetoed the actor who created the role, and to whom he owed the success of the production.

CR receiving his medal for "Good Speech on the American Stage" for his performance in Darkness at Noon.

The 1950-51 Broadway season was remarkable: Continuing runs included *Call Me Madam* with Ethel Merman; *Bell, Book and Candle* with Rex Harrison; *Where's Charley?* with Ray Bolger; *The Member of the Wedding* with Ethel Waters; *South Pacific* with Mary Martin; *Gentlemen Prefer Blondes* with Carol Channing; and *Twentieth Century* with Gloria Swanson. Among the new plays were *The Country Girl* by Clifford Odets, *Billy Budd* by Louis O. Coxe and Robert H. Chapman, *The Lady's Not for Burning* by Christopher Fry, and *The Rose Tattoo* by Tennessee Williams.

On March 25, 1951, the American Theatre Wing's 5th Annual Tony Awards were held at the Waldorf Astoria Grand Ballroom. And the Antoinette Perry Award for Best Actor in a Play went to Claude Rains for *Darkness at Noon*. In fact, Rains made theatre history by winning every award on Broadway: the Best Actor Award from the New York Drama Critics, the Drama League of New York's Delia Austrian Medal, the Bronze Medal from the Comedia Matinee Club, and the Donaldson Award from *Billboard* for the Best Performance by an Actor.

The American Academy of Arts and Letters, recognizing good speech on the American stage, additionally honored Rains. For his *Darkness at Noon* performance, "and above all, for his magnificent rendering of the English language, we count it a joy to present the Academy Medal for Good Speech on the American Stage to a great actor: Claude Rains." This was his favorite honor; it reminded him of those eighteen months he had practiced the letter "r." He took all the awards, including a large loving cup from the theatre company, home to Stock Grange and placed them on the mantle in his library. Thirteen-year-old Jennifer, in typical teenage fashion, teased her father about the decorations, calling them "a vulgar display..."

CR approaching the stage door of the Forrest Theatre for a preview performance of Darkness at Noon, *with his friend-assistant Charles Brown. (Photo taken by Toby Cohen.)*

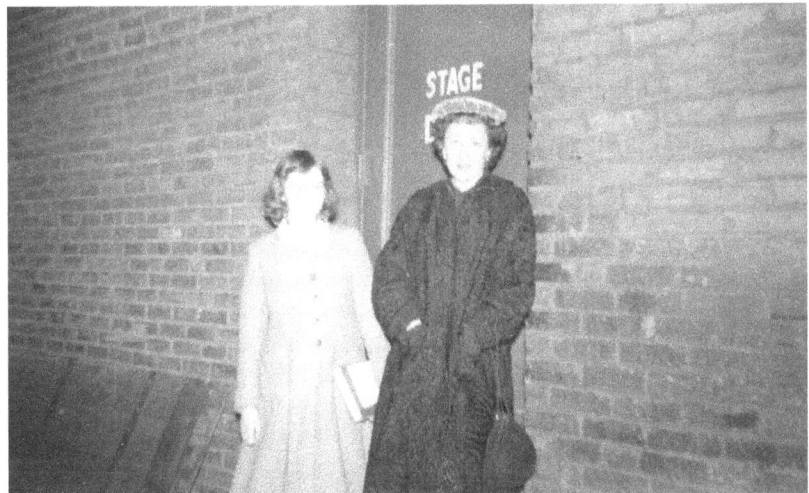

CR's wife Frances and their daughter Jennifer. (Photo taken by Toby Cohen.)

CR walking to the Forrest Theatre. (Photo taken by Toby Cohen.)

Darkness at Noon had physically and emotionally devoured him, but he had emerged with unanimous respect in a supreme stage performance that had demonstrated his talent and skills in a manner no movie ever could.

****

More than seven decades later, this author has never forgotten what it was like to see Rains (as related in the book's preface) completely dominate a theatre stage at the peak of his powers. Photographs she took at the time aren't necessary to bring back memories.

"And the Tony Award for Best Performance by an Actor in a Play goes to..."

CHAPTER 22
After the Show Was Over

Rains rested at Stock Grange for several days before taking Jennifer to camp in New Hampshire. Then he and Frances decided to extend the vacation and visit friends in the New England area.

Normally, after a strenuous project like *Darkness at Noon*, Rains would have remained at the farm, just puttering around his large vegetable garden. He told the *Philadelphia Evening Bulletin*: "I feel so content and relaxed, I don't care right now whether I ever do another stroke of work…" This time, however, he felt the need to get away, hoping for some emotional rejuvenation with Frances. There was no denying *Darkness* had had a serious impact on their marriage. Initially, Frances had been so helpful as they worked together toward a common goal and shared moments of creativity. Then all the difficulties arose, with the eventual estrangement from the Kingsleys. All during the New York run, Rains was tense and exhausted, spending each day alone in his hotel until about two hours before curtain. On Sunday and Monday, days the theatre was "dark," if the weather permitted, he might make the two-hour train trip back to Stock Grange. But once there, usually he was so tired, he couldn't engage in any activity. Evidently (and understandably), Frances was lonely, which may have inflated discontent.

Being the wife of a celebrity had its compensations, occasionally Frances herself was in the limelight because of her famous husband. Through the years she became socially active in Chester County society, but often gatherings required the attendance of a spouse and Rains disliked these affairs, even if he didn't prefer to go to bed very early. Then, too, most of these events were for a younger crowd. In December 1950, Frances was honored as one of the ten best dressed women of Philadelphia's Main Line. It was a prestigious recognition in a world of wealthy society, but she was still "Mrs. Claude Rains."

It was wonderful for the two of them to leave the theatre, the movie business, the telephone, everything behind as they set off on their holiday. They both looked forward to being together in a relaxed atmosphere. After dropping Jennifer off at camp, they first visited Dr. Uhle and his wife Janet, who had a small summer cottage in Sandwich, New Hampshire. Mrs. Uhle remembered the couple staying at the only inn in town, the Corner House, which still stands today. In the years since her husband had performed prostate surgery on Claude, the two men had become friends. This was Rains' first exposure to the area, and he fell in love with the town. Frequently, he and Frances would visit Sandwich whenever the Uhles went. Mrs. Uhle recalled:

I always thought of Claude as two people. I remember he invited us for cocktails at the Bellevue [a Philadelphia hotel] and there were a few people there. When we arrived, he met us on the steps with a big red ribbon across his chest and wearing a cape. He was quite a character that way, and in his booming voice nobody could miss he was Claude Rains. There was no possibility of a quiet cocktail. I think he used to like to think he didn't want to be in evidence, but at the same time he did. The other part of the man was a gentle sensitive one. He did have a gentle voice when he wanted to.

In July, Claude and Frances went to Maine to visit other old friends: first, John and Ann McCoy. In addition to being the sister of the famous American artist Andrew Wyeth, Ann McCoy had married a man who was an artist in his own right. Ann, living in the Chadds Ford area, met Frances through some social activity in the Brandywine vicinity; the two couples became friends and often had dinners together. The Wyeth family homes were nearby to Stock Grange and get-togethers were fairly frequent. Rains met Ann's famous brother once or twice at Ann's home, but it was actually John McCoy's watercolor paintings the actor admired. The entire Wyeth clan, including Ann and her husband, spent their summers on the Maine coast and the McCoys had a beautiful home near Wheeler Bay. Ann remembered the visits, and especially those of Rains, with great fondness:

> He was a special person and we loved him. Frances was very pleasant, but it was hard to know what to do with her. He loved music and painting; she didn't have the same interests. We had a more interesting time with Claude when he came alone. He was devoted to her — there was always a feeling of love, but I think he was beyond her. He was an intelligent person and enthusiastic. She was different — they were of a different ilk. I do remember he was blind in one eye. We were using a telescope, and I noticed how he looked at things. I could tell just by the way he looked — he never told us. I just knew … He told us how fearful he was about Palance [in *Darkness at Noon*] — that Palance actually pushed him around [on stage]; he admitted he was scared of him.

Ann especially remembered their visit that summer of 1951: "Claude was one of the nicest guests I've ever had! So helpful! Believe it or not, he washed dishes…" While at Wheeler Bay, the couples enjoyed a lobster feast outdoors, and afterwards, Claude decided to gather up the leftover scraps and take them down to the sea gulls flying around the rocks. In the process of walking on the stony path, he twisted his ankle, necessitating a consult with a doctor who prescribed bathing his foot in warm water and staying off it for a few days. According to Ann McCoy: "At the time, he was supposed to be visiting Bette Davis and her new husband Gary Merrill near Portland. They were furious with him because he upset their plans. I know because I talked with Merrill by phone!" She also described another occasion when Rains came to Wheeler Bay by himself: "He washed out his shirt

CR and friend Ann Wyeth McCoy. Annotated on the back: "CR with lady cook in Maine. I should have taken my apron off. PS: It was blowing a gale!" (Photo courtesy Ann Wyeth McCoy)

(Photo courtesy Ann Wyeth McCoy)

and hung it on the line to dry. It needed redoing and ironing, so I just did it again for him, but he never once asked. I was astonished that a man would do his own laundry." A few days after his minor ankle injury, Claude and Frances drove to Prouts Neck,

Maine, to visit Bette. Writing about his life with the formidable actress in his 1988 autobiography, Gary Merrill recounted this visit:

> Claude Rains and his wife Frances … said they would stop by for dinner on their way home to Pennsylvania. I arranged for them to stay at the inn [Black Point Inn]. This would be my first meeting with Rains, a friend of Bette's, and she advised me to get some Irish whiskey for his visit…. Bette arranged to have a few people come in after dinner…. When the Rainses arrived, Claude was using a cane … and was ready for a drink. I asked how he'd like his whiskey and he said, "Just give me a glass and put the bottle beside it." As we were having drinks and hors d'oeuvres, I watched the whiskey go down in the bottle as it went down Claude. After dinner, when the other guests had arrived, I heard a loud exclamation from Claude above the general chatter, "That's a lot of bullshit!" Since the Prouts Neck people were pretty straight, this cleared the house quickly… Claude and Frances spent one night at the hotel and left the next morning. Several days later, Bette received a card from Claude saying, "Frances tells me I used the word 'bullshit.' I know that 'shit' is a household word, but 'bullshit' — my apologies."

Frances described the visit in more detail in a letter to Ann McCoy. Her words reveal the depth of her understanding of her husband's friendship with the star actress, and the fact that Bette could offer Claude a demonstrative warmth and pampering that was difficult for Frances to extend. Frances obviously felt she could share things with Ann:

Ann Dear, (near Portland)

> This is one of those elegant and snobbish hotels that wouldn't stoop to the vulgarity of making itself attractive. Lovely water from this window and a beautiful beach.
>
> We found Bette in a rented cottage on the hotel grounds where they keep house… Gary entertained us and gave us drinks (he's nice) until Bette came down… They said

> she was so upset at our not coming Thursday that they both got roaring drunk. Their friends from N.Y. came for dinner and some ghastly Boston blue bloods came after.
>
> We think she is very unhappy. Claude went to talk to her in the kitchen and said (right to the point), "Are you happy, Bette?" She said, "Oh, I'm all right," but with a very discontented inflection….
>
> Claude is over there having breakfast. I had mine in bed and will go over when I'm finished this. It's raining. Bette wants to do a play with Claude. God forbid! Movies are offering nothing, but she is scared to come back and yet thinks she must, to survive. So, we talked a lot about the horrors and glories of returning to the theatre after so long an absence.
>
> Bette is really charming with Claude and loving and understanding and careful in handling him. With everyone else she is the one to be catered to. But with Claude she is completely different, and it makes her much more attractive.
>
> Well, I can almost hear Claude scream for help so will close after I've said that we both are thrilled with our heavenly visit with you and that we love you all madly.

After Claude and Frances returned to Stock Grange, she again wrote to Ann about the first week in August, lamenting:

> Claude's holiday has completely demoralized him, and he even loses things now. Heretofore, an unheard of thing…
>
> I've been so busy that I have only had one brief session down at the pond and my tan is in a bad way. I'm trying to achieve some semblance of order in [Jennifer's] domain by throwing things away. This is impossible to do when she is around. Also, we've had guests and you know how much time that takes up, don't you dear? Although you never once showed the strain.
>
> I never finished about the visit with Bette. The next morning, she looked attractive in blue jeans cut short and an old shirt…

On our way to N.H. we stopped at Kennebunkport and had lunch on a dock there. My last lobster roll. Then two nights in Wolfeboro. We watched [Jennifer] rehearse her ballet and Claude was so touched, he wept. She can't really dance but she has grace and incredible aplomb on a stage, and she convinces you that this is a performance…

My garden was a jungle and I'm slowly getting it cleaned up. Also, Lily (our cook) is going away for a while and Claude's theatre valet is coming down to help me during her absence. This means getting a room ready for him and planning his work as he will probably do jobs she can't do and I will do the ones he can't.

We still talk about the perfect time we had at Wheeler Bay.

(This "valet" helped Rains during the run of the *Darkness at Noon*. A theatre dresser by profession, he only assisted Rains for about two weeks.)

Since there were only three people to cook for if the Rainses did not have company, why a cook was necessary is perplexing, unless it was because Frances simply did not want the daily task of preparing three meals: she was an excellent cook and enjoyed preparing very fancy dishes, especially when the couple entertained. Lily Brown was not hired for this position specifically, but as the wife of Rains' right hand man, it was fitting that she become part of the household.

Ann McCoy remembered Frances frequently expressing admiration at her friend's ability "to keep the place in such good shape and what a wonderful housekeeper and mother she seemed to be." She also recalled Frances saying she felt she ought to be doing a better job at those same things and was going to make an effort and try "to be a better wife." This comment, taken together with noticing how Bette was able to "handle" her husband, perhaps indicates that Frances may have felt her shortcomings in her marriage. During the visit with the McCoys, Rains had admired a water-color painting of John's and arranged to purchase it, sending the artist a check and a short note on August 20: "Here you are, John. Please do not acknowledge it for it is to be a surprise for Frances… There are a lot of things I'd like to say to you two, but I won't. However, as Frances said as we

drove away three weeks ago, 'Aren't they the sweetest people?' I concurred. Love and kisses."

During the remaining weeks of summer, Rains' continued uneasiness made him consider a previous offer of a film to be shot in England, but the project was postponed and then eventually scrapped. He underwent another minor operation for a hernia condition aggravated by the physical ordeal of *Darkness*. The vacation helped, but Rains still felt tired and apprehensive. He was pleased that offers continued to come in — several plays, television episodes, radio broadcasts and a Hollywood movie — but quantity didn't mean quality. At sixty-two, he was in the latter phase of his career. He had earned a decent sum for *Darkness at Noon*, but certainly not an exorbitant figure (the exact earnings are unknown as the 1951 income tax forms are missing from his files).

Jennifer was growing up quickly. When Rains was fifty, it had been sheer delight to play with a three-year old; when she was seven, she would greet him with "Hi ya, Bub" as she blew bubble gum in his face. He adored her antics. Although his love was deep, he was less and less able to show affection as Jennifer matured. When she was a baby, their age disparity made little difference, but now he appeared and acted more like her grandfather, so that as Jennifer approached her teens, the girl grew closer to Frances. Even though her father spoiled her with gifts, as a sensitive and shy teenager she felt more comfortable with her mother. Jennifer had always felt the power of her father's presence. Her cousins, when they spent time on the farm during the summers, remembered that whenever Claude called his daughter, he would bellow as if he were on stage so that it sounded like a command. This was his demeanor, and softness was never an outward attribute of this man, perhaps because he had never experienced tenderness in his own life. Jennifer never doubted her father's affection for her. Whenever Rains was conversing or during interviews, he talked about her and the farm as those things most dear to him. He was quite proud of his daughter's activities, bragging to an interviewer: "She swims well, has a nice touch on the piano, attends ballet school, and is good with the paint and brush. She's just a lovely, decent human being." But it was, Jennifer admitted, very difficult to say "no" to him for any reason: "You just did what he said, you didn't argue, he had a powerful presence."

Even though Rains was physically undemonstrative, he could be thoughtful in so many other ways. Whenever he was away from the farm for any period of time, he sent his daughter postcards every day, signing with terms of endearment such as "Poopie" or "Cloudy" or addressing her sometimes as "My dear Little Pot of Beans" because it was Lily's nickname for her. He bought her anything she desired — all those things that had been missing from his own childhood. As Jennifer grew older, he felt a great reluctance to display a kiss or a hug, it just did not seem "proper" now that she was a young lady.

In the remaining months of 1951, Rains became involved with a project very dear to his heart. Any work connected with American history had special appeal, and he loved portraying any of the founding fathers and was happy to be cast as Thomas Jefferson. The National Association of Educational Broadcasters consisted of universities, colleges, school systems and public services agencies which were engaged in non-commercial educational broadcasting. They approached Rains with a program funded by the Ford Foundation: a series of non-commercial radio programs based on the research and advice of Professor Dumas Malone of the Department of History at Columbia University. The project totaled seven long-playing albums, all of which were recorded in New York City. Rains earned only a small salary, along with royalties each time the program aired. After this experience, Rains conceived the idea of going on tour with his own readings. Or, if he could find a sponsor, he preferred broadcasting his own program.

In early 1952, Rains got another chance to make a film overseas: the British-American *The Man Who Watched Trains Go By*, based on a 1938 novel by Georges Simenon, creator of the hugely popular Inspector Maigret series. Many of the prolific writer's stories were adapted into films, but as interesting as they were, with characters built around vivid descriptions of their thoughts, something was usually lost when they were brought to the screen. (In 1949, during the making of *The White Tower*, Rains, Cedric Hardwicke and a producer named Irving Allen had set up a company and planned to make *Man Who Watched Trains Go By*, with Rains starring and Hardwicke directing.)

In his final big-screen starring role, Rains plays a meek Dutchman who bicycles every morning to his job as head clerk at a venerable Amsterdam firm in which he has invested 18 years of his life and all his

CR and Ferdy Mayne in The Man Who Watched Trains Go By.

savings. When he learns that his buttoned-up boss (Herbert Lom) has bankrupted the company keeping his mistress living the high life in Paris, the two men have a late-night waterfront scuffle which results in Lom accidentally taking a fatal fall into the canal. Rains snaps and, clutching Lom's valise crammed with stolen money, boards the Paris Express, intent on finding Lom's girl (Marta Toren) and picking up where Lom left off (!). By this point in Rains' career, he had established a suave, rational, highly intelligent persona in too many movies for audiences to now accept him as a pathetic little clerk who transforms into a doubly pathetic simpleton, hopelessly in love with a woman who is a total stranger. Referring to the movie by its American title, *The New York Times* sniffed, "A very low quality of service is provided by *The Paris Express*…." Despite Rains' star presence and attractive Technicolor hues, it was a box-office failure.

Shooting again in England meant Claude and Frances would enjoy a grand vacation together. He rented a car and they began touring the countryside — all very different from their last visit in 1948 when rationing was still in effect. The first excursion was to

Dorset and all the little towns around the coast. He chose inns and old hotels that were typically English. Frances had read a lot about the area and was quite knowledgeable about many historical sites, which greatly impressed her husband. They went to Amberley in Sussex, then on to Arundel, Chichester and the little village of Bosham, then off to Winchester and parts of Hampshire, spending a night with friends in Boars Hill, Oxford. They toured the Cotswolds and then made their way back to London, staying at the stately old Mayfair rather than at one of the lavish new West End hotels. Rains joked that the entire time, all Frances could say was "Wow! Just look at that, Claude!" One historic site she never saw was the East End house in which Rains was born. On their adventures, Rains bought a reproduction virginal for Jennifer, one of his favorite old instruments (an actual antique would have been too expensive). As with so many things, he was quick to interject humor: "When [Jennifer] plays Bach on it, I weep, and I don't know whether I'm weeping for Bach or [Jennifer]. For Bach, I think."

Rains continued to read film and theatre scripts submitted to him but found nothing really exciting, and wisely refused to become involved in another heavy drama. Just prior to the overseas trip, in the spring of 1952, the Playwrights Company had contacted Rains about a new play titled *Jezebel's Husband*. Serving as producers, Roger Stevens, William Fields and actor Hume Cronyn wanted Rains for the lead. It was intended for the show to play the "straw hat circuit" over the summer before any decisions about a New York run were finalized. Unlike his previous arrangement for *Darkness at Noon*, Rains had his lawyer draw up a contract stating he was to be the star, and had the right to approve audience capacity, as well as the location, of the theatres. The actor was guaranteed three weeks rehearsal with compensation of $1,500 per week minimum. Remembering his ordeal with Jack Palance, there was also a clause giving him right of approval in casting. Furthermore, if there was going to be a Broadway run, he would have a seven-day option to decide if he wanted to be a part of the production. A tentative New York opening was set for November 3. Meanwhile, Rains could have an enjoyable summer on the circuit and not have to make any major decisions until the fall.

Jezebel's Husband had an excellent cast: Carmen Mathews, Eileen Heckart, a 21-year-old Ben Gaz-

zara, four years before his breakout in *Cat on a Hot Tin Roof*, and Ossie Davis, a veteran at thirty-five. While the script was light, the story, drawn from the Bible, was pleasant and enjoyable: Learned prophet Jonah is plagued by his wife, Jezebel, to charge money for his prognostications. Eventually, neither Rains nor the producers felt *Jezebel's Husband* worth the gamble of a New York commitment, and it closed after its summer run. Gazzara, on the threshold of his own great career, spoke very highly of Rains: "One night, at supper, after the show, he actually said that I could make a great actor one day, disparaging himself as he said so. That was 'style' and I have thought of him often ever since. He was a great actor, a sensitive man — a good man."

Forty years later, Ossie Davis retained special memories of the experience:

I remember the entire tour with fondness, but there was one incident — one time — that still lives very vividly in my memory and it still says to me who Claude Rains was.

I had known about Mr. Rains as a motion picture-goer and had admired that tremendous voice ever since he did *The Invisible Man*. I was quite glad to be working with him in *Jezebel's Husband*. We toured in the New England area, and in New Haven, the theatre was in one of those huge buildings owned by the insurance companies. After one matinee show I stayed in, and the two of us found ourselves alone backstage between the matinee and the evening performance. So, we talked a bit. He was not a very talkative man. Very private, very shy and a very sad and sensitive man. I always felt Mr. Rains was visited a lot by his past. I remember he would use the words "sad," "wounded" and "hurt" a lot when talking.

On this occasion we were chatting with each other and having nothing else to do and no place else to go, I suppose we just sort of let things hang out. He told me his wife had come to see him and his daughter — at any rate, she was there, and he told me what great friends and companions they were, and how they loved to shop and go places together and do things. Now I seemed to get the feeling he had expected them to show up so they could have a bite between shows, but they didn't.

At any rate, it didn't seem to trouble him; he assumed they were out shopping, and I soon got the feeling he was expressing an opinion that they were much fonder of each other than they were of him. They might have loved him and all, but they seemed to have more fun together than they had with him. He said this himself — that his wife and his daughter were close and didn't have a great deal of time for him. He didn't seem to mind it too much, but he certainly mentioned it to me, but I had no reason to ask him any questions about it.

…It was the kind of joking that husbands tell each other when they discover a truth about their relationship that is sensitive and tender. That is what I brought away from it — that he loved them both and they loved him, but they found more fun in each other's company than they found in his… I had a feeling that this was something that he would hardly tell anyone else.

At any rate, the thing that moved me most was I remember him standing against the racks in the dressing room, and he was leaning against them and he still had on his costume, a tunic, and he was talking about his life and some of the things he'd done and eventually he got to *Richard II*. And I remember him standing there and drifting into a recitation of some of the soliloquies, and being deeply moved as this voice, subtle and sad soothing, carried me. He did the speech so beautifully and so movingly that at the end of it, I was in tears and so was he. And there was nothing more to say after that, but I always had a very tender and affectionate feeling for him that grew out of that.

While Rains never had the opportunity to perform *Richard II* on stage, it remained his favorite play. When Davis learned this, he continued:

[That] sounds a bit in keeping with the person he was… Even when he played Jonah, there was something in his voice and manner that came from *beyond* the character that was in the play. He brought a lot of his own — or he was visited by a lot of his own past. I guess tragedies or lost loves or whatever — it all informed the play without in any way changing it whatever, but you always knew that something deep and mysterious was going on inside the Jonah he presented to us. …I got the feeling he was hurt, and I could understand it. You know, as a husband waiting on his wife and daughter. And in the way he described they had such fun together and by implication that 'it would be so wonderful if they had a little fun with me sometime.' I read that in the intonations of his voice…. This great soul had opened a door to his interior being to me for a moment and closed it again. I respected the privacy and I never spoke of it. It was always something I wanted to share with someone who would understand, but there was never an occasion and I'm glad [of] this opportunity because I loved him and saying this makes me feel better. I owed him that.

Poignantly, after the close of *Jezebel's Husband*, the two actors never met or spoke again. Did Rains realize Davis now knew a secret about him, and therefore wanted no further penetration of his protective shell? He could easily disguise a great deal beneath his tremendous self-deprecating sense of humor, but like the great clowns, even the greasepaint of a painted-on smile cannot hide their sadness. Bette Davis felt things had happened in Rains' life over the years which caused him to assume this protective stance: "[He] seemed wide open to the human experience, quite capable of being hurt in a relationship and therefore I think he withdrew … not to be snobbish or to be secretive. Whenever he took the risk of revealing himself, evidently something happened."

Back at Stock Grange, Rains received a telegram on September 19 from the Theatre Guild's Lawrence Langer about a new play, but after the exchange of many telephone calls and letters, Rains returned the script. The family would spend Christmas together at the farm. By the end of the year, as Rains readied his tax forms, he realized that 1952 had been a financial disaster and the worst year of his career since 1933. Because he made no motion pictures, his only professional income was approximately $10,000 for *Jezebel's Husband* and about $19,500 from the National Association of Educational Broadcasters. That was a total gross of $47,621, which included the sale of stocks and bonds along with a personal loss of $5,000 and a significant farm loss of nearly $8,400. The only luxury he allowed himself in 1952 was the purchase of two pedigree English Setter dogs which he intended to breed, but never did.

Rains had always run his home and farm with economy — now he became even more frugal, but also practical. He might limit himself to three new suits a year, but these were of high quality, and made

THEATRE MASTERWORKS

AN EVENING WITH
WILL SHAKESPEARE
on L.P. RECORDS

Original Gala Hartford Performance

ALL STAR CAST

CLAUDE RAINS   FAYE EMERSON
NINA FOCH   LEUEEN MacGRATH
Arnold Moss — Wesley Addy — Staats Cotsworth
E V A   L E   G A L L I E N N E
Selected Shakespearian Songs By
RICHARD DYER-BENNET
Directed and with Narrations By
MARGARET WEBSTER

ON SALE IN THE LOBBY

Or Use Order Form Below
Album of 4 L.P. Sides — $11.90
Scenes from RICHARD II—MACBETH—TWELFTH
NIGHT — HENRY V — MERCHANT OF VENICE

Please send .... albums of "An Evening With Will Shakespeare" to me postpaid.
Name...
Address...
For which I enclose check for $11.90.
Or for your convenience hand your check to attendant in the lobby and your album will be mailed to you promptly.
THEATRE MASTERWORKS - 30 ROCKEFELLER PLAZA - NEW YORK CITY

Program for An Evening with Will Shakespeare, *a December 1952 benefit for the American Shakespeare Festival and Academy.*

to his measurements on London's exclusive Savile Row. He also had his shoes hand-made in England at Harrods, preferring ankle-height boots of soft English leather. (These created the impression that he liked to ride, but he had not done so since the 1930s in Hollywood. Why he stopped is unknown, but he let this impression linger and when photographers came out to the farm, he would shine Frances' saddle under the pretense that they kept horses.) Rains' one sartorial weakness was quality shirts (he always had to have the sleeves shortened), which he ordered

CLAUDE RAINS

Distinguished Star of Stage and Screen

IN PERSON

THE PLAYHOUSE THEATRE
WILMINGTON, DELAWARE

November 21, 1953   Curtain, 8:30 p.m.

Program

CLAUDE RAINS
"WORDS AND MUSIC"
Jack Maxin at the piano

ENOCH ARDEN .... *Alfred Lord Tennyson*
Pianoforte arrangement by Richard Strauss

INTERMISSION

ON THE HARMFULNESS OF TOBACCO .... *Anton Tchekhov*

JOURNEY OF THE MAGI .... *T. S. Eliot*
Pianoforte arrangement by Marian Brinton

Scene from RICHARD II .... *Shakespeare*

APRIL MORNING .... *Robert Hillyer*
Pianoforte arrangement by Marian Bauer

Excerpts from THE CANTERBURY TALES .... *Chaucer*
Translated by Nevill Coghill

Words and Music *program.*

from conservative Abercrombie & Fitch. He had little vanity about his appearance, but he was always impeccably clean and well-dressed when working.

Rains' frugality was a part of his lifestyle and except for the antiques, there was little that was fancy in the decor of his home. He hated the idea of closed windows in the summer, refusing to permit air conditioning to be installed in his Colonial "palace." In the winter, he kept the thermostat at about 65 degrees. From his background in England, he was used to lower temperatures and felt Americans overheated their homes. Frances, always chilly, wore a sweater and warm tweeds and grumbled. There were moments of extravagance, especially towards people he was fond of; this often included gifts to the crew on a set or hotel employees. The Plaza Hotel doorman in New York City, Joseph Szorentini, remembered Rains staying there during the run of *Darkness at Noon*, and commenting that the actor was an impeccable dresser. One evening in early April on his way to the theatre, Rains greeted Joseph, asking him why he looked so sad. The doorman replied, "I'm not sad, I'm tired — my wife had a baby, and she is at the hospital." The actor offered his congratulations, asking which hospital. That evening, when Joseph went to visit his wife, he discovered a large, beautiful bouquet of flowers, sent by Rains. In telling the story four decades later, the old doorman's eyes filled with tears: "Mr. Rains was a gentleman — I never forget that — those beautiful flowers."

With no film or play offers tempting him, Rains hit on an idea: create a series of live readings and tour the country. The program consisted of Tennyson's "Enoch Arden," Shakespeare (Rains' favorite, *Richard II*), poetry by Robert Hillyer, an excerpt from *The Canterbury Tales*, T.S. Eliot's "Journey of the Magi" and selections from the Bible. He contacted Aaron Copland, requesting that the famous composer write a musical background for the show, but Copland was committed to another project. Instead, the musical

Author-poet Edward Shelton and composer Harl McDonald (manager of the Philadelphia Orchestra) in a publicity photo with CR for the Orchestra's program Builders of America.

accompaniment for the series, called *Words and Music*, was provided by an acclaimed pianist, Jack Maxin, only in his mid-twenties at the time. The tour went out under the auspices of the National Concert and Artist Corporation, which made all arrangements and bookings for performances in a different city nearly every other day for eight weeks. Rains earned $1,000 for each performance; however, if he was scheduled into a city for a few days and had five or six performances in any one week, then his salary was only $3,500 for the week, not $6,000. Gross earnings for the tour were $33,000. During interviews, Rains confessed he liked traveling for a change and boasted that he did his own laundry, washing out his nylon shirts by hand.

He was scheduled to go abroad again in April for another movie, but the shoot was postponed. This was to his advantage, because it allowed him to be-

come involved with another project closer to home. The venture would bring together two of his artistic friends, Edward Shenton and Harl McDonald. Shenton had attained prominence as an illustrator, author and editor; his poem "Artisans," an evocative depiction of the growth of America as seen through the eyes of Washington and Lincoln, had appeared in a national magazine a few months earlier. Shenton expanded the poem into a cantata, with music composed by McDonald (manager of the Philadelphia Orchestra) and supplemented by the Pennsylvania Collegiate Choral Association. Both Shenton and McDonald remembered Rains' amazing performance of Copland's "Lincoln Portrait" winning critical acclaim for the Orchestra. Rains wanted to be a part of this musical creation, which would provide him with the opportunity to pay tribute to his adopted country. *Builders of America*, as the show was titled, was performed on April 20 at Philadelphia's Drexel Institute. Columbia Records released a ten-inch LP of the composition for distribution to public schools. (Rains received no fee for the performance but must have been paid for the recording.)

Two other events occurred in 1953 that were firsts for Rains, both personally and professionally: He served on jury duty and made his television debut. In mid–June, he received notice that, as a Chester County resident, he was to appear in the Common Pleas Court for jury duty, in a case involving an auto accident. Rains reported to the courthouse fifteen minutes prior to opening and was in his juror's chair five minutes before court convened. "I like to be on time," he mentioned on another occasion. "This 'vice' has caused me embarrassment at times, it is true, but I just can't help being punctual and I like others to be that way too." He told an inquiring reporter: "I'm not missing a thing in show business by serving on the jury, but I could find plenty to do on the farm. It's been good weather for the past two days and there's some hay out there that needs attention." Asked why he didn't request to be excused as a farmer who needed to bring in the hay, he replied: "I wouldn't do that. I regard jury service as a civic duty. This is my first experience as a juror, and I find it very interesting. Even though my name was not called until yesterday afternoon, I enjoyed being in the courtroom while trials were under way."

TV-wise, Rains made his small-screen debut. First, he appeared on an episode of *Omnibus*, reading a poem by Sandburg. Then he starred in an episode of the CBS series *Medallion Theatre*, "The Man Who Liked Dickens." To his surprise, the actor found it a positive experience:

> I very much enjoy acting on television, but I do wish the pressure was a bit less. There is such a short time to get ready, and I must have time for preparation…. Usually there isn't enough time to learn the part and develop the character. You just learn the words and hope for the best, and if, like me, you're trying for some form of perfection, this can be very frightening…. You have to worry about words when you should be worrying about interpretation. Once the words are out of the way and come naturally, you can concentrate on your character.

Television seemed to combine Rains' love for live acting along with the magic intensity of the camera which brought out the best in him. But he did miss the director calling "cut" if there was a miscue.

In the fall, he signed a contract for another *Medallion* episode, playing a barrister on "The Archer Case." The only other activity in 1953 was a December 17 local (Philadelphia) broadcast, together with MET mezzo-soprano Risë Stevens and the Temple University Chorus. Rains read verses from the gospel according to St. Luke.

Nineteen fifty-three matched 1952 as a financial low. Between the farm's loss of $4,877 and lack of substantial work, Rains grossed only $49,000. This was a crucial turning point: He began to accept film roles no matter the merits of the project. Luckily, as 1954 approached, a wonderful opportunity came to the actor's rescue: another chance to return to Broadway, in T.S. Eliot's *The Confidential Clerk*.

Eliot had made a dramatic impression on Broadway with two previous plays, *Murder in the Cathedral* and the provocative *The Cocktail Party*. His most recent work had been commissioned for the 1952 Edinburgh Festival; Broadway producer Henry Sherek wanted to bring the play to New York. Initially Eliot was reluctant, partly because the play had been created for the festival, and because it was decidedly British in approach and dialogue. Sherek convinced Eliot to let him produce *Cocktail Party* in London first. When it opened in August and was well-received, Sherek was in a more persuasive position. However, several American investors were apprehensive, believing it was safer to have both American and British actors in the cast, and book tryouts in New Haven, Boston and Washington, D.C. Sherek was able to convince his backers that *The Confidential Clerk* would be a hit, especially with a star heading the cast.

The American production was under the auspices of the Producers' Theatre (Roger Stevens, Robert Whitehead and Robert Dowling). Stevens immediately contacted Rains to play the male lead. After *Darkness at Noon*, the actor's participation ensured advance ticket sales. Even though Rains may have considered himself American, there's no question he was still thoroughly British as far as audiences were concerned. Douglas Watson and Joan Greenwood were in the cast; vibrant and beautiful Ina Claire, returning to the theatre after her own seven-year absence, completed the four-person company. Rehearsals were set for mid–December.

For Rains, it was an experience totally different from the unpleasantness of *Darkness at Noon*. The

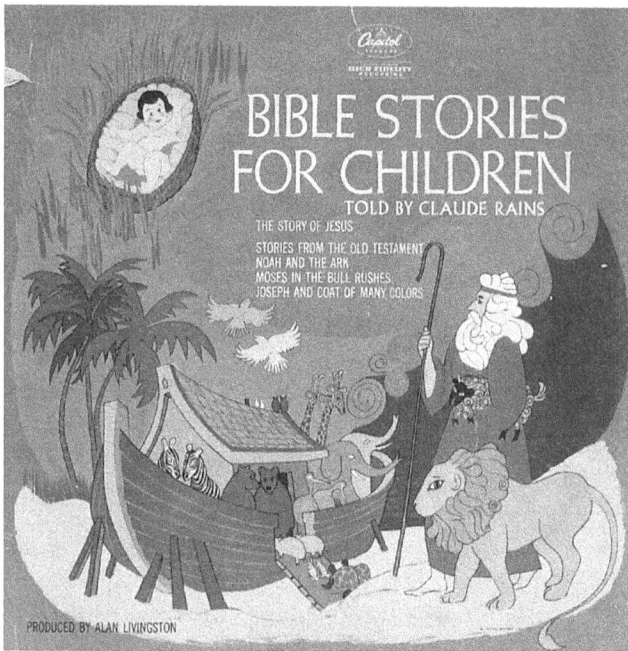

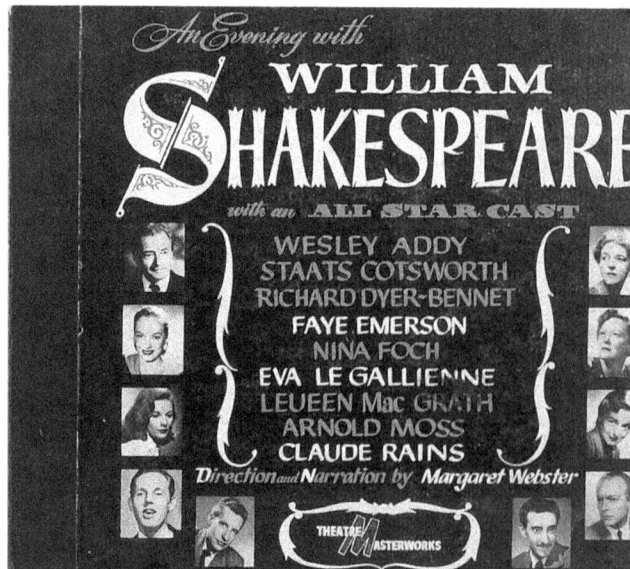

Rains' distinctive voice made recordings – of all subjects – a natural.

small company was amiable, cooperative and very professional; there was no infighting among egos. He loved the stylized dialogue and the subject matter: individuals must make inner peace with their souls, especially when the success they achieve in life is far removed from their original goals. Things progressed so smoothly it was almost relaxing. *The Confidential Clerk* opened in New Haven at the Shubert on January 7, 1954, moving on to Boston and Washington. Although the play was called "talky," all agreed that Rains was splendid. "Eliot's play is an intellectual exercise and not a sentimental journey despite its touches of very real sentiment which Claude Rains brings in with his superior talent for acting character roles," wrote the *Connecticut Record*. "The play had elegance, exercised the intellect and displayed admirable performances by all concerned," said the *Boston Herald*.

The Confidential Clerk did a good job of expressing the hunger of the human heart for understanding, love and fulfillment. Into a rather unrealistic situation in which Rains' character and his wife both mistakenly believe the young man they have hired as their confidential clerk is their illegitimate son, Eliot weaves the more important plot of self-disillusionment and ever-lasting frustration in not being able to fulfill our true desires regardless of our other successes in life.

What no one else would have known was that Rains' character was espousing many of the actor's own yearnings. Although he had achieved great success in Hollywood, movie roles never seemed to have afforded him complete fulfillment or deep satisfaction as an actor; he always felt he was not really recognized until the ordeal of *Darkness at Noon*, which had come so late in his life and at such an emotional cost. It's easy to read into one of Rains' speeches what he himself must have felt about his profession:

> If it's an escape, it's an escape into living.... I want a world where the form is the reality, of which the substantial is only a shadow.... There are moments, contemplating some masterpiece when I seem to be united with the soul of the maker.... I sometimes have that sense of identification with the maker, that I spoke of — an agonizing ecstasy which makes life bearable. It's all I have. I suppose it takes the place of religion.... There are others, it seems to me, who have at best to live in two worlds: each a kind of make-believe. That's you and me…

Under the efficient direction of E. Martin Browne, *The Confidential Clerk* opened in New York at the Morosco Theatre on February 11, 1954. There it also met with favorable, although not ecstatic, reviews, plenty good enough to ensure a run through the season. The March issue of classy *Vogue* magazine featured a lavish full-page photo spread of Rains with Joan Greenwood and Ina Claire at his side. Newspaper ads incorporated solid pull quotes, like the *Christian Science Monitor*'s "Play mingles light and serious dialogue and Mr. Rains is consistently dignified and he becomes genuinely touching when the final revelations appear." If some felt Eliot's new work lacked intellectual depth, the first-rate cast impeccably handled the author's elaborate and witty lines, which carried the show through May. Just as *Notorious* was Rains' last great supporting role in a great motion picture, *The Confidential Clerk* was the final superior play in which he performed on the New York stage.

CHAPTER 23
A Family Divided

After the run of *The Confidential Clerk* ended, Rains returned to Stock Grange in a good mood to relax and enjoy the summer. It was during these months that he met a young man who, like the *Confidential Clerk* character, was caught in the trap of wanting to do something else with his life, but who needed someone to support and encourage him in his dream. It was because of Rains' interest and friendship that Dick Berg eventually became a successful television producer.

Married with two sons and running an art gallery in New Jersey, Berg longed to write and produce shows for TV. He had what he considered a unique idea for a weekly series: The basic plots would examine the lives of people from a high school yearbook twenty years after graduation. Believing there was only one actor who could give his work credence, Berg contacted Rains' agent at William Morris, who suggested the young man take his scripts directly to the actor. Receiving approval for the visit, Berg, nervous, sat outside in his car while Rains went into his library and read. "He was very gracious, and I was overwhelmed," remembered Berg decades later. "He was warm and receptive and liked the program." Rains agreed to narrate the series; Berg credited the actor's positive reaction with giving him the confidence to undertake his new career.

Now it was all up to Berg. He sold his art gallery, took his savings and raised money for a pilot. At Rains' suggestion, William Morris tried to sell the series to various sponsors. Unfortunately, Berg's unrealistic endings were sometimes harsh and true-to-life, unlike most popular programs of the 1950s, and he was unable to sell the series. But in the months that followed, Rains continued to express confidence that Berg would eventually achieve his goal — which he did, moving his family to Los Angeles and succeeding in a new career as a TV producer. Berg and Rains stayed in touch, seeing each other occasionally,

but they didn't work together until many years later. Berg never forgot Rains' enthusiasm for a young, untried gallery owner's dream of breaking into the entertainment business. To show his appreciation of Rains' kindness, Berg named his third child after the actor: Anthony Rains Berg was born in October 1954 and Rains was the boy's godfather. (Another of Berg's children, A. Scott Berg, won the Pulitzer Prize for his 1999 Charles Lindbergh biography.)

During the remainder of 1954, Rains received no additional offers, but did have two large expenses. In August, Frances accompanied Jennifer abroad with her French class; in just a year's time, the girl would be off to Bennington College as a freshman. During their absence, Rains' brother-in-law and friend, Walter Propper, invited the actor to attend the wedding of his son Eric, who had spent many summers at Stock Grange. Walter had been the only Propper family member who approved of the actor's proposal of marriage to his sister; Rains became the only member of Frances' family to loan Walter money when he needed it for his roofing business, telling his brother-in-law not to worry about repayment. Eric remembered how much his father and Claude enjoyed each other's company, and that they could easily finish off a bottle of whiskey between them. Photos prove Claude had a good time at the wedding, partly due to the fact that he was able to show off his new car — an expensive reward he bought for himself that summer, the second large expense. The purchase of the car – an elegant Bentley – may have been to ward off depression he was feeling due to lack of work, or the inescapable fact he was approaching 65. He was not feeling very happy about the waning days of his life: At this age, he should be basking in success with financial security. He even considered retirement. His life had been consistently hectic ever since he was ten years old, and now he was tired. Maybe it was time to settle back and take things easy, reduce the energy expended in his profession. Time to enjoy life with Frances, possibly do new things, take trips together, attend the theatre as an audience member for once. He decided to give this matter serious thought, occasionally even mentioning it to a reporter. Still, Rains was conditioned by his past; he absolutely needed to act, not as a livelihood as much as a way to manage his personality. Preoccupied — with his age, the need to keep working, with the futility of finding decent work, and his self-absorption in this quest — Rains failed to notice, or to realize, that his wife was also experiencing her own serious crisis.

When not working, the summers were enjoyed as a quiet time for Rains, but over the years they may have been too quiet for Frances. She had provided elaborate meals for the small dinner parties they hosted, but often she attended many social events without Claude. A young girl friend of Jennifer's, who spent many happy days on the farm, was Jan Dekker, the daughter of actor Albert Dekker. "I remember when Jennifer and I would be asleep at Stock Grange, Frances would come into the room and we'd awake to bowls of fruit. She groomed a lot, and he always wore a suit. …Frances may have become restless at Stock Grange. You can love someone and still outgrow the relationship."

Dekker remembered that at times, the tension between the couple was palpable. Until Jennifer graduated high school, she grew up in a happy home with a secure parental relationship. Even though his daughter was sometimes afraid of Rains, her friend never was. "It wasn't that he was a controlling person; he just had his way. And there was a shyness. I think he would have been open to contact, but his manner was so forbidding." Upon reflection years later, Dekker suggested that Rains could not readjust to changes in his relationship other than those of his own devising; he could not acclimatize his personality to a new situation and only felt comfortable in an environment he had established.

In a way, by 1955 Frances and Claude were each caught in a personal midlife crisis. Intimacy can take many forms: A person can be made to feel attractive or wanted by no more than a smiling glance. Perhaps, now in her early forties, Frances needed to feel she was still desired. In the early days of their marriage, Rains was open about his love for his wife to the point where sometimes she would be embarrassed. But as he grew older, he may have made assumptions

that she "understood" how he felt. He probably was not the type to reflect upon a relationship, and there probably were times when he was too absorbed in himself to even imagine that Frances was drifting away. After all, he was faithful and never flirted; there was no need to constantly reassure her of his love. But Frances did need reassurance, more than Claude realized.

Compounding these emotional insecurities were mounting financial ones. Nineteen fifty-four was a terrible year; Rains' gross income was only $36,810 (approximately $26,000 for *The Confidential Clerk*, and about $500 for each episode he recorded for his 15-minute NBC radio series *Claude Rains Presents*). Some annuities and government bonds matured; however, he was now incurring medical expenses. And once again the farm failed to make a profit, in 1954 suffering its largest loss, nearly $8,500, almost double that of 1953. Rains began to feel a sense of panic. It seemed as if a prophecy he had made to critic Laura Lee in September 1951, following his triumph in *Darkness at Noon*, was coming true: "Where can I go but down?" The ordeal of *Darkness at Noon*, coupled with his tendency to seldom take a vacation, had taken a toll both physically and mentally. As he approached his mid-sixties, he grew moodier and more irascible. The devilish, mischievous twinkle in his eyes vanished and he laughed less often. General exhaustion may have prevented him from being as attentive and loving a husband as he had been during the early days of his marriage.

But friends noticed that Frances seemed restless and at times even bored; things that had once given her great pleasure were no longer fulfilling. Even though the couple took occasional trips to Sandwich and the New England region, for the most part when he wasn't working, Rains was perfectly content with the quiet, scenic beauty of the Brandywine area. All of this gave him great satisfaction and, more importantly, had a calming effect on his psyche. More than likely he assumed Frances shared his love of the pastoral life, and for many years she did, often expressing her happiness about living at Stock Grange.

Frances' nephew Eric believed that she was very happy with Claude for about fifteen years, but as the actor aged, he seemed less responsive to the younger woman's needs. Although Frances had generally been a very quiet and conventional woman, in her forties but still attractive, with a daughter now grown, she may have felt something missing from her life.

Initially Frances liked the fact that her husband was twenty years older: he was mature, and she, so quiet and diplomatic, was easily able to accommodate herself to his whims as well as his idiosyncrasies. Always reluctant to create a scene or get into arguments, Frances understood that Claude's strong-willed manner was a part of his artistic personality. Rains was admittedly complex, and many people marveled at her ability to maintain a tranquil home life. Even though their personalities were so different, they got along splendidly. Claude was drawn to and admired his wife's soft-spoken and undemanding manner. She seldom challenged him on any issue and consequently the relationship never seemed strained. Lacking the nature to convey her feelings openly, Frances accepted her husband's wishes. Undoubtedly, their childhood upbringings — diametrically opposed — had much to do with their maturing relationship. As the youngest member of the Propper clan, Frances had been spoiled and pampered, showered with attention and affection. Her mother and father, as well as siblings, indulged her. She was even allowed to leave high school early to become an actress.

Rains, however, lacked the stability of growing up in a solid family unit, with its associated emotional security. As an adult, his single crucial need was a dedicated, caring and obedient companion; he could not bear to be alone. This pitiful state must have been hard for others to understand. (In his book, Paul Henreid unkindly commented: "Claude was a prima donna — a big baby — he always expected women to serve upon him.")

Of utmost importance in their relationship was Frances' respect for Claude's integrity. She accepted his flair for the theatrical because he was an artist with great talent, and she was philosophical about his moodiness. She never doubted that he would always provide for her and her child. Above all, her husband was faithful. The strongest bond of their marriage was that they trusted each other. As a famous actor, Rains had actresses throwing themselves at him; it would have been quite easy to indulge in a fling, but fidelity and virtue were of paramount importance to him. His loyalty to the woman he married would not be compromised — ever. Rains expected the same from his wife; but then, he always expected others to act as he would in any given situation.

As with any relationship, there may have been niggling little things which Frances found annoying over the years and which grew into increasingly insurmountable irritations. Top of any list would probably have been her husband's inordinate frugality, even when he made a great deal of money, and his continuing anxiety over financial security. Perhaps as she grew older, Frances felt deprived, or possibly even humiliated, that she had so little independence. For many years, she rationalized that her husband's behavior didn't come from selfishness, but the insecurity fostered by the memory of his childhood, and while she was young, she could indulge this aspect of his character. However, it was to be hoped and even anticipated that, when he earned more money, he would eventually relax about finances. But he held fast. Yet, when it came to the farm's constant need for upkeep, Rains never hesitated to spend freely.

And finally, those who knew the couple felt without qualification that while Claude loved and respected Frances, it was Jennifer who made his life complete. Rains spoiled his daughter, spent money on gifts for her — he felt life flow from her into his soul. Oddly, while Rains loved his daughter, his wife and his farm, he seldom participated in any traditional family events. While he was under contract to Warner Bros., the studio PR department did its part to try and position Rains as an average dad. In one publicity still, Rains is helping his daughter with a long division problem, but Jennifer admitted he couldn't do complicated math because of his lack of schooling.

Jennifer's friend Jan Dekker remembered spending several summers at Stock Grange. She said that the actor was usually in his study and "never came to the pond." Dekker also recalled his quiet but decidedly authoritarian manner:

> In his presence, we kids would behave. We would dress for dinner; it was formal. I remember once after we had been playing, I changed clothes and was sitting with Claude in the study opposite him and he looked at me and said, "The frock is clean, but the knees beneath it need attention." I whipped out of there and washed my knees better than I ever had in my life. His word was definitely law. I wasn't scolded, but there was the oblique approach with

humor in it, but it was law, coming from Claude. I wasn't afraid of him, but very respectful. He had a commanding speech and spoke as if he were seven foot tall and he also had a very erect being.

There's no question that Stock Grange was the foundation of the family at that point. It always amazed the Propper family how a city girl like Frances came to love living on the farm. She once told a neighbor: "I love it here; I never want to live anywhere else." Yet as the years passed, and especially when her husband was in Hollywood, the neighbor realized: "She seemed to be groping for friendship — I'm sorry now I didn't pay more attention to that. Looking back, I realize now that is what it was — she was lonely. I never ever saw them doing things together as a couple, you know. I'd see him or I'd see her and except for their entertaining, they never did things together." Mrs. Jeffers recalled a time she went over to the farm on her horse:

We were supposed to go riding. He came out and said, "She was at a party last night and hasn't got herself together yet." I turned around and came home. I always tried to do whatever she wanted to do because I sorta felt sorry for her. She loved the farm but seemed bored. Frances told me he had to be alone because in a lot of parts he would play, he would shout as he rehearsed…

She did not talk about Claude much…. She loved Stock Grange, but she wasn't a farmer's wife like most of us. She did take me through the house. I was teaching school at that time and she did volunteer work at the Chester County Hospital. When I and a nurse friend of mine came out she invited us over and served us lemonade and cookies. I'll always remember that; she was very hospitable. I don't know what else she did with her time. Now, my brother had contact with him. I remember when Claude would drive here to get some tools. And I remember he always rode with one foot out when he drove the Jeep and my brother said, "He does that because he's afraid someone will hit him and then he'll

be halfway out of the Jeep!"

The Rainses … well, they had their parties with their friends, but neighbors weren't invited. Now my brother, who was a farmer, well, Claude would go out to the barn and they would talk a lot. We tried to respect their privacy. Evidently Claude gave off two signals to his neighbors and they were never certain as to where they stood in their circle of friends. They were not considered "friends," just neighbors. In that respect, he remained very English…

Like her parents, Jennifer loved Stock Grange but unlike her mother, she never felt lonely and had a great many friends. As a teenager in the mid–1950s, she was unaware that her mother and father were drifting apart. Everything seemed harmonious; even if there was friction, the couple always concealed it from their daughter. There was always laughter at Stock Grange. The good times of her young life seemed to linger more than any negative images. "We all loved that place," she repeated with a sigh.

One summer afternoon in 1954, Rains returned to the farm from a trip. He found Frances entertaining a guest invited in his absence: a clothing store merchant from nearby West Chester, Henry Feder. Jennifer and her mother had bought things in his store; he seemed very pleasant and interesting. If Rains was upset by the male "guest," he said nothing in front of their daughter, nor was there any additional comment about the visit. According to Jennifer: "My parents never fought and never spoke loudly to each other. I never heard them quarrel." However, knowing the world in which Rains grew up, and understanding his values, it was undoubtedly disturbing for him to discover another man in his home, uninvited by him and during his absence. But he had always trusted his wife just as she trusted him. To Rains, that was the most important aspect of their marriage.

Various persons who were around the couple at this time, who knew them and had firsthand knowledge of the situation, suggest that Frances had occasionally seen Feder socially. He must have satisfied something she felt was missing in her life; there is enough consistency in comments made by these observers to substantiate such an assumption. Their marriage lacked the vital element of compromise. Frances told an old friend, "Claude never really knew what it meant to be a husband." She had changed; she was "ready:" Frances made the monumental decision to leave her husband. She felt it was more prudent to wait until Jennifer had graduated high school and gone off to college, in order to try and protect her from any local scandal. However, evidently something happened which caused Frances to feel she could no longer remain at Stock Grange.

Much of this is based upon reports of observers and educated assessments. Whenever anyone approached Frances about her life with Claude or the reasons she left, she insisted, "I could never talk about it — I just couldn't do it." And she never did — not even to her daughter later in life. The only person from that time who knew Frances' reasons, and who remained silent, was her confidant, her older sister Martha. Perhaps Frances had reached the point where she wanted to be recognized for her own individuality and not solely as "Mrs. Claude Rains." Or perhaps it's that people inevitably change as they grow older. Or was it the excitement of a new admirer? Henry Feder was younger than Rains, tall, attractive and intelligent. He was jovial and laughed a lot. He seemed warm, friendly and outgoing. He owned a dress shop; Jennifer had purchased some items there. (Did Jennifer know who he was, what he meant to her mother?) Was Frances attracted to his demeanor and character? One of Jennifer's friends noticed that Henry was very attentive to Frances. Ironically, Rains appeared to regard this as an immature flaw; he confided to a friend after the divorce, "Some women never grow up."

Whatever the reason, or reasons, on an evening in early summer 1955, all of their lives changed forever. According to Jennifer, her parents engaged in a very loud and serious argument. She had never before heard them quarrel in this manner — screaming at each other with frightful accusations. Fearful, Jennifer stayed in her room until things grew quiet. Then her mother came to tell her that she was leaving Stock Grange; did Jennifer want to come with her or stay? The teenager elected to stay, for several reasons: She had many friends in the area, she loved the farm, and soon she would be off to college. So Frances

Jennifer and her father in a Downingtown, Pennsylvania, store in the mid–1950s.

drove off, without saying goodbye and without any of her personal effects. Rains fell apart. "My father got drunk that night, really drunk. It was the only time I heard them fight — the only time I saw him drunk." It was a harrowing experience intensified by the fact that, prior to this, there had only been the happiness and the laughter they all shared. Many years later, Frances stated only that the marriage had started to sour about five years before she decided to leave. As Rains viewed it, her departure was the ultimate act of betrayal. He would marry again, but he was never the same man.

Because Rains was so absorbed with his own pain, he was oblivious to the fact that Jennifer was likely overwhelmed by events, too. It had always been difficult to talk to her father; now it was almost impossible to meet his demands or feel comfortable with him. Aware of the effect the divorce could have on their daughter, both Claude and Frances were relieved she would enter Bennington College in September. The awful choice of which parent to live with would be avoided, and embarrassing local gossip would be tempered. However, Frances had left in such anger and haste she made no arrangements for Jennifer during the summer months, and so except for a few weekends away, she lived at Stock Grange. She could not help but notice her father had lost interest in the farm, nor could she ignore a recent arrival — his newly established drinking companion.

It was extremely difficult for Rains to be without the companionship of a woman, so he took up with a married female neighbor whose husband traveled frequently and who, like him, enjoyed a glass. Her almost daily visits to Stock Grange became the talk of the area. Jennifer referred to the woman as "his drinking buddy." Nothing came of the relationship.

In the meantime, Frances went to the Bronx, New York, to stay with her sister Martha; she never returned to Stock Grange anytime Rains was there. Her cousin, a lawyer, arranged for her to establish a pseudo-legal residence in the state of Alabama, Cullman County, in absentia. She decided not to go through the publicity of a Reno "quickie divorce"; she had always protected Claude's privacy. A divorce a year later from a Southern state would generate less press. Rains permitted his wife to state in the legal papers that "he had abandoned her bed," regardless of the facts.

To keep busy, Rains contracted to do a series of radio shows for NBC, which he recorded on tape at the farm and mailed to New York for broadcast. Robert Jennings produced the show, which aired weekdays in a 3:30 p.m. time slot. *Variety* reviewed the first one as interesting and deserving of attention. However, the NBC sales department had difficulty finding commercial sponsors and the project was canceled after the summer months.

At times, especially when he was alone, Rains became overwrought and irrational. Jennifer remembered that during her freshman year, he telephoned her at college and demanded she return to Stock Grange "to take care of him." She hardly knew how to react. "I was frightened. I didn't know what to do and phoned my mother [in New York] who stated firmly to me that I remain at Bennington." In all likelihood, his action was a response to the depression that had descended on him and he phoned her in a moment of panic and loneliness.

In November, Rains was offered a part in a color-widescreen Republic film to be shot on location in

Maureen O'Hara and CR in Lisbon.

Portugal, with his friend Ray Milland as producer-director-star. Anxious to get away from Pennsylvania and think about something other than his personal problems, Rains accepted. In *Lisbon*, the wife (Maureen O'Hara) of an elderly millionaire wrongly imprisoned overseas is assured by international crook Rains that, for a steep price, her husband can be sprung and returned to her. Milland, a happy-go-lucky American smuggler using his yacht to ply his trade in the waters off Lisbon, is drawn into the plot, which takes several unexpected twists.

Rains' character Aristides Mavros calls himself "a citizen of the world" but admits to Milland that he's Greek. ("I was born on the island of Mytilene, once called Lesbos. Delightful legend, that!") His palatial Lisbon home is staffed by a gloomy black-clad hit man (Francis Lederer) and a pair of young beauties "[that] Rains keeps around to satisfy his esthetic tastes" (*Variety*). When he learns that one of them (Yvonne Furneaux) had drinks with Milland, he instructs his secretary, "Burn two of her newest gowns." A sly silver-haired rogue in the now-classic Rains tradition, the character has the full supply of wry, sophisticated banter but a heart as black as his name (*mavros* is Greek for black). In a dinner table scene, he's the perfect host, telling O'Hara that he

THE PHILADELPHIA ORCHESTRA

Forty-ninth Season, 1948-1949

THIRD PROGRAM

Friday Afternoon, October 15, at Two-thirty
Saturday Evening, October 16, at Eight-thirty

EUGENE ORMANDY Conducting
GINETTE NEVEU, Violinist
CLAUDE RAINS, Speaker

MOZART . . . . Symphony No. 35, in D major
(K. 385)—"Haffner"
    I Allegro con spirito
    II Andante
    III Menuetto
    IV Presto

COPLAND . . . . A Lincoln Portrait
CLAUDE RAINS, *Speaker*
(First performance at these concerts)

INTERMISSION

BEETHOVEN . . . . . Concerto in D major, Opus 61,
for Violin and Orchestra
    I Allegro ma non troppo
    II Larghetto
    III Rondo: Allegro
         GINETTE NEVEU

The Steinway is the official piano of The Philadelphia Orchestra
Columbia Records   Victor Records
COLUMBIA BROADCASTING SYSTEM

69

inherited his love of beauty from his father: "He was a connoisseur of fine jewels, and only stole the best." O'Hara quails at his candor but the rascal remains all-smiles: "We have been thieves for six generations, Mrs. Merrill. Very *successful* thieves!" O'Hara remembered Rains as withdrawn: "[He] was a very private person. He did not socialize with the members of the company. He was a kind and charming gentleman, and a fine actor. I was honored to work with him." *Lisbon* had a weak script unworthy of the talents of the three leads, but Rains pocketed $30,000 for six weeks of work.

When Rains returned to the U.S., Alfred Hitchcock wanted the actor to guest star on his new television series, and on February 12, 1956, the actor appeared in the first of five *Alfred Hitchcock Presents* episodes. It was one of his best performances, as the possessed ventriloquist in "And So Died Riabouchinska," based on a story by Ray Bradbury. The author was more than pleased with the performance, calling Rains "assured, self-aware, humorous, dynamic!"

At Chicago's Ravinia Festival, Rains recited Aaron Copland's "A Lincoln Portrait" while Copland himself conducted the orchestra. Then in March, the actor (in a snappy suit and wearing glasses) appeared in wraparounds in addition to narrating the TV adaptation of Walter Lord's famous saga of the *Titanic*'s sinking, "A Night to Remember," for NBC's *Kraft Television Theatre*. The show's director was George Roy Hill, a young man who had begun as a writer for *Kraft* and went on to make movie classics like *Butch Cassidy and the Sundance Kid* and *The Sting* (in which Rains' daughter had a bit part). "A Night to Remember" was an unusual and arduous undertaking when those early days of live television presented such difficult technical challenges. There were seven cameras, over one hundred performers and thirty different sets — a huge production for the time. Not surprisingly, it earned spectacular ratings. *Variety* noted that Rains "was excellent as the narrator, his script hitting the right note of questioning and moralizing." Hill admired Rains' reading and acknowledged the impact the actor's delivery had on the production. He remembered Rains as humble and unpretentious, and very interested in learning more about the medium of television. He and Rains "became friends, but not close or intimate, no one did. Claude was completely absorbed in his work."

Television provided a great deal of work for Rains during the late 1950s. The young television playwrights were churning out good material, and seasoned artists like Rains could cope with the fluffs and glitches of live performance. Rehearsals were often limited to a week; during broadcasts, viewers could frequently hear scenery being moved and props dropped off camera. The hot lights literally would melt makeup. For audiences raised on a film medium that had matured over the past decades, live television sometimes seemed like amateur theatrics in one's own living room. Regardless, even with the drawbacks, some of the finest television drama ever produced appeared on the tiny black and white screen in millions of homes across the country. For Rains, television proved a life saver at the time he needed one, and as soon as he finished one television play, he signed on for another. Seven days of rehearsals, one performance, and he collected his usual $5,000 fee. Plus, he was once again working in front of a camera where he felt comfortable.

One such show which aired in May 1956 was *The Alcoa Hour*'s "The President." With a script by David Davidson and directed by Robert Mulligan, the absorbing episode featured Rains as Justice Paul Westman, a popular, retired Supreme Court Justice who is drafted to run for president to save his party. It was one of Rains' best TV performances, aided by an excellent supporting cast featuring Everett Sloane and Rains' friend Larry Gates. The moral of the story was that a presidential candidate cannot afford to limit the support he receives to only groups he likes. Politics involves distasteful compromises, and if a man runs for high office, he will be corrupted sooner or later. (Shades of *Mr. Smith Goes to Washington*'s Senator Paine.) Initially, Rains' character will not compromise his lofty principles, but in the course of the campaign, the idea of being president bewitches him. Then comes the moment of redemption. Just before the election, the opposition learns that one of the former justice's trusted clerks once belonged to a club with Communist leanings, about the worst allegation that could be made against anyone in the 1950s. The party bosses demand their candidate denounce the young man rather than chance losing the election. He refuses, instead offering an explanation to the public. In the end he wins and becomes "Mr. President," but it is clear that the victory is psychologically and morally costly. In the future, he will compromise again and again to remain in power. Rains was still an impressive actor — this short, muscular man who stood ramrod straight, with his throaty imperious voice. It was an intelligent and tightly controlled performance and won critical praise: "[Rains] held the play firmly together with an excellent performance. His persuasively drawn portrait corrected any tendency of the script to fall into generalizations about the conflict of ambition and idealism. Rains made the abstractions come alive…."

Professional successes aside, the enormity of what had occurred in his personal life became overpowering. For a man of Rains' temperament, divorce was more than devastating — it was the end of all he had hoped and planned for during the last twenty-five years. He was sixty-six-years old; his wife had walked out on him; his daughter was now in college and soon would be off to a career. He would be totally alone. With so few close friends, he had no way to come to terms with Frances' desertion or how to overcome his intense loneliness. His emotional disintegration was apparent to those few who knew him; he was inconsolable and seemed unable to deal with what he regarded as a devastating wound to his ego. As he saw it, all during his life it had been others who hurt and abandoned him. As a friend of both Claude and Frances for ten years, Ronald Neame reflected that Rains was like any other human being, with imperfections, problems and sometimes bad thoughts. As an actor, Rains was an acknowledged genius, but Neame concluded that he must have been a very, very difficult man to live with:

> I would think Frances must have been long-suffering, but prepared (and willing) to accept it. But after she met Henry [Feder], she became closer and preferred to be with Henry…. Claude had tremendous insecurity, most actors do, and when he would drink, well, it could be occasionally become upsetting. He'd have a great deal to drink at dinner and then a brandy; he had to be careful because if he drank much more it could be a problem. He seemed to know when to stop. When I knew him, it seemed he cared about Frances a great deal. I can only think it became too much for her, but I also think he went downhill from the time they parted. The divorce from Frances shattered his ego. I never saw him after that.

Rains felt betrayed, abandoned and humiliated at the hands of the one person who had meant the most to him for the past twenty-seven years of his life, spiritually depleted because of his failure to sustain the intimacy that was so crucial to him. As a result of increased alcohol intake, anger replaced reason. He was totally fixated on the idea that his loyalty to and trust in his wife had been violated. Reporters had often quoted him declaring that above all he hated insincerity, that he "could not stand a lie." If Frances had left him but remained unmarried, possibly, in time, Rains could have adjusted. But she had replaced him — a great actor — with a shopkeeper. This was more than his pride could accept. His personal failures with women now completely upset his psychological equilibrium. His self-esteem had experienced a fatal blow because he could not overcome the inevitable emptiness of life as he grew older.

CHAPTER 24
"He's not the same man."

In late May 1956, the divorce decree was granted to Frances, and by mid–July she divested her property joint ownership in Stock Grange as part of the settlement. She wanted and took nothing else from Claude except her personal effects. When the divorce was finalized, Rains took his Bentley convertible coupe and left the farm for a drive. He returned late in the evening, emotionally distraught and overcome by events, and couldn't maneuver the large automobile around the bend in the gravel road near his neighbor's farm. Though not driving fast, he lost control; the car careened off into a stream bed and crashed on its side, with some wires catching on fire. Rains was thrown out before the car overturned. When the neighbor heard the crash and came running, she realized that the mud-covered actor must be intoxicated as he tried to make his way up the embankment. Everyone who converged at the scene realized the sensitivity of the situation and agreed not to call the police or the fire department. It was Rains' own car on his own property, and he was un-injured. The neighbor remembered the actor ranting that he had almost drowned: "It was very dramatic, the way he carried on … it was difficult not to laugh at his comments and his appearance. We watched him try to walk up Chestnut Lane toward his farm with one shoe, dirty and disheveled, muttering and weaving from side to side." Charles Brown helped the disoriented actor home and put him to bed. Quite early the next morning, Brown returned to the site of the crash with the tractor and hauled out the destroyed Bentley, which he towed back to the farm. Rains called Jennifer and told her about the incident, insisting he had only sprained his arm. As usual, he did not make a report to the insurance company but wrote off the loss of the car on his income tax.

Now officially divorced from her mother, Rains decided to establish an irrevocable trust for Jennifer, committing to yearly contributions to ensure her future financial security whatever happened to him. He also made her the beneficiary of his life insurance policies and sole heir. Aggravated by his drinking, a series of serious physical illnesses began to assail Rains. His doctor suggested the actor think about selling the farm to relieve stress, an idea which began to appeal to him because of the intense loneliness he felt wandering around the once happy rooms by himself. His sanctuary of peace, the pleasure he had taken in homegrown food raised by his own hands, such joy as he had never known — ghosts of happy times haunted him. He couldn't cope with the pain and memories in Stock Grange, the home he and Frances had loved and restored together. Even though Charles and Lily Brown, also growing older, were loyal to him and remained, it was all too much to endure. In the scribbled notes he compiled for his autobiography, there is one word in the margins which leaps out when he writes of this period: "Crying." Rains did not elaborate; the word stood alone. He knew he had to leave. "I loved that farm," he said. "It was something to come home to. When the play closed or the movie was finished, I went right back to the farm. Knowing it was there sustained me." Stock Grange was no longer home.

With his health deteriorating, his depression worse, no family to share it with, it seemed logical to sell. He rationalized the decision by claiming it was doctor's advice. Jennifer would come back only for holidays and perhaps a few weeks during summers. She was beginning a new life with new friends and it was only a matter of time before she, too, departed permanently. The loss of Stock Grange would be a great sadness for Jennifer as well; she spent some of the happiest times of her life there. She repeated frequently that, as a child, her father was "a happy man. I remember lots of laughter and jokes; he loved life, the farm and farming. I'm sure he had bad times, I do remember that, but he got tremendous satisfaction from his work and his family, running the farm and telling stories to anyone who would listen. He was also a very private person and did not open up emotionally to people…"

That August, Harrison Wetherall expressed interest in buying Stock Grange, offering less than the asking price, probably knowing that Rains was less concerned with money than he was with who would be the future caretaker of his precious farm. The Wetheralls were prominent in Chester County and knew about Stock Grange's long history — including the care with which Rains had restored it. Wetherall agreed to all requested stipulations and promised to preserve it in the same manner.

Acting was the only thing that could save him now. Rains went to New York to ready himself for the *Kaiser Aluminum Hour*'s "Antigone," another excellent live TV production of the period. It was a particularly difficult work to condense into less than sixty minutes, but as *Variety* commented, "in essence it's an idea play dealing with the inhuman corruption of power and the spirit of man to resist tyranny. Claude Rains, the royal devil's advocate, was far more convincing in his arguments and [his] performance was excellent. It had authority, sweep and insight."

Late in September, Rains returned to Pennsylvania to make arrangements to complete the sale of Stock Grange, the final date for the deed transfer set for January 1957. He was back at work in November, in a new stage play by his old friend Arch Oboler. Producer Kermit Bloomgarden had talked to Theresa Helburn of the Theatre Guild about sponsoring the oddly titled *Night of the Auk*. But even with Rains as the star, the Guild thought the script was weak and declined to produce it, leaving the producer with the choice of finding his own investors or dropping the project. Bloomgarden went ahead, hired a thirty-five-year-old director named Sidney Lumet, and managed to raise $70,000, enough to produce the play and guarantee the first night's box office. Rains was supported by Christopher Plummer, Wendell Corey and Dick York. *Night of the Auk* was pure Arch Oboler: A doomed rocket ship, trying to return home from its Moon mission, is unable to land back on Earth because of a global nuclear attack. The piece was an unusual, futurist work and Rains had doubts about its possibilities, much as he wanted Oboler to have a hit. Things went smoothly during rehearsals, although Lumet remembered the first time Rains

viewed the raked set of the rocket ship's interior, he blanched, because he suffered from vertigo. After several days of walking rather timidly, he managed to overcome the angled stance and his performance was, according to Lumet, "immaculate." *Auk* opened in New York on December 3. The cast was praised for their efforts, but good acting could not overcome the problems of the script. The show itself garnered unfavorable reviews and closed after four days.

Nineteen fifty-seven began in sorrow: Harrison Wetherall became the new owner of Stock Grange, almost sixteen years to the day since Rains had bought it on January 4, 1941. The original farm Rains bought consisted of 294 acres; he had added 183. The sale price for the 477 acres was $130,657. It had cost the actor $133,370 to restore and maintain throughout his ownership. But Stock Grange had never been an investment. Wetherall remembered Rains calling on January 7 to advise that his broker would bring the deed transfer for signature — that he could not come himself because he was so upset, it had broken his heart. Wetherall confided that his wife was scared to death of Rains after they moved into Stock Grange: The old actor would telephone frequently, often in the middle of the night, to tell them something about the farm. One night, about two in the morning, Mrs. Wetherall answered the phone. Rains was shouting and she literally dropped the receiver. "No question in my mind," Wetherall said, "that he was drinking."

On a temporary basis, Rains moved into a new high-rise luxury apartment building on City Line in Philadelphia, putting most of his antiques in storage. Charles Brown, the man who had run Stock Grange for sixteen years, returned with his wife to a small cottage he owned in Darby, Pennsylvania, but he remained Rains' friend and continued to do odd jobs when the actor finally moved into a large West Chester house later that year. But Charles' farming days were over.

Rains never again returned to Stock Grange, but Frances and Jennifer had no reservations about visiting from time to time during the twenty-nine years Wetherall lived there. Wetherall remembered Frances visiting with her new husband Henry Feder and said that she seemed happy. "[Henry] was a person who you could talk to, and I would think that Claude would be a very difficult man to live with," Wetherall admitted.

Just before Rains left Stock Grange, Ronald Neame and his wife arrived in New York City and telephoned, hoping to visit Claude and Frances. Lily Brown informed the Englishman that Mrs. Rains was no longer living there and gave him another phone number. When he finally contacted Frances, she said: "Oh, Ronnie, I hope you won't be upset with me. You may not want to be friends any longer — you see, I have left Claude." Was that how she saw her life, only as an extension of him — the great, venerated actor Claude Rains? She provided no further information, and Neame, a divorcee, asked for none. He tried to reach Rains, but the actor did not return his calls: "Somehow my friendship with him waned," Neame remembered regretfully. "You know how that goes." It was as if Rains wanted to eliminate from his current life any vestiges of the past. Ash McDonnell, who had helped restore and maintain Stock Grange, commented that the divorce had an overwhelming impact on the actor. McDonnell's son remembered his father telling him that Rains "would have a drink or two, but not the way he did after he moved into West Chester." To those few persons who had personal contact with him during this time, all agreed Rains was never the same man.

When not working, Rains began to socialize. Gossip columnists in the local newspapers rumored he was seen with several prominent women; tactfully, no names were ever mentioned but Jennifer confirms that her father was "dating." In the spring of 1957, a well-known artist in the Wayne, Pennsylvania, area, Quita Brodhead, met Rains at a cocktail party and asked if he would pose for a portrait. Rains obliged, even though the task required several long sittings at her studio. While she felt Rains had a tender side to his personality, nonetheless she added, "He had quite an ego — much too big for his physical size." As a rule, Brodhead did not like her subjects to talk while she worked. Rains chatted constantly; she admitted it was all interesting and amusing. Furthermore, she was rather amazed at the intimate nature of some of the stories he related, so he must have felt relaxed in her presence as he talked freely and "never stopped talking about Jennifer." In the end, the actor didn't purchase the portrait. Perhaps he didn't care for Brodhead's modern style or her quiet colors, or perhaps he simply did not want to hang a portrait of himself. She remained a casual friend; he later attended an art opening at her home. According to

Brodhead, he talked quite loudly at the event, as if he needed to project himself so that everyone would know he was in the room.

Rains worked in television several times during 1957, including an *Alfred Hitchcock Presents,* "The Cream of the Jest," based on a story by Frederic Brown and directed by Herschel Daugherty. There was an eerie resemblance between Rains and his character, a drunken, has-been actor. It was difficult to get depth into these thirty-minute episodes, but he gave another polished, sensitive performance. One reviewer stated that Rains handled the assignment "with his usual smooth effectiveness."

In the fall, he again flew to Hollywood to play the evil mayor in a made-for-television version of Browning's epic poem "The Pied Piper of Hamelin." A musical, with a script almost entirely in verse and songs derived from Edvard Grieg compositions (notably *Peer Gynt*), the 90-minute special with Van Johnson in the title role aired on NBC on November 26. (Victor Borge was the producer's first choice for the role of the mayor; after that, his next choices were Rains or Cedric Hardwicke.) Rains had often remarked that he had done everything in his career "except play a woman and the hind end of a horse." Now he was going to be a song-and-dance man, contributing several solo verses of a drinking song called "Prestige," and even a few gallant dance steps. As Rains commented later in a *TV Guide* interview: "After the producers sent me the script, they phoned from Hollywood and asked me if I sang. Of course, I answered, 'No.' Once I got out there, they suggested they just play the music for me — the melodies are very tenacious. I found myself humming along with the piano and within a week, I was bawling the music as loudly as any of them." In fact, Rains does sing pleasantly on pitch and keeps in rhythm for his lengthy number. Reviews were mixed, but work was work. "Kids will like it," he wrote in a note to his daughter, "but what fans I have are going to wonder what the hell has happened to Rains. The guy's a comic." He admitted he had been having "terrible headaches each morn, but they wear off as the day proceeds."

Fortunately for Rains' reputation, he appeared in another superior television effort which aired one week prior to *Pied Piper*. On November 17, *Hallmark Hall of Fame* presented a ninety-minute production of the 1938 Paul Osborn play *On Borrowed Time*, adapted for TV by James Costigan with young George Schaefer as producer-director. In addition to Rains, who was listed as a guest star, it featured a splendid cast of veterans: Ed Wynn, Beulah Bondi, Margaret Hamilton and Rains' friend Larry Gates. Rains enjoyed working with Schaefer: "He never tries to confine your movements on the set to match his camera positions. He gives you perfect freedom, as far as the cameras go." The broadcast suffered marginally from the usual ordeals of live television, such as the obvious noises of prop movements, and an audible cough from an off-stage crew member. Schaefer remembered Rains as a professional, very quiet on the set, always in control. He admired Rains, commenting: "[He was] up there with the best — he wasn't a romantic leading man, but he had such a style and dignity. He was very different in every role except for his incredible voice which allowed you to realize who it was." Rains' professional income for 1957 was less than $22,000 — the worst year in the last twenty-five of his career.

Early in 1958, his real estate broker showed Rains a West Chester Colonial mansion built in 1839 and known as the Hawthorne House. (His only criteria to the realtor had been that the residence be at least a century old.) Rains was fascinated by a sealed passageway in the rambling home, once part of the heroic and historic Underground Railroad. Old friend Ash McDonnell was hired to do the restorations, and on occasion, Charles Brown returned to do odd jobs. While the townspeople knew Rains had moved into the area, when he took walks or went to the post office, he was seldom bothered. The strong influence of Quaker values and philosophy prevailed; people did not pry and were, to a large degree, unfazed by celebrities. However, he soon gained the reputation of being "a character," especially when he paraded around in dark glasses and a cape, as one of his Sandwich neighbors remembered.

Apparently, the cape attire was a favorite. Mrs. Hester Girvin, who grew up in Middlebury, Connecticut, during the 1940s, remembered a local family who owned the Chase Brass & Copper Company. The Chases had been large landowners, farming many acres and keeping cows, but had sold off most of their holdings, retaining their old summer house and a converted barn. The children referred to the barn as the Palace and had great respect for patriarch Frederick Chase, whom they all called Grandfather.

Rains visited Chase, and Mrs. Girvin remembered the two of them, "Grandfather tall, with a hook nose and lots of white hair parted in the middle," and Rains, "small, wearing gloves and a cape, as they strolled about inspecting the Chases' overgrown former gardens or fields."

Despite the occasional theatrical trappings, Rains' neighbors were always genuinely impressed by his behavior toward working people. A housepainter's wife, whose husband did some interior work for Rains, remembered that when the actor sent the check to pay for services rendered, there was a note attached thanking the man for doing such a nice job. Residents felt "he never acted like a celebrity," but one person (who, years later, himself bought from subsequent owners the Hawthorne House) commented: "He could be a rascal, he could be malicious, but he wasn't mean. He often had two meanings for his comments and a person was never certain which he meant." The actor made a greater impression on locals with his frequent automobile accidents. Once he hit a neighbor's parked car, and on other occasion he plowed through and smashed his own closed garage doors. Both times, neighbors recalled, he was "under the influence," but most were quick to add that while he may have been "tipsy," he was "not drunk."

During the summer months, Jennifer stayed with her father in West Chester. These visits enabled her to see her mother, now married to Henry Feder and living just outside of town. At times, Rains' acquaintances — from the Chester County area, or Hollywood, or New York — might arrange to come by. Although the actor created the illusion of having "recovered" from his divorce and the loss of Stock Grange, many who knew him could see he had changed enormously. When Jennifer returned to college in the fall, he again became depressed.

In mid-September 1958, his new agent from William Morris, Bill Joyce, secured a role for Rains in Universal-International's *This Earth Is Mine*. Based on the book by Alice Tisdale Hobart, the screenplay was adapted by Casey Robinson, who was also producing and wanted Rains in the cast. Henry King was directing and when production began in California's Napa Valley on September 2, 1958, it was touted as the biggest-budgeted picture in Universal's history. The handsome production boasted a good cast: Rock Hudson, Jean Simmons,

Henry King's 40 years as a movie director were celebrated on the set of This Earth Is Mine. *Left to right, Kent Smith, Dorothy McGuire, CR, King, Rock Hudson and Jean Simmons.*

Dorothy McGuire and Kent Smith. Rains' part wasn't large, but it was nice: With his own natural salt-and-pepper hair and sporting a beard, he played John Philippe Rambeau, French-American head of an intermarried clan of Napa Valley vintners, slowly going broke during Prohibition. Unfortunately, the story is packed with soap opera melodramatics and sex; occasional respites spent with Rains' "Grand Old Man of Wine," who walks among the vines at night to find peace, are a pleasant diversion. Despite lush Technicolor and CinemaScope photography of the scenic Northern California wine country, the movie did not fare well upon release.

On February 22, 1959, Rains appeared in his third *Alfred Hitchcock* episode, "The Diamond Necklace," and once again Herschel Daughtery directed. Rains

was wonderful as a charming and clever second-generation thief who gets away with his ultimate crime — which he commits with the help of his daughter (Betsy Von Furstenberg), the next in the family line. *Variety* considered the episode intriguing and well done: "[Rains and Von Furstenberg have themselves] a thesping ball enacting it. Rains goes through all the fake misery and repentance in the book with a relish…"

This light résumé credit was followed by one considerably more weighty: that of the small-town American judge in CBS's highly regarded *Playhouse 90* production of "Judgment at Nuremberg," written by Abby Mann. Director George Roy Hill always admired Rains, remembering how he handled the narration for the "Night to Remember" TV episode, and asked that the actor, now nearly seventy, be hired. Others in the exceptional cast included Paul Lukas, Melvyn Douglas and Maximilian Schell.

Hill remembered Rains worried constantly about his lines, which were rather dry and judicial; he would come to the director's New York apartment to discuss the script. The actor put a great deal of effort into his role of Judge Haywood, who presides at the trial of Paul Lukas' Nazi official, with Lukas defended by Schell and prosecuted by Douglas. At issue was an individual's responsibility when given immoral orders to be carried out out under the guise of misplaced patriotism. For the very first time, actual film shot at the liberation of the German concentration camps was shown to millions of television viewers. Rains felt his character would be a quiet kind of man and underplayed the part; there are few of the familiar gestures, no raising of eyebrows, no implied subtext in the dialogue. Props were limited to his own heavy black-rimmed glasses, which he used for dramatic effect, and a wedding band which he fingers when he wistfully talks about being home with his wife. For most of the film, Rains is seated at the bench, but Hill knew when to focus the camera on the actor's expressive face to underscore the drama. When he has no lines and is merely listening to the heart-wrenching testimony, the actor's pain and emotion are evident. At the end, condemned to death, the defendant asks to see the judge. This was the most important scene in the production, the two men representing the heart of the play's meaning, and in these moments, Rains delivers the crucial important line: "To be logical is not to be right — the laws of humanity are always above the laws of any country." It was a very powerful summation.

For everyone connected with the production, the most difficult moment, strangely, came from the sponsors, who, in a rather ghastly coincidence, were the Gas Companies of America. They refused to permit the words "gas chamber" to be used in the courtroom dialogue. Knowing this, CBS higher-ups secretly ordered the audio engineer to turn off the sound as the words were uttered; even the cast only learned afterwards of the censorship. Trade papers quickly picked up on the absurdity: "The blanking out of the references to Nazi Gas chambers ranks as an act so childishly outrageous and inconsistent with the high moral tone of the drama … immature med-

Agi Jambor, Rains' fifth wife, was a respected pianist.

dling by the sponsors." The production won acclaim from nearly all outlets. *Variety* wrote: "*Playhouse 90* added another glowing chapter to its growing stature with this production. A stunning balance of drama and documentary. Claude Rains, as the honest, perceptive, outraged Chief Justice, creates a remarkable incisive study of a man who must make a monumental decision. It is a role that demands, and gets, from Rains the most subtle and significant shadings."

Two years later, a stellar international cast was brought together when *Judgment at Nuremberg* was produced as a major motion picture. Sadly, Rains was not recast in his pivotal role. Both the producer and director stated they wanted a "younger" actor and a "box office star" to play the judge, and Spencer Tracy (ten years younger than Rains) was eventually cast. It was a hard blow for Rains to absorb in the waning days of his career, along with all his other difficulties.

In June 1959, Jennifer graduated from Bennington College with a major in Art History. Electing to follow in her father's professional footsteps, she had made plans for a season of summer stock. Her father was pleased by her independence.

In the early autumn, Rains' long-time friend

CR and Agi Jambor at home a few days after their November 4, 1959, wedding.

Adolph Vogel, a music publisher in Philadelphia, hosted a dinner party at which he introduced the actor to a 50-year-old pianist named Agi Jambor. A native of Budapest, Hungary, she had lived through the horrors of World War II and came to the U.S. in 1947 with her scientist husband, who died in 1949. Because Rains liked classical music, Vogel thought the two artists might find each other's company interesting. Agi was a graduate of the Royal Academy of Music in London and had studied at schools in Berlin. Her career as a concert pianist was interrupted by the war, but now she performed occasionally, especially at the Academy of Music in Philadelphia, while teaching music at Bryn Mawr College where she was considered a Bach specialist.

The initial attraction between Claude and Agi was their mutual love of music; she remembered how impressed she was by his understanding and appreciation, given he had no formal musical education.

Also, as a European, she admired his formal gentlemanly demeanor and extreme politeness. They could easily have stayed merely good friends, but Rains had always been impetuous when it came to his romantic inclinations. Moreover, he had always avoided close friendship with a woman that could develop into an affair: When he desired an intimate relationship, he refused to become seriously involved outside marriage. Agi was shy and not extremely attractive, but she liked Claude and may have felt flattered by his attention. They got along during dinners together and seemed to feel comfortable with one another. Both were lonely. Each later claimed the other suggested marriage within a month after meeting. Rains was now seventy, two decades older than Jambor.

On November 4, 1959, the couple was married.

According to the local paper, Justice George Bonsall performed the ceremony in Rains' home. Jennifer, then 21, and "two friends of the couple, Adolph Vogel of Merion and Edward Lower of West Chester, were in attendance." By Thanksgiving, Claude and Agi were settled into the Hawthorne House; they had a small photograph taken on the porch made into announcement cards with the words "Happy and at peace," and sent them to several friends, including Bette Davis.

Rains obviously hoped, and expected, this would be a new beginning for him. Tragically, within only a few weeks, both he and Agi realized the marriage was a dreadful mistake, the result of a rash decision based on the anxiety of loneliness. Agi also discovered that Claude was an alcoholic, something he had heretofore been able to conceal from her. Now she understood his strange behavior at times. Most shocking was his unpredictable temperament and moodiness. She was totally unprepared for her husband's uncharacteristic nastiness when he had had too much to drink. "It was not Claude's fault — he was ill. I think alcoholism is an illness and you don't criticize anyone with cancer."

Agi believed her companionship would decrease Rains' depression, and time would provide the healing he needed. But she sadly admitted it was "too late" — he had been through too much. Rains was incapable of dealing with personal issues. So many things continued to oppress him: He was still not reconciled about his divorce from Frances and the loss of Stock Grange. And now he had to face the truth that he and his fifth wife were not compatible. Rains claimed that Agi had begun to indulge in her own odd behaviors, like practicing piano on a paper cardboard with keys printed on it, and that her cooking was too spicy for him. Even Rains' good friends, Dr. and Mrs. Uhle, knew something was amiss. Just before the marriage, they dined with Rains at the Hawthorne House. They had not yet met Agi and expected to be getting together for dinner with the couple during the holidays, but it all turned out rather bizarrely as Mrs. Uhle remembered: "Claude wanted us to meet his new wife, so we suggested they dine with us. He seemed delighted and we mentioned two other couples whom they might enjoy meeting. He replied, 'Fine, and Agi will play for you.' I protested she need not 'sing for her supper' but he insisted." In anticipation of the visit, Mrs. Uhle had a piano tuner come to make sure their instrument was ready, just

in case. Then the Uhles received a call from Agi that Claude suddenly "went out of town" and the couple would not be attending the dinner; strange, since it was he who initiated the recital. In an effort to apologize, Agi invited Mrs. Uhle to tea the following week, but this meeting also never took place.

In the few weeks they were together, Agi was disturbed when Claude seemed unable to focus on reality; he was not behaving in a manner which reflected emotional stability. She stated that Claude often retreated into a world that sustained him — an imagined reality where he could control all outcomes. Once he sat by the window in the house at Church and Dean Streets, discussing the people passing by and reacting to them with varied emotions: anger, sympathy, joy. Initially, she thought he must have known them, because of the way he spoke about them. But she then realized that he was in some world of his own, a world of make-believe. He would comment: "Here a woman who goes to work to feed her four fatherless children. She is worn out and tired but wants to make fine human beings out of her children. There is a man who betrays his wife with the wife of his best friend. There, a young woman with an old face, who takes care of her old, paralyzed mother, sacrificing her own young life."

The first week in December, Rains went to New York to appear in an NBC holiday show based on Paul Gallico's fable *Once Upon a Christmas Time*. Also starring were veteran comic actor Charlie Ruggles, singer Kate Smith, and a twelve-year-old actress, Patty Duke. Director Kirk Browning recalled Rains as a "sweet and quiet man," not entirely focused, who didn't look well. "Rains had a terrible time remembering his lines and he was in trouble even when we were on the air. I felt sorry for him in his difficulty." The usually letter-perfect Rains was in an emotional turmoil, unable to handle the matter, and too embarrassed to discuss it.

Instead of dissolving the marriage in an amiable and cordial manner, Rains committed a draconian act, disastrous for everyone concerned. In early January 1960, Rains left for Hollywood to make a film for which he had hurriedly contracted, Irwin Allen's adaptation of the adventure story *The Lost World*. Once there, he called his old friend Charles Brown and instructed him to change all the door locks to the Hawthorne House while Agi was out teaching or shopping. She came home to find herself shut out of her home — and her marriage. Understandably, she became somewhat hysterical, immediately phoning Jennifer in New York. Rains' daughter could do nothing, mainly because she had always been afraid to confront her father on any issue. Even outraged, even as Agi's friend, she would not interfere. Meanwhile, Rains had a local lawyer in West Chester inform his wife that she needed to agree to an immediate divorce in order to gain access to her personal belongings. There was nothing the blindsided woman could do, outside of suing. During this terrible time, she stayed with friends in Chester County who were appalled by Rains' actions. In all probability, Adolph Vogel helped Agi as much as possible, feeling responsible because he had introduced the pair.

While Rains was in Hollywood making *The Lost World*, George Roy Hill visited Philadelphia. Knowing he was Rains' friend, Agi contacted the director, inviting him for lunch. She was quite distressed, cried a lot, begging him to help her understand what she had done to warrant such inexcusable behavior. He too was astonished by the events she related, but confessed that, while he had been friendly with Rains while working with him, he had never become close with the actor. He had no advice to offer.

By May 20, local newspapers were reporting that Agi had filed for a divorce, which was granted by a Chester County court on July 28. The couple had lived together as man and wife less than six weeks. Newspapers quoted some of the testimony, in which Agi called her husband "vile and nasty," especially when he was drinking, and stating that when he was in a temper, he would throw things around the house. In one drunken episode, he ordered her to go out to work because he was broke; in another, he refused to give her money for groceries, saying she could use her own. To Agi's credit, whenever approached by the media, she remained silent, realizing that her relationship with Rains had been a victim of his drinking. Years later, she admitted she was totally unprepared for her husband's mercurial temperament but insisted: "I always thought of Claude as two people, really. One was flamboyant, and the other was a gentle quiet man when he wanted to be. At times he would use his booming voice and at other times he would speak so quietly." He was two separate people — the man and the actor. It certainly seems that something was psychologically wrong with Rains. While it's true he had a temper, being deliberately cruel was

out of character. His behavior to Agi, who had done nothing to warrant such irrational and vindictive actions, had to have been a symptom of the pain he was still feeling about the manner in which Frances had left him. Rains' vindictiveness was horrifying and unforgivable to Jennifer, who liked Agi very much and remained upset and angry. It may have been difficult for her to comprehend the depth of her father's emotional instability. Perhaps Rains had descended into paranoia, worrying that Agi might leave him as had all his other loves. To protect himself, he would hurt her first. While this is conjecture, all evidence indicates that Rains' emotional life was highly precarious until he met Frances. Only then did he have a sense of stability; now all that was gone.

Years later, when she was eighty-seven, Agi Jambor agreed for the very first time to discuss her short relationship with Claude Rains, remembering most vividly his idiosyncrasies:

> Claude started the day every morning shining his shoes. It was a kind of dedicated work he didn't like to share with anyone. I think it was a gesture of infinite trust when he permitted me — 20 years his junior — to take over that chore from him. Lovely English shoes, riding boots, summer shoes, winter shoes, all like soldiers standing orderly in the shoe closet of his dressing room. One day I shyly asked him: "How did you happen to become such a devoted shoeshiner? The answer was: "My mother told me that I should have dirty feet rather than dirty shoes." The intriguing part of this little story is not his neatness, but that at age of 70, the world-renowned actor, spoiled artist, the great movie star, still humbly carried out the wishes and instructions of his mother.
>
> Claude was a very strict man, but also a good man — he was not the type to associate with a crowd of people. What made a great impression on me was his modesty as a man, and that his success as an actor never turned him into an overbearing snob.

Although she was bewildered and frightened by Claude's behavior, Agi was never angry at him. She, who had lived through the horrors of a world war, could understand his terrible insecurity when he talked about his ghastly boyhood. She explained that even though Claude was a mature man of 70 and successful, he was always conscious of his lack of education and extremely sensitive about it. She was amazed that a man so respected and admired had no close friends. He was always reading and listening to music; he liked to listen to her practice piano. He was easily embarrassed, modest, and while very severe in his professional self-criticism, he was very understanding of his colleagues' professional mistakes. She remembers one incident when he wrote a motto on a blackboard, spraying it with varnish — a reminder so that he would not feel sorry for himself: "I wept because I had no shoes, until I saw a man who had no feet."

Claude did discuss his marriage to Frances with Agi, but she would not divulge any comments said to her in trust. It was her opinion that Frances may not have been mature enough to realize how monumental her husband's needs were. After all, he had been a father figure to Frances; also, she had her own needs and desires which Claude may not have been able to satisfy as he aged. Agi insisted Claude was a good man, but ill emotionally, which is why he drank so much. He frequently voiced self-doubt and constantly criticized himself as an actor. He regularly brought up what he saw as career failures: lamenting that his success had been limited; that while he had made a few good films, he had accepted too many terrible scripts. He believed that many of his colleagues had surpassed him in wealth and fame, and that he wasn't held in the same high regard as, for example, his one-time pupil, Sir John Gielgud. He felt he did not command the same respect, or reap the same rewards, as actors whose personalities alone made them into "stars." As an artist with great potential herself, Agi could understand and empathize, especially with Rains' awareness of his "limited" status among his peers. Claude Rains was alone inside himself, and he kept his pain and self-doubts invisible to others. Of those who did try to befriend him, more often than not his formidability made them hesitate to draw closer. His fifth wife summed up her experience: "I don't think Claude believed that anyone could really love him. I did then and I do now. But I could not live with him."

In reflection, and after a series of her own serious illnesses, Agi Jambor related her story without bitterness. On May 27, 1967, she and several friends were playing with a Ouija board, when she found the pointer guiding her hands to the letters which spelled out the word "good-bye." She was unnerved for she knew what it meant. Claude Rains died three days later. She had loved him but could not help him. She never remarried.

After the divorce, Agi and Jennifer remained friends for many years, but Agi never told Rains' daughter about her father's strange behavior or his violent temper. She never shared any details about the marriage with anyone except this author. Her sad summation: "Somehow success and happiness did not enter simultaneously into his life."

CHAPTER 25
A New Family, Ready-Made

Rains initially agreed to make *The Lost World* just to keep himself occupied during the divorce from Agi. Meanwhile the actor notified his agent, Bill Joyce at William Morris, that he was interested in eventually doing a play. Joyce had decided to retire because of ill health, but before leaving the agency, he wanted to be certain just the right person would represent Rains.

He approached Ed Robbins, a young man with a pleasant personality who would give the veteran actor the time, respect and understanding he needed and deserved. Joyce told Robbins that, if he declined, the retiree would advise Rains to sign with another agency. As it happened, Robbins was a Rains fan and delighted by the opportunity. It was a positive association. Robbins remembered the actor as quiet, extremely courteous, and a person who never displayed self-importance. Once Rains phoned the office, informing the secretary, "This is Claude Rains." When she offered to get Robbins, the actor replied: "No need, he may be busy. You can just relay the message that I telephoned." "I'll always remember his graciousness," Robbins reflected.

The terrific success that 20th Century–Fox's *Journey to the Center of the Earth* enjoyed with movie-goers in 1959 seemed to bring forth a renaissance of science fiction and fantasy films based on classic literature: among others, *The Time Machine, The 3 Worlds*

As *Prof. Challenger* in The Lost World. (Photo courtesy John Antosiewicz)

of Gulliver, Mysterious Island, The Wonderful World of the Brothers Grimm and *Master of the World. The Lost World* was a science fiction novel by Arthur Conan Doyle, the creator of Sherlock Holmes. Published in

1912, the rousing tale follows an expedition to a plateau in South America's Amazon basin where they discover living prehistoric creatures. The book was first adapted for the screen in 1925, with Wallace Beery starring as the intrepid Professor Challenger, and stop-motion effects provided by legendary animator Willis O'Brien. The decision to remake the film — in Technicolor and CinemaScope — was that of 20th Century–Fox producer-director Irwin Allen, who wanted O'Brien to again work his magic. Unfortunately, budgetary restrictions mandated instead the use of much-abused live reptiles for the land beyond time discovered by the explorers.

Allen and Charles Bennett wrote a new screenplay for a deluxe production which was expected to do well with summer (1960) family audiences. The cast featured Michael Rennie, Jill St. John, Fernando Lamas and Richard Haydn. To portray the "fiery" George Edward Challenger, Rains' hair, slightly permed, and beard were dyed an improbable shade of reddish orange. He wore safari clothing and high riding boots — all he lacked was a pith helmet. (The closed umbrella he carries throughout the adventure, with which he pokes and prods everything and everybody, wasn't just for effect. He uses it like a cane in the trekking scenes, some of which were truly treacherous for the actors.) Rains made the most of his over-the-top dialogue, acting with an almost adolescent enthusiasm which fit the character: an arrogant, cantankerous, but oh-so-lovable old geezer. In an interview with Hedda Hopper, Rains explained why the part interested him:

> When Irwin Allen suggested I do the part, I read the Conan Doyle book before I read the script. Then I went to the library and found out everything I could about the character. I learned Doyle considered Challenger second only to Sherlock Holmes. He used to dress like Challenger at times when the character had such hold on his imagination, and he appears in many of his books.

Although critics didn't think much of *The Lost World*, members of the National Screen Council voted it the Blue Ribbon award for August 1960,

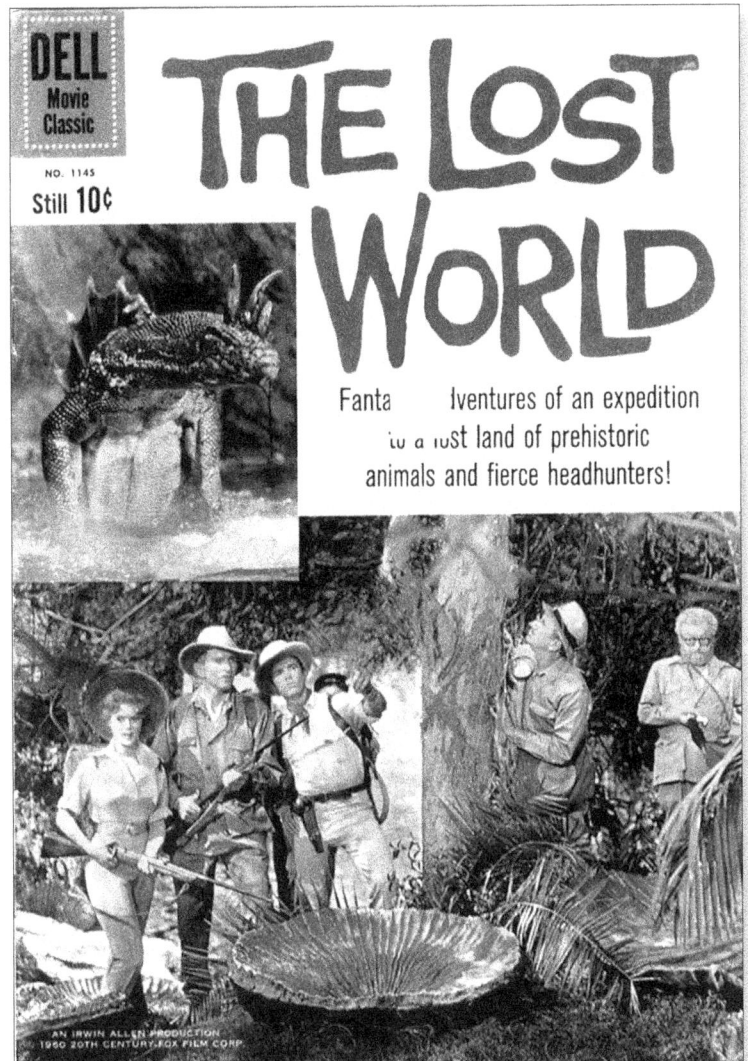

A comic book tie-in with the 1960 Lost World.

calling it an "outstanding picture" and "good entertainment for the whole family." Shortly before the picture's nationwide July release, there was a special preview at 20th Century–Fox's enormous screening room on Manhattan's 56th Street. Among the attendees was a 20-year-old college student named Sam Sherman, who would become a writer and cult filmmaker-distributor. As Sherman recalled for film historian Tom Weaver:

> They called it a screening room, but it was a theatre – 500 seats, maybe 700 seats, and every seat filled. I sat toward the back and I was waiting for the picture to start, and as I looked down toward the screen, I noticed a door open on the left wall – and in came Claude Rains. And he had the dyed-red hair, like he did in the movie. He came

in by himself, I believe, and all eyes saw him. And it was as if the audience was programmed: Everyone stood to their feet as one and burst out into cheers and applause. Including me! How many actors would get that? The ovation was for his body of work, it was for a man whose presence brought forth the feeling of great theatrical quality. I don't remember his reaction, just that as soon as he sat, the lights went down, and the picture started. The way he walked in and the whole theater erupted – it was a wonderful moment and I'll never forget it.

Around this time, Jennifer had some wonderful news for her father: she was engaged to be married. Her fiancé, Edward Brash, was a graduate of Williams College who had received a scholarship to continue his studies in England; Jennifer had arranged to take an assistant position there with British producer John Bolton. Rains' wedding gift was the couple's plane fare. He felt lonelier than ever.

One thing that helped slightly was the fact that he hadn't been forgotten by fans and still received a great deal of mail. One day he happened to read a letter from a woman who introduced herself as a neighbor, working with a theatre group in the area, and who wondered if the stage and film star would consider speaking to them one afternoon. Intrigued, Rains telephoned the woman and invited her to stop by his home. When she took him up on the invitation and they conversed, he became interested, delighted by her vivaciousness and good looks. He said he would get back to her when he finished his next film in Hollywood. However, on his return, he discovered he had misplaced the letter with her phone number.

Rosemary Clark Schrode (*née* McGroarty) was forty-two, thirty years younger than Rains. A native of Wilkes-Barre, she was an amateur painter who had attended Moore Institute of Art and the Pennsylvania Academy of Fine Arts. Recently divorced from her third husband, she had left her home in nearby Paoli and moved into a small apartment in town with her nine-year old son Schuyler and eighteen-year-old daughter Angela (sometimes called Angel), who was attending Bryn Mawr.

Later that summer, Rosemary was walking her dog in the area and Rains happened to be outside taking to a mechanic about his Mercedes 450 SL

convertible. The pair reconnected; she was often invited for tea. Rains felt comfortable with Rosemary; she seemed to renew his spirit. As the relationship developed, they couldn't be seen in public until his divorce from Agi was finalized, but once that occurred, they became an official couple. Rains took her out to dinner, and if he had to go to Hollywood for a television appearance, she would write and telephone him. Rains was missing Jennifer, now married, and he appreciated Rosemary's attention. It was not unexpected when Rains proposed to make Rosemary his wife, which was what Rosemary had been waiting for. Within two weeks of his July final divorce decree from his fifth wife, Rains married for the sixth time. On August 24, newspapers in West Chester and Philadelphia ran a story that the actor "disclosed his marriage to a West Chester woman who has been collaborating with him on his autobiography."

There are several different versions of how the couple met: Rosemary's son heard one from his mother; Rains told his own daughter something different; and then recounted a different version when he recorded his autobiographical tapes.

Rosemary's son Schuyler was told by his mother that she was walking a small French poodle in the neighborhood where Rains lived. Rains, also out walking, noticed her and commented on the dog. The two began to chat, which led to their becoming friends.

Rains' version was that Rosemary knocked on the door of the Hawthorne House, introduced herself, and asked him to consider addressing the local theatre group. They continued to meet, and later, she suggested she could help him write his memoir.

After the marriage, Rosemary told a reporter she had long admired the movie star and was in fact determined to marry him: "I'd been a fan of his for years and when we met, he thought all I was interested in was the book [his autobiography], but I had a much bigger and better idea."

During their brief courtship, Rains had refrained from drinking — it seemed he was able to abstain for periods, especially when he was happy. But when something bothered him, or something caused him to retreat into one of his "black moods," he renewed the one long-term relationship of his life. After the actor was involved in another of his frequent auto accidents, Rosemary realized he had been drinking. (He never filed an insurance claim for any incidents, despite paying hefty premiums to Lloyds of London, especially if they were due to incapacitation. Rather than have the company realize the truth, Rains consistently bore the expensive repairs out of his own pocket to avoid an escalation of premiums and, more importantly, any possibility that the news might be leaked to the press.) Alarmed, Rosemary talked to Bob Gawthrope, a lawyer and friend to the couple. He confirmed the extent of her husband's habit, which came as a shock to her. Gawthrope remembered that Rosemary found it particularly upsetting that other people were aware of her husband's problem, and yet she had been ignorant. Rosemary believed (as those who love alcoholics do) that if she could keep him happy and their relationship stable and free of stress, Claude would feel comfortable and safe and be less likely to drink so heavily.

Rosemary did her best to deal with Claude's sensitive ego. She praised him constantly, made a fuss over him, never argued, was in high spirits all the time and shared his interests in music, books and art. Unlike his former wives, it appeared that Rosemary somehow understood Claude's inner loneliness, and the insecurity that plagued him despite all his artistic success. People found her ebullient and interesting. She would often state to reporters that she and Claude were "very much in love — I go everywhere with him." Her son described the relationship: "She was his youth in many respects, and she gave him a sense of manly worth. She knew how to handle him and could make suggestions in such a manner so that he would always feel he was in control." A caring woman, Rosemary was sensitive where his previous series of disastrous relationships was concerned.

Because of all this, and perhaps reasonably, Rains believed this marriage would be different. Rosemary was a dazzler, full of life and good humor. She tried her utmost to become his trusted friend and listened attentively when he spoke of his past life and marriages. He called her "my Rosie" when he spoke of her. He had never addressed Frances with an endearment: it had always been "my wife." For her part, Rosie was proud to be Mrs. Claude Rains, the wife of a famous movie star, proudly bragging of his accomplishments, even to taxi drivers, and enjoying immensely the social circle of celebrities and artistic people. When the couple attended small social gatherings, she was lively and fun; everyone who met her found her personality appealing. Relaxed and happier

than he had been in many years, Rains put on weight, looked healthier, and limited his drinking.

Rosemary often handled her husband's paperwork and helped him organize his life, but it was not an easy role to fill. Claude's old habits and traits remained. He was still paranoid and very tight about money matters, but Rosemary understood that his difficult childhood had inflicted deep scars. Divorced herself, she knew how painful the experience he had been through with Frances was. She seemed to recognize he needed to be married to someone who adored him, who would look up to him. She hoped she could create happiness for a husband who was complicated, talented, fearful and aging. Over time, Rosemary's companionship and behavior seemed to soften him.

That summer, ten-year-old son Schuyler was away at camp. After their wedding ceremony that August afternoon, she and Claude arrived to inform the youngster of their marriage. In September, when the boy returned to West Chester, he and his college student sister lived in the Hawthorne House. As the boy's stepfather, Rains assumed all financial responsibility for his welfare, which included private boarding school, summer camp, medical expenses and clothing. Generous when giving gifts to people he cared for, Rains often bought the boy books to encourage reading of the classics. He took him for drives in the car. His relationship with the youngster was one of genuine fondness, but it was difficult for the seventy-year-old man to show affection. Instead, he believed it was his duty to "build character" and instill discipline in the boy. To this end, Schuyler was given chores in an effort to give him a sense of responsibility. To some extent Rosemary agreed to this arrangement and did her best to maintain harmony when her son grew resentful of Rains' ordering him about. She also felt her husband could be too strict in his approach. Without doubt, the elderly man had a strong impact on the youngster, which Schuyler acknowledged as an adult. Rains' influence turned out to be positive and helpful, although at times he was unnecessarily harsh.

Rains called the well-behaved boy "my man." He even considered adoption but the proceedings were never initiated, mostly because the boy's biological father objected. Rains continued to act as a grandfather figure toward his stepson and the three of them shared many wonderful times. Whenever the actor made a trip to New York City for a radio show, they stayed at the Plaza Hotel where, according to Schuyler, "Claude tipped very frequently and flamboyantly, [dollar] bills were always being pulled out, for the doorman, the bellboy." (When it came to courting the public and showing gratitude to working people, Rains was liberal.)

Above all, the boy was intrigued by the actor's method of rehearsing a role, wandering around the house muttering his lines to himself or reciting them to the boy. "'Rainey' [Rains] would sometimes stand at his desk saying a line with various inflections until he found the one he liked. In other words, each word in a sentence would be stated with certain emphasis until it sounded right: *You* must come home immediately. You *must* come home immediately. You must *come* home immediately. You must come *home* immediately. You must come home *immediately*. Then he would repeat and repeat the line until it flowed naturally." Schuyler never ceased to admire and respect Rains' discipline.

Some of Rains' ideas about proper attire for his stepson were hopelessly outdated; inevitably, they had unpleasant repercussions. Seeking to create a model English schoolboy (from a previous century), Rains ordered all Schuyler's school clothing from England: shorts, shirt and tie, jacket, knee-high stockings and a small beanie cap, with heavy English laced oxfords instead of the stylish penny loafers of his peers. The look was topped off with a bowl-type haircut. Caught in the middle, Rosemary understood what her husband was trying to do, but she knew her son was miserable. The boy's appearance invited jeers from classmates, not surprisingly leading to fights and him coming home with a bloodied nose. Rains was unconcerned; the boy had to learn to stand up for himself. Showing good sense and adult tact, not to mention a bit of ingenuity, Schuyler managed the problem by keeping "American" clothing in his locker at school and changing before classes.

Rosemary's daughter Angela was considerate of her mother's new marriage, but the truth was, she felt uncomfortable about the thirty-year age difference and was bewildered by her mother's relationship with such a complex personality. However, unlike Jennifer Rains, she was not deterred by or apprehensive about Rains' formidable presence. Angel and her stepfather would remain strained but polite.

Rains' joy in his new relationship was marred by one important thing: Jennifer was still outraged by her father's treatment of his previous wife. Additionally, she was suspicious of Rosemary's motives, believing she only wanted to be married to Rains because he was a celebrity. Jennifer refrained from expressing such feelings to her father, but she never sent the couple congratulations, and afterwards, became more emotionally distant from her father. This estrangement did not lessen with time. Rains and his grown daughter had never been at such odds; it was difficult for him to absorb. Perhaps Jennifer, as a young woman, resented Rosemary replacing her mother Frances as her father's wife. It had been hard for her, watching her parents divorce and then both remarry; and his father remarry again. The atrociously orchestrated divorce from Agi had upset her. While Rains never discussed any details of his previous divorces with her, he had exacted a solemn promise from Jennifer that she would never make any attempt to contact his former wives, with the obvious exception of her mother. Then too, Jennifer was experiencing her own marriage problems at the time, especially after returning from abroad. This inability to communicate their feelings to one another prevented father and daughter from ever resolving issues that created barriers. According to Angela, Jennifer handled herself diplomatically and was always extremely polite on her infrequent visits, but as a daughter she had no interest in her father's new situation and never accepted it.

Claude and Rosemary's marriage seemed to be working, depending on Rosemary's diplomacy, tactfulness and patience. She accepted his peculiarities, the habits usually associated with older men set in their ways, and did not try to change him. She jokingly called him "Tidy Tim" because "he was fussier than a woman! He would empty all the ashtrays personally before going to bed; couldn't bear anything not in its proper place, was very exacting about things in the house." She was sensitive to his changing moods. When he spent days on end in his library, even wanting his meals served there, she accommodated him. Perhaps she was less a dutiful wife and more a friend and companion. Rains had many positive traits that Rosemary admired: he had good taste, he was witty and scholarly, he exhibited good manners, he loved antiques, classical music and paintings. The house was full of beautiful old things, mostly from Stock Grange: silver, pewter, copper, furniture, pottery, fine china, a baby grand piano (originally purchased for Agi). Moreover, she respected him for what he had achieved.

The actual writing of Rains' autobiography was shelved during the first year of their marriage. Rather than making written notes, Rains — a man of the spoken word — decided to record his memories on audio tapes, which Rosemary would then transcribe. The reminiscences consisted mostly of the same anecdotes about his early days in the theatre he had been relating for decades.

In mid–October, Rains appeared as the High Lama in NBC's *Hallmark Hall of Fame*'s production "Shangri-La," based on James Hilton's classic novel *Lost Horizon*. George Schaefer directed, and Richard Basehart had the lead role made famous by Ronald Colman in the 1937 film. *Hallmark Hall of Fame* was noted for quality and "Shangri-La" had an excellent cast, but this production was a disaster. The live television of the time was incapable of the special effects required by the plot, such as the initial plane crash. The usual and careless background noises were quite audible (creaks from camera wheels, coughs, props being dropped). All of this couldn't help but distract from the timeless adult fairy tale of a place where no one ages and all live comfortably in paradise. Schaefer remembered rehearsals went for fifteen days, unusual for the time. He was struck by the professionalism of the veteran actors, and recalled that Rains had a terrible time trying to impersonate a five-hundred-year-old Tibetan elder when the pasty makeup made him appear grotesque instead of wizened. The bald cap didn't fit, and together with the heavy makeup and a costume of flowing robes, the actor perspired profusely and breathed heavily. His voice quavered, his eyes seemed glassy and teary. Nevertheless, Schaefer remembered the old actor's style and dignity, his valiant effort to give a quality performance.

After this arduous assignment, Rains appeared on an episode of the hard-hitting crime drama *Naked City*, and a week later, made a recording for children titled "Remember the Alamo," written by the prolific Michael Avallone (creator of the Nick Carter spy series). The *New York Herald Tribune* wrote that, while there were many recordings available on the subject, Rains' dramatic voice created "the liveliest and most listenable … exciting yet unexaggerated narration.… Mr. Rains creates as much drama by simply telling the stories straightforwardly as a cast of 200 might

have done by acting out individually the roles of the brave Texans." *Billboard* also praised the recording, giving four stars to "a fine and inspiring reading of the story.… Claude Rains does a superb job."

Writer Avallone had vivid memories of the day Rains made the master recording:

> "Pistol shot," said Mr. Claude Rains in that cultured husky voice of his. "Pis-tol shot … I should like to change that to read 'pistol ball.' Is that all right with the author?" He turned around in the control room of one of the largest recording studios in Manhattan. A little man with wide shoulders, a white sweep of orator's hair and a pair of enormous black framed glasses poised on his intellectual nose. I nodded from the desk where I sat, the forty-five odd pages of script of "Remember the Alamo" laid out before me.
>
> "Forty-five pages," I said. "and you've touched only three words. Be my guest."
>
> I had counted myself lucky that one of the greatest voices on or off a movie soundtrack or Broadway stage had consented to do a Spoken Word LP of [mine]. Claude Rains had said he would like to narrate the 60-minute script and here he was, ready to record, going over the script and apologizing and asking permission for mere trifles like "pistol ball." He was right too. The Rains voice, remarkably controlled and huskily strong, reduced the two words "pistol shot" to a sibilant run-on that sound like ssshhhhhh.
>
> …After a few warm-ups, Mr. Rains disappeared behind the wide glass of the recording studio. He sat alone at the big table, as small as a child, glasses resettled over his eyes. The script was held before him, gently, as though it was something far more precious than a mere sheaf of typewriter paper. [Producer Lyle Kenyon Engel] sat down next to me. "He's nervous. Can you imagine?"

Rains followed this with another *Alfred Hitchcock Presents*, a sweet comedy titled "The Horseplayer," in which he played a kindly priest from an impoverished

P R O G R A M

**THE PHILADELPHIA ORCHESTRA
PENSION FOUNDATION CONCERTS**

Monday evening, March 20, 1961

EUGENE ORMANDY Conducting

Claude Rains, Narrator

*HAYDN . . . . Symphony No. 7, in C major—"Le Midi"
    I   Adagio; allegro
    II Adagio
    III Adagio
    IV Menuetto
    V Finale: Allegro
    ANSHEL BRUSILOW and DAVID MADISON, *Violins*
    LORNE MUNROE, *Violoncello*

INTERMISSION

†RICHARD STRAUSS . . . "Enoch Arden", for Narrator and Orchestra
Poem by Tennyson—Orchestrated by Lucien Cailliet
CLAUDE RAINS, *Narrator*

†*Orchestra materials and premier performance of this transcription
contributed by Elkan-Vogel Co., Inc., Philadelphia, Penna.*

*Columbia Records   *The Baldwin is the official
piano of the Philadelphia Orchestra*

The Directors of The Philadelphia Orchestra Pension Foundation wish to extend their cordial gratitude to Claude Rains, Eugene Ormandy and the members of the Orchestra for contributing their services on this occasion. The Directors also wish to thank The Baldwin Piano Company for their generous assistance in defraying the cost of this program.

"Enoch Arden" program.

parish, forced reluctantly to resort to the sinful act of betting on the ponies. The episode required only a week's work.

Returning home, Rains offered his services to the Philadelphia Orchestra to help raise money for their pension fund by performing in concert the long narrative poem "Enoch Arden" by his favorite poet, Tennyson. Rains' reading would be accompanied by the Philadelphia Orchestra playing the lovely music of Richard Strauss. On the night of March 20, in an Academy of Music filled to capacity, the audience was captivated. "In voice, enunciation, emotional dynamics and projection, Rains gave a superb reading," enthused the *Philadelphia Inquirer*. Rains considered it one of the proudest events of his professional life, confiding to an interviewer that a recitation and recording of "Enoch Arden" had been one of his secret desires. "I like Tennyson because he was not afraid of sentiment, not afraid of emotion. He was not afraid of being melodramatic." Neither was the actor, as he

put forth boundless exuberance, with precise pronunciation and his voice rising and lowering in pitch like musical phrases from the orchestra. The event was such a success that Eugene Ormandy urged Columbia Records to record it. Schuyler Chapin, head of the Classical Division of the company, insisted on only the Strauss original piano accompaniment, which was performed by the artist Glenn Gould. In Chapin's memoir, he recalled the recording session:

> The studio was arranged with a series of screens around Rains and a series of baffles around Gould. They could look over at one another but pursue their individual parts without distraction. At the outset I think the fastidious Rains was offended by Gould's casualness. Mrs. Rains was quickly to imagine slights to her husband and right away she picked up the idea that the atmosphere was not right. They set to work with mutual suspicion. Gould would romp through the florid piano part while Rains rolled out the language with suppressed chokes and sobs that were so much a part of 19th-century declamation. Mrs. Rains was constantly furious and the conversations between the two artists was peppered with her comments. The studio temperature rose as the work progressed.... But they did finish it and at the end stiffly acknowledged that they had both done some service to Tennyson and Strauss.

Just exactly what Rosemary was "furious" about is not explained, but both Gould and Rains were possessed of gigantic egos and each may have thought the other was trying to upstage him, creating a tension-filled atmosphere. Nevertheless, with Gould's sensitive interpretation of the music and Rains' dramatic intonation of the verse, the result was a superb achievement. The album, released in 1962, sold well.

In the summer of 1961, Rains bought himself a Mercedes convertible sports coupe for the summer drive to Sandwich, New Hampshire, to see their friends, the Uhles, and others nearby. The Uhles went to the Sandwich area during the summer months and lived in West Chester for the rest of the year. A urologist, Mr. Uhle had become Rains' friend as well as his doctor, and the two couples got along well. Squam

ENOCH ARDEN

MUSIC BY RICHARD STRAUSS / POEM BY ALFRED TENNYSON

GLENN GOULD   CLAUDE RAINS

For his work on the "Enoch Arden" album, Rains was awarded a certificate by the National Academy of Recording Arts & Sciences for Best Spoken Word Recording of the year

Lake was remarkably beautiful and still undiscovered by tourists who spent more time in the Lake Winnipesaukee region, which appealed to the actor. On the last day of their visit, Rosemary inscribed a fitting tribute in the guest book: "When social intercourse brings to persons respect for one another' strengths, acceptance of one another's weaknesses, and enjoyment of one another' differences, there results that rare and precious alchemy which is called friendship. May we enjoy this enriching fulfillment of time spent together. [signed] Rosemary and Claude."

Although Rains liked living in the manor house in West Chester, he sorely missed the remoteness of country life. Then, too, there was the painful knowledge that both Stock Grange and Frances were physically and uncomfortably nearby. Rains loved this part of New Hampshire and began to feel that Sandwich was where he wanted to spend the rest of his life. Rosemary, on the other hand, enjoyed annual summers in Sandwich, but living there all year round was another matter. The small village was isolated and had none of the cultural advantages of Philadelphia. She voiced concern about relocating somewhere so remote from airports, trains

and, most importantly, Rains' doctors. The idea was tabled for the time being.

When Rains was contacted by director Antonio Margheriti (who worked under the name of Anthony M. Dawson) about playing the lead in an Italian science fiction film, the actor hesitated. The emotional upheavals of the last few years had exhausted him. He wanted to relax and enjoy his garden and the company of his new wife. The nervous urge to *work, work, work* was subsiding, and now he acted for pleasure. But Rosemary, excited by the opportunity to see Rome, pressured her husband; he acquiesced, even though it meant uprooting the family and the expense of finding an English school in Italy for Schuyler, whom Rosemary would not leave alone all summer.

Items in *Variety* in May and June 1961 refer to the film as *Il Pianeta degll Uomino Spenti (The Planet of Spent Men)* and *The Arrival of the Outsider,* "the Outsider" being the name scientists give to a rogue planet on a crash course with Earth. A plan is devised to preemptively destroy the Outsider in space, but unexpectedly it goes into orbit around the Earth and unleashes a fleet of flying saucers. Rains plays Prof. Benson, a misanthropic and (of course) imperious mathematician who lives in a seaside botanical garden; he seems to have genuine contempt for everyone around him, both scientific and military, and his comments aren't amusing, they're boorish ("There's only one opinion that interests me; my own!" he snarls). He attempts to fight off the alien invasion, but his desire for knowledge leads to his explosive demise. Apart from the extremely strange sight of the veteran co-star of *The Adventures of Robin Hood* and *Casablanca* in a silver spacesuit and helmet, the film (eventually seen in America as *Battle of the Worlds*) had nothing to recommend it. For Rains, the job was physically draining and an embarrassing credit. (To top it off, a staged promotional party somehow attracted his old nemesis, Jack Palance.

One can only imagine the awkwardness, but in publicity photos, Rains manages to appear unruffled.) Rosemary, of course, was overjoyed to be in Italy: She was seeing new celebrities, she was traveling in style, she was Mrs. Claude Rains.

Although looking forward to a rest, Rains was happy when he heard from his old friend David Lean, and even happier that the respected director was offering him work. Lean was in the ancient Moorish city of Seville, Spain, and wanted Rains to take a small but pivotal role in his current motion picture. Tired as he was, Rains so admired and so enjoyed working with Lean, he accepted the assignment on the phone. As both Frances and Rosemary said about the actor: When he picks up a script, the years vanish. Rains was

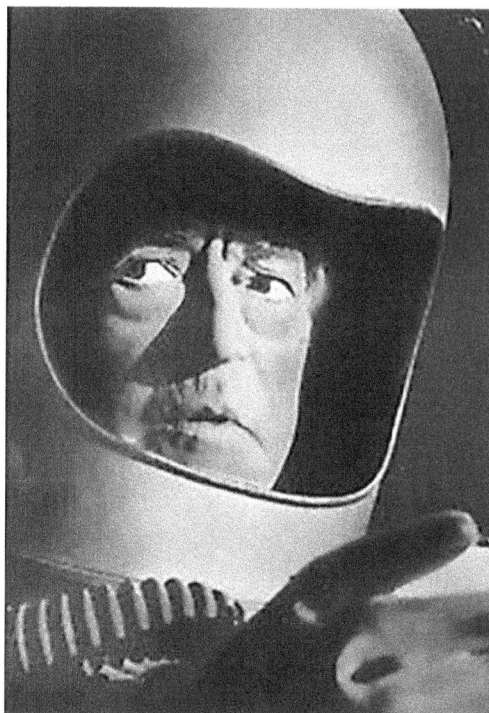

Battle of the Worlds.

While making Battle of the Worlds *in Italy, Rains had a brief encounter with* Darkness at Noon's *Jack Palance.*

looking forward to working on a quality film, and Lean's picture, a biography of the remarkable British adventurer T.E. Lawrence, had every indication of being all that and more.

In mid–December 1961, the Rains entourage left for Spain. As usual, Lean was fanatical about everything on his shoot being perfect, so although Rains didn't have a large part in *Lawrence of Arabia*, and none of his scenes were shot on the difficult desert locations, he was still working for a remarkable ten weeks. Unfortunately, the actor became quite sick with an intestinal infection which took a toll on his usually robust appearance.

All the major characters in *Lawrence* are based on historical persons except for Rains'. While fictitious, the character of Dryden is quite pivotal: It is Dryden who selects Lawrence for the amazing real-life adventures depicted in the film. Lean wanted an "instigator" in the plot, and after scriptwriter Robert Bolt had created such a linchpin, he needed an actor who could play the part with subtlety and adroit timing. Rains' Dryden is a quiet, cultivated, scholarly yet tricky official, the chief of the Arab Bureau for the British in the Middle East during World War I. But Rains is more — he is the epitome of dignified control, quiet subterfuge and masterful intrusion. He offers ideas or solutions when consulted but, like a puppet master, lets the actual decisions come from the other "more important" officials. In the scene where Lawrence (Peter O'Toole) is attempting to convince his superior (Jack Hawkins) to assign him to the Arab Bureau, the young man displays an unseemly eagerness. Dryden discreetly squashes it with just a suspicion of a frown and a small wag of his fingers.

Throughout the shoot, director Lean's demanding attitude caused many scenes to be redone. Lean could be relentless. One witness to the production told the following anecdote to Kevin Brownlow: "When an actor had a difficult scene coming up, David made sure that nobody — crew,

Rains' family joined him on location in Spain during the shoot of Lawrence of Arabia: *right to left, CR, his stepson Schuyler and their driver-translator. (Photo courtesy Schuyler Schroeder)*

publicity, producers — approached them. One day, Claude Rains … had waited all day to do a close-up. David said, 'Claudie, so sorry, we'll do it in the morning.' Claude replied, 'Dear boy, that's what we're paid for. Let's do it now.' A rather tired old man became a bright ten years younger."

After a long day's work, Rains, true to form, did not join the cast for the usual late afternoon cocktails, instead retiring to the hotel for a nap — often without Rosemary, who remained and enjoyed socializing with the movie people. When he was working, Rains was careful about his drinking. Because his stomach remained upset, he was even more cautious than usual. Added to this was the tension of being in a foreign country, eating strange food and enduring the brutal heat. Rains was continuously tired and not interested in socializing. Rosemary, however, delighted in interacting with everyone on the set, thrilled to have an opportunity to mingle with celebrities, especially the men. Those who met her remembered her vivacity, finding her enjoyable and

interesting. She would have drinks with Lean, Jack Hawkins, Anthony Quayle and Omar Sharif, with whom she enjoyed long conversations about art. Peter O'Toole, then a brash young man, openly flirted with her, irritating her husband who did not approve of such conduct. Rosemary loved it all. According to Jennifer, at one point during filming, Lean took Rosemary to lunch to discuss a problem: Edmond O'Brien, playing the obnoxious reporter based loosely on Lowell Thomas, had suffered a heart attack and needed to be replaced. Lean was quite upset. Rosemary suggested Arthur Kennedy, which Lean thought was a splendid suggestion. He immediately wired the actor's agent, and Kennedy assumed the role.

At first, Schuyler enjoyed being in Seville, especially when Rains took him sightseeing, but as usual, the age difference and the old man's formal manner inhibited real closeness. A typical ten-year-old, Schuyler loved "horsing around" on the set between takes, and he found himself the object of attention since he was the only child; Jack Hawkins, two decades younger than Rains, rough-housed with the boy. Even though by contrast Rains was at times

Peter O'Toole, CR, unidentified actor, Jack Hawkins and Anthony Quayle in Lawrence of Arabia.

Lawrence of Arabia.

stern, the boy liked being with his stepfather and was pleased to be confided in, "man to man," and be taught bawdy limericks.

While in Spain, Rains was provided with a car and driver. On days when he wasn't working, the three family members would go off touring together. Pleasant excursions notwithstanding, by the end of

six weeks, Schuyler grew bored; he missed his sister and got very homesick. Rains was still working on the picture, and because he wasn't well, Rosemary felt it best to remain with him. So arrangements were made for Schuyler to fly home alone and be met by Angela. The trips to Rome and Seville, and the time spent with such famous stars, had all been very exciting for the youngster, a wonderful experience he remembered all his life with great fondness.

CR and Peter O'Toole in Lawrence of Arabia.

CHAPTER 26
Twilight Years

Jennifer and her husband had been living abroad in London and Paris. Returning to the States, they settled in New York so she could concentrate on her acting career. She never expressed her feelings to her father, but he recognized that an estrangement existed between the two of them; sadly, he did nothing to alleviate the situation. When she appeared in a production of Arthur Miller's *A View from the Bridge* in Buffalo, he did attend some of her performances, once even traveling to Buffalo in a terrible snowstorm. Yet true to form, when he took Jennifer to dinner after the show, instead of engaging in conversing, the actor held court, inviting a group of cast members over to his table where he talked only of himself.

Rightly or wrongly, Jennifer still felt her stepmother was more interested in the spotlight that shone on the wife of a star than in her husband's personal needs. Friends acknowledged that Rosemary enjoyed the glamour, but believed she had deep feelings for Claude and truly cared about him. Rosemary sold her property holdings in Paoli, Pennsylvania, and seems to have consolidated some of her funds with her husband's. She established a trust for her daughter Angela, who continued to live at the Hawthorne House, but who remained even more unsettled than Jennifer about her mother's marriage. Angela felt that Rains (whom she also called "Rainey," at his request) was too harsh with her younger brother, and could be duplicitous, especially about his drinking.

While Rains was abroad, the poet Robert Hillyer died. Rains had known Hillyer, who had won a Pulitzer Prize in 1934 for his collected verses, for a long time, and was asked to speak at the May memorial service. Appropriating some of his stepson's school notepaper, Rains composed his speech. He seldom did anything extemporaneously, and being used to a completed script, he underlined and accentuated. He wrote,

Robert gave me this little book. The inscription reads, "For Claude Rains with love from his old friend, Robert Hillyer" — from Robert to me. We met in Hartford in 1928. It is too presumptuous for me to attempt to choose words to express a relationship sensitive and tender when speaking of him. From Robert's pen flew the gift of selecting words ... saying for us those things imprisoned in our inarticulate souls.... I am so conscious of my own limitations.... We have an interval, and then our place knows us no more — the wisest among us spend this interval in art and song....

This exercise in pen-to-paper notwithstanding, Rains made no further progress on his autobiography. Rosemary kept herself busy painting, attending cultural and social events and, since they had no servants, maintaining the house. Now and then Rains enjoyed getting together with some of his few friends, like Ash McDonnell, the contractor who had done so much of the Stock Grange restoration. McDonnell invited the Rainses to dinner, but Rosemary declined; she did not seem to care for people her husband knew from the Stock Grange days, or those who were not "notables" or artistic people. McDonnell's son remembered Rains mentioning this during a dinner, and also how upset he was about his estrangement from Jennifer. The actor admitted that he had not felt strong enough to undertake *Lawrence of Arabia*, but did so because he wanted to work, and especially to work again with David Lean, and because Rosemary wanted to go to Seville. He talked about how affected he was by the terrible heat, and how ill he felt during the shoot. McDonnell told his son how horrified he was to see the degree to which Rains had aged in the few years since selling Stock Grange.

As the fallen, alcoholic judge in the Rawhide episode
"Incident of Judgment Day."

The year 1962 would be one of the actor's busiest in quite a while. In Hollywood, he did his fifth (and last) *Alfred Hitchcock Presents*, "The Door Without a Key," and appeared on the popular Western series *Rawhide* in an episode titled "Incident of Judgment Day." *Rawhide* was filmed at Republic studios, which still had numerous Western sets and props from its 1930s-40s heyday. Many of the show's stories centered around the character Rowdy Yates, played by an up-and-coming Clint Eastwood. In "Incident of Judgment Day," Rowdy agrees to accompany several Confederate comrades to a rundown, deserted town, where they plan to stage a trial for Eastwood's alleged betrayal of them. The verdict is a foregone conclusion — until Rains staggers down the stairs as the town's sole occupant, a judge, disillusioned by the one fatal error he made in his career which led to a woman's death and his guilty retreat into the bottle. Rains has pages and pages of dialogue, mostly with Eastwood, quoting Shakespeare and Latin maxims, discussing morality and the unavoidable end to which Fate leads us all. By the denouement, the judge has regained both his physical and moral strength, standing up to the misguided men and their obsessed leader in a final defense of the truth which helps save Eastwood,

but brings his own journey to a bittersweet, poignant end: "Boy … lawyer … judge … man." Disheveled, the whiskey bottle clutched tightly in his hand until he has the nerve to throw it away, Rains delivers his lines with style and panache, and gives a strong, convincing portrayal. The episode's director, Tommy Carr, vividly remembered how Rains addressed his craft, compared to younger, unpolished actors whose stardom depended more on personality than talent. "I worked with a lot of actors in my time, and there is no question Claude was one of the greatest. He never acted like a prima donna. He would listen to you — most big stars wouldn't listen, but Rains was a joy to work with. He always knew his lines. We were supposed to have six days to shoot, but he was so good, we finished in five. And he had a big share of the dialogue and he did it like it was nothing." One particular incident demonstrated what a trooper the aging actor still was:

> [Claude] was coming down the steps and using a handrail, and it was an old rickety Western set at the Republic studios. In doing that, he got a really bad splinter in his finger…. But he said nothing to me about it. Nothing until I saw his hand bleeding, and he said, "Oh, that's part of it," and he went right on doing what he was supposed to in the scene without any problems at all. Ordinarily another actor, especially a star, would have made a big fuss. Not Rains — and with his finger bleeding with this big splinter. He insisted, "No, no, let's go on with the scene." I wanted him to go to the hospital, but he replied, "Let's finish this scene and then we'll tend to it." He got the splinter pulled out there on the set and they put a bandage on it and that was all there was to it.

Rains remained in Hollywood for a guest shot on another popular TV Western, *Wagon Train* (coincidentally again playing a judge), before returning to West Chester in the spring. In late May, he received a script for a series debuting on NBC in September: *Sam Benedict*, starring Edmond O'Brien, now fully recovered from the heart attack he had suffered during *Lawrence of Arabia*. While the episode was apparently broadcast as "Nor Practice Make Perfect,"

CR and star Edmond O'Brien in an episode of the TV series, Sam Benedict.

Rains' script was titled "Nice Little Doggie, Bite the Lawyer's Leg." The series was shot at MGM in Hollywood. As he had in several recent roles, Rains played a boozy drunk — here, an aging lawyer whose suicide attempt prompts Sam Benedict to help his old friend rediscover purpose in life. What is significant about this particular show is that in the entire script, Rains made no notations except to underline a single line: "Home is where the hurt is." Perhaps the words brought back memories of Stock Grange and the night Frances left him. Critics thought Rains did an admirable job but noted that the actor appeared exhausted. In one scene, not yet sober, the lawyer tries to hold a cup of black coffee in trembling hands; he sips it and has a hard time swallowing. Unfortunately, this screen action wasn't far from what was happening off-camera. Yet even with deteriorating health, Rains still managed a semblance of dignity with his venerable presence.

No other offers came that summer and the actor again became moody. Shut up in the library, he could only be coaxed out by Rosemary, who understandably found his behavior disconcerting. To help lift his spirits, he purchased a new Mercedes SL convertible sports car which he drove extremely fast, frightening his wife, who considered it dangerous. She pronounced the only demand she ever made of him: Get rid of the car and buy a sedan. In the meanwhile, he sported dark sunglasses and put the top down, and the two of them zoomed around the back roads of New Hampshire, visiting friends like the Uhles. The break did him good: His complexion became ruddy, he put on some weight, and he seemed happy again.

That summer after their visit to Sandwich, Rains made the surprising decision to relocate there. He contacted a local real estate broker, Denley Emerson, expressing his interest in purchasing something directly on the lake, preferably a small mansion similar to the Hawthorne House. In 1962, Squam Lake had nothing but small cottages and bungalows (as seen in the 1981 movie On Golden Pond which was filmed there). Emerson suggested the actor seek a larger house in the village, especially since Rains wanted to live there all year. Although Rosemary liked to visit Sandwich, she wanted to remain in West Chester, close to friends and to her daughter. The Squam Lake area is quite beautiful, but in 1962 was isolated and sparsely populated — which, of course, is exactly why Rains loved it. Approaching his seventy third birthday, he was well aware this would be his final move.

In most every respect, relocating was ill-advised. Isolation had been pleasant on the farm at Stock Grange, but trains into Philadelphia and New York City, hospitals and doctors, were still all close at hand. He knew no one in Sandwich except the Uhles, who were there only during the summer months. But Rosemary knew better than to try to reason or argue with Rains once he made up his mind.

CR and Rosemary. Photos courtesy Mrs. Janet Uhle.

Beginning on August 16, Rains was reporting to NBC's Brooklyn studios for rehearsals and taping of an episode of the *The DuPont Show of the Week*. Airing on September 16 to open the series' second season, "The Outpost" was directed by Fielder Cook and boasted a terrific five-person cast: Rains, Richard Conte, Everett Sloane, Keir Dullea and Neville Brand. The eerie, allegorical drama takes place at an isolated military outpost — in limbo, or purgatory, or worse. Four deeply flawed soldiers and their commander, a colonel (Rains), await the arrival of a replacement lieutenant. The unit's mission is strictly observational: Scrutinizing the horizon in perpetuity, they search for signs of an enemy invasion ten miles away, at the border with another country (which went unnamed). When the new lieutenant (Dullea) reaches the outpost, he demands action from the sluggish, guilt-wracked quartet, insisting he be al-

lowed to execute a reconnaissance mission in search of evidence of an imminent invasion. But if the enemy is ever sighted, the unit will have outlived their purpose. The group is so rotten (with cowardice or spite or envy or greed) that it becomes the colonel's job to tear the lieutenant down to size, dragging him through an abasement ritual that is part cross-examination, part–sacramental Confession. In the end, the young man realizes that he has become one with his equally twisted peers; the outpost is the place where hopelessly degraded soldiers go to live out a pointless existence. *Variety* wrote that the episode was well-done, "its total impact on the viewer enhanced by the believable performances of the cast, particularly in the case of Rains."

Some 45 years later, a fascinating anecdote about the show was posted on the Internet Movie Database website by a contributor with the screen name MikeMagi:

There was a time when superb drama was presented on television, by shows like *Playhouse 90* and *The DuPont Show of the Week*. Admittedly, I'm prejudiced because back in that golden era, I served as the *DuPont* series publicist. And among its best plays was Roger Hirson's brilliant allegory, "The Outpost." The tale centered on a group of soldiers … sent to a desert outpost, each having committed an act of brutality or cowardice. Commanding the outpost was Claude Rains as a character simply labeled "The Colonel."

Claude had been seriously ill and just before a major scene, while we were lunching in the commissary at NBC's Brooklyn studios, he suddenly began to weep. I asked what was wrong and he said, "I shouldn't have taken on this role. I'm too sick. I can't remember one damn line of the next scene. I'm going to humiliate myself." He was a wreck by the time he was called to the set where he proceeded to give a magnificent performance in the climactic scene in which the Colonel breaks down and confesses that he is the worst villain of the five. Over drinks afterward, I asked him, "What was that all about, all that hysteria?" He smiled at me and said, "Read *An Actor Prepares* by Stanislavsky. You'll understand." We became friends and remained so until his death just a few years later. If you ever have a chance to catch "The Outpost," do so. You'll see acting at its best.

Director Fielder Cook, who had previously met Rains during the making of "A Night to Remember," became friends with the actor: "He was, in my memory, an elegant man, and a prince to me. I do know he loved his home [in Sandwich] which I visited after 1965." Cook and his wife invited Rains for dinner whenever Rains was in New York. Cook remembered Rains' ability to concentrate totally on the task at hand and loved listening to stories of his days in London.

Rains still enjoyed working in TV, telling a reporter: "Broadcasting is the real miracle of entertainment. The theatre hasn't substantially changed in 400 years. Movies have progressed from silent to talkies to widescreen epics. But against this, broadcasting has in less than four decades grown from local radio broadcasts to network color television — and now Telstar…"

He returned to West Chester again suffering from health problems. In fact, from August 30 to September 8, he was admitted to nearby Coatesville Hospital for a complete exam, having suffered a sudden and severe weight loss. According to hospital records, he was diagnosed with gout, cirrhosis of the liver and a hernia. For the remainder of the month he rested, recovering from the gout, but his diseased liver was untreatable. Unless he stopped drinking totally, it would only get worse.

In October, Rains received a movie script from director George Stevens. But pre-production on his Biblical epic *The Greatest Story Ever Told* was way behind schedule, and it wasn't clear when Rains would be required. He remained active in the local community, contributing his services to the Calvary Lutheran Church which was celebrating a World Community Day program. Evidently the wife of his good friend Robert Gawthrope asked the actor to participate and he obliged. The Gawthropes were church members; the Rainses had dined at their home several times. Gawthrope remembered, "Rosemary was quite a woman," and it seemed to him that she and her husband were very fond of each other.

For Rosemary's son Schuyler, the few years in West Chester were wonderful. His mother seemed very happy: He remembered Rains buying her a beautiful pin in the shape of an artist's palette which he himself had designed — with two brushes in the thumb hole and seven colored precious stones as the paints (diamond, emerald, amethyst, ruby, emerald, sapphire, topaz, spelling out the word "Dearest"). Rains also commissioned a portrait of Rosemary which was hung in the living room. Schuyler recalled many "good times" traveling with Rains on trips to New York and staying at the Plaza Hotel (the elevator man let him operate the controls). When the youngster was ordered to shine several pairs of Rains' handmade English shoes each day, he did it obediently, but with a certain annoyance: "Every morning I did it and then he would only wear the one pair of ankle boots."

Over the Christmas–New Year's holidays, the Rainses made another trip up to Sandwich to see what their new home was like in winter. The excur-

The Greatest Story Ever Told.

sion ended unpleasantly – and *could* have ended fatally.

Schuyler remembered vividly that a fierce winter storm caused a pileup of cars on the ice-coated Connecticut turnpike. While heading home to Pennsylvania, Claude, Rosemary, Schuyler, Angela and Angela's boyfriend were all in the new Mercedes Benz sedan. Everyone was tired and upset by the strain of the conditions; even in fair weather, Rains was not a good driver. As Schuyler recalled: "All of a sudden as we came over a hill, the car went out of control. It was all ice and the brakes and the steering would not react. As we literally slid down, we saw cars smashed into each other. It was too late to try and stop — we hit someone, and we were hit. The car was thrown from here to there; we were hit in the side and front. The impact was so great, the windshield fell out and the window on the driver's side of the car fell out." No one was seriously hurt, thanks to the solid structure of the Mercedes, but it was caught in between other wrecks. It was bitterly cold. The dead and injured had to be taken care of first; it took nearly seven hours for emergency crews to get all the vehicles untangled and the road cleared. The Rainses' car wasn't in terrible shape, but the front fender was bent so severely into the tire well that the wheel could not be turned; it had to be towed out of the pile-up. Rains and his family made it to a small local motel, absolutely exhausted, but Rains refused to stay at the dingy place overnight. Rosemary tried to reason with him, but he insisted that the fender could be fixed and they could drive back to West Chester. It was insensitive not to appreciate the stress

the others were feeling, but he wanted to get home, and that was that. According to Schuyler, "It was the most horrifying experience of my life. My mother tried to be the referee but to no avail. This is what he wanted and what we had to do. We were freezing, we were scared, we were in a wrecked car with no windows — but we did get home." According to Schuyler, Rains believed the sturdy Mercedes had saved their lives in the accident: he admired integrity even in the form of an automobile.

On March 4, 1963, MGM announced its decision to add Rains to the cast of an upcoming project scripted by Rains' old friend Henry Denker and directed by Boris Sagal. Now Rains would be working in two movies being shot at the same time during that spring of 1963: MGM's *Twilight of Honor* and, finally, George Stevens' depiction of the life of Jesus, *The Greatest Story Ever Told*. However, when Rains arrived on the *Greatest Story* set in Hollywood, it was not Stevens in the director's chair but the actor's old friend, David Lean. Fifteen million dollars over-budget, plagued with problems shooting in the Utah and Nevada deserts, Stevens was so far behind schedule that he had arranged for Lean (who was in Los Angeles to receive his *Lawrence of Arabia Oscar*) to lend a hand with the second unit, shooting interior sequences at the former Selznick Studios in Culver City, now Desilu-Culver. Lean volunteered to direct some sequences as a "courtesy gesture" to Stevens, as *Variety* put it. He would take no screen billing, work for the Screen Directors Guild minimum (as did Jean Negulesco, who helmed the nativity scene), and then donate that salary to the Guild pension plan.

Lean's section of the picture comprised the scenes dealing with King Herod's terrible decree to murder every male Hebrew child. In general, Lean didn't like interiors and initially he was not thrilled about remaining in Hollywood, but he wanted to help out the troubled Stevens and was especially glad to work again with Rains. The director admitted that he learned a lot about filmmaking within the confines of a studio set and was impressed by the professionalism displayed by production crew members. Because Lean was a perfectionist, retakes were frequent. The entire first day's shoot resulted in three minutes and twenty seconds of screen time. Rains started on April 22 and worked for ten days. Under another director, Rains could easily have overplayed the part, but his Herod was a carefully underplayed performance. The *Greatest Story Ever Told* finally reached theatre screens in February 1965. Several months later, when Lean was about to begin working in Hollywood a second time (putting finishing touches on *Dr. Zhivago*), he admitted to Variety columnist Army Archerd that he never saw *Greatest Story* and asked if his sequence was still in the movie.

Ironically, the title of Rains' final film, *Twilight of Honor*, was figuratively and literally true for the actor. Playing the lead role was handsome Richard Chamberlain, in the middle of his huge success starring as Dr. Kildare in the hit TV series. When a young drifter (Nick Adams) goes on trial for murder in a New Mexico city, his court-appointed defense attorney (Chamberlain) seeks help for his first trial from his old professor, a former trial lawyer (Rains). Retired following a stroke and now using a cane, the old man is cantankerous and feisty but the wily legal mind has lost none of its brilliance and his heart is still in the courtroom. With his mentor's assistance, Chamberlain finds loopholes in the case and the jury acquits. The old lawyer has his "twilight of honor."

Chamberlain remembered the film as a wonderful opportunity to work with veteran star Rains, whose endless stories he found fascinating. Rains wasn't well but had lost none of his sense of humor. According to Chamberlain:

> On a low-budget film such as this, we'd often shoot in the evening and have overruns, and this was hard for Claude.... He would get tired and sometimes have trouble remembering his lines. It was unusual, but it would happen. I remember one evening he complained about the script and the way the lines were written — in a rather nice, but slightly irritated way, and the lighting and the camera were wrong, and he made a whole bunch of excuses for having flubbed a line. And then there was a little pause and he smiled and looked quite sad as he confessed, "Alibi Ike" — because he knew he was making excuses for being tired. He was so endearing. It was kind of a sad moment for all of us.

There are many good moments in the film, and Rains was as skillful as ever. The elderly lawyer is no longer permitted to drink but tells Chamberlain to pour himself one. Watching enviously as Chamberlain imbibes, Rains twitches his face ever so slightly, vicariously downing the contents. He inhales the aroma of the liquor and murmurs rapturously, "Mmmm, it's beautiful, beautiful!" It was a splendid example of finesse, and a situation with which he could identify only too well, having been advised many times himself to give up alcohol. His physical appearance reflected his long-term illness: face deeply lined, hair almost white, and he could see very little without his glasses. But there is still that twinkle in his eye when, on the last day of the trial, he enters the courtroom in a wheelchair, shocking everyone present. Chamberlain hurries to his side and expresses concern, prompting Rains to quietly growl, "Oh, it's just for effect, ya damn fool. Now wheel me down that aisle. Like a pallbearer!" With its Southern-style setting, a pitiable defendant, townsfolk in a lynching mood and a prosecutor with his eye on the governorship, there was plenty in *Twilight of Honor* to keep Rains fans flashing back to one of his earliest successes, *They Won't Forget*, although his frequent use of "hell" and "damn" is surprising to those accustomed to his dialogue in earlier, tamer films. In the end, *Twilight of Honor* was not a moneymaker, with Chamberlain attributing the failure to a poor screenplay, while co-producer William Perlberg put the blame on Chamberlain (a TV actor that the public expected to see for free). Rains later guest-starred on the *Dr. Kildare* episode "Why Won't Anybody Listen?"

While Rains was in Hollywood, his old friend Dick Berg, now a successful TV producer, asked him to take a role in a *Bob Hope Presents the Chrysler Theatre* episode, "Something About Lee Wiley"; the part required only two days of shooting. Sydney Pollack,

CR and Richard Chamberlain in Twilight of Honor.

a relative newcomer to the business, directed the show, which aired on October 11. Berg was pleased to be working with Rains in the elaborate production. Piper Laurie played the lead in a true story about a girl from Oklahoma, part–Cherokee, who was one of the great jazz singers of her time. Rains was the wealthy father of a ne'er-do-well son (Steven Hill) who drinks too much and wants to marry Lee. Because the singer has had such a positive effect on his only son, the father is willing to pay her handsomely if she will go through with the marriage (she needs the money for an expensive eye operation which could restore her failing sight and help her ailing mother). All in all, the plot was an unusual mélange, with sultry night club singing interspersed with high drama. The plot was saved by David Rayfiel's sophisticated script, filled with double entendres which Rains loved. The show was provocative and interesting enough to receive two Emmy nominations.

Director Pollack remembered that at times Rains required special attention because he became breathless quite easily and was perspiring heavily. Between takes, the actor rested while the makeup artist covered his face with Seabreeze to cool him down. "Claude had tremendous elegance and an ability to handle the dialogue and language in an incredibly graceful way. Not many actors do. He did things with ease and wisdom. It was a pleasure to watch him." Pollack told Rains, "I'm so grateful that you came out of retirement to do this." Talented and intelligent, Piper Laurie was only twenty-five when she appeared in what she remembered as "a terrific and really interesting show. Sydney was extremely good to work with and had a light touch with the actors.... The best part for me was working with Ruth White again and with that warrior Claude Rains, whose body of work continues to thrill me."

I had been forewarned about him from a friend who heard tales about him and Bette Davis — that she who adored working with him found him to be very

CR and James Gregory in Twilight of Honor.

competitive, and that it was a real exercise in trying to hold your own. I came to the project quite terrified because I was not all that experienced, and he was somebody I admired. I mean, I never thought of him as an actor — he was just a presence, a very strong presence. And so, we started to work and sure enough, he was trying to steal the scene. I can't put it any other way and I found myself involved in one of [my] most exhilarating acting experiences … and quite stimulating. And so, whenever he would do something, in positioning himself or an approach to a moment, I had to be stronger than him, and it was very good for the scene and it was like that all day.

We had a couple of scenes together, but there was one major one and quite

CR and Piper Laurie in "Something About Lee Wiley," on Bob Hope Presents the Chrysler Theatre.

important when we confront each other. It was very exciting for me as an actor to be challenged like that. And he was so intelligent — every time I'd find something, he'd find something more interesting to do, you know, and I would try to find something else, so I wouldn't disappear in the scene. It was more an ego thing, although that was part of it — it was like a sporting match. I don't think I ever experienced that before, and I don't think so since. It was exciting — exhausting, I must say, but also so exhilarating. I always had the feeling he would have worked with me again.

...I've worked with actors who literally try to upstage you. I know what conventional scene-stealing is, but this was something different, something quite different — just because it was done by someone, I think so superbly clever and talented, and it was always within the context of the character.

Before returning east, Rains had dinner at Dick Berg's home. The producer recalled a strange incident during the meal. Rains asked his young godson, "Tony, do you believe?" It was not the sort of question usually asked in that secular household, and particularly by someone like Rains. Everyone was a bit startled. The boy was equally bewildered: "Believe in what?" The actor made no reply, and the subject was dropped. Berg remained puzzled by this totally uncharacteristic remark: "There had never been a private expression from him to me about personal matters. Because I respected the fact that if he wanted to talk to me, he would. But he chose not to and that was cool — any more than I did with him about my personal life except in a most superficial way." Rains was now very sensitive about his mortality, and there would be brief, intimate moments when he revealed his feelings, as he had with Ossie Davis. These memorable insights into his character suggest that, so close to the end of his life, the severe reserve which he always cultivated was beginning to dissipate.

In May, the New Hampshire realtor called about a property near Squam Lake. Claude and Rosemary traveled to Sandwich, staying at the Lord Hampshire House on Lake Winnipesaukee, just south of Laconia. There, the broker escorted them to view a manor house similar in Greek Revival style and size to the home in West Chester: the Weed House, built in 1850 and recorded in the National Register of Historic Places. When Rains saw the stately building with square columns across the front, standing behind two huge old willow trees like a retiring grande dame, he put down a deposit on the spot. Rosemary was less enthusiastic: She could see that the old place needed a lot or work, and she didn't really want to move. However, she thought and hoped that being in a totally new environment might be a good thing for her husband — getting him away from Chester County and all of its memories — so as usual, she let him have his way. On June 6, Claude sold off a small tract of land he still owned at Stock Grange and made arrangements to have contractors start repairs on the Sandwich house.

Later that month, Rains did another *DuPont Show of the Week* in New York. It was titled "The Takers," again under the direction of his friend, Fielder Cook. The cast included twenty-year-old Shirley Knight, Walter Matthau, Larry Hagman and Frederick Rolf. Script changes meant three weeks of rehearsals during hot June weather. Knight and Matthau both remembered Rains talking endlessly about Warner Bros. and his work with Bette Davis, his early days with Herbert Beerbohm Tree and the meeting with George Bernard Shaw. By now these stories had become a personalized script, from which he acted out his own life before his audiences.

Knight remembered how methodical Rains was, that his delivery was "clear and clean" even in rehearsal. "He worked and it showed, especially his concentration. He would practice his lines out loud to hear how the words sounded.... It's different today — today's big stars are 'selfish' in a way — their concentration is not on their lines as much as their position in the film." Matthau was so impressed, he admitted: "I would have paid to be in a movie with Claude Rains."

Of his co-stars, Frederick Rolf was able to get closest to Rains; they had worked together a decade earlier in *An Evening with Will Shakespeare*, produced by the Theatre Guild's Lawrence Langer. In the fundraiser for the American Shakespeare Festival, Rains had played Richard III. As Rolf remembered the event:

How refreshing it was to see a Richard with none of the effeminacy and foppishness

CR, *William Hansen and unidentified actor in the*
DuPont Show of the Week *episode "The Takers."*

that had become the traditional trappings of the role. [Claude] had sensitivity, poetry, whimsy and a child-like openness, which were quite winning and gave a unique vulnerability to the part. And he read the lines like no one else. His asthma prevented him from ever speaking long phrases or becoming mellifluous; he had to take a breath after every short phrase. But because his thought was continuous and carried right through every pause, there was no impression of choppiness. His spirit was elegant and the effect more lyrical than that achieved by more melodic "singers" of the verse.

Ten years later, Rains was clearly unwell, but remained a professional, even when performing in a trite television play:

The cast, the crew, the staff all loved him; and all were concerned for his health. He seemed quite old, breathed with obvi-

ous effort … This dedication to his job was the keynote to the man. I never heard him express any of the contempt that the rest of us felt for the obviousness of this script, the cheapness of the dialogue. He gave the role as much commitment and passion as if he were playing King Lear.

The script called for Rains to use crutches. I don't recall the reason, but they were an unfortunate choice, for many people who saw the show, assumed they were a reflection of the actor's infirmity, rather than just a character touch. Any other actor of Claude's age would have anticipated this and insisted on cutting the crutches. I don't believe it ever occurred to Claude. He saw them as a chance to work on this specific handicap and made that so convincing, that many people believed he used crutches in the last years of his life.

By now, Rains was sometimes legitimately confusing past events, but he also altered his stories and anecdotes purposely for effect. Rains talked to Rolf about his ordeal with Sidney Kingsley during *Darkness at Noon*, but then mentioned "his terrible accident with the Bentley in the winter of 1962 on a lonely country road in Pennsylvania, which had been a horrible experience. He related he 'crawled out and limped for a mile through the blizzard before reaching help in the nearest house.'" (In fact, the accident occurred in August 1956 when Frances divorced him and it was only a quarter of a mile from Stock Grange. Neighbors were on the scene immediately, and farm overseer Charles Brown helped Rains walk back.) Rains told Rolf that he went to England in 1944 on a destroyer, instead of the British Lancaster bomber, and changed details about his meeting with Shaw. Probably the actor's memory, and even his mind, were by now seriously affected by his drinking (Rolf knew nothing about that at the time). Yet of everything he recalled about those three weeks in June 1963, what Rolf actually witnessed was more important than the confused relating of life stories:

> It was a blazing hot June day. We had been cooped up in NBC's Brooklyn studios since early morning and everyone was exhausted and nervously keyed-up. Especially Claude, worried, as always, about remembering his lines.
>
> The opening shot was a close-up of Claude's face. Then the camera pulled back to reveal a hotel lobby full of reporters crowding around him in an impromptu news conference. He was dressed in heavy tweed, with vest, muffler, overcoat and those crutches. He sweated profusely, as he stared at the big camera, inches from his face and with forty actors surrounding him. We waited for the cue to start taping the first act, which Fielder Cook had announced he wanted to shoot "in one take, no fluffs!"
>
> There was tension in the boiling hot studio and no sound other than Claude's heavy, effortful breathing and the mechanical voices from the control room coming over the headphones of the cameramen. Apparently, there was some technical delay and we had to wait in place. One minute. Two minutes. The makeup man requested and got permission to reach past the camera and mop Claude's wet face with tissues and then to add some more powder. Claude hardly seemed to notice. His mind

> was obviously racing through the lines. Ten seconds later he was again covered in sweat. The minutes ticked by. Any other actor of his standing would have exploded at this torture or walked off the set with a "Call me when you're ready!" Not Claude Rains. He stood and sweated and rehearsed his lines to himself and gasped for breath. All eyes were on him. He looked so old and so ill. The voices over the earphones droned on. This must have gone on for seven or eight minutes of tension and agony. Claude seemed near collapse. Finally, he raised his eyebrows, took a deep breath and said in a plaintive little treble: "I want my mother."
>
> The tension was broken, he was invited to go to his dressing room and cool himself off, there were apologies for the delay.... His gentle humanity achieved more than the tantrums of a star could ever have done. A beautiful man.

One day during a break, Rains mused, "It was Isabel Jeans who caused me in the end to marry all those other women." He did not elaborate, and it seemed impolite to pursue the topic. Just as Rolf gathered the courage to inquire further, the director called them back to the set. "Of all the comments he made to me," remembered Rolf, "I wish we could have discussed that more, but we never did."

During the filming in New York, Rosemary spent some time with her husband at the Plaza and did some shopping. One evening "Mrs. Claude Rains" was a guest on The *Jack Paar Show*, a proud and exciting moment for her. She discussed how they met, and stated she was helping her celebrated husband with his autobiography.

Rains sold the Hawthorne House in West Chester to Mr. and Mrs J Lanier Jordan for $40,000. He had paid $37,500 for it, painted and made repairs, which meant he made no profit on the sale, but then, he habitually sold his homes in haste, usually under great emotional stress or pressure. It still needed work, which may have been the reason for the low price. Mrs. Jordan remembered that each time she came to the house to itemize the work needed to be done, Rains was quite gracious, but followed her about, chattering about himself constantly.

Quite soon thereafter, things became chaotic.

CHAPTER 27
Tragedy

The huge move to New Hampshire changed all their lives. On June 27, 1963, Rains signed the deed papers for his manor home in Sandwich. He wanted the painting, papering and the updating of the kitchen completed before moving in. Of course, they were not done on time, so Claude and Rosemary stayed in nearby Moultonborough for a few weeks. Rains was pleased by the workmanship and gave a Christmas party for the people who remodeled the house.

Rosemary began to frequently find herself growing tired easily, and attributed it to the stress of the tremendous task at hand. She handled much of the interior decorating and chose a textured rose wallpaper for the stairway and most of the second floor. She also created an upstairs hideaway for herself: a small room next to the master bedroom. It had lavender-colored wallpaper with small leaves and branches, bringing nature inside. It was furnished with a four-poster canopy bed and a "fainting couch" by the one window, where she would sit and look out over the garden.

Downstairs, the small living room or receiving area had French wallpaper dating to when the house was built in 1850, small flowers surrounded by fleurs de lys. This was one room Rains did not wish to remodel, believing that the original wallpaper was rare. He contacted the Metropolitan Museum of Art in New York and learned that he was correct; in fact, the museum offered to purchase the paper and pay for all costs involved. Rains refused: "There it is, and there it will stay as it should be."

The actor supervised the landscaping of the grounds and the alterations of outbuildings. He had lilac bushes, crab apple trees, magnolias and hydrangeas planted by the local nurserymen. A small porch, at one time a potting shed, was enclosed. The icehouse, once attached to the barn, was converted into an art studio for Rosemary. The library was near the back corner of the house, painted in the same dark green color he had chosen for the West Chester residence. Once again, his precious books lined the plain wooden shelves from ceiling to floor. Rosemary had the front door painted a bright red and attached a large antique lion-headed knocker, the kind found on better homes in London. In addition to the main manor house located on six acres, Rains soon purchased an additional ninety-three acres of adjacent wooded land as well as a sixty-foot beachfront on the lake.

Rains was very happy with the new home and felt he would find the peace and solitude he sought in this beautiful area. Like many New England towns, Sandwich has a strong sense of history impervious to time; residents take great pride in their heritage, which is reverently incorporated into the present. This meant a great deal to Rains, with his affinity for American history. The small village existed unconcerned with the "future." More than anything, it was the attitude of the residents and the quality of life, creating a continuum between past and present, that made the actor feel so comfortable.

By late summer, the Rainses were more or less established in their new old home. Rosemary became active in area social affairs, and because she was the wife of a noted celebrity, she was invited to become a board member of Belknap College, a small private institution nearby. Soon after the Rainses arrived, a neighbor named McQuade knocked on the door and "reintroduced" himself. He was the man who had flown in the bomber across the Atlantic when Rains traveled to England in 1944 to make *Caesar and Cleopatra*. Rosemary soon became very close to the McQuades. Although not overly religious, as a Catholic, she sought the friendship of the few Catholic families in the area who were socially active. On occasion, she and Rains attended cocktail parties, although more often than not Rosemary went alone because she enjoyed such get-togethers and Claude did not.

At times, however, Rains enjoyed being the center of attention. At a cocktail party at the home of a neighbor, the actor became bored and asked the hostess if he could look around her new house. After Rains left the room, Rosemary leaned over and smiled, "He'll look in your closets." Everyone laughed. When the actor returned, the host remembered him making "a grand entrance" as if he were coming on from the wings. He stood in the doorway, struck a pose and waited until everyone's attention was on him — silent and expecting. Then in his booming voice, he reported: "Those two bedrooms for the children, they are so simple — so virginal," and he pointed upwards as if he is delivering a significant line from a play. His flair for the dramatic and his use of the word "virginal" to describe the bedrooms caused laughter among the guests, but Rains was not amused and brooded for the remainder of the evening. He often insisted he did not want to be noticed or given the recognition of a celebrity, but then he would walk around town with a black cape lined in red, dark glasses and a broad-rimmed black hat, attire that was guaranteed to make him conspicuous in the small New England village. On top of this, he had vanity license plates made for his Mercedes that announced: **RAINS**.

But for the most part, Rains seemed to enjoy the quiet life. Denley Emerson recalled that the actor would come to the coffee shop after going to the post office, pick up the local paper, sit and chat: "It was the simple existence that he liked … and he had a great sense of humor."

It seemed to Dr. Uhle's wife Janet that Claude "did not want to share his wife with anyone else in Sandwich. He wanted her to be home for him and she wanted to go out and be with people. She liked to paint outside, but Claude insisted she paint in the studio he built for her, so that she would be close by." She remembered Rosemary admitting, "Claude just doesn't want me to get involved in the activities around here. He wants me close to home." Rosemary knew how much it pleased her husband to relate tales and she would encourage him at dinners or social affairs. According to Janet: "She could really bring him out, but she was also anxious for him. It must have been hard on her at times later when she was in Sandwich — she must have been lonely."

In relocating to New Hampshire, Rains expected to enjoy the peace and quiet of New England, sharing the rest of his life with a woman who showered him with affection and understanding. He had to expect that he didn't have many years left. Tragically, it was not his life which was shortly to end.

During the fall, Rosemary liked to drive into Laconia to go shopping, but as the holidays neared, she still did not seem like herself, to the point that an extensive physical examination was called for. A series of intensive tests in a Boston hospital revealed advanced pancreatic cancer, inoperable and incurable. It was just a matter of time.

The shock was profound. Rains was almost paralyzed by the news. At seventy-four, he was more or less resigned to his own deteriorating health, but his wife was only forty-eight, a vibrant and active woman — who now was terminally ill. At first, he refused to accept the diagnosis, but other doctors confirmed the deadly prognosis. Rosemary was the strongest member of the family. She elected not to enter a treatment center, but instead returned home with her husband so they could be together in the time she had left. Just prior to learning the news, Rains had contracted for two television appearances; now he wanted to cancel, but Rosemary encouraged him to meet the obligations, accompanying him to New York in November for the tapings.

By March 1964, Rains had hired a local nurse to check in on Rosemary almost daily. Consulting a lawyer in New Hampshire concerning the legal ramifications of the death of his spouse and confused by the technicalities of power of attorney (an issue they had neglected), he sought advice from his friend in Philadelphia, Judge Winnett. Increasingly overwhelmed, Rains began to drink more frequently during the day.

On the morning of April 17, he telephoned the judge's home. Winnett was not in; Rains became confused and proceeded to discuss his problems with the secretary. She sensed he was not himself as he rambled on about unrelated issues; she decided to document the call so the judge could understand the extent of Rains' decline. He talked of his insurance policies totaling $50,000, and that he had named his loving daughter as his beneficiary. Then his tone abruptly changed, and he insisted his only child did not care about him at all. He brought up annuities and seemed confused about future premiums, insisting he was running short of money because of Rosemary's illness. Undoubtedly this incident was a serious indication that Rains was mentally unwell and required some kind of oversight. Judge Winnett's secretary summed up her report: "He really had tears in his voice." Obviously, Winnett was disturbed. He phoned Rains to reassure him that no further payments were necessary for either the insurance policies or the annuities. This seemed to calm the actor. However, Winnett remained very concerned because there was little he could actually do for his friend, since it would be very difficult to travel back and forth to Sandwich easily.

As the spring warmed into June, Rosemary asked Claude if they could spend that summer on Squam Lake. Since he only owned a small parcel of undeveloped land, Rains arranged to rent a cottage. It required some important repairs, and Rosemary's nurse's husband, an electrician and handyman, was brought in to work as quickly as possible; the place was finally ready in August. However, when this man invoiced Rains for materials only, not for his labor, Rains sent back a check in a greater amount, along with a note of thanks: "I see nothing re the trip to the cottage and time worked there. And all those little bellies to feed!!!!!" Rains repaid the debt in another way: When it seemed the nurse and her husband were going to have to cancel a weekend excursion because their car broke down, Rains offered them the use of his station wagon.

Rosemary's condition worsened, but she insisted she did not want to go to a hospital. Rains saw that she would have everything she needed at home; he wanted to help, but when the doctor tried to demonstrate how to administer opioids by hypodermic, he simply couldn't do it — his eyesight was too poor and his hands trembled (whether from nerves, age or alcohol). Clearly, someone else needed to be in the house after the nurse left for the night. Rosemary's daughter Angela took a leave of absence from the University of Pennsylvania, where she was doing graduate work on a fellowship, to come to Sandwich and help take care of her mother, arranging to teach French parttime at local Belknap College during the day. When Rains' daughter Jennifer learned this, she wrote her father, offering to visit. Rains responded in a letter dated June 16:

> You would not find it in any way comfortable to visit here at this time. Our home has become a clinic, everything revolving around Rosie — an atmosphere you would not enjoy at all. The house is holding its breath and hope. Rosie has cancer — it may kill her. I take her to the hospital again today. When you lunched with us in N.Y. [during the TV taping] you saw a very gallant woman — she knew then, and it has been hell to watch. [Her daughter] has been a wonderful help and turned down two fellowships to be with us. The garden is full of flowers … but they don't mean anything anymore.

Because of Rosemary's condition, Rains became even more withdrawn, and his anguish developed into nastiness in his behavior toward her son. That terrible summer of 1964, Schuyler was completely bewildered by the personality change in "Rainey," who had always been exacting in his commanding manner, but never cruel as he was now. Rains ordered his stepson to do all sorts of menial tasks around the garden, in addition to other chores. Every third day, the boy had to cut the grass with an old-fashioned hand mower because Rains refused to buy a power machine (too noisy and smelly), and water the rose bushes and flower beds. Once he overwatered and Rains scolded him severely. Another time, Schuyler accidentally cut the hose with the mower; Rains lost his temper and threatened to reduce the boy's allowance. In addition, the youngster had to make breakfast for his stepfather every morning — two poached eggs with tea in a big white cup — and then clean up the kitchen, including the stainless steel sink which Rains would then "inspect." There were frequently times when the boy would be yelled at for minor offenses and then sent to his room for "punishment." As Angela watched Rains' treatment of her brother, a great deal of tension and anger built up. Schuyler was just twelve years old and about to lose his mother. His only release from the doom and gloom of the house was to go swimming with his friends in Squam Lake, but with all the tasks assigned to him, there was little freedom to get away. Rosemary lacked the strength to intervene. When Angela attempted to step in, arguments ensued which upset everyone. Although Rosemary understood why her husband was so irrational, she was much too weak to act as a mediator. Instead, she explained to her son that Rains meant well in "training him to be a man." Showing great compassion, Schuyler did not hold Rains' behavior against him:

> I realize now he was damaged and acted differently with those he worked with and those he lived with. I don't think he was harsh with me because it was his character so much as he was from the traditional British school which meant that children were to be trained and disciplined and put to work. He had made something of himself and when I came into the picture, he thought it was time to train me, you know, times are tough — you have to struggle and fight for yourself. So therefore I didn't really have a childhood with him — I was just a laborer…. My mother and my sister were horrified because all the other kids were at the beach, which is where I belonged, and instead, I was home doing all this labor…. I was told that it would be a mistake to rebel. I probably got angry a few times. Both my sister and mother tried to make me understand, "You know he's not angry with you; that's just the way things are supposed to be and he is trying to form you into a proper person" … and I think there was a fear that if I rebelled against him, it would disrupt everything….

In late August, arrangements were made for the boy to attend sixth grade at a boarding school at Cardigan Mountain in New Canaan, New Hampshire, the next month. Living in Sandwich was increasingly difficult for the youngster, who now referred to his stepfather as "Grumplestiltskin."

On September 2, Rains wrote to Jennifer in reply to another query about a visit:

> You could come here but it wouldn't make you happy. I have got a little cottage — isolated on the water with its own beach. If I can get [Rosemary] into the water waist high — it may be good for her. I'll be running to and fro for flowers in the garden and the Post Office…. I turn down many offers — abroad and in California. Mustn't be too far away. [Schuyler] comes back from a vacation tomorrow. I didn't

want him to see her slowly day by day falling to pieces. She is a very brave soul; makes me feel like a pigmy. Keep your chin up. Love, The Dean (X) That is what Alec Guinness calls me.

Rains received two scripts from Hollywood producers but appeared to never read them; he also turned down work from a company in London. Within two weeks of Jennifer's letter, he was writing to Judge Winnett: "Rosie is weaker, resigned, but still a noble spirit — eight months of it — I don't think I could suffer (for her) more…" He sold some government bonds at a loss to pay for the mounting medical expenses. He also purchased a grave site for the two of them at a small cemetery in nearby Moultonborough. Five days later, he informed Winnett: "Today the doctor said Rosie is fading fast."

By October, with the weather turning damp and chilly, Rosemary was too ill to remain at the cottage; the couple returned to the Weed House in Sandwich. She was now bedridden, so a hospital cot replaced the four poster in the small bedroom with the lavender paper. Other notes and letters written by Rains during this terrible time indicate his dread of the inevitable; in each, he stresses how much he admires his wife's strength. His only escape from watching his beloved Rosie slowing dying day by day was to retreat to his study and drink. Everyone was suffering: physical pain for Rosemary, emotional upheaval for her children, and irreversible psychological damage to her husband who, anticipating abandonment once again, became angry, remorseful and more withdrawn.

Into this tragedy came a friend to Rosemary and later to Claude. As a practicing Catholic, Rosemary had attended Sunday services with the McQuades. Once she became bedridden, a local priest, Father Tom, came to the home twice a week to give her communion. At first Rains considered this an intrusion, but he soon realized how important the ceremony was to his wife and received the priest politely. During one visit, Rains called up to the nurse that his wife was "keeping God waiting" in the foyer. Rains would greet the priest at the door in the formal Irish tradition, bearing a candle and escorting him upstairs, a theatrical but respectful performance. In years previous, Rosemary had told Claude a lot about her faith and he was very moved, especially by the formality of the ceremonies and the comfort it seemed to give her.

Rosemary's best friend in the community, Mrs. McQuade, came often to offer some cheer; the professional nurse, Fran Mauck, was another source of help and great comfort, also becoming close to the dying woman. She recalled how Rosemary would spruce up in the afternoon, comb her hair and put on a little makeup, in preparation for her husband's daily "visit." Rains rarely stayed for any length of time; he quickly became either agitated or depressed by the mounting ravages of the cancer. Somehow Rosemary understood how difficult this for her older husband, who no longer had any capacity for resilience to deal with her illness. After his visit, full of despair and feeling guilty about his inability to spend more time with his dying wife, Rains would simply go back into his library and drink. Embarrassed by his behavior and lack of resilience in the crisis, he would later tell Jennifer that he had in fact remained by Rosie's side all day long, holding her hand. This was how it should have been; this is how a movie would depict the tragedy. But by now, Rains simply lacked the mental and emotional fortitude to deal with a situation over which he had no control. The one time when his skills as an actor might have enabled him to exhibit style and grace, he simply could not pretend. His few notes from this period are painful and very revealing. What tore him to pieces was Rosemary's rapid physical disintegration, and the pain she was suffering. At times Rains' seemingly uncaring behavior was misinterpreted by those close to Rosemary; perhaps she alone could appreciate that his actions stemmed from fear, and she never spoke negatively about it to anyone. Rains wanted to cancel his November commitment to the CBS-TV series *The Reporter*, but

Rosemary again coaxed him to fulfill the assignment, reminding him of his "professional obligations" to his craft. Unfortunately, few others were aware that this was her wish, and consequently thought that Rains leaving his wife, even for a few days, was heartless. Rosemary knew that only work could offer distraction and some much-needed relief.

That Thanksgiving, the Uhles arrived at their Sandwich cottage and invited Rains for dinner. He ate little. Early in the evening, there was a terrible ice storm. The distance to his home was short but very dangerous to drive, so they persuaded Rains to stay overnight. Early the next morning, Janet Uhle found the actor in her kitchen looking to make himself a cup of tea, because he did not want to disturb her.

By the first week in December, it was evident to everyone that Rosemary was close to death. When Schuyler arrived home from school for the Christmas holidays, both his sister and stepfather felt it would be better for the boy not to be present to watch his mother die, so arrangements were made for him to go skiing with friends in the northern part of the state. On New Year's Eve, Rosemary seemed to be resting comfortably and Nurse Mauck left to spend the evening with her husband. Within hours, there was a frantic telephone summons from Rains: "Rosie's gone into a coma, she's bad, please come." He then called Father Tom. Both came immediately, the nurse holding her friend's hand until the end.

Rains was shattered. He was an old man, ill himself. His much younger wife, his companion, his Rosie, was gone. As Schuyler commented sadly: "'Rainey' died that evening too. When she died, he died — he just wasn't pronounced dead for a couple of years."

CHAPTER 28
Alone

On a very cold winter day, Rosemary was buried under the inscription "The Beloved Wife of Claude Rains," with a polished black granite headstone he designed. The text combined a line from Christina Rossetti's popular poem "Song" with a variation on the refrain of a traditional hymn: "When I am dead, my dearest/ Sing no sad songs for me./ Rather in thy gracious keeping/ Leave me now/ Thy servant sleeping."

Rains quickly became a recluse: in his house, his drinking increased to the point where he was often out of control and would lock himself in his library for hours. Angela became frightened by his frequent outbursts of anger and strange behavior, and on several occasions, she and Schuyler spent the night with the McQuades. Angela was also furious about the issue of Rosemary's tombstone, erected without any reference to her children or words like "Beloved Mother." She regarded it as a "disgusting affair."

Father Tom did all he could to help, visiting the elderly actor as often as his schedule would allow. With the exception of Judge Winnett in Philadelphia, the priest was the only friend Rains could talk to. But there were times when Father Tom felt that the actor was replying as if he were listening for a cue. Rains, overwhelmed, often incoherent, was unable to deal with his wife's legal affairs. It cannot be emphasized enough how frantic the man's mind was. Unfortunately, his financial matters had worsened: In 1964, his income dropped to $30,971, and much of that went for the nurse and medical expenses. Everything that had given him pleasure was gone.

In his reflective brooding, Rains came to feel he had been a failure as an artist. Oh, he had achieved success in the movies but being a "movie star" never satisfied him. Rains loved acting for many reasons, it gave him the freedom to act out different personas and earn a decent living, but it provided him with neither great wealth nor a sense of personal fulfillment.

There always remained an element of emptiness: as a man, a husband, and a father, an emotional burden which certainly contributed to his excessive drinking. More unbearable in his bitter reflections were the multiple marriages, and that he had never established a close relationship with his only child. And when he had finally met someone who fawned and fussed over him and seemed to genuinely care about him, she died a lingering death at a young age. This final blow eradicated any hope that he would finally find the inner peace that had always eluded him.

After the holidays, Schuyler returned to boarding school and Angela went back to her graduate work. Jennifer was working in New York. All winter, Rains was alone in that big house in a remote area of New Hampshire. Word of Rosemary's death reached a few people in Hollywood who telephoned condolences, but no one offered to come to see him. But then that was his own fault, since he never tried to develop a dependable circle in his industry. When his old producer friend Dick Berg called about a role in a television play, Rains hesitated, feeling guilty, but he knew that if he didn't accept, he would only be home alone and drink. He sought guidance from Father Tom, who counseled that if Rosemary were alive, she would encourage him to return to his craft. Rains left for Hollywood if only to escape the cold weather and the quiet house.

On January 11, 1965, he began a week of rehearsals in Los Angeles for the *Bob Hope Presents the Chrysler Theatre* production "Cops and Robbers." When he arrived on the Universal set, few people recognized him. He was extremely thin, his hair, though still full, was completely white, and throughout rehearsals the famous voice cracked. But the comedic part was quite light, and he had two wonderful character actors to work off of, Bert Lahr and Billy De Wolfe. The story was unabashedly silly: A group of old men spend their days playing cards while waiting to die. They decide to have one last daring fling at life by playing a game of "cops and robbers" and knock over a bank. They manage to pull off the heist but, realizing that small depositors, ordinary people like themselves, will be hurt, they decide to return the money in an equally slapstick fashion.

The evening he was to return east, Rains had dinner with Berg, who was shocked to see a very gaunt, elderly man whose appearance reflected the ordeals of the terrible past year. In the audio tapes Rains recorded for his never-completed autobiography, he claimed: "I got drunk and [Berg] drove me to the airport. I restrained myself, didn't let him know what was going on inside me. I don't even remember getting on the plane." Perhaps this is truly how Rains remembered the night, since he had by his own account been drinking. Or perhaps it's how he wanted to remember it. Berg had quite a different recollection of events. After their dinner, because of stormy weather, the actor wanted to take a taxi to the airport, but Berg insisted on driving his old friend.

I was slowing the car down to let him off. He turned to me and said, "Dick, I don't know if I can get over the loss of Rosie." And I said, "Well, I'm sure you will in time." And then he said, "Rosie was not the only woman I loved in my life, but she was the only one who loved me back." As he said this, he pounded on the windshield with his fist and almost went through the glass. With each word he struck the windshield with his fist. Here was a usually totally controlled human being whose [hand] almost went through the windshield. ...It was as if he was saying something he had been holding within him for months, or years. That's the last time I saw him. We were extremely close that night — it was a cry into the night. I was shocked. I was shaking after I left him off. I had to pull back over to the curb and just sat in the car for a couple of minutes.

This man took all his clothes and skin off, after a superficial relationship over years. Well, it was more than superficial, but we were talking about him all the time, about his biography and that sort of thing, but to move from low gear into 110 miles

an hour in one moment was blinding. There were tears in his eyes and boy, the passion all came out — it was jolting — a shattering moment. He was extremely circumspect and very proud. This outburst I got was the earthquake. It was a short burst, but it was volcanic.

Rains may have been drunk, but he was coherent. For the first time, "the invisible man" revealed himself. Berg realized that his old friend was, in every sense — physically, spiritually, emotionally — dying. The actor's self-imposed isolation made him vulnerable to dark thoughts, and his memory was now unreliable. It was as if everyone he knew and everything he had done had been a part of that world of celluloid — they were only images of what he knew. He thought perhaps if he wrote about his life, he could somehow make sense of it and possibly discover facets he had never seen before. Rains asked Berg to suggest a writer to help him with the autobiography. Berg named Jonathan Root, a young *San Francisco Chronicle* reporter who had authored several books. For several months, Root and the actor corresponded and talked on the phone, but nothing was contracted, although Root did seek out possible publishers. In April, the writer phoned Rains in Sandwich to advise that any progress would be limited until they could meet. Rains telegraphed back that the two of them should begin work in June. However, in May, Root wrote Rains that he was going to Europe and would get in touch on his return. He also explained to the actor that making a record of any life is difficult, but in Rains' case, it would be even harder due to the actor's "profound personality," and that he wanted to delve into the elderly man's personal life as much as his career, especially his marriages. Notes were compiled, the tapes made. Then Root went abroad and sadly suffered a fatal heart attack. Whether or not Rains retained any enthusiasm for his autobiography remains unknown.

That summer, Angela decided that, rather than have her brother remain with Rains, she would take the boy on a trip to Europe. Rains agreed; he wrote to Judge Winnett that he was paying for the trip and taking care of all their expenses. Rosemary's estate consisted of a small trust for her son, designated for private schooling, but there was little spare money. Financial disputes now arose frequently, even though

Rains had legal power of attorney; the intricacies of Rosemary's estate were muddled. Given Rains' emotional state, he could hardly deal with the complications and had to rely on advice he received from an attorney in New Hampshire. Initially, others believed that Rains was handling everything himself, coherently and logically.

Rains knew his only salvation lay in working, and he considered an offer from the Theatre Guild he had received just before his wife's death. Producer and friend Henry Denker had remained in touch because he wanted a "star" personality to assure financial backers of advanced ticket sales. The play was *So Much of Earth, So Much of Heaven* by Ugo Betti, considered the greatest Italian playwright after Pirandello. Director Joel Schenker had seen the play in London and decided to produce it in summer theatres with Eric Portman and Signe Hasso to gauge the feasibility of a Broadway production. Although that venture was not well received, the Guild felt Denker could make revisions in the script and, with a forceful lead like Rains and a supporting cast which included Leueen MacGrath and Rains' friend Larry Gates, the play might have a successful run.

Rains' role was that of a dictator who has renounced power and retired but is persuaded to resume leadership of the government because of a political crisis. The action revolved around the last twelve hours of the man's life. Rains liked the part: "It had much to say about the perversion of idealism when it falls into the hands of corrupt politicians and about crime and destruction in the name of expediency." Forty-year-old Edward Parone, in the middle of a successful career as a stage and film director, was hired by the Guild for its 1965-66 season; he was not ecstatic about the play but he felt privileged to work with Rains. Denker too had doubts about the drama's potential, considering it pretentious. Previews in June and July included short runs at a theatre on Long Island, at the famous Westport Country Playhouse in Connecticut, and two weeks at the Bucks County Playhouse in New Hope, Pennsylvania. The New York opening was scheduled for October.

It soon became painfully evident that Rains was not the actor he had once been. He constantly talked of Rosemary and, in Denker's opinion, was still grieving. He began to doubt himself. He had been through so much and hadn't been on a stage for nearly a decade. Could he still manage a Broadway run of eight shows a week? He had never shied from a challenge, but he now openly admitted his apprehension:

> [The dictator's role is] emotionally disturbing, a magnificent part, something like the Old Bolshevik in *Darkness at Noon*. It must be true. I've got to suffer it. The man is terribly disturbed in it. Yet there is a religious note — and some hope for the future. I know what I can do with the role; the only question is, am I going to be able to do it? No matter how much the director can do for you, you always wonder if you can project what you know you are capable of projecting. I think I can do it. It is the sort of thing I do best — highly emotional.

But to a friend, he confided: "I pray I can survive." Knowing how much depended on him, the veteran actor did his utmost to live up to everyone's expectations. As Denker recalled:

> [He] never lost his temper on the set for any reason, especially on the road when so many unavoidable changes can occur, but Claude would be accommodating. He spoke softly, almost like a whisper, yet with power. And when he walked on the set, all five foot six inches (or less), he became over six feet tall. He had fantastic power, especially in his eyes. But when he became so ill, I was distraught. If he had trouble with his lines, well, he had a way of making pauses that were better than the lines.

The hard truth was that Rains simply wasn't up to it. In the past fifteen months, his physical condition had deteriorated; he was quite thin and seemed frail and unsteady. Worst of all, he had trouble hearing his cues. The director recalled that Rains seemed to be able to remember his lines in rehearsal, but when he went before an audience, stage fright paralyzed him. Forgetting his lines and missing cues was shameful and humiliating. As his anxiety increased, he drank even more, claiming it helped "to steady his nerves."

Old friend Bette Davis saw the play in Westport and went backstage after the performance, but Rains was exhausted and not up to talking. Later she wrote him: "Claude dear, You can't know how greatly I admire you — your performance — your courage — and just you! I wish you so much success with the play — watching you give a performance is always a privilege to me — I am so lucky I have worked with you so many times. It made me homesick for those days. Always my love — and I look forward to New Hampshire one day." Nevertheless, Davis told a friend it had been extremely painful to see Rains, always precise and methodical, losing control and struggling to maintain his dignity.

Toward the end of the Westport run, Rains sent a short note to Bertha Gotshall, the Sandwich postmistress who lived directly across the street from him and who had been taking care of small matters, including forwarding mail. "Thank you and thank you. Here is a check. I got myself a cold and it went to my tummy — so much so, I could just about stand up — getting better now. I miss my home and all concerned. I doubt the play will be a success in N.Y. How I miss my Rosie. God Bless You and my best to your good man. Your neighbor." The "cold" was an excuse for his chronic failing health and while he knew this, he made no attempt to see a doctor. Whatever the consequences, "the show must go on" — he had lived by that credo all his life and wasn't going to desert it at the end. In another short note to the postmistress, he wrote: "Say a little prayer for me. This is a tough job I've got myself. God Bless."

Rains managed to complete the week in Connecticut on a Saturday night. His next performance was Tuesday in Bucks County, Pennsylvania. Reviewers had panned the play but were polite about the legendary actor: "Rains' performance is not yet the sure, polished work he will be doing later, but it has many moments of both charm and power. Because the star is feeling his way, director Edward Parone's fine efforts to give the play a sense of menace and to infuse it with crackling pace are deferred for the time being. In this state of things, Larry Gates becomes the most important figure on the stage. He gives a crisp and convincing performance of a cynical warmonger." If Claude was going to be outshone by anyone, he was glad it was his good friend Gates.

The Bucks County Playhouse had 432 seats, and every one of them was sold in anticipation of the famous star's performance. Just before crew and cast arrived, theatre manager Walter Perner, Jr., received word that Rains was having trouble "with his lines, with his energy, and he was very, very frail." As a pre-

caution, Perner hired a dependable backup, veteran stage and television actor Walter Coy, as stand-by. Perner recalled the events:

> [Rains] seemed very, very tired, and was not talkative or demonstrative, and he seemed to be conserving his energy as much as he possibly could. I do not mean to imply that Mr. Rains was either temperamental or unpleasant; he was not. He simply seemed to be close to exhaustion and doing everything he could to stay the course.
>
> Opening night was a revelation. For the first act that night, what we had was vintage Claude Rains. His energy was high, he didn't miss a beat or a line, and he drove the play magnificently. At the intermission, everyone (including the audience) was excited. The show was playing like a smash hit, and one could hardly wait for the intermission to end. Alas, he couldn't keep it up. In the second act, his energy waned, and he began missing cues and forgetting lines and blocking. He got through it, but that was about all. The show received polite applause at its end, and polite reviews the following day. Although he played at least several more performances, he never again approximated that first act.

Then the inevitable happened. After the fourth night's performance, Larry Gates noticed that a pallid Rains appeared ready to collapse. Concerned because the elderly man looked "like death warmed over," Gates wanted to contact Rains' doctor friend in Chester County. When Rains didn't protest, Gates knew things were serious. He called Dr. Margolis at his home late at night and, after describing Rains' condition, was told to drive the actor to the Coatesville hospital immediately. It was well after midnight when they arrived; Rains was officially admitted on September 9 with severe internal hemorrhaging. Rains admitted to the doctor that prior to the performance, he had vomited blood. The first item on his diagnosis sheet was advanced cirrhosis of the liver, the cause of multiple other issues. Rains had blood clots on his esophagus, blood in his stomach, and was severely anemic; doctors were especially concerned because they could not stop the bleeding. Rains' liver was beyond repair; a diseased liver prevents the normal flow of blood and the veins that line the stomach and esophagus easily rupture. This would have caused the blood in the stomach which made him sick. If this condition grew worse, the toxicity would pass into the brain. There was no effective treatment for advanced cirrhosis, and liver transplants were unknown in 1965.

It was around this time that Rains' daughter changed her name for professional reasons, and as Jennifer Rains was working and living in New York City, still married to Edward Brash, a Time-Life researcher. (She will continued to be referred to as Jennifer, for clarity.) Both Dr. Margolis and Dr. Uhle, as well as representatives from the Theatre Guild, contacted her about her father's serious illness. No medical details were divulged to reporters; the hospital administrator advised only that the actor was suffering from a bleeding ulcer and severe anemia. It was anticipated that Rains would spend two weeks in the Coatesville hospital; instead, he was confined for thirty-five days, and not discharged until October 14, largely because the doctors could not stem the continuous intestinal bleeding. Another staff member, Dr. McChesney, recalled that, even though the ordeals of treatment were very uncomfortable, Rains was not in constant pain. He remembered the actor as mentally competent and alert, even though he was quite ill: "He still had that voice and was a gentleman all the way."

Of course, Rains' incapacitation was the death knell for *So Much of Earth, So Much of Heaven*; the show was canceled at a large financial loss. News of the actor's hospitalization spread quickly; the *Times* even telephoned the New Hope police station at four in the morning from London to obtain details. Because patient rooms at the small Coatesville hospital had no phones, Bette Davis sent her dear friend a note. Rains' fifth wife, Agi Jambor, who always had a warm spot for her ex and bore him no ill will, telephoned the hospital; she had read about his illness in the West Chester paper and wanted to wish him a speedy recovery. Old farm hand and friend Charles Brown visited often, and undoubtedly Judge Winnett came, but for the most part Rains had no company. He was allotted a private room and paid for private nurses, which the doctor encouraged, especially at night to monitor his condition. One who worked the 3 p.m. to 11 p.m. shift, a Nurse Robinson, remembered the old actor as a "character," pleasant and polite to the staff, never making a fuss about tests or treatment. "He was delightful to work for." She continued:

I did nothing for the man in that he needed no care. He had a large checkbook and he had an awful lot of mail, so I was his private secretary. I paid all his bills that came in. He would make a big fuss over a very small amount. I would open the bills and we'd discuss them and then I'd write the check and it was like he didn't want to pay that bill. I answered notes and that is all I did. At night I rubbed his back. I would go down to supper in the evening and all the nurses would beg me to let them rub his back. So I asked him if it would be all right and he agreed. He had a different nurse rub his back every night and he never got better back rubs in his entire life. It took twenty minutes doing it, but he knew and he laughed about it, so eventually I didn't even rub his back — I just took care of his mail. …Most of it had to do with the liver problem. I'd walk him down the hall after all visitors left just for some exercise.

I think he just about came up to my shoulder and he had flat slippers on, and I remember commenting to him, I said, "Lord in Heaven, how did you play those great love scenes?" and he said, "I stood on a box all the time." He got two letters from Bette Davis while he was there and his comment to me was: "That woman has been chasing me from the day we met." And he went on that he never would have married her because his life would have been miserable, saying, "I tried to stay clear of her."

Nurse Robinson remembered vividly that the actor was very lonely, and wanted to talk and talk:

He would use that voice of his real loud and people would come flying in thinking he was beating me to death or something, you could hear that voice all over the floor, you know, like he was in a playhouse with no microphone. Sometimes pretending as if he were on the stage. I mean, really shout at the top of his lungs, just anything. It didn't happen all the time but enough to make people wonder what was going on. He just loved attention. I also remember the black man with blue eyes [Charles Brown] who came to see him often. But I knew that his liver was not functioning properly, a progressive thing, usually fatal.

As fast as transfusions were pumped into him, Rains would hemorrhage out through his bladder or bowels. His condition worsened and after six weeks, Dr. Margolis realized that his facility could do nothing more and agreed to release the elderly actor on the condition that Rains get in touch with the top doctor in Laconia, New Hampshire, and a liver specialist in Boston. A major operation was an absolute necessity, or Rains would bleed to death. Before returning home to Sandwich, Rains spent several days as a guest of Judge Winnett in Philadelphia.

Larry Gates and his wife Judy were helpful to Rains during his long hospitalization. Although the two men were colleagues, there was never a real familiarity. Larry referred to Rains as "Claudie" in conversation with others, but he would never use this endearment in front of the actor. (It's too bad, because Rains would probably have enjoyed it, similar as it was to his stepchildren's nickname for him, "Rainey." Such intimacies were his manner of "anointing" a friendship by permitting the use of or employing a diminutive, just as he had done with others, for example, "Rosie" for his wife and "Jenni" for his daughter.) Gates also remembered that Rains was very vain about the fact that he had become hard of hearing and tried to camouflage it just as he had always done with the blindness in his one eye. What upset Gates most was how enfeebled Rains appeared — that grand and commanding presence was gone, and only a whisper of greatness remained in the once powerful voice that for decades reached the back of every house. During rehearsals of the play, while management was openly annoyed and impatient, everyone in the cast had done their best to help the old veteran if he missed cues. As Gates explained it: "You confront a younger actor with an icon like

Rains, and he'll doing anything to help him through the performance because you love him and because of his achievements."

Before leaving Coatesville hospital, Rains told Gates that some of his personal belongings were still at the Algonquin Hotel in New York City. Judy Gates was attending Hunter College at the time, so Gates asked her to collect Rains' things and send them on to Sandwich. Gates received a thank you note from Rains which stated quite frankly: "I took on a play too soon. I wanted to get out of the house and get over her death." In the same note, he invited the couple to Sandwich during the summer of 1966.

Judy Gates was quite honest about Rains' stage performance: "[What] I saw was certainly not the Claude Rains I knew from the films. He was a little old man who wasn't doing a very good job of making the play work. I realize now, of course, he was quite ill." When she went to the hotel to fetch his belongings, "I was surprised at the shabbiness of the baggage. …When I walked into the Algonquin and said I was here for Claude Rains, I got some wonderful obsequiousness — they were so nice and helpful to me for him."

Rains was wistful about Sandwich, as he indicated in the many short notes he sent to his friend, the postmistress: "I miss my house and garden and soon I hope to be walking up the brick path again." Other notes to her indicate how much he still grieved for Rosemary and how much Sandwich meant to him. "Thank you for your nice thoughts — did you ever have a nasty one? I don't think so. Home soon. Uncle C." In a postscript, he continued to insist that his condition was not serious: "I had become too concerned re: the doings of others (not my Jenni); result a bloody ulcer. Naught to do with cracking ice."

Rains was finally released from hospital but within a few days awoke to find himself lying in bloody sheets. His local doctor sent him by ambulance to the Laconia Hospital for more transfusions and the discussed esophagus treatment. The doctors wanted to send Rains to New England Baptist Hospital in Boston for a liver operation, but his condition did not stabilize. File notes indicate that he had private nurses from November 16 through 22, day and night. One nurse remembered that Rains never showed concern about the impending operation. He surely knew he was dying.

CHAPTER 29
"The Rest Is Silence"

At the end of November 1965, Rains seemed to be stabilizing, but the Laconia Hospital doctors hesitated to release him for the Boston trip until they could stop the bleeding. As of December 10, he was still in the New Hampshire hospital, and as his physical condition began to affect his mind, he grew confused easily. Very unwisely, Rains had never designated power of attorney to anyone. As he attempted to attend to his own affairs, he made a $250 overdraft on his Philadelphia bank account. Luckily, the bank manager had known the actor for years and discreetly contacted Judge Winnett, who soon straightened out the matter. This was only one of several embarrassing incidents. With no one to help, financial matters became more chaotic. Rains gave his local attorney in Sandwich the names and phone numbers of people to be notified in the event of his demise. Letters indicate that this attorney and Dr. Uhle both called him about the upcoming operation in Boston.

Complications arose concerning financial arrangements for the trust established for Schuyler's boarding school tuition. Because Rains had been in hospital in Coatesville during most of September and had been tied up with the play prior to that, he turned over the matter to his lawyer. The money from the trust was to come to Rains, who would write a check. However, because the actor was in the hospital, the lawyer held up the trust payments. This only intensified the resentment and friction between Angela and the ill actor, in that there was no executive to properly handle finances. Rains tried attending to things from his sickbed, but in his condition, things only became more confused, aggravating an already tension-filled atmosphere. Judge Winnett came to Rains' aid again.

Legal matters became messier. After Rosemary's death, Rains revised his will more than a dozen times. He was torn between his daughter by blood and his emotional obligations to the children of his late wife. Jennifer sought a reconciliation with her father, on account of his illness and the emotional trauma he had experienced since Rosemary's passing. In the meantime, Jennifer was desperately trying to get her own life in order; she and her husband were on the brink of divorce. Even when Rains was well, she found it difficult to talk to him about her life; seeking his advice now was out of the question. The ghosts of memories haunted him, interfering with rational and logical thinking. As if matters were not bad enough, Rains' income for 1965 consisted of $14,290 from two television shows and $4,150 from annuities and dividends, etc., totaling $20,488. His medical expenses far exceeded this amount.

The new year of 1966 started off with Rains still in Laconia Hospital. Over the holidays, as the tension between him and Angela intensified, so did his paranoia. In several letters to Judge Winnett, Rains accused Angela of spreading "stories" about him in connection with administration of her mother's will. Winnett was Rains' only confidant but could do little when it came to legal matters in the New Hampshire courts. He expressed concern about Rains' obvious depression and his isolation in Sandwich, advising the actor to refrain from making accusations. Trying to be helpful, he invited Rains to stay at his Philadelphia home for several weeks after the upcoming surgery.

Meanwhile, the doctors, wary of further delays and agreeing that a major procedure was Rains' only chance, made arrangements to have their patient taken by ambulance to the Boston hospital. Prior to the perfection of organ transplants, surgical intervention for Rains' condition consisted of a bypass of the liver with an internal shunt. As Jennifer signed all the necessary papers, doctors explained that her father could die on the operating table, but if he survived, it was possible he could live from six months to several years. The problem with the procedure was that it often resulted in the swelling of other veins, causing further bleeding, but there was no alternative for the treatment of cirrhosis.

Fortunately, all went well, but recovery was slow and Rains remained in the hospital for a month. He continued to bleed internally and was given frequent transfusions. Rains wrote short notes to only a few people, but kept in touch with Bertha Gotshall, the kindly Sandwich postmistress. One note to her went: "Hi! When I get back, I'll show you my stitches. My best to the lot of you." Another: "They are to 'stick' me on Monday and I should walk up the brick path two weeks after." With very few visitors, it was a lonely time, but also a time of reflection.

In the early spring, Rains returned to Sandwich to recuperate. He now realized his would be a tragic exit from the world of acting he had known for sixty-five years. His end would not come with a standing ovation, but instead a slow fade-out. For years, he had been warned to cut down or stop abusing alcohol — why did he continue? After Frances left him and he sold Stock Grange, his intake increased drastically. When Rosemary became terminally ill, he knew he was poisoning himself, but didn't seem to care. He continued to deny that there was any problem in scribbled notes to friends, insisting that his reputation was undeserved.

He was alone in that empty house. Everything was gone — his wives, his farm, his career and, to some extent, his daughter. Rains began to have delusions, or at best, exhibit exceedingly strange behavior. His English friend and fan, Audrey Homan, who knew him when he made *Caesar and Cleopatra*, came to the U.S. and wanted to visit him. When Rains met her at the Boston airport, he was surrounded by autograph seekers. "These are students at the university where I teach English," he told her, which was patently untrue. During the drive back to Sandwich, he talked about preparing his autobiography *The Love Habit*, a title he said he had selected to help the book sell.

That June, when Jennifer went to Judge Winnett for advice about obtaining a divorce, the judge contacted Rains about the situation. The expedient approach was a Mexican divorce, which Edward Brash agreed to only if he was compensated financially — an expense Rains claimed he could not afford. Judge Winnett saw how precarious the situation was and in August, he made the trip to remote Sandwich to convince Rains to return to the Philadelphia area.

By now, however, Rains was completely unable to undertake the complications of relocation. Moreover, he had come to like Sandwich and took comfort in its environment, which offered a peace that was impossible when living in a city. Winnett's visit helped to lift the actor's spirits but did little to alleviate the problems he faced alone.

That same summer, Warner Bros. sent Rains the screenplay for a film version of the hit Broadway show *Camelot*, but it's unlikely the actor ever read it. (There are no marks in the script and he never bothered to return it as he usually did when he turned down a part.) On August 15, he wrote Jennifer in Calumet, Michigan, where she was performing in a play. She must have proposed they take a trip together as he replied: "I am in bed with a dreadful cold. I doubt I'll make it to Calumet, much as I want to… Don't forget you are planning a visit. …[Maybe] South America in December. Irving Rapper called me — they want me for a Bishop. WOW. …Love and kisses. Your naughty old (young) FaFa." (The South American film to which Rains refers was *Ceferino Namuncura*. *Variety* reported on September 28, 1966, that Rapper, director of *Now, Voyager* and *Deception*, was in Argentina scouting locations for the movie, which was to have featured Anthony Quinn, Rains, Ricardo Montalban and Yma Sumac.)

As summer cooled into fall, Larry and Judy Gates drove to Sandwich for a brief visit that left the couple with indelible memories. Despite the colorful countryside, Judy experienced an unsettling and eerie feeling, a gloom she could not shake off. She remembered the old house with its large garden as a magnificent New England dwelling: "I associated it with a poem by Swinburne, 'A Forsaken Garden.'" She remembered the inside as dark and cluttered, and that Rains appeared quite enfeebled, very unhappy, and very frail. "At dinner, I was quite shy and felt pity for Mr. Rains because he seemed so lonely and so ill. It was impossible to talk to him. There was nothing he wanted to hear and nothing he wanted to say. I could never imagine a more uncomfortable evening." Her husband added: "There was a formality in the visit, but Claude's hospitality was excellent. Yet as much as I admired and loved him, I never felt comfortable with him for any length of time; he seemed to me to be a very private person and didn't seem to want to share. He was a forbidding personality, very austere in his demeanor."

This comment echoes what so many others had felt: Because of their respect, they maintained the distance Rains imposed and didn't dare intrude on his privacy. Gates had a further, wistful reflection: "Of course, it may have been a misunderstanding — he may have wanted people to talk with him." During their visit, Judy got the impression that Rains was disappointed and disillusioned about his life. "I don't think he wanted to communicate with anyone. And yet he would never have invited us to come up unless he wanted to see Larry. I am certain it was an obligation on his part, [but] Claude would never have invited Larry unless he really wanted to see him. But it was not a happy house and I felt sorry for anyone in it." She saw Rosemary's children, who had little to say during the visit. Several days after the couple returned to their Connecticut farm, Gates sent a very warmly worded thank you letter to which Rains responded with a postcard: "Bless you Larry. 'What joy or sadness often springs from just the simple little things.' Love to you both. C."

Come September, Schuyler and Angela again returned to their respective schools, leaving Rains alone in the house with a day housekeeper whose personality he disliked: She was a strong-willed, bossy person who was quite strict about his diet and medications. He wailed and complained of her treatment and called her a witch. Living in Sandwich was inconvenient for an elderly and ill person on his own. Even if Rains wanted to visit Judge Winnett in Philadelphia, it was over an hour's taxi drive to Manchester to board a commuter plane for a connection in Boston, followed by another flight to Philadelphia. Most importantly, Rains wanted to be close to his doctors because of his precarious health. The few people he knew casually in Sandwich tried to be accommodating in the only way they knew how with such a reserved man. Rains wandered into his old age without the will to survive. Regardless of the consequences to his health, he continued to drink heavily. It was a paradoxical situation. While he wanted privacy, he needed intimacy — revealed by the many short notes, written in a scrawl, to various individuals about his despondency and loneliness.

One evening a Sandwich neighbor gave a cocktail party and in kindness invited the lonely celebrity. A local woman who attended remembered,

For three hours straight, he talked about his youth, his moviemaking days, his friendship with Bette Davis, etc., etc. When he left the party, he thanked his hostess profusely. As she returned to her guests, she made an insightful but sarcastic comment: "You know what he said to me? 'Thank you very much, I have enjoyed myself immensely.' No wonder he enjoyed himself — all he did was talk about himself!

The hostess added, "He absolutely needed an audience," and commented that no one could relax until Rains departed. She also remembered that the actor was so lonely, he would telephone other locals and chat with them about trivial matters. No one ever visited him at the Weed House, but Rains would call different residents and "complain about his housekeeper and then ring off."

At least once or twice a week, Rains needed to cash a check; he never kept more than $25 in the house. Since there was no bank in the village, he would send the housekeeper to deliver a short note to his friend, the postmistress. These little communiques reflected his self-pity in a self-deprecating manner: "Please, Granny, I'm broke again…" and "I'm a poor old man, so will you please give me $25.00? Uncle C." Another went: "Please — I have a bin, but there ain't no dough in it."

The only bright moment in this dark year came in the late fall. On November 21, 1966, Claude Rains was made an honorary fellow of Boston University, "in recognition of [his] contribution to the arts." This event had come in a rather roundabout way. The new director of the Boston University Mugar Memorial Library collections division was a man named Howard Gotlieb. It was his goal that the Mugar should become renowned for its collection of important archives and private papers, and he began to solicit donations from celebrated individuals, especially in the humanities.

It happened that Bette Davis knew Gotlieb and had already designated in her will that all of her personal papers were to be donated to the Mugar Library. During one of her conversations with Gotlieb, she mentioned the extensive collection of signed scripts and books, especially those by George Bernard Shaw, owned by her friend and colleague, Claude Rains. Gotlieb wrote Rains to arrange a meeting in hopes of convincing the actor that this memorabilia should be bequeathed to Boston University. In dogged pursuit of this objective, he went out of his way to befriend Rains, having dinner with him monthly. Even though Rains indicated to his daughter that he was aware of the transparent motive behind the relationship, it pleased him to be courted; he welcomed Gotlieb's visits, which afforded an opportunity to tell his favorite stories. The agreement to make the donation may have been verbal, as there is no written authorization among Rains' private papers in their archives. However, Rains did mention the arrangement in letters to Judge Winnett.

The more time Gotlieb spent with Rains, the more he came to appreciate the actor's obvious intellect, his humor and profound courtesy. He noted a rare "courtliness" in Rains' demeanor. He also came to believe that Rains, despite (or perhaps, because of) his lack of formal academic education, deserved some kind of scholastic recognition for his profound knowledge of English literature. Born in Britain, Rains had chosen to become an American citizen; he had mastered the King's English in an extraordinary manner; he had performed to great acclaim on the stages of London and New York and appeared in over fifty motion pictures, as well as on radio and television. Gotlieb proposed that Boston University make Rains an honorary fellow in recognition of his achievements in the world of arts and letters, and that the award be presented during the dedication ceremony of the new library. It was a fitting tribute to a great artist — and an irresistible carrot to dangle in order to secure his remarkable collection of signed Shaw plays, as well as other treasures and personal effects.

On November 21, Boston University hosted a gala with many eminent dignitaries and personalities present. Arthur Fiedler, Cleveland Amory, Eric Ambler, General Matthew B. Ridgeway, Alec Waugh, F. Van Wyck Mason, Hans Habe and Rains (the only actor) were among thirteen celebrities who pledged to donate their private papers to the library, and were named fellows of the Boston University library. With such prestigious contributions, the Mugar was on its way to becoming a noted repository of the papers of distinguished 20th century writers, artists and other public figures. A photograph of the actor at the event harshly reveals how emaciated and frail he had become. Jennifer did not attend; Rains was driven to the event by a woman in her late forties, who was referred to in reports as a "companion."

During the last year of Rains' life, there were two frequent visitors to the Sandwich home — his doctor and Father Tom. Rains had been so impressed by the comfort his wife had found in her faith as she was dying, that he had queried the priest about the possibility of becoming a Catholic. Undoubtedly, as Father Tom admitted, Rains was attracted to the formalities and ceremonies involved, especially the solemnity of the liturgy, with its flowing Latin language. Catholicism has the trappings and flair of the theatrical and is quite dramatic, which would have appealed to the actor. As Rains' health declined, he repeatedly asked the priest to begin the necessary lessons for conversion. Father Tom took the matter to his superiors, but they all felt the elderly actor was much too ill to undertake, or possibly even comprehend, the psychological preparations of such a procedure, which could involve many months. Rains grew weaker and thinner. The severe varicose veins on the wall of his esophagus, caused by the liver operation in Boston, worsened. Since his damaged liver could no longer detoxify his blood supply, he was always tired and at times very confused. Father Tom gave him materials to read, and remained a close friend, visiting often.

During one of their conversations, Rains voiced bitterness about his marriages, even describing Rosie's death as a kind of abandonment. He was particularly remorseful that Fate had robbed him of his last opportunity to know happiness by taking from him, in a cruel manner, the only woman who ever loved him. Even Rosemary's daughter Angela (who never understood why her mother married Rains) remembered how patient and forgiving her mother was of Rains' caustic behavior, which she considered an outward manifestation of his having been hurt and disappointed so frequently in his life.

In the months that followed, Bette Davis wrote and telephoned often. She asked if she could visit, but Rains repeatedly told her it was "a bad time." Bette loved Claude but she would not have had a calming effect on him at this time. He was fearful she might dwell on the past. Additionally, he knew that the presence of the great movie star would bring unwanted media to the quiet town. So she never went to Sandwich but, a true friend, she understood and respected Rains' wishes and continued to feel strongly about him even after death.

Dr. Nadeau of Laconia Hospital made frequent house calls (a common practice in the 1960s) because the actor would telephone that he felt quite ill. (It was Nadeau who signed the actor's death certificate.) According to the physician: "Rains would open the door all dressed in an ascot, a smoking jacket and elevated shoes and take me into a beautiful library. I never saw him in bed. The most I did was listen to his heart, but I realized he was deteriorating rapidly. He'd repeat stories and they began to lose some of their impact and were less fascinating. He did go downhill fast after his wife died." The stories were getting more and more improbable: Rains claimed that, when a young man, he was corresponding with a girl in the United States, but because he knew he wasn't sufficiently eloquent, Oscar Wilde offered to write the letters for him. This was an obvious fabrication, as Wilde died when Rains was only eleven.

Because Rains continued to lose blood, Nadeau arranged for him to take an ambulance-taxi to Laconia Hospital for transfusions. Even though the actor argued that he was a controlled drinker and not an alcoholic, the doctor realized that depression and loneliness impaired any ability to regulate intake.

During the last six months of his life, Rains composed many different legal documents and was in constant contact with Judge Winnett about his estate. His paranoia about money disturbed his final days. As 1966 drew to a close, and his annual tax return was prepared, it's hard to imagine this once great star now had a total gross income of $11,830, of which only $440 was from his profession (television reruns or royalties from recordings); the rest came from dividends and annuities. Rains once again revised his will on December 1, and decided to reestablish a relationship with his daughter. Jennifer was still trying to obtain a divorce from Edward Brash. She had gone to Sandwich to discuss the matter with her father; as usual, intimate interaction regarding such matters was difficult. He was in bed with a bad cold and when she told him of her separation and upcoming divorce, he responded with a thunderous query: "Was it sex?" Attempting to maintain composure in the wake of such an awkward question, she explained that she required a financial agreement because Edward was demanding money. Rains relented and provided his remaining savings for his daughter's needs. By this time, Jennifer was seeing a young actor named Rick Lenz. (Lenz had understudied, and eventually taken

over the juvenile lead in the Broadway hit *Cactus Flower*, and would recreate the role for the 1969 hit movie with Goldie Hawn. His other credits would include *The Shootist* in 1976 and *Melvin and Howard* in 1980.) Jennifer decided that she and Lenz would visit her father the following spring.

All over the country, people were concerned about the condition of the beloved performer. On January 3, 1967, the director of the Boston University Libraries sent Rains a two-page letter in reply to a Christmas note from Rains in which the elderly man had sounded despondent: "[You are] one of the greatest and most beloved actors of our time and you have a great deal of pleasure to give people in the future." He invited Rains to visit with him and his family in Boston.

All during January and February, Rains was housebound by the severe cold weather and snow. He had given up the ghost psychologically; physically, there was no fight left in him as he continued to lose blood but did not inform the doctor because he did not want to endure the ordeal of going to the hospital for more transfusions.

As planned, Jennifer and Rick Lenz drove up to Sandwich in March to spend the weekend. Jennifer fluttered around her father, who enjoyed their visit. Meeting Lenz was an opportunity to tell all his old stories. Rick realized Rains was giving a performance of sorts: "My impression — he was very lonely and very ill. He took such pleasure in having company. Jennifer had brought him an audience, but his voice was shaky and wavering. He seemed so genuinely happy to have us there." Lenz remembered one humorous incident when he was staying with Jennifer in New York and the telephone rang at seven in the morning. He picked up the call, to the obvious surprise of Jennifer's father. After Jennifer took the receiver from him, Rains reprimanded her that it wasn't appropriate for her to have "guests" at such an early hour (meaning, male visitors to whom she wasn't married), a reflection of how unalterable his Victorian mindset was. Jennifer and Rick Lenz would shortly make their relationship legal in a marriage that lasted a decade.

In the latter part of March, Judge Winnett advised Jennifer to return to Sandwich and make an inventory of her father's possessions to prevent future legal problems. During that visit, Rains told her he wanted a private funeral with a closed coffin made of

666

plain pine wood. After she left, he composed his final will, dated March 29. He realized that his daughter was the only person who now mattered to him, and he made her his sole heir.

The old man lingered on, awaiting the coming of spring; once it arrived, he could leave in peace. The last letter he wrote to his old friend Judge Winnett was on April 19, 1967. It is a letter of pain and rage, reflecting a confused state of mind as Rains ranted on about how good he had been to his late wife's children in providing a home and paying for their European trip, and that now there was nothing from them but ingratitude. Rains' paranoia makes it difficult to understand what really happened between him and Angela. He insisted he had lived up to his obligations, and that in the last year when he had paid all expenses, he had done so in Rosemary's memory. As if tying up loose ends, he wrote to the Screen Actors Guild on April 29 to state his intention to retire from his nearly seventy-year career; his SAG pension and insurance would go to his daughter. Just as he prepared so diligently for his acting roles, now Rains did so for his death.

When the doctor visited Rains on May 10, he was so alarmed that he ordered an ambulance. But this time Rains was adamant: He had had enough of hospitals and no longer wanted to delay the inevitable. On May 23, he was able to take a morning walk in the beautiful spring morning sunshine, greeting a few neighbors. But on his return to the house, he looked pale and by the early afternoon he fainted. He was now so thin that the female housekeeper was able to lift him into his bed. His attending doctor, however, was out of town. Frightened, the housekeeper called the doctor's colleague who, unfamiliar with both the seriousness of Rains' condition and the urgency of the situation, didn't arrive until 11:30 that evening. When he saw how close to death Rains was, he ordered an ambulance to take the actor to the Lakes Region General Hospital in Laconia, a 45 minute drive. All this time, Rains was hemorrhaging. On arrival, he was given nine units of blood in the ER, in a body that probably held about ten. Surprisingly, his blood pressure held at 110/40 and there was some improvement and stabilization.

The doctor notified Jennifer to drive up immediately, and she remained by her father's bedside for two days. Rains feigned irritation and told her not to worry. Complaining that he saw no reason for stay-

ing in the hospital, he demanded his clothes so he could leave and ordered Jennifer back to New York City. The great actor's final performance was quite convincing. After assurances from the doctors that her father seemed to be stabilizing, Jennifer obligingly left. Rains returned to his Sandwich house by ambulance.

On May 29, a lovely spring day, Rains took a short walk before noon. About one p.m., he collapsed. The housekeeper phoned Dr. Nadeau, who ordered an ambulance to return the actor to Laconia Hospital. Records indicate he suffered epigastric pain radiating to his back as his condition worsened; he lapsed into a coma and was placed in an oxygen tent. When Father Tom arrived, the dying man did not know him. Doctors contacted Jennifer, telling her to return. When she explained she didn't think she could get there quickly enough, she was told it was unlikely her father would recognize her anyway. In the end, Jennifer didn't arrive in time.

At 8:20 am on the morning of May 30, 1967, Claude Rains gave up his long struggle. On the day previous, Judge Winnett had written that he hoped to visit soon, a letter Rains never saw. The actor's diseased liver was the cause of his physical death, but spiritually, his soul had died ten years earlier when he left Stock Grange. Jennifer contacted Judge Winnett, who in turn asked Father Tom to work with the Mc-Quades on funeral arrangements. Bad feelings (over obscure financial disagreements) had developed over the last year, regardless, John and Ruth commendably acted decently, in honor of their friendship with Rosemary and her children.

Because her father always loved wildflowers, Jennifer managed to cut daisies from the florist's own garden (all he had in his shop were special hot house flowers). These she placed on Rains' coffin, but the funeral director considered them weeds and thoughtlessly removed them. In attendance at the burial were Jennifer; Angela and Schuyler; the McQuades, and Father Tom. There was no cortege, no long line of friends, no Judge Winnett, no Dr. Gotlieb, no Bette Davis. The haste and apparent secrecy of the funeral puzzled and upset many people in Sandwich.

By the end of his life and career, Claude Rains — the actor who represented the epitome of culture and sophistication — had become a semi-recluse, living alone in a large house on a quiet rural road in a very small remote area in New Hampshire. His once beautiful home and its lands were sold off as part of his estate; the small printed advertisement read "House and its lands contained 120 acres with 80 ft. of frontage on Squam Lake" and it was listed at $65,000. On September 16, an executor's auction was held to dispose of the remaining items. As Jennifer prepared for this ordeal, a woman in her forties came to the house and asked for the actor's dressing gown. Possibly this was the "companion" during the last two years of his life who sometimes chauffeured him places, such as to Boston for the honorary fellowship ceremony. Jennifer charitably obliged her; they never exchanged any information. All of Rains' pewter and numerous antiques, and those things that Jennifer did not wish to keep, were designated for a large auction at Parke-Bernet Galleries in New York. (Rains had bequeathed the antique silver to Judge Winnett, for all his kindness.) The auction netted $43,908. Proceeds from the household auction came to a mere $10,000; the actor's new Mercedes sold for $4,750. These monies were added to the trust that had been established for Jennifer. There was life insurance at $163,000, along with $3,200 from some stocks and bonds. In his will, Rains had bequeathed a gift of $25,000 to the Actor's Fund of America. To commemorate his contribution, a room at the Retirement Home for Actors in Englewood, New Jersey, was dedicated in his honor and a bronze plaque is mounted in the corridor. After the funeral expenses, taxes, lawyers' fees and unpaid medical bills, etc., Rains' estate totaled $326,213. At the end of 1967,

the judge filed the last income tax form for Claude Rains, writing in as occupation: actor. In the final year of the veteran performer's life, there was one last check, from Universal Studios, for royalties amounting to $471.25.

In February 1968, as his old friend had directed him, Judge Winnett sent a few personal effects, together with autographed books, manuscripts and other items, to the new Research Center at Boston University. Some legal matters were more complicated, and it was not until April 30, 1969, that the Weed House in Sandwich was sold — for $45,000, at a loss of $3,344. Rains' estate was finally settled.

The sole mention of Rains' funeral had gone through the wire services to the various newspapers stating, "[O]nly close relatives and friends attended the private services." Perhaps more puzzling was that there was never a memorial service. It was as if Rains strolled off into the fog, just as he had done with Bogart at the end of *Casablanca*. In his final scene, Claude Rains disappeared just like the invisible man he always was.

As he requested, he is buried beside Rosemary in the small cemetery near Sandwich. Like hers, his gravestone is of black polished marble, with a gothic design. His epitaph reads as the final credit of his longest performance:

> All things once
>> Are things forever.
> Soul, once living,
>> Lives forever.

Epilogue

You never knew who was beneath the civility and the charm and the beauty of the voice, but you thought that inside was a sad and lonely spirit, maybe wounded, maybe hurt. And out of those sad eyes … you know the fire that burned … that, you could feel.

— Ossie Davis

I suppose life is just a business of knowing what to do with it. I suppose I was somewhat a prey to my emotions, and they can be awfully misleading. You can get hurt — and you can hurt other people. I had something of both.

— Claude Rains (*Silver Screen*, 1946)

Sometimes when I'm in my room, I go to the mirror and I look into it, trying to see who I am…. I talk to myself, and all the characters I've ever played pass in front of me, and I'm every one of them. But that's *all* I am, there's no real me, only the characters! …I'm only real when I'm acting. The rest of the time, I'm *nothing*! That's why I drink!

— Claude Rains, "The Cream of the Jest," *Alfred Hitchcock Presents*

By the end of his life, Rains was exhausted from an inner struggle to understand why he could not hold on to a loved one. His failed marriages weighed heavily, evidence of the emotional discord in his life. The actor's psychological state can't be fully understood without further hard evidence, so only reasonable assumptions can be made and suggestions offered. Rains had never understood the necessity of give and take in a relationship, and he had only a limited capacity for understanding the needs of others.

Neither did he ever examine his own behavior. Each of his marriages is a reflection of where and who he was at the time.

When he was growing up in the early 1900s, emotional security — that normal, essential element of childhood development — was denied young "Willie Wains." Rains suffered from a near-desperate desire for companionship, denied the usual pattern of emotional development, child to young adult. But that instability seemed to have set the foundation for lifelong insecurity, especially when coupled with the cliched but often accurate trope of British stoicism and formality. Consequently, that aspect of his psyche needed and sought attention the rest of his life. While being egocentric is normal for a youngster, being egotistical is a defect in an adult. As he grew older, Rains remained self-focused, a quality which inevitably fostered a constant sense of loneliness. It would always remain difficult for him to release, in a safe and satisfying manner, any tension caused by his insecurities. And so he drank. Rains once insisted: "I must have a woman," but when it was suggested he find "companionship without marriage," he replied adamantly, "No, it's marriage or nothing." He referred to his romantic passions as his "love habit," and had told Jonathan Root that this should be the title of his autobiography.

His first experience with Isabel was pure romance; nevertheless, it was genuine and had a profound influence on his subsequent behavior with women. The marriage to Marie was undertaken in haste, to fend off loneliness and disappointment. The union with Beatrix was a kind of "fatal attraction" — they were both too self-obsessed to give in to the other, and to a degree, Beatrix wanted the upper hand, which he could never relinquish. He once commented to a friend at the Theatre Guild that "Trixie" (as she was known) did not want to have children and lamented how very much he wanted to be a father.

He was confident his marriage to Frances would

work, and for twenty years he was right. She willingly gave up her independence, she was a woman who would be a servile, dutiful wife, and because of her youth, she would also represent the obedient daughter. Perhaps she encompassed everything Rains needed in a companion. However, protected and spoiled as a girl, she didn't realize she was tying herself to such an egocentric and insecure older man. As she grew older, her needs changed, and when she moved on, it was with a man whose demeanor was the complete opposite of her husband's. Rains' years with Frances, and the birth of their daughter, represented the happiest of his life, so what he perceived as her betrayal and infidelity was the greatest wound of all, especially coming as it did so unexpectedly. To add to the psychological trauma, when he sold Stock Grange, he no longer had physical roots to sustain him – but the pain associated with his "haunted palace" was too great for him to remain there alone.

He married Agi at a very precarious time in his life, and believed he had found a mature partner who, as an artist herself, could understand his temperament and needs. But he was still in great pain from the divorce from Frances and the loss of Stock Grange, all of which complicated his emotional state. Belatedly, Agi realized that Claude was simply too complex a personality and too wounded for her (or anyone) to help at such a late stage. Even when she became the victim of his strange and vindictive actions, she made excuses for him, blaming everything on his drinking. Of all his wives, perhaps it was Agi who suffered most from the ordeal of the "invisible" Claude Rains.

At last, in Rosemary, Rains was convinced he had found someone fun to be with, who really cared about him, with all of his faults. She made him the center of her attention, she wooed him, pumping up his ego. Rains seemed to open up and enjoy himself, even appearing to mellow. The terrible tragedy of her fatal illness was something from which he himself could not recover. When she "left" him, he seemed to have little strength to continue, and disappeared into a world of alcohol.

If, as facts would seem to bear out, Rains was uncomfortable with, or even fearful of, anyone knowing or penetrating his inner feelings, playing different characters allowed his psyche a release. Rains buried himself in his roles. It was as if the fictional personas replaced his own – as if his identity could be expressed only through the characters he portrayed. Undoubtedly, he felt it was safer to stay within himself and in a reality he seemingly could control. Perhaps assuming a false persona gave him a means of emotional armor, and so he excelled as an actor.

And what an actor he was.

Sadly, like all his theatre colleagues prior to the era of talking pictures, Rains' stage work is only the stuff of memory, of contemporary reviews and blurry photographs. Few audience members remain who have memories even of his twilight triumph, *Darkness at Noon*. But this author is one. And she has never forgotten the brilliance.

Like most artists, there were movies in his career in which it was hard for him to overcome a weak script or inadequate supporting players; but he always made the bad, better. And he delivered so many unforgettable performances – creating classic characters in all-time classic films like *Casablanca* and *The Adventures of Robin Hood*, emotional mastery in a lesser-known but not lesser quality movie like *Mr. Skeffington*, finding the nuance to garner sympathy for the villain in *Notorious*. That unique voice, coupled with the arch of a perfect eyebrow, could heighten the most insignificant line. He might have been "invisible" as a personality, but as an artist, his genius couldn't be masked.

One evening in 1971, Bette Davis was a guest on Dick Cavett's talk show. After discussing *Now, Voyager*, with Davis reiterating her conviction that her character, Charlotte, eventually married Rains' Dr. Jaquith, Cavett asked, rather startlingly, "Was he a happy man? I like to think so, he gave me so much pleasure." Davis was slow and deliberate in her reply. "Well, I think as happy as any…" She paused for several seconds; her face very thoughtful as she searched for words. "I don't think, as a group, actors are what I'd call happy people. I think we're very … moody people…. I think we're terribly peculiar that way, and rather lonely people, actually. So, Claude, I could not say, was a happy person. He was witty, amusing and beautiful, really beautiful. Thoroughly enchanting to be with. And brilliant." Her answer was a fitting tribute to her friend.

Claude Rains' personality was an enigma even to those who wanted to love him. For such a man, whose only sense of life and deep feelings came through his acting, it was difficult to find peace. His complexity was a contributing factor to his greatness.

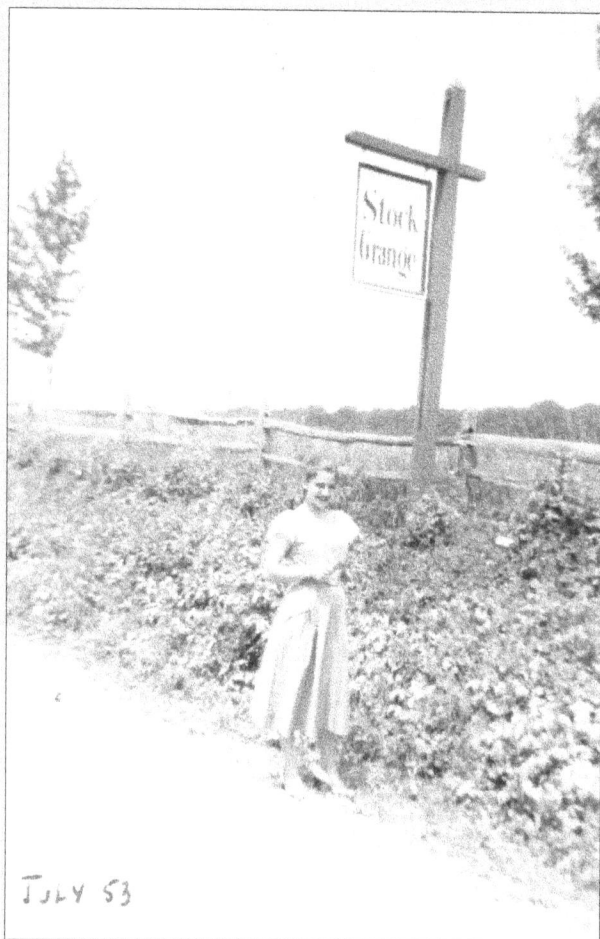

July 53

"On Visiting the Gravesite of
Claude Rains"

It is quiet here
only the leaves speak
as they gently caress
the black polished stone,
whispering words of comfort.

In life we were strangers,
here we are together in the
brilliance of the autumn sun,
the living and the dead
embracing each other in memories.

— Toby I. Cohen
Sandwich, 1995

Appendices

The Films of Claude Rains
* - Oscar nomination
Year Title and Studio
      Director(s)
1920 *Build Thy House* (Ideal Film Co.)
      Fred Goodwins
1933 *The Invisible Man* (Universal)
      James Whale
1934 *Crime Without Passion* (Paramount)
      Ben Hecht and Charles MacArthur
1935 *The Man Who Reclaimed His Head* (Universal)
      Edward Ludwig
      Mystery of Edwin Drood (Universal)
      Stuart Walker
      The Clairvoyant (Gainsborough-Gaumont)
      Maurice Elvey
      The Last Outpost (Paramount)
      Louis Gasnier and Charles Barton
1936 *Hearts Divided* (Warners)
      Frank Borzage
      Anthony Adverse (Warners)
      Mervyn LeRoy
1937 *Stolen Holiday* (Warners)
      Michael Curtiz
      The Prince and the Pauper (Warners)
      William Keighley
      They Won't Forget (Warners)
      Mervyn LcRoy
1938 *Gold Is Where You Find It* (Warners)
      Michael Curtiz
      The Adventures of Robin Hood (Warners)
      William Keighley and Michael Curtiz
      White Banners (Warners)
      Edmund Goulding
      Four Daughters (Warners)
      Michael Curtiz
1939 *They Made Me a Criminal* (Warners)
      Busby Berkeley
      Sons of Liberty (short)   (Warners)
      Michael Curtiz
      Juarez (Warners)
      Willian Dieterle

Daughters Courageous (Warners)
Michael Curtiz
Mr. Smith Goes to Washington (Columbia)
Frank Capra
Four Wives (Warners)
Michael Curtiz
1940 *Saturday's Children* (Warners)
      Vincent Sherman
      The Sea Hawk (Warners)
      Michael Curtiz
      Lady With Red Hair (Warners)
      Curtis Bernhardt
1941 *Four Mothers* (Warners)
      William Keighley
      Here Comes Mr. Jordan (Columbia)
      Alexander Hall
      The Wolf Man (Universal)
      George Waggner
1942 *Kings Row* (Warners)
      Sam Wood
      Moontide (20th Century-Fox)
      Archie Mayo
      Now, Voyager (Warners)
      Irving Rapper
1943 *Casablanca* (Warners)
      Michael Curtiz
      Forever and a Day (RKO)
      various directors
      Phantom of the Opera (Universal)
      Arthur Lubin
1944 *Passage to Marseille* (Warners)
      Michael Curtiz
      Mr. Skeffington (Warners)
      Vincent Sherman
1945 *Strange Holiday* (PRC)
      Arch Oboler
      This Love of Ours (Universal)
      William Dieterle
1946 *Caesar and Cleopatra* (Rank Organization)
      Gabriel Pascal
      Notorious (RKO)
      Alfred Hitchcock

Angel on My Shoulder (United Artists)
Archie Mayo
Deception (Warners)
Irving Rapper
1947 *The Unsuspected* (Warners)
Michael Curtiz
1949 *The Passionate Friends* (Pinewood/Cineguild)
David Lean
Rope of Sand (Paramount)
William Dieterle
Song of Surrender (Paramount)
Mitchell Leisen
1950 *The White Tower* (RKO)
Ted Tetzlaff
Where Danger Lives (RKO)
John Farrow
1951 *Sealed Cargo* (RKO)
Alfred Werker

1953 *The Man Who Watched Trains Go By* (Eros Studios)
Harold French
1956 *Lisbon* (Republic)
Ray Milland
1959 *This Earth Is Mine* (Universal)
Henry King
1960 *The Lost World* (20th Century-Fox)
Irwin Allen
1961 *Battle of the Worlds* (Ultra Films/Sicilia)
Anthony Dawson (Antonio Margheriti) (released in the U.S. in 1963)
1962 *Lawrence of Arabia* (Columbia)
David Lean
1963 *Twilight of Honor* (MGM)
Boris Sagal
1965 *The Greatest Story Ever Told* (United Artists)
George Stevens (David Lean directed Rains' scenes)

This copy of the rules and regulations for His Majesty's Theatre was given to actor Cecil Yapp during the period that Claude Rains worked there. (Billy Rose Collection, Library)

His Majesty's Theatre, Proprietor and Manager: Mr. Tree
Rules and Regulations

1. Salaries are not paid for Ash Wednesday nor Good Friday nor for such other days as the theatre may be closed during Holy Week, or for Christmas Day, nor for such weekdays (Not exceeding six) as The Theatre may be closed prior to Christmas Day, nor for such period as Theatrical Performances may be suspended on account of Fire, the death of any member of the Royal Family, Public Calamity, Public Festival, Epidemic, etc., nor during the illness of the Performer engaged whereby the Manager is deprived of his or her services.

2. Any member of the company not playing an Evening Performance will not be paid extra for any Morning Performance for which he or she would otherwise be entitled to extra payment.

3. Any member of the Company refusing to act a part cast by the Manager, such part being agreeable to the terms of his or her engagement, incurs a penalty of one week's salary for every such refusal or his or her engagement may be cancelled by the Manager.

4. No member of the company is allowed to act, sing, or appear publicly at any other theatre or place of Entertainment, without the permission of the Management. A breach of this Rule will entitle the Manager to cancel the engagement.

5. No song, dance or dialogue (or any portion of either of the same) in any performance is allowed to be omitted without the permission of the Management.

6. No member of the Company is allowed to address the Audience without the consent of the Management.

7. At Rehearsal ten minutes' grace is allowed for the first piece rehearsed, but not for any subsequent one.

8. Any member of the company not attending to fulfill his or her duties, be it at a performance or at a rehearsal, except in case of illness, may incur forfeiture of engagement. Illness not admitted as an excuse for absence unless a doctor's certificate is sent to the Management.

9. Any Member of the Company be intoxicated in the Theatre, either before or behind the curtain, or whose conduct in or out of the theatre shall be such as to bring discredit to the Management, may be instantly dismissed.

10. No Member of the Company is permitted to go to the front of the house, when engaged in any part of the entertainment, without leave from the Management.

11. No Member of the Company shall give any orders to the carpenters, property-men, or other servants of the Theatre.

12. Smoking is forbidden in the dressing rooms.

13. No Member of the Company shall be photographed in character without the permission of the Management.

14. No stranger is allowed to pass the Stage Door without the consent of the Management.

15. Members of the Company are required to obtain permission of the management before consenting to be interviewed by the Press, excepting when no reference is to be made to the Management or to the part or the play in which they are appearing.

16. Salary of one pound/11 shillings/six pence per week of seven performances. One/14th of this sum to be paid for every additional performance.

The engagement to be for the term as follows (the run of <u>Name of Play</u>).

Special conditions: Mr. Tree reserves the right of terminating this agreement at any time by giving two weeks' notice of such his desire.

Acknowledgments

This book has been a life-long ambition. I dedicate it to the many people (and creatures in nature) who instilled something within me that helped me develop as a human being. Deepest gratitude to my deceased sister Jaye (June), who not only shared with me a love of Hollywood's "Golden Age," and foreign films of the 1950s and '60s, but who helped me in the early stages to delete repetitive text in the manuscript. Homage to a dear friend from my days at Harvard Graduate School of Teaching, Sue Fisher-Moran, who supported my efforts and read chapters in progress, but sadly died from brain cancer.

Over the decades, I was fortunate to be able to interview many important surviving friends, family and colleagues of Claude Rains. Some of these people requested anonymity; I have honored their request by either omitting names or providing pseudonyms. Many are long gone. I have tried to remember them all.

Thanks to Rains' fellow artists in the entertainment industry for interviews, photographs and copies of correspondence: Dick Berg, Lloyd Bridges, Corinne Calvet, Tommy Carr, Richard Chamberlain, Fielder Cook, Ossie Davis, Jan Dekker, Susanna Foster, John Garland, Larry and Judy Gates, Ben Gazzara, Doris Hall, George Roy Hill, Kim Hunter, Stanley Kauffman, Shirley Knight, Piper Laurie, Rick Lenz, Walter Matthau, Roddy McDowall, Ronald Neame, Maureen O'Hara, Sydney Pollack, Allan Rich, Frederick Rolf, George Schaefer, Vincent Sherman, Gloria Stuart, Audrey Totter and Fay Wray.

Thanks to the directors, curators and staff at libraries, research centers, museums and institutions, both in the U.S. and in England: The Archival Research Center of the Boston University library, formerly the Mugar Reference Center, then the Howard Gotlieb Center, which houses Rains' personal papers; The New York Public Library, Billy Rose Theatre Collection; The Academy of Motion Pictures Arts and Sciences, Beverly Hills; The New York Museum of TV and Radio; The Chester County Historical Society in West Chester, PA (material on the Brandywine area and Stock Grange farm); The Sandwich, NH Historical Society, Robin Dustin, director (Thank you, Robin, for introducing me to the citizens of your town who knew Rains, and for allowing me to stay with you when I visited Sandwich); The London Scottish, Regimental Headquarters, London; Public Record Office, Kew, Richmond, Surrey; Ministry of Defense, Hayes, Middlesex; Yale University Library, Theatre Guild Collection; Warner Bros. Film Collection at University of Southern California Library, Los Angeles.

Indispensable contributions were made by Swami Tom Weaver, including text proofing/error correction *ad infinitum*, colorful "antidotes" and rare photo acquisition.

Kevin Brownlow kindly shared background on the making of *Caesar and Cleopatra*, as well as other vital sources, and gracious support over the years. Essential services were provided by Pat H. Broeske (essential proofing, Karen Chacon (front and back cover design), Jim Nemeth (text conformation from obsolete formats) and Laura Wagner (indexing). BearManor resident designer, Robbie Adkins, rolled up her sleeves to tackle the enormous manuscript with great good grace.

Other experts and authors involved include David Thomson; and John Antosiewicz, Ted Bohus, Gibby Brand, Mike Brunas, Martin Grams, Richard Heft, Mark Martucci and Fred Rappaport.

Heartfelt thanks to Jessica (Jennifer) Rains for reminiscences about life with a famous and loving father, and for access to her memorabilia collection. A special expression of deep gratitude to Agi Jambor, Rains' fifth wife, for memories of her short and extraordinary marriage. A very special thank you to the children of Rains' sixth wife, Rosemary Schroeder: Schuyler and Angela (Angel). For a boy of ten, Schuyler's memories were charming; Angel's input provided insight on Rains' personal behavior. Also to Eric Propper, and Tony and Dirk Partridge, Frances' nephews, who spent many summers at Stock Grange — their mostly fond memories were extremely informative.

A very special note of gratitude to Ann Wyeth McCoy, who knew Claude and Frances as personal friends while they lived at Stock Grange, and provided wonderful personal photos, seen here for the first time; to Mrs. Janet Uhle, wife of Rains' doctor, who as a summer resident of Sandwich, NH knew both Frances and Rosemary; to Harrison Wetherill, for remembrances of buying Stock Grange from Rains — and for continued caretaking of the farm for twenty-five years; Terry McDonnell, the son of Ash McDonnell, the original contractor who worked with Rains to restore Stock Grange, who provided many details about the relationship the two men had and himself worked on the project as a young man; to Mrs. Henry E.I. duPont, owner of Stock Grange in the 1990s, who granted me permission to visit the historic farm and grounds.

Thank you to all the neighbors in the area from 1940 to 1957 for amusing, honest, and sometimes bittersweet anecdotes of their famous neighbor: Mrs. Jeffers, who went riding with Frances; Mary Crocker, whose husband did odd jobs for Rains in his West Chester house; Mrs. Emmy Jordan, who purchased Rains' house when he left for Sandwich; Quita Brodhead, who painted an oil portrait of the actor; and Joseph Szorentini, doorman at the Plaza Hotel in New York City, where Rains stayed from January to June 1951, who recalled the actor's kindness in great detail.

Thanks to the wonderful, kind people of Sandwich, NH, who knew either Rains or Rosemary as a neighbor or friend, especially Mrs. Bertha Gotshall, the postmistress from 1963 to 1967, who shared many sweet personal notes.

I am grateful to staff at Laconia Hospital, NH and at the hospital in Coatesville, PA. All medical personnel interviewed remained professional while discussing their famous patient, especially Nurse Fran Mauck, Dr. Nadeau, Dr. Margolis, Dr. McChesney, Nurse Robinson.

Finally, profound thanks and deep gratitude to Jim Hercules and Lucy Chase Williams, whose commitment made publication of this book possible.

Jim: whose tireless efforts to aid me with word processing, technical issues and computer problems frequently included coming to my rescue after putting in a hard day's work. He taught me computerese though many generations of Apples, formatting text from obsolete word processing programs. He has been a loyal and understanding friend for many, many years.

Lucy: whom I met in 1994 when we were both conducting research in the Academy Library, who understood my heartfelt desire to write this biography and promised the book would be published in my lifetime. She committed countless hours to the project: editing the author's lengthy manuscript; identifying errors and content repetition unavoidable after multiple software incarnations and years of revisions. She also located the bulk of the career photographs, and solicited invaluable contributions from a few kind colleagues. Her extensive knowledge of Rains' career was an asset in interpreting my intentions. Her dedication to the project was above and beyond.

Bibliography

Books

Ayars, Barbara. *Window on West Bradford.* Pennsylvania: Chester County Historical Society, 1976.

Basinger, Jeanine. *A Woman's View.* New York: Alfred Knopf, 2013.

Behlmer, Rudy, ed. *Inside Warner Bros. (1935-1951).* New York: Viking Adult, 1985.

Brownlow, Kevin. *David Lean: A Biography.* New York: St. Martin's Press, 1996.

Callow, Simon. *Charles Laughton: A Difficult Actor.* New York: Grove Press, 1988.

Chapin, Schuyler. *Musical Chairs: A Life in the Arts.* New York: G.P. Putnam Sons, 1977.

Curtis, James. *James Whale: A New World of Gods and Monsters.* London: Faber & Faber, 1998.

Davis, Bette. *The Lonely Life: An Autobiography.* New York: G.P. Putnam Sons, 1962.

Deans, Marjorie. *Meeting at the Sphinx: Gabriel Pascal's Production of Bernard Shaw's* Caesar and Cleopatra. London: Macdonald & Co., 1946.

____. Unpublished manuscript, *Nero's Fiddle* (wartime experiences with Shaw and Pascal).

Dewey, Donald. *James Stewart: A Biography.* Nashville TN: Turner Publishing, 1997.

Dunning, John. *Tune in Yesterday: The Ultimate Encyclopedia of Old-Time Radio, 1925-1976.* New Jersey: Prentice-Hall, 1976.

Eaton, Walter. *The Theatre Guild: The First Ten Years.* New York: Brentano, 1929.

Eliot, T.S. *The Confidential Clerk: A Play.* London: Faber & Faber, 1954.

Finler, Joel W. *Hitchcock in Hollywood.* New York: Continuum Publishing, 1992.

Fraser, George M. *The Hollywood History of the World.* New York: Beechtree Books, William Morrow, 1988.

Gabler, Neal. *An Empire of Their Own.* New York: Crown Publishers, 1988.

Gatiss, Mark. *James Whale: A Biography.* London: Cassell, 1995.

Gielgud, John. *Backward Glances.* London: Hodder & Stoughton, 1989.

____. *Distinguished Company*, Chapter 2, "Two Forceful Actors." London: Heinemann, 1972.

____. *Early Stages: 1921-1936.* Revised Edition. New York: Taplinger Publishing, 1976.

Glut, Donald. *Classic Movie Monsters.* Metuchen NJ: Scarecrow Press, 1978.

Gordon, Ruth. *My Side: The Autobiography of Ruth Gordon.* New York: Harper & Row, 1976.

Harmetz, Aljean. *Round Up the Usual Suspects: The Making of* Casablanca. New York: Hyperion, 1992.

Henreid, Paul, with Julius Fast. *Ladies Man: An Autobiography.* London: St. Martin's Press, 1984.

Higham, Charles. *Bette: The Life of Bette Davis.* New York: Macmillan, 1969, 1981.

Holroyd, Michael. *Bernard Shaw: The Lure of Fantasy, Vol. III.* London: Chatto & Windus, 1992.

Jensen, Paul M. *The Men Who Made the Monsters,* London: Twayne Publishers, 1996.

Langer, Lawrence. *The Magic Curtain.* New York: E.P. Dutton, 1951.

Laurie, Piper. *Learning to Live Out Loud.* New York: Crown, 2011.

Leff, Leonard J. *Hitchcock & Selznick.* New York: Weidenfeld & Nicholson, 1987.

Lorenz, Janet, edited by Nicholas Thomas. "Claude Rains," *International Dictionary of Films and Filming 3: Actors & Actresses.* Chicago, IL: St. James Press, 1986 and 1992.

Mank, Gregory William. *The Hollywood Hissables.* Metuchen NJ: Scarecrow Press, 1989.

____. *Women in the Horror Genre 1931-48.* Jefferson NC: McFarland, 2005.

McClelland, Doug. *Forties Film Talk.* Jefferson NC: McFarland, 1992.

Merrill, Gary. *Bette, Rita, and the Rest of My Life.* New York: Yankee Books, 1988.

Miller, Frank. Casablanca: *The Fiftieth Anniversary (Limited Collector's Edition)*. Nashville TN: Turner Publishing, 1992.

Mordden, Ethan. *The Hollywood Studios.* New York: Alfred Knopf, 1988.

Morris, L. Robert, and Lawrence Raskin. Lawrence of Arabia: *The 30th Anniversary Pictorial History*. New York: Doubleday, 1992.

Nadel, Norman. *A Pictorial History of the Theatre Guild.* New York: Crown Publishing, 1969.

Peary, Danny, ed. *Close-Ups, 10th Anniversary 1978-1988.* New York: Simon & Schuster.

____, ed. *Close-Ups,* "Claude Rains: Astute Craftsman." New York: Simon & Schuster, 1978, 1988.

Phillips, Gene D. *Alfred Hitchcock.* Boston MA: Twayne Publishers, 1984.

Priestley, J.B. *Particular Pleasures,* Feature on Claude Rains. London: Heinemann, 1975.

Robertson, James. *The* Casablanca *Man: The Cinema of Michael Curtiz.* London: Routledge, 1993.

Sherman, Vincent. *Studio Affairs: My Life as a Film Director.* University Press of Kentucky, 1996.

Shipman, David. *The Great Movie Stars: The Golden Years.* New York: Crown Publishers, 1970.

Skal, David, with Jessica Rains. *Claude Rains: An Actor's Voice.* University Press of Kentucky, 2008.

Slide, Anthony. *The American Film Industry: A Historical Dictionary.* Westport CT, Greenwood Press, 1986.

Soister, John T., with Joanna Wioskowski. *Claude Rains: A Comprehensive Illustrated Reference.* Jefferson NC: McFarland, 1999.

Spoto, Donald. *The Life of Alfred Hitchcock: The Dark Side of Genius.* Little, Brown, 1995.

Stine, Whitney. *Mother Goddam: The Story of the Career of Bette Davis.* New York: Hawthorn Books, 1974.

Swindell, Larry. *Body and Soul: The Story of John Garfield.* New York: William Morrow, 1975.

Terrace, Vincent. *Radio's Golden Years, 1930-1960.* New York: A.S. Barnes, 1987.

Thomson, David. *Showman: The Life of David Selznick.* New York: Knopf, 1992.

____. *A Biographical Dictionary of Film,* 3rd ed. New York: Knopf, 1994.

Waldau, Roy S. *Vintage Years of the Theatre Guild 1928-1939.* Cleveland OH: Case Western Reserve University Press, 1972.

Walker, John, ed. *Halliwell's Film Guide,* 8th edition. New York: Harper-Collins, 1992.

Wallis, Hal B., and Charles Higham. *Starmaker: The Autobiography of Hal Wallis.* New York: Macmillan, 1980.

Weaver, Tom, *Science Fiction Stars and Horror Heroes.* Jefferson NC: McFarland, 1991.

Young, Freddie. *Seventy Light Years: A Life in the Movies.* London: Faber & Faber, 1999.

Newspapers and Periodicals

Abel, Richard. *Wide Angle,* Vol. 4, No. 1, "The Male System of Hitchcock's *Notorious,*" Samford University, Birmingham AL 1980-81.

Agate, James. *London Sunday Times,* theatre reviews, Aug. 17, 1924, p.4; Sept. 30, 1923, p.4; Aug. 9, 1925, p.4; March 14, 1926, p.5.

Agnew, Ewan. *Spectator,* London, U.K. theatre reviews, March 20, 1926; Oct. 16, 1926, p.625.

Atkinson, Brooks. *The New York Times,* theatre reviews, Dec. 6, 1927; March 17, 1931; Feb. 22, 1934.

Beebe, Lucius. *New York Herald Tribune,* interview, March 13, 1932.

Benchley, Robert. *New Yorker,* review, Feb. 22, 1934.

Birrell, M. *The Nation,* U.K. Theatre review, July 19, 1924, p. 509.

Boston Herald, Jan. 12, 1954.

Boston Post, Jan. 12, 1954.

Brown, Ivor. *Saturday Review,* London, UK, review, March 1925; Sept. 26, 1925, pp.334-5; Feb. 1934.

Brown, John Mason. *New York Evening Post,* Nov. 27, 1929; Feb. 26, 1930; March 1, 1932.

Brown, John Mason. *Saturday Review,* review of *Darkness at Noon,* Feb 3, 1952.

Chadbourne, Mary. *Modern Movies,* "He's Never Himself," 1939, Museum of the city of New York.

Cole, Herbert. *Picturegoer,* "Doesn't He Have Fun," December 28, 1940.

Cole, Herbert. *Picturegoer,* interview, December 28, 1940, p.9.

Connecticut Record (Meridan), Jan. 9, 1954.

Contratti, Lawrence. *Classic Film Collector*, "*The Invisible Man*," Fall, 1974.

Creelman, Eileen. *Universal Weekly* (Hollywood), "Claude Rains Made Invisible," Dec. 9, 1933.

Creelman, Ellen. *New York Sun*, NY, Review of *Caesar and Cleopatra*.

Cross, Brenda. *Picturegoer*, "Claude Rains," July 31, 1948.

Day, Barry. *Film*, "*Casablanca*: The Cult Movies," August 1974, p. 22.

The Era, London, theatre reviews, Mar. 21, 1920, p.7; Apr. 18, 1920, p.11; Jan. 17, 1921; Apr. 4, 1923, p.11; May 9, 1923, p.11; June 27, 1923, p.11; Aug. 14, 1924, p.16; Sept. 3, 1924, p.4; Aug. 14, 1924, p.16; Sept. 3, 1924, p.4; Mar. 17, 1926, p.1.

Etheridge, Ann. *American Classic Screen 5*, No. 3: "Bette Davis and Claude Rains: Two Opposites That Attracted," pp. 9-13.

Film Weekly, reviews of *Crime Without Passion*, Feb. 22, 1935, pp.8-9; Aug. 9, 1935, p.7; Dec. 28, 1940, p. 9.

Franchey, John. *Hollywood Magazine*, "Vivid Villain," Dec. 1938.

Fulton, John P. *American Cinematographer*, "How We Made *The Invisible Man*," Sept. 1934.

Grein, J. T. *Illustrated London News*, theatre reviews, Jan. 14, 1920; Jan. 17, 1920; April 24, 1920, p.122; Jan. 22, 1921, p.126; Oct. 6, 1923, p.638; March 14, 1925, p.428; July 4, 1925, p.44.

Hall, Gladys. *Silver Screen* magazine, "Claude Rains is Frightened," December 1947.

Hopper, Hedda. *Los Angeles Times*, "Claude Rains Still Suffers from the Jitters," Sept. 28, 1947.

Ibid. *Evening Bulletin*, Philadelphia, Sept. 14, 1947.

Ibid. *Saturday Review*, "Two on the Aisle," Feb. 23, 1934.

Ibid. *Film Comment*, "Acting English," May-June 1982.

Ibid. *Wide Angle*, Vol. 1, No. 1, "*Notorious* per Version par Excellence," 1976-77.

Isaacs, Edith. *Theatre Arts Magazine*, Vol.18., 1934, pp.323-24.

Kean, J.H. *Philadelphia Daily News*, June 17, 1932.

Kerr, Walter. *Herald-Tribune*, New York, theatre review, Jan. 15, 1952.

Lahr, John. *New Yorker*, "Glamour," March 21, 1994.

Lee, Laura. *Sunday Bulletin*, Philadelphia, "Meet Farmer & Mrs. Rains of Chester County," April 6, 1942; "In the Movies," Aug. 26, 1944.

LeJeune, C.A. *London Movie News*, London, June 16, 1944.

Lindsay, Lt.-Col. J.H., ed. *The London Scottish in the Great War*, Regimental Headquarters, London, October 1925.

London Sunday Times, theatre reviews, Jan. 16, 1921, p.10; Jan. 20, 1921, p.16; March 6, 1921, p.6; March 28, 1921, p.4; Nov. 19, 1921, p.6; Nov. 20, 1921, p.4; Feb. 8, 1923, p.8; May 6, 1923, p.14; June 24, 1923, p.6; Sept. 8, 1923, p.8; Sept. 30, 1923, p.4.

Lonergan, Phil. *Picturegoer Weekly*, "Close-up of Claude Rains," June 24, 1934.

Los Angeles Times, article, Sept. 28, 1947.

Manchester Guardian, U.K., *Darkness at Noon* review, Jan. 1952.

Manners, Dorothy. *Herald Examiner*, Los Angeles, Sept. 16, 1935.

Mantle, Burns. *New York Daily News*, review Feb. 22, 1934.

McCaleb, Kenneth. *Philadelphia Record*, review, Feb. 16, 1932.

McIlvaine, Jane S. *Philadelphia Inquirer* (Sunday Magazine), "Farmer Rains on Stage Again," Sept. 3, 1950.

Mooring, W.H. *Film Weekly*, "He Hates Humbug," April 2, 1938, p.11.

Morehouse, Ward. "Claude Rains Recalls Stage Greats," article found in Claude Rains' papers.

Morley, Cassidy. *Evening Bulletin*, (Philadelphia), "An Actor's Haven — 3,000 miles and 195 Years from Hollywood," April 2, 1941.

Murdock, Henry T. *Evening Bulletin* (Philadelphia), review, Feb. 16, 1932.

New Republic magazine, review, May 11, 1942.

New Yorker magazine, Jan. 25, 1952; April 11, 1970; July 8, 1996; Aug. 16, 1999.

Newsweek magazine, May 4, 1942.

Observer, U. K., article, April 18, 1920, p.11; April 28, 1923, p.11; June 11, 1924, p.11; Aug. 31, 1924, p.9.

Philadelphia Evening Bulletin, review, June 16, 1932.

Philadelphia Inquirer, "Rains Impressive," June 17, 1932.

Pollock, Arthur. *Daily Eagle*, Nov. 26, 1929.

Porter, Katherine. *Colliers*, "The Plow and the Star," November 19, 1938.

Price, Michael H. *American Cinematographer*, "Fun, Games and *Crime Without Passion*," October 1985, p. 35.

Rains, Claude. *Evening Bulletin*, Philadelphia, article on proper diction, May 24, 1935.

Rains, Claude. *New York Sunday Times*, Theatre Section, "My Most Difficult Role," January 1952.

Richards, Jeffrey. *Films and Filming*, "In Praise of Claude Rains," Hansom, U.K., February 1982.

Ruhl, Arthur. *New York Herald Tribune*, "Second Nights," March 1, 1932.

Rylands, George. *Nation*, U.K. review, Sept. 6, 1924.

Sennwald, Andre D. *The New York Times*, "That Invisible Actor," Dec. 3, 1933.

Service, Faith. *Silver Screen* magazine, "A Villains Love Story," December 1940, pp. 42, 88-90.

Shanklin, Gertrude. "Claude Rains — Out of Character," 1946 article found in Rains' file in Warners Collection at Academy of Motion Pictures.

Sobel, Bernard. *New York Mirror*, Feb. 22, 1931.

Stage, London U.K., Jan. 20, 1921, p.16; Aug 14, 1924, p.16; Sept. 24, 1924, p.16; Mar. 12, 1925, p.18.

Watts, Jr., Richard. *New York Herald Tribune*, review, Mar. 21, 1935.

Williams, Hershel. *Theatre Arts Magazine*, Jan. 1933.

West, John C. *Panorama* of *Chicago Daily News*, "*The Invisible Man*, 40 Years Later," November 10-11, 1973.

Winsten, Archer. *New York Post*, "*Caesar and Cleopatra*," May 26, 1946.

Wray, Fay. *Film Weekly*, "Claude Rains as I Know Him," August 9, 1935.

End Notes

It's not an exaggeration to state that contributions to this project were made over seven decades, with dedicated research, interviewing and writing extending for some thirty years. Research trips were made to Los Angeles; New York; Boston; Stock Grange farm in Chester County, Pennsylvania; the Brandywine area; and Sandwich, New Hampshire. Interviews were conducted by the author in person, by telephone, and through correspondence.

Several major collections and libraries were visited. Main sources were the Howard Gotlieb Archival Research Center at Boston University, the repository of Claude Rains' personal papers, and the private collection of Rains' daughter. Archives at the Motion Picture Academy Library and Warner Bros. Studios were also extremely useful.

Late in life, Rains tape recorded thirty hours of autobiographical background for a proposed book with writer Jonathan Root. He also scribbled memories on notes and legal tablets. These items, as well as innumerable print articles, press releases and personal letters throughout the decades, are the source of most of the quotes. Additional information about Rains' early career came from a contemporary scrapbook compiled by Rains' great admirer, Englishwoman Audrey Homan. The author herself compiled personal scrapbooks.

Unfortunately, over the years, transference of material from one proprietary word processing system to another led (perhaps inevitably) to loss of data and some confusion of sourcing. The decision was made to omit publication dates of print materials in the End Notes; complete information is included in the Bibliography.

Legend:

ACADEMY . . . Motion Picture Academy Library, Los Angeles, CA.

BOSTON . . . . . Howard Gotlieb Archival Research Center at Boston University.

BROWNLOW . Brownlow, Kevin, *David Lean, A Biography*, 1996, St. Martin's Press, NY.

HOMAN. . . . . . Audrey Homan scrapbooks.

JRAINS . . . . Jessica Rains collection.

ROOT . . . . Audio tapes made by Rains; additional notes by Jonathan Root for never completed autobiography.

SKAL. . . . . Skal, David, with Jessica Rains: *Claude Rains, An Actor's Voice*, University of Kentucky Press, Lexington, KY, 2008.

SOISTER . . . . . Soister, John T., *Claude Rains: A Comprehensive Illustrated Reference*, McFarland, 1999.

WARNERS . . . . Warner Bros. Studios archives.

YALE . . . . Theatre Guild file, Yale University.

Gielgud/Company . . . Gielgud, John, *Distinguished Company*. Heinemann, London 1972.

Gielgud/Stages. . Gielgud, John, *Early Stages*, Revised Edition. New York: Taplinger Publishing, 1976.

Chapter 1
BOSTON, JRAINS, SKAL, BROWNLOW, ROOT.
Publications: *Philadelphia Inquirer, The Evening Bulletin.*
Anne Slavitt letter to author dated 3/9/95.

Chapter 2
BOSTON, JRAINS, HOMAN, Gielgud/Company, Gielgud/Stages.
Books: Simon Callow, *Charles Laughton: A Difficult Actor*, Grove Press, NY, 1988; Ruth Gordon, *From My Side*, Harper & Row, NY, 1976.
Publications: *The Evening Bulletin; The New York Times; Colliers.*
Author interview with Frederick Rolf.
Military information provided by: Records of the London Scottish, Regimental Headquarters; County Records Office, Bedford, Bedfordshire County Council; Lindsay, Lt. Col. *The London Scottish in the Great War*, 1925; Public Records Office, Kew, Richmond, England; Katharine Roberts, "The Plow and the Star," *Colliers*, 11/19/38, quoted in SOISTER.

Chapter 3
BOSTON, JRAINS, HOLMAN.
Publications: *London Sunday Times; The Observer; The Nation; The New York Times; The Era; The Nation; Stage; Star, Sunday Review; Illustrated London News; Westminster Gazette; Saturday Review; London Telegraph; Spectator, Evening Standard; Film Comment.*

Chapter 4
JRAINS, YALE.
Books: Larry Swindell, *Body and Soul: The Story of John Garfield*, William Morrow, NY, 1975; Roy S. Waldau, *Vintage Years of the Theatre Guild 1928-1939*, Case Western Reserve University Press, Cleveland OH, 1972; Norman Nadel, *A Pictorial History of the Theatre Guild*, 1969, Crown Publishers, New York.
Publications: *The New York Times; Evening World; Daily Eagle; Saturday Evening Post; The Public Ledger; The New York Tribune; Philadelphia Evening Bulletin; Philadelphia Enquirer.*

Specific articles: Alexander Woollcott, *Theatre Arts*, Dec. 17, 1927, vol. 39; Mary Chadbourne, "He's Never Himself," *Modern Movies.*

Chapter 5
The Hearst Collection at the University of Southern California.
Books: Gregory Mank, *The Hollywood Hissables*; James Curtis, *A New World of Gods and Monsters*, Faber & Faber, London, 1998; Mark Gatiss, *James Whale: A Biography*, Cassell, London, 1995; Paul M. Jensen, *The Men Who Made the Monsters*, Wayne Publishers, 1996.
Author interviews: James Curtis; Gloria Stuart (4/4/94 and the above books).
Publications: *Classic Film Collector; Herald Examiner; Variety* (West Coast Edition); *Los Angeles Times; New Yorker Magazine; Classic Movie Monsters.*
Specific articles: Eileen Creelman, "Claude Rains Made Visible," *Universal Weekly*, 12/9/33; Andre D. Sennwald, "That Invisible Actor," *The New York Times*, Dec. 3, 1933. For those interested in a detailed photographic technical explanation see: John P. Fulton, "How We Made the Invisible Man," *American Cinematographer*, Sept. 1934.

Chapter 6
YALE, BOSTON, JRAINS.
Books: Gregory Mank, *Hollywood Hissables*; Roy S. Waldau, *Vintage Years of the Theatre Guild 1928-1939*, Case Western Reserve University Press, Cleveland, 1972; Eaton, Walter P, *The Theatre Guild: The First Ten Years*, Brentano's NY; Lawrence Langer, *The Magic Curtain*, E.P. Dutton, 1951.
Publications: *Variety; Saturday Review; New York Post; The New York Times; The New York Daily News; Theatre Arts; Film Weekly; American Cinematographer; American Film Institute Catalog: Films of the 1930s; Los Angeles Herald; The New York Herald Tribune; Motion Picture Herald; New Republic; Silver Screen; Picturegoer.*
Deed book 973, page 343; Delaware County Courthouse, Emily Scott, Recorder of Deeds, Delaware County Historical Society Broomall, PA.

Chapter 7 and 8
BROWNLOW, BOSTON, SKAL, Billy Rose Theatre Collection, New York Public Library.
Books: David Thomson, *Showman: The Life of David Selznick*, Knopf, NY 1992; *Leslie Halliwell's Film Guide*, (8th edition), New York: Harper-Collins, 1992.
Publications: *Silver Screen*; *Picturegoer*; *Philadelphia Evening Bulletin*; *Philadelphia Enquirer*; *The Herald Examiner*; *The New York Times*; *The New York Herald Tribune*; *Variety*; *Picturegoer*; *Film Weekly*; *The Daily Mail*.

Chapter 9
ACADEMY.
Books: Neal Gabler, *An Empire of Their Own*; Gregory Mank, *In the Horror Genre, 1931-1948*, McCutheson Press, NJ; Rudy Behlmer, *Inside Warner Bros. (1935-1951)*, Simon & Schuster; Anthony Slide, *The American Film Industry: A Historical Dictionary*, Greenwood Press, NY, 1986.
Publications: *The Los Angeles Herald Examiner*; *New York Journal*; *Variety*; *The New York Herald Tribune*.
Specific articles: W. Mooring, "He Hates Humbug," Pen portrait, *Film Weekly*, April 2,1938; Katherine Roberts, "The Plow and the Star," *Colliers*, November 19, 1938.

Chapter 10
WARNERS, ACADEMY.
Books: Neal Gabler, *An Empire of Their Own*; Ethan Mordden, *The Hollywood Studios*, Alfred Knopf, NY, 1988; William K. Everson biography on Michael Curtiz; James Robertson, *The Casablanca Man*.
Publications: *Variety*; *Film Weekly*; *Silver Screen*; *Time*; *New Republic*; *New York Herald Tribune*; *The New York Times*; *New York Daily News*; *New York Sun*; *Indianapolis Times*; *Modern Movies Magazine*.
Specific article: John T. McManus, "Traffic Is Jammed by Heavy Rains," in *The New York Times* 7/11/37.

Chapter 11
WARNERS, ACADEMY, SOISTER.

Books: Nicholas Thomas (ed.) *International Dictionary of Films and Filmmakers -- 3 Actors and Actresses*, chapter on Claude Rains by Janet Lorenz, St. James Press, Detroit, 1986 and 1992; James Robertson, *Casablanca Man*; Sidwell's *John Garfield*; Robert A. Juran, *Old Familiar Faces*, Movie Memories Publishing, Sarasota FL 1995; Rudy Behlmer, *Inside Warner Bros. (1935-1951)*, Simon & Schuster, NY, 1985; Bette Davis, *The Lonely Life: An Autobiography*, New York: G.P. Putnam Sons, 1962; Charles Higham, *The Life of Bette Davis*, Macmillan NY 1981.
Publications: *Silver Screen*; *The New Yorker*; *Picturegoer*; *The Hollywood Reporter*; *Variety*; Box Office.
Specific articles: John Franchey, "Vivid Villain," *Hollywood Magazine*; Jeffrey Richards, "Films of Claude Rains," *Films and Filming*, Feb. 1982; Anne Etheridge, "Bette Davis and Claude Rains," *American Classic Screen*, Vol. 5, No.3.

Chapter 12
ACADEMY, BOSTON, WARNERS, JRAINS.
Books: Swindell, *Body and Soul: The Story of John Garfield*, 1975, William Morrow, NY; Robert A. Juran, *Old Familiar Faces*, Movie Memories Publishing, Sarasota FL, 1995; James Robertson, *Casablanca Man*; Donald Dewey, *James Stewart: A Biography*, 1997, Turner Publishing, Atlanta GA; Vincent Sherman, "Claude Rains: Astute Craftsman," in *Close-ups*, edited by Danny Peary, Simon & Schuster, NY, 1978 and 1988; Jeanine Basinger, *A Woman's View*, Alfred Knopf, NY, 2013.
Publications: *Punch*; *New York Journal of Commerce*; *Philadelphia Inquirer*; *Philadelphia Record*; *Hollywood Spectator*; *Evening Bulletin*; *Film Weekly*.
Specific article: Jeffrey Richard, "Claude Rains: A Career to Remember," *Films and Filming*, March 1982.

Chapter 13
Information pertaining to the history of Stock Grange came from various sources, including the Chester County Historical Society and interviews with neighbors in the area.

Inventories of the farm equipment purchased, and the pro yields were found in BOSTON.

Interviews: Jessica Rains; Terry McConnell; Stock Grange neighbors.

Details of the buildings (some of which still stand) as well as factual details of the house interiors can be verified by the author who visited the site and spent several days in October 1994 walking and touring their land and the interior of the buildings. The gentleman who purchased the farm from Mr. Rains made very few changes and maintained the restorations as he vowed he would do. The only main difference is the glorious barn no longer exists, only the stone wall foundation. There was a terrible fire, and all the wooden part of the barn was destroyed. Charles Stone wrote an epic poem, "Stories of Stock Grange," out of historical respect for the ancestral home which reflected his childhood.

Book: Aljean Harmetz, *Round Up the Usual Suspects—The Making of* Casablanca, 1992.

Specific articles: Barbara Ayars, "A Window on West Bradford," 1976, Chester County Historical Society, West Chester PA; Morley Cassidy, "An Actor's Haven—3000 miles and 195 years from Hollywood," *Evening Bulletin*, Philadelphia, Pa. April 2, 1941; Laura Lee, "Meet Farmer and Mrs. Rains of Chester County," *Sunday Bulletin*, Philadelphia, Pa. 1942; Jane McIlvaine "Farmer Rains on Stage Again," *Philadelphia Inquirer*, Sept. 3, 1950.

Chapter 14

ACADEMY, JRAINS, WARNERS, BROWNLOW, SOISTER, UCLA Theatre Arts Library, 20th Century-Fox Collection.

Books: Hal B. Wallis and Charles Higham, *Starmaker: The Autobiography of Hal Wallis*, Macmillan, 1980; Ethan Mordden, *The Hollywood Studios*, Alfred Knopf, NY, 1988; Frank Miller, Casablanca: *The Fiftieth Anniversary (Limited Collector's Edition)*, 1992; Doug McClelland, *Forties Film Talk*, section on Julius Epstein, 1992, McFarland, Jefferson, NC; Paul Henreid, *Ladies Man*, St. Martin's Press, New York, 1984; Aljean Harmetz, *Round Up the Usual Suspects*; Howard Koch, *As Time Goes By*, Harcourt, Brace and Jovanovich, 1979;

Frank Miller, Casablanca*'s 50th Anniversary*, 1992; Rudy Behlmer, *Inside Warner Brothers*; John Walker, *Halliwell's Film Guide, 8th Ed.*, Harper Collins, Great Britain, 1991; Charles Higham, *Bette Davis*; Whitney Stine, *Mother Goddam*, 1974.

Publications: *Philadelphia Evening Bulletin*; *Newsweek*; *New Republic*; *American Classic Screen*; *Variety*; *The Hollywood Reporter*.

Specific articles: Gertrude Shankin interview with Claude Rains, American Film Institute print out record 3291; "Here Comes Mr. Jordan," *Chicago Daily News*; Barry Day, "*Casablanca*: The Cult Movies," *Films and Filming*, August 1974.

Chapter 15

WARNERS, SKAL.

Interviews: Susanna Foster, Vincent Sherman.

Books: David Shipman, *The Great Movie Stars: The Golden Years*, Crown Publishers, 1970; Danny Peary (ed.), *Close-Ups 10th Anniversary Edition*, Simon and Schuster, 1978, 1988; Donald F. Glut, *Classic Movie Monsters*, Scarecrow Press, Metuchen NJ, 1978; Richard Schickel, *Good Morning, Mr. Zip, Zip, Zip*, Ivan R. Dee Publishers, Chicago, 2003; Rudy Behlmer, *Inside Warner Bros. (1935-1951)*, Simon and Schuster, NY, 1985; Vincent Sherman, "Claude Rains: Astute Craftsman," in *Close-Ups*, Simon & Schuster, 1978 and 1988; Charles Higham, *The Life of Bette Davis*, Macmillan, 1981.

Publications: *The New Yorker*; *New York World Telegram*; *The Hollywood Reporter*; *Boston Christian Science Monthly*; *New York Post*.

Specific article: Laura Lee "In the Movies," *Evening Bulletin*, Philadelphia, August 26, 1944.

Chapter 16

SKAL, BROWNLOW, JRAINS, ACADEMY.

Interview: Doris Hall.

Unpublished manuscript of Marjorie Deans, *Nero's Fiddle: My Wartime Experiences with Bernard Shaw and Gabriel Pascal*, literary executor, Michael Santoro.

Books: Marjorie Deans, *Meeting at the Sphinx: Gabriel Pascal's Production of Bernard Shaw's* Caesar and Cleopatra, Macdonald & Co.,

London, 1946; Michael Holroyd, *Bernard Shaw, The Lure of Fantasy, Vol. III*, London: Chatto & Windus, 1992; Freddie Young, *Seventy Light Years: A Life in the Movies*, Faber & Faber, London,1999; *Forties Film Talk*, by Doug McClelland, McFarland, Jefferson, NC.
Publications: *Philadelphia Inquirer, London Movie News; Life; The New Yorker; The New York Times; Esquire; The New York Herald Examiner.*
Specific article: Jeffrey Richards, "In Praise of Claude Rains," *Films and Filming*, Feb. 1982.

Chapter 17
SKAL, ACADEMY, JRAINS, WARNERS, UCLA RKO Archive.
Interview: Audrey Totter.
Books: John Dunning, *Tune in Yesterday: The Ultimate Encyclopedia of Old-Time Radio 1925-1976*, Prentice-Hall, Englewood Cliffs, NJ 1976; Leonard J. Leff, *Hitchcock & Selznick*, Weidenfeld & Nicolson, NY, 1987; *Hitchcock/Truffaut*, 1983, Simon & Schuster, NY; Joel Finler, *Hitchcock in Hollywood*, 1992, Continuum Publishing, NY; Gene D. Phillips, *Alfred Hitchcock*, Twayne Publishers, Boston, MA, 1984.
Publications: *Picturegoer, Silver Screen; Philadelphia Evening Bulletin; The New York Times; The Philadelphia Inquirer, The Philadelphia Evening Bulletin.*
Specific articles: Anthony Lane, "In Love with Fear," *The New Yorker*, 8/16/99; "From Identification to Ideology: The Male System of Hitchcock's *Notorious*," *Wide Angle*, Vol. 4, No. 1, 1980-81; Richard Abel, "Notorious Perversion par Excellence," *Wide Angle*, Vol. 1, No. 1, 1976-77.

Chapter 18
WARNERS, SKAL, ACADEMY, YALE, BROWNLOW.
Books: Aljean Harmetz, *Round Up the Usual Suspects: The Making of Casablanca*; Charles Higham, *Bette Davis, The Life of Bette Davis*, Macmillan, NY, 1981; Whitney Stine, *Mother Goddam: The Story of the Career of Bette Davis*, Hawthorne Books, NY, 1974.
Publications: *Forties Talk; Los Angeles Examiner; New York Post; Showman's Trade Review;*

The Hollywood Reporter; Gene Handsker's The Hollywood Column; The San Francisco Times; Evening Bulletin; Philadelphia Enquirer.
Specific article: Gertrude Shanklin, "Claude Rains Out of Character," 1946.

Chapter 19
BROWNLOW, SKAL, ACADEMY, BOSTON, UCLA RKO Archive.
Interviews: Corinne Calvet, Lloyd Bridges.
Book: Vincent Terrace, *Radio's Golden Years, The Encyclopedia of Radio Programs 1930-1960*, 1987, A.S. Barnes, NY.
Publications: *The Philadelphia Evening Bulletin; Picturegoer, The Evening News/London; London Times; The New York Times; The Los Angeles Times; The Hollywood Reporter.*

Chapter 20
JRAINS, BOSTON, YALE.
Interviews: Kim Hunter, Allan Rich. Set designer Frederick Fox's son.
Book: Tom Weaver, *Science Fiction Stars and Horror Heroes*, McFarland, 1991.
Publications: *The New York Times; The Evening Bulletin; Variety; Manchester Guardian; The Newark New Jersey News; The Cleveland Ohio Press; The New York Herald Tribune; The World Telegram; New York Sunday Herald Tribune; New York Telegraph; Vogue.*
Specific article: John Mason Brown, "The Iron Transparency," *The Saturday Review*, Feb 3, 1951.

Chapter 21
BOSTON, JRAINS.
Interviews: Ann Wyeth McCoy, Ossie Davis, Ben Gazzara, Janet Uhle.
Book: Gary Merrill, *Bette, Rita and the Rest of My Life*, New York: Yankee Books, 1988.
Publications: *The Evening Bulletin; The Sun; The Philadelphia Inquirer Magazine; Connecticut Record; The Boston Herald; The Boston Post; Variety; The Christian Science Monitor; New York Times; Boston Herald; New York Herald.*

Chapter 22, 23 and 24
BROWNLOW, JRAINS, BOSTON, ACADEMY, Museum of Radio & TV.

Interviews: Dick Berg, Aji Jambor, Schuyler
Schroeder, Jan Decker, Maureen O'Hara,
George Roy Hill, Ronald Neame, Harrison
Weatherall, Terry McConnell, Quita Brod-
head, George Schaefer, Michael Avallone, Ed
Robbins, Kurt Browning.
Books: Donald F. Glut, *Classic Movie Monsters*,
Scarecrow Press, Metuchen NJ, 1978; Schuy-
ler Chapin, *Musical Chairs: A Life in the Arts*,
G.P. Putnam Sons, NY, 1977.
Publications: *Philadelphia Evening Bulletin*; *Herald
Tribune*; *Billboard*; *Cash Box*; *The Philadelphia
Inquirer*; *Variety*.

Chapter 25, 26 and 27
BOSTON, RAINS, SKAL, BROWNLOW.
Interviews: Mrs. Jordan (who bought Hawthorne
House). Richard Chamberlain, Tony Carr,
Fielder Cook, Sydney Pollack, Piper Laurie,
Dick Berg, Shirley Knight, Walter Matthau,
Frederick Rolf, Dudley Emerson, Janet Uhle,
Henry Denker, Warner Perner, Jr., Larry
Gates, Dr. Margolis, Dr. McChesney, Nurse
Robinson, Nurse Fran Mauck, Father Tom.
Publications: *Concord New Hampshire Monitor*;
The New York Herald Tribune; *The Philadelphia
Evening Bulletin*; *The New Yorker Magazine*.

Chapter 28, 29 and Epilogue
BOSTON, JRAINS.
Interviews: Judy Gates, Rick Lenz.
Organization: The Actor's Fund.
Publication: *Screenland Magazine*.

Index